# Learning ActionScript 3.0

Second Edition

**Rich Shupe with Zevan Rosser**

O'REILLY®

Beijing · Cambridge · Farnham · Köln · Sebastopol · Tokyo

# Learning ActionScript 3.0, Second Edition

by Rich Shupe with Zevan Rosser

Published by O'Reilly Media, Inc., 1005 Gravenstein Highway North, Sebastopol, CA 95472.

O'Reilly Media books may be purchased for educational, business, or sales promotional use. Online editions are also available for most titles (*http://my.safaribooksonline.com*). For more information, contact our corporate/institutional sales department: 800-998-9938 or *corporate@oreilly.com*.

**Editor:** Mary Treseler

**Production Editors:** Rachel Monaghan and Teresa Elsey

**Development Editor:** Linda Laflamme

**Technical Reviewers:** Anselm Bradford, Chrissy Rey-Drapeau, Tim Goss, Xingyi Guo, Sonia Garbès Putzel, and Bently Wolfe

**Proofreaders:** Nancy Kotary and Chris Niemiec

**Indexer:** Ron Strauss

**Interior Designer:** Ron Bilodeau

**Cover Designer:** Mark Paglietti

**Compositor:** Nancy Kotary

**Print History:**

| | |
|---|---|
| December 2007: | First Edition. |
| October 2010: | Second Edition. |

ISBN: 978-1-449-39017-4
[TI]

Adobe Developer Library, a copublishing partnership between O'Reilly Media Inc. and Adobe Systems, Inc., is the authoritative resource for developers using Adobe technologies. These comprehensive resources offer learning solutions to help developers create cutting-edge interactive web applications that can reach virtually anyone on any platform.

With top-quality books and innovative online resources covering the latest tools for rich-Internet application development, the *Adobe Developer Library* delivers expert training, straight from the source. Topics include ActionScript, Adobe Flex®, Adobe Flash®, and Adobe Acrobat® software.

Get the latest news about books, online resources, and more at *adobedeveloper-library.com*.

# CONTENTS

## Part II    Graphics and Interaction                49

# Part V    Input/Output    359

## Chapter 13
## Loading Assets ......................................... 361

## Chapter 14
## XML ................................................... 385

## Index ................................................. 421

# PREFACE

When deciding if the book in your hands will be a good resource for your library, it might help you to know why we, the authors, wrote this particular book. We are both developers who use ActionScript extensively in our everyday work, but we are also teachers. Collectively, we have taught thousands of students at multiple universities, training facilities, and conferences, and yet we share one significant common experience. We were consistently told that no feature-rich ActionScript book existed that didn't assume readers already had extensive programming experience and an understanding of object-oriented programming.

So, we started to research how we could fill this void and provide a book to our students that would really help them beyond the classroom. We talked with a lot of students, user groups, and instructors and began to sketch out a book that would put what we learned into practice.

When ActionScript 3.0 was released, the interest in the language grew dramatically. In the Flash community reactions ranged from excitement to uncertainty to fear, as the ActionScript 3.0 learning curve became apparent. Talk of the Flash Platform splintering into Flex ("developer") and Flash ("designer") camps left many designers and programmers more uncertain than ever about their futures. When Flash CS3 Professional was released, the need for a guiding resource increased, and we knew it was time to write the book you hold in your hands.

We hope this book will help ActionScript coders of all kinds—from curious to intimidated, from eager to experienced—embrace the power and performance of ActionScript 3.0. We hope these pages will ease the transition from whatever prior version of ActionScript you may have used (if any) to 3.0—the biggest architectural change to the language since its inception.

# Who This Book Is For

This book is aimed at designers and developers without extensive ActionScript 3.0 experience. Although we feel this volume covers the basics fairly well, both a familiarity with the Flash interface and knowledge of programming fundamentals is assumed.

We've tried to explain the material herein clearly and concisely enough for any reader with at least this minimal background. However, we recommend that you skim Chapter 2 to see if you think we've provided enough core programming fundamentals to fill any gaps in your knowledge base. Throughout this book we cover relevant syntax with extensive comments, but the first two chapters serve as a foundation upon which the rest of the chapters are built.

Similarly, if you are a relatively experienced ActionScript 2.0 programmer, you may wish to glance at a few chapters of interest before deciding whether or not this book is for you. Migration from ActionScript 2.0-to-ActionScript 3.0 is not our primary focus, so we want you to be happy with the tone and straightforward approach we've adopted before you decide to rely solely on this book.

If you need additional support with the Flash Professional interface, want solutions to specific problems, or would benefit from a quick look at migration issues, consider augmenting this book with the *ActionScript Quick Reference Guide* by David Stiller, Rich Shupe, Jen deHaan, and Darren Richardson (O'Reilly). The book is divided into two halves, starting with interface-centric material and culminating with a series of recipe-style problem-solving chapters, including one that focuses on ActionScript 2.0 to 3.0 migration.

## Push Yourself

Although this book was written for a reader still finding his or her way with ActionScript 3.0, we've tried to include exercises throughout the book that encourage you to push yourself. When exercises move somewhat beyond the basics of a topic, we've identified them with this icon:

We've also tried to mention additional exercises and resources from the companion website (which we'll talk about in a moment) that may help you continue your explorations. In most cases, these exercises and notes are not central to understanding syntax or a topic as a whole. If you find any of these inclusions to be too much to digest, feel free to skip them and come back to them later.

Between these two supplemental efforts, we hope this book will be useful to a wide variety of scripters and allow you to progress along the ActionScript 3.0 learning curve quicker than expected.

## ActionScript Editors

Although we try to remain ActionScript-editor neutral whenever possible, the examples in this book were created in Flash Professional. We've provided source files that are compatible with the oldest version of Flash Professional that the applicable feature will allow. Most are compatible with Flash CS3 Professional, some require later versions of the tool, and some require Flash Player 10.1, the latest version as of this writing.

However, we've also tried to provide files for users that are working with other ActionScript editors, like Adobe's Flash Builder, Powerflasher's FDT, or the open-source FlashDevelop (Windows-only). These class-based files may also be useful to readers who already have experience with object-oriented programming.

*Despite these efforts, it's very important to understand that these supplemental files will not be actively supported.* You should buy this book knowing that many of the source files are in FLA format and, even if you typed in the scripts yourself, some rely on assets found in the libraries of these FLA files. If you are not a Flash Professional user, you may need to recreate these scripts and assets as best you can.

## How This Book Is Organized

Unlike any other book on ActionScript 3.0 that we've seen, this book does not rely extensively on object-oriented programming (OOP) principles. If you are unfamiliar with this term, don't worry. You have the correct book in your hands, and you'll learn more with each successive chapter.

We demonstrate key chapter concepts using focused syntax that's executable within the Flash Professional timeline and gradually introduce OOP concepts along the way. The first five chapters—including coverage of the new ActionScript 3.0 event model and means of displaying content (the display list)—do not introduce more than a modicum of content that is class- or OOP-related. Starting in Chapter 6, we provide increased object-oriented coverage, beginning with an OOP primer, and continuing for the remaining chapters with select class- or OOP-based applied examples.

This book was designed to be read linearly. Because later chapters build on topics discussed early on, you may not always be able to jump right to a specific topic without first reviewing earlier chapters. If you're looking for specific solutions to specific problems, take a look at the *ActionScript 3.0 Cookbook* by Joey Lott, Darron Schall, and Keith Peters (O'Reilly).

# What Is—and Isn't—In This Book

We've tried to design a book that covers as many ActionScript essentials as we could include, even while being constrained by a page count designed to keep the book affordable.

## What's In

*Part I: Getting Started*

Part I begins with Chapter 1, discussing ActionScript 1.0, 2.0, and 3.0, and how the different versions are used in the Flash Professional application and Flash Player. It concludes with Chapter 2 looking at the building blocks that are ActionScript's version-neutral core fundamentals.

*Part II: Graphics and Interaction*

Chapter 3 leads off Part II with explanations of the basic vocabulary of ActionScript: properties, methods, and events (including ActionScript 3.0's significantly different event model). Chapter 4 focuses on displaying content dynamically, which is also a big departure from prior versions of the language. Chapter 5 covers timeline control, and Chapter 6 introduces OOP. Chapter 7 discusses animating objects using ActionScript, and Chapters 8 and 9 explain drawing with code.

*Part III: Text*

Chapter 10 is the only chapter in Part III and focuses on text formatting, HTML support, and the use of Cascading Style Sheets.

*Part IV: Sound and Video*

Chapter 11 opens Part IV with a discussion about sound. In addition to manipulating internal and external sounds, it touches on parsing ID3 metadata and culminates with a sound visualization exercise, drawing a sound's waveform during live playback. Chapter 12 wraps up Part IV by demonstrating how to play video both with and without components, as well as how to subtitle your videos for accessibility.

*Part V: Input/Output*

Part V focuses on loading assets into Flash and sending data out to a server or another client. Chapter 13 covers loading SWF files, images, text, URL variables, and binary data, as well as communicating between loader and loadee SWFs. Chapter 14 covers XML and the new standard for working with XML that makes the task as easy as working with other ActionScript objects, methods, and properties.

*Part VI: 3D (Download)*

A special bonus chapter, available for download from the companion website, takes a short look at the 3D capabilities built-in to ActionScript 3.0.

## What's Not

As mentioned previously, this book focuses on ActionScript 3.0 (which applies to most segments of the Flash platform), but is presented within a Flash Professional context. As such, it does not include coverage of Flex, AIR, Flash Media Server, or other evolving Flash platform technologies.

As a basic text, this book has understandable constraints that limit the extent of coverage we can offer. Browsing through the Table of Contents will tell you what we include and, in some cases, the depth in which we'll cover the material. While it does include coverage of object-oriented programming techniques, for example, it does not address this material in great depth. (For more information about this point, please see the previous section, "How This Book Is Organized.") When you want to continue your OOP studies, we recommend *Object-Oriented ActionScript 3.0* by Peter Elst, Todd Yard, and Sas Jacobs (Friends of Ed).

We didn't intend this text to be a reference book, but rather a learning tool. If you're looking for a comprehensive reference volume, we recommend *Essential ActionScript 3.0* by Colin Moock (O'Reilly). Our book may serve as a useful companion to this title, particularly if you are not an advanced user, but it's not a substitute.

## Companion Website

All the exercises included in this book are available for download from the book's companion website, *http://www.LearningActionScript3.com*. Supplemental materials are also available, including additional exercises, self quizzes, extended examples, ongoing learning suggestions, a list of additional resources, reader comments, errata, and more. The source file archives for each chapter are available from the Downloads page, and you can sort posts by category or use the search feature to find posts by name. Both authors can be reached directly through this website.

## Typographical Conventions Used In This Book

The following typographical conventions are used in this book:

Plain text

> Indicates menu titles, menu options, menu buttons, and keyboard modifiers (such as Alt and Command).

*Italic*

> Indicates new terms, URLs, email addresses, filenames, file extensions, pathnames, and directories.

**NOTE**

*A note gives additional information, such as resources or a more detailed explanation.*

**WARNING**

*This box indicates a warning or caution.*

Constant width

Indicates ActionScript code, text output from executing scripts, XML tags, HTML tags, and the contents of files.

**Constant width bold**

Shows commands or other text that should be typed literally.

*Constant width italic*

Shows text that should be replaced with user-supplied values.

## Using Code Examples

This book is here to help you get your job done. In general, you may use the code in this book in your programs and documentation. You do not need to contact us for permission unless you're reproducing a significant portion of the code. For example, writing a program that uses several chunks of code from this book does not require permission. Selling or distributing a CD-ROM of examples from O'Reilly books does require permission. Answering a question by citing this book and quoting example code does not require permission. Incorporating a significant amount of example code from this book into your product's documentation does require permission.

We appreciate, but do not require, attribution. An attribution usually includes the title, author, publisher, copyright holder, and ISBN. For example: *Learning ActionScript 3.0*, Second Edition, by Rich Shupe with Zevan Rosser (O'Reilly). Copyright 2011 Rich Shupe and Zevan Rosser, 978-1-449-39017-4.

If you feel your use of code examples falls outside fair use or the permission given above, feel free to contact us at *permissions@oreilly.com*.

## We'd Like To Hear From You

Please address comments and questions concerning this book to the publisher:

O'Reilly Media, Inc.

1005 Gravenstein Highway North

Sebastopol, CA 95472

(800) 998-9938 (in the United States or Canada)

(707) 829-0515 (international or local)

(707) 829-0104 (fax)

We have a web page for this book, where we list errata, examples, and any additional information. You can access this page at:

*http://www.oreilly.com/catalog/9781449396558*

To comment or ask technical questions about this book, send email to:

*bookquestions@oreilly.com*

For more information about our books, conferences, Resource Centers, and the O'Reilly Network, see our website at:

*http://www.oreilly.com*

# Acknowledgments

We would like to give thanks to our talented O'Reilly team: Linda Laflamme, Ron Bilodeau, Nellie McKesson, Rachel Monaghan, Teresa Elsey, Nancy Kotary, Mary Treseler, Betsy Waliszewski, Anselm Bradford, Chrissy Rey-Drapeau, Bentely Wolfe, Tim Goss, Robyn Thomas, Steve Weiss, Michele Filshie, Matthew Roberts, Jill Steinberg, Joy Dean Lee, Phil Dangler, Linda Seifert, Mark Paglietti, Karen Montgomery, and Laurie Petrycki. Extra thanks to Linda, Ron, and Rachel for their endless patience and support.

Zevan would like to thank: Rich Shupe, The School of Visual Arts, Jesse Reznick and the creative team at SOM, Ann Oren, all of his students, and his family.

Rich would like to thank: Zevan Rosser, Jodi Rotondo, Sally Shupe, Claire Shupe, Mike Wills, Steven Mattson Hayhurst, Thomas Yeh, Anita Ramroop, and his family.

Rich would also like to show his appreciation for:

- Bruce Wands, Joe Dellinger, Russet Lederman, Mike Barron, Jaryd Lowder, Diane Field, Jenny Lin, Annie Wang, all at The School of Visual Arts, and all my students.

- Mark Anders, Paul Burnett, Mike Chambers, Mike Downey, Richard Galvan, Mally Gardiner, Stefan Gruenwedel, Jeff Kamerer, John Nack, Michael Ninness, Pete Falco, Nivesh Rajbhandari, and all at Adobe.

- John, Jo, and Amy Davey, Joe Franklin, Hippy Wright, and everyone at Flash on the Beach and Geeky By Nature; Dave Schroeder and everyone at Flashbelt; Susan Horowitz, William Morrison, and the University of Hawaii's Outreach program; Kelly Sanders, Tomo Kuriyama, and Julie Loo of Sheraton Hotels.

- Alex Taylor (Eltima); Gaby Ciordas, Alin Dogar, Raul Popa (Jumpeye Components); John Pattenden (Screentime Media); Coby Rich (Sorenson Media); Jerry Chabolla, Richard Blakely, and Grant Garrett at Influxis (the only streaming media host you'll ever need).

- Lynda Weinman, Bruce Heavin, and everyone at Lynda.com; everyone at Flashcoders NYC.

- Aral Balkan, Pete Barr-Watson, Rob Bateman, Brendan Dawes, Julian Dolce, Stephen (Tink) Downs, Joa Ebert, Hugh Elliot, Peter Elst, Hardy Fox, Homer Flynn, Jared Ficklin, Jesse Freeman, Chris Georgenes, Hoss Gifford, Bruce Gilbert, Brandon Hall, Ralph Hauwert, Robert Hodgin, Thibault Imbert, Scott Janousek, Penn Jillette, Mike Jones, Lisa Larson-Kelley, Philip Kerman, Mario Klingemann, Seb Lee-Delisle, Graham Lewis, Richard Lord, Jobe Makar, Niqui Merret, André Michelle, Stacey Mulcahey, Erik Natzke, Colin Newman, James Paterson, Chris Pelsor, Keith Peters, Robert Reinhart, Lou Reed, Tim Saguinsin, Grant Skinner, David Stiller, Craig Swann, Jared Tarbell, Teller, Jer Thorpe, Carlos Ulloa, (and no doubt others that I'm forgetting) for support and/or inspiration.

- (Extra special thanks to) Hudson Ansley, Tim Beynart, Anselm Bradford, Lee Brimelow, Veronique Brossier, Thaylin Burns, Xingyi Guo, Colin Holgate, Tyler Larson, Chris Niemiec, Sonia Garbès Putzel, Kevin Suttle, and Josh Tynjala.

- (Supreme nod to) Scotty and Kat Meltzer, Steve and Cindy Shupe, Dennis and Elaine Rotondo, Mari Howard, and Brian and Abigail Shupe. You know why.

Welcome Lucas Robert Bilodeau! Best wishes to Tom Kelley. I wish I could say this book is for whomever Kyle Baker is going out with now, but that was done long ago. This book is for Sally and Claire.

## About the Authors

**Rich Shupe** is the founder and president of FMA—a full-service multimedia development company and training facility in New York City. Rich teaches a variety of digital technologies in academic and commercial environments, and has frequently lectured on these topics at conferences all over the world. He is currently on the faculty of New York's School of Visual Arts in the MFA Computer Art department. Rich has written or co-written multiple books, including *Learning Flash CS4 Professional*, *The ActionScript Quick Reference Guide*, and *Flash 8: Projects for Learning Animation and Interactivity* (all O'Reilly), *Flash CS3 Professional Video Training Book* (Lynda.com/Peachpit), and the *CS3 Web and Design Workflow Guides* (Adobe). He also presents video training for Lynda.com. Visit Rich's website at *http://www.fmaonline.com*.

**Zevan Rosser** is a freelance designer/programmer/consultant and computer artist. He teaches ActionScript and Flash animation at New York's School of Visual Arts in the Undergraduate and Continuing Education programs, and has acted as thesis advisor for a handful of Masters students. He also teaches ActionScript and Flash at FMA in New York. When he's not working on commercial projects, he works on his personal site, *http//www.shapevent.com*.

# Colophon

Our look is the result of reader comments, our own experimentation, and feedback from distribution channels. Distinctive covers complement our distinctive approach to technical topics, breathing personality and life into potentially dry subjects. The text font is Linotype Birka; the heading font is Adobe Myriad Pro.

# GETTING STARTED

Part I starts this book off with a collection of basic overviews, spanning Chapters 1 and 2. It begins with a survey of ActionScript, providing a list of new feature highlights, a brief explanation of procedural versus object-oriented programming, and gets you started right away with your first script.

It concludes with a review of core language fundamentals, most of which remain consistent across all versions of ActionScript. The material at the outset of the book serves as an introduction to ActionScript for those new to the language, or as a refresher for those already familiar with it, and allows you to focus later on ActionScript 3.0–specific syntax.

# WHAT IS ACTIONSCRIPT?

While you likely know that ActionScript is the main scripting language of the Flash Platform, and you're no doubt eager to begin working with the new version, a brief overview of its development will give you some insight into its use—particularly as related to Flash Player and how it handles different versions of ActionScript. This brief introductory chapter will give you a quick look at where ActionScript 3.0 fits into your workflow.

Before we get started, it might help to understand how you get from ActionScript code to a finished file that you can put into a website. If this isn't news to you, bear with us for just a paragraph or two.

When you publish a Flash file—using Flash Professional's File→Publish or Control→Test Movie—all of the internal graphics and other assets used in your movie, as well as all of the ActionScript code, are *compiled* into a final file format called a *SWF* (pronounced "swiff" or "S-W-F"). That is, a part of your Flash Platform application of choice (such as Flash Professional) contains software called the *compiler*. This software converts all of your human-readable scripts into an optimized, machine-readable format. It combines that code with your assets into a single SWF file that Flash Player can decode and play back for all to see.

Although your SWF can load external assets not already compiled into your SWF (such as an MP3 or a video), any asset that you imported or embedded and all scripts—even if they originate outside the FLA (pronounced "flah" or "F-L-A") file—must go through this compilation process to be included in the SWF. This is why you must publish a new SWF every time you make a change to your code. It's also why you don't have to distribute ActionScript files with your SWF, even if you created external files, such as classes, when coding. Distributing ActionScript files with your SWF won't affect playback, but it may expose your source code to the public. This is fine when you're contributing code for others to learn from, but it won't make a client happy if you're doing work for hire!

For most users, the compilation process occurs behind the scenes and is handled by Flash Professional. At the time of this writing, the current version is Flash Professional CS5, but most of this book is compatible with versions dating back to Flash Professional CS3.

Other applications, such as Adobe's Flash Builder (or its predecessor Flex Builder), Power Flasher's FDT, the open source FlashDevelop, and even text editors in combination with a command-line compiler, can transform ActionScript into SWFs. However, this book focuses primarily on Flash Professional as an ActionScript editor.

Many examples will work seamlessly in any ActionScript editor; other examples will rely on symbols found in the library of a sample Flash file (FLA). This will be discussed briefly in the "Flash Platform" section of this chapter, but be sure you're comfortable with this workflow before investing any time in these examples. If your primary goal is to become a Flex developer, for example, with an equal emphasis on that technology's MXML syntax, you may want to pick up a companion to this text that focuses more significantly on Flex, such as *Learning Flex 4* (O'Reilly).

- **What Is ActionScript 3.0?** Every new version of ActionScript introduces new features. ActionScript 3.0, however, was written from scratch (not built on prior versions of the language) and is handled entirely separately from previous versions of ActionScript anywhere the language is used. This intentional branching allows for syntax improvements and significantly improves performance, but also makes it more difficult to use multiple versions of ActionScript at the same time.

- **The Flash Platform.** ActionScript 3.0 can be used in Flash, Flex projects, and AIR (Adobe Integrated Runtime) desktop applications, each of which are part of what is collectively known as the Flash Platform. Although they affect only a small portion of the language, differences in these environments prevent ActionScript 3.0 from working exactly the same way in every application that is part of the Flash Platform. The fundamentals, however—indeed, the bulk—of the language, are the same throughout.

- **Procedural Versus Object-Oriented Programming.** A lot of attention has been focused on the object-oriented programming (OOP) capabilities of ActionScript 3.0, and the language's power really shines in this area. However, embracing ActionScript 3.0 doesn't mean that you must become an expert in OOP. Using Flash, it is still possible to write scripts in the timeline, using functions to organize more complex code. This is commonly called *procedural programming*. If you prefer object-oriented programming, enhancements to ActionScript's OOP structure make version 3.0 more robust and bring it more in line with the features of other OOP-based languages (such as Java). This also makes moving between such languages a bit easier.

- **The Document Class.** Object-oriented programming is not for everyone, but for those starting on the OOP journey, Flash offers a simple stepping off point in the Document class. Using this feature, you need only specify an external ActionScript class file as your starting point, and no timeline script is required.

- **Legacy Code Compatibility.** Because ActionScript 3.0 can't mingle with previous versions of the language in the same file, developing projects that support older code is a challenge. We'll briefly introduce the issues involved and point to a technique that makes possible some communication between ActionScript versions.

- **Hello World.** This chapter will conclude with you writing your first ActionScript 3.0 application. We'll dive into some syntax for text manipulation, but don't worry: we'll cover the material in more detail in a later chapter. This exercise is just to get you started and build a little confidence.

# What's New in ActionScript 3.0?

If you're familiar with ActionScript or you're learning it based on experience with another programming language, you may want to know what ActionScript 3.0 has to offer. Although the third major version of the Flash Platform's primary scripting language contains much that will be familiar to users of prior versions, it's probably best to think of ActionScript 3.0 as entirely new, for a few simple reasons.

First, a few things are quite different, such as how events are handled and the way assets are displayed. Second, subtle changes run throughout the language. (These are usually small concerns, such as a slight change in the name of a property, but if you are used to ActionScript 2.0, for example, old habits can die hard.) Most importantly, ActionScript 3.0 has been rewritten from the ground up and uses a different code base than prior versions of the language. This optimization provides relatively dramatic performance increases, but it means that ActionScript 3.0 code cannot be mixed with prior versions of the language in the same file.

Regardless of your experience level, don't let the newness of ActionScript 3.0 intimidate you. It's true that its learning curve is steeper than that of prior versions, but that is usually a function of its robustness more than one of difficulty. Typically, whether you are coming to ActionScript 3.0 from a prior version of ActionScript or another language altogether, there is an adjustment period during which users must occasionally adapt to a new way of doing things.

Here's a look at some of the highlights of ActionScript 3.0. Keeping these benefits in mind may help make it easier to learn a robust language, or accept change—particularly when that change may initially seem tedious or overly complicated. Select new features include:

### Detailed error reporting

ActionScript 3.0 supports strict data typing of variables, arguments, values returned from functions, and so on. Chapter 2 discusses data typing in depth, but it boils down to telling the compiler and Flash Player which kind of data you want to work with at different points within your project code. This allows the compiler to warn you if you use the wrong data type, catching related errors. ActionScript 3.0 supports *static* data type checking, which occurs at compile time (when publishing your SWF), and improves *dynamic* data type checking, which checks for errors at runtime. In ActionScript 3.0, errors will no longer fail silently. Understanding this fully in this overview isn't important, and the benefits of data typing will become apparent after reading Chapter 2—and even more so after gaining a little experience with ActionScript 3.0. For now, just take heart knowing that error checking and reporting are more vigilant than in any prior version of ActionScript.

### Syntax improvements

Syntax issues have been unified and cleaned up throughout the language. For instance, some property names have been clarified and made consistent by removing leading underscores. (Setting the x coordinate of a movie clip, for example, now uses **x** instead of **_x**.). Also, former multiple and varying ways of approaching the same or similar tasks have been simplified and made consistent.

### New display architecture

The many previous approaches to displaying assets are now consolidated. ActionScript 3.0 has simplified how visible assets, such as movie clips and text fields, are handled, using a new display architecture called the *display list*. Chapter 4 examines this major change introduced by ActionScript 3.0.

### New event architecture

Still another example of improved consistency, all events—such as a mouse click or key press—are handled by event listeners in ActionScript 3.0—essentially listening for a specific event to occur, and then reacting accordingly. The new event model is very powerful when combined with the display list, allowing mouse and keyboard events to propagate through multiple display objects. The event model is discussed in Chapter 3.

### Improved XML handling

Working with complex XML documents is a pleasure with ActionScript 3.0. It allows you to reference XML data the same way you reference properties of other objects, such as movie clips or buttons, using a similar syntax.

You'll learn more about this in Chapter 14, but a simple example is referring to an XML node called *phone*, nested inside a node called *user*, as `user.phone`. This is comfortable territory when you remember that a movie clip called *mc2*, nested inside a movie clip called *mc1*, is referenced as `mc1.mc2`.

### Additional text options

New text-processing options now allow for much finer control over text manipulation. For example, you can now find the contents of a particular line in a text field, the number of characters in that line, and the character at a specified point (such as under the mouse). Flash Professional CS5 also introduces a brand new text feature called the Text Layout Framework (TLF). This new engine provides a greater degree of text control, including traditional typographic features, automatic text flow, and even support for right-to-left and vertical text layouts and double-byte languages (such as Chinese, Japanese, and Korean, among others). Text is discussed in Chapter 10.

### More sound management options

ActionScript 3.0's sound capabilities are among the jazziest changes to the language. On a practical level, they improve programmatic control over both individual sounds and all sounds playing. Sounds are now placed into separate channels, making it easier to work with more than one discrete sound. Sounds are also funneled through a sound mixer for collective control. You can get the amplitude and frequency spectrum data from sounds during playback, as well as from microphone input. Chapter 11 covers sound in detail.

### New access to raw data

For more advanced needs, you can access raw binary data at runtime. Individual bytes of data can be read during download, during sound playback, or from bitmap data, to name a few examples. These bytes can be stored in a large list and still be accessed quickly and efficiently. We'll show an example of this technique in Chapter 11 when discussing sound visualization.

### New automatic scope management

In a programming language, the word *scope* is sometimes used to define the realm in which an object, such as a movie clip, lives. A movie clip might exist in one part of a Flash movie but not another. For example, a child movie clip might be nested inside one of two movie clips found in the main timeline. That nested movie clip exists within one clip but not the other. Its scope, therefore, is restricted to the movie clip in which it lives, or its *parent*. Programming structures have specific scopes, as well, and ActionScript 3.0 greatly simplifies this concept by automatically keeping track of where a particular block of code was defined—so you don't have to.

### Improved object-oriented programming

If you're familiar with object-oriented programming, you'll be glad to know that ActionScript 3.0 supports this structure well. *If you're new to OOP*, don't worry: we'll introduce it in this book at a comfortable pace. We'll focus on syntax throughout by using simple examples, and we'll start to discuss OOP in greater detail in Chapter 6. *If you're already familiar with OOP*, you may be happy to know that sealed classes and new namespaces, among other things, have been added to ActionScript 3.0. Most classes are sealed by default, meaning the compiler recognizes only those properties and methods defined at compile time. This improves memory usage and performance. However, if you need to add properties to an instance of a class at runtime (for example), you can still use dynamic classes such as the `MovieClip` and `Object`, and you can make your own custom classes dynamic. Additionally, namespaces, including the ability to define custom namespaces, allow finer control over classes and XML manipulation.

## The Flash Platform

It's important to note that this book focuses primarily on developing ActionScript 3.0 applications using the Flash Professional application (also commonly referred to as an *integrated development environment*, or *IDE*). However, ActionScript 3.0 is the programming language used in Flash Platform technologies, as well—notably AIR and Flex.

AIR is the Adobe Integrated Runtime application, a sophisticated way of delivering your applications to the computer desktop, rather than through a web browser. Flex is another technology for creating SWFs that includes not only the ActionScript 3.0 language, but also *MXML*, a tag-based language that is part of what is commonly called the Flex Framework. This book will not discuss MXML or the Flex Framework at all, but most of the ActionScript you learn herein can be used in ActionScript-only Flex projects.

The existence of AIR and Flex means that the scripting skills you develop using Flash Professional will be largely applicable in other areas of the Flash Platform, extending your reach as a programmer. There are, however, some differences between these technologies that are important to understand when examining the big picture of cross-application scripting.

For instance, each technology adds some features that are not available to the others. Using a feature that is specific to AIR or Flex, for example, means that your code may not compile in Flash Professional. The thing to keep in mind is that the ActionScript 3.0 language skills you develop will ease your move between these applications and even allow you to work with different authoring tools or compilers to create your finished product.

**NOTE**

*AIR projects can also be created from HTML, JavaScript, and PDF, but ActionScript 3.0 is a large part of its appeal and the language most relevant to this discussion.*

**NOTE**

*This book is written for readers who have some familiarity with scripting but are new to ActionScript 3.0, and it assumes a working knowledge of the Flash Professional interface. See the Preface for more information about this expectation.*

*While virtually all of the code in the book applies to any tool that supports ActionScript 3.0, some of the examples use assets that are embedded within FLA files—the main document format used by Flash Professional. The companion website, http://www. LearningActionScript3.com, contains information about using the examples with applications other than Flash Professional. See the "Using the Book Examples" post as a starting point for learning more about this process.*

# Procedural Versus Object-Oriented Programming

Much discussion has been made over the pros and cons of procedural and object-oriented programming, and many who are new to ActionScript 3.0 have been led to believe that using OOP is the only way to program in ActionScript 3.0. This is not the case. Object-oriented programming is very powerful, and you'll probably want to use it when you're more comfortable with the language. However, it's just one possible way to write ActionScript. We'll introduce OOP slowly throughout the book, and we'll try to encourage you to learn OOP by presenting some exercises that use its methodologies. We'd like to reassure you, however, that OOP isn't required to program the Flash Platform, or to use this book.

To put this into an ActionScript perspective, consider a little background on the language's evolution. ActionScript started as a *sequential* programming language, meaning that scripting was limited to a linear sequence of instructions telling Flash what to do in a step-by-step manner. This approach to scripting was not very flexible and did not promote reuse.

As the language evolved, it became a *procedural* programming language. Like sequential programming, procedural programming relied on a step-by-step set of instructions, but introduced a more structured, modular approach to scripting. Procedures, otherwise known as *functions* (or sometimes subroutines), could be executed again and again as needed from different parts of a project, without copying and pasting copies of the code into the ongoing sequence of instructions. This modularity promoted reuse, and made the code easier to edit and more efficient.

Scripters in search of an even greater degree of modularity and reuse gravitated toward *object-oriented* programming. OOP languages create programs that are a collection of objects. Objects are individual instances of *classes*—collections of code that are self-contained and do not materially alter or disrupt each other. Creating an instance of a class, also referred to as *instantiation*, is much like creating an instance of a library symbol in Flash Professional. Just like movie clips dragged from the library onto the stage, multiple instances of that movie clip symbol can be altered without affecting one another, and without affecting the original from which they were derived.

Using OOP, however, you can extend this idea much further. One example of extending an object-oriented system is the use of *inheritance*—the ability to derive classes from other classes, passing on specific characteristics from the base class, or *parent* class.

Consider, for instance, designing an OOP application that simulates a set of transportation vehicles. You might start with a generic `Vehicle` class that includes traits common to all vehicles, such as the basic physics of movement. You might then extend `Vehicle` to create three *subclasses*: `GroundVehicle`,

**NOTE**

*The programming terms* parent, child, sibling, ancestor, *and similar words and phrases mean much the same as they do when used to describe families.*

*One simple example occurs when referring to symbol instances such as movie clips, which can be nested within each other. The upper- or outermost movie clip is sometimes referred to as the parent (there is even an ActionScript 3.0 property called* parent*), and the clips nested inside are sometimes called children. Similarly, two movie clips at the same hierarchical level are siblings, and clips that are more than one parent up the chain of nested clips are called ancestors.*

*In general, if you liken these terms to their everyday uses, referring to families, you will readily grasp their meanings.*

`WaterVehicle`, and `AirVehicle`. These classes would alter or introduce vehicle traits, making them specific to ground, water, and air travel, respectively. However, these classes might not yet be complete enough to represent an actual vehicle. Further derived classes might be `Car` and `Motorcycle` (descending from `GroundVehicle`), `Boat`, and `Submarine` (descending from `WaterVehicle`), and `Plane` and `Helicopter` (descending from `AirVehicle`). Depending on the complexity of your system, you can carry on this process, creating individual models with individual settings for fuel consumption, friction, and so on.

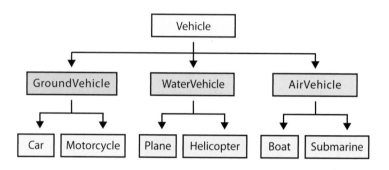

*Figure 1-1. An example of inheritance*

As you can probably imagine, this approach to development adds additional power, flexibility, and prospects for reuse. These benefits, among others, sometimes position object-oriented programming as the best approach to a problem. However, as we implied at the start of this section, there is a tendency among some programmers to believe that OOP is the best solution to *all* problems or, effectively, the *only* solution. This is flat-out untrue.

OOP is often best for large projects or for working with a team of programmers, but it can be overkill for small projects. Additionally, for the uninitiated, it can significantly increase the learning curve and distract from key topical concepts during your studies. In short, OOP is not always the best tool for the job. Procedural programming still has its place, and Flash Professional allows you to explore and employ both programming paradigms.

This book attempts to introduce material using both procedural and OOP approaches where appropriate. Using object-oriented practices is a fine goal, and one that we will encourage. However, we will try first to use simple procedural syntax to focus on the material central to each chapter, highlighting syntax and explaining how and why each topic should be addressed in code.

In general terms, we will focus on procedural programming prior to Chapter 6. Chapter 6 introduces OOP using a simplified version of the vehicle metaphor and serves as a transition chapter between procedural and OOP practices. Beginning with Chapter 7, chapters will introduce new concepts using simple timeline syntax and, when appropriate, include an applied OOP example.

This is our preferred approach to presenting material for all possible users—in both procedural and OOP formats. It is our hope that, regardless of your skill and experience, you will hone in on the topics at hand, and then choose to work using the timeline or classes based on your comfort level.

## The Document Class

If you want to start thinking in OOP terms right away, you can easily take a step in that direction. Remember that this is not necessary to get started and that you should feel free to skip this section if you don't want to be exposed to classes yet. You won't lose any momentum if you decide to skip ahead, as all of this material will be discussed again in Chapter 6.

**NOTE**

*If you don't plan to start using OOP until we roll it out in later chapters, feel free to skip this section as the material is discussed again in Chapter 6. We will provide minimal explanation here just to get you going using document classes, and will explain these concepts in greater detail in later chapters throughout the book.*

Flash Professional introduced a new feature that simplifies associating a main class, or primary entry point for your application, with your FLA. In Flash Professional, this class is called the *document class*, and it does all the work of instantiating the class for you. This means you don't need any code in the timeline at all and can edit your code not only in Flash Professional, but also in the external text editor or development environment of your choice.

Let's start with a simulated chapter example that you might use in the timeline. It does nothing more than use the **trace()** statement to display text in your authoring environment. In Flash Professional, this text will appear in the Output panel, an authoring-only panel that accepts text output from your file for diagnostic purposes.

**NOTE**

*As discussed previously, this book focuses strictly on ActionScript and assumes a familiarity with the Flash Professional application. If you are unfamiliar with the Actions, Timeline, or Output panels, please consult a reference on the Flash Professional application, such as this book's companion volume, Learning Flash CS4 Professional (O'Reilly). If you are using another script editor, please consult similar references for your editor of choice.*

In Flash Professional, use File→New and create a new ActionScript 3.0 FLA file. Select frame 1, and add the following to the Window→Actions panel:

```
trace("Flash");
```

To accomplish this using a document class, you essentially need to create an external file and enclose this instruction in the correct class syntax.

Users of Flash Professional CS3 and CS4 should use File→New and create a new *ActionScript File* (rather than a new FLA document). Users of Flash CS5 Professional will see this option as *ActionScript 3.0 Class* and most of this will be taken care of for you (Figure 1-2).

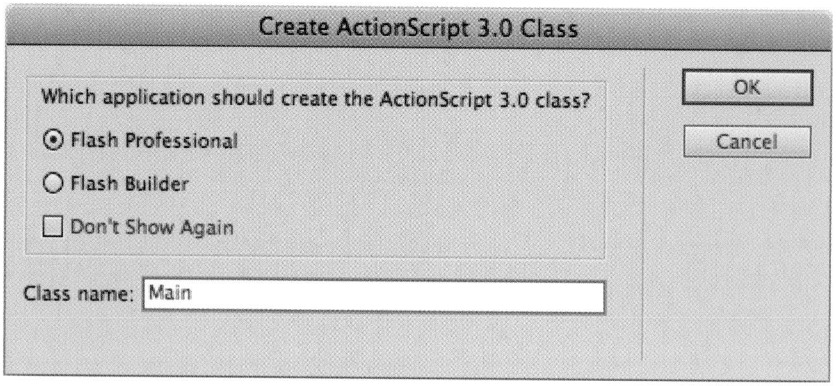

*Figure 1-2. Creating a new class in Flash CS5 Professional*

In the new file, type or edit the following:

```
1   package {
2
3       import flash.display.MovieClip;
4
5       public class Main extends MovieClip {
6
7           public function Main() {
8
9           }
10
11      }
12  }
```

The first line, along with the closing brace in line 12, defines the class's *package*. This is a mandatory structure that tells the compiler where your class resides. For simplicity, you will save your file in the same directory as the FLA that will use this class, so no further syntax is required.

Next, you must import any additional classes that your class will reference. The **import** keyword doesn't actually import anything; it just provides the location of a class to the compiler so it can validate your code and include the class when creating the SWF. Ordinarily, because this simple example uses only the **trace()** statement, you wouldn't need any additional classes to accomplish your goal. However, a document class is essentially a *replacement* for your main timeline. Behind the scenes, the compiler will use an instance of this class, instead of the main timeline, as the starting point for your SWF. Therefore, your document class should *extend*, or be derived from, the **MovieClip** class so that it inherits all the functionality of the main timeline. So, as a result of extending the **MovieClip** class in line 5, you must import the **MovieClip** class, as seen in line 3.

Line 5, along with its closing brace on line 11, is the class definition. What you decide to call your class (in this case, "Main") is up to you, but when naming it you should follow a few basic rules and conventions. The name can't contain spaces, it can't already exist in ActionScript, it should start with an

## NOTE

*When creating a document class, you can also extend the* **Sprite** *class, which is essentially a movie clip without a timeline. However, using the* **MovieClip** *class for this purpose offers more flexibility.*

*For example, although it's not a good idea to combine timeline code with a document class (it's best to think of the document class as replacing the timeline), it is possible only when the document class extends* **MovieClip**.

*For more information, see the "Sprite versus MovieClip" post at the companion website.*

alpha character (rather than a number or other character), and it is typically capitalized.

You must add **public** to line 5 when declaring the class, so that other parts of your program can access it. We'll cover this in detail in Chapter 6, but you can control which parts of your class are accessible to other areas of your project. For example, if you make something private, it will be accessible only from within the class. Doing so can protect portions of your class from outside manipulation and reduce conflicts with similar functionality that may exist elsewhere in your project. The class, itself, however, must be public so that it can be instantiated.

Line 7, along with its closing brace on line 9, define what is called the class *constructor*. This is the main function that automatically runs when creating an instance of this class. It, too, must be public and must have the same name as the class. Other functions (if any) can, and must, have unique names, but using the same name as the class identifies this function as the class constructor, so it is executed upon instantiation.

All that remains to complete this document class is to add the lone instruction required to replicate the timeline example discussed previously. The constructor must trace "Flash" to the Output panel, so add the following to line 8:

```
7          public function Main() {
8               trace("Flash");
9          }
```

Now that you're finished writing your class, name your file *Main.as* and save it to a location you'll remember. (In a moment, you'll need to save an FLA to this same location.) When creating a class, you must give the class, constructor, and file the same name—the notable exception being that the file must bear the *.as* extension.

Now, in Flash Professional, use File→New and create a new ActionScript 3.0 FLA file. Because this simple example included no custom path instructions in the package declaration in line 1 of your class, save your file in the same directory as your class file. The name of the FLA is unimportant, so you may as well call it *main.fla*.

Finally, open the Properties panel in the FLA and add the name of your class to the document class field. (It's labeled "Class" and appears in the Publish section of the panel.) Use the name of the class, not the name of the file. In this case, type Main instead of Main.as, as seen in Figure 1-3.

*Figure 1-3. Adding a document class to your FLA*

Now compile your FLA file using the Control→Test Movie menu command in Flash Professional, or Cmd-Return (Mac)/Ctrl-Return (Windows). (For Flash Professional CS5 users, the command is now Control→Test Movie→Test.) When your SWF runs, you should see "Flash" appear in the output panel, and your test application will be complete. You can compare your work to the files found in the *document_class_example* directory in the accompanying source code.

Hereafter, you can try any of our timeline code in a document class of your own. Initially, you probably won't know which classes to import or how to make any possible changes to variables or similar structures to conform to the class syntax. However, all the sample code will come with an accompanying class file for testing. You can use those files whenever you wish until you get used to the document class format.

## Legacy Code Compatibility

If you've worked with ActionScript 1.0 or 2.0 in the past—or even if you find yourself updating legacy code created by someone else—it's very important to understand that you cannot mix ActionScript 1.0 or 2.0 code with ActionScript 3.0 code in the same SWF. You are unlikely to do this if you're learning from scratch, but you may run into this limitation if you attempt to update legacy projects by adding ActionScript 3.0 code.

If you ever have the need to run a discrete mixture of ActionScript 3.0 and a prior version of the language, such as showing a legacy file within a new demo interface shell, you can do so by loading a SWF. An ActionScript 3.0 file can load a SWF created in ActionScript 1.0 or 2.0, but it cannot directly access the older SWF's code. A SWF created in ActionScript 1.0 or 2.0, however, cannot load an ActionScript 3.0 SWF.

In Chapter 13, we will discuss how to communicate between these two discrete SWFs using a special process. For now, however, just remind yourself again that you cannot combine ActionScript 3.0 with older versions of the language in the same file.

## Hello World

Now it's time to write your first ActionScript 3.0 application. If you learned about the document class earlier in this chapter, you've already done this. That exercise, however, displayed text only within an authoring application like Flash Professional—a technique used for testing and debugging, but not for displaying text in your finished files. In this section, we'll expand the example to show you how to display text in the SWF files you send out into the world. Using a text field makes a small leap, because we won't discuss text at length until Chapter 10, but our needs are meager for this example, and you should have no problem at all. Our main goal is to give you a big-picture view of the script-writing process and to give you some experience coding.

# Timeline Example

First you'll create your Hello World application using a simple timeline script to focus on the basic syntax. Then we'll show you how to use a document class to achieve the same result.

Create a new ActionScript 3.0 FLA file and type the following into a script in frame 1 of the file.

*Throughout this book, any time you want to create a timeline script, select a keyframe in which you want the script to reside, open the Window→Actions panel, and write your code.*

```
1  var txtFld:TextField = new TextField();
2  addChild(txtFld);
3
4  txtFld.text = "Hello World!";
```

When you're finished, test your movie choosing Control→Test Movie in Flash Professional. You should see the phrase, "Hello World!" in the upper-left corner of your published file.

**NOTE**

*Because you use variables to store information for later retrieval, naming them in a clear and meaningful way is important. Ideally, the name you choose should convey the purpose of the variable whenever practical. You have a lot of freedom when determining what to call your variables, but there are a few simple guidelines to follow. We'll discuss variables, including naming requirements and conventions, in Chapter 2.*

Line 1 of the script creates a new text field using the **TextField** class and places a reference to that field into the variable **txtFld**. Note the colon and reference to the **TextField** class immediately following the variable name. This is called a *data type* and makes sure that only a compatible type of data can be put into that variable—in this case, a **TextField** instance. If you try to put something else into this variable, an error is displayed, which can help you spot problems with your code. Using data typing will save you lots and lots of time, and we'll talk about it in greater detail in Chapter 2.

Line 2 adds the text field to the display list so it can be seen at runtime. Chapter 4 will explore this further, but put simply, the display list contains everything you can see in your file. For example, a text field is a visual asset, but a sound is not. For the user to see the text field, you must add it to the display list, but this does not apply to the sound. Finally, line 4 puts the phrase "Hello World!" into the text field. Default values for font, size, and color are used to display the text in the field. You'll learn how to manipulate those characteristics in Chapter 10.

**NOTE**

*When writing your own class files, you'll see that other classes referenced therein (such as **MovieClip**) must be imported so the compiler knows where to find them when publishing your SWF. There are no import statements in this script, however, because Flash Professional does not require that you import any class that is built into Flash player when coding in the timeline.*

*In short, when referencing a class in the timeline, if that class appears in a **flash** package—such as the **flash.text** package in which **TextField** resides—it doesn't have to be imported. On the other hand, classes in packages not starting with **flash**—such as class you write or a class used with a component like **fl.controls.Button**—must still be imported, even in the timeline.*

*For brevity, we will follow this guideline, but importing classes does no harm. In fact, as an interface improvement, Flash Professional CS5 will often automatically add import statements to your scripts when you use a class in the timeline—including those from the **flash** package. If you are using CS5, consider these automatic imports when comparing line numbers between your code and the book.*

## Document Class Example

To recreate this example using a document class, place the same code inside the constructor of the class—the only function included in this example. Take the following steps to create the files required:

First, create a new ActionScript 3.0 file and type or edit the following code. Save the file as *HelloWorld.as* and remember where you saved it.

```
1   package {
2
3       import flash.display.MovieClip;
4       import flash.text.TextField;
5
6       public class HelloWorld extends MovieClip {
7
8           public function HelloWorld() {
9               var txtFld:TextField = new TextField();
10              addChild(txtFld);
11
12              txtFld.text = "Hello World!";
13          }
14
15      }
16  }
```

Next, create a new ActionScript 3.0 FLA and save it in the same directory in which you saved your class. The name of the FLA is not critical. In the Properties panel in that FLA, add `HelloWorld` to the document class field.

Finally, test your movie. You should see the small phrase, "Hello World!" on the stage in the upper-left corner.

The class syntax here conforms to the syntax described in "The Document Class" section of this chapter, with two small exceptions. (If you want to complete this portion of the Hello World exercise, and haven't already read that section, please do so now.) The main difference is that the code in the class constructor differs because its purpose differs. Like the timeline code used to create the first Hello World example, this code uses a text field to display text, instead of the Output panel. The second difference results from this change. Because you are now using the `TextField` class to create a new text field, you must also import this class in line 4 so the compiler knows to include it.

## Success

Congratulations! If you completed one or both of these Hello World examples, you just created an ActionScript-only application. You can compare your work to the *hello world_timeline.fla* file and/or the files in the *hello_world_document_class* directory, both found in the accompanying source code at *http://www.LearningActionScript3.com*.

# What's Next?

Now that you know a little more about ActionScript 3.0 and the Flash Platform, it's time for a look at some of the fundamentals of the language. By reviewing version-independent concepts at the outset, we can focus on new syntax in subsequent chapters. If you have a lot of experience with ActionScript 1.0 or 2.0, you may wish to skim Chapter 2.

**In the next chapter**, we'll discuss:

- Basic concepts to bring you up to speed quickly, including using the **trace()** statement as a diagnostic tool to see immediate feedback from your scripts

- Using variables to store data (including arrays and custom objects that allow you to easily manage more than one value) and data typing to improve error reporting

- Structures such as conditionals for decision making and loops for simplifying repetitive tasks

- Functions that can isolate code into convenient blocks that will be executed only when instructed

- Ways to address Flash objects with ActionScript, including using absolute and relative paths, and the identifier **this**

## CHAPTER 2

# CORE LANGUAGE FUNDAMENTALS

ActionScript 3.0 is a complete rewrite of the language—so much so that ActionScript 3.0 doesn't even share the same Flash Player code base as prior versions of ActionScript. But that's all behind the scenes. The truth is that all versions of ActionScript to date have quite a bit in common. This is because ActionScript is based on a scripting language standard (called ECMA-262) that grew from the success of JavaScript, and ongoing versions of ActionScript are as backward-compatible as possible in an effort to support legacy projects.

Of course, each new update to ActionScript introduces new features and, because the decision was made to create ActionScript 3.0 from scratch, an opportunity presented itself to tidy up a few messy things that lingered from previous versions. Among these improvements are tightening up and requiring best practices that had been optional, and restructuring how events and graphical assets are handled (the Event Model and Display List, respectively). All of this progress, however, didn't steamroll over the standard upon which ActionScript is based, and most of the language fundamentals remain intact.

With the intention to focus on new ActionScript 3.0 features later on, we want to cover some of the more commonly used fundamentals up front. We do not intend to ignore these ideas throughout the rest of the book. However, we hope to explain them in sufficient detail here and spend less time on them as we proceed.

This book doesn't assume that you're well versed in any prior version of ActionScript, but its size and purpose requires that we assume a basic understanding of general scripting concepts. If you haven't already, please look over the Preface for a good idea of whom this book is for, as well as a few alternative references if you need more background information.

If you're already comfortable with ActionScript and are reading this text as an introduction to version 3.0, you may want to skim this chapter. In any case, you can refer to it as a point of reference when an underlying programming concept needs further explanation.

You can also look at the source files, which can be downloaded from the companion website at *http://www.LearningActionScript3.com*. As we have not yet discussed some of the essentials of ActionScript required to manipulate assets, we'll use a common testing and debugging technique to display text while reviewing each example.

In these pages, we'll look at the following topics:

- **Jump Right In.** Add core logic to your Hello World! example with a conditional, a loop, and random number generation.

- **Miscellaneous Basics.** This section includes a few essential items and techniques used throughout this book that don't necessarily warrant sections of their own.

- **Variables and Data Types.** Information must be stored in containers called variables if it is to be recalled for later use, and declaring which type of data will be stored in each variable can help Flash check for errors during development.

- **Operators.** ActionScript uses characters called *operators*, such as plus (+) and less than (<), that combine, compare, or modify values of objects, properties, or expressions.

- **Conditionals.** Often, when a decision must be made in the course of a script's execution, a conditional is used to evaluate an outcome. We'll look at the `if` and `switch` conditional statements.

- **Loops.** When you must execute an instruction multiple times, it is sometimes handy to do so within a loop structure. We'll look at the commonly used `for` and `while` loops and also at alternatives to explicit loops, including frame and timer events.

- **Arrays.** Although a basic variable can contain a single value only, it is frequently efficient, or even necessary, to store more than one value at a time. Imagine a shopping list, for example, with several items written on a single piece of paper rather than many individual paper slips. In ActionScript, you can use an array to store several values in a similar manner.

- **Functions.** Functions are essential to just about any programming language, and allow you to execute code only when you are ready to do so and reuse that code efficiently.

- **Custom Objects.** A custom object is essentially an advanced kind of variable that allows you to store lots of information as well as to consistently and easily retrieve it.

- **this and parent.** The **this** keyword is used as a shorthand reference, much like a self-referential pronoun, typically referring to the current object or scope of a script. Similarly, **parent** refers to an object immediately higher up in the ActionScript family tree, if you will. These ideas will become clearer in context, but understanding how these keywords work can save you much repetitive typing and reduce the need for more complex references in your scripts.

- **Absolute versus Relative Addresses.** ActionScript can reference objects using absolute paths, such as starting from the root timeline and including every object between it and your destination, or relative paths, such as going up to a parent and down to a sibling, no matter where you are.

Again, this chapter is not meant to act as the only reference to bring you up to speed if you have absolutely no experience with ActionScript. It will likely serve the bulk of your needs, but other basics—such as reviewing where scripts are created in Flash Professional or another application—require a text dedicated to the editor of your choice.

For the most part, this chapter—along with the context and supplemental explanations presented in subsequent chapters—should provide you with enough to understand the topics and to get the sample exercises working.

**NOTE**

*As the Preface mentioned, we recommend* Learning Flash CS4 Professional *by Rich Shupe (O'Reilly) for a starter book on the Flash interface and* Essential ActionScript 3.0 *by Colin Moock (O'Reilly) for a more complete ActionScript 3.0 resource. The latter is decidedly an intermediate to advanced reference but, at nearly three times the size of this volume, it is also substantially more comprehensive.*

## Jump Right In

Before we cover some of the fundamental structure and logic of ActionScript 3.0, let's write another script to help get the feel of the language and build a little confidence. Specifically, we'll build on the Hello World! exercise from Chapter 1 to introduce some of the material explained in detail in this chapter. We'll give you a brief explanation here and then expand on each relevant topic as you read on. Create a new ActionScript 3.0 FLA file and type the following code into frame 1 using the Actions panel. You can compare your work with the *hello_world_if_loop.fla* source file.

```
1   var str:String = "Hello World!";
2
3   if (Math.random() < 0.5) {
4       var txtFld:TextField = new TextField();
5       addChild(txtFld);
6       txtFld.text = str;
7   } else {
8       for (var i:int = 0; i < 3; i++) {
9           trace(str);
10      }
11  }
```

Line 1 creates a variable and tells the ActionScript compiler that it will contain a *String*, which is simply text. Telling the compiler what kind of data you intend to put into a variable will help it warn you if something attempts to manipulate the data in an incompatible way later on—such as trying to treat text as if it were a number.

The **if** statement in line 3 does what its name implies. It tests to see *if* something is true and, if so, executes the code within its braces. In this case, the braces are balanced on line 7, but the statement continues with an **else**. This means that if the test is false, the next set of instructions, balanced with the last brace on line 11 (lines 8 through 10), is executed. The test in this example, added to show how easy it can be to randomize an outcome in ActionScript, is whether a random number is less than 0.5. **Math.random()** will create a random number between 0 and 1.

If that number is less than 0.5, the first block of code (lines 4 through 6) will execute. This code creates a text field, makes it visible by adding it to the display list, and puts the contents of the variable into the field—just as you saw in Chapter 1. If the test fails, the second block (lines 8 through 10) will execute. This code is a loop that will run through three times, tracing the value of the string to the Window→Output panel.

We'll explain the syntax of this script in greater detail as this chapter progresses, but if you test your movie using Control→Test Movie, you'll see the result immediately. Based on the random number selection, you'll either see text on the stage or in your Output panel. You can test your movie repeatedly to see various outcomes. Now, let's dig in to some language fundamentals!

## Miscellaneous Basics

Some basic topics don't require a section devoted to their discussion, but should still be mentioned due to their use throughout the book. For example:

*Case sensitivity*

> ActionScript 3.0 is a case-sensitive language, so you have to be careful with capitalization. For example, the keyword **true** is all lowercase. If you type **TRUE** or **True**, in the same context, you will get an error.

*Use of the semicolon (;)*

> The official use of the semicolon in ActionScript is to execute more than one statement on a single line. This is rare in the average script, but we will look at this technique when discussing loops. The semicolon is also used to indicate the end of a line. This is not typically required, but it is recommended for clarity and to ease any possible transition into learning other languages in which the semicolon at the end of a line is required.

*Use of* **trace()**

> As a means of getting quick feedback in an example, or as a testing and debugging technique when writing scripts, **trace()** can be very helpful. This instruction places text into the Output panel of the Flash Professional interface. As such, this is an option that is available only when creating your file, and has no use in your distributed SWF. ActionScript 3.0's version of **trace()** supports tracing multiple items at once by separating them with commas. These items are then traced with a space separating the content.

Typing the following into a script, for example, will display "Learning ActionScript 3.0 Shupe Rosser" in Flash Professional's Output panel:

```
trace("Learning ActionScript 3.0", "Shupe", "Rosser");
```

# Variables and Data Types

Variables are best described as containers into which you place information for later recall. Imagine if you were unable to store any information for later use. You would not be able to compare values against previously described information (such as user names or passwords), your scripts would suffer performance lags due to unnecessarily repeating calculations, and you wouldn't be able to carry any prior experiences through to the next possible implementation of a task. In general, you wouldn't be able to do anything that required data that your application had to "remember."

Variables make all this and more possible. In the most basic terms, you need only create a variable with a unique name and then populate it with a value. However, for an ActionScript 3.0 compiler to know you are creating a variable, rather than mistyping some other ActionScript keyword, you must also declare the variable using the **var** keyword. A simple example is remembering the number 1 with the following:

```
var myVariable = 1;
```

Keep in mind that variable names:

- Must not contain spaces

- Should not already be a keyword or reserved word in the ActionScript language specification

- Should not start with a number

- Can include only alphanumeric characters along with the dollar sign ($) or underscore (_)

To help ensure that you are using variables (and other ActionScript language elements) appropriately, ActionScript can check your efforts and warn you when you go awry. Not every mistake can be detected, of course, but every little bit helps. For example, your ActionScript compiler can warn you if you try to perform a mathematical operation on a passage of text. Dividing the text "Flash" by 17, for example, doesn't make much sense, and it really helps when you are told of such errors.

To make this possible, you must use what is called *data typing* when you write your code. That is, you must tell the compiler that a variable will contain a specific type of data. To accomplish this, you must follow your variable name with a colon (:) and then the type of data that you want to store in that variable. For example, to data type the previous sample code write:

```
var horizontalLocation:Number = 4.5;
```

**NOTE**

*Throughout this book, code samples will be presented in full color. Most ActionScript editors, including Flash Professional, can apply colors, based on your preference, to specific ActionScript structures. As the average reader of this book is likely to use Flash Professional, we have adopted the default color scheme used by that application. Other editors may use different colors, but you will rapidly adjust to any such differences. In this context, key ActionScript terms are in blue, strings (or text values) are in green, comments are in gray, and more basic elements, (such as parentheses, semicolons, and the like) are in black. Anything that is not already predefined in ActionScript, such as names of variables that we create, will also be in black.*

This insures that any type of number, be it positive or negative, whole number or decimal value, is the only type of data that can ever be stored in **horizontalLocation**. (In just a few moments, we'll show you what would happen if you tried to put something other than a number into this variable.)

ActionScript supports several basic data types including, but not limited to, those listed in Table 2-1.

*Table 2-1. Variable types*

| Data type | Example | Description |
| --- | --- | --- |
| Number | `4.5` | Any number, including floating-point values (decimals) |
| int | `-5` | Any integer or whole number |
| uint | `1` | Unsigned integer or any nonnegative whole number |
| String | `"hello"` | Text or a string of characters |
| Boolean | `true` | Values true or false |
| Object | `{name:"Claire", age:2}` | The basic structure of every ActionScript entity, typically used to store multiple name-value pairs of data |

In addition to these basic data types, it's very common to store variable references to ActionScript objects, such as a movie clip, text field, or sound, and to use type checking to make sure your code contains fewer errors. For example, the following instruction places a **MovieClip** into the variable **logo**. The data type insures that the compiler will warn you if you do anything with this variable that is not compatible with the **MovieClip** type.

```
var logo:MovieClip = new MovieClip();
```

Let's revisit our **horizontalLocation** variable and see what happens if we try to perform an operation on it that is incompatible with the **Number** data type. Here's an example of trying to reassign the variable to a **String**:

```
horizontalLocation = "ActionScript";
```

Having told the compiler to expect only numbers in this variable, this will yield the following error:

```
1067: Implicit coercion of a value of type String to an unrelated type
    Number.
```

This means your code is trying to change a value of type **Number** to a value of type **String**, without first explicitly telling the compiler you want to do so. The compiler warns you about this because you may not have intended to change the data type and it wants a clearer instruction before allowing the switch. While this is usually a huge benefit, you may sometimes want a type change to occur. In these cases, you just need to be more direct by *casting* the data.

# Casting

Casting is the overt act of telling the compiler to treat a value of one data type as if it's a value of another data type. When discussing type conversion previously, we showed that trying to assign a **String** to a variable with a **Number** data type would cause an error. This is pretty clear when you're trying to overwrite a variable called `horizontalLocation`, which contains a value of 1, with a new value of "ActionScript."

But what if you want to assign the text "300" to that variable? For example, what if you want to create a horizontal location value from something a user typed into a text field? Although text entered into a text field originates as having a data type of **String**, you need to be able to tell the compiler to treat that information as having a data type of **Number**.

There are two ways to cast data, both shown here, and both with pros and cons.

```
horizontalLocation = Number("300");
horizontalLocation = "300" as Number;
```

The first example, using the format *type(data)*, is simple and, best of all, will generate an error if you try to cast to an incompatible data type. On the other hand, it could be confusing because it resembles other ActionScript syntax that we'll discuss a bit later (such as the name of a function or instantiation of a class). There are also isolated cases where this approach won't work because it conflicts with syntax reserved for another purpose. For example, later in this chapter we'll discuss *arrays* (objects designed to contain multiple values), and you'll learn that the **Array()** syntax creates a new array. As such, this form can't be used to cast data to an array.

The second example, using the format *data as type* will work where the prior syntax fails, but it won't generate an error if the casting fails. Instead, it will simply return **null** as the resulting value.

You can check whether an object is of a certain type using the **is** operator.

```
var userName:String = "Aubrey";
trace(userName is String);
//traces true to the Output panel
```

> **NOTE**
>
> *Our personal preference is to use the type(data) form of casting because we want to take advantage of the error reporting to correct any problems. If a resulting error points to a conflict with this format, we then switch to data as type for specific needs.*

# Strict Mode

Once you start data typing your variables, you can be warned of related errors when your application runs or, better yet, when you compile your file—such as when testing your movie in Flash Professional. Whether you check for errors at runtime or when compiling your code is determined by your ActionScript compiler's *Strict Mode* setting.

In Flash Professional, the Strict Mode setting is on by default and is a per-file preference, rather than an application preference. As such, it's found in the Publish Settings of each file (File→Publish Settings). Flash Professional CS5 users will find shortcuts to this destination in the File menu (File→ActionScript Settings) and in the Publish section of the Properties panel. In the Flash option at the top of the Publish Settings dialog is a pull-down menu that lets you choose which version of ActionScript to use in each file. Next to that menu is a Settings button, as seen in Figure 2-1. Clicking this button will reveal the Strict Mode option in the Advanced ActionScript 3.0 Settings dialog, as seen in Figure 2-2.

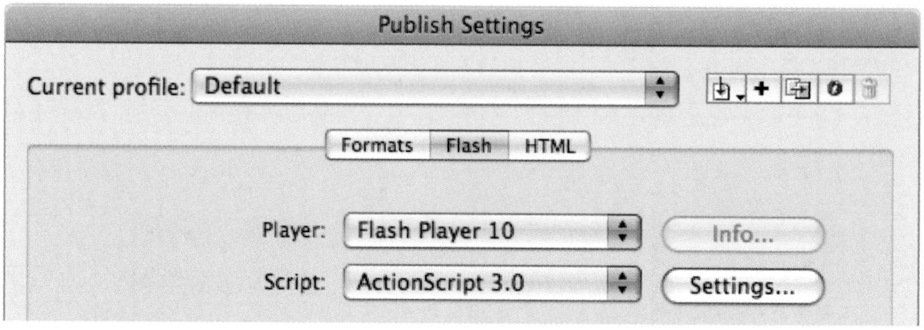

*Figure 2-1. A detail from the Flash section of the Publish Settings dialog*

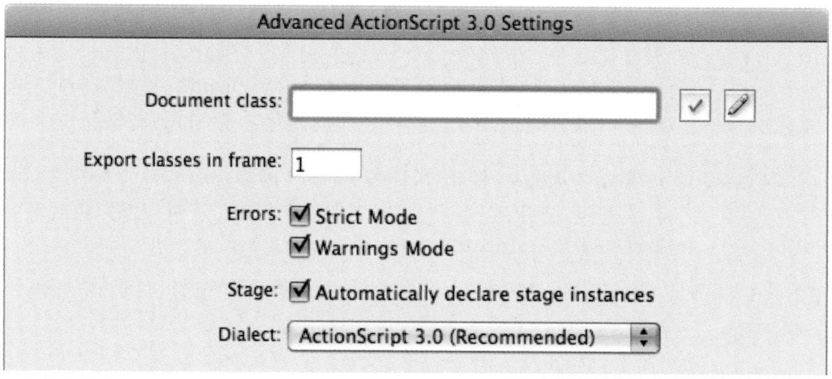

*Figure 2-2. A detail from the Advanced ActionScript 3.0 Settings dialog, where the Strict Mode preference is found*

If Strict Mode is enabled, you will be notified of errors when you compile your file as well as when your SWF is running. If you disable Strict Mode, you will rely solely on runtime error warnings to catch mistakes. We recommend keeping Strict Mode enabled because the compiler will not only help you catch problems as you code, but will even try to tell you where the problem is in your scripts.

# Operators

Operators are characters that dictate how to combine, compare, or modify values of objects, properties, or expressions. Table 2-2 lists most of ActionScript 3.0's operators, focusing on the operators you're likely to use when working with this book's examples.

*Table 2-2. A partial list of ActionScript 3.0 operators*

| Arithmetic | | |
|---|---|---|
| + | addition | Adds numeric expressions. |
| - | subtraction | Negates or subtracts numeric expressions. |
| * | multiplication | Multiplies two numeric expressions. |
| / | division | Divides two numeric expressions. |
| ++ | increment (1) | Adds 1 to a numeric expression. |
| -- | decrement (1) | Subtracts 1 from a numeric expression. |
| % | modulo (2) | Calculates remainder of *expression1* divided by *expression2*. |
| **Assignment** | | |
| = | assignment | Assigns value at right of operator to variable, array element, or object property at left of operator. |
| **Arithmetic compound assignment** | | |
| += | addition assignment (3) | Assigns expression1 the value of *expression1* + *expression2*. |
| -= | subtraction assignment | Assigns expression1 the value of *expression1* – *expression2*. |
| *= | multiplication assignment | Assigns expression1 the value of *expression1* * *expression2*. |
| /= | division assignment | Assigns expression1 the value of *expression1* / *expression2*. |
| %= | modulo assignment | Assigns expression1 the value of *expression1* % *expression2*. |
| **Comparison** | | |
| == | equality (4) | Tests two expressions for equality. |
| != | inequality | Tests for the exact opposite of the equality (==) operator. |
| > | greater than | Compares two expressions and determines whether *expression1* is greater than *expression2*; if so, the result is true. |
| >= | greater than or equal to | Compares two expressions and determines whether *expression1* is greater than or equal to *expression2*; if so, the result is true. |
| < | less than | Compares two expressions and determines whether *expression1* is less than *expression2*; if so, the result is true. |
| <= | less than or equal to | Compares two expressions and determines whether *expression1* is less than or equal to *expression2*; if it is, the result is true. |
| **Logical** | | |
| && | AND (4) | Tests two expressions to see if both are true. |
| \|\| | OR | Tests two expressions to see if either is true. |
| ! | NOT | Inverts the Boolean value (truth) of a variable or expression. |

*Table 2-2. A partial list of ActionScript 3.0 operators*

| Type | | |
|------|------|------|
| **as** | as | Casts data to left of operator as data type to right of operator. |
| **is** | is (5) | Evaluates whether an object is compatible with a specific data type. |
| **String** | | |
| + | concatenation (6) | Concatenates (combines) strings. |
| += | concatenation assignment | Concatenates value to right of operator. Assigns *string1* the value of *string1 + string2*. |

You're probably familiar with many of ActionScript 3.0's arithmetic, assignment, and comparison operators. Other operators may be new to you, and many will be explained and used throughout the coming chapters. Here are some quick notes referred to in Table 2-2 covering some of the operators you may be less familiar with:

1. Increment and decrement operators add 1 to or subtract 1 from an expression. For example, **i++** is the same as saying **i = i + 1**. They come in postfix (**i++**) and prefix (**++i**) flavors. The difference between them is that the postfix version alters the value of the variable after a related expression is evaluated, and the prefix version alters the value before the expression is evaluated. This can be seen by tracing both operators at work:

   ```
   var i:int = 0;
   trace(i++);
   //0
   trace(i);
   //1

   var j:int = 0;
   trace(++j);
   //1
   trace(j);
   //1
   ```

   In the first example, the postfix increment operator is used within a **trace()** statement. Because the postfix flavor of the operator increments after the statement is executed, the first trace is 0 and the second is 1. The prefix flavor of the operator increments before the **trace()** statement is executed, so both traces show the value of 1.

2. Modulo calculates the remainder of a division, not how many times the numerator goes into the denominator. In other words, **4 % 2** is 0 because 2 goes into 4 two times, and leaves no remainder. However, **5 % 2** is 1 because 2 goes into 5 two times and leaves a remainder of 1.

3. Compound assignment operators work a bit like increment and decrement operators, but they are not restricted to altering an expression by a value of 1. Instead, they alter the original based on whatever is to the right of the equal sign. For example, `10 += 5` is 15 and is equivalent to saying `10 = 10 + 5`.

4. Note the difference between the assignment operator (=, a single equal sign) and the comparison equality operator (==, a double equal sign). The first assigns a value to an expression; the second tests whether two values are equal. Both comparison and logical operators are discussed later in the "Conditionals" section of this chapter.

5. The `as` and `is` operators are discussed earlier in the "Casting" section of this chapter.

6. When used in the context of strings, the plus symbol (+) is a concatenation operator, which joins two strings together. The expression `"Sally" + "Claire"` evaluates to "SallyClaire".

**NOTE**

*Additional ActionScript 3.0 operators can be found at* http://www.adobe.com/livedocs/flash/9.0/ActionScriptLangRefV3/operators.html.

## Arithmetic Operator Precedence

Arithmetic and arithmetic compound assignments are evaluated in order of precedence. Multiplication, division, and modulo are executed first, and addition and subtraction are executed second. For example, 1 + 2 / 3 + 4 is equivalent to five and two-thirds because the division is evaluated before the addition.

Parentheses can alter the order of precedence by evaluating their contents first. Changing the previous expression to (1 + 2) / (3 + 4) is equivalent to three-sevenths because the addition is evaluated before the division.

## Conditionals

You will often need to make a decision in your script, choosing to do one thing under one circumstance and another thing under a different circumstance. These situations are usually handled by *conditionals*. Put simply, a test asks whether a condition is met. If the condition is met, the test evaluates to **true** and specific code is executed accordingly. If the condition is not met, either no further action is taken or an alternate set of code is executed. We'll now take a look at the **if** and **switch** conditional structures.

You can try this code for yourself, or look at the *conditionals.fla* source file from the chapter archive found in the Downloads section of the companion website. This section provides multiple examples of conditionals to teach the logic behind their use. For an additional practical example, revisit the opening of this chapter, which uses a conditional to perform one of two tasks based on a random number value.

# if

The most common form of the conditional is the **if** statement. The statement's basic structure is the **if** keyword, followed by parentheses in which the conditional test resides, and braces that contain the code that is executed when the statement evaluates to true. The first three lines in the following example create and populate a set of variables. These variables will be used for this and subsequent examples in this section, but will not be repeated.

```
var num:Number = 1;
var str:String = "hello";
var bool:Boolean = false;

if (num == 1) {
    trace("num equals 1");
}
```

**NOTE**

*The test in this example uses a double equal sign. This is a comparison operator that asks, "Is this equal to?" This distinction is very important because the accidental use of a single equal sign will cause unexpected results. A single equal sign is an assignment operator and assigns the value on the right side of the equation to the object on the left side of the equation. Because this assignment naturally occurs when an assignment operator is used, the test will always evaluate to true.*

To evaluate the truth of the test inside the parentheses, conditionals often make use of *comparison* and *logical operators*. A comparison operator compares two values, such as equals (==), less than (<), and greater than or equal to (>=), to name a few. See Table 2-2 for more examples of operators.

Logical operators allow you to build complex tests by combining multiple conditional expressions. The AND (&&), and OR (||) operators allow you to combine two or more tests into one. They allow you to ask if "this *and* that" are true, if "this *or* that" is true. The NOT (!) operator will negate the results of a test, or ask if "this" is *not* true. Table 2-3 is a Boolean truth table that shows several possible outcomes of conditional tests. The first two columns represent the initial outcome of two separate conditional tests, *a* and *b*. Using our given variables, these columns might represent the questions, "is **num** equal to 1?" and "is **str** equal to 'hello'?" The rows show various permutations of true and false results of these tests. Column 3 shows the effect of the NOT operator, negating the results for test *b*. Columns 4 and 5 show the results of using the AND and OR operators on the outcomes in each row.

*Table 2-3. A Boolean truth table*

| a | b | !b | a && b | a \|\| b |
|---|---|----|--------|---------|
| true | true | false | true | true |
| true | false | true | false | true |
| false | true | false | false | true |
| false | false | true | false | false |

Looking at some ActionScript syntax, the following snippet uses the AND operator and will evaluate to false because only one of the conditions is true. When using the AND operator, *both* conditions must be true. As a result, nothing would appear in the Output panel.

```
if (num == 1 && str == "goodbye") {
    trace("both tests are true");
}
```

In the next example, the test will evaluate to true, because *one* of the two conditions (the first) is true. As a result, "one test is true" will be traced.

```
if (num == 1 || str == "goodbye") {
    trace("one test is true");
}
```

Finally, the following would also evaluate to true, because the NOT operator correctly determines that **bool** is not true. (Remember, that every **if** statement, at its core, is testing for truth.)

```
if (!bool) {
    trace("bool is not true");
}
```

The logical NOT operator should not be confused with the != comparison operator. The NOT operator reverses the truth of a test (returning false where true was expected, or true instead of false); the != operator is the reverse of the == operator, and tests whether something is "not equal to" a value. The following will evaluate to false because **num** does equal 1, and nothing will be traced.

```
if (num != 1) {
    trace("num does not equal 1");
}
```

Additional power can be added to the **if** statement by adding an unconditional alternative. That is, an alternative set of code is executed any time the main test fails, without a need for any additional evaluation. This is accomplished by adding an **else** to the **if** block. With the following new code added to the previous example, the last trace will occur:

```
if (num != 1) {
    trace("num does not equal 1");
} else {
    trace("num equals 1");
}
```

Finally, the statement can be even more flexible by adding a conditional alternative (or an additional test) to the structure. To add another test, you must add an **else if** section to your conditional. In this example, the second trace will occur:

```
if (num == 2) {
    trace("num does not equal 1");
} else if (num == 1) {
    trace("num equals 1");
}
```

The **if** statement requires one **if**, only one optional **else** can be used, and any number of optional **else if** tests can be added. In all cases, however, only *one result* can come from the structure.

Consider the following example, in which all three results could potentially execute—the first two because they are true, and the last because it is an unconditional alternative:

```
if (num == 1) {
    trace("num equals 1");
} else if (str == "hello") {
    trace("str equals 'hello'");
} else {
    trace("other");
}
```

In this case, only "num equals 1" (the first option) would appear in the Output panel. Because only one result is possible from an **if** statement, the first time a test evaluates to true, the conditional is exited and the script continues. If you need more than one execution to occur when using **if** statements, you need to use two or more conditionals. The following structure is based on the prior example in which all tests evaluate to true. However, because the code has been broken into *two separate* **if** statements, the first and second traces will occur.

```
if (num == 1) {
    trace("num equals 1");
}
if (str == "hello") {
    trace("str equals 'hello'");
} else {
    trace("other");
}
```

## Logical Operator Precedence

When more than one logical operator is used, they are evaluated in a particular order. NOT is evaluated first, then AND, and finally OR. For example, considering the expression *a* **&&** *b* **||** *c*, the expression would evaluate as, "are both *a* and *b* true?" and then "is either the outcome of the *a* **&&** *b* test or *c* true?" Because of operator precedence, the following expression would evaluate the same way: *c* **||** *a* **&&** *b*. That is, the operators are not evaluated from left to right. In this last example, *a* **&&** *b* would still be evaluated first, and the outcome of that test would be compared with *c*.

It's possible to build more complex conditional tests by overriding this precedence with parentheses. Table 2-4 contains all the possible outcomes of three tests in the first three columns. Column 4 checks the outcome of two tests, using operator precedence. Column 5 tests the outcome of the same tests, but gives the OR test precedence using parentheses.

*Table 2-4.* Logical operator precedence truth table

| a | b | c | a && b \|\| c | a && (b \|\| c) |
|---|---|---|---|---|
| true | true | true | true | true |
| true | true | false | true | true |
| true | false | true | true | true |
| true | false | false | false | false |
| false | true | true | true | false |
| false | true | false | false | false |
| false | false | true | true | false |
| false | false | false | false | false |

# switch

An **if** statement can be as simple or as complex as you need. Long **if** structures can be difficult to read, however, and are sometimes better expressed using the **switch** statement. In addition, **switch** has a unique feature that lets you control which results are executed—even when a test evaluates to false—and can be a simpler way to execute multiple results.

Imagine an **if** statement asking *if* a variable is 1, *else if* it's 2, *else if* it's 3, *else if* it's 4, and so on. A test like that quickly becomes difficult to read, so use **switch** instead:

```
switch (num) {
    case 1 :
        trace("one");
        break;
    case 2 :
        trace("two");
        break;
    case 3 :
        trace("three");
        break;
    default :
        trace("other");
        break;
}
```

A **switch** statement begins with an expression in the parentheses of its first line. Because this is an expression, rather than a test, it does not have to evaluate to true. For example, the contents of the parentheses could be 5 + 5. Possible *results* of the expression are included in as many **case** statements as necessary. If the result of the expression matches the contents of a particular case statement, the instructions following the colon of that case are executed. Each **break** statement prevents any subsequent instructions from executing once a test is successful. We'll talk more about **break** in just a moment.

NOTE

*If you need to evaluate the truth of more than one expression in a switch structure, you can restructure it by swapping the result and expression between* **switch** *and* **case**. *That is, you can place a single result, true, in the* **switch** *statement, and each expression in the* **case** *statements. The following example can be found in the* switch_2. fla *source file.*

```
switch (true) {
    case num == 1 :
        trace("one");
        break;
    case str == "hello" :
        trace("two");
        break;
    case bool :
        trace("three");
        break;
}
```

Meanwhile, the example code asks: is it the case that **num** equals 1 is true? Is it the case that **num** equals 2 is true? This continues with all remaining case statements. The equivalent of an unconditional alternative (or **else**, in an **if** statement) is **default**. In other words, this is the default response in the event that no case evaluations are true.

The result of the example is that the word "one" appears in the Output panel because **num** is equal to 1 and a **break** follows the **trace()** statement.

Now back to the **break** feature. Use of **break** is *optional* and, when you don't use **break**, the next instructions will execute *regardless* of the outcome of the case evaluation. That is, the next instruction will execute even if the prior case already evaluated to true and even if the following case evaluates to false.

For example, note the absence of **break** in the first case of the following code. This structure will trace both "one" and "two" to the Output panel, even though the first evaluation is true, and even though **num** does not equal 2.

```
switch (num) {
    case 1 :
        trace("one");
    case 2 :
        trace("two");
        break;
}
```

This **break** feature does not exist with the **if** statement and, if used with care, makes **switch** an efficient alternative to a more complex series of multiple **if** statements. **Switch** statements must have one **switch** and one **case**, an optional unconditional alternative in the form of **default**, and an optional **break** for each **case** and **default**. The last **break** is not needed, but may be preferred for consistency.

## Loops

It is quite common to execute many repetitive instructions in your scripts. However, including them line by line, one copy after another, is inefficient as well as difficult to edit and maintain. Wrapping repetitive tasks in an efficient structure is the role of *loops*. A programming loop is probably just what you think it is: it goes through the structure and then loops back to the start and does it again until its task is concluded. There are a few kinds of loops, and the type you choose to use can help determine how many times your instructions are executed. The examples in this section can be found in the *loops. fla* file, which is downloadable from the companion website. This section explains two kinds of loops: **for** and **while**. The first **for** loop example will look familiar from the opening of this chapter.

# for Loop

The **for** loop executes its contents a finite number of times of your choosing. For example, you may wish to create a grid of 25 movie clips or check to see which of 5 radio buttons has been selected. The first example here uses a **for** loop to trace content to the Output panel three times.

To loop through a process, as in the case of our three traces, you must first start with an initial value, such as 0, so you know you have not yet traced anything to the Output panel. The next step is to test to see whether you have exceeded the limit you set (in this case, 3). The first time through the loop, 0 does not exceed the prescribed limit. The next step is to trace the content, and the final step is to increment your initial value, registering that you've traced the desired content once. The process then starts over until, ultimately, you exceed the limit of the loop. The syntax for a basic **for** loop is as follows:

```
for (var i:int = 0; i < 3; i++) {
    trace("hello");
}
```

The first thing you may notice is the declaration and typing of the counter, **i**. This is a common technique because the **i** variable is often used only for counting and is therefore created on the spot and not used again. If you have already declared and typed the counter previously, that step can be omitted. (This is true in the next example, as these code passages are in the same source file.)

Next is the loop test. The counter variable must have a value that is less than the limit, in this case 3, for the loop to execute. Finally, the double plus sign (**++**) is the *increment operator* and is equivalent to **i = i + 1**, or adding 1 to the current value of **i**.

The result is three occurrences of the word "hello" in the Output panel. The first time through the loop the value of **i** is 0, that value is less than 3, a trace occurs, and **i** is incremented by 1. The second time through the loop, **i** is 1, that value is less than 3, a trace occurs, and **i** is again incremented. This continues until the value of **i** fails the loop test. The third time through the loop **i** is incremented to a value of 2. The fourth time through, the loop test fails because 3 is not less than 3, and the loop concludes.

If desired, you also can count down by reversing the values in the test, starting with a maximum initial value, and then decrementing the counter. In other words, instead of starting with 0 start with 3, then test to be sure **i** is greater than 0, and decrement by subtracting 1 each time through the loop using the decrement operator (**--**) (which is equivalent to **i = i - 1**). Here's the code:

```
for (i = 3; i > 0; i--) {
    trace("hello");
}
```

**NOTE**

*As stated earlier, the variable **i** is intentionally not declared (using the **var** keyword) in this loop because it is in the same source file as a loop that previously declared **i**. Once a variable has been declared in a scope, it need not be declared again. If it is declared a second time, a duplicate variable declaration warning will be displayed.*

## while Loop

The other kind of loop that you are likely to use is a `while` loop. Instead of executing its contents a finite number of times, a `while` loop executes as long as something remains true. As an example, consider a very simple case of choosing a random number.

To create a random number, use the syntax `Math.random()`. Just like the `MovieClip` class discussed in Chapter 1, `Math` is a class, or collection of code. It contains instructions for performing mathematical tasks, including picking a random number. This method always generates a decimal number greater than or equal to 0 and less than 1. So, let's say you wanted to choose a random number greater than or equal to 0.5. Because of the random factor in this exercise, you may end up with the wrong choice several times in a row. To be sure you get a qualifying number, you can use this code:

```
var num:Number = Math.random();
while (num < 0.5) {
    trace(num, "is less than 0.5");
    num = Math.random();
}
trace("final num:", num);
```

Starting with a default value of 0, `num` will be less than 0.5 the first time into the loop, so the contents of the loop are executed. A random number is then put into the `num` variable and, the structure loops back to test the new value. The loop will continue to execute as long as the random numbers chosen are less than 0.5. When that test fails, because a number chosen is greater than or equal to 0.5 (and, although not material to the test, less than 1 by restrictions of the `Math.random()` method) the loop concludes.

## A Loop Caveat

It's very important to understand that loop structures, although compact and convenient, are not always the best method to use to achieve a repetitive outcome. This is because loops are very processor-intensive. Once a loop begins its process, nothing else will execute until the loop has been exited. For this reason, you may be wise to avoid `for` and `while` loops when you require interim visual updates.

In other words, when a `for` or `while` loop serves as an initialization for a process that is updated only upon the loop's completion (such as creating a grid of 25 movie clips), you are less likely to have a problem. The script enters the loop, 25 clips are created, the loop is completed, a frame update can then occur, and you see all 25 clips.

If you want each of the 25 clips to appear one by one, however, those interim visual updates cannot occur while the processor is consumed by the `for` or `while` loop. In this situation, another type of looping—one that does not interfere with the normal playhead updates—is desirable. Two such loops, `frame` and `timer` loops, are commonly used for this purpose. A `frame` loop is not a defined ActionScript structure, but rather simply a repeating `frame` event, executing an instruction each time the playhead is updated. A `timer` loop is similar, repeating a timer event, but is not tied to the frame tempo. Instead, an independent timer triggers a `timer` event at a set frequency.

In both cases, the events occur in concert with any other events in the ordinary functioning of the file, so visual updates, as one example, can continue to occur. Both `frame` and `timer` loops will be explained, complete with examples, in Chapter 3. The first exercise in that chapter is a great example of using a frame event as an alternative to a loop.

# Arrays

Basic variables can contain only one value. If you set a variable to 1 and then set that same variable to 2 in the following line of code, the value would be reassigned, and the value of the variable would be 2.

However, there are times when you need one variable to contain more than one value. Think of a hypothetical set of groceries, including 50 items. The standard variable approach to this problem would be to define 50 variables and populate each with a grocery item. That is the equivalent of 50 pieces of paper, each with one grocery item written on its face. This is unwieldy and can be created only at authoring time—at which point the process is fixed— and you'd have to recall and manage all variable names every time you wanted to access the grocery items.

In real life, you handle the problem by writing a list of 50 grocery items on one piece of paper. You can add to the list while at the store and cross each item off once it is acquired, and you only have to manage one piece of paper. In ActionScript, you handle the problem by creating an *array*, the code equivalent of that sheet of paper.

Creating an array is quite easy. Like many objects in ActionScript 3.0, you can create an array using the `new` keyword—either prepopulating the array with a comma-separated list of items, or as an empty array that you intend to populate at runtime. You can also create an array by wrapping your list of items in brackets. Creating an empty array with brackets requires only an empty set of brackets. Both techniques are illustrated here:

```
var needToBuy:Array = new Array("eggs", "flour", "milk");
var impulseItems:Array = new Array();

var needToBuy2:Array = ["eggs", "flour", "milk"];
var impulseItems2:Array = [];
```

An array of comma-separated values is called a *linear array* because it contains a series of items in linear order. Whether the array is prepopulated or empty, you can add to, or remove from, the array at runtime. For example, you can add a value to an array using the `push()` method, which pushes the value into the array at the end.

**NOTE**

*A* method *is an action performed by an object—in this case adding something to an array—and will be discussed in detail in the next chapter.*

The **push()** method is a handy way to add something to an array because it also tells you how long the new array is, and you can choose to use that information or ignore it. In the following example, the second line of code uses **push()** without any regard for the feedback the method returns. All that matters is adding the item to the end of the array. The second time **push()** is used, however, the entire statement is placed inside a **trace()**. As a result, when **push()** returns a value of 2 to indicate that there are now two items in the array, that value will be traced. Finally, the resulting array is displayed in the last executed instruction.

```
var cake:Array = new Array();
cake.push("sugar");
trace(cake);
// sugar appears in the Output panel
trace(cake.push("vanilla"));
// 2 appears in the Output panel
trace(cake);
// sugar,vanilla appears in the Output panel
```

You can remove an item from the end of an array in a similar manner, using the **pop()** method. This method also returns a value that you may wish to use but, instead of returning the new length of the array, it returns the item removed from the array.

The next code passage continues the previous example, in which the last value of **cake** was "sugar, vanilla". The first line removes the last item in the array and, because it does so from within the **trace()** statement, the removed item appears in the Output panel. Finally, the entire array is then traced.

```
trace(cake.pop());
// vanilla appears in the Output panel
trace(cake);
// the final one-item array, sugar, is traced
```

You can add values to or retrieve values from locations within the array by using brackets and including the *index*, or position, of the array item you need. To do so, you must understand that ActionScript uses what are called *zero-based* arrays. This means that the first value is at position 0, the second is at position 1, the next at position 2, and so on. As an example, to retrieve the existing third value from an array, you must request the item at index 2:

```
var newArray:Array = ["chocolate", "lemon", "red velvet"];
trace(newArray[2]);
//"red velvet" appears in the Output panel
```

To determine the number of items in an array, use the **length** property:

```
trace(newArray.length);
//"3" appears in the Output panel
```

You can also create arrays inside arrays. These are typically called *multi-dimensional arrays* and are used to create multiple levels of data. A typical database is a multidimensional array because it is a list of records (such as users), each of which contains fields (such as name, phone, email). If such

**NOTE**

We'll further discuss the idea of ActionScript returning values upon receiving instructions when we get to functions later in this chapter.

**NOTE**

Methods (like **push()** and **pop()**) are added to the end of objects (the **cake** variable) with a dot separating the two words. This is the syntax used to navigate the ActionScript object model, and is sometimes referred to as *dot syntax* or *dot notation*. This describes a parent-child relationship among the objects.

Consider an example where you may wish to check the width of a movie clip that is inside another movie clip. The first, or most senior item in this familial chain is the container movie clip, or parent. Let's call it **mc1**. A reference to the child clip nested inside, called **mc2** in this example, follows, and the width property concludes the statement:

```
mc1.mc2.width;
```

This dot syntax will be used in virtually every example for the rest of the book, and it will soon become quite easy to understand just what each object references along the way.

**NOTE**

A *property* describes an aspect of an object—in this case how long the array is, or how many items it contains—and will be discussed in detail in the next chapter.

a database had three records, it would be equivalent to one array of three arrays.

Creating this arrangement is as simple as using an inner array as a value for one of the indices of the outer array. You can do this at the outset, or add it using **push()**—both of which are demonstrated here:

```
var mdArray1:Array = ["a", "b", ["c", "d"]];
var mdArray2:Array = ["e", "f"];
mdArray2.push(["g", "h"]);
```

To access values in a multidimensional array, you must use multiple brackets to go into the nested arrays. For instance, continuing the prior example to retrieve the first item in the array **mdArray1**, you need only the standard single bracket syntax:

```
trace(mdArray1[0]);
//traces "a" to the Output panel
```

However, to access the values in the nested array requires two components. First, you must identify the nested array as the third item of **mdArray1** (at index 2). Then you must reference the item within that nested array with another pair of brackets. So, to retrieve "c", which is the first item in the nested array, the syntax is as follows:

```
trace(mdArray1[2][0]);
//traces "c" to the Output panel
```

This makes sense, if you think about it in steps, because not only is **mdArray1** an array requiring bracket syntax to retrieve an item therein, but **mdArray1[2]** is also an array requiring its own brackets to retrieve an item.

**NOTE**

*There is another kind of array, called an* associative array, *which is often used interchangeably with custom objects. We'll discuss both in the "Custom Objects" section later in this chapter.*

## Vectors

*Vectors* (not to be confused with the precise lines, curves, and shapes created by such object-drawing tools as Adobe Illustrator) are *typed* arrays. Arrays like those in the previous section can contain data of any type. The following example array includes a **String**, **Number**, and **Boolean**:

```
var arr:Array = new Array();
arr[0] = "avocado";
arr[0] = 2;
arr[0] = true;
```

A vector, however, can contain data of only one type, which is determined at the time the vector was created. Although vector syntax may look a little odd at first, its principle uniqueness is the addition of the data type to the vector creation process. The following example vector contains only integers.

```
var vec:Vector.<int> = new Vector.<int>();
vec[0] = 1;
vec[0] = 2;
vec[0] = 3;
```

If you try to add an incompatible data type to a vector, you will receive a type coercion error. The following example tries to add a **String** to the integer vector from the previous snippet:

```
vec[3] = "guacamole"
//Error 1067: Implicit coercion of a value of type String
//            to an unrelated type int.
```

From a syntax and use perspective, vectors function the same way arrays do. Vector syntax is typically identical to array syntax. However, because they can contain only one data type, they support more restrictive error checking. When working with vectors, you can be certain that any data you retrieve will be the correct data type for your needs, and any data you add will be checked to be sure it conforms to the desired type. In addition, vectors can be significantly faster than arrays—particularly with large data sets.

## Functions

Functions are an indispensable part of programming in that they wrap code into blocks that can be executed only when needed. They also allow code blocks to be reused and edited efficiently, without having to copy, paste, and edit repeatedly. Without functions, all code would be executed in a linear progression from start to finish, and edits would require changes to every single occurrence of any repeated code. We'll look at functions in three parts: minimal structure, use of arguments, and returning values. Figure 2-3 identifies examples of each of the parts of a function that we'll discuss.

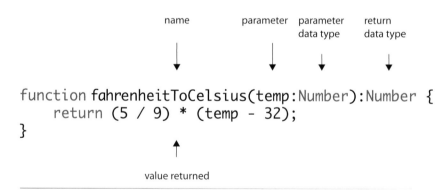

*Figure 2-3. Parts of a function*

Creating a basic function requires little more than surrounding the code you wish to trigger at will with a simple syntax that allows you to give the block of code a name. Triggering that function later requires only that you call the function by name.

> **NOTE**
>
> *One thing to remember about data type checking when populating vectors is that content added with the* **push()** *method will be type checked at runtime. For this reason, you should use bracket syntax when adding elements to a vector, as in the example in this section, to receive the benefits of compile-time error checking.*

The following syntax shows a function that traces a string to the Output panel. The function is first defined and then, to illustrate the process, immediately called. (In a real-world scenario, the function is usually called at some other time or from some other place, such as when the user clicks a button with the mouse.) The actual output is depicted in the comment that follows the function call, without any added quotation marks. This code can be found in the *functions_simple.fla* source file.

```
function showMsg() {
    trace("hello");
}
showMsg();
//hello
```

If reusing code and executing code only when needed were the only advantages of functions, you'd already have a useful enhancement to the linear execution of ActionScript, because it would allow you to group your code into subroutines that could be triggered at any time and in any order. However, you can do much more with functions to gain even greater power.

## Local Variables

For example, you can define a variable that exists only inside a function. These are called *local variables* because they are local to the function. The syntax to declare and use the variable is the same; to make it local, simply declare the variable inside the function. These variants on the prior example can be found in the *functions_local_var.fla* source file.

```
function showMsg() {
    var msg:String = "hello";
    trace(msg);
}
showMsg();
//hello
```

If you tried to trace the value of **msg** at the end of this script, you would receive an error because ActionScript thinks it doesn't exist outside the function. The following syntax is what the same example might look like using a variable that is available to the entire script, not just a single function:

```
var msg2:String = "hello";
function showMsg2() {
    trace(msg2);
}
showMsg2();
//hello
```

Declaring **msg2** outside the function means it is not local to **showMsg2()**. In this case, tracing **msg2** at the end of the script would successfully show "hello" in the Output panel of Flash Professional.

**NOTE**

*Commenting your code to explain as much about what it does as is practical can help you greatly if you return to a project after a prolonged absence. It's also vital to projects with multiple programmers and when distributing your code to others, like clients or the public.*

*You can comment a single line of code using two slashes (//), and multiple lines of code using a balanced pair of slash-asterisk (/\*) and asterisk-slash (\*/).*

```
//single-line comment

/*
multi-line
comment
*/
```

**NOTE**

*Unlike some other languages, ActionScript 3.0 does not support block-level local variables. That is, declaring a variable within a logical block, such as a conditional or loop, does not confine the life of that variable to the block itself. In ActionScript 3.0, variables are either accessible to an entire script or restricted to a function, depending on where they're declared.*

## Parameters and Arguments

Even when defining a local variable to hold content, your function is still "hard-wired." That is, it can't change from the effect of some outside influence. Let's say you need to trace ten different messages. To do that without any new features, you'd have to create ten functions and vary the string that is traced inside each function.

However, this can be more easily accomplished with the use of *parameters* and *arguments*—words that are often used interchangeably but that have a subtle distinction. Parameters are like local variables in that they exist only inside a function, but they are easier to use because they do not have to be declared. Instead, you just place them inside the function's parentheses and use them inside the function as you see fit. Arguments are the values that are passed into those parameters. By passing data into a function, you can vary its execution.

When using parameters, it is a great idea to use the same data typing practices as you would with variables, so the ActionScript compiler knows how to react and can notify you of errors. Simply follow the parameter name with a colon and data type. The same rules that apply to naming variables, apply to naming parameters. Furthermore, because parameters are local to a function, you can reuse parameter names in different functions without ill effect. Just be sure not to confuse yourself!

In the following example, the function no longer traces "hello" every time it is called. Instead, it traces whatever text is sent into the function. To send data in, you need only include the data in the parentheses used when calling the function.

```
function showMsg(msg:String) {
    trace(msg);
}
showMsg("goodbye");
//goodbye
```

You can even use multiple parameters separated by commas and pass multiple arguments to the function. To avoid errors, the order of the arguments must match the order of parameters. This example expands on the previous code by adding a second parameter. In this case, the function uses the plus operator (+) to *concatenate*, or join, strings together.

```
function showMsg2(msg:String, user:String) {
    trace(msg + ", " + user + "!");
}
showMsg2("Welcome", "Sally");
//Welcome, Sally!
```

Default values can also be supplied for a parameter. This makes sending an argument into the parameter optional because, if no value is sent, the default will be used. When using parameter default values, you must place them at the end of the parameter list so they always follow any parameters for which values are required. For example, the following code requires a message but the user name is optional. As a result, **user** must appear after **msg** in the order of parameters.

```
function showMsg3(msg:String, user:String="User") {
    trace(msg + ", " + user + "!");
}
showMsg3("Welcome", "Claire");
//Welcome, Claire!
showMsg3("Welcome");
//Welcome, User!
```

The code in this section is in the *functions_parameters.fla* source file.

## Returning a Value from a Function

Finally, it is also possible to return a value from a function, increasing its usefulness even further. Having the ability to return a value to the script from which it was called means you can vary both the input *and* output of a function.

The following examples are used to convert temperature values from Celsius to Fahrenheit and Fahrenheit to Celsius. In both cases, a value is sent into the function and the result of a calculation is returned to the script. The return value is sent back to the exact same location as the function call.

For instance, in the first of the two following cases, the **return** keyword returns the value to the inside of a **trace()** statement, which consequently traces the result. In the second case, the **return** keyword returns the value to the right side of an equation, thereby populating a variable. This mimics real-life usage in that you can immediately act upon the returned value or store and process it at a later time. In both cases, the actual trace is shown as a comment. This code can be found in the *functions_return.fla* source file.

```
function celciusToFarenheit(temp:Number):Number {
    return (9 / 5) * (temp + 32);
}
trace(celciusToFarenheit(20));
//68
```

```
function farenheitToCelcius(temp:Number):Number {
    return (5 / 9) * (temp - 32);
}
var temperature:Number = farenheitToCelcius(68);
trace(temperature);
//20
```

**NOTE**

*Values are returned from a function immediately, so any code inside the function that appears after the return statement is not executed.*

Note that when returning a value from a function, you should also declare the data type of the return value. This is achieved the same way you type data in variables or parameters—with a colon followed by the data type. This time, the data type is placed between the closing parenthesis of the function's declaration and its opening curly brace. This position symbolizes output, rather than input, of the function.

Once you get used to this practice, it is best to specify **void** as a return data type to indicate when your function does *not* return a value. By telling the ActionScript compiler that nothing should be returned (by using **void** as a data type), it can warn you if you inadvertently add a return statement later.

# Custom Objects

After working with ActionScript for just a short while, you will realize that you are immersed neck-deep in objects—whether you're using procedural or object-oriented programming. In addition to the numerous objects that are already predefined in the ActionScript language (such as movie clips, text fields, sounds, and more), you can create your own objects and give them *properties*—the adjectives of the ActionScript world, describing an object's general characteristics, the way you might describe a movie clip's width, location, rotation, and so on.

To demonstrate this, we'll create a custom object called **villain**, and give it properties for **health**, **armor**, and **lives**. None of these terms—villain, health, armor, or lives—are already part of the ActionScript language. However, the syntax for using custom objects conforms to the same dot syntax used throughout ActionScript, so it will seem like those properties have always been there. The following snippet creates an object, and then creates and populates properties:

```
var villain:Object = new Object();
villain.health = 100;
villain.armor = 100;
villain.lives = 3;
```

**NOTE**

*You will use objects later in the book, in Chapter 10 when working with cascading style sheets and in Chapter 12 when working with video.*

These values can be called up at any time, by querying the properties the same way they were created.

```
trace(villain.health);
//100
```

## Objects and Associative Arrays

Another way to create a custom object is type its properties and values explicitly at the time of definition:

```
var obj:Object = {msg:"Hello", user:"Jodi"};
```

This structure is sometimes also called an *associative array* because it associates a value with a property (also called a *key* in this context). The object syntax to retrieve a key value is the same as described in the prior section. Using associative array syntax, you substitute a string of the key, in place of the integer index used with linear arrays. Both of the following examples trace "Hello":

```
//object syntax
trace(obj.msg);
//associative array syntax
trace(obj["msg"]);
```

You can find both object examples in the *custom_objects.fla* source file.

# this and parent

Although potentially a bit nebulous when you're starting with ActionScript, **this** can be your friend. It is essentially a self-referential pronoun and is shorthand for "whichever object or scope you're working with now." *Scope* is the realm or space within which an object lives. For example, think of a movie clip inside Flash's main timeline. Each of these objects (the movie clip and main timeline) has a unique scope, so a variable or function defined inside the movie clip will not exist in the main timeline, and vice versa.

It is easiest to understand the usage of **this** in context, but here are a couple of examples to get you started. If, from the current scope, you wanted to check the x location of a movie clip with the instance name **mc**, you might say:

```
this.mc.x;
```

Conversely, if you wanted to send the main timeline to frame 2, but do so from within the movie clip, you might say:

```
this.parent.gotoAndStop(2);
```

The latter example uses the **parent** keyword, which refers to the object that is immediately above the current scope in the object hierarchy. In this case, it refers to a movie clip (or main timeline) in which another movie clip resides, and this will be discussed a wee bit more in the following section.

In both cases, **this** is a reference point from which you start your path. It's very common to drop the **this** keyword when referencing properties and methods in the current scope. Many programmers include the keyword for clarity, but it's also sometimes particularly useful or even required—such as when some ActionScript editors color various parts of your script for improved legibility. In any case, keeping **this** in your code will help you remember that you're referencing an object—a concept easy to forget if you frequently omit the friendly pronoun.

**NOTE**

*Depending on how you set up your file, it is often necessary to specifically declare what kind of parent you are referencing. For example, you may need to explicitly say the parent is a movie clip before you can work with its timeline. A little more background is probably needed to grasp this, as covered in detail in the "Clarifying or Changing the Data Type of a Display Object" section of Chapter 4.*

# Absolute Versus Relative Addresses

Much like a computer operating system's directory, or the file structure of a website, ActionScript refers to the address of its objects in a hierarchical fashion. You can reference an object address using an absolute or relative path. Absolute paths can be easy because you most likely know the exact path to any object starting from the top of your application—such as Flash Professional's main timeline. However, absolute paths are quite rigid and will break if you change the nested relationship of any of the referenced objects. Relative paths can be a bit harder to call to mind at any given moment, but they are more flexible. Working from a movie clip and going up one level to its parent and down one level to a child will work from anywhere—be that in the root timeline, another movie clip, or nested even deeper—because the various stages aren't referenced by name.

Tables 2-5 and 2-6 draw analogies to uses found in more familiar computer operating system and website analogies.

*Table 2-5. Absolute (from main timeline to mc3, a nested movie clip inside mc2)*

| ActionScript | Windows OS | Mac OS | Website |
|---|---|---|---|
| `root.mc2.mc3` | *c:\folder2\folder3* | *Macintosh/folder2/folder3* | `http://www.domain.com/dir/dir` |

*Table 2-6. Relative (from a first-level movie clip called mc1, up to its root, and down to the child of a sibling)*

| ActionScript | Windows OS | Mac OS | Website |
|---|---|---|---|
| `this.parent.mc2.mc3` | *..\folder2\folder3* | *../folder2/folder3* | *../dir/dir* |

## Put It All Together

To end this chapter, let's look at a script that brings together much of what we've discussed to create a randomizing sentence builder. This code can be found in the *build_a_sentence.fla* source file. To begin, lines 1 through 7 create a series of arrays of adjectives, nouns, and verbs, imagined by my children, Sally and Claire.

Lines 9 through 22 define the **buildASentence()** function, which takes the adjective, noun, and verb arrays as arguments. Lines 10 through 12 store the number of items in each array, and then the conditional in lines 13 through 15 check to make sure there is at least one item in each array. If any array has 0 items, a warning is returned in line 14 and the function is at an end.

Lines 17 through 19 create a random number between 0 and 2. The **Math. random()** method generates a random number between 0 and 1, which is then multiplied by the length of each array. The resulting numbers will be used in line 21 as indices to retrieve values from the arrays that were passed into the function. Because array indices must be integers, we must round the random number created.

However, a random number between 0 and 3 might round to a value of 3. Traditional rounding techniques round up when the number is 0.5 or above, and round down for anything under 0.5. So, value of 2.9 would round up to 3. In this case, you'd receive an error because only items 0, 1, and 2 exist in the array. There is no fourth item (that would be retrieved with an index of 3).

To skirt this possibility, we force the rounding operation to round down, using the **Math.floor()** method, allowing only numbers 0, 1, and 2.

The function then ends by returning a sentence. It combines "The ", a random adjective, a space, a random noun, a space, a random verb, and " away!" and returns it to the caller of the function. We'll look at that process, after the code.

```
1   var adjsSally:Array = ["hairy", "funny", "bouncy"];
2   var nounsSally:Array = ["daddy", "mommy", "sister"];
3   var verbsSally:Array = ["drove", "swam", "ran"];
4
5   var adjsClaire:Array = ["tall", "snuggly", "clean"];
6   var nounsClaire:Array = ["duck", "birdy", "chipmunk"];
7   var verbsClaire:Array = ["ran", "jumped", "tip-toed"];
8
9   function buildASentence(adj:Array, noun:Array, verb:Array):String {
10      var aCount:int = adj.length;
11      var nCount:int = noun.length;
12      var vCount:int = verb.length;
13      if (aCount == 0 || nCount == 0 || vCount == 0) {
14          return ("not enough words provided");
15      }
16
17      var a:int = Math.floor(Math.random() * aCount);
18      var n:int = Math.floor(Math.random() * nCount);
19      var v:int = Math.floor(Math.random() * vCount);
20
21      return "The " + adj[a] + " " + noun[n] + " " + verb[v] +
                "away!";
22  }
23
24  for (var i:int = 0; i < 3; i++) {
25      var sallySays:String = makeASentence(adjsSally, nounsSally,
                                    verbsSally);
26      trace(sallySays);
27
28      var claireSays:String = makeASentence(adjsClaire, nounsClaire,
                                    verbsClaire);
29      trace(claireSays);
30  }
```

To call the function, we use a **for** loop in lines 24 through 30. The loop executes 3 times, calling the function with Sally's arrays (line 25) and Claire's arrays (line 28). The function returns a sentence in each line, and the loop then traces the results in lines 26 and 29. The results are random, but here is a sample:

```
The funny mommy drove away!
The snuggly birdy ran away!
The funny sister swam away!
The tall duck tip-toed away!
The hairy daddy swam away!
The clean chipmunk jumped away!
```

**NOTE**

*Here are some examples of the rounding features of the* **Math** *class, with the results listed as comments following each method:*

```
Math.round(0.8); //1
Math.round(0.2); //0
Math.floor(0.8); //0
Math.floor(0.2); //0
Math.ceil(0.8); //1
Math.ceil(0.2); //1
```

*The* **Math.round()** *method rounds up when the value is 0.5 and above and down when the value is below 0.5.* **Math.floor()** *always rounds down, and* **Math.ceil()** *(short for ceiling) always rounds up to the nearest whole number.*

# What's Next?

Ideally, we've provided just enough background (or review) of key ActionScript fundamentals to now focus on topical syntax. Although we won't entirely ignore basic elements within the scripts of future chapters, we will spend more time describing the collective goal of a script, and highlighting new issues introduced or updated by ActionScript 3.0.

Next, we start off the ActionScript 3.0-specific material with a look at the three essential building blocks of most ActionScript objects: properties, methods, and events. Events are one of the most significantly changed elements of ActionScript with the introduction of version 3.0.

**In the next chapter**, we'll discuss:

- The descriptive properties, such as `width`, `height`, `location`, `alpha` (opacity), `rotation`, and more, of each object that define its major characteristics

- The actions you may exert on objects, or that objects may take on other objects, in the form of methods

- The events issued by the user or aspects of your program or environment and, perhaps more directly, the *reactions* to those events

# GRAPHICS AND INTERACTION

Part II represents the largest section of the book, spanning Chapter 3 through Chapter 9. This part covers many significant features that distinguish ActionScript 3.0 from prior versions. It focuses on graphics and interactions and includes the new event model and display list.

Chapter 3 is a discussion of properties, events, and methods—the items responsible for manipulating just about anything in Flash. Chapter 4 goes on to explain the display list, a great new way to display visual assets in Flash. Chapter 5 discusses timeline control, including various navigation techniques.

Chapter 6 marks an important transition in the book. Chapter 6 discusses object-oriented programming and, while still introducing syntax in the timeline, the remaining chapters in the book will focus increasingly on OOP. Chapter 7 takes a look at various ways to animate graphics with ActionScript. Chapters 8 and 9 round out the presentation of graphics and interactivity with tutorials covering drawing with vectors and pixels. Included are demonstrations for creating vectors with ActionScript and manipulating a variety of bitmap properties in your projects.

# PROPERTIES, METHODS, AND EVENTS

In addition to the core language fundamentals reviewed in the previous chapter, you will find that the majority of your scripts are written using properties, methods, and events. These are the basic building blocks of most scripted tasks and allow you to get and set characteristics of, issue instructions to, and react to input from, many assets.

This is what we'll be covering in this chapter:

- **Jump Right In.** Get your feet wet right away by starting the chapter with a simple practical example. Adapt the Hello World! example by conveying your greeting one character at a time.

- **Properties.** Properties are somewhat akin to adjectives, in that they describe the object being modified or queried. For example, you can check or set the width of a button. Most properties are read-write, in that you can both get and set their values. Some properties, however, are read-only, which means you can ask for, but not change, their values.

- **Events.** Events are the catalysts that trigger the actions you write, setting properties and calling methods. For instance, a user might click the mouse button, which would then result in a mouse event. If you write code to react when that event is detected, the event can then cause a function to execute performing the desired actions.

- **Methods.** Methods are a bit like verbs. They tell objects to do something, such as play and stop. In some cases, methods can be used to simplify the setting of properties. You might use a method called `setSize()`, for example, to simultaneously set the width and height of something. Other methods are more unique, such as `navigateToURL()`, which instructs a browser to display a web page.

In this chapter, you will build a utility that will demonstrate each of these ActionScript structures. Using mouse and keyboard events, you will manipulate several properties, as well as execute a few methods. The majority of ActionScript objects—from visual assets like movie clips to code-only objects like timers—have properties, methods, and events.

For simplicity, we'll focus primarily on the movie clip. Using the movie clip to centralize our discussion will make it easier for you to expand your examples on your own, as you look for other attributes to manipulate. Once you are comfortable with how properties, methods, and events work, it will be relatively easy to learn about other objects.

## Jump Right In

This chapter's first script again builds on the Hello World! theme, this time concentrating on properties, methods, and events. In this example, we'll display our salutation one character at a time. As with prior chapters, we'll explain this code briefly, and elaborate as the chapter continues. This script is found in the *hello_world_prop_event.fla* source file.

```
1    var txtFld:TextField = new TextField();
2    addChild(txtFld);
3
4    txtFld.textColor = 0xFF0000;
5
6    var str:String = "Hello World!";
7    var len:int = str.length;
8    var i:int = 0;
9
10   this.addEventListener(Event.ENTER_FRAME, onEnter, false, 0, true);
11   function onEnter(evt:Event):void {
12       txtFld.appendText(str.charAt(i));
13       i++;
14       if (i > len) {
15           removeEventListener(Event.ENTER_FRAME, onEnter);
16       }
17   }
```

**NOTE**

*ActionScript 3.0 uses hexadecimal notation to express colors as numbers. The format of a simple color is 0xRRGGBB. 0x tells the compiler the number is a hexadecimal value and replaces the # symbol used to express the same value as a string, as in HTML. The next three character pairs represent red, green, and blue and must represent values from 0 to 255. To do this, hexadecimal numbers use base 16 (instead of base 10 like a decimal number) and each character uses not only 0–9 but also A–F. 00 is no color and FF is all color, for each pair. 0x000000 is black (no colors), and 0xFFFFFF is white (all colors). The color used in this script is all red, no green, and no blue.*

Lines 1 and 2 again create a text field and add it to the display list so the user can see it. Line 4 sets **textColor**, a basic property of the text field, coloring the text red. This approach to text coloring is a quick solution, but it colors all text in the field. In Chapter 10, you'll learn how to exercise more precise control over text, allowing you to color individual segments of text.

Lines 6 through 8 create and populate variables including a string, the number of characters in that string, and a counter's initial value. The remainder of the script is an enter frame event listener to add the string text to the end of the field, character by character. Each time the event is received, line 12 uses the string method **charAt()** to determine the character at position *i* in the string, and the **appendText()** method to add that character to the field. The *i* counter is then incremented and, if it exceeds the number of characters in the field, the listener is removed, halting the process. The result is that "Hello World!" is added to the field, one character at a time.

# Properties

If you think of properties as ways of describing an object, they become second nature. Asking where a movie clip is, for example, or setting its width, are both descriptive steps that use properties.

In Chapter 2, we briefly discussed the object model and dot syntax that bring order and structure to ActionScript as well as many other scripting and programming languages. The first step in using a property is to determine which object you want to manipulate. For example, you might want to affect a movie clip on the stage with an instance name of *box*. The instance name is important because there may be multiple movie clips on stage, but you may want to alter only one. So you need to be able to differentiate which clip to change.

It's easy to give a movie clip on the stage an instance name. Select it and type the name in the upper portion of Flash Professional's Properties panel, as seen in Figure 3-1. (You've also learned how to create objects, such as text fields, entirely from code, and you'll be doing that more and more as the book progresses.)

box.x += 10;
box.y += 10;

box.scaleX = 0.5;
box.scaleY = 0.5;

box.rotation = 20;

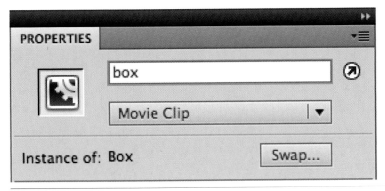

*Figure 3-1. Giving a movie clip an instance name in Flash Professional CS5's Properties panel*

box.alpha = 0.5;

The syntax for manipulating a property with ActionScript requires that you follow the instance name with a dot (period) and the property name. To get you started, we'll show you the syntax for making several changes to movie clip properties in the following table. Then, when we demonstrate how to handle events in the next section, we'll change these properties interactively. The following examples assume that a movie clip with an instance name of *box* is on the stage, and Figure 3-2 demonstrates the visual change made by each property. The light-colored square is the original state before the movie clip is affected. (The **alpha** property shows only the final state, and the dashed stroke for the visible property is only to show that the box is not visible.)

Table 3-1 shows nine movie clip properties with sample syntax and notes on each property's unit of measure and possible sample range of values.

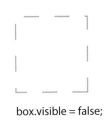

box.visible = false;

*Figure 3-2. Changes to movie clip properties*

*Table 3-1. Movie clip properties*

| Description | Property | Syntax for Setting Value | Units and/or Range |
|---|---|---|---|
| Location | `x, y` | `box.x = 100;`<br>`box.y = 100;` | Pixels |
| Scale | `scaleX, scaleY` | `box.scaleX = 0.5;`<br>`box.scaleY = 0.5;` | Percent / 0–1 |
| Dimensions | `width, height` | `box.width = 72;`<br>`box.height = 72;` | Pixels |
| Rotation | `rotation` | `box.rotation = 45;` | Degrees / 0–360 |
| Transparency | `alpha` | `box.alpha = 0.5;` | Percent / 0–1 |
| Visibility | `visible` | `box.visible = false;` | Boolean |

**NOTE**

*In Chapter 2, you learned that ++ adds 1 and -- subtracts 1 from a variable. You can also use these operators with properties.*

*The following code uses += to change the rotation of the box movie clip. Rather than adding just 1 to the left side of the equation, += will add whatever value is on the right side of the equation. The operators -=, \*=, and /= function similarly—subtracting, multiplying, or dividing the left side of an equation by the value on the right of the operator. These are called* compound assignment operators *because they simultaneously alter and assign values.*

*This code will add 20 degrees to the movie clip's rotation:*

```
box.rotation += 20;
```

*This is equivalent to, but shorter than:*

```
box.rotation = box.rotation + 20;
```

If you have experience with prior versions of ActionScript, you may notice a few changes in the property syntax. First, the properties do not begin with an underscore. This is a beneficial consistency introduced with ActionScript 3.0. Rather than varying property syntax, some with and some without leading underscores, in 3.0 no properties begin with the underscore character.

Second, some value ranges that used to be 0–100 are now 0–1. Examples include **scaleX**, **scaleY**, and **alpha**. Instead of using 50 to set a 50% value, specify 0.5.

Finally, the first scaling method uses properties **scaleX** and **scaleY**, rather than **_xscale** and **_yscale**, which are their ActionScript 1.0 and 2.0 equivalents. Typically, ActionScript 3.0 properties will cite the x and y version of a property as a suffix to make referencing the property easier.

Table 3-1 shows syntax only for setting properties for the *box* movie clip. Getting the value of a property is just as easy. For example, if you wanted to trace the movie clip's **alpha** value, or store it in a variable, you could write either of the following, respectively:

```
trace(box.alpha);
var bAlpha:Number = box.alpha;
```

# Events

Events make the Flash world go 'round. They are responsible for setting your scripts in motion, causing them to execute. A button can be triggered by a mouse event, text fields can react to keyboard events—even calling your own custom functions is a means of issuing a custom event.

Events come in many varieties. In addition to the obvious events like mouse and keyboard input, most ActionScript classes have their own events. For example, events are fired when watching a video, working with text, and resizing the stage. To take advantage of these events to drive your application, you need to be able to detect them.

In previous versions of ActionScript, there were a variety of ways to react to events. You could apply a script directly to a button, for example, and use the **on(Release)** approach. As the language matured, you could create event handlers and apply them remotely using instance names—for example, using **myButton.onRelease**. Finally, you could use *event listeners*, structures that listen for the occurrence of an event and execute a function, primarily with components or custom objects.

In the latest version of ActionScript, reacting to events is simplified by relying on one approach for all event handling. The ActionScript 3.0 event model uses event listeners regardless of the type of event or how it is used.

## Using Event Listeners

The concept of event listeners is pretty simple. Essentially, you tell an object to listen for an event and react if that event occurs. Imagine that you're sitting in a busy airport. Lots of things are going on around you, all of which can be thought of as events. If you had no particular reason to be at the airport, you might ignore all of these events. They would still occur, but you would not listen for them.

However, if you're scheduled to depart on an upcoming flight, you might establish a few listeners. For example, you might listen for a loudspeaker announcement about your flight number but ignore everything else. Or, you might also listen for a loudspeaker announcement about your destination city. You might even plan to listen for a third event: the inclusion of your airline in an announcement.

In all cases, the reaction to these events would be to pay attention to the announcement hoping to learn more about your flight. Other events might still occur in the airport, including other announcements, but without listening for those events, they would wash over you without reaction.

ActionScript 3.0 event listeners work much the same way. Creating an event listener, in its most basic form, is fairly straightforward. The first item needed is the object that will listen for the event. A button is a good example to start with. The **addEventListener()** method is then used to assign a listener to that object. This method requires two arguments. The first argument is an event to listen for—one that is appropriate for your goal. For example, it makes sense for a button to listen for a mouse event, but less so to listen for the end of a video or a resizing of the stage. The second argument is a function to execute when the event is heard.

Here's an example of code that uses a button with the instance name *rotate_ right_btn* and a function called **onRotateRight()**. This can be found in the *simple_event_listener.fla* source file.

```
1  rotate_right_btn.addEventListener(MouseEvent.MOUSE_UP, onRotateRight);
2  function onRotateRight(evt:MouseEvent):void {
3      box.rotation += 20;
4  }
```

*Separating mouse events into discrete up and down events allows you to react independently to each event. That is, you can assign one listener to the down event and another to the up event. This can be useful when creating draggable objects. You can start dragging on mouse down, and then stop dragging on mouse up, as you'll see later in this chapter.*

*You can also use a simpler mouse event called* **CLICK***, which requires both the down and up stages of the user's click process to trigger a listener.*

The event this code is listening for is a mouse up event—that is, when the mouse button is released while over the button. In ActionScript 3.0 syntax, events are typically grouped together in classes, and the event itself is usually defined as a *constant*—a variable that cannot be changed after it's defined. Using constants, when you know a value will never change, reduces errors because the compiler will warn you if you try to change them. Constants are usually typed in all uppercase letters, with multiple words separated by underscores.

The **MouseEvent** class contains constants that refer to mouse events like **MOUSE_UP** and **MOUSE_DOWN**. Other examples of events are **ENTER_FRAME**, found in the **Event** class and used to react to playhead updates, and **KEY_UP**, found in the **KeyboardEvent** class, for reacting to user keyboard input. We'll look at both of these events later on in this chapter.

The second argument in the **addEventListener()** method, the function that is called when the event is received, is listed by name only, without the trailing parentheses. This is because you are referring to the function, not actually calling it. The listener will do that for you when the event is received. In this example, **onRotateRight** refers to the **onRotateRight()** function, defined in lines 2 through 4.

You will probably be familiar with the structure of this function from the discussion about functions in Chapter 2. To review the syntax, the braces define the function's contents. In this case, line 3 adds 20 degrees to the current rotation value of the movie clip *box*. Also explained in Chapter 2, the *void* that follows the function name and parentheses indicates that no value is returned by the function.

However, new to our discussion of functions (see Chapter 2 if needed) is the fact that when functions are used in event listeners, the function requires a single parameter. This parameter receives information not from any ActionScript you write, but rather from the event. In this case, we arbitrarily named the parameter **evt**. (You may also see **e** or **event** used in other resources, but any valid parameter name will work.)

Without a parameter in place to receive that incoming data, you will get an error that says something like, "Argument count mismatch. Expected 0, got 1." It will also tell you which function has the problem to make it easier to find. The error means that the function expected no arguments coming in, because no parameters were defined. Instead, one argument was received, resulting in a mismatch.

You'll get used to this quickly, and reap the benefits. The data received usually contains useful information about the event and element that triggered the event. You can parse this information for use in the function. In keeping with good error reporting, the parameter should have a data type that matches the type of data being sent into the function. In this case, the event that triggered the listener was of type **MouseEvent**. Using this as the parameter data type will make sure that the listener receives only a **MouseEvent**, or the compiler will warn you to the contrary.

To illustrate the use of this argument data, let's look at another mouse event example, found in the *start_stop_drag.fla* source file. This time, however, we'll use two events, and use the incoming information to identify the **target** of the event—speaking generically, the object at which the event occurred. Specific to this case, the target is the object that was clicked.

```
1  myMovieClip.addEventListener(MouseEvent.MOUSE_DOWN, onStartDrag);
2  myMovieClip.addEventListener(MouseEvent.MOUSE_UP, onStopDrag);
3  function onStartDrag(evt:MouseEvent):void {
4      evt.target.startDrag();
5  }
6  function onStopDrag(evt:MouseEvent):void {
7      stopDrag();
8  }
```

> **NOTE**
>
> *It is also possible to type an event listener parameter with the more generic* **Event** *class, from which other built-in ActionScript 3.0 event classes are extended. This will allow more than one type of event to call the same function.*

In this example, two event listeners are assigned to a movie clip in lines 1 and 2. One listens for a mouse down event, another listens for a mouse up event. They each invoke different functions. In the first function, the **target** property of the event, which is parsed from the function argument, is used to identify which object received the mouse event. This allows the **onStartDrag()** function in lines 3 through 5 to start dragging the movie clip that was clicked. The **onStopDrag()** function in lines 6 through 8 then stops all dragging when the movie clip receives a mouse up event.

The best thing about this example is that the **target** property identifies the movie clip without an instance name. This generic approach is very useful because it makes the function much more flexible. The function can act upon any appropriate object that is clicked and passed into its parameter. In other words, the same function could start and stop dragging any movie clip to which the same listener was added. The following additional lines, adding the same functionality to a second movie clip called *myMovieClip2*, demonstrate this:

```
9   myMovieClip2.addEventListener(MouseEvent.MOUSE_DOWN, onStartDrag);
10  myMovieClip2.addEventListener(MouseEvent.MOUSE_UP, onStopDrag);
```

> **NOTE**
>
> *A similar event property is* **currentTarget**, *which references the object to which the event listener is attached. When a listener is attached to a single movie clip (as in the cited example),* **target** *and* **currentTarget** *are the same because you click on the object with the listener. However, you'll learn in the next chapter that events can pass from a parent clip down to any child clips within. When the listener is attached to the parent and you click on the child, target will still refer to the child, because that's what you clicked. The* **currentTarget** *property, however, will refer to the parent movie clip because that's the object to which the listener is attached. For more information, see "The Event Object," an event-related post at http://www. LearningActionScript3.com.*

Finally, this example's last modification demonstrates that more than one object can also call the same listener function. It is possible, while dragging an object, to move your mouse so quickly that the mouse up event occurs outside the bounds of the object you're dragging. If that occurs, the object would not receive the mouse up event, and the drag would not be stopped.

One way to get around this is to attach another listener to the stage, and set that listener to also call the **onStopDrag()** function. This way, whether your mouse up occurs over the movie clip or over the stage, the dragging will cease.

```
11  stage.addEventListener(MouseEvent.MOUSE_UP, onStopDrag);
```

## Using Mouse Events to Control Properties

Now we can combine the syntax we've covered in the "Properties" and "Events" sections to set up interactive control over properties. In the *chapter03* directory of the accompanying source code for this book, you'll find a file called *props_events_methods_ui.fla*. It contains nothing more than the example movie clip *box* and two buttons in the library that will be used repeatedly to change the five properties discussed earlier. The movie clip contains numbers to show which of its frames is visible, and the instance name of each copy of the button on the stage reflects its purpose. Included are *move_up_btn*, *scale_down_btn*, *rotate_right_btn*, *fade_in_btn*, and *toggle_visibile_btn*, among others. Figure 3-3 shows the layout of the file.

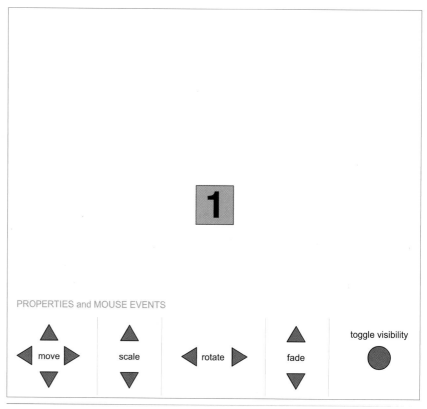

*Figure 3-3. Layout of the props_events_ui.fla file*

Starting with movement, we need to define one or more functions to update the location of the movie clip. There are two common approaches to this task. The first is to create one function in the keyframe in frame 1 for all movement that uses a conditional to decide how to react to each event. We'll demonstrate that when we discuss keyboard events. For now, we'll use the simpler direct approach of defining a separate basic function for each type of movement, as shown in the following script:

```
1   function onMoveLeft(evt:MouseEvent):void {
2       box.x -= 20;
3   }
4   function onMoveRight(evt:MouseEvent):void {
5       box.x += 20;
6   }
7   function onMoveUp(evt:MouseEvent):void {
8       box.y -= 20;
9   }
10  function onMoveDown(evt:MouseEvent):void {
11      box.y += 20;
12  }
```

Once the functions are defined, all you have to do is add the listeners to the appropriate buttons.

```
13  move_left_btn.addEventListener(MouseEvent.MOUSE_UP, onMoveLeft);
14  move_right_btn.addEventListener(MouseEvent.MOUSE_UP, onMoveRight);
15  move_up_btn.addEventListener(MouseEvent.MOUSE_UP, onMoveUp);
16  move_down_btn.addEventListener(MouseEvent.MOUSE_UP, onMoveDown);
```

This simple process is then repeated for each of the buttons on stage. The remaining script collects the aforementioned properties and event listeners to complete the demo pictured in Figure 3-3. The resulting file wires up one or more buttons for each property, all of which manipulate the movie clip in the center of the stage. The finished script can be found in the *prop_events. fla* source file.

```
17  scale_up_btn.addEventListener(MouseEvent.MOUSE_UP, onScaleUp);
18  scale_down_btn.addEventListener(MouseEvent.MOUSE_UP, onScaleDown);
19
20  rotate_left_btn.addEventListener(MouseEvent.MOUSE_UP, onRotateLeft);
21  rotate_right_btn.addEventListener(MouseEvent.MOUSE_UP,
22                              onRotateRight);
23
24  fade_in_btn.addEventListener(MouseEvent.MOUSE_UP, onFadeIn);
25  fade_out_btn.addEventListener(MouseEvent.MOUSE_UP, onFadeOut);
26
27  toggle_visible_btn.addEventListener(MouseEvent.MOUSE_UP,
28                              onToggleVisible);
29
30  function onScaleUp(evt:MouseEvent):void {
31      box.scaleX += 0.2;
32      box.scaleY += 0.2;
33  }
34  function onScaleDown(evt:MouseEvent):void {
35      box.scaleX -= 0.2;
36      box.scaleY -= 0.2;
37  }
38
39  function onRotateLeft(evt:MouseEvent):void {
40      box.rotation -= 20;
41  }
42  function onRotateRight(evt:MouseEvent):void {
43      box.rotation += 20;
44  }
45
46  function onFadeIn(evt:MouseEvent):void {
47      box.alpha += 0.2;
48  }
```

```
49    function onFadeOut(evt:MouseEvent):void {
50        box.alpha -= 0.2;
51    }
52
53    function onToggleVisible(evt:MouseEvent):void {
54        box.visible = !box.visible;
55    }
```

# Methods

Methods, the verbs of the ActionScript language, instruct their respective objects to take action. For example, you can tell a movie clip to stop playing by using its **stop()** method. Like properties, methods appear consistently in the dot syntax that is the foundation of ActionScript, following the object calling the method. One way to tell methods apart from properties is that methods always end with parentheses—even when no values are required for the method to work. For example, if the movie clip *box* in the main timeline calls the **stop()** method, the syntax would be:

```
box.stop();
```

As they have properties, most ActionScript classes also have specific methods, and you can define your own methods by writing functions in your own custom classes. For the following demonstration, we'll again focus on the movie clip from the prior example. This time, however, we'll introduce another event class and show you how to control your movie clips with the keyboard.

## Using Keyboard Events to Call Methods

Listening for keyboard events is very similar to listening for mouse events, with one significant exception: The target of the event listener is not always the object you wish to manipulate. When working with text, the text field may indeed serve well as the target of the keyboard events. When controlling movie clips, however, the stage itself is often a useful, centralized recipient of keyboard events.

Adding an event listener to the stage means that you can process all key events with a single listener, and then isolate only the desired key events with a conditional, issuing instructions accordingly. To simplify the syntax of this demonstration, we'll use the *switch* form of conditional statements. The **switch** statement, discussed in Chapter 2, is simply a more easily readable **if/else-if** conditional structure.

This script in the following example can be seen in the *methods_events.fla* file in the accompanying source code. We'll start by adding the listener to the stage. In this case, we'll be looking for the key down event, which is specified using a constant like all predefined events, **KEY_DOWN**. This time, however, it's part of the **KeyboardEvent** class. When the event is heard, our listener will call the **onKeyPressed()** function.

```
1    stage.addEventListener(KeyboardEvent.KEY_DOWN, onKeyPressed);
```

Next, we define the **onKeyPressed()** function, being sure to type the incoming argument value as **KeyboardEvent**. Finally, we parse the incoming event information for the **keyCode** property. The **keyCode** is a unique number assigned to each key and allows you to determine which key was pressed.

To specify each key in our script, we'll use constants defined in the **Keyboard** class that each contain key codes. Using these constants, when they suit your purpose, is easier than having to know the **keyCode** value for each key. For example, you can reference the Enter/Return key as **Keyboard.ENTER**, the left arrow key as **Keyboard.LEFT**, and so on.

We'll use five keys to execute five methods. When each desired key is pressed, it will execute the appropriate method, and then break out of the switch statement. We'll also add a default state that will trace the **keyCode** of any other key pressed. The final script segment looks like this:

```
2   function onKeyPressed(evt:KeyboardEvent):void {
3       switch (evt.keyCode) {
4           case Keyboard.ENTER:
5               box.play();
6               break;
7           case Keyboard.BACKSPACE:
8               box.stop();
9               break;
10          case Keyboard.LEFT:
11              box.prevFrame();
12              break;
13          case Keyboard.RIGHT:
14              box.nextFrame();
15              break;
16          case Keyboard.SPACE:
17              box.gotoAndStop(3);
18              break;
19          default:
20              trace("keyCode:", evt.keyCode);
21      }
22  }
```

The first four methods are basic movie clip navigation options: playing, stopping, or sending the movie clip to the previous or next frame in its timeline. The last method sends the movie clip to a specific frame and then stops its playback. The methods are probably self-explanatory, with only the last method even using an argument—in this case, the frame number. If you do want additional information, however, we'll put these and other navigation options to use in Chapter 5 when we discuss timeline control.

The combined source file, *props_methods_events.fla*, includes both the properties and methods examples in this chapter.

**NOTE**

*One* **keyCode** *value is assigned to a key, so this value can't be used directly for case-sensitive key checking—that is, uppercase "S" has the same* **keyCode** *as lowercase "s." In case you need to analyze case sensitivity, the* **charCode** *property has a unique value for each character in each case. Finally, not all keys trigger keyboard events, as some keys are reserved for operating system use.*

**NOTE**

*Depending on your computer setup, some key events may not function properly in Flash Professional when using the Control → Test Movie command. This is probably not an error but instead a result of Flash Player using keyboard shortcuts just like the Flash Professional application does. To test your key events, simply use the Control → Disable Keyboard Shortcuts menu command to disable keyboard shortcuts in the Flash Professional integrated player (that is, after invoking Test Movie). Be sure to reenable the shortcuts, or you won't be able to use Cmd+W (Mac) or Ctrl+W (Windows) to close the window, or use other familiar shortcuts.*

*Alternatively, you can test the movie in a browser using Cmd+F12 (Mac) or Ctrl+F12 (Windows). Also, the keyboard shortcut conflicts do not apply to the standalone Flash Player, in case you choose to use it for testing. Typically, double-clicking an SWF will open the SWF in the standalone player, but your system may be configured differently.*

# Event Propagation

So far in this book, we've been working primarily with movie clips, which are visual assets, or *display objects*. A display object is any ActionScript object that can be seen by the eye. That is, a movie clip is a display object, but a sound is not. For your audience to see a display object, it must be part of the *display list*—a list of everything a user can see at any given time. That is, you can create a display object (such as a text field), but not add it to the display list. This means the text field will exist, but the user won't be able to see it.

The display list includes the stage, buttons, text fields, shapes, and bitmaps, as well as visual assets loaded at runtime like images and other SWFs—everything you can see, right down to the most deeply nested clip. We'll explain the display list in greater detail in the next chapter, but we need a little background to get the most from our introduction to events. (It's hard to talk about one without the other!)

One of the best things about ActionScript 3.0 is the way that events and the display list work together. This includes *event propagation*, in which events flow through objects in the display list, making it possible for multiple display objects to react to the same event. Certain events, such as mouse and key events, are not sent directly to the target of the event. That is, a button doesn't immediately receive a mouse event when clicked. Instead, events are dispatched to the start of the display list, and the event propagates down to the event target, and then bubbles back up through the display list again. You can react to the event anywhere along this path.

Consider two movie clips (*mc2* and *mc3*) within another movie clip (*mc1*) that is on the stage. Next, imagine that you click on the nested movie clip, *mc2*, making it the target of the event. When the event occurs, it is not dispatched directly to *mc2*, but rather to the display list. For a simple look at the route the event takes, the stage receives the event first, then the main timeline (also called the **root**), then the parent movie clip, *mc1*, and then the target of the event, *mc2*. After the target receives the event, it then propagates back up through the display list to *mc1*, the main timeline (root), and stage. Figure 3-4 depicts the journey of the event.

Not every display object is a part of this path, however—only those in the hierarchical line of the event flow. For example, *mc3* is not a child or parent of any of the objects between the stage and the event target. Therefore, it's outside this event flow, as seen in Figure 3-4.

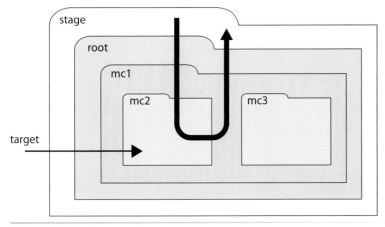

*Figure 3-4. Event propagation process*

Event propagation can be used to great advantage with just a little bit of planning. For example, let's say both nested movie clips in Figure 3-4, *mc2* and *mc3*, were designed to react to **mouse over** and **mouse out** events. Whenever the user rolled the mouse over either of the clips, it would change its **alpha** value. In the most direct case, you would attach a listener for each event to each movie clip. The following code shows the script for this scenario using two movie clips, *folder0* and *folder1*, and Figure 3-5 depicts the result.

```
1   folder0.addEventListener(MouseEvent.MOUSE_OVER, onFolderOver);
2   folder0.addEventListener(MouseEvent.MOUSE_OUT, onFolderOut);
3   folder1.addEventListener(MouseEvent.MOUSE_OVER, onFolderOver);
4   folder1.addEventListener(MouseEvent.MOUSE_OUT, onFolderOut);
5
6   function onFolderOver(evt:MouseEvent):void {
7       evt.target.alpha = 0.5;
8   }
9
10  function onFolderOut(evt:MouseEvent):void {
11      evt.target.alpha = 1;
12  }
```

*Figure 3-5. The effect of the changing alpha values using* mouse over *and* mouse out *events*

*It's important to note that not all events propagate through the display list. Frame events, for example, which we'll discuss in the next section, are dispatched directly to the event target. Before relying on event propagation, check the documentation to see how the event behaves. In particular, the* **bubbles** *property of an event class is a Boolean that indicates whether an event bubbles back up through the display list after reaching its target.*

*For more information, see the companion website, which includes discussions about event phases, priority of execution, stopping event propagation, and more. Consult* Essential ActionScript 3.0, Chapters 12 and 21, *for more discussions on event propagation.*

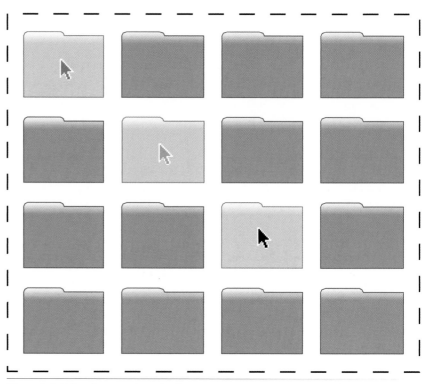

*Figure 3-6. Using the parent movie clip to propagate events*

Now imagine having to use the same approach for many folders, as seen in Figure 3-6. The code could get quite extensive with all those listeners for each folder. However, with event propagation, it's possible to attach the listener to the parent movie clip. In this example, all of the folders are inside a movie clip called *folder_group*, symbolized by the dashed line in Figure 3-6. If we attach the listener to the parent movie clip, the event will cascade through the display list, and the listener functions will be able to determine the object target from the data sent into the function. The code that follows is significantly simplified, thanks to event propagation, and can be seen in the source file *event_propagation2.fla.*

*To see another example of the difference between the* **target** *and* **currentTarget** *event properties, change target in lines 5 and 9 to* **currentTarget** *in the code at right. Because the listener is attached to the parent movie clip, which contains all the folders,* **currentTarget** *causes the parent clip to fade, affecting all its children. Used judiciously, these properties could be used to highlight a single folder, or all folders as a group.*

```
1    folder_group.addEventListener(MouseEvent.MOUSE_OVER, onFolderOver);
2    folder_group.addEventListener(MouseEvent.MOUSE_OUT, onFolderOut);
3
4    function onFolderOver(evt:MouseEvent):void {
5        evt.target.alpha = 0.5;
6    }
7
8    function onFolderOut(evt:MouseEvent):void {
9        evt.target.alpha = 1;
10   }
```

# Frame and Timer Events

We've been using mouse and keyboard events because you're almost certainly familiar with them to some degree, and they are ideally suited to this tutorial context. However, there are many events in the ActionScript language. While it's not possible to cover every one, we would like to round out the chapter with two other significant event types: *frame* and *timer*.

## Frame Events

Frame events are not triggered by user input the way mouse and keyboard events are. Instead, they occur naturally as the SWF plays. Each time the playhead enters a frame, a frame script is executed. This means that frame scripts execute only once for the life of the frame, making them an excellent location for seldom executed tasks, such as initializations. In other words, for a frame script to execute more than once, the playhead must leave the frame and return—either because of an ActionScript navigation instruction, or a playback loop that returns the playhead to frame 1 when it reaches the end of the timeline. Single-frame FLA files, therefore, execute their single frame scripts only once.

However, using an event listener, you can listen for a recurring enter frame event that some display objects have, including the main timeline, movie clips, and even the stage. An enter frame event is fired at the same pace as the document frame rate. For example, the default frame rate of an FLA created by Flash Professional CS4 and later is 24 frames per second, so the default enter frame frequency is 24 times per second. Using the enter frame event allows your file to update frequently—a handy thing for updating visual assets.

The *frame_events.fla* file in the accompanying source code demonstrates this event by updating the position of a unicycle every time an enter frame event is detected. It places the unicycle at the location of the mouse and, as a further review of properties, it rotates the child movie clip in which the wheel resides. Figure 3-7 demonstrates the effect. As you move your mouse to the right on the stage, the unicycle will move to the right, and the wheel will rotate clockwise.

The code for this example follows. The first line adds an enter frame event listener to the main timeline, specifying the event using the **ENTER_FRAME** constant of the **Event** class. The function sets the unicycle's x coordinate and rotation to the x coordinate of the mouse.

```
1   stage.addEventListener(Event.ENTER_FRAME, onFrameLoop);
2
3   function onFrameLoop(evt:Event):void {
4       cycle.x = mouseX;
5       cycle.wheel.rotation = mouseX;
6   }
```

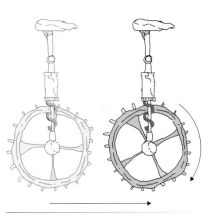

*Figure 3-7. Visual depiction of the unicycle movements*

**NOTE**

*This example demonstrates a scripting shortcut aided by ActionScript. When specifying a rotation higher than 360 degrees, ActionScript will understand the fact that an angle of rotation cannot exceed 360 and use the correct value. That is, 360 degrees is one full rotation around a circle, bringing you back to degree 0 (720 degrees is twice around the circle and also equates to 0). Similarly, 370 degrees is equivalent to 10 degrees, as it is 10 degrees past degree 0, and so on. This allows you to set the rotation of the wheel movie clip to the x coordinate of the mouse, without worrying about rotation ceasing after moving past the 360th pixel on the stage.*

## Timer Events

An alternative to using enter frame events to trigger actions on a recurring basis is to use time-based events. Although it's among the most straightforward options, using the enter frame event exclusively for this purpose has disadvantages. For example, Flash Player can reliably achieve only moderate frame rates—somewhere between the default 24 frames per second (fps) and perhaps 60 or so fps on the high end. Your mileage may vary, but that's fairly accurate when averaging the CPU population at large. More importantly, the rate at which the enter frame fires is not always consistent.

On the other hand, time-based events are measured in milliseconds and can therefore sometimes fire more quickly. Further, time-based events don't vary as much from scenario to scenario, so they are more reliable and consistent.

Previous versions of ActionScript used the **setInterval()** method for ongoing recurring events and the **setTimeout()** method for finitely recurring events. ActionScript 3.0 wraps up these approaches neatly behind the scenes of the new **Timer** class, simplifying the process of using timers.

The first step in using the **Timer** class is to create an instance of the class. Fortunately, creating instances in ActionScript 3.0 is very consistent, so this may look familiar. A variable is declared and typed using a data type that matches the class being instantiated. The new keyword creates a new instance of the class and that instance is stored in the variable:

```
var timer:Timer = new Timer(delay, repeatCount);
```

In this case, the class constructor can take two arguments. The first is mandatory and specifies the delay, in milliseconds, before the timer event is fired. The second is optional and is the number of times the event fires. Omitting the second argument will cause the event to fire indefinitely, each time after the specified delay. Using a positive value, such as 3, will cause the event to fire that finite number of times (again, after the specified delay).

In the sample *timer_events.fla* in the accompanying source code, the timer event (consistently specified as the constant **TIMER** in the **TimerEvent** class), occurs every second (or, in **Timer** units, every 1,000 milliseconds) and calls a function that increases the rotation of a hand nested inside a watch movie clip. The rotation increases 6 degrees every second, making one full 360-degree journey in 60 seconds.

```
1  var timer:Timer = new Timer(1000);
2  timer.addEventListener(TimerEvent.TIMER, onTimer);
3  timer.start();
4
5  function onTimer(evt:TimerEvent):void {
6      watch.hand.rotation += 6;
7  }
```

One important thing to note is line 3. The timer you instantiate does not start automatically. This gives you greater flexibility and control over your timer events. You can also stop the timer using the **stop()** method, and reset the timer using the **reset()** method. The latter stops the timer and also resets the repeat count to zero. For example, if you specified that the timer call a function five times, but reset it after the third call, the timer would begin counting again from zero rather than picking up from three at the point when it was reset. Figure 3-8 shows the watch used in *timer_events.fla*.

# Removing Event Listeners

Though event listeners make most event handling easy to add and maintain, leaving them in place when unneeded can wreak havoc. From a logic standpoint, consider what could happen if you kept an unwanted listener in operation. Imagine a weeklong promotion for radio station 101 FM, which rewards customer number 101 who enters a store each day of that week. The manager of the store is set up to listen for "customer enter" events, and when customer 101 enters the store, oodles of prizes and cash are bestowed upon the lucky winner. Now imagine if you left that listener in place after the promo week was over. Oodles of prizes and cash would continue to be awarded at great, unexpected expense.

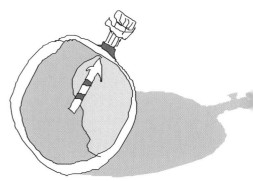

*Figure 3-8. Use of the timer event in a stopwatch*

Unwanted events are not the only problem, however. Every listener created occupies a small amount of memory. Injudiciously creating many event listeners, without cleaning up after yourself, uses memory without releasing it, which reduces available memory over time. This effect is called a *memory leak*. Therefore, it's a good idea to remove listeners when you know they will no longer be needed.

To do so, just use the **removeEventListener()** method. This method must be invoked by the object to which the listener was originally attached and requires two parameters: the event and function specified when the listener was created. Specifying the correct object, event, and function is important because you may have multiple listeners set up for the same object or event and you'll want to remove the correct listener.

Let's show how this works by adding to the previous example and removing the timer event listener when the rotation of the watch hand meets or exceeds 30 degrees of rotation. The new code is in bold and can be found in the source file *removing_listeners.fla*.

```
1   var timer:Timer = new Timer(1000);
2   timer.addEventListener(TimerEvent.TIMER, onTimer);
3   timer.start();
4
5   function onTimer(evt:TimerEvent):void {
6       watch.hand.rotation += 6;
7       if (watch.hand.rotation >= 30) {
8           timer.removeEventListener(TimerEvent.TIMER, onTimer);
9       }
10  }
```

## Checking ActionScript Angles

The code in the "Removing Event Listeners" section of this chapter is a simple extension of the prior example, rotating a watch hand every second. However, it was chosen to demonstrate one of the efficiencies of ActionScript: using the shortest angle possible to get to a specific degree of rotation. This is best explained by showing that 270-degrees is the same as –90 degrees.

Rotation angles in ActionScript start with 0 at East on the compass, or three o'clock on a watch face. If you start at three o'clock on a watch face, and travel around a circle for 270 degrees, you'll move three-quarters of the way around the circle and end up at twelve o'clock. However, if you start at the same original position and travel counter-clockwise, or a negative angle, you need travel only –90 degrees, or one quarter of the way around the circle to end up at the same location.

Setting an angle is easy because, as noted previously, ActionScript will automatically adjust the value over 360 degrees to a compatible angle. However, getting an angle can be more difficult. For example, if you changed the angle used in the conditional in the cited example from 30 to 270, the listener would never be removed. Why? Because ActionScript rotation angles span 0 to 180 degrees and 0 to –180 degrees, so 270 never occurs.

You can compensate for this in one of two ways. You can write functions that take negative angles and convert them to their positive equivalents (so you can ask for a familiar 270 degrees but really ask ActionScript for –90 degrees behind the scenes), or you can just use a variable, instead of checking the rotation property directly. This variant of the existing example can be found in the *removing_listeners_2.fla* source file.

```
1    var angle:Number = 0;
2    var timer:Timer = new Timer(1000);
3    timer.addEventListener(TimerEvent.TIMER, onTimer);
4    timer.start();
5
6    function onTimer(evt:TimerEvent):void {
7        angle += 6;
8        watch.hand.rotation = angle;
9        if (angle >= 270) {
10           timer.removeEventListener(TimerEvent.TIMER, onTimer);
11       }
12   }
```

This can be accomplished using a repeat count in the timer, like this:

```
var timer:Timer = new Timer(1000, 5);
```

However, the point of the example is to show you how to remove the listener from your logic flow and, equally important, from memory, when it is no longer needed. We briefly discuss an additional scenario for removing listeners in the upcoming "Garbage Collection" sidebar, but in all cases, it's good practice to remove any listeners that you know you'll no longer need.

# Garbage Collection:
# A Recommended Optional Parameter for Event Listeners

Garbage collection is the method by which Flash Player purges from memory objects that you no longer need. Garbage collection and memory management typically are not topics you need to concern yourself with when just getting started with ActionScript 3.0. However, garbage collection frees up memory so it's available for your SWF to use throughout its runtime life, so it's a good thing to be aware of. There are some coding practices that you can adopt immediately, and relatively painlessly—even at the outset of your learning—that may prove to be useful habits in the long run. Using *weak references* is such a practice.

We want to just scratch the surface of this subject, laying the groundwork for conventions that we'll use throughout the remainder of this book, and then refer you to additional resources for more information.

There are three optional parameters that you can add to the end of the `addEventListener()` method. Here is the syntax of the method, which will look partly familiar. The optional parameters we'll discuss are in bold.

```
eventTarget.addEventListener(EventType.EVENT_
    NAME, eventResponse, useCapture:Boolean,
    priority:int, weakReference:Boolean);
```

The first two optional parameters control when the listener function executes. You may never need to adjust these values often, but here's a quick snapshot of what they do.

The first optional parameter, `useCapture`, allows you to handle the listener event before it reaches its target (if set to `true`) or once the event has reached its target (if set to `false`) and is bubbling back up through the display list. The default (`false`) behavior is to react to all events captured at or after the event reaches the target, and this is the configuration you will use most of the time. Using `true` is akin to clicking on a button but capturing the event before it reaches the button. It will appear as if nothing happened. (The only practical use of this feature that we've found is preventing any mouse clicks from registering, as in the case of a modal dialog.)

The second optional parameter, `priority`, allows you to order the execution of multiple listeners set to respond to the same event in the same phase. In other words, if the same button used three mouse down listeners, you could set their order of execution. This, too, is unlikely to be a common issue, and the default parameter of **0** will serve you well in the vast majority of circumstances. When you need this feature, the highest number will execute first.

The third optional parameter, `weakReference`, is the option we want you to understand and start using. In a nutshell, this

parameter helps with memory management in the event that you're not careful about removing unneeded listeners.

Briefly, in ActionScript 3.0, memory management that you don't explicitly control is handled behind the scenes by the garbage collector, using the *mark and sweep* process. When you are no longer referencing an object in your application, it is marked for cleanup, and the garbage collector periodically sweeps through your application discarding unneeded items, freeing up memory along the way. If a reference to an object remains, however, the garbage collector can't know that the object should be purged from memory.

Try as we might to be good, it's not uncommon for developers to forget to remove event listeners in their code (see the section "Removing Event Listeners" earlier in this chapter). However, a distant next-best thing is a weakly referenced listener. Simply put, weakly referenced listeners aren't supervised by the garbage collector and therefore don't have to be manually marked for removal. If only weak references to an object remain after you have finished using it, then the object is eligible for collection.

Using this option is very simple. All you need to do is change the `weakReference` setting of the `addEventListener()` method from its default value of `false`, to `true`. Because it's the third optional parameter, values for the first and second arguments must be included so that ActionScript knows which parameter you are trying to set. You will rarely need to change those values, so you can use their aforementioned defaults (`false` for `useCapture` and 0 for `priority`).

So, our preference, and the convention we will use hereafter in this book, is to use the `addEventListener()` method with this syntax:

```
eventTarget.addEventListener(EventType.EVENT_NAME,
    eventResponse, false, 0, true);
```

If you get in the habit of using this syntax, you will be less likely to run into memory management problems due to lax code maintenance. Remember, this is not a substitute for removing your unneeded listeners explicitly. However, it's a backup plan and a best practice that is easy to adopt.

Additional discussion of the event flow—including event phases, setting listener priority, stopping propagation along the way, manually dispatching events, and more—is featured on the companion website. Flash developer Grant Skinner also wrote a helpful series of articles on resource management on his blog (*http://www.gskinner.com/blog*) that got us thinking about this in the first place. Finally, event flow is discussed in depth in Chapters 12 and 21 of *Essential ActionScript 3.0*.

# What's Next?

This chapter has demonstrated ways to manipulate ActionScript objects, but in the case of our example movie clip, we have assumed that the movie clip already existed on the stage. This is an acceptable assumption for projects authored primarily using the timeline, but it's limiting. If all files are to be constrained by using only elements manually added to the stage at time of authoring, and used only in the manner and order in which they were originally added, the files cannot be as dynamic as the ActionScript language allows.

Coming up, we'll talk more about the display list—an excellent means of managing visual assets. Understanding the basics of the display list is instrumental not only in dynamically adding elements at runtime, but also inn manipulating existing stage-bound objects to their fullest potential.

**In the next chapter**, we'll discuss:

- Adding new children to the display list

- Removing existing children from the display list

- Swapping depths of objects in the display list to change their visual stacking order dynamically

- Managing the hierarchical relationship of display list objects and how to change that relationship through reparenting

# THE DISPLAY LIST

One of the most dramatic changes introduced by ActionScript 3.0, particularly for designers accustomed to prior versions of ActionScript, is the way in which visual elements are added to an application at runtime. In prior versions of ActionScript, a separate approach was used to add most kinds of visual assets at runtime, requiring varied syntax. Management of those assets—particularly depth management—and creating and destroying objects, were also fairly restrictive and could be relatively involved, depending on what you were trying to accomplish.

ActionScript 3.0 brings with it an entirely new way of handling visual assets. It's called the *display list*. It's a hierarchical list of all visual elements in your file. It includes common objects such as movie clips, but also objects such as shapes and sprites that either didn't previously exist or could not be created programmatically.

The biggest difference between the ActionScript 3.0 display list display techniques used in prior versions of ActionScript is that the display list can't have any gaps. If the display list contains 10 display objects (such as 10 movie clips), you can't add a new display object to position 20. Furthermore, if something is removed from the display list, any display objects at a higher position will all drop down to fill in the gap.

That is, if display objects *a*, *b*, and *c* were added to the display list in that order, *a* would be at the bottom of the list (and, therefore, at the bottom of the SWF's visual stacking order), and *c* would be at the top of the list. Their positions in the display list would be 0, 1, and 2, respectively. Objects with higher indices are above objects with lower indices in the visual stacking order of the SWF. If *b* were removed, *c* would drop down and the new display list would be *a*, *c*. This makes working with the display list much easier because you don't have to worry about any empty positions in the list.

In this chapter, we'll look at the following topics:

- **Jump Right In.** Say hello to the world using three separate display objects.

- **The Sum of Its Parts.** Understanding the display list means understanding its parts. In addition to knowing the kinds of objects that can be part of the display list, it's also important to grasp the simple difference between display objects and display object containers—objects that can contain other display objects.

- **Adding and Removing Children.** The best part of the display list is how easy and consistent it is to add objects to, and remove objects from, the list.

- **Managing Object Names, Positions, and Data Types.** In addition to adding and removing display objects, you will need to manipulate existing members of the display list. You will likely need to find an object, either by name or position in the list, or even identify an object's data type as a particular kind of display object.

- **Changing the Display List Hierarchy.** It's also much easier than ever before to manage asset depths (z-order, or the visual stacking order controlled by ActionScript rather than timeline layers), and to change the familial relationship of assets. Moving a child from one parent to another is a breeze.

- **A Dynamic Navigation Bar.** As a quick demonstration of using the display list, we'll show you how to dynamically generate a very simple navigation bar.

## Jump Right In

Adapting the Hello World! examples of previous chapters, this exercise focuses on the display list and the very useful technique of relative positioning. It creates three text fields and positions them horizontally adjacent to each other, using only the display list for references to the fields. As in prior chapters, this script is provided up front just to get you started and give you a little experience with the material you'll be covering. The code used in these examples is designed to focus on the chapter at hand while presenting as little unfamiliar territory as possible. Content will be further explained in this chapter as well as later in the book. This script can be found in the *hello_world_display_list.fla* source file.

```
1   var i:int;
2   var parts:Array = ["Hello", "World", "!"];
3
4   for (i = 0; i < 3; i++) {
5       var txtFld:TextField = new TextField();
6       txtFld.text = parts[i];
```

```
7      txtFld.autoSize = TextFieldAutoSize.LEFT;
8      if (i > 0) {
9          txtFld.x = getChildAt(i-1).x + getChildAt(i-1).width;
10     }
11     addChild(txtFld);
12  }
```

Lines 1 and 2 create an integer counter and an array with three strings. Line 4 defines a **for** loop that executes three times. Lines 5 and 6 create and populate a text field, using each string from the array, consecutively. As the value of *i* increases with each iteration, the next string in the array is used. Line 7 uses the **autoSize** property to automatically adjust the size of the field to the minimum required to display the text, anchoring the resizing process to the upper-left corner.

Line 8 ensures that the first field exists because *i* is incremented after the first iteration of the loop. If the first field has already been added to the display list, line 9 positions the remaining fields relative to the prior field's position and width. The power of the display list allows us to do this without any instance names or preexisting object references because we can get a child from the any position in the list. For example, the second time through the loop, line 9 positions the new field based on the position and width of the display object at position 0 in the display list (*i* equals 1, so *i* – 1 equals 0 in the **getChildAt()** method). Finally, line 11 adds each field to the display list so the user can see it.

If you want to see the boundaries of the three separate text fields, you can add the following bold line of code to your file:

```
1      txtFld.autoSize = TextFieldAutoSize.LEFT;
2      txtFld.border = true;
3      if (i > 0) {
4          txtFld.x = getChildAt(i-1).x + getChildAt(i-1).width;
5      }
```

## The Sum of Its Parts

If you think about the display list by considering what you see in any given application, you're halfway home. In addition to contributing to the structure of the new event model, discussed in Chapter 3, the display list is responsible for maintaining the visual assets in your file. You will use the display list to create and destroy visual assets, and manage how they interrelate.

Let's take a look at the contents of the display list of a simple file. Figure 4-1 shows that this file has a shape, a text element, and a movie clip, and inside the movie clip is a bitmap. You can see this example in the *sample_display_list. fla* source file.

Figure 4-2 shows the display list of the same structure.

**NOTE**

*By default, text fields are 100 pixels wide and 100 pixels tall. The **autoSize** property can resize a field to match its contents, based on the left, center, or right edges of the field.*

*Figure 4-1. The visual layout of the simple file structure*

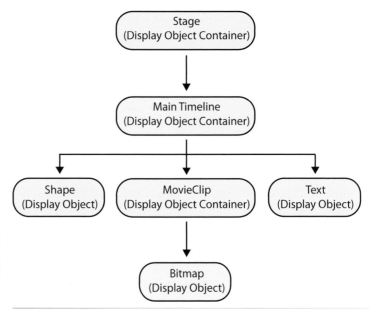

*Figure 4-2. The display list of the sample file*

## _root versus root

If you have experience with ActionScript 1.0 or 2.0, you may have heard that you should avoid using the _root property. That's because the value of the property was subject to change. Before ActionScript 3.0, _root referred to the timeline of the original host SWF no matter how many SWFs got loaded.

_root was the equivalent of an *absolute* address, like referring to an image in a website as *http://www. yourdomain.com/image*, or a file on your computer as *C:\directory\ file*, instead of a more flexible *relative* address such as "image" (or "../image," for example).

Because _root was an absolute address, if a SWF using the property was loaded into another SWF, _root was redefined to become the timeline doing the loading, rather than your original SWF as intended. This then broke any object path references that originated with _root.

In ActionScript 3.0, the display list changed that prevailing logic, the new root property is safer to use. root is now relative to the context in which it's used and doesn't always refer to the main timeline. As a result, it behaves more like a relative address. The root of a movie clip in SWF A, is the same if it stands alone or is loaded into SWF B. The same goes for the root in SWF B, whether it stands alone or is loaded into SWF C, and so on.

At the top of the list is the stage. Although you can access the stage from many objects in the display list, it's easiest to think of the stage as the foundation on which everything is built. It also helps to think of the stage as the ultimate container within which all your visual assets reside at runtime. The container analogy is central to this discussion. The stage contains everything.

Next is the main timeline, which can also be referenced using the **root** property. (See the sidebar "_root versus root" for more information.) An FLA file has a main timeline within which all other assets are contained. Because of event propagation, it is common to use the main timeline as a location to add event listeners when writing scripts in the timeline. In that context, the main timeline is typically referenced using the **this** identifier, as in "this object being currently referenced within the context of the script." (For more information about event listeners and event propagation, see Chapter 3. For more information about **this**, see Chapter 2.)

Below the main timeline in the display list hierarchy are all the visual assets in the file. Included in our sample display list are the aforementioned shape, text, and movie clip assets, and inside the movie clip is the bitmap.

You may notice in Figure 4-2 that everything is subtitled as a display object or display object container. This is key to understanding and working with the display list effectively. It probably follows that everything in the display list is a display object. However, some display objects can contain other elements and therefore are also display object containers.

For example, a shape is a display object, as are bitmaps and videos. However, none of these items can have children, so the display list lineage ends there.

That is, it doesn't make sense for a bitmap to have a nested object. A movie clip can have children, however, so it is also a display object container.

## Display List Classes

In just a moment, we'll walk through a typical ActionScript display list that demonstrates the distinction between display objects and display object containers. First, however, take a look at the individual classes that contribute to the display list, as shown in Figure 4-3.

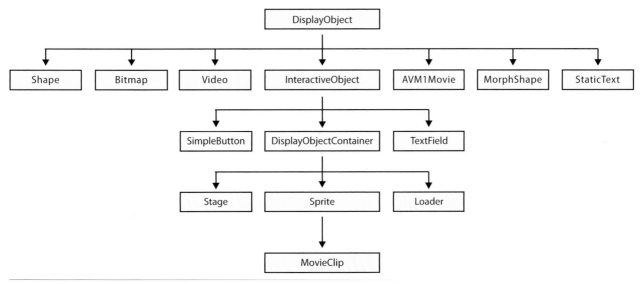

*Figure 4-3. The display list classes*

We discussed classes in Chapter 1, and we'll be using them extensively as you delve deeper into the book. In this context, however, just think of these classes as blueprints for objects that can be part of the display list. As you look through Figure 4-3, for instance, you'll recognize **Shape**, **Bitmap**, **Video**, and so on.

Note however, that, unlike Figure 4-2, this is not a depiction of an average display list. For example, it is possible for shapes, bitmaps, videos, and static text, among other items, to exist inside movie clips. Figure 4-3 merely shows all the possible object types that can be a part of *any* display list, and displays the hierarchical relationship among display list classes. Here is a quick description of the classes in Figure 4-3, rearranged slightly for clarity of discussion:

**DisplayObject**

> Anything that can exist in the display list is a display object, and more specialized classes are derived from this class.

**NOTE**

*When using ActionScript to refer to an image that has been manually added to the stage, such as when dragging it to the stage from the library, ActionScript will see the object as a* **Shape**. *However, you can still create a* **Bitmap** *object from an imported image using the* **BitmapData** *class.*

Shape

> This is a rectangle, ellipse, line, or other shape created with drawing tools. New to ActionScript 3.0, you can now create these at runtime.

Bitmap

> This is an ActionScript bitmap created at runtime using the **BitmapData** class.

Video

> This is a video display object, the minimum required to play a video, rather than using a video component for this task. This can also now be created dynamically at runtime.

InteractiveObject

> This class includes any display object the user can interact with using the mouse or keyboard. You can't create an instance of this class. Instead, you work with its descendants.

Skipping a bit, temporarily, and moving down a level:

SimpleButton

> This class is used to manipulate buttons created in the Flash Professional interface, so you don't have to rely solely on movie clips. Introduced in ActionScript 3.0, this class also allows you to *create* a button with code. You can assign display objects to properties of a **SimpleButton** instance to serve as the button's up, over, down, and hit states, and the instance will swap these states automatically as well as automatically show the finger cursor state, when responding to mouse interaction. This class is different from the **Button** class, which is used with Flash Professional's Button component.

TextField

> This class includes dynamic and input text fields. Both are controllable from ActionScript and input fields can also be edited by the user.

DisplayObjectContainer

> This class is similar to **DisplayObject** in that it refers to multiple display object types. The difference here, however, is that this object can contain children. All display object containers are display objects, but display only objects that can have children are display object containers. For example, a video is a display object, but it cannot have children. A movie clip is a display object, and it can have children, so it's also a display object container. Typically, you will work directly with this class when traversing the display list, looking for children or ancestors. Usually, you will manipulate one or more of its descendant classes.

There are four kinds of display object containers:

### Stage

Remember, the stage itself is part of the display list. Any interactive object can reference the stage, which is a display object container itself.

### Sprite

New to ActionScript 3.0, a sprite is simply a movie clip without a timeline. Many ActionScript manipulations typically performed using movie clips require only one frame. So the size and administrative overhead of the timeline is unnecessary. As you become more accustomed to ActionScript 3.0, and begin to consider optimization more frequently, you may find yourself using sprites more often.

### Loader

This class is used to load external assets destined for the display list, including images and other SWFs.

### MovieClip

This refers to the movie clip symbol you might create using drawing tools in Flash Professional. They can also be created with ActionScript.

We left three items from the second tier for last, as you will probably use these classes least often:

### AVM1Movie

This class is for working with loaded SWFs created using ActionScript 1.0 or 2.0. AVM1, (which stands for ActionScript Virtual Machine 1) is reserved for SWFs that use ActionScript 1.0 and/or ActionScript 2.0, while AVM2 is used for SWFs that use ActionScript 3.0. Because Flash Player uses two discrete code bases, these virtual machines are not compatible. The **AVM1Movie** class provides a way of manipulating display properties of legacy SWFs, but does not facilitate communication between ActionScript 3.0 and older SWFs. This must be accomplished by other means, such as a **LocalConnection**. We will discuss this approach in Chapter 13.

### MorphShape *and* StaticText

These two classes represent a shape tween and a static text element, respectively. You can't create a shape tween, or do very much with the text in a static text element, with ActionScript. However, they are part of the display classes because they inherit properties, methods, and events from their **DisplayObject** parent class. This makes it possible to rotate a static text element, for example.

Once you begin using the display list frequently, you will quickly become enamored with its power, flexibility, and simplicity. We will show you how to perform several common display list tasks in this chapter but, if you take one thing away from this initial discussion, it should be a basic understanding of display object versus display object container. To demonstrate this effectively, let's look at a short segment of code that traces display list content to the output window.

## Displaying the Display List

It's sometimes useful, especially when you're creating many display objects with potentially complicated nested objects, to walk through the display list and analyze its contents. The *trace_display_list.fla* file from the companion source code, will trace the contents of any display object that you pass into it, and indent each child and successive grandchild to help convey its position in the display list hierarchy.

This function introduces our first display list property and method—numChildren and getChildAt(), respectively—both used for retrieving information. As the name implies, numChildren returns the number of children within the object being analyzed. If, for example, there is one movie clip in the main timeline, and that movie clip contains two nested buttons, the main timeline has one child and the movie clip has two children. Grandchildren are not considered in this property.

The getChildAt() method retrieves a reference to a display object in the desired scope. For example, myMovieClip.getChildAt(0) will return the first child of the *myMovieClip* object, while getChildAt(1) will return the second display object of the current scope.

This source file also makes practical use of some of the skills we've discussed, such as sending arguments into (and returning a value from) a function, default argument values, and using a **for** loop, among others. Here's the code:

```
1   function showChildren(dispObj:*, indentLevel:int=0):void {
2       for (var i:int = 0; i < dispObj.numChildren; i++) {
3           var obj:DisplayObject = dispObj.getChildAt(i);
4           trace(padIndent(indentLevel), obj.name, obj);
5           if (obj is DisplayObjectContainer) {
6               showChildren(obj, indentLevel + 1);
7           }
8       }
9   }
10
11  function padIndent(indents:int):String {
12      var indent:String = "";
13      for (var i:Number = 0; i < indents; i++) {
14          indent += "    ";
15      }
16      return indent;
17  }
18
19  showChildren(stage);
```

Lines 1 through 9 define the function **showChildren()**, which has two parameters. The first receives the display object you want to inspect. This parameter uses a special value for its data type. Specifying an asterisk as a data type means the type will *not be checked*. This makes the function more flexible and is required in this case because you may pass different data types into the function: `DisplayObject` or `DisplayObjectContainer` (a display object that can contain children).

The second parameter is used by the function itself, and its value will ultimately indent each level of child objects, formatting the output to show the hierarchical relationships in the file. Here is a sample output of a file that contains two movie clips. We'll walk through another example after we discuss the code.

```
root1 [object MainTimeline]
    myMovieClip [object MovieClip]
    myMovieClip [object MovieClip]
```

Note that the second parameter of the `showChildren()` function has a default value of 0, so you don't have to pass anything into the function for this parameter to work. Line 19 shows the syntax for calling the function and passes in the stage for analysis, but no second argument. Therefore, the default value of the argument will be used. In this example, the function will trace the contents of all children of the stage.

Lines 2 through 8 of the function define a `for` loop, which will loop until there are no more children in the display object passed to the function. The number of loops is determined by the aforementioned `numChildren` property. Each time through the loop, line 3 populates the *obj* variable with the next child in the display list using the `getChildAt()` method. This determines the child object at the display list index indicated by the loop counter (`i`). The first time through the loop, when `i` is 0, the first child will be returned—equivalent to `getChildAt(0)`. The second time, when `i` is 1, the second child will be returned, and so on.

Once a display object reference is obtained, line 4 traces the object name and the reference itself, as arguments 2 and 3 of the `trace()` statement. The latter is handy because the type of object will also be displayed. For example, if the object is a movie clip called *logo*, the output will say "logo [object MovieClip]." But line 4 also does something else. The first item in the `trace()` is a function call to `padIndent()` and passes one argument to the function: the level of indent desired. The first time `showChildren()` is called, the initial value of this argument is 0, which comes from the default value of the `indentLevel` parameter. You'll soon see that this value can change as the function continues and progressive indents are needed for successive children. But first, let's jump down to look at how `padIndent()` works, in lines 11 through 17.

The `padIndent()` function begins by initializing a local variable as an empty string in line 12. It then enters a loop in lines 13 through 15 that adds four spaces to this variable. The indent level desired determines the number of loops. Once the loop is completed, this string of empty spaces is returned to the `showChildren()` from line 16, so the spaces can be added to the beginning

**NOTE**

*You can also omit a data type to prevent the compiler from testing an object's type. However, using an asterisk is considered a best practice because it reminds you, and others who may read your code, that preventing type checking was intentional.*

**NOTE**

*See the "Functions" section in Chapter 2 for a review of argument default values.*

of every trace. The end result is that, for each level of indent, these accumulated spaces push the output to the right, resulting in an outline format.

Lines 5 through 7 are what make this function powerful. Line 5 checks to see whether the display object currently being analyzed is also a display object container. It does so by using the **is** operator, which checks the data type of the object in question, and comparing it against the **DisplayObjectContainer** type. If the object is a container, *the function calls itself again*, in line 6. When doing so, it passes in that current object, and increments the indent level so any children found will be further indented during the trace.

This idea of a function calling itself is called *recursion*. It may seem redundant, but it can be very useful. In this case, it's the most efficient way for the **showChildren()** function to continue introspecting every display object it finds, no matter how deeply nested. The result is a complete walkthrough of all display objects, no matter how many children each may have.

### The showChildren() function in action

Take a look at the function in action. Figure 4-4 shows a sample file that will be analyzed. The rectangle and circle movie clips, with their instance names, are indicated in the figure. Within each rectangle, a shape is used to create the fill and stroke appearance. Inside each circle, a shape again provides the fill and stroke and a static text element is added to display the word "child."

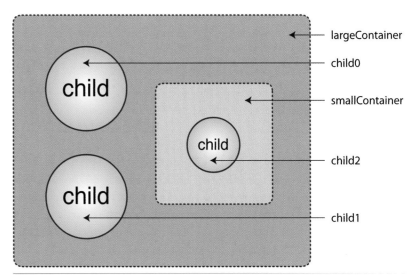

*Figure 4-4. A look at the stage of trace_display_list.fla*

When the function runs, the following is traced to the output window, showing all children of the stage. Note that whenever a display object has no name, "instance" is combined with an incrementing integer to create a unique name.

```
root1 [object MainTimeline]
    largeContainer [object MovieClip]
        instance1 [object Shape]
        smallContainer [object MovieClip]
            instance2 [object Shape]
            child2 [object MovieClip]
                instance3 [object Shape]
                instance4 [object StaticText]
        child0 [object MovieClip]
            instance5 [object Shape]
            instance6 [object StaticText]
        child1 [object MovieClip]
            instance7 [object Shape]
            instance8 [object StaticText]
```

# Adding and Removing Children

The previous section described the parts of the display list and how to analyze an existing list. But you'll also need to know how to add to, and remove from, the display list at runtime. In previous versions of ActionScript, you needed to rely on varying methods to add items to the stage. For example, you needed to use separate methods for creating a movie clip, placing a library movie clip on stage, or duplicating a movie clip. Using the ActionScript 3.0 display list, you need only one approach to create a movie clip: **new MovieClip()**. Even adding a precreated movie clip from the library is consistent with this syntax, as you'll soon see.

## Using addChild()

Adding a display object to the display list requires just two simple steps. The first is to create the object—in this case, an empty movie clip (a movie clip created dynamically, but without content). Commonly, this reference to this object is stored in a variable.

```
var mc:MovieClip = new MovieClip();
```

This creates the movie clip but does not display it. To display the movie clip, you must add it to the display list using the **addChild()** method:

```
addChild(mc);
```

Without any additional syntax, this adds a child to the current scope of the script. That is, if you typed this into a frame script in the main timeline, it would add the movie clip to the main timeline. You can also add a child to another display object container. So, if you instead wanted to add the mc movie clip nested inside another movie clip called **navBar**, you would change the second step to:

```
navBar.addChild(mc);
```

**NOTE**

*Remember, you can't add children to display objects like shapes, videos, text elements, and so on, because they are not display object containers.*

We've been adding movie clips to the display list in our examples, but it's just as straightforward to add other display objects. Two simple examples include creating a sprite and a shape:

```
var sp:Sprite = new Sprite();
addChild(sp);

var sh:Shape = new Shape();
addChild(sh);
```

You don't even have to specify a depth (visible stacking order) because the display list automatically handles that for you. Remember, the display list can't have any gaps, so the **addChild()** method always adds the object to the end of the display list no matter how long it is. You never need to know how many items are in the display list to use this method.

## Adding Custom Symbol Instances to the Display List

In the previous examples, we created display objects without any visible content. In Chapter 8, we'll show you how to draw with code so you can create art for these movie clips solely with code. This keeps file size down and allows more dynamic control.

However, you will frequently need custom art in your files, which would be difficult or virtually impossible to create with code. So we're going to show you how to dynamically add movie clips that already exist to the display list. In this chapter, we'll focus on adding instances of symbols that exist in your Library, using Flash Professional. In the accompanying source file, *add_child_linkage.fla*, you will find a unicycle in the library. To add this movie clip to the display list using ActionScript, you must first prepare the library symbol for ActionScript use.

In prior versions of ActionScript, there were two ways of doing this. The first approach was to assign the symbol a linkage identifier name—a name unrelated to symbol and instance names, specifically for use in ActionScript. The second way was to assign your own class to the movie clip so that it could be created when you created an instance of the class.

**NOTE**

*This improved approach to dynamically creating custom symbol instances also allows you to add classes easily later on for these instances to use—without having to edit your library. See the "Adding Classes to Pre-Existing Symbols" post at http://www.LearningActionScript3.com for more information.*

In ActionScript 3.0, these two approaches are unified into a single *linkage class*. This name allows you to create runtime instances of the symbol, but also allows you to create a class of the same name that will give the movie clip autonomous behavior. The most important thing to know at this point is that you don't have to write your own class to control the symbol instance if you don't want to. Before defining your own class, Flash will automatically create an internal placeholder class for you, so you can use its name to dynamically create the symbol when requested.

To prepare a movie clip for ActionScript use, select it in your library, and then click the Symbol Properties button (it looks like an "i" at the bottom of the library) to access the clip's properties, as shown in Figure 4-5. You can also right-click (Windows) or Ctrl-click (Mac) on the symbol and choose Properties from the pop-up menu.

In the resulting dialog, seen in Figure 4-6, click to enable the Export for ActionScript option (click the Advanced button if this option is not visible), and add a name to the **Class** field. When naming classes, it's common practice to begin the name with an uppercase letter. This is a bit different from naming a variable, where you might choose to use a lowercase first letter, so it's a good idea to get into this practice now. In the provided source file, we've already used the class name **Unicycle**.

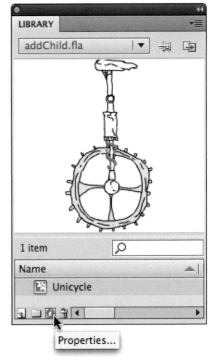

*Figure 4-5. Accessing a symbol's Properties dialog*

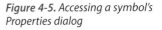

*Figure 4-6. Entering a class name for a movie clip in the library Properties dialog*

You will also likely notice that Flash adds the **MovieClip** class (in this case) to the Base Class field for you. A *base* class is a class from which other classes can be derived. A base class is also sometimes called a parent class because this is a form of inheritance. You'll learn more about inheritance in Chapter 6, but basically, this makes it possible for your new class to automatically inherit the accessible properties, methods, and events available to the **MovieClip** class. For example, you can automatically manipulate the x and y coordinates of your new custom movie clip.

Now that you've given your movie clip a class name, you can create an instance of that class the same way you created an instance of the generic movie clip class. Instead of writing **new MovieClip()**, however, you will write **new Unicycle()** to create the movie clip. The same call of the **addChild()** method is used to add the newly created unicycle to the display list, as seen in the following code:

```
var cycle:MovieClip = new Unicycle();
addChild(cycle);
```

## Using addChildAt()

The **addChild()** method adds the display object to the end of the display list, which places the object at the top-most position in the visible stacking order. This makes it very easy to place items on top of all other items. However, it's also useful to be able to add a child at a specific position in the display list. For example, you may wish to insert an item into the middle of a stack of display objects.

To accomplish this, the **addChildAt()** method takes as its arguments not only the object to add, but also the position in the display list where you want the object to appear. The following example, found in the *add_child_at.fla* source file, adds a movie clip with the class name **Ball** to the *start* of the display list (position 0) with every mouse click. The effect is that a new ball is added *below* the previous balls (and positioned down and to the right 10 pixels using additional code), every time the mouse is clicked.

Remember, you can't add an object to a position greater than the number of items already in the display list because the display list can't have gaps.

```
1   var inc:int = 0;
2
3   stage.addEventListener(MouseEvent.CLICK, onClick, false, 0, true);
4
5   function onClick(evt:MouseEvent):void {
6       var ball:MovieClip = new Ball();
7       ball.x = 100 + inc * 10;
8       ball.y = 100 + inc * 10;
9       addChildAt(ball, 0);
10      inc++;
11  }
```

Line 1 creates a variable that will be incremented each time the mouse is clicked. This variable will be used to help position each ball. Line 3 adds an event listener to the stage, listening for a mouse click, so that any mouse click will trigger the listener's function in lines 5 through 11.

In line 6, a new movie clip is created, using a library symbol with a linkage class of **Ball**. Lines 7 and 8 manipulate the x and y coordinates, setting **x** and **y** to 100 and adding a 10-pixel offset for each ball added. The offset is calculated using the incrementing variable. For example, when the first ball is added, **inc** is 0 so the additional pixel offset is 0 multiplied by 10 or 0. Then **inc** is incremented at the end of the function, in line 10. The next mouse click will offset the new ball to 1 multiplied by 10 or 10 pixels. The third click offset will be 2 multiplied by 10 or 20 pixels, and so on. Most importantly, line 9 adds the ball to the display list, but always at position 0, making sure the newest ball is always on the bottom.

**NOTE**

*It is possible to issue more than one assignment instruction in a single line. For example, this code assigns 100 to both the x and y coordinate of a movie clip:*

```
ball.x = 100;
ball.y = 100;
```

*Because both values are 100, the same task can be expressed this way:*

```
ball.x = ball.y = 100;
```

*This is handy for making code shorter for less scrolling, but some may think this form is harder to read or understand. The result is the same, whichever syntax you choose, so use what is most comfortable for you.*

## Display Objects and References to Stage and Root

It's usually possible to manipulate display objects before or after adding them to the display list. For example, you can set the x coordinate of a display object before adding it to the display list and the object will appear at the desired location when added. You can also change the object's x coordinate any time after appearing in the display list to update the object's position later.

However, some display object properties or methods may not be valid when the object is not part of the display list. Good examples of this scenario include the root and stage instances of any display object.

Once a display object is added to the display list, its stage and root properties are valid. However, if the object is not part of the display list, these properties will return null. Try the following example, in which trace output is shown in comments:

```
var mc:MovieClip = new MovieClip();

trace(mc.stage); //null
trace(mc.root); //null

addChild(mc);

trace(mc.stage); //[object Stage]
trace(mc.root); //[object MainTimeline]
```

The first line creates a new movie clip. However, the clip is not added to the display list, so the traces in the next two lines return null. After adding the movie clip to the display list, though, the properties return references to the Stage and MainTimeline, respectively.

Invalid stage and root properties can be a common problem if you don't plan ahead. For example, the following code tries to set the location of a movie clip to the center of the stage prior to adding the object to the display list:

```
var mc:MovieClip = new MovieClip();
mc.x = mc.stage.stageWidth / 2;
addChild(mc);
```

This will fail, however, because the stage property is null. This problem can be corrected by transposing the last two lines of the script.

It's very easy to fall into this trap if you often code in the timeline, because the stage *appears* to exist without referencing a display object, as seen here without error:

```
var mc:MovieClip = new MovieClip();
mc.x = stage.stageWidth / 2;
addChild(mc);
```

However, this only works because the stage *is* referencing a display object. It's just an implied reference. This can be illustrated by rewriting the second line of the previous code this way:

```
mc.x = this.stage.stageWidth / 2;
```

The code works only because, in this example, the this keyword refers to the main timeline. In Flash Professional, the main timeline is always automatically part of the display list. (See Chapter 2 for more information on this.) The this keyword is usually omitted when the scope of the script is obvious, but its use here illustrates that stage must always be accessed through a display object.

# Removing Objects from the Display List and from Memory

It's just as important to know how to remove objects from the display list after they've been added. The processes for adding to and removing from the display list are similar. To remove a display object, you can use the **removeChild()** method, which takes only one argument: a reference to the child that must be removed:

```
removeChild(ball);
```

You can also remove a display object from a specific position in the display list using **removeChildAt()**. However, this method will remove any object from the specified position, so, unlike **removeChild()**, no object reference is needed.

```
removeChildAt(0);
```

The following example, found in the *remove_child_at.fla* source file, is the reverse of the **addChildAt()** script discussed in the prior section. It starts by using a **for** loop to add 20 balls to the stage, positioning them with the same technique used previously. It then uses the event listener to remove a child with each click.

**NOTE**

*For more information on **for** loops, please review Chapter 2. For more information on simultaneous assignment, as seen in line 3 of this script, see the note on page 85.*

```
1  for (var inc:int = 0; inc < 20; inc++) {
2      var ball:MovieClip = new Ball();
3      ball.x = ball.y = 100 + inc * 10;
4      addChildAt(ball, 0);
5  }
6
7  stage.addEventListener(MouseEvent.CLICK, onClick, false, 0, true);
8
9  function onClick(evt:MouseEvent):void {
10     removeChildAt(0);
11 }
```

This script works if something's in the display list because there is always something at position 0. After removing the last ball, however, a click will result in an error like, "the supplied index is out of bounds" because no object is in position 0.

To avoid this problem, check to see if there are any children in the display object container you are trying to empty. Making sure that the number of children exceeds zero will prevent the aforementioned error from occurring. The following is an updated **onClick()** function; it replaces lines 9 through 11 used in the previous code with a new conditional, which is shown in bold here. (For more information on conditionals, please review Chapter 2.)

```
1  function onClick(evt:MouseEvent):void {
2      if (numChildren > 0) {
3          removeChildAt(0);
4      }
5  }
```

The `numChildren` property, in this scope, references the main timeline. You can check the number of children in any display object container by preceding the property with your object of choice.

## Removing objects from memory

It's always a good idea to try to keep track of your objects and, when you're sure you no longer need them, to remove them from memory. This not only uses less memory and helps keep your projects efficient, but can also prevent unexpected errors that come from using old objects or values left in memory.

This is particularly relevant when discussing the display list because removing an object from the display list does not remove it from memory. The following script, found in the *remove_child.fla* source file, is a simplification of the previous example and will both remove a movie clip from the display list and from memory. Trace outputs are shown here as comments.

```
1   var ball:MovieClip = new Ball();
2   ball.x = ball.y = 100;
3   addChild(ball);
4
5   stage.addEventListener(MouseEvent.CLICK, onClick, false, 0, true);
6
7   function onClick(evt:MouseEvent):void {
8       removeChild(ball);
9       trace(ball); //[object Ball]
10
11      ball = null;
12      trace(ball); //null
13
14      stage.removeEventListener(MouseEvent.CLICK, onClick);
15  }
```

Lines 1 through 5 are derived from the previous example, creating and positioning the ball, adding it to the display list, and adding a mouse click listener to the stage. The first line of the function, line 8, removes the ball from the display list. Although it's no longer displayed, it's still in memory, as shown by the trace in line 9. Line 11, however, sets the object to **null**, allowing it to be removed from memory. Line 12 shows that the *ball* variable is null.

# Managing Object Names, Positions, and Data Types

As any display list grows, it will likely become desirable to traverse its contents and work with individual display objects. This may require simple tasks such as identifying a display object by name or position in the list, or even by referencing existing objects as a specific display object type. (For example, you may need to refer to an existing object as a movie clip if you want to use a movie clip method like **play()**).

**NOTE**

*If you want to use a* **for** *loop to remove all children of a container (such as everything in the display list or all children of a specific movie clip), it is easiest to remove the objects from the bottom, as discussed here. This prevents out of range errors that might be caused by removing objects from a specific position using the loop counter.*

*For example, this code will cause an error because the display list updates itself to remove gaps and, after children 0 through 4 are removed, there are no longer objects at positions 5 through 9.*

```
for (var i:int = 0; i < 10; i++) {
    removeChildAt(i);
}
```

*Use this approach, instead:*

```
for (var i:int = 0; i < 10; i++) {
    removeChildAt(0);
}
```

**NOTE**

*As an added review of best practices, line 14 emphasizes the concept of removing event listeners covered in Chapter 3.*

# Finding Children by Position and by Name

In most of the example scripts in this chapter, references to the display objects already exist and are known to you. However, you will likely need to find children in the display list with little more to go on than their position or name.

Finding a child by position is consistent with adding or removing children at a specific location in the display list. Using the **getChildAt()** method, you can supply a position in the list and retrieve a reference to that object. For example, you can work with the first child found using this familiar syntax:

```
var dispObj:DisplayObject = getChildAt(0);
```

If you don't know the location of a needed child, you can try to find it by name using its instance name (or value of its **name** property). Assuming a child had a name of circle, you could store a reference to that child using this syntax:

```
var dispObj:DisplayObject = getChildByName("circle");
```

Finally, if you need to know the location of a display object in the display list, but only have its name, you can add the **getChildIndex()** method to accomplish your goal. The first line of the following snippet retrieves a reference to the desired object, and the second line uses that reference to determine its index in the display list.

```
var dispObj:DisplayObject = getChildByName("circle");
var doIndex:int = getChildIndex(dispObj);
```

## Clarifying or Changing the Data Type of a Display Object

Note that, in the preceding discussion, we used **DisplayObject** as the data type when retrieving a reference to a display object—rather than **MovieClip**, for example. This is because you may not know if a child found in the display list is a movie clip, sprite, shape, and so on.

For example, if you call a function that adds a display object to the display list, what is the data type of that item? Without knowledge of what the function does, you can't know if the item is a movie clip, text field, or video. Similarly, what if you reference the parent of a display object, without giving the compiler any additional information? The only thing the compiler knows is that the parent is a display object container (because it's part of the display list and has children).

This can be a problem because the compiler can't know if a property or method is legal if it doesn't know the object's data type. The following creates a movie clip, adds it to the display list, and tells the movie clip's parent to go to frame 20 and stop:

```
var mc:MovieClip = new MovieClip();
addChild(mc);

mc.parent.gotoAndStop(20);
```

However, the ActionScript compiler doesn't know if **gotoAndStop()** is a legal method of *mc*'s parent because it doesn't know the parent's data type. For example, the parent might be a sprite and a sprite doesn't have a timeline. As such, you can't very well go to frame 20 of a sprite. If the data type of the parent is unknown to the ActionScript compiler, you will get an error similar to:

```
Call to a possibly undefined method gotoAndStop through a reference with
    static type flash.display:DisplayObjectContainer.
```

You can avoid this error by *casting* the object. Previously discussed in Chapter 2, casting is particularly important when manipulating the display list and warrants another mention. Casting means you are explicitly telling the ActionScript compiler the data type of the object—changing the compiler's understanding of the data from one type to another. Casting does not actually change data. In our example, to make sure the compiler doesn't object to the **gotoAndStop()** method, you must cast the parent from **DisplayObjectContainer** to **MovieClip**. You can do this by surrounding the object of unknown type with the desired class name. The following syntax tells the compiler that *mc*'s parent is of data type **MovieClip**:

```
MovieClip(mc.parent).gotoAndStop(20);
```

**NOTE**

*Another way to cast an object is by using the* as *operator. Continuing the example on this page, this syntax will also cast mc's parent as a movie clip:*

```
var mc2:MovieClip = mc.parent as MovieClip;
mc2.gotoAndStop(20);
```

*Although this is more verbose, it has advantages. For example, the <ClassName>() syntax may be confusing because it looks like you are calling a function or instantiating a class. Also, some conversion or creation functions takes precedence over casting and prevents casting from working. For example,* **Array()** *will not cast to an array because that syntax is equivalent to* **new Array()**, *which creates an array. This means it's possible to cast an object to Array only using the* **as** *operator.*

*One reason we like to use the <ClassName>() syntax is that the compiler will display an error if the casting is incorrect. The* **as** *operator will return* **null** *in this case, but not issue an error.*

If you need to tell the compiler that a display object is of another type, the syntax is consistent. The following syntax examples tell the compiler that a variable named *obj* is a text field, and that an item retrieved from the display list is a sprite, respectively:

```
TextField(obj);
Sprite(getChildAt(0));
```

**NOTE**

*It's possible to change the data type of an object implicitly, or even inadvertently. This is called* coercion. *You will sometimes see this in error messages similar to "Type Coercion failed," or "Implicit coercion of type X to type Y." When you see this, you should look in your code for possible data type errors or incompatible operations performed on a specific data type.*

# Changing the Display List Hierarchy

In addition to improving consistency over previous versions of ActionScript, the display list also makes managing assets much easier. Particularly simplified are: changing the visual stacking order (depth management) and dynamically changing the familial relationship between visual assets (reparenting, or moving a display object from one parent to another).

## Depth Management

Adding items to the display list does not require that you specify which level the new child should occupy, because all of that is handled for you automatically. This also makes managing the depths of display objects much easier than ever before.

To begin with, you can simply use the **addChild()** or **addChildAt()** methods to alter the order of display list items. As we discussed, adding a child to a display list position below other elements using the **addChildAt()** method will automatically push the other elements up in the list. But you can also use the **addChild()** method on an object that *already* exists in the display list. This step will remove the object from its original position and move it to the top of stack, pushing the other elements down.

For example, consider the following simple code, found in the source file *add_child_trace.fla*. Lines 1 through 6 use the standard approach of creating and adding movie clips to the display list, with the added step of giving each clip an instance name. Lines 7 and 8 display the results at this point and, as expected, the traces (indicated by comments here) show **mc1**, or "clip1," at position 0, and **mc2**, or "clip2," at position 1.

```
1    var mc1:MovieClip = new MovieClip();
2    mc1.name = "clip1";
3    addChild(mc1);
4    var mc2:MovieClip = new MovieClip();
5    mc2.name = "clip2";
6    addChild(mc2);
7    trace(getChildAt(0).name); //clip1
8    trace(getChildAt(1).name); //clip2
```

However, if you add **mc1** to the display list again, it is moved from position 0 to the end of the list, and **mc2** gets pushed to position 0. Adding the following lines to the script will demonstrate this process.

```
9    addChild(mc1);
10   trace(getChildAt(0).name); //clip2
11   trace(getChildAt(1).name); //clip1
```

This is demonstrated further in the following script, found in the *bring_to_top.fla* source file (Figure 4-7). This example takes advantage of the event propagation discussed in Chapter 3 to automatically bring any display object that is rolled over with the mouse to the top of the visual stacking order:

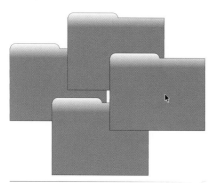

*Figure 4-7. In bring_to_top.fla, rolled-over items pop to the top*

```
1   addEventListener(MouseEvent.MOUSE_OVER, onBringToTop,
2                    false, 0, true);
3
4   function onBringToTop(evt:MouseEvent):void {
5       addChild(MovieClip(evt.target));
6   }
```

If adding or moving an item to the top of all others is not specific enough for your needs, there are also direct methods for swapping the depths of objects that are already in the display list. The **swapChildren()** method will swap the depths of two display objects regardless of where they are in the display list. For example, the following code, found in the *swap_children.fla* source file, will swap positions between the movie clip at the top of the display list—no matter how many display objects exist—and the movie clip that is clicked—no matter where in the display list that clip may be:

```
1   var gs:MovieClip = new GreenSquare();
2   gs.x = gs.y = 0;
3   addChild(gs);
4   var rs:MovieClip = new RedSquare();
5   rs.x = rs.y = 25;
6   addChild(rs);
7   var bs:MovieClip = new BlueSquare();
8   bs.x = bs.y = 50;
9   addChild(bs);
10
11  addEventListener(MouseEvent.CLICK, onClick, false, 0, true);
12  function onClick(evt:MouseEvent):void {
13      var clickedChild:MovieClip = MovieClip(evt.target);
14      var topChild:MovieClip = MovieClip(getChildAt(numChildren-1));
15      swapChildren(clickedChild, topChild);
16  }
```

Lines 1 through 9 repeat the same process three times. First, new instances of library symbols, using the **GreenSquare**, **RedSquare**, and **BlueSquare** linkage classes, respectively, are created. (See the "Adding Custom Symbol Instances to the Display List" section in this chapter for more information.) Next, the x and y coordinates of each instance are set 25 pixels apart. Finally, each instance is added to the display list.

Line 11 creates an event listener that is attached to the main timeline and listens for a mouse click. Any time an object in the main timeline is clicked, the **onClick()** function is called. Line 13 casts whatever is clicked as a movie clip, line 14 does the same with the last object in the display list, and line 15 swaps those display objects.

ActionScript identifies the bottom item in the display list using 0. Therefore, Line 14 can't use the **numChildren** property by itself to identify the last item in the display list. For example, if you have three items in the display list, **numChildren** returns 3, but the indices (positions) of those items are 0, 1, and 2. So, to retrieve the last item in the list, you must use **numChildren - 1**, which correctly identifies the last item in the list.

**NOTE**

*This script is written in the main time-line, so that is the script's scope. By using methods like* **addChild()** *and* **addEventListener()** *without attaching them to a specific object, the scope of the script is the implied object. Using the* **this** *keyword to refer to the current scope is another way to make this clear. Considering line 3 as an example, the syntax is* **this.addChild(gs)**. *See Chapter 2 for more information.*

You can also swap the contents of any two depths, no matter what's in them, using the **swapChildrenAt()** method. This example snippet will swap whichever display objects are in display list positions 0 and 10:

```
swapChildrenAt(0, 10);
```

Finally, you can move a child to a specific depth using the **setChildIndex()** method. It requires two arguments: the child you want to move, and its intended depth. The following code adjustment to the swap children example, found in the *set_child_index.fla* source file, changes line 15 to set the index of the clicked child to 0.

```
12  function onClick(evt:MouseEvent):void {
13      var clickedChild:MovieClip = MovieClip(evt.target);
14      var topChild:MovieClip = MovieClip(getChildAt(numChildren-1));
15      setChildIndex(clickedChild, 0);
16  }
```

## Reparenting Children

Another task made easy by the display list is moving a child from one parent to another. In the *reparenting.fla* source file, a moon can be moved to either of two night skies, just by clicking that sky (Figure 4-8). Both skies are also draggable, demonstrating that the moon will automatically move with each sky because it is a child object inside the parent.

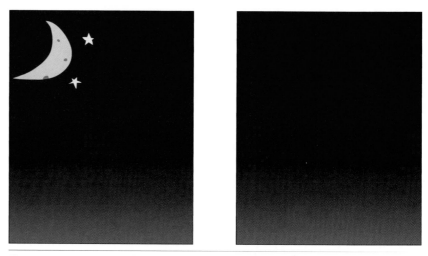

*Figure 4-8. In reparenting.fla, the moon becomes a child of the clicked sky*

This exercise again demonstrates the bubbling of events by attaching both listeners to a parent container once, instead of to each sky. (See Chapter 3 for more information.) However, a side effect of this efficiency is that the moon, as a child of that parent container, will also react to the events. So, it's possible to add the moon *to itself*, resulting in an error. To prevent this from happening, line 1 disables mouse interaction with the moon.

In the default layout of the file, the three siblings (moon and two skies) are all on the stage. The first reparenting process is demonstrated in line 2 by adding the moon to the first sky (on the left) as its starting position. Lines 4 and 5 then add two event listeners to the main timeline. Note that the listeners are not attached to a specific object in lines 4 and 5. The **this** object is the implied responsible party, indicating the current scope, or main timeline. As a result, *any* child display object that receives a **mouse down** event will call **onDrag()** and a child **mouse up** event will call **onDrop()**.

```
1    moon.mouseEnabled = false;
2    sky0.addChild(moon);
3
4    addEventListener(MouseEvent.MOUSE_DOWN, onDrag, false, 0, true);
5    addEventListener(MouseEvent.MOUSE_UP, onDrop, false, 0, true);
6
7    function onDrag(evt:MouseEvent):void {
8        evt.target.addChild(moon);
9        evt.target.startDrag();
10   }
```

Line 8 then adds the moon to the sky that was clicked. This process removes the moon from its previous parent and adds it to the clicked item, reparenting the moon. The last line of the function then enables dragging of the clicked item.

Finally, when the **mouse up** event is received, the **onDrop()** function disables dragging.

```
11   function onDrop(evt:MouseEvent):void {
12       stopDrag();
13   }
```

As you can see, by using the **addChild()** method, you can move a display object from one parent container to another. As a result, the child will inherit basic display attributes from its parent. For example, in addition to the x and y coordinates demonstrated in this file, the child will also be affected by any changes to rotation, scale, or alpha values of the parent.

## A Dynamic Navigation Bar

Now it's time to tie much of this together and create a dynamic navigation bar. This project will create a five-button navigation bar that will be centered on the stage as shown in Figure 4-9. To simulate functionality, each button will trace its name to the Output panel when clicked. Later in the book, you'll combine additional skills to create a similar navigation bar that will use XML and load external assets.

*Figure 4-9. A dynamically generated navigation bar*

This script can be found in the *dyn_nav_bar.fla* source file. Lines 1 and 2 initialize the number of buttons used and the space between each button (in pixels). Line 4 creates a container that will hold not only the buttons, but also background art. The container doesn't need a timeline, so for efficiency (and practice), a sprite is used rather than a movie clip. Next, line 5 adds the sprite to the display list.

```
1    var btnNum:int = 5;
2    var spacing:Number = 10;
3
4    var navBar:Sprite = new Sprite();
5    addChild(navBar);
```

**NOTE**

*The* **SimpleButton** *class, used to create custom buttons, is so named because a* **Button** *class already existed. The latter is used to create instances of the* **Button** *component.*

Lines 6 through 15 create the buttons. Line 6 types a variable as **SimpleButton**, which allows you to use (or create) button symbol instances, rather than relying solely on movie clips. The loop defined in line 7 creates five buttons, based on the value of **btnNum** assigned in line 1.

```
6    var btn:SimpleButton;
7    for (var i:int = 0; i < btnNum; i++) {
8        btn = new Btn();
9        btn.name = "button" + i;
10       btn.x = spacing + i * (btn.width + spacing);
11       btn.y = spacing / 2;
12       btn.addEventListener(MouseEvent.CLICK, onTraceName,
13                            false, 0, true);
14       navBar.addChild(btn);
15   }
```

Each time through the loop, a new button is created from a button symbol in the library with the linkage class, *Btn* (line 8). The button is given a name by combining the string "button" and the loop counter value (line 9). The first button is called *button0*, the second is called *button1*, and so on.

Each button is positioned horizontally (line 10) using the spacing gap set in line 2, plus the width of the button (in this case, 65 pixels) and another spacing gap. Figure 4-10 shows the measurements in use. The first button is positioned only 10 pixels to the right of the container's edge, while the second button is positioned 85 pixels to the right of the container's edge. In both cases, the spacing is 10, and the button width (65) plus spacing is 75. So, the first result is 10 plus 0 * (65 + 10), or 10 + 0, or 10. The second result is 10 plus 1 * (65 + 10), or 10 + 75, or 85. This process continues for each button. The vertical position is also set for each button, moving the button down 10 / 2, or 5 pixels.

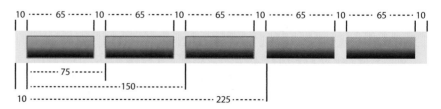

*Figure 4-10. Object positioning in the dynamic navigation bar*

The last lines in the loop add a mouse click event listener to the button (line 12) that will call the **onTraceName()** function when the event is received, and add the button to the **navBar** parent container (line 14).

```
16   var bg:MovieClip = new NavBarBack();
17   bg.width = spacing + btnNum * (btn.width + spacing);
18   bg.height = btn.height + spacing;
19   navBar.addChildAt(bg, 0);
```

Starting with line 15, a background is added to the **navBar**. Similar to the calculation used to position each button, its width is set to an initial spacing gap plus the total number of buttons times the sum of the button width and **spacing** (line 16). It's height is set to the button height plus **spacing** (line 17). The background is then added to the **navBar** at position 0, ensuring that it's placed *behind* all the buttons (line 18). The result is, no matter how many buttons you need, or what the button size is, the buttons will be spaced uniformly within the background, both horizontally and vertically.

Finally, the last script block positions the finished **navBar** and creates the listener function. The bar is centered horizontally by subtracting its width from the stage width, and dividing that value by two for a left and right margin (line 19). It is also positioned vertically at a y coordinate of 20 pixels (line 20). The **onTraceName()** function (lines 22 through 24) traces the name of each button when the user clicks on it.

```
20   navBar.x = (stage.stageWidth - navBar.width) / 2;
21   navBar.y = 20;
22
23   function onTraceName(evt:MouseEvent):void {
24       trace(evt.target.name);
25   }
```

This exercise demonstrates how to create a simulated navigation bar using the display list, when no assets previously existed on the stage. Later in the book, you'll also learn how to create the buttons and draw the background shape entirely with ActionScript, removing the need to precreate these assets as library symbols. You'll also learn how to create a class-based version of this system to control the playhead of a movie clip (Chapter 6), and load images or SWFs (Chapter 13).

## What's Next?

The display list is among the most important new introductions to ActionScript 3.0. It is worth the effort to explore the properties, methods, and events of the various display list classes—starting with the contents of this chapter, and then delving into the Flash help system, and additional resources, as you gain experience. Experimenting with the display list will show you that it is easy to use and, if you have experience with prior versions of ActionScript, you will soon find that it's much simpler and more consistent than equivalent methods in ActionScript 1.0 or ActionScript 2.0.

**NOTE**

*Push Yourself: A bonus file in this chapter's source archive expands on this example. It's called **dyn_nav_bar_urls. fla** and shows how to load web pages based on this dynamic navigation bar example. It uses information explained in Chapter 13, but if you want to learn more at the same time you put this chapter into practice, give the file a look!*

Next, we'll discuss timeline control. Regardless of whether you are creating lengthy linear animations or single-frame applications, you are likely to require some degree of control over the main timeline or movie clips. ActionScript 3.0 offers a few new features for you to try out.

**In the next chapter**, we'll discuss:

- Controlling playback of your animations and applications by moving the playhead with ActionScript

- Parsing frame label names from timelines and scenes

- Changing the frame rate of movie playback for the first time

## CHAPTER 5

# TIMELINE CONTROL

In this chapter, you'll learn some basic approaches to controlling timelines—both that of the main Flash movie and the movie clips it contains. We'll divide our focus into three main areas:

- **Jump Right In.** Change the frame rate of your SWF at runtime.

- **Playhead Movement.** This includes stopping and playing the file, and going to a specific frame.

- **Frame Labels.** Including improved playhead movement techniques without relying on frame numbers.

- **Frame Rates.** Changing the movie's frame rate to increase or decrease animation speed during playback.

- **A Simple Site or Application Structure.** We'll wrap up the chapter by building a project that combines timeline animation with ActionScript navigation. The project can be used as an example template for a multi-state application or Flash-based website.

We'll also take a look at an undocumented feature that allows you to add frame scripts to movie clips at runtime and show you a demo of how to create a flexible structure for a Flash website or application.

## Jump Right In

We'll start off with one of the most-desired features in the evolution of ActionScript: the ability to adjust the frame rate of a file with code. Consider a simple example that switches a SWF's frame rate between 1 and 24 frames per second, with every click of the mouse. This script can be found in the *frame_rate_trace.fla* source file.

```
1    stage.frameRate = 24;
2
3    this.addEventListener(Event.ENTER_FRAME, onEnter, false, 0, true);
4    function onEnter(evt:Event):void {
5        trace(stage.frameRate);
6    }
7
```

**NOTE**

*Real-world frame rates vary based on many factors including the processing power of your computer, how hard it's working at any given moment, and what your SWF is trying to do. Depending on these circumstances, among others, you're likely to achieve a maximum frame rate between 60 and 120 frames per second.*

*Although you're unlikely to see this performance anytime soon, it's theoretically possible to assign a frame rate up to 1000 fps. Any assignment above that number will fall back to 1000.*

**NOTE**

*To review the basics of movie clips, consult Chapters 3 and 4.*

```
8   stage.addEventListener(MouseEvent.CLICK, onClick, false, 0, true);
9   function onClick(evt:MouseEvent):void {
10      if (stage.frameRate == 24) {
11          stage.frameRate = 1;
12      } else {
13          stage.frameRate = 24;
14      }
15  }
```

Line 1 shows a new stage property called **frameRate**, which is assigned to 24 frames per second. Lines 3 through 6 contain an enter frame listener that traces the current frame rate. Lines 8 through 15 contain a mouse click listener that will toggle the frame rate between 1 and 24 frames per second.

Once you get this example working, experiment by adding visual assets, as in *frame_rate_timeline_tween.fla*, and watch your animations change. A similar example later in the chapter will show the speed of an animation change in response to buttons that increase or decrease the frame rate.

## Playhead Movement

One of the most basic ActionScript skills you need to embrace is the ability to navigate within your Flash movies. You will often use these skills to control the playback of movie clips nested within your main movies.

The code in this chapter is straightforward enough that you can create your own examples to test the functionality discussed, if you want to use your own assets. We'll cover the structural necessities for each example to make it easier for you to follow along using your own assets. In each section, we'll also cite the sample file we're using so you can consult that file if preferred.

Let's start by covering the basic concept of stopping and starting playback of the main timeline or movie clip, and then add an initial jump to another frame. If you're creating your own file, be sure it has a linear animation in one layer of the main timeline, and four buttons in one or more other layers that span the length of the animation. In other words, your buttons must be visible throughout the animation. Alternatively, you can open the sample file *navigation_01.fla*.

Figure 5-1 shows *navigation_01.fla*, which contains four timeline tweens of black circles. For added visual impact, the circles use the *Invert* blend mode (seen in the Display section of the Properties panel) to create an interesting optical illusion of rotating cylinders. We'll be starting and stopping playback at any point, as well as jumping to a specific frame to start and stop playback (frame 1, in this example). Initially, we'll rely on frame numbers to specify where to start and stop.

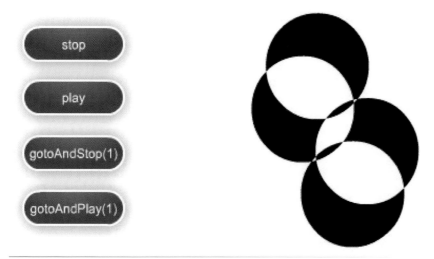

*Figure 5-1. navigation_01.fla demonstrates simple navigation*

Placing a **stop()** action in any frame script is a means of halting playback of that timeline without user interaction—perhaps at the end of an animation or to support a menu or similar need to display a single frame. Only the timeline in which the **stop()** action is used will stop, so if the main timeline is stopped, movie clips will continue to animate.

Let's take a more interactive approach and look at invoking the **stop()** action via user input, such as clicking a button. Line 1 of the following script is an event listener added to a button named *stopBtn*. It uses a mouse click to call **onStopClick()**, the function defined in Lines 3 through 5.

**NOTE**

*If you don't know about event listeners or typed arguments, consult Chapter 3 for more information. Be sure to pay particular attention to the sidebar "Garbage Collection" on weak references.*

```
1    stopBtn.addEventListener(MouseEvent.CLICK, onStopClick,
2                           false, 0, true);
3    function onStopClick(evt:MouseEvent):void {
4        stop();
5    }
```

All playback of the main timeline will cease when the user clicks the button. Adding the following lines to the script will allow you to restart playback. The new code is similar to the previous example, but invokes the **play()** method from the *playBtn* instead. Using this pair of buttons, you can start and stop playback at any time without relocating the playback head in the process.

```
6    playBtn.addEventListener(MouseEvent.CLICK, onPlayClick,
7                           false, 0, true);
8    function onPlayClick(evt:MouseEvent):void {
9        play();
10   }
```

Using **stop()** and **play()** in this fashion is useful for controlling a linear animation, much in the same way a YouTube controller bar might control video playback. However, it's less common when using interactive menus, for example, because you typically want to jump to a specific point in your timeline before stopping or playing.

For example, you might have generic sections that could apply to any project, such as home, about, and help. If you were restricted to the use of **stop()** and **play()**, you would be forced to play through one section to get to another.

Adding again to the previous script, the following content adds a slight variation. The buttons in the new script function in similar ways. However, instead of stopping in (or playing from) the current frame, the new buttons move the playhead to a specific frame first. For example, if you had previously stopped playback in frame 20, triggering **play()** again would send the playhead to frame 21. However, if you used **gotoAndPlay()** and specified frame 1 as a destination (as seen in line 16 of the script that follows), you would resume playback at frame 1, rather than at frame 21. If you use **gotoAndStop()** (as in line 19), the playhead will go to that frame but not continue to play through the rest of the timeline. There are no structural differences in this code, so simply add the following content to your existing script:

```
11  gotoPlayBtn.addEventListener(MouseEvent.CLICK, onGotoPlayClick,
12                              false, 0, true);
13  gotoStopBtn.addEventListener(MouseEvent.CLICK, onGotoStopClick,
14                              false, 0, true);
15  function onGotoPlayClick(evt:MouseEvent):void {
16      gotoAndPlay(1);
17  }
18  function onGotoStopClick(evt:MouseEvent):void {
19      gotoAndStop(1);
20  }
```

Once you get a navigation system working, it may sometimes be useful to know where you are in a timeline, or how many frames the timeline contains. For example, you can determine if you're in the last frame of a timeline by checking to see if the current frame matches the total number of frames. Tracing this information to the Output panel can help you track your movements during development. Tracing **totalFrames** will display the number of frames in the timeline, and tracing **currentFrame** will show the frame number in which the playhead currently sits.

```
trace("This movie has", totalFrames, "frames.");
trace(currentFrame);
```

The companion sample file, *navigation_02.fla*, demonstrates the use of these properties, tracing **totalFrames** in frame 1, and **currentFrame** each time a button is clicked.

# Frame Labels

Using frame numbers with `goto` methods has advantages, among them simplicity and use in numeric contexts (such as with a loop or other type of counter when an integer is at hand). However, frame numbers also have disadvantages. The most notable disadvantage is that edits made to your file after your script is written may result in a change to the number of frames, or frame sequence, in your timeline.

For example, your help section may start at frame 100, but you may then insert or delete frames in a section of your timeline prior to that frame. This change may cause the help section to shift to a new frame. If your navigation script sends the playhead to frame 100, you will no longer see the help section.

One way around this problem is to use frame labels to mark the location of a specific segment of your timeline. As long as you shift content by inserting or deleting frames to all layers in your timeline (maintaining sync among your layers), a frame label will move with your content.

This is a useful feature when you are relying heavily on timeline tweens for file structure or transitions (as we'll see in our demo site in a short while), or when you think you may be adding or deleting sections in your file. Frame labels remove the need to organize your content linearly and free you to rearrange your timeline at any point.

The sample file, *frame_labels_01.fla*, demonstrates the use of frame labels instead of frame numbers when using a `goto` method. It also illustrates another important and useful concept, which is that you can use these methods to control the playback of movie clips as well as the main timeline.

Instead of controlling the playback of a linear animation, the sample file moves the playhead between the frames of a movie clip called *pages*. This is a common technique for swapping content in a Flash file because you can keep your main timeline simple, and jump the movie clip from frame to frame to reveal each new screen. Figure 5-2 displays the "page1" frame of the *pages* movie clip in *frame_labels_01.fla*, after jumping to the frame by specifying the frame label. The timeline inset shows the frame labels.

The initial setup of this example requires that we prevent the movie clip from playing on its own, so we can exert the desired control over its playback. There are several ways to do this. The first, and perhaps most obvious approach, is to put a `stop()` action in the first frame of the movie clip.

**NOTE**

*A frame number is always an integer equal to, or greater than 1. A frame label is always a string.*

Button *one*

Button *two*

Button *three*

*Figure 5-2. The "page1" frame of the pages movie clip in frame_labels_01.fla*

The second technique is more flexible and easier to maintain because it centralizes your code into fewer frames. Use the **stop()** method, but in your main timeline, targeting the movie clip instance. To do this, precede the method with the object you wish to stop, as seen in line 1 of the following script. In this case, we are stopping the movie clip called *pages*. Immediately upon starting, the SWF stops the *pages* movie clip in line 1. Each button causes the movie clip to change frames in lines 8, 11, and 14.

```
1   pages.stop();
2
3   one.addEventListener(MouseEvent.CLICK, onOneClick, false, 0, true);
4   two.addEventListener(MouseEvent.CLICK, onTwoClick, false, 0, true);
5   three.addEventListener(MouseEvent.CLICK, onThreeClick,
6                           false, 0, true);
7   function onOneClick(evt:MouseEvent):void {
8       pages.gotoAndStop("page1");
9   }
10  function onTwoClick(evt:MouseEvent):void {
11      pages.gotoAndStop("page2");
12  }
13  function onThreeClick(evt:MouseEvent):void {
14      pages.gotoAndStop("page3");
15  }
```

To test the effectiveness of using frame labels, add or delete frames across all layers before one of the existing frame labels. Despite changing the frame count, you will find that the navigation still works as desired.

## New Timeline ActionScript

ActionScript 3.0 provides a few new features relevant to timelines. The first is an associative array of all frame labels in a file. This array is called `labels`, and contains `name` and `frame` properties that provide the text of the frame label and the frame number to which it is applied.

The second is a `scenes` array that contains each scene's name and number of frames, stored in the array's `name` and `numFrames` properties, respectively. The scenes array also has its own `labels` object so you can check the label names and frame numbers as described previously, in all the scenes in your file.

The sample file, *frame_labels_02.fla*, demonstrates several of these features, as well as illustrates a couple uses of the available frame label options. It uses the same *pages* movie clip as in the prior file, but with adapted functionality and buttons. Figure 5-3 shows the direct navigation to a frame *that is four frames after a specified label*.

**NOTE**

*In case you're unfamiliar with scenes, they're essentially a way of organizing very long timelines into smaller manageable chunks. At runtime, all scenes are treated as one giant timeline, and the playhead can move freely between scenes either automatically during linear playback, or with ActionScript.*

*We don't use scenes much in the work we do, but we've had students who rely on scenes to tell long stories through linear animation. Adding a new scene to a file (Window→Other Panels→Scene) effectively resets the interface to a new timeline, making it easier to work with the relevant frames without being distracted by prior or future scenes in your file. Another advantage of scenes is that you can test single scenes during development, rather than having to test your entire movie.*

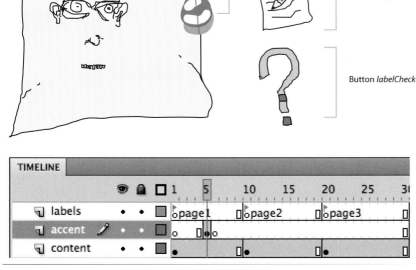

*Figure 5-3. The **pages** movie clip of frame_labels_02.fla jumping to a frame relative to the location of a label*

We're going to start by highlighting the functionality of the second button, *output*, which collects many of the features in one information dump to the Output panel. Looking at the following script, the first new item you'll see is a main movie **stop()** action on line 1. This has been added because this file has a second scene to demonstrate the new **scenes** array and **currentScene** property. Line 3 stops the movie clip as in the prior example, and line 5 creates a mouse click listener for the button.

```
1   stop();
2
3   pages.stop();
4
5   output.addEventListener(MouseEvent.CLICK, onOutputClick,
6                           false, 0, true);
7   function onOutputClick(evt:MouseEvent):void {
8       trace("The main movie has " + scenes.length + " scenes.");
9       trace("The current scene is 0" + currentScene.name + "0.");
10      trace("It has " + currentScene.numFrames + " frame(s),");
11      trace(" and " + currentScene.labels.length + " label(s). ");
12      trace("The second scene's first label is 0" +
13          scenes[1].labels[0].name + "0,");
14      trace(" which is in frame " + scenes[1].labels[0].frame + ".");
15      var numLabels:int = pages.currentLabels.length;
16      trace("Movie clip 'pages' has " + numLabels + " labels.");
17      trace("Its last label is 0" +
18          pages.currentLabels[numLabels-1].name  + "0.");
19  }
```

**NOTE**

*In ActionScript 3.0, you can trace multiple items to the Output panel by separating them with commas when using the* **trace()** *statement. However, that will automatically put a space between each item in the trace. So, when you want to build a string with adjacent items, such as the single-quotation marks that surround some of the values in this script, it's better to use the string concatenation operator (**+**) to join the items together, rather than use commas.*

Lines 7 through 19 contain this button's goodies, tracing the number of scenes (line 8), the name and number of frames of the current scene (lines 9 and 10), and the total number of labels in the current scene (line 11). The script also traces the name and frame number of the first label of the second scene (lines 12 through 14). Line 14 uses the array syntax discussed in Chapter 2, with indices starting at 0 to represent the first item in an array. Thus the code targets the second scene, first label, frame number.

Finally, lines 15 through 18 look at the **currentLabels** array of the *pages* movie clip, getting the number of labels through the **length** property, and the name of the last label in the clip.

This series of trace commands offers a half dozen or so variants on the new scene and label features and should stimulate your imagination. Try to figure out interesting ways to make use of these properties. To get you started, we've provided two examples, included on the other two buttons.

Attached to the first button, **onePlus** is a way of reaching a frame relative to a frame label. For instance, you may want to revisit a section of your file, but without retriggering an initialization routine found in the frame marked by your frame label. For example, a section may have an intro animation that you want to see the first time, but skip thereafter. In that case, you may want to go to the "label frame plus one."

Perhaps more common is a uniformly structured file, such as a character animation cycle (walk, run, jump, duck, and so on), or an interface of drawers or tabs that slide in and out from off-stage. In these cases, each action might consist of the same number of frames. You may want to interrupt one sequence and jump to the same position in another sequence. Imagine, as an example, interrupting a timeline tween of an interface drawer sliding open, and wanting to jump to the same location in the timeline tween of the drawer sliding closed.

To avoid relying strictly on frame numbers, it helps to be able to start from a frame label and jump to a specific number of frames beyond that label. As an addition to your ongoing script, look at the following. This code sends the *pages* movie clip to a frame returned by the **getFrame()** function. In Line 21, the script passes in a label and a movie clip. The function, which we'll look at in just a moment, returns the frame number that matches the label provided. In line 22, if the value returned is greater than zero (as all timelines start with frame 1), the movie clip is sent to that frame plus a relative offset of four additional frames.

```
20  onePlus.addEventListener(MouseEvent.CLICK, onOnePlusClick,
21                           false, 0, true);
22  function onOnePlusClick(evt:MouseEvent):void {
23      var frameNum:int = getFrame("page1", pages);
24      if (frameNum > 0) {
25          pages.gotoAndStop(frameNum + 4);
26      }
27  }
28
29  function getFrame(frLabel:String, mc:MovieClip):int {
30      for (var i:int = 0; i < mc.currentLabels.length; i++) {
31          if (mc.currentLabels[i].name == frLabel) {
32              return mc.currentLabels[i].frame;
33          }
34      }
35      return -1;
36  }
```

The aforementioned **getFrame()** function appears in lines 27 through 34. The function accepts a **String** parameter containing the name of the original frame label, and the movie clip within which the label resides. Note the **int** data type of the return value so the compiler knows to expect an integer from the function. Lines 28 and 29 loop through all the labels in the referenced movie clip, comparing the name of each label to the label desired. If a match is found, the frame in which the label resides is returned in line 30. If no match is found after looping through all the labels, –1 is returned in line 33. The desired result, in our sample file, is that the playhead jumps to frame 5 instead of frame 1 where the "page1" label resides.

A similar coding technique is to use these features to check whether a specific frame exists. This option can be used for navigation error checking or simply to make sure you're working with the correct movie clip among many that may be available.

**NOTE**

*Although not universal, returning –1 when something isn't found is a common technique. It may sound counterintuitive, but it came into popular use because zero is often a meaningful value. For example, both the first item in an array and the first character in a string have an index of zero.*

*In this example, you might choose to return 0 because you know there is no frame 0. However, maintaining consistency with other methods that return –1 when nothing is found will make things easier the more you code.*

The following code adds such a function and triggers it from a mouse click listener defined in lines 35 through 39. As before, the function call passes a label and movie clip to the function, as seen in line 38. The function itself is defined in lines 41 through 48, and is explained following the code.

```
37  labelCheck.addEventListener(MouseEvent.CLICK, onLabelCheckClick,
38                              false, 0, true);
39  function onLabelCheckClick(evt:MouseEvent):void {
40      trace(frameLabelExists("page3", pages));
41  }
42
43  function frameLabelExists(frLabel:String, mc:MovieClip):Boolean {
44      for (var i:int = 0; i < mc.currentLabels.length; i++) {
45          if (mc.currentLabels[i].name == frLabel) {
46              return true;
47          }
48      }
49      return false;
50  }
```

The functionality of **isFrameLabel()** is nearly the same as the **getFrame()** function discussed previously, except that this function returns **true** if a queried frame label is found, or **false** if it is not found. In our sample file, the third button will trace **true** to the Output panel, because the "page3" frame label does exist in the *pages* movie clip. This subtle variant is just another simple example of how you might use the frame label and scene arrays and properties introduced in ActionScript 3.0.

## Frame Rate

As seen in the chapter's opening script, you can now dynamically change the frame rate at which your file plays at runtime. In Flash Professional CS5, the default frame rate of an FLA is 24 frames per second, which can be adjusted in the Properties panel. Prior to ActionScript 3.0, the frame rate you chose was locked in for the life of your SWF. It is now possible to update the speed at which your file plays by changing the **frameRate** property of the stage, as demonstrated in the sample file *frame_rate.fla*.

Figure 5-4 shows the interface of *frame_rate.fla*, which visualizes the runtime reassigning of frame rates.

**NOTE**

*For more information about referencing the stage in ActionScript 3.0, see Chapters 3 and 4.*

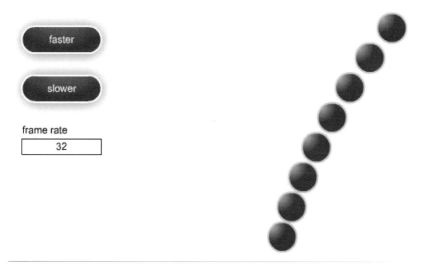

*Figure 5-4. frame_rate.fla with buttons on the left that increase and decrease the frame rate, which controls the speed of the animation on the right*

The script in this file, shown in the following code block, increments or decrements the frame rate by five frames per second with each click of a button. You may also notice another simple example of error checking in the **onSlowerClick()** function, to prevent a frame rate of zero or below. Start the file and watch it run for a second or two at the default frame rate of 24 frames per second. Then experiment with additional frame rates to see how they change the movie clip animation.

```
1   info.text = stage.frameRate;
2
3   faster.addEventListener(MouseEvent.CLICK, onFasterClick,
4                           false, 0, true);
5   slower.addEventListener(MouseEvent.CLICK, onSlowerClick,
6                           false, 0, true);
7   function onFasterClick(evt:MouseEvent):void {
8       stage.frameRate += 5;
9       info.text = stage.frameRate;
10  }
11  function onSlowerClick(evt:MouseEvent):void {
12      if (stage.frameRate > 5) {
13          stage.frameRate -= 5;
14      }
15      info.text = stage.frameRate;
16  }
```

The **frameRate** property requires little explanation, but its impact should not be underestimated. Other interactive environments have long been able to vary playback speed, and this is a welcome change to ActionScript for many enthusiastic developers—especially animators. Slow motion has never been easier.

# A Simple Site or Application Structure

As the final demo file in this chapter, we want to provide a very simple example of one of our most commonly requested uses of navigation to add visual interest. The *demo_site.fla* source file shows how to design a basic site or application skeleton that gives you the freedom to combine your timeline animation skills with ActionScript coding.

This file intentionally uses detailed, and varied, timeline tweens—with inconsistent frame counts—to transition between three separate sections of this sample site or application (Figure 5-5). The idea is to take advantage of frame label navigation, but freely move from any section to any other section without concern of interrupting (or matching) the entrance or exit animations.

As you look through the sample file, you'll see that a virtual gamut of property manipulations add visual interest. Section 1 rotates in and skews out, section 2 bounces in and zooms out, and section 3 wipes in and fades out. Each section stops in the middle of the transitions to display its placeholder content. Moving unencumbered between any sections is achieved through a combination of the **play()** method and a variable.

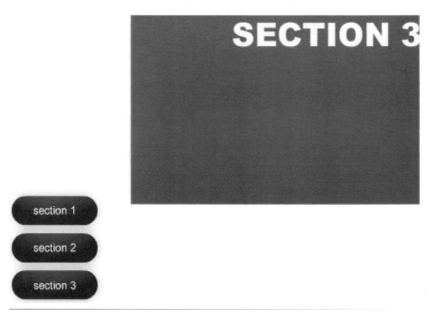

*Figure 5-5. The file demo_site.fla demonstrates navigation with transitions*

The first script of this file is in frame 1 of the main timeline. Line 1 initializes the **nextSection** variable, typing it as a String. We will store the destination frame label in this variable. Scripts in other keyframes (which we'll look at in a moment) will use the **gotoAndPlay()** method to jump to the frame stored in this variable.

```
1    var nextSection:String = "";
2
3    section1.addEventListener(MouseEvent.CLICK, navigate,
4                              false, 0, true);
5    section2.addEventListener(MouseEvent.CLICK, navigate,
6                              false, 0, true);
7    section3.addEventListener(MouseEvent.CLICK, navigate,
8                              false, 0, true);
9    function navigate(evt:MouseEvent):void {
10       nextSection = evt.target.name;
11       play();
12   }
```

The remainder of the script is similar to the previous examples, creating three buttons that all access the same listener. Line 10 populates the **nextSection** variable using the name of the button that was clicked. Knowing that the **target** property can identify the button that was clicked, we can further query its **name** property to determine the name of the button. By naming buttons with names that match frame labels, we can set up our file cleanly and efficiently. Clicking the **section1** button will take us to the corresponding "section1" frame label.

**NOTE**

*Chapter 3 discussed the use of the event argument in event listeners, and the ability to learn about the event trigger by querying its* **target** *property.*

How, then, do we prevent the entry and exit animations from being interrupted or from overlapping? First, each button click populates the **nextSection** variable with the desired destination frame label. Then we use **play()** to play the file from that point forward. This plays through the entry animation of the first section, and then another script halts the playhead in the content keyframe of the section with a **stop()** action.

```
//at end of entry animation
stop();
```

Using the **play()** method prevents repeated clicks on a button from starting an entry animation over and over again—a possible side effect of using **gotoAndPlay()**. Instead of every click first jumping to a specific frame before playing, each click just continues to tell the timeline to play, which it's already doing, and so has no ill effect.

Having stopped at the content frame of the section, the user is free to view that screen. Any subsequent button clicks will first populate the **nextSection** variable and then again call the **play()** method. This sets the playhead in motion, carrying it through the concluding animation until it hits the last frame script in the section:

```
//at end of exit animation
gotoAndPlay(nextSection);
```

This script is the last piece of the puzzle. After playing the prior section outro animation, this method sends the playhead to the new section entry animation. The cycle then repeats as the playhead dutifully stops at the content frame of the new section.

This structure allows you to be as creative as you want with timeline tweens and still move in and out of any section no matter how many frames each animation requires. Because you're using frame labels, you can easily change any sequence without having to adjust your scripts to update new frame numbers.

## Undocumented: Adding Frame Scripts to Movie Clips at Runtime

To finish off our discussion of timelines, we want to show you an undocumented method for adding frame scripts to movie clips at runtime. As always, be careful using undocumented ActionScript, testing your implementation thoroughly and trying not to rely on its use for final production, if possible. In addition to making no warranties as to current reliability, there's no guarantee that future versions of Flash Player will support an undocumented feature.

To implement this feature, you need to create a movie clip with two or more frames, and give it an instance name of *mc*. Alternately, you can use the *addFrameScript.fla* source file. The method we will use is:

```
<movieclip>.addFrameScript(<framenum1>, <function1>,
                           <framenum2>, <function2>,
                           ...rest);
```

By adding the method to a movie clip instance, you can dictate that any function be called when the specified frame number is reached. The ellipsis followed by "rest" is a special case that indicates this function will accept an unlimited number of comma-delimited arguments. In this case, the structure requires pairs of frame number, function; frame number, function; and so on. In the following example, only one frame script is added.

First, a function is defined that will stop the movie clip and trace the frame on which it stopped.

```
function onStopMC() {
    mc.stop();
    trace(mc.currentFrame);
}
mc.addFrameScript(mc.totalFrames - 1, onStopMC);
```

Then the addFrameScript() method is used, specifying that the onStopMC() function be added to the last frame. This can be a bit confusing because the totalFrames property returns a number that corresponds with the last frame, yet this script subtracts one from that value. The addFrameScript() method consistently functions on the premise that a first item in most ActionScript structures (such as an array, the display list, a string, and more) is item 0. Therefore, totalFrames - 1 is the last frame of the movie clip.

When you run the sample file, the movie clip animates and, when it reaches frame 40, the script stops and traces 40 to the Output window.

# What's Next?

By now you should have a relatively firm grasp of how to navigate timelines, be able to manipulate display objects (including their properties and methods), and understand the fundamentals of the ActionScript 3.0 event model. Up to this point, we've been focusing primarily on syntax and approaching each task using simple procedural programming techniques.

As you'll read in Chapter 6, you may find this sufficient for many of the projects you create. However, larger projects, and projects developed in a workgroup environment with multiple programmers, can significantly benefit from OOP techniques. From this point on, we'll be using a little OOP in our demos, and you will eventually end up with a final project that is built entirely using object-oriented programming. This content design allows you to learn at your own pace, choosing when to use procedural programming and when to use OOP.

**In the next chapter**, we'll introduce some basics of OOP, including:

* Using encapsulation and polymorphism
* Writing your first class
* Creating a subclass that demonstrates inheritance
* Organizing your classes and packages

## CHAPTER 6

# OOP

Object-oriented programming (OOP) is an approach to coding that uses classes to create individual objects and control how those objects interrelate. It's sometimes described as a problem-solving technique—a programming style that addresses issues that procedural programming (which is also referred to as *timeline programming* in Flash Professional) can't handle well. It's a way of organizing your code into small, specific, easily digestible chunks to make project or application development more manageable. These objects are typically designed to be as self-contained as possible, but are also usually designed to play well with other objects.

Whether you know it or not, you've been flirting with object-oriented programming for some time now. You've been creating objects from classes, calling methods, getting and setting property values, and so on. Each time you create a movie clip with ActionScript, for example, you're creating an object by instantiating the **MovieClip** class. But although you may be using objects fluently while coding in the timeline, this is only the tip of the OOP iceberg. To really embrace OOP, you need to write your own custom classes, guided by a few basic object-oriented principles that we'll discuss in this chapter. For our discussions, we'll further define OOP as using classes primarily, if not entirely, rather than simply using objects in procedural programming.

Choosing OOP as a programming methodology is a decision that is sometimes fairly obvious, such as when working with large projects or with a team of collaborating programmers. At other times, however, adopting OOP as a development strategy can be less obvious, and even debated. In still other cases, using OOP can be like driving a finishing nail with a sledgehammer—overkill that just doesn't make sense for quick experiments or proofs of concept.

The goal of this chapter is to give you a high-level view of object-oriented principles, as well as supporting examples, to help prepare you to make these decisions on a project-by-project basis. Each subsequent chapter in this book will continue to introduce syntax in concise, timeline-based exercises, but also make increasing use of classes. Ultimately, we hope you will continue your learning using the book's companion website, where a cumulative project will collect much of what you've created along the way into a "lab" of experiments. The larger project will be OOP-based, but also will contain exercises that you create throughout the book using procedural techniques, exposing you to both programming paradigms.

Knowing when to opt for an object-oriented model depends largely on understanding the benefits of OOP. Among the highlights we'll cover in this chapter are:

- **Classes.** Classes are collections of related functions and variables (called *methods* and *properties*, respectively, in class vernacular) gathered to facilitate one or more specific goals. They are the foundation of OOP, and we'll look at a few ways to use them.

- **Inheritance.** Inheritance is one of OOP's greatest sources of power, especially in ActionScript 3, as it allows you to add functionality to an existing feature set without reinventing the wheel. This is known as *extending* an existing class to create a *subclass*, rather than originating a new class. Inheritance can save you time and labor, as well as improve project design.

- **Composition.** Inheritance isn't appropriate for every situation, and composition is often a useful alternative. Using composition, new classes are assembled using other classes, rather than inheriting from parent classes.

- **Encapsulation.** It's usually not a good idea to expose all aspects of a class to other classes or the surrounding application. Encapsulation isolates most elements of a class from the outside world, allowing only a select few elements, if any, to be seen by other classes.

- **Polymorphism.** Polymorphism is a design practice that allows you to use objects of different types in a uniform manner. For example, it allows you to have methods that share the same name but that behave differently (if desired) when called. Considering a method responsible for motion, you can name it `move()` everywhere instead of `drive()` for a car and `fly()` for a plane. This makes it easier to document, write, and even change your code.

It's important to understand that OOP is not appropriate for everyone, and it is not even appropriate for every situation. OOP can dramatically improve the development cycle of large projects or projects to which more than one programmer can contribute. OOP can even be ideal for smaller projects that are particularly suited for object-based coding (such as some kinds of arcade games, as one example).

The common thread is that object-oriented programming benefits from economies of scale. The time, labor, and learning investments begin to pay off over time. Procedural programming is often more appropriate for small tasks and is sometimes less time-consuming for smaller-scale projects, resulting in code that is simpler to maintain.

You don't *need* to learn OOP to use ActionScript 3.0. The benefits and buzz of object-oriented programming—particularly the continuing swell of interest in design patterns—sometimes lead to almost fetishistic adherence to their principles, without context and at the cost of practicality.

The key to adopting any programming paradigm is finding the right tool for the job. It's certainly a good idea to learn OOP as soon as your schedule and skill set permits, simply because it gives you more options to choose from. Remember, however, that there is more than one way to skin an interface. Before embracing your next significant project, try to set aside some time for planning, information architecture, and programming design. You may find that your goals will be more easily achieved by adopting an object-oriented approach.

If your typical production schedule or project budget cannot allow the inevitable time and resource stumbles associated with attempting new challenges, try learning OOP through a series of fun experiments or artistic endeavors. You may find that the things you learn, the mistakes you make, and the epiphanies you experience will improve your next project.

Having said all that, we'll hit the high points in this introduction to object-oriented programming. This chapter is meant to be a transition between prior and future chapters. As mentioned, we'll continue to show simple procedural examples for syntax, but we'll make more frequent use of OOP techniques—particularly in applied examples at the end of the chapters, and even more so in the supplemental source code and enhanced learning available on the companion website.

## Classes

In Chapter 1, we discussed the three most common programming paradigms: sequential, procedural, and object-oriented. We described procedural programming as an improvement over sequential programming because, instead of being limited to a linear sequence of statements, you can group related tasks together into procedures (called functions, in ActionScript).

Classes offer a similar improvement over procedural programming, in that they collect related functions (methods), variables (properties), and other relevant items. They are the foundation of object-based programming, yet you have probably been working with them for some time. Even if you are new to programming, if you have followed this book through to this chapter, you already have some experience with classes but may not realize it. This is because most of what goes on behind the scenes in ActionScript is accomplished through the use of classes.

To start off with, Chapter 1 of this book gave you a quick peek at classes, and introduced the first use of the document class. We'll look at that again in just a moment, as a quick review.

Beyond that, you learned how to use events (using several event classes, including `Event`, `MouseEvent`, and `Timer` in Chapter 3), how objects are displayed (using a large number of display classes, including `TextField`, `MovieClip`, `DisplayObject`, `DisplayObjectContainer`, and more in Chapter 4), and how to control navigation and timelines (including `FrameLabel`, among others in Chapter 5). Even in Chapter 2, when discussing basic language fundamentals, you were using classes when learning about data types.

If you're suddenly concerned that you've missed a lot of material, don't be. In part, that's the point. All of these examples make use of classes. You just may not be aware of it because it's happening behind the scenes.

Take a look at the movie clip, for example. Throughout the preceding chapters, you've worked fairly extensively with movie clips. You've set numerous properties (such as `x`, `y`, `rotation`, `alpha`, and more), called methods (`play()` and `stop()` among them), and handled events (like `Event.ENTER_FRAME`)—all while making use of the `MovieClip` class. You even learned how to create a movie clip dynamically by creating an instance of the class—a fundamental step in working with classes:

```
var mc:MovieClip = new MovieClip();
```

So, with all that experience, what's the big deal about classes? A bit of a flippant thought, perhaps, but not entirely off the mark. The fact is, you can apply that history to learning OOP. You may not have a lot of experience writing classes, but you do have some experience using them. In fact, it isn't until you begin working with custom classes that things begin to look new.

## Custom Class Review

Start by revisiting the structure of the first custom class introduced in this book, all the way back in Chapter 1—a very basic use of Flash Professional's *document class*. A document class is little more than a timeline replacement—allowing you to move timeline code into a class. But it eases you into OOP because it's a simple way to start using classes. Moving from timeline to class not only points you in the direction of object-oriented programming, it makes your code easier to reuse, share, and archive.

If you need to, you can review Chapter 1 for more information about the document class, including how to create it and how to reference it in Flash Professional's Properties panel. Here, however, we'd like to quickly review the formatting of the class, as you'll use this format for many classes in the future. Consider the following class code:

```
1   package {
2
3       import flash.display.MovieClip;
```

```
4
5        public class Main extends MovieClip {
6
7            public function Main() {
8                trace("Flash");
9            }
10
11       }
12   }
```

Line 1 and the balancing brace in line 12 surround the class in a *package*. Packages help organize your code and are the programming equivalent of your computer's folders or directories. We'll discuss this in a moment or two, but for now, think of a package as a wrapper for your class. While getting started, you don't need to concern yourself with packages if you place all your classes in the same directory as your *.fla* file. The ActionScript compiler will automatically look for classes in this location.

Line 3 is an import statement. It doesn't really import anything: it just tells the compiler where to find the classes needed by your code. The compiler can then use the class to validate your code and add the needed class to your SWF when it is compiled. This gives your class access to all the properties, methods, and events needed by your script.

Line 3 also demonstrates the use of a package. This document class requires the `MovieClip` class, which is found in the `flash.display` package. In other words, the *MovieClip.as* file is inside a "display" directory, which is inside a "flash" directory, which is in a *classpath*, or location of classes known to the compiler. Your ActionScript editor of choice, such as Flash Professional, already knows about a few such locations, and you'll learn to create your own in the next section of this chapter.

None of the timeline examples in the previous chapters included import statements because the examples used only items found in `flash` packages. Importing classes from these packages is not required when writing Flash Professional timeline scripts, but you *must* import them in classes. As a rule of thumb, import all classes used when writing your own classes.

Line 5 declares the class. The first thing you may notice about this is the word `public` beginning the declaration. This is called an *access control modifier* and determines how something can be accessed by code elsewhere in your project. Using `public` makes the class available to the rest of your project. Additional modifiers are covered in the "Encapsulation" section of this chapter.

The next thing you may notice is the phrase `extends MovieClip` following the name of the class, `Main`. This is called *inheritance* and means that the publicly accessible events, methods, and properties of the `MovieClip` class will also be available to (are inherited by) this class. This use of the `MovieClip` class requires the import in line 3. We'll talk more about extending classes in the "Inheritance" section of this chapter.

**NOTE**

*Some ActionScript editors, such as Adobe's Flash Builder, PowerFlasher's FDT, and even Flash Professional as of version CS5, will automatically add class import statements as you edit your code.*

**NOTE**

*We should reinforce from Chapter 1 that the name of an external class file must match the name of the class and constructor. In the class being discussed, the file must be called **Main.as**. It is common practice to start class names, and therefore their file and constructor names, with a capital letter.*

Finally, lines 7 through 9 are the *class constructor*. This is a function that's executed automatically when an instance of the class is created. Just as you can create instances of a library symbol in the Flash Professional timeline, you can create instances of a class. Although Flash Professional instantiates a class for you when you use a document class, you can also do this manually:

```
var main:Main = new Main();
```

Does this manual instantiation look familiar? It should. This is the same format used to instantiate the vast majority of classes in ActionScript 3.0, including the recently cited example of creating a movie clip. So, you already have some of the skills required for working with custom classes!

## Classpaths

You have a few choices when deciding where to place your custom classes. The ActionScript compiler will automatically look for a class in the same directory as the file (FLA or other class) making use of the class. This is the easiest way to store classes because it's easy to transport them with your project by just moving the parent directory.

However, you can also organize your classes into directories, grouping classes of similar functionality for easier management. This technique was detailed when using existing ActionScript classes, as in the cited movie clip example, but applies to custom classes as well. When using classes in a package, you must import them—including classes in the flash package.

It's usually a good idea to import every class needed so you can see all *dependencies* of your class—other files your class relies on—at a glance. However, you can also import all classes in a package by using an asterisk (*) as a wildcard. This saves a little time and reduces the number of lines in your script so you can focus more on your code. (We'll use this approach as a space-saving technique from time to time in this book.) It's also no less efficient, because the compiler will include only classes required by your code, rather than the entire package, when compiling a SWF.

Here are examples of a full package and wildcard used with built-in ActionScript 3 classes, as well as a full package for a custom class:

```
import flash.display.MovieClip;
import flash.events.*;
import com.mycompany.effects.Water;
```

Naming the parent directory of a class library *com* stems from what is called reverse domain naming. It breaks your domain into folder names in reverse order, starting with your domain extension (.com, .org, .edu), then the next portion of your domain, and so on, until you want to stop. This is common but only a convention. It's helpful to think of this when you work with other programmers, but you can organize your package folders any way you like and your code will still work.

Here is an example structure of the fictional **Water** class cited in the prior import statement. Note the path—up to, but not including, the class name—in the package declaration. Forgetting to include this will result in a compiler error telling you that the package declaration of the class does not reflect the location of the file.

```
package com.mycompany.effects {

    public class Water {

        public function Water() {
        }
    }
}
```

Finally, the ActionScript compiler needs to know where to start looking for these packages and classes. Because the compiler will automatically look in the same folder as the file using the class, you can put package directories (as well as individual classes) next to your FLA file. This is often called a *local* or *relative* classpath (local or relative to your FLA). For most situations, this is all you need to worry about. Figure 6-1 shows an example parent directory for a project that uses the aforementioned **Water** class.

Figure 6-1. A sample directory structure using the local classpath

However, this approach can be somewhat impractical if you intend to build a library of classes that you will reuse often. In this case, you can store frequently reused classes in a centralized location, and add that location to the list of classpaths your compiler will search.

You can add paths to folders, or SWCs if you have them (Flash Professional CS4 and later)—the latter being compressed collections of classes and assets that can be used for compilation but can't be edited. You can also add paths of runtime shared libraries, which we'll demonstrate in Chapter 10 when we discuss the Text Layout Framework, the new text options introduced in Flash Professional CS5.

You can add your own classpath to Flash Professional either at the application or project level. To make a classpath available to all projects, you can go to Flash Professional's Preferences (Macintosh: Flash→Preferences; Windows: Edit→Preferences), select ActionScript from the left menu, and click on the ActionScript 3.0 button at the bottom of the ActionScript preferences. Using the resulting dialog, seen in Figure 6-2, you can browse to the directory in which you will be maintaining your class libraries, and Flash will thereafter also search in that directory when importing your classes.

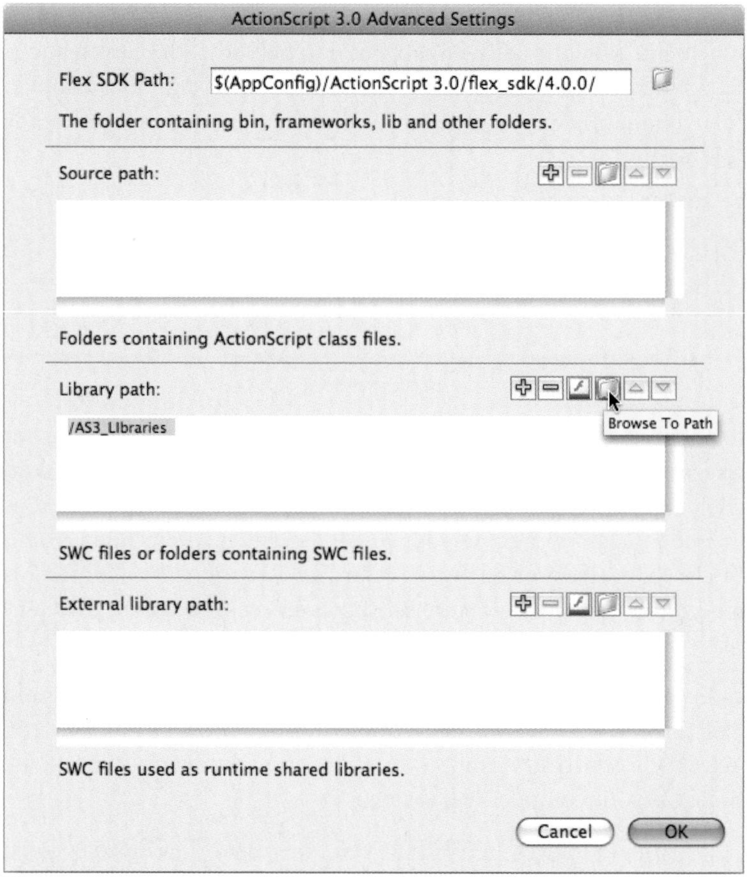

*Figure 6-2. Adding your own application-wide classpath to Flash Professional CS5's ActionScript preferences*

To add a file-specific classpath, the process is very similar and begins in the dialog, File→Publish Settings→ActionScript 3.0 Settings. (In Flash Professional CS5, the new menu item File→ActionScript Settings accesses this dialog immediately.) As seen in Figure 6-3, choose the Source Path section of the dialog and again browse to the directory you want to add.

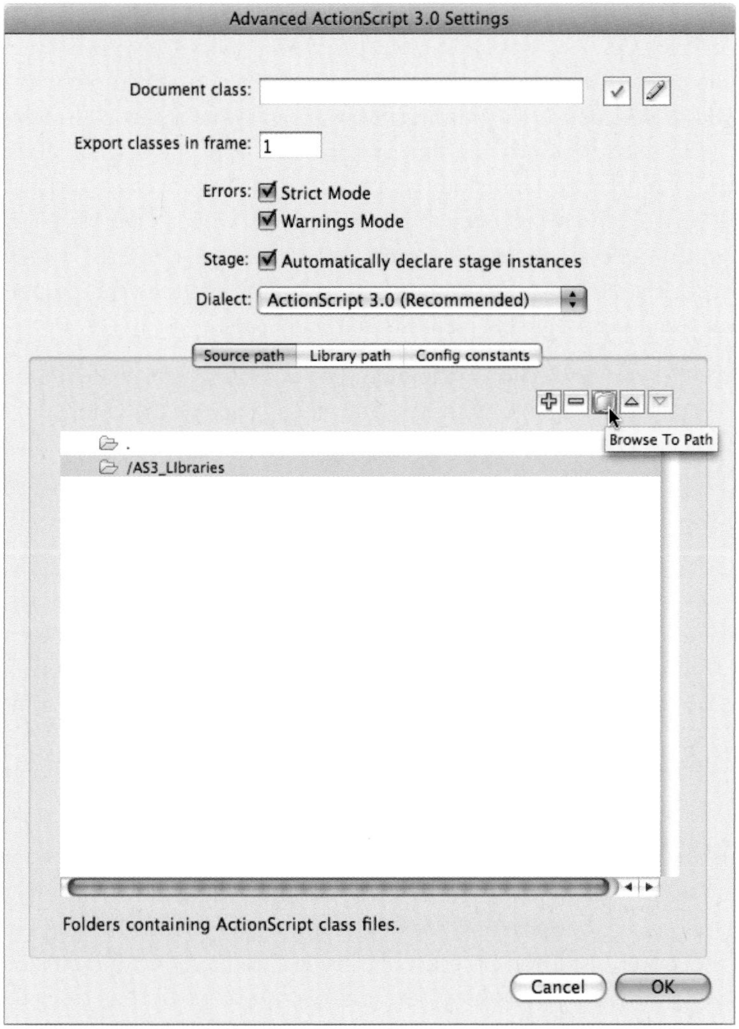

*Figure 6-3. Adding your own file-specific classpath to Flash Professional CS5's ActionScript Settings dialog*

## Note to Flash Professional CS5 users

Flash Professional CS5 now offers code completion and color syntax highlighting for custom classes as well as built-in ActionScript classes. It accomplishes this by parsing all known classpaths and building a cache of all classes in these paths. A side effect of this feature is that the process of building the cache can become overwhelmed if there are too many classes to analyze. Therefore, try not to collect every class you have into one giant folder. Move applicable classes in and out of your folder, or create classpaths for smaller folders on a project-by-project basis. See the companion website for more information about this issue.

# Inheritance

Among the most easily explained concepts of an object-oriented programming model is *inheritance*. This means that you can create a new class, typically called a *subclass*, which can inherit attributes from the original class, also called the *superclass*. This is similar to the way you inherit characteristics from your parents. You share many things in common with a parent but also have several unique attributes. The same can be said of classes. Through inheritance, a class can acquire from its parent useful methods and properties, as well as add entirely new methods and properties.

The source files for this section are found in the *inheritance_mc* folder in the Chapter 6 archive—available from the Downloads page at the companion website, *http://www.LearningActionScript3.com*. Ultimately, you'll test the FLA file, *inheritance_mc_01.fla*, but you'll be working primarily with the *Box.as* and *Square.as* class files.

The following script creates a class called **Box**, found in the *Box.as* source file, that is a subclass of **MovieClip**. As a result, it has access to all the properties, methods, and events accessible in a movie clip, including the **x** property seen in line 22, and the **graphics** property used in lines 13 through 16 to draw a blue box. We'll discuss drawing vectors with code in Chapter 8, but the script sets a 1-pixel black line style, sets a fill color stored in the **color** variable, draws a rectangle from x,y coordinate point (0, 0) to the coordinate point (100, 100), and ends the fill.

The **color** variable is declared in line 9. This is an example of a class property. As you can see, it uses the same syntax as the variables you create in the timeline, with one exception. Like timeline programming, it is defined within the scope of the script (inside the class just like inside a frame script), but outside all methods, so it can be available to the entire script scope (in this case, the entire class, similar to the entire frame script in the timeline). The declaration uses a **var** keyword and data type and is given a color value that produces a dark blue. The only exception is that here the **public** access modifier is added, which makes the variable available to code outside the class. We'll continue our explanation after the code.

```
1    package {
2
3        import flash.display.MovieClip;
4        import flash.display.Graphics;
5        import flash.events.Event;
6
7        public class Box extends MovieClip {
8
9            public var color:uint = 0x000099;
10
11           public function Box() {
12               this.graphics.lineStyle(1, 0x000000);
13               this.graphics.beginFill(color);
```

```
14              this.graphics.drawRect(0, 0, 100, 100);
15              this.graphics.endFill();
16
17              this.addEventListener(Event.ENTER_FRAME, onLoop,
18                                    false, 0, true);
19          }
20
21          public function onLoop(evt:Event):void {
22              this.x += 5;
23          }
24
25      }
26  }
```

The **Box()** method is a special kind of method called a *constructor*. In the class, it appears no differently than any other, but it's unique because this code will automatically be executed the moment an instance of the class is created. A class instance is created using the **new** keyword or, in the case of a document class in Flash Professional, when a SWF is launched. In ActionScript 3.0, if a constructor is used, it must always be available to other parts of your program, so it must always use the **public** access control modifier.

In this class, the constructor draws a box at runtime and adds an event listener. The event listener created in lines 17 and 18 calls the **onLoop()** function on every enter frame event, which adds five pixels to the current horizontal location of the class.

But what does it draw the box into? This class extends **MovieClip**, so **Box** is, essentially, a movie clip. **Box** is still unique, because it has visual content and a new movie clip does not, but creating an instance of this class is just like creating an instance of **MovieClip**.

As discussed in the "Classpaths" section of this chapter, the ActionScript compiler must know where your class resides. The **Box** class does not include a path in its package declaration, so if you place this class into the same directory as your FLA, the compiler will find it. Therefore, all that is required to create an instance of this class in the timeline is using the **new** keyword. Finally, just like a movie clip, you must add the instance to the display list to see the box on the stage. The *inheritance_mc_01.fla* source file demonstrates this code, in the first keyframe:

```
var box:Box = new Box();
addChild(box);
```

With these two lines, an instance of the **Box** class will be created and added to the display list, and the drawn square will move across the stage at 5 pixels per enter frame event. Very much a benefit of OOP, this box is given autonomous behavior. With just the two preceding lines of code, the box can create its own appearance and control its own movement. This class can also easily be reused elsewhere with the same result.

## Symbol Base Classes

We can take further advantage of inheriting from the **MovieClip** class by linking a class directly to a movie clip library symbol. You did this more than once in Chapter 4 when adding symbol instances to the display list. (See "Adding Symbol Instances to the Display List" in Chapter 4.) At that time, however, you had not written a class to link up with the symbol instance, so you let Flash create a placeholder class just for the purpose of supporting runtime creation.

Now, you can make use of this existing link by providing the symbol with a custom class to execute when instantiated. As described, creating an instance of the symbol either by manually dragging it to the stage, or using the **new** keyword, will execute the constructor in the linked class.

The following example is nearly identical to the previous class but excludes visual content, focusing only on motion. Similarly, in the *inheritance_mc_02. fla* source file, no timeline code is used to create the movie clip. This demonstrates the automatic link between a linkage class assigned in the symbol's property dialog, and a custom class with the same name. Simply by adding an instance of the symbol to the stage, the class is applied. This code is in the *Square.as* class.

```
1   package {
2
3       import flash.display.MovieClip;
4       import flash.events.Event;
5
6       public class Square extends MovieClip {
7
8           public function Square() {
9               this.addEventListener(Event.ENTER_FRAME, onLoop,
10                                  false, 0, true);
11          }
12
13          public function onLoop(evt:Event):void {
14              this.x += 5;
15          }
16
17      }
18  }
```

## Can You Figure Out Why?

As a fun break, and a bit of review, take a look at the *inheritance_mc_03.fla* source file. This file combines both the **Square** class, instantiated by virtue of the *Square* symbol placed on the stage, and the **Box** class, instantiated through its use as a document class. Each class moves itself 5 pixels to the right every enter frame. Why then does the *square* instance (red) move twice as fast as the *box* instance (blue)? Look for the answer to the left.

*ANSWER: In the file inheritance_mc_03. fla, why does the square instance (red) move twice as fast as the box instance (blue)? Because square is a child of box.*

*Remember that a document class is a timeline replacement. As such, the reference **this** in the Box document class refers to the entire timeline. Updating its x coordinate moves the timeline (document class) and all its children. Because square is placed manually, it is a child of the timeline so it moves accordingly. However, square also moves on its own, due to the Square class. So, for every enter frame event, the entire timeline (thus both movie clips) is moved 5 pixels and then square is updated 5 pixels again, effectively moving square 10 pixels every enter frame event.*

*For comparison, take a look at inheritance_mc_04.fla, in which Box is instantiated using the new keyword, rather than via the document class. In this example, both movie clips update themselves and the timeline is not affected. For further reference, you can also see the entire timeline move without any classes in play by looking at time- line_move.fla.*

# A More Traditional Look at Inheritance

Now that you have a basic idea of how a custom class inherits the attributes of a movie clip, let's look at a more traditional example with a bit more substance. The files in this section are found in the *inheritance* folder of this chapter's source. We'll also build on this example throughout the remainder of the chapter, adding features as we go, to demonstrate the various tenets of object-oriented programming.

We described inheritance earlier by discussing how a child inherits from a parent. The same analogy can be made from other real-world scenarios. A **Puppy** class might inherit from a **Dog** class, a **Ball** class might inherit from a **Toy** class, and a **Car** class might inherit from a **Vehicle** class.

Consider a very simple execution of the vehicle metaphor. Whether a vehicle is a car or a truck—or even a plane or a boat, for that matter—it's still a vehicle and shares much in common with other vehicles. It makes sense, then, to create a class that contains basic methods and properties that are common to all vehicles. For simplicity, think about fuel availability (the number of gallons of fuel the vehicle has in its tank) and fuel efficiency (gas mileage, in miles per gallon, for our purposes). Also, a calculation based on that information could result in miles traveled and the resulting reduction in the amount of fuel. Obviously not every vehicle uses gas (such as a glider or bicycle), but this limited scenario will suit our purposes.

## Vehicle class

Here is a basic class you can use to represent a generic vehicle. We'll call this class **Vehicle**, so the document name will be *Vehicle.as*, and the class will be saved in the same directory as your FLA. This class creates a vehicle and, when activated (by calling the **go()** method), increases the number of miles traveled and decreases the remaining gallons of gas after each enter frame event, tracing the result. It will show in the Output window how many miles the vehicle traveled, and how much fuel remains until it runs out of gas.

The class has four public properties, representing: gas mileage, available fuel, miles traveled, and a Boolean property called **moving**. The latter will enable functionality when true, and disable functionality when false. All the properties and methods in the class are public so other classes can see them. We'll discuss that in further detail in a little while.

The constructor does only two things. It sets the properties for gas mileage and available fuel to the arguments passed in when the class was instantiated, and adds a listener to the vehicle that reacts to the enter frame event and calls the **onLoop()** method. Here's what this portion of the class looks like:

**NOTE**

*Note that default values have been added to the parameters in the **Vehicle** class constructor in line 13. If an instance of the class is created without passing in arguments, the default values will be used.*

```
1   package {
2
3       import flash.display.MovieClip;
4       import flash.events.Event;
5
```

```
6    public class Vehicle extends MovieClip {
7
8        public var gasMileage:Number;
9        public var fuelAvailable:Number;
10       public var milesTraveled:Number = 0;
11       public var moving:Boolean;
12
13       public function Vehicle(mpg:Number=21, fuel:Number=18.5) {
14           gasMileage = mpg;
15           fuelAvailable = fuel;
16           this.addEventListener(Event.ENTER_FRAME,
17                                 onLoop, false, 0, true);
18       }
```

Now let's talk about the listener function in the next segment of the script. When the **moving** property is true, the **onLoop()** method first decrements the **fuelAvailable** property and increases the **milesTraveled** property by the value of the **gasMileage** property. So, if a vehicle claims a gas mileage rating of 21 miles per gallon, the car will travel 21 miles using 1 gallon of gas.

Next, the method checks to see if there's less than one gallon of gas remaining. If so, the listener is removed. While the listener remains, the class will trace the vehicle object, miles it's traveled, and remaining fuel to the output panel. In addition, the x coordinate of the class instance will be set to the current number of miles traveled, so any visual asset associated with this class will move. Because **Vehicle** inherits from **MovieClip**, the **x** property is accessible to **Vehicle** so it doesn't have to be added anew. The effect is that a corresponding movie clip will move across the stage by pixels that correspond to miles driven.

Finally, the **go()** method, when called from outside the class, sets the **moving** Boolean property to **true** and allows the frame loop to work. This could be likened to starting the engine of the vehicle and driving. A more complex system might also provide a method for stopping the vehicle, as well as other features, but let's keep this example simple.

```
1    public function onLoop(evt:Event):void {
2        if (moving) {
3            fuelAvailable--;
4            milesTraveled += gasMileage;
5            if (fuelAvailable < 1) {
6                this.removeEventListener(Event.ENTER_FRAME,
7                                         onLoop);
8            }
9            trace(this, milesTraveled, fuelAvailable);
10           this.x = milesTraveled;
11       }
12   }
13
14   public function go():void {
15       moving = true;
16   }
17
18   }
19 }
```

## Simple example

To see this class in action, all you need to do is create an instance of the class, and call the **go()** method from that instance. If desired, you can also pass in a new value for gas mileage and available fuel. If there is a visual component to the instance (and we'll see that soon), you would also add the instance to the display list. Here is an example of all three steps, including new values for the **mpg** and **fuel** parameters, as seen in the *vehicle_only.fla* source file. This is the last time in this chapter that we'll use the timeline. For future examples, we'll use a document class, moving all aspects of each example from the timeline to classes.

```
var vehicle:Vehicle = new Vehicle(21, 18);
addChild(vehicle);
vehicle.go();
```

When testing this file, the resulting trace lists the **Vehicle** class instance, the accumulating miles traveled, and the decreasing fuel available. After several iterations (condensed with the ellipsis in the sample that follows), the trace stops and shows the final number of miles traveled and less than one gallon of gas remaining.

```
//output
[object Vehicle] 21 17
[object Vehicle] 42 16
[object Vehicle] 63 15
...
[object Vehicle] 336 2
[object Vehicle] 357 1
[object Vehicle] 378 0
```

That's fine if every vehicle you ever create is exactly the same kind of vehicle. However, the principle of inheritance allows you to subclass this **Vehicle** class, inheriting the attributes of **Vehicle**, but customizing each subclass into a specific kind of vehicle, like car and truck, as in the following examples.

The following two classes, **Car** (*Car.as*) and **Truck** (*Truck.as*), both extend **Vehicle**, so they inherit the properties and methods of **Vehicle**. Because the properties are inherited, they're not included in the subclasses. Although these classes extend **Vehicle**, you can add unique properties and methods to make each class further specialized. For simplicity, we'll add a method to each class to control an accessory—a sunroof for the car and a tailgate for the truck.

**NOTE**

*Although not used in these example classes, both* **Car** *and* **Truck** *can take advantage of* **MovieClip** *properties and methods by virtue of inheritance because* **Vehicle** *inherits from* **MovieClip** *and* **Car** *and* **Truck** *inherit from* **Vehicle**. *This is just like passing DNA on from grandfather to father to son. The inheritance chain is not limited to the immediacy of superclass and subclass.*

## Car class

```
1   package {
2
3       public class Car extends Vehicle {
4
5           public function Car(mpg:Number, fuel:Number) {
6               gasMileage = mpg;
7               fuelAvailable = fuel;
8           }
```

```
9
10          public function openSunroof():void {
11              trace(this, "opened sunroof");
12          }
13      }
14  }
```

## Truck class

```
1   package {
2
3       public class Truck extends Vehicle {
4
5           public function Truck(mpg:Number, fuel:Number) {
6               gasMileage = mpg;
7               fuelAvailable = fuel;
8           }
9
10          public function lowerTailgate():void {
11              trace(this, "lowered tailgate");
12          }
13      }
14  }
```

Because of inheritance, the **Vehicle** class constructor is called implicitly when you create instances of the **Car** and **Truck** classes. This adds the enter frame listener so the cars and trucks can move, and then the **Car** and **Truck** class instances redefine the **gasMileage** and **fuelAvailable** public properties from the **Vehicle** class. It's also possible to explicitly call the constructor, or other accessible method, of a superclass, which we'll demonstrate when we discuss encapsulation.

## Document class and revised FLA

Now we can revisit the FLA and, instead of instantiating the **Vehicle** class, we can create instances of the new **Car** and **Truck** subclasses. We can also create car and truck movie clips in the FLA's library and associate those symbols with **Car** and **Truck** by adding their names as linkage classes in each symbol's Library Properties dialog. The new symbols will add a visual element to the example because they will be updated by the classes automatically. Because the **Vehicle** class extends **MovieClip**, and the x coordinate of **Vehicle** is updated, any subclass of the **Vehicle** class will also update its x coordinate.

In this example, we're going to move away from the timeline and use a document class instead. So start by creating a new ActionScript 3.0 file (ActionScript 3.0 Class file in the New Document window in Flash Professional CS5). We'll discuss its contents in a moment, but first save the file as *Main.as* in the same directory as your FLA file, and reference this class, Main, as the FLA's document class. If you'd rather use the source file provided to get you started, it's called *car_truck.fla*.

Lines 1 through 7 create the package, import the necessary class dependencies and create this class. Remember a document class should extend **MovieClip** so they can behave as a timeline. Lines 9 and 10 create two properties, *compact* and *pickup*, and type them as **Car** and **Truck**, respectively.

Lines 14 and 20 create instances to these classes, passing in values for gas mileage and fuel available. Both *compact* and *pickup* are set to the same initial **x** value (lines 15 and 21), and *pickup* is given a different **y** value (line 22) so you can easily see both vehicles once they are added to the display list (lines 17 and 23).

The custom methods for both instances are called right away (lines 18 and 24), but the vehicles don't move because the **go()** method calls are inside an event listener function (lines 38 through 41) waiting for you to click the stage. Setting up the event listeners in lines 26 through 36 is very important, and we'll discuss this after the code and a description of this example's output.

```
1   package {
2
3       import flash.display.MovieClip;
4       import flash.events.Event;
5       import flash.events.MouseEvent;
6
7       public class Main extends MovieClip {
8
9           public var compact:Car;
10          public var pickup:Truck;
11
12          public function Main() {
13
14              compact = new Car(21, 18);
15              compact.x = 0;
16              compact.y = 20;
17              addChild(compact);
18              compact.openSunroof();
19
20              pickup = new Truck(16, 23);
21              pickup.x = 0;
22              pickup.y = 100;
23              addChild(pickup);
24              pickup.lowerTailgate();
25
26              this.addEventListener(Event.ADDED_TO_STAGE,
27                                    onAddedToStage,
28                                    false, 0, true);
29          }
30
31          public function onAddedToStage(evt:Event):void {
32              this.removeEventListener(Event.ADDED_TO_STAGE,
33                                    onAddedToStage)
34              stage.addEventListener(MouseEvent.CLICK, onClick,
35                                    false, 0, true);
36          }
37
38          public function onClick(evt:MouseEvent):void {
39              compact.go();
40              pickup.go();
41          }
42      }
43  }
```

The first thing to appear in the Output panel when testing your FLA is the initial trace caused by the custom method calls:

```
[object Car] opened sunroof
[object Truck] lowered tailgate
```

When the stage is clicked, the **go()** methods start the car and truck moving, and traces like the one seen in the vehicle-only example will now compare the miles traveled by the car and truck instances. Which will travel the farthest on a tank of gas? The car gets better gas mileage, but has a smaller gas tank. Try it and see!

## Accessing the Stage in a Class

In the document class from the preceding section, you may have noticed that we didn't just add the mouse click event listener to the stage inside the class constructor. This is because the stage usually doesn't yet exist in a constructor and this technique will typically result in an error.

When referencing a display object outside this class, such as the stage or root, the document class is a special exception to this rule. Because the document class is a timeline replacement, it automatically becomes a part of the display list. If the very same class is not used as a document class, however, this exception will not apply. Therefore, when referencing a display object outside this class, it's important to set up your listeners as we are about to describe to make your classes more flexible.

In the display list (the new display architecture of ActionScript 3.0 discussed in Chapter 4), the stage is the senior-most item, and you must access it through a display object. We discussed this in the Chapter 4 sidebar, "Display Objects and References to Stage and Root," but this is particularly important when writing classes. Remembering that you must access the stage through a display object, knowing when the class is instantiated, and when the stage is referenced in a class, play a big part in the success of your script.

Recall how to instantiate a display object class: you first use the **new** keyword and then add the instance to the display list. The prior example of creating a **Vehicle** instance is repeated here for reference:

```
var vehicle:Vehicle = new Vehicle(21, 18);
addChild(vehicle);
```

Earlier we told you that the class constructor executes immediately upon instantiation. In other words, it executes *before* adding the instance to the display list. As you may have read in the "Display Objects and References to Stage and Root" sidebar, this means that you can't access the stage in the constructor.

So, when we need to access a display object like the stage, we must add an event listener to the constructor that listens for the **ADDED_TO_STAGE** event. This listener will be executed when the class instance is added to the display list, with the stage as its senior-most object. At that point, the class instance is a part of the display list and access to the stage or root is possible.

# Composition

Although inheritance is a common practice in object-oriented programming, it's not the only way to build OOP projects. *Composition* is more appropriate in some cases. Composition says that an object is composed of other objects, rather than descending from other objects. The best way to decide when to use inheritance or composition is to follow the "is a/has a" rule.

Consider how to add tires to the car example. You might be able to use inheritance ("is a"), but composition ("has a") is likely better. A car "is a" vehicle, meaning inheritance will work well, but tires don't fit the "is a" vehicle, or car, or truck model. However, a car (or truck) "has a" set of tires, making this model suited to composition. In a real-world scenario, this might be particularly useful in an expanded version of our vehicle metaphor. For example, land vehicles typically have tires, but water vehicles usually don't.

Composition makes it easier to switch out items that compose a class. If a car is extended from a vehicle, you can't change that any more than you can change your parents. However, if a car is composed of things, you can easily remove one object and substitute another. Now let's use composition to put tires onto our car and truck.

Continuing our work on our vehicle example, this time using the files in the *composition* folder of the source archive, let's set up the process by adding a **tires** property to the **Car** and **Truck** classes, as seen in line 5 of the following code excerpts. This will hold an instance of the **Tires** class we'll create, and is typed accordingly. Next, we'll create an instance of the new **Tires** class. The new class will be able to equip vehicles with different kinds of tires so we'll pass in a different tire type for car and truck, as seen in line 10 of both excerpts that follow. The class will also trace the kind of tire used, by querying a public property called **type**, shown in line 11 of both excerpts.

### Car class

```
3      public class Car extends Vehicle {
4
5          public var tires:Tires;
6
7          public function Car(mpg:Number, fuel:Number) {
8              gasMileage = mpg;
9              fuelAvailable = fuel;
10             tires = new Tires("highperformance");
11             trace(this, "has", tires.type, "tires");
12         }
```

### Truck class

```
3    public class Truck extends Vehicle {
4
5        public var tires:Tires;
6
7        public function Truck(mpg:Number, fuel:Number) {
8            gasMileage = mpg;
9            fuelAvailable = fuel;
10           tires = new Tires("snow");
11           trace(this, "has", tires.type, "tires");
12       }
```

### New Tires class

This basic **Tires** class simulates functionality by putting the type of tire requested into a property. In a real-world situation, the new class might affect the performance of a car or truck object. For example, using snow tires might reduce fuel efficiency, and upgrading to high-performance radials might improve mileage. In our simplified example, the **Car** and **Truck** classes will just trace the value of this property.

```
1    package {
2
3        public class Tires {
4
5            public var type:String;
6
7            public function Tires(tire:String) {
8                //simulated functionality change based on tire type
9                switch (tire) {
10                   case "snow" :
11                       type = "storm-ready snow";
12                       break;
13                   case "highperformance" :
14                       type = "high-performance radial";
15                       break;
16                   default :
17                       type = "economical bias-ply";
18                       break;
19               }
20           }
21       }
22   }
```

As you try out the amended classes, the most important thing to understand is that inheritance is not used to introduce the **Tires** class. Instead, the car and truck are composed of objects. In this simplified case, only the tires were added, but a complete car (for example) would consist of seats, windows, and so on, all composed rather than inherited from **Car** or **Vehicle**. Again, this satisfies the "is a/has a" rule, which should be your guide when deciding whether inheritance or composition is optimal.

## Document class

No change is required to the document class, but testing the *car_truck.fla* file again will show a new element to the trace output. In addition to the use of the accessories (sunroof and tailgate) and the resulting miles traveled until fuel is depleted, the tires used will also be traced, as shown:

```
[object Car] has high-performance radial tires
[object Car] opened sunroof
[object Truck] has storm-ready snow tires
[object Truck] lowered tailgate
[object Car] 21 17
[object Truck] 16 22
[object Car] 42 16
[object Truck] 32 21
...
```

# Encapsulation

In the preceding examples, all class properties and methods were public. This is convenient in that it allows code outside the classes to see properties and methods inside classes. However, this is also risky because other elements of the application can change property values or execute methods—intentionally or even accidentally—when not desired.

The way to avoid this possible problem is through *encapsulation*. Put simply, encapsulation is the practice of hiding class properties and methods from other areas of your project while still allowing you to manipulate them in a controlled fashion.

There are a handful of built-in namespaces in ActionScript 3.0. They are also called *access control modifiers* because they control how outside objects access properties and methods. Although we'll focus primarily on **private** and **public** modifiers in this book, Table 6-1 describes some of the other access control modifiers available.

**NOTE**

*There is another access control modifier, called* **static***, which is a bit different. The static modifier indicates that a property or method is accessed from a class reference, but not an instance of the class. For example,* **random()** *is a static method of the* **Math** *class. You call this method not from a class instance, but from a reference to the class directly. Compare this syntax of an instance method, like* **play()** *from the* **MovieClip** *class, and a static method, like* **random()** *from the* **Math** *class.*

```
var mc:MovieClip =
    new MovieClip();
mc.play();

trace(Math.random());
```

*In the first case, the method is called from* **mc***, the class instance. By contrast no instance is created before invoking the* **random()** *method. Instance methods and properties are not aware of static methods or properties, and vice versa.*

*Table 6-1. ActionScript 3.0 access control modifiers*

| Example | Description |
|---|---|
| public | Accessible to all objects, inside and outside the class |
| private | Accessible to objects only inside the class |
| protected | Accessible to objects inside the class and any derived class |
| internal | Accessible to objects inside the class and all classes in the same package |

A loosely related analogy might help describe the ideas behind encapsulation. If you include your email address in the text of an HTML page, spam bots will likely harvest it and flood you with unwanted solicitations. However, if you keep your email entirely private, potential contacts won't be able to reach you. One solution to this problem is to use a contact form that connects to a server that, in turn, sends information to your email address. This allows you to keep your email address private, but provide some sort of public access. This control is the basis of encapsulation.

## Getters and setters

How, then, can you provide public access to private information? This is accomplished with a special group of methods called *getters* and *setters*. These public methods are used to retrieve from, or reassign values to, private properties. In their simplest use, getters and setters can provide a friendly or consistent public name for a possibly more obscurely named property. For example, a property named "registeredUserEmail" could be referenced outside the class as "email."

Beyond that use case, getters and setters can also add functionality. A simple example includes wanting to allow a programmer to get, *but not set*, the value of a property. Or, you might want to convert a property value behind the scenes when requested or supplied, without requiring a custom method or two to do so. For instance, a currency value might be stored as a number but, when retrieved with a getter, might be formatted as a string with a leading currency symbol (such as a dollar sign, $), commas, and a decimal point. Neither example is possible when just exposing a property as public.

**NOTE**

*A property that a programmer can get, but not set, is called a read-only property.*

Getters and setters are also special because they behave like properties as far as the rest of your application is concerned. This simplifies what is typically called an *application programming interface (API)*—all the public properties and methods of your class (and, by extension, all the classes that make up your application) that a programmer can access.

Let's revisit our email address discussion to show how this works. The first step in changing from using a public property to using getters and setters is to change the property from public to private. This requires only changing the access modifier, but a common naming convention advocates preceding private properties with underscores. This is a personal choice, and some favor it because you can see at a glance if access to the property is limited to the class. We'll follow this convention in this book. This first snippet shows both changes:

```
private var _registeredUserEmail:String = "person1@example.com";
```

Next, to provide access to the property, a getter/setter pair is added to the end of the class. Let's discuss the content of the functions first. The public getter will return the value of the private property, and the public setter will assign a new value, sent in as an argument, to the private property:

```
public function get email():String {
    return _registeredUserEmail;
}
public function set email(newEmail:String):void {
    _registeredUserEmail = newEmail;
}
```

Note, however, that both methods are named "email." This would ordinarily cause a conflict error because all methods within the same scope must have unique names. However, this is part of how getters and setters work. The matching method names are preceded by identifiers **get** and **set**, and both methods work together to appear as a single property in the code that is referencing the class. That is, instead of having to remember and document two functions, perhaps called **getUserEmail()** and **setUserEmail()**, all you need is one property: **email**. Getting and setting are both shown in the following snippet (assuming an example class instance called *user*):

```
user.email = "person2@example.com";
trace(user.email);
```

As you can see, property syntax, rather than method syntax, is used. Which version of the method in the class is called is determined by usage. In the first line, a value is being assigned to the property, so the class knows to call the setter. In the second line, no value is assigned, so the class calls the getter, and the property value is retrieved. Now that you have a brief background on implementation, let's put that information to use in our ongoing vehicle example.

**NOTE**

*The use of getters and setters, versus using public properties, is often debated. You may find it interesting to search online resources for discussions about this concept, and the companion website may have additional information about this and related topics in the future.*

## Vehicle class

Let's move to the encapsulation folder of this chapter's source archive. The first thing we'll do to adapt our existing code is make the properties in lines 8 through 11 and the method defined in line 20 in the **Vehicle** class private. All constructors in ActionScript 3.0 must be public, and the **go()** method should remain public so it can easily be executed from other areas of your project.

```
1    package {
2
3        import flash.display.MovieClip;
4        import flash.events.Event;
5
6        public class Vehicle extends MovieClip {
7
8            private var _gasMileage:Number;
9            private var _fuelAvailable:Number;
10           private var _milesTraveled:Number = 0;
11           private var _moving:Boolean;
12
13           public function Vehicle(mpg:Number=21, fuel:Number=18.5) {
14               _gasMileage = mpg;
15               _fuelAvailable = fuel;
16               this.addEventListener(Event.ENTER_FRAME, onLoop,
17                                    false, 0, true);
18           }
19
20           private function onLoop(evt:Event):void {
21               if (_moving) {
22                   _fuelAvailable--;
23                   _milesTraveled += _gasMileage;
24                   if (_fuelAvailable < 1) {
25                       this.removeEventListener(Event.ENTER_FRAME,
26                                    onLoop);
27                   }
```

```
28                    trace(this, _milesTraveled, _fuelAvailable);
29                    this.x = _milesTraveled;
30                }
31            }
32
33        public function go():void {
34            _moving = true;
35        }
```

Now that the properties are private, getters and setters must be added to access them. Lines 37 through 55 add a getter and setter pair for each of the private properties in the class.

```
36        //new getters and setters
37        public function get gasMileage(): Number  {
38            return _gasMileage;
39        }
40
41        public function set gasMileage(mpg:Number):void {
42            _gasMileage = mpg;
43        }
44
45        public function get fuelAvailable():Number {
46            return _fuelAvailable;
47        }
48
49        public function set fuelAvailable(fuel:Number):void {
50            _fuelAvailable = fuel;
51        }
52
53        public function get milesTraveled():Number {
54            return _milesTraveled;
55        }
56    }
57 }
```

Getters and setters are used to update properties, but subclasses can also update properties of a superclass directly. Remember that when **Car** and **Truck** instances were created, the constructor of these subclasses updated the **gasMileage** and **fuelAvailable** properties of **Vehicle** class. If those properties are no longer public, this isn't possible using the same techniques.

A subclass uses the **super()** method to call the corresponding method in its superclass. For example, placing **super()** in a subclass constructor will call the constructor in the superclass. You can even pass arguments into the superclass method, if the superclass constructor normally accepts the same arguments. We will modify the **Car** and **Truck** classes to use this technique.

When building instances of these classes, you can pass arguments in to create custom miles per gallon and available fuel values for each car or truck. Because the classes inherit properties from **Vehicle**, these properties are not recreated. However, now that we're exploring encapsulation, and the properties are private, a direct assignment is not possible. Instead, you can use the syntax **super()** to pass the incoming values on to **Vehicle** where the properties are assigned. The object **super** refers to the superclass, and the **super()**

statement explicitly calls the constructor of the superclass. Line 8 in both of the following excerpts uses this technique.

Also note that, just like in the **Vehicle** class, we've changed the property from public to private (line 5 in both **Car** and **Truck** classes), and added an underscore to the start of the property name (line 5, and again when used in lines 9 and 10, of both classes).

**NOTE**

*Another way to access properties from a superclass, without making them public, is to use the* **protected** *access control modifier. For more information, see the companion website.*

## Car class

```
3    public class Car extends Vehicle {
4
5        private var _tires:Tires;
6
7        public function Car(mpg:Number, fuel:Number) {
8            super(mpg, fuel);
9            _tires = new Tires("highperformance");
10           trace(this, "has", _tires.type, "tires");
11       }
```

## Truck class

```
3    public class Truck extends Vehicle {
4
5        private var _tires:Tires;
6
7        public function Truck(mpg:Number, fuel:Number) {
8            super(mpg, fuel);
9            _tires = new Tires("snow");
10           trace(this, "has", _tires.type, "tires");
11       }
```

## Tires class

The **Tires** class (*Tires.as*) is adjusted in much the same way the **Vehicle** class was altered, shown in the bold lines that follow. First, the lone property becomes private, and its uses are updated to add the underscore reserved for private properties. Next, a getter and setter pair is added to make the property accessible outside the class.

```
1    package {
2
3        public class Tires {
4
5            private var _type:String;
6
7            public function Tires(tire:String) {
8                //simulated functionality change based on tire type
9                switch (tire) {
10                   case "snow" :
11                       _type = "storm-ready snow";
12                       break;
13                   case "highperformance" :
14                       _type = "high-performance radial";
15                       break;
16                   default :
17                       _type = "economical bias-ply";
```

```
18              }
19          }
20
21          public function get type():String {
22              return _type;
23          }
24
25          public function set type(tire:String):void {
26              _type = tire;
27          }
28      }
29  }
```

## Document class

The only changes required to the document class to complete our encapsulation example are to make the properties and methods private, and add an underscore to the property names. Only the class and constructor remain public. Note these changes in bold:

```
7       public class Main extends MovieClip {
8
9           public var _compact:Car;
10          public var _pickup:Truck;
11
12          public function Main() {
13
14              _compact = new Car(21, 18);
15              _compact.x = 0;
16              _compact.y = 20;
17              addChild(_compact);
18              _compact.openSunroof();
19
20              _pickup = new Truck(16, 23);
21              _pickup.x = 0;
22              _pickup.y = 100;
23              addChild(_pickup);
24              _pickup.lowerTailgate();
25
26              this.addEventListener(Event.ADDED_TO_STAGE,
27                                    onAddedToStage,
28                                    false, 0, true);
29          }
```

The property names also appear in the **onClick()** method.

```
30          private function onClick(evt:MouseEvent):void {
31              _compact.go();
32              _pickup.go();
33          }
34
```

# Polymorphism

The last important concept of object-oriented programming that we want to discuss is *polymorphism*. Although we'll expand the explanation as this section evolves, you can start by thinking of polymorphism as a design practice that allows you to use objects of different types in a uniform manner. For example, for our vehicle exercise, you might create classes for land-, water-, and air-based vehicles and write code to move each type of vehicle. In this scenario, it's better to use one method name for moving all of these vehicle types (such as "move"), instead of separate method names (like "drive," "pilot," and "fly," for moving a car, boat, and plane, respectively). Doing so makes your code more flexible, more reusable, and easier to read and document.

In ActionScript 3.0, polymorphism is commonly used with inheritance and/or *interfaces*. We'll work with interfaces in a moment but, for now, think of them as rulebooks for classes. An interface is nothing more than a list of public methods that must be present in any class that conforms to the interface. For example, you might continue to develop our vehicle exercise and eventually end up with vehicles that contain public methods that activate (start up), go, stop, and deactivate (shut down) your vehicles. You can create an interface that includes these method names and requires classes to adhere to that interface. This makes certain all of those classes can be controlled consistently.

An interface doesn't restrict your class to those methods, either. Classes can have their own public methods that are not in the interface, without consequence. As long as the interface methods are present, everyone will be happy. We'll discuss the further role that interfaces play in polymorphism a little bit later. For now, let's extend what you already know and show how to use polymorphism with inheritance.

## Polymorphism and inheritance

Employing polymorphism with inheritance allows you to design subclasses that can use the same method names as their superclasses, but without creating a conflict. For example, a superclass can have a public method called "turn," which multiple subclasses use. One subclass, however, might also have a public method called "turn," that is either entirely different or enhanced. Ordinarily, the fact that a subclass inherits public methods from a superclass means that the subclass would effectively have two methods called "turn" and a conflict would exist.

However, polymorphism allows the subclass method to replace or augment the superclass method of the same name by *overriding* it. Overriding a method tells the compiler that the new version of the method (in the subclass) takes precedence over the previous version of the method (in the superclass).

To demonstrate this process, let's begin by adding two methods to our **Vehicle** class. If you want to look at the source files, they are in the *polymorphism* folder of the chapter archive. The new methods can be seen in lines

**NOTE**

*Only public and protected methods can be seen by ActionScript 3.0 subclasses, so they are the only kinds of methods that can be overridden.*

33 through 39 in the following excerpt, and are named **useAccessory()** and **changeGear()**. Both of the new methods are available to the **Car** and **Truck** subclasses through inheritance and notice that the functionality of the **useAccessory()** method is to turn on a vehicle's lights.

## Vehicle class

```
20        private function onLoop(evt:Event):void {
21            if (_moving) {
22            _fuelAvailable--;
23            _milesTraveled += _gasMileage;
24            if (_fuelAvailable < 1) {
25                    this.removeEventListener(Event.ENTER_FRAME,
26                                            onLoop, false, 0, true);
27                }
28                trace(this, _milesTraveled, _fuelAvailable);
29                this.x = _milesTraveled;
30            }
31        }
32
33        public function  changeGear(): void  {
34            trace(this, "changed gear");
35        }
36
37        public function useAccessory():void {
38            trace(this, "vehicle lights turned on");
39        }
```

Next let's see how to override the **useAccessory()** method in the **Car** and **Truck** classes so we can customize its functionality without having to change our API.

## Car class

A public method also named **useAccessory()** is added to the **Car** class, seen in lines 17 through 19 of the following excerpt. Remember that this would ordinarily conflict with the method of the same name in the **Vehicle** superclass, because of inheritance. As discussed previously, we avoid this by preceding the method declaration, including its access control modifier, with the **override** keyword.

The functionality of the method is the same in both classes: to use an accessory. So the **useAccessory()** method in the Car class can call its existing **openSunroof()** method.

```
13        public function openSunroof():void {
14            trace(this, "opened sunroof");
15        }
16
17        override public function useAccessory():void {
18            openSunroof();
19        }
```

The beauty of this arrangement is that you've created an API that employs the flexible "use accessory" idea to . . . er . . . use accessories. Hereafter, you can write **instancename.useAccessory()** and be free to change your **Car** class without having to change the rest of your application. For example, you might have many method calls using the syntax **useAccessory()** that all open car sunroofs. If you later decide to change the accessory to something else, you would need to edit only the **Car** class, not the many existing method calls, to update your application.

## Truck class

Now we'll do the same thing with the Truck class, but with a twist. In some cases when overriding, you may not want to entirely replace the original behavior that exists in the superclass. When needed, you can execute the custom code in the subclass method *and* call the same method in the superclass. To do this, add an instruction in the subclass method to explicitly call the original superclass method, as seen in line 18 of the **Truck** class. In this case, you can't simply use the **super()** statement the way you did earlier, because that only works in the constructor. Within a method, you must reference the superclass using the **super** object, and follow it with the superclass method you want to call. The edit is in bold.

```
13        public function lowerTailgate():void {
14            trace(this, "lowered tailgate");
15        }
16
17        override public function useAccessory():void {
18            super.useAccessory();
19            lowerTailgate();
20        }
```

## Tires class and Document class

No change to the **Tires** class is required, but we'll make two changes to the document class **Main** to show the outcome of your efforts. First, in both **Car** and **Truck** instances (*compact* and *pickup*), we'll call the other method we added, **changeGear()** (lines 18 and 25). This will show that the outcome of a public method called from either car or truck will be the same if polymorphism is not in play.

Next, we'll follow the example discussed and change our code from calling **openSunroof()** and **lowerTailgate()**, for *compact* and *pickup* respectively, to both instances calling **useAccessory()** (lines 19 and 26). This will make our code a bit more flexible, as we can later change the accessories in one or both classes and not have to change our FLA to benefit from the adjustment.

```
12        public function Main() {
13
14            compact = new Car(21, 18);
15            compact.x = 20;
16            compact.y = 20;
17            addChild(compact);
18            compact.changeGear();
19            compact.useAccessory();
20
```

```
21              pickup = new Truck(16, 23);
22              pickup.x = 20;
23              pickup.y = 100;
24              addChild(pickup);
25              pickup.changeGear();
26              pickup.useAccessory();
27
28              this.addEventListener(Event.ADDED_TO_STAGE,
29                                    onAddedToStage,
30                                    false, 0, true);
31          }
```

An abbreviated output follows. As you can see, the car class traced its tires, the *compact* instance changed gear, and then used its accessory. This opened the sunroof, but nothing more because the **Car** class override replaced the functionality of the **Vehicle useAccessory()** method, which turned on the vehicle's lights. The *pickup* behaved similarly, but in addition to lowering its tailgate, also turned on its lights. This is because the **Truck** class also called the **useAccessory()** method in the superclass, rather than just overriding it.

```
[object Car] has high-performance radial tires
[object Car] changed gear
[object Car] opened sunroof
[object Truck] has storm-ready snow tires
[object Truck] changed gear
[object Truck] lowered tailgate
[object Truck] turned on lights
[object Car] 21 17
[object Truck] 16 22
[object Car] 42 16
[object Truck] 32 21
...
```

## Polymorphism and interfaces

Earlier, we said there's another way to use polymorphism that doesn't focus on inheritance. Because it's not based on method overriding between subclass and superclass, it's applicable to more situations. The general idea is the same, in that your coding is simplified by using the same method names across different object types. However, it's even more useful in that it adds additional flexibility by not requiring that you type your object to a specific class.

To help explain this, let's sideline a bit to revisit two important ActionScript 3.0 topics: compile-time error checking and the display list. The benefit of using data typing with your objects is that the ActionScript compiler will warn you if you do something that's incompatible with your stated data type. By design, the simplest case means that you can only work with one data type. (A look at Chapter 2 will reinforce this idea if you need a quick review.)

However, there are times when you may want things to be a bit more flexible. For example, you may want to put either a **MovieClip** or **Sprite** into a variable. If you type the variable as **MovieClip**, only a movie clip will be accepted. To get around this, you can type a variable as the base class **DisplayObject**, from which both **MovieClip** and **Sprite** descend (see Chapter 4 for more information), and the compiler won't object.

The downside to this is that it can be a bit *too* generic. If, for example, you used a movie clip method on an object that the compiler only understood as a **DisplayObject**, an error would occur:

```
var thing:DisplayObject = new MovieClip();
thing.play();
```

Why? Because, although **play()** is a legal movie clip method, the compiler doesn't understand that **thing** is actually a movie clip. It might be a sprite (and that flexibility is the very reason we're discussing this), and a sprite doesn't have a timeline.

This can be addressed by casting (also discussed in Chapter 4), but that kind of defeats the purpose of what we're doing. Instead, what if you could specify a data type that was flexible enough to work with different kinds of objects, but also knew which methods those objects supported? That's where interfaces come in.

As we explained earlier, an interface is simply a list of public methods that must be present in a class. The following is an example of an interface that might be used with classes for devices that play music (like a radio or CD player). All of the code for this discussion can be found in the *polymorphism_interface* source code directory. The interface is called **IAudible** and is found in the *IAudible.as* source file. It's a very common practice to start the name of all interfaces with a capital I, to differentiate them from classes.

```
1   package {
2
3       public interface IAudible {
4
5           function turnOn():void;
6           function playSelection(preset:int):void;
7           function turnOff():void;
8
9       }
10  }
```

As you can see, not even the content of a method is included. Only the name, parameters and data types, and return data type (which are collectively called the method's *signature*) are included. Also, any import statements needed to support included data types are required. (In this case, the compiler automatically understands the **int** data type. However, if a data type represents a class, such as **MovieClip** or **Event**, that class must be imported.)

Once you've created an interface, you can require a class to adhere to it by *implementing* it using the **implements** keyword in the interface declaration, as shown in line 3 of the following simple **Radio** class (*Radio.as*):

```
1   package {
2
3       public class Radio implements IAudible {
4
```

```
5        public function Radio() {
6            trace("radio added");
7        }
8
9        public function turnOn():void {
10           trace("radio on");
11       }
12
13       public function playSelection(preset:int):void {
14           trace("radio selection: channel", preset);
15       }
16
17       public function turnOff():void {
18           trace("radio off");
19       }
20   }
21 }
```

All this class does is trace appropriate diagnostic statements, identifying itself as "radio" each time. It complies with the interface because every method required is present. Here is a **CDPlayer** class (*CDPlayer.as*) that also implements, and complies with, the same interface. The purpose of the class is similar, but it identifies itself as "cd player" in each trace to demonstrate unique functionality.

```
1  package {
2
3      public class CDPlayer implements IAudible {
4
5          public function CDPlayer() {
6              trace("cd player added");
7          }
8
9          public function turnOn():void {
10             trace("cd player on");
11         }
12
13         public function playSelection(preset:int):void {
14             trace("cd player selection: track", preset);
15         }
16
17         public function turnOff():void {
18             trace("cd player off");
19         }
20
21         public function eject():void {
22             trace("cd player eject");
23         }
24
25     }
26 }
```

Although the **Radio** and **CDPlayer** classes do different things (demonstrated simply by the unique traces), the method names required by the interface are present in both classes. This means that you can write a full application using a radio, later swap out the radio with a CD player, but not have to change any of your basic method calls—a key benefit of polymorphism.

The **CDPlayer** class also demonstrates that additional methods, not referenced by an interface, can appear in classes—as shown by the **eject()** method in lines 21 through 23. An interface is only designed to enforce a contract with a class, making sure the required methods are present. It doesn't restrict the functionality of a class.

## Simple example

All that remains is putting this into practice. The following basic implementation is found in the *sound_system.fla* source file. The key step in using interfaces in this context is typing to the interface. If you type to **Radio**, you can't switch to **CDPlayer** later. However, if you type to **IAudible**, the compiler will nod approvingly at both **Radio** and **CDPlayer**. Also, because the interface rigidly enforces that all public methods are present, you don't run into situations where the compiler is unsure if a method is legal. This is polymorphism at its best. The following script starts with a radio and then switches to a CD player, using methods in both cases without error.

```
var soundSystem:IAudible = new Radio();
soundSystem.turnOn();

soundSystem = new CDPlayer();
soundSystem.turnOn();
soundSystem.playSelection(1);
```

## Adding a sound system to your vehicles through composition

Now let's practice what you've learned by composing the sound system example into the ongoing vehicle exercise. This will review encapsulation, composition, and polymorphism.

First, add another private property to the **Vehicle** class to hold the sound system, just like we did when we composed **Tires** into the exercise. It's typed to the interface to allow a vehicle to have any sound system that implements **IAudible**. The property can be seen in line 12 of the following excerpt from the *Vehicle.as* source file:

```
8        private var _gasMileage:Number;
9        private var _fuelAvailable:Number;
10       private var _milesTraveled:Number = 0;
11       private var _moving:Boolean;
12       private var _soundSystem:IAudible;
```

Next, provide public access to this property by adding a getter and setter, again typed to the **IAudible** interface. The following excerpt, still in the *Vehicle.as* source file, shows this addition in lines 64 through 70:

```
60       public function get milesTraveled():Number {
61           return _milesTraveled;
62       }
63
64       public function get soundSystem():IAudible {
65           return _soundSystem;
66       }
```

```
67
68            public function set soundSystem(device:IAudible):void {
69                 _soundSystem = device;
70            }
```

The last class changes involve adding an instance of **CDPlayer** in the **Car** class, and a **Radio** instance in the **Truck** class—just as we did when adding **Tires** in the composition example. This excerpt from the **Car** class (*Car.as*) shows the change at the end of the constructor:

```
7             public function Car(mpg:Number, fuel:Number) {
8                 super(mpg, fuel);
9                 _tires = new Tires("highperformance");
10                trace(this, "has", _tires.type, "tires");
11                soundSystem = new CDPlayer();
12            }
```

This excerpt from the **Truck** class (*Truck.as*) also adds the sound system at the end of the constructor. The edits in both classes appear in bold at line 11:

```
7             public function Truck(mpg:Number, fuel:Number) {
8                 super(mpg, fuel);
9                 _tires = new Tires("snow");
10                trace(this, "has", _tires.type, "tires");
11                soundSystem = new Radio();
12            }
```

Finally, the document class is modified to use the sound system in both the **Car** instance (*compact*) and **Truck** instance (*pickup*) when you click the stage. Shown in bold in the *Main.as* excerpt below, lines 42 through 44 access the CD player and radio through the **soundSystem** property. This triggers the getter method in the respective classes and returns the car's CD player and the truck's radio.

```
39            public function onClick(evt:MouseEvent):void {
40                compact.go();
41                pickup.go();
42                compact.soundSystem.turnOn();
43                compact.soundSystem.playSelection(2);
44                pickup.soundSystem.turnOn();
45            }
```

The trace immediately reflects the fact that the car has a CD player and the truck has a radio. Once you click the stage (shown by the gap in the output that follows), the sound systems are used and the vehicles drive off into the sunset.

```
[object Car] has high-performance radial tires
cd player added
[object Car] changed gear
[object Car] opened sunroof
[object Truck] has storm-ready snow tires
radio added
[object Truck] changed gear
[object Truck] lowered tailgate
[object Truck] turned on lights
```

```
cd player on
cd player selection: track 2
radio on
[object Car] 21 17
[object Truck] 16 22
...
```

# Navigation Bar Revisited

Chapter 5 concluded with the start of a simple navigation bar created using procedural programming techniques. We'll now step through a new exercise to demonstrate one way to approach the same task using OOP. This exercise combines the use of standalone classes with classes that are linked to movie clips in the main Flash file, *LAS3Lab.fla*—found in the *nav_bar* folder of the chapter source archive.

This exercise is also the start of the navigation system for the cumulative book/companion website collective project. In this chapter, we'll use a basic array to create five main buttons. Later, in Chapter 14, we'll add submenus to this system and load all the content dynamically through the use of XML.

The files and directories you create here will continue to be used and enhanced throughout the remainder of this book, so establishing a logical directory structure now will be very helpful. The FLA and document class should reside in the top level of a new directory. Adjacent to the FLA, you'll eventually create two directories for classes. In later versions of the exercise, you'll create a *com* folder for general packages that you may use in multiple projects. At this point, you're ready to create an *app* folder for classes specific to this project that you are less likely to reuse. As always, adopting naming conventions and organization recommendations are personal choices that you can adapt when your comfort increases.

The FLA requires two symbols in the library (included in the source):

*MenuButtonMain*

In our example, this is a movie clip that looks like a tab. (Its name was influenced by the fact that submenus will be introduced to this example, later in the book.) The symbol's linkage class is called `MenuButtonMain`, too. However, we'll be using a custom class this time, rather than just relying on the automatic internal class created by Flash Professional for the sole purpose of birthing the object with ActionScript. Therefore, the fully qualified path name, which includes not only the class name but also its package, is used as the symbol's linkage class: `com.learningactionscript3.gui.MenuButtonMain`.

*HLineThick*

This is simply a thick line, approximately 8 pixels tall and the width of your file. This serves as the horizontal plane on which the main menu buttons reside to form the navigation bar. Unlike the button symbol, there's no

**NOTE**

*Push Yourself: A great way to make sure you understand packages is to reorganize the source files in the polymorphism_inheritance exercise by putting the sound system files in their own package. Pick a package name such as* `app.las3.soundsystem`, *or try your own reverse domain path. Don't forget to revise the package declaration line in each affected class, and add import statements to the other classes referencing your sound systems. An example of this kind of organization can be found in the polymorphism _packages directory.*

external class for this line, as it has no functionality. Still, we'll give it a linkage class that includes a package location anyway: `com.learningactionscript3.gui.HLineThick`. The result will be the same as using a class name without package information; Flash Professional will still create a placeholder class in the SWF. However, the nice thing about preplanning this way is that if you ever want to add functionality to this asset, you can create a class in this location and perhaps avoid additional edits to the FLA.

## Document class

The entry point to this project is the document class, *LAS3Main.as*, which follows. Lines 3 and 4 import the **MovieClip** class and custom **NavigationBar** class, which you'll create in a moment. Line 6 declares the class and extends **MovieClip**. Lines 8 through 14 contain the class constructor.

This navigation bar can feature a variable number of buttons, determined by the contents of an array seen in lines 9 and 10. Lines 11 and 12 creates an instance of the **NavigationBar** class and passes in the array of labels for the new buttons. Finally, line 13 adds the navigation bar to the display list.

```
1   package {
2
3       import flash.display.MovieClip;
4       import com.learningactionscript3.gui.NavigationBar;
5
6       public class LAS3Main extends MovieClip {
7
8           public function LAS3Main() {
9               var menuData:Array = ["one", "two", "three",
10                                     "four", "five"];
11              var navBar:NavigationBar =
12                  new NavigationBar(menuData);
13              addChild(navBar);
14          }
15      }
16  }
```

## NavigationBar

Next we need to create the **NavigationBar** class (*NavigationBar.as*), which will be the home for our buttons. Here we'll focus on the times that are appreciably different in purpose from the prior class, or are otherwise noteworthy. Line 1, for example is the package declaration discussed several times previously in the book, but is worthy of mention because it reflects the location of the class—in the *gui* directory, within the *com* directory, found in the same folder as the FLA. Lines 9 through 12 contain the class constructor, populate the properties with the incoming argument data, and call the **build()** method:

```
1   package com.learningactionscript3.gui {
2
3       import flash.display.MovieClip;
4
```

```
5     public class NavigationBar extends MovieClip {
6
7         private var _navData:Array;
8
9         public function NavigationBar(navData:Array) {
10            _navData = navData;
11            build();
12        }
```

In the next code segment, the **build()** method uses a **for** loop to add each button to the navigation bar. The loop first creates an instance of the **MenuButtonMain** class, passing the name of the button as a string for the button's label. This string comes from the button array passed into the constructor from the document class, and can be seen in line 9 of the prior class. Next, the button is positioned horizontally by starting with a 20-pixel offset, and then multiplying the width of the button plus a 2-pixel space for each button. That is, the first button starts at 20 pixels because *i* begins as 0 and no further offset is added. The second button starts at 20 and then 1 * (button width + 2) is added, and so on. A fixed y location is also used, and each button is added to the display list.

Finally, the aforementioned horizontal bar from the FLA library is added to the bottom of the menu buttons (lines 22 through 25). Two things are important here. First, the line is typed as **MovieClip** to give you a bit more flexibility. We haven't yet created a dedicated class for this object, and it's a movie clip in the FLA. Second, as a display object, this line movie clip can be a target of mouse events. Because it has no active role in the navigation bar, we disable it from interacting with the mouse by setting its **mouseEnabled** property to false.

```
13        private function build():void {
14            for (var i:uint; i < _navData.length; i++) {
15                var menuBtn:MenuButtonMain =
16                    new MenuButtonMain(_navData[i]);
17                menuBtn.x = 20 + i * (menuBtn.width + 2);
18                menuBtn.y = 75;
19                addChild(menuBtn);
20            }
21
22            var hline:MovieClip = new HLineThick();
23            hline.y = 100;
24            hline.mouseEnabled = false;
25            addChild(hline);
26        }
27    }
28 }
```

## MenuButtonMain

Finally, we present the **MenuButtonMain** class, which creates the button for each menu added to the navigation bar. In addition to the previously explained package declaration and imports, this class also uses two text classes originally discussed in Chapter 4—the display list class **TextField** and the text automatic sizing and alignment class, **TextFieldAutoSize**. The text field goes into a private property called _btnLabel, and the remainder of the functionality will be explained after the code.

```
1    package com.learningactionscript3.gui {
2
3        import flash.display.MovieClip;
4        import flash.events.MouseEvent;
5        import flash.text.TextField;
6        import flash.text.TextFieldAutoSize;
7
8        public class MenuButtonMain extends MovieClip {
9
10           private var _btnLabel:TextField;
11
12           public function MenuButtonMain(labl:String) {
13               _btnLabel = new TextField();
14               _btnLabel.autoSize = TextFieldAutoSize.CENTER;
15               _btnLabel.textColor = 0xFFFFFF;
16               _btnLabel.text = labl;
17               _btnLabel.mouseEnabled = false;
18               addChild(_btnLabel);
19
20               buttonMode = true;
21               useHandCursor = true;
22               addEventListener(MouseEvent.CLICK, onClick,
23                                 false, 0, true);
24           }
25
26           private function onClick(evt:MouseEvent):void {
27               trace(_btnLabel.text);
28           }
29       }
30   }
```

Lines 13 through 18 apply to the text label inside the button. When a button is created, a string that will serve as the button text is passed into the **labl** parameter (custom-named to differentiate it from an ActionScript property called **label**). Line 13 creates a new text field and line 14 sizes the field to the minimum dimensions required to display the text—reducing the field at left, right, and bottom, effectively centering the text. Line 15 colors all text in the field white, and line 16 places the string from **labl** into the field.

Line 17 is particularly important in this example. The default mouse behavior for a dynamic text field is to display a standard I-beam text cursor and allow a varying degree of text editing (depending on properties we'll discuss in Chapter 10). As such, a text field used inside a button will follow this behavior and intercept mouse events, preventing the button from behaving properly. Line 17 disables mouse interaction with the text field, so it won't interfere, and so the mouse will display a pointer cursor when interacting with the button. Line 18 adds the field to the button.

Lines 20 through 23 apply to the button itself. Although a movie clip will react to mouse events, it will not exhibit the mouse cursor feedback associated with a button. For example, it won't switch from a pointer to a finger. Line

## CHAPTER 7

# MOTION

From your very first experiment to the umpteenth time you've performed a familiar task, moving assets with code can be very gratifying. In addition to creating more dynamic work by freeing yourself from the permanency of the timeline, there is something very immediate and pleasing about controlling the motion of an object purely with ActionScript.

Because programming motion can cover many concepts, we've chosen to focus on a few key topics in this chapter. For each group of ideas we introduce, we offer what we call *simplified simulations*—that is, we don't maintain that our examples accurately reflect real-world scenarios. When discussing physics, for example, we won't be accounting for every force that can act on an object. On the contrary, we'll try to provide simple implementations that you can easily integrate into your own projects.

We also hope to show that math can be your friend. To some of you, this may be a given, but to others, math can be a little intimidating. If you're in the latter group, we hope to reduce what may be a knee-jerk reaction to nothing more than working with numbers. Understanding just a few practical applications of mathematical or scientific principles can really go a long way. Before you know it, you'll be creating what seem like complex animations with little effort. You'll be building grids of movie clips, animating planets in elliptical orbits, shooting projectiles in games, building novel navigation systems, and more.

In this chapter, we'll look at the following topics:

- **Basic Movement.** We'll start with simple movement, updating x and y coordinates using velocity, acceleration, and easing.

- **Physics.** Gravity, friction, and elasticity add a bit of realism to animations, and you may be surprised how easy they are to simulate.

- **A Basic Particle System**. Learning by doing is important, so we'll combine movement, physics, and object-oriented programming to create a class-based particle system.

- **Collision Detection**. Next we'll discuss how to detect collisions with other objects, points, and the boundaries of the stage.

- **Geometry and Trigonometry.** Even basic geometric and trigonometric principles can make animated objects move in wonderful ways. We'll show you how to determine the distance between two points, how to move an object along a specific angle, how to animate objects in a circular path, and how to rotate objects to point at a specific location. We'll also combine some of these skills to create a novel navigation widget and another basic particle system.

- **Programmatic Tweening.** Scripting movement entirely from scratch affords the greatest flexibility but also requires a fair amount of labor. Sometimes, a prewritten method or two can satisfy a basic need for motion. We'll demonstrate ActionScript's Tween class and its occasional partner in crime, the Easing package.

- **Using a Tweening Engine: TweenLite.** Finally, we'll show you an alternative to ActionScript's built-in tweening options (and, at the same time, give you some experience using third-party ActionScript 3.0 packages) by introducing the fabulous TweenLite tweening engine.

## Basic Movement

When discussing scripted motion, a good place to begin is simple movement through updating x and y coordinates of a display object. Whether you realize it or not, you're probably already used to thinking of points in two-dimensional space as x and y coordinates. However, you're probably used to thinking about positive x values moving to the right and positive y values moving up, the way simple graphs are usually expressed.

The Flash coordinate system differs a bit from the typical x-, y-coordinate system with which you may be familiar. The x values still increase to the right, but the (0, 0) point of the stage is in the upper-left corner, and the y values increase when moving *down*. This becomes important when you want an object to travel up, because you must subtract from the **y** property. For example, if a MovieClip starts at an x, y position of (100, 100), getting it to move up by 10-pixel increments means changing its **y** property to 90, 80, 70, and so on. This inverted y axis also makes a difference when creating practical user interface elements, such as sliders. We'll create a slider in Chapter 11 to control sound volume, in which the inverted y value plays a part.

To increase or decrease a value, you simply add to, or subtract from, the previous value. You may recall from Chapter 2 that the increment operator, two plus signs (**++**), are equivalent to value = value + 1, and two minus signs (**--**) represent value = value – 1. We also discussed the compound assignment operators **+=** and **-=**, which add or subtract (respectively) whatever is on the right of the equal sign from the existing value of the variable or property on the left of the equal sign. Assuming two movie clips begin at (0, 0), where will they be after this code?

```
mc.x++;
mc.y--;
mc2.x += 10;
mc2.y -= 10;
```

The *mc* movie clip ends up at (1, −1) and the *mc2* movie clip ends up at (10, −10). In this chapter, you'll be moving objects around the stage in this way, as well as by using more involved formulas and variables. To give you some perspective on what lies ahead, it will help to understand the terms *speed*, *velocity*, and *acceleration*, which we use throughout the chapter:

*Speed*

Speed, or how fast an object is moving, is a *scalar* quantity, which means it's a value that can be expressed with magnitude alone. That is, you can drive your car at 60 miles per hour, but that speed doesn't imply a direction. We can create a variable or object property called **speed**, but it won't help animate a display object until we add a direction to the mix.

*Velocity*

Velocity is a constant speed of motion, but adds direction. It's called a *vector* quantity because it's expressed with both magnitude and direction. One easy way to do this when animating objects in ActionScript is by referring to the **x** and **y** properties of a display object. For example, moving a movie clip 20 pixels in the x direction sends it to the right, representing speed and direction.

*Acceleration*

Acceleration is the rate of *change* in velocity and is also a vector quantity, requiring both magnitude and direction. For example, an object that accelerates to the right has an ever increasing change in its **x** property.

These distinctions may be subtle, but they are helpful when understanding how to get from point a to point b. You certainly don't have to memorize them, but understanding the basics of each term will help you plan, and even troubleshoot, your code. If a display object is moving at a constant rate of speed when it's meant to move faster over time, you may realize that you forgot to add acceleration before updating your x or y values.

## Velocity

Starting out, velocity will be expressed as an increase or decrease of x and y coordinates. Later on, we'll show you how to move an object using an angle but, for now, remember that incrementing the x property by 4 means a velocity of 4 pixels to the right. Breaking this update into separate components for position and velocity can make this clearer and easier to work with— particularly when additional factors enter the equation such as acceleration, gravity, friction, and so on.

**NOTE**

*See the "Adding Custom Symbol Instances to the Display List" section of Chapter 4 to review how to use a linkage class.*

The following code, found in *velocity.fla* in the companion source files, creates a ball from a library movie clip with the linkage class, **Ball**. It then adds 4 pixels to the ball's x and y coordinates each time the enter frame event occurs. This means the ball moves down and to the right, as depicted in multiple frames in Figure 7-1.

```
1   var ball:MovieClip = new Ball();
2   ball.x = ball.y = 100;
3   addChild(ball);
4
5   var xVel:Number = 4;
6   var yVel:Number = 4;
7
8   addEventListener(Event.ENTER_FRAME, onLoop, false, 0, true);
9   function onLoop(evt:Event):void {
10      ball.x += xVel;
11      ball.y += yVel;
12  }
```

If the ball's x velocity is 4, how far does the ball move along the x axis in one second? This an important question because the ball's speed is dependent upon the FLAs frame rate. Because the function is executed every time an enter frame event is received, a frame rate of 20 frames per second (fps) yields a distance of 80 pixels per second—approximately one inch on a 72-pixel-per-inch monitor—in the x direction. Next let's look at how to *change* that ball's velocity.

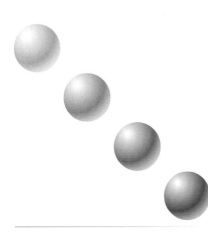

*Figure 7-1. Simulated movement of a movie clip, at a constant velocity, down and to the right*

## Acceleration

Changing the velocity over time accelerates or decelerates an object. Consider a ball that moves 4 pixels in the x direction every time an enter frame event occurs; you can easily calculate the ball's movement as 4 + 4 + 4 + 4 and so on. In 3 seconds the ball would travel 240 pixels (4 pixels per frame * 20 frames per second * 3 seconds). If we accelerate the object 1 pixel per enter frame event, however, the ball's changing velocity would be 4 + 5 + 6 + 7, and so on. At the same frame rate of 20 frames per second, the ball would travel 2070 pixels in the same 3 seconds! Acceleration is the compound interest of motion.

Figure 7-2 illustrates the effect of acceleration by depicting an increasing distance traveled by a ball each time an update occurs. You can illustrate this change more dramatically by changing acceleration in only one direction. All you have to do is increment velocity by acceleration every time the function executes. The source file *acceleration.fla* demonstrates this idea by adding acceleration to the x velocity. This file augments the velocity example by adding lines 7 and 14, shown in bold:

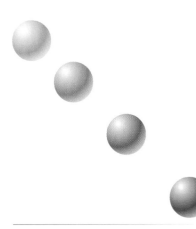

*Figure 7-2. Acceleration increasing the velocity over time, simulated by increased movement in each frame*

```
1   var ball:MovieClip = new Ball();
2   ball.x = ball.y = 100;
3   addChild(ball);
4
5   var xVel:Number = 4;
6   var yVel:Number = 4;
```

```
7   var xAcc:Number = 1;
8
9   addEventListener(Event.ENTER_FRAME, onLoop, false, 0, true);
10  function onLoop(evt:Event):void {
11      ball.x += xVel;
12      ball.y += yVel;
13
14      xVel += xAcc;
15  }
```

# Easing

One of the biggest challenges to creating good animated sequences is bringing realism to your work. As any animator will tell you, this is a lifelong effort, but adding *easing* to your animation is a very quick way to take a big step towards that goal. Easing is so named because when used, an object appears to "ease in" to an animation, accelerating as the animation progresses, or "ease out" of an animation, decelerating as the animation finishes. As a crude real-world example, think about merging onto a highway. As you approach the highway from the on ramp, you slowly increase your speed looking for a chance to join the stream of vehicles. You continue to add acceleration, find an opening, and ease into the highway traffic.

Later in this chapter we'll show you how to use preexisting easing equations but it's very useful to first understand the basics behind easing. For one thing, writing your own simple easing code helps you learn more about programming motion. More importantly, however, integrating easing into your scripts is also more flexible. The most common use of easing is when adding it to *tweens*—sequences where the computer calculates the interim property values between starting and finishing frames. However, these starting and finishing values are typically preset in tweens. Writing your own easing code means you can add it to any other scripted motion, even when values are changing on the fly.

The simplest easing equation is a formula akin to *Zeno's paradox*. This philosophical idea says that, when moving from one point to another, you never really reach your ultimate destination because you're dividing the remaining distance with every movement. If you divide the distance between point a and point b in half with every step, theoretically, you could never reach point b. As a philosophical idea this may be interesting, but in practical terms, objects reach their intended destinations all the time. In fact, we can use a formula derived from Zeno's paradox in animation, to slow down an object as it approaches its new location, as shown in Figure 7-3.

*Figure 7-3. Zeno's paradox, a simple way to depict friction or easing*

The following example, found in the *easing.fla* source file, demonstrates this principle; it first creates a ball movie clip from the library, and then calls the **onLoop()** function every enter frame. This updates the movie clip's x and y coordinates every enter frame by calling the **zeno()** function, where the easing equation does its work:

```
1   var ball:MovieClip = new Ball();
2   ball.x = ball.y = 100;
3   addChild(ball);
4
5   addEventListener(Event.ENTER_FRAME, onLoop, false, 0, true);
6   function onLoop(evt:Event):void {
7       ball.x += zeno(ball.x, mouseX, 2);
8       ball.y += zeno(ball.y, mouseY, 2);
9   }
10
11  function zeno(orig:Number, dest:Number, reducer:Number):Number {
12      return (dest - orig) / reducer;
13  }
```

The **zeno()** function starts by subtracting the starting location (the ball's current x or y location) from the ending location (the mouse x or y location) to determine the distance that must be traveled. It then divides that distance by an amount used to slow the progress. Finally, it adds that diminished value to the current coordinates of the ball and the process begins again. The result is that every time you move the mouse, the ball begins moving again and slows down as it approaches the new mouse position.

In this example, the amount is cut in half every time simply to relate back to the explanation of Zeno's paradox. Discussing only the horizontal position for simplicity, if the ball must move from an x coordinate of 100 to an x coordinate of 200, the first few updated positions are as follows. (Also shown are the formula values used to calculate each position.) The effect is that the ball eases in to the final destination.

```
starting point        :100
100 += (200 - 100) / 2 :150
150 += (200 - 150) / 2 :175
175 += (200 - 175) / 2 :187.5
```

You don't always have to cut the remaining distance in half, of course, when using this formula. In fact, this is how you vary an animation's deceleration. Numbers higher than 2 require more time for the object to reach its destination, and lower numbers finish the animation more quickly. The *easing.fla* source file in the companion source code demonstrates this by passing 8 into the reducer parameter of the **zeno()** function.

Best of all, every time you move the mouse in this example, the equation automatically adjusts because the starting and ending locations are dynamic. The starting point will always be the current location of the ball, and the ending point will always be the mouse location.

**NOTE**

*Although the examples in this book are necessarily general and concise for tutorial purposes, you may sometimes want to add tolerance factors when applying them to your own projects. When easing, for example, you may want to add a conditional statement that removes an event listener when your display object comes close enough to your destination. This will eliminate unnecessary activity in your scripts, and you can also use the opportunity to snap your display object to your exact destination, if important.*

*The upcoming section "A Basic Particle System" shows a variant of this approach by removing a listener when a particle leaves the stage.*

# Simple Physics

In the quest for more expressive animation, you will find that adding physics to animations, games, and similar projects can really elevate them to another level of user enjoyment. The visual appearance and, in interactive scenarios, even the user experience of a project are sometimes dramatically enhanced by surprisingly small code additions.

We're going to be discussing some basic physics principles in this section, but it's more important for you to understand their *effects* than to focus minutely on the math and science behind them. This is because the formulas offered here are necessarily simplified, or even adapted, from their real-world counterparts. Once you're comfortable with the principles in general, you can refine formulas, account for additional variables, and so on, to improve their realism. For example, it's often helpful to first simulate the simple orbit of a planet before considering the orbit's decay, the gravitational attraction of other bodies, and so on.

## Gravity

What happens when you toss a ball into the air? It goes up, starts to slow down as gravity affects its rate of ascent, it stops momentarily at the top of its journey, and then the ball starts moving faster again as gravity starts to accelerate its trip downward.

If you think about it carefully, a simple ActionScript simulation of gravity requires little more than acceleration in the y direction. The following code, found in the *gravity.fla* source file, requires only minor changes to the previous acceleration example. Here we'll focus on acceleration in the y direction, and we'll start with a negative y velocity to start the ball moving upward:

**NOTE**

*Remember that, in the ActionScript coordinate system, increasing y values move an object downward.*

```
1   var ball:MovieClip = new Ball();
2   ball.x = ball.y = 100;
3   addChild(ball);
4
5   var xVel:Number = 4;
6   var yVel:Number = -10;
7   var yAcc:Number = 1;
8
9   addEventListener(Event.ENTER_FRAME, onLoop, false, 0, true);
10  function onLoop(evt:Event):void {
11      ball.x += xVel;
12      ball.y += yVel;
13
14      yVel += yAcc;
15  }
```

The ball begins moving at 10 pixels per enter frame event, but acceleration adds 1 to the y velocity each iteration. As such, the velocity decreases from −10 to −9 to −8, and so on, slowing the ball's ascent, just as if gravity were counteracting the upward force of the toss. Eventually, the y velocity reaches zero at the height of the toss, where the upward force and gravity reach equilibrium.

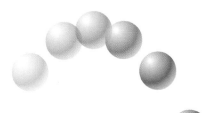

*Figure 7-4. The effect of gravity on acceleration*

**NOTE**

*To continue your exploration of gravity, velocity, and acceleration, visit the book's companion website. The "More Motion (Gravity)" post includes a file called* **wall_bounce.fla** *that demonstrates all these concepts and adds several additional features. Included are conditionals to change the ball's direction when hitting a stage boundary (which we'll discuss in a moment), bounce behavior, and even a texture to simulate rotation during bouncing.*

Then, as we continue to add 1 to the y velocity, its value becomes 1, then 2, then 3, and so on, as the ball begins to accelerate downward due to the effect of gravity. Figure 7-4 shows the effect of the simulated gravity by depicting several frames of the animation at once. When a ball is tossed in the air, gravity slows its rate of ascent and then increases the rate at which it falls.

## Friction

All other things being equal, if you slide a hockey puck along three surfaces—a street, a marble floor, and an ice rink—the puck will travel three different distances due to friction. Friction will be highest on the street, building up resistance to motion between the puck and the street surface, limiting the progress of the puck. Friction will be reduced on the marble surface, and lowest on the ice, allowing the puck to travel the farthest.

A simple way to add friction to an animation is to create a friction *coefficient*. A coefficient is a modifier that alters an object's property, the way friction alters the speed of the hockey puck. It's often a multiplier, which we'll use in this example, multiplying by a value less than 1 to reduce an effect, or by a value grater than 1 to exaggerate an effect.

To demonstrate this, we'll adapt the prior velocity and gravity examples to create the *friction.fla* source file. The example begins with x and y velocities of 10 in lines 5 and 6. Like the gravity example, we'll update the velocity before adding it to the ball's **x** and **y** properties. This time, however, instead of accelerating the ball in the y direction only, we're going to decelerate the ball's movement in both directions, as if friction was slowing its movement.

Remember that friction hinders movement, so you want to choose a friction value between 0 and 1 to slow down the motion. If you choose a value greater than 1, the motion would speed up, while a negative friction coefficient would move an object in reverse. Depending on the application, you can vary the number. Perhaps you might use 0.95 for ice, 0.90 for marble, and 0.60 for asphalt. With a friction coefficient in place in line 7, we can then multiply the x and y velocities by this value in lines 11 and 12. Then we can update the ball's x and y positions in lines 13 and 14.

```
1   var ball:MovieClip = new Ball();
2   ball.x = ball.y = 100;
3   addChild(ball);
4
5   var xVel:Number = 10;
6   var yVel:Number = 10;
7   var frCoeff:Number = 0.95;
8
9   addEventListener(Event.ENTER_FRAME, onLoop, false, 0, true);
10  function onLoop(evt:Event):void {
11      xVel *= frCoeff;
12      yVel *= frCoeff;
13      ball.x += xVel;
14      ball.y += yVel;
15  }
```

In addition to simulating friction, this formula is another type of easing. The big difference here is that you don't need a final value for the formula to work. That is, in the previous "Easing" section, the formula diminished the distance between two known points by adding ever decreasing values to an object's current location. In this case, all you need to know is the degree to which the velocities of an object will be reduced. Where that object ends up depends on the velocities and coefficients used.

## Elasticity

The last simple physics principal we'll look at is elasticity. Elastic properties can be applied to simulate springs, of course, but can also be used as yet another easing method.

The following example uses elasticity to settle a movie clip into a new location. The movie clip moves from a starting position to the mouse location, bouncing around the destination until settled. Figure 7-5 simulates this by showing that each successively larger position gets closer to the final location, indicated by the red crosshairs.

**NOTE**

*Developer extraordinaire Seb Lee-Delisle is developing an ActionScript animation library called Tweaser, based on easing coefficients that alter property values over time. Other animation libraries work by using the starting and ending points of the motion. Tweaser, on the other hand, works by using a starting point and an easing coefficient so you don't have to have a final destination for the animated object. This adds a bit of freedom to the task of animation. Tweaser was in beta at the time of this writing, but you can learn more at http://www.tweaser.org.*

origin        2    4   5   3    1

*Figure 7-5. A basic depiction of easing using Hooke's law of elasticity*

The ball in the figure overshoots the destination just like a spring, stopping at position 1. It then bounces back, but not quite as far, to position 2. This continues, bouncing to position 3, then 4, and ultimately settling at position 5.

Elasticity is calculated using *Hooke's law*. Hooke's law says that the force exerted by a spring is linearly proportional to the distance it's stretched or compressed. It's expressed with the formula $F = -kx$. F is the resulting force of the spring, $-k$ is a spring constant (the strength of the spring, so different springs can have different elasticities), and x is the distance to which the spring is stretched or compressed. This formula determines the power of the spring but eventually all springs return to their original state due to conservation of energy. So we'll also add a damping factor to reduce the bounce of the spring over time.

**NOTE**

*Although not vital to this discussion, the elasticity equation is expressed as a negative because the force given off by the spring is not in the same direction as the force applied to the spring. This is called a restorative force because it helps restore a property to its prior value.*

The following script, found in the *elasticity.fla* source file, starts as the prior examples have begun, by creating and adding a movie clip to the display list (lines 1 through 3), and initializing x and y velocity variables (lines 5 and 6). It then creates a listener in line 8, which calls the listener function in lines 9 through 14, every enter frame. In turn, the **velElastic()** function determines the x and y velocity of the movie clip, and the clip's **x** and **y** properties are updated.

Passed to the function in lines 10 and 11 are the movie clip's starting and ending positions, the spring constant and damping factor, and the current velocities that will be changed by the formula. The last part of the listener function includes updates to the x and y locations of the movie clip, using the newly calculated velocities. The elasticity calculation follows in the **velElastic()** function, which we'll discuss after the code.

```
1   var ball:MovieClip = new Ball();
2   ball.x = ball.y = 100;
3   addChild(ball);
4
5   var xVel:Number = 0;
6   var yVel:Number = 0;
7
8   addEventListener(Event.ENTER_FRAME, onLoop, false, 0, true);
9   function onLoop(evt:Event):void {
10      xVel = velElastic(ball.x, mouseX, 0.3, 0.8, xVel);
11      yVel = velElastic(ball.y, mouseY, 0.3, 0.8, yVel);
12      ball.x += xVel;
13      ball.y += yVel;
14  }
15  function velElastic(orig:Number, dest:Number,
16                      springConst:Number,
17                      damp:Number, vel:Number):Number {
18      var elasticForce:Number = -springConst * (orig - dest);
19      var newVelocity:Number = (vel + elasticForce) * damp;
20      return newVelocity;
21  }
```

All that remains is the elasticity calculation itself. Line 18 uses Hooke's law to calculate the force of the spring by multiplying the spring constant (the strength of the spring) by the distance between the starting point and the mouse location (the distance the metaphorical spring is stretched). Line 19 calculates the new velocity affected by the spring. It adds the newly calculated elastic force to the velocity, but reduces the value due to conservation of energy. If this dampening effect were not in place, the spring would bounce infinitely.

Both the strength of a spring (the spring constant), and the dampening effect on its force, are arbitrary values that can be adjusted to fit the needs of your projects. In this example, each successive force of the spring will be only 80 percent (0.8) of the prior force.

## A Basic Particle System

Now let's combine several of the things you've learned—including velocity, acceleration, gravity, and object-oriented programming—to create a class-based project. Particle systems are a way of simulating complex objects or materials that are composed of many small particles, such as fluids, fireworks, explosions, fire, smoke, water, snow, and so on.

Complex systems are achievable because individual particles have their own characteristics and behave autonomously. Further, the particles themselves are typically easy to adjust, or even replace, making it possible to alter the appearance or functionality of the system relatively easily. These are also characteristics of object-oriented programming, so it's not surprising that particle systems are often written using this approach.

As you're just getting started, this is a simple particle system using only two classes, which looks a little bit like a primitive water fountain. Blue circles shoot up out of the "fountain" and then fall down under the effect of gravity. Figure 7-6 shows what the system looks like, and you can get a look for yourself by testing the *particle_system.fla* source file.

## The particle

The first step in creating the system is to create a **Particle** class, found in the *Particle.as* class file. This class will give life to each individual particle. Reviewing class syntax, line 1 creates the class package, lines 3 and 4 import the required classes, and line 6 declares the class and extends **Sprite** to inherit display object properties like **x** and **y**. Lines 8 through 12 declare the position, velocity, and gravity properties that are private to this class.

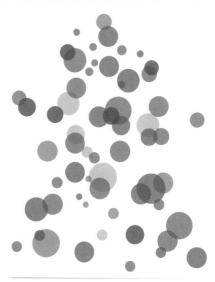

*Figure 7-6. A particle system simulating a primitive water fountain*

```
1    package {
2
3        import flash.display.Sprite;
4        import flash.events.Event;
5
6        public class Particle extends Sprite {
7
8            private var _xPos:Number;
9            private var _yPos:Number;
10           private var _xVel:Number;
11           private var _yVel:Number;
12           private var _grav:Number;
```

Next, the class constructor creates and initializes the particle. Lines 17 through 21 populate the private properties with values passed into the constructor when the particle is instantiated. These parameters all have default values, but our example will vary their values when creating each particle.

Next, the constructor adds visual content to the particle by creating an instance of the **Ball** class from the FLA library and adds it to the display list. This ball movie clip is nothing more than a blue circle with a radius of 20 pixels. Five particle properties are then populated in lines 26 through 29: **x**, **y**, **alpha**, **scaleX**, and **scaleY**, their values coming into the class during instantiation. The last line of the constructor adds an enter frame event listener to the particle.

```
13           public function Particle(xPos:Number=100, yPos:Number=100,
14                                    scale:Number=1, opacity:Number=1,
15                                    xVel:Number=4, yVel:Number=-10,
16                                    grav:Number=1) {
17               _xPos = xPos;
18               _yPos = yPos;
19               _xVel = xVel;
20               _yVel = yVel;
```

```
21            _grav = grav;
22
23            var ball:Sprite = new Ball();
24            addChild(ball);
25
26            x = _xPos;
27            y = _yPos;
28            alpha = opacity;
29            scaleX = scaleY = scale;
30
31            addEventListener(Event.ENTER_FRAME, onRun,
32                                   false, 0, true);
33        }
```

The event listener function, **onRun()**, uses the techniques discussed in the velocity and gravity examples of this chapter—first altering the y velocity with the effect of gravity, and then updating the **x** and **y** properties of the particle every enter frame. It also adds one new thing. A conditional statement determines whether the particle position is off the stage on the left or right (line 41), or top or bottom (line 42). If so, the event listener is removed in line 43, and the particle is removed from the display list in line 44.

```
34        private function onRun(evt:Event):void {
35            _yVel += _grav;
36            _xPos += _xVel;
37            _yPos += _yVel;
38            x = _xPos;
39            y = _yPos;
40
41            if ( _xPos < 0 || _xPos > stage.stageWidth
42                || _yPos < 0 || _yPos > stage.stageHeight) {
43                removeEventListener(Event.ENTER_FRAME, onRun);
44                parent.removeChild(this);
45            }
46        }
47    }
48 }
```

**NOTE**

*Because particle systems can create hundreds or even thousands of particles a second, it's very easy to run out of memory if you don't remove listeners, display objects, and particle storage (such as a variable or array).*

Note, in line 44, that an object can't directly remove itself using syntax like **removeChild(this)**. A display object to be removed must be a *child* of the object calling the **removeChild()** method, and an object can't be a child of itself. One way to remind yourself about this is to precede the method call with the optional **this** reference to clarify which object is calling the method. Ideally, writing **this.removeChild(this)** shows that **this** can't be a child of **this**. Instead, the object instructs its parent to remove itself and, as the object is a child of its parent, the syntax works just fine.

## The system

The following simple document class **ParticleDemo** is responsible for creating the particles. It creates a particle every time an enter frame event is received and adds it to the display list. The variance in the system comes from the values passed into the **Particle** class in the listener method **onLoop()**.

```
1    package {
2
3        import flash.display.MovieClip;
4        import flash.events.Event;
5
6        public class ParticleDemo extends MovieClip {
7
8            public function ParticleDemo() {
9                addEventListener(Event.ENTER_FRAME, onLoop,
10                                    false, 0, true);
11            }
12
13            private function onLoop(evt:Event):void {
14                var p:Particle = new Particle(mouseX,
15                                        mouseY,
16                                        (Math.random()*1.8) + 0.2,
17                                        (Math.random()*0.8) + 0.2,
18                                        (Math.random()*10) - 5,
19                                         Math.random()*-10,
20                                        1);
21                addChild(p);
22            }
23        }
24    }
```

Recalling the signature of the **Particle** class, its parameters are **xPos**, **yPos**, **scale**, **opacity**, **xVel**, **yVel**, and **grav**. The corresponding order of arguments passed into the class when a particle is instantiated (starting in line 14), determine its appearance and behavior. To begin with, the particle is born at the mouse location (**mouseX**, **mouseY**).

The formulas for **scale**, **opacity**, **xVel**, and **yVel** are then randomized within specific ranges. The **random()** method of the **Math** class always generates a random number greater than or equal to 0 and less than 1. Therefore, to pick a random value greater than or equal to 0 and less than a number other than 1, you must multiply the decimal value generated by the desired maximum value. Jumping ahead to the y velocity, for example, the ultimate value will be greater than or equal to 0 and less than −10. If a range that does not start with 0 is desired, an offset must be applied.

For example, the scale value is not just a random number times 2. This may result in a scale of 0 and the particle would disappear. The 0.2 offset guarantees this will not happen. If the random number selected is 0 or very near 0, the minimum size of 0.2 will be used (0 + 0.2). If the random number chosen is near 1, the ultimate outcome is 2 (1.8 + 0.2). The opacity of the particle is determined the same way with the next formula, yielding a value between 0.2 and 1 (20 and 100 percent, respectively).

The x velocity is calculated in a similar manner, but this time the offset value is subtracted from the possible range of random numbers. If the random number is near 0, the resulting value is 0 minus 5, or −5. If the random number is near 1, the outcome will be 10 minus 5, or 5. Therefore, the possible x velocity values are between −5 and 5.

The last argument represents gravity, for which a constant value of 1 is used.

**NOTE**

*A signature describes a constructor or method by including its name; parameters, data types, and possible default values; and return data type. This lets a programmer know how to invoke the constructor or method.*

### The FLA file

The *particle_system.fla* source file uses the **ParticleSystem** class as a document class, so there is no additional code therein. If you prefer not to use the document class approach, however, all you need to do is instantiate the **ParticleSystem** class and add it to the display list.

```
1    var ps:ParticleSystem = new ParticleSystem();
2    addChild(ps);
```

Particle systems are a lot of fun and can lead to many fruitful experiments. Run this system several times, modifying the values sent to the **Particle** class. Increase the range of x and y velocities for a larger spread of particles, or decrease the force of gravity to see what particle life is like on the moon. Let your creativity flow.

## Simple Collision Detection

Once you get your display objects on the move, you can add code that will react when objects collide. For example, games like pool, pinball, and platform scrollers wouldn't be possible without collisions. We'll show you three collision types in this section: collisions between two objects, between an object and a point, and between an object and the boundaries of the stage.

## Collision with Objects

Collisions between two objects are detected using the **hitTestObject()** method. It determines whether the object calling the method collides with another object passed in as an argument in the method call. The following code, found in the *collision_objects.fla* source file, will remove two objects from the display list when they collide. This is handy, for example, when bullets hit spaceships and they must disappear. Lines 1 through 11 give us two balls and an event listener to work with. Every enter frame, line 12 moves the ball to the right, and line 13 checks to see if *ball* collides with *ball2*. If so, the listener is removed in line 14, and both *ball* and *ball2* are removed from the display list in lines 15 and 16.

```
1    var ball:MovieClip = new Ball();
2    ball.x = ball.y = 100;
3    addChild(ball);
4
5    var ball2:MovieClip = new Ball();
6    ball2.x = 100;
7    ball2.y = 400;
8    addChild(ball2);
9
10   addEventListener(Event.ENTER_FRAME, onEnter, false, 0, true);
11   function onEnter(evt:Event):void {
12       ball.x += 5;
13       if (ball.hitTestObject(ball2)) {
14           removeEventListener(Event.ENTER_FRAME, onEnter);
```

```
15          removeChild(ball);
16          removeChild(ball2);
17      }
18  }
```

It's important to note that the **hitTestObject()** method uses the minimum bounding rectangle of both objects to detect collisions. Figure 7-7 shows two circles that appear to not collide. However, the minimum bounding rectangles of the circles overlap and, therefore, a collision is reported.

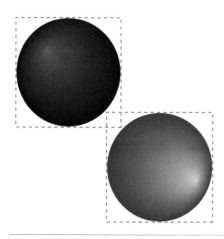

*Figure 7-7. The pictured overlap of circles would cause a collision using* **hitTestObject()** *because the method uses the minimum bounding rectangle of each object*

## Collision with Points

Similarly, collisions between an object and a point are detected using the **hitTestPoint()** method. It determines whether the object calling the method collides with a point specified in the method call. The script in the *collision_points.fla* source file, will move an object to a random location when it comes in contact with the mouse. After creating the ball and listener in lines 1 through 6, line 7 checks to see if *ball* collides with the mouse, and sets the optional *shape flag* to true. When true, the shape flag uses nontransparent pixels to test for collisions with the point, rather than the minimum bounding rectangle of the object. If a collision occurs, the ball is relocated.

```
1   var ball:MovieClip = new Ball();
2   ball.x = ball.y = 100;
3   addChild(ball);
4
5   addEventListener(Event.ENTER_FRAME, onEnter, false, 0, true);
6   function onEnter(evt:Event):void {
7       if (ball.hitTestPoint(mouseX, mouseY, true)) {
8           ball.x = Math.random() * stage.stageWidth;
9           ball.y = Math.random() * stage.stageHeight;
10      }
11  }
```

**NOTE**

*Checking for more accurate collisions of nonrectangular assets requires significantly more advanced programming—typically using precise pixel analysis with the* **BitmapData** *class, which we'll introduce in Chapter 9. Fortunately, Corey O'Neil has done most of the work for you by creating his fantastic Collision Detection Kit. Now, instead of programming all the collision detection yourself, you only have to implement his code in your projects. Documentation and examples can be found at http:// code.google.com/p/collisiondetectionkit/.*

**NOTE**

*Any alpha value above 0 will register a collision using the* **hitTestPoint()** *method. Only when a pixel is **completely** transparent will no collision be detected. To register collisions with nontransparent alpha values, use Corey O'Neil's Collision Detection Kit. See the previous note.*

**NOTE**

*Placing a display object on the stage within a given area ensures only that the registration point of the object is in the area prescribed. If, for example, the object is placed adjacent to a stage edge, part of the object may be out of view. Later in the chapter, we'll show you how to be sure the entire object is always visible, even with random placement.*

Figure 7-8. No collision is detected here because only nontransparent pixels collide with a point (such as the mouse location) when the shape flag of the hitTestPoint() method is true

Figure 7-8 shows the mouse overlapping the bounding rectangle of the circle, but not touching any nontransparent pixels. In this case, because the shape flag is true, no collision would be detected.

## Collision with Stage Boundaries

The following code, found in the *collision_stage_boundaries.fla* source file, moves the movie clip instance, *ball*, to the right 5 pixels every enter frame. For this example, the movie clip added in lines 1 through 3 has a center registration point. *Before* moving the ball, however, the conditional in line 7 checks to make sure the ball hasn't passed the right side of the stage. If not, the ball's position is updated. If it has passed that boundary, the listener is removed and the ball stops moving.

```
1    var ball:MovieClip = new Ball();
2    ball.x = ball.y = 100;
3    addChild(ball);
4
5    addEventListener(Event.ENTER_FRAME, onEnter, false, 0, true);
6    function onEnter(evt:Event):void {
7        if (ball.x + 5 < (stage.stageWidth - ball.width / 2)) {
8            ball.x += 5;
9        } else {
10           removeEventListener(Event.ENTER_FRAME, onEnter);
11       }
12   }
```

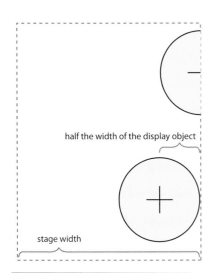

half the width of the display object

stage width

Figure 7-9. When testing for boundary collisions on display objects with a center registration point, the collision value must be inset by half the width of the object from the stage dimensions

Notice that the right stage boundary is detected using the width of the stage, but that's not the only value used in the conditional. Instead, half the width of the ball is subtracted from the boundary value first to prevent the ball from leaving the stage before the test fails. If this adjustment were not made, at least half of the ball would need to leave the stage before its center registration point caused the conditional to fail. Figure 7-9 shows the point at which a boundary collision is detected without accounting for a display object's center registration point (top) and when subtracting half the width of the object from the test value (bottom).

A similar equation is used to detect movement beyond the bottom of the stage, using **stage.stageHeight** in the conditional. To check whether an object is about to leave the left or top of the stage, the test must start with a value of 0, but *add* half the width of the display object to inset the boundary from each edge. Later in this chapter, a more complete example will be used to reverse the direction of a particle's movement before leaving the stage.

**NOTE**

*If you create a display object with a noncenter registration point, your collision detection code will need to change. For example, using a registration point in the upper-left corner of a display object, you will need to subtract the full width of the object to see if it leaves the left or top sides of the stage, and subtract nothing to see if it leaves the right or bottom sides of the stage.*

# Geometry and Trigonometry

Although many people find geometry and trigonometry intimidating, the small investment required to understand a few basic principles in these disciplines can pay large dividends. For example, what if you needed to find the distance between two points, or rotate one object around another? These small tasks are needed more often than you may think, and are easier to accomplish than you may realize.

## Movement Along an Angle

Earlier we discussed velocity as a vector quantity because it combined magnitude and direction. However, the direction in the previous example was determined by changing x and y coordinates. Unfortunately, such a direction is easily identifiable only when moving along simple paths, such as along the x or y axis. A much better way to indicate a direction is to specify an angle to follow.

Before we discuss angles and their different units of measure, you need to understand how angles are indicated in the ActionScript coordinate system. As you might expect, angles are commonly referenced using degrees, but it's important to note that 0 degrees is along the x axis pointing to the right. The 360-degree circle then unfolds clockwise around the coordinate system. This means 90 degrees points down along the y axis, 180 degrees points left along the x axis, and so on, as shown in Figure 7-10.

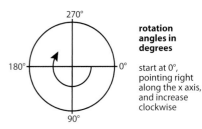

*Figure 7-10. How Flash angles are referenced*

Now that you have a correct point of reference, the next important concept to understand is that most of ActionScript, like most computer languages and mathematicians, does *not* use degrees as its preferred unit of measurement for angles. This is true for just about all common uses of angles, except for the **rotation** property of display objects and one or two more obscure items also related to rotation. Predominately, ActionScript uses *radians* as the unit of measure for angles. A radian is the angle defined by moving along the outside of the circle only for a distance as long as the circle's radius, as seen in Figure 7-4. One radian is 180/pi degrees, which is approximately 57 degrees.

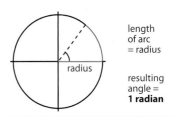

*Figure 7-11. How radians are calculated*

Though some of you may find that interesting or helpful, memorizing this definition isn't vital. Instead, all you need to do is remember a handy conversion formula: radians = degrees * (**Math.PI**/180). Conversely, to convert radians to degrees use: degrees = radians / (**Math.PI**/180). (You may also see a degrees-to-radians conversion that looks like this: degrees = radians * (180/ **Math.PI**)). In the upcoming example, we'll write utility functions for this purpose that you can use throughout the rest of the examples.

Now we're prepared to address the task at hand. We must send a movie clip off in a direction specified by an angle (direction) at a specific speed (magnitude). This will be the resulting velocity. This script, found in the *movement_along_angle.fla* source file, starts by creating a movie clip and positioning it on stage at point (100, 100). It then specifies the speed and angle at which the

movie clip will travel, and converts commonly used degrees to ActionScript-preferred radians using the utility function at the end of the script.

```
1   var ball:MovieClip = new Ball();
2   ball.x = ball.y = 100;
3   addChild(ball);
4
5   var speed:Number = 12;
6   var angle:Number = 45;
7   var radians:Number = deg2rad(angle);
```

With both a direction (angle) and magnitude (speed), we can determine the required velocities relative to the x and y axes. To do so, we use the **sin()** and **cos()** methods of the **Math** class, which calculate the sine and cosine of an angle, respectively. If this dredges up bad memories of high school math class, just relax and picture a right-angle triangle with one point at the origin of the x/y axes (Figure 7-12).

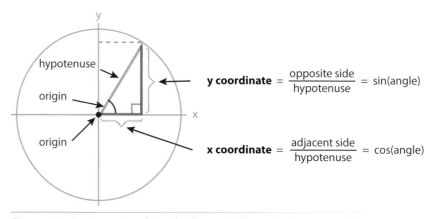

*Figure 7-12. A point on a circle can be determined by using the cosine and sine of an angle and the circle's radius*

The *sine* of an angle is the length of the *opposite* side of the triangle (shown in blue in Figure 7-12) divided by the length of the triangle's hypotenuse (the longest side, opposite the triangle's right angle). The *cosine* of an angle is the length of the *adjacent* side of the triangle (shown in red in Figure 7-12) divided by the length of the triangle's hypotenuse. In terms more applicable to our needs, the x component of the direction we're looking for is the cosine of an angle (in radians), and the direction's y component is the sine of the same angle.

Multiply each value by a speed and you get x and y velocities, as seen in lines 8 and 9 of the following script block, respectively. All that remains is to add those velocities to the x and y coordinates of the ball (in the listener function at lines 13 and 14) and it's on the move.

```
8    var xVel:Number = Math.cos(radians) * speed;
9    var yVel:Number = Math.sin(radians) * speed;
10
```

```
11  addEventListener(Event.ENTER_FRAME, onLoop, false, 0, true);
12  function onLoop(evt:Event):void {
13      ball.x += xVel;
14      ball.y += yVel;
15  }
16
17  function deg2rad(deg:Number):Number {
18      return deg * (Math.PI / 180);
19  }
```

Lines 17 and 18 contain the conversion function called in line 7. It takes an angle in degrees and returns the same angle in radians.

## Distance

Let's say you're programming a game in which a character is pursued by an enemy and must exit through one of two doors to safety. However, the enemy is close enough that the character must choose the *nearest* exit to survive. The player controls the character, but you must make sure the enemy catches the character if the player makes the wrong decision. To do that, the enemy must know which exit is closest.

To determine the distance between the enemy and a door, all you need to do is imagine a right triangle between those points and use a formula called the Pythagorean theorem. The theorem states that the square of the longest side of a right triangle is equal to the sum of the squares of the other two sides. This is illustrated in the top of Figure 7-13.

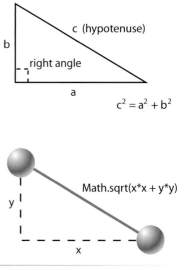

The bottom of Figure 7-13 shows this theorem in use, determining the distance between two movie clips, or, in our metaphorical case, between an enemy and a door. The triangle appears beneath the two points, and the differences between the x and y coordinates of points 1 and 2 are shown in dotted lines. These lengths correspond to the a and b sides of the triangle, so we need to square (x2 − x1) and square (y2 − y1) to satisfy the theorem.

The linear distance between the two points is shown as a solid red line. This linear distance corresponds to the length of the longest side of the triangle, but we don't want the square of this length. So we must take the square root of both sides of the equation. In other words, we need the square root of (x2 − x1) * (x2 − x1) + (y2 − y1) * (y2 − y1).

*Figure 7-13. Calculating the distance between two points using geometry*

Once you determine the distance between the enemy and one door, you repeat the process for the distance between the enemy and the other door. You can then determine which door is closest.

In the source file, *distance.fla*, the **getDistance()** function calculates the distance between two balls and returns that value as a **Number**. Line 3 determines the distance between the x coordinates, and line 4 determines the distance between the y coordinates. Line 5 uses the **sqrt()** method of the **Math** class to calculate the square root of the sum of those squares.

It compares the distance between **ball0** and **ball1** to the distance between **ball0** and **ball2**:

```
1   function getDistance(x1:Number, y1:Number,
2                        x2:Number, y2:Number):Number {
3       var dX:Number = x2 - x1;
4       var dY:Number = y2 - y1;
5       return Math.sqrt(dX * dX + dY * dY);
6   }
7
8   var dist1:Number = getDistance(ball0.x, ball0.y,
9                                  ball1.x, ball1.y);
10  var dist2:Number = getDistance(ball0.x, ball0.y,
11                                 ball2.x, ball2.y);
12
13  if (dist1 < dist2) {
14      trace("ball1 is closest to ball0");
15  } else {
16      trace("ball2 is closest to ball0");
17  }
```

**NOTE**

*In Chapter 8, we'll show you another way to calculate the distance between two points using a simple method of the* **Point** *class.*

## More Particles: Collision and Distance

Now it's time for another project to put your latest knowledge to the test. This second particle system, found in *particles_angle.fla*, will again create particles that move around on their own. This time, however, they'll bounce off the edges of the stage and a line will be drawn between any particles that are within 100 pixels of each other.

This exercise will combine skills you've developed in moving objects along angles, collision detection, and distance calculation. It also uses such language fundamentals as **for** loops, conditionals, array structures, and random numbers, as well as reviews the display list and event listeners.

Finally, it makes use of the **Graphics** class to draw lines at runtime. We'll cover this class in greater depth in the next chapter, but briefly, it allows you to draw vectors, including lines, curves, fills, and shapes, into display objects. In this script, we'll just define line characteristics, connect points, and periodically clear what we've drawn.

Lines 1 through 4 of the following code create variables for use throughout the script. Line 1 creates an array to hold all the particles created. Line 2 creates a single particle so its diameter (line 3) and radius (line 4) can be determined. Lines 6 and 7 create a container sprite and add it to the display list. This will be a container into which we'll draw lines that connect our particles. Line 8 makes this process a bit easier and more efficient by storing a reference to the **graphics** property of the container. This is the virtual canvas into which we'll draw.

Lines 10 through 20 create 20 particles. Line 11 creates a new **Particle** instance, and lines 12 and 13 position the particles randomly on stage. Like the previous discussion about stage boundary collision testing, these lines guarantee that the particle is placed wholly within the stage. They do so by reducing the available area by the diameter of the particle, and insetting the left- and topmost positions by the radius.

```
1    var particles:Array = new Array();
2    var particle:Particle = new Particle();
3    var pD:Number = particle.width;
4    var pR:Number = particle.width / 2;
5
6    var container:Sprite = new Sprite();
7    addChild(container);
8    var g:Graphics = container.graphics;
9
10   for (var i:int = 0; i < 20; i++) {
11       particle = new Particle();
12       particle.x = Math.random() * (stage.stageWidth - pD) + pR;
13       particle.y = Math.random() * (stage.stageHeight - pD) + pR;
14       particle.speed = Math.random() * 5 + 1;
15       particle.angle = Math.random() * 360;
16       updateParticleVelocities(particle);
17
18       container.addChild(particle);
19       particles[i] = particle;
20   }
```

Line 14 creates a random speed, between 1 and 6, for each particle, and line 15 creates a random angle for movement, in degrees. This angle will be converted later into radians. Note that these are properties specific to each particle, not variables available to a function or the entire script. This is a useful practice because the values are created randomly when the particle is instantiated, and they are easily stored this way within each particle.

Line 16 calls the **updateParticleVelocities()** function found in lines 57 through 61. In line 58, the function converts the particle's angle into radians using the conversion function at the end of the script. It then uses the formulas from the "Movement Along an Angle" section in lines 59 and 60 to update the x and y velocities for each particle. The particle is passed into the function as an argument, so these velocities can be stored in the particle object, as described in the previous paragraph. The velocities are calculated using the cosine and sine, respectively, of the angle, multiplied by the particle's speed. Finally, the particle is added to the container (line 18), and to the array we'll use to keep track of all the particles (line 19).

The remainder of the script is an event listener that's executed every time an enter frame event is received. The listener function begins with line 23 by clearing the graphics property of any previously dynamically drawn lines. Next a loop executes once for every particle upon every enter frame. The loop first stores a reference to the next instance in the particles array (line 26). Lines 28 through 37 then determine if the *next* location of the particle is beyond the bounds of the stage; they check the current location plus the current velocity to see if the resulting point is outside the area available for placement.

The conditional uses the same technique explained in the "Collision with Stage Boundaries" section of this chapter. It first takes the appropriate stage edge (top or bottom in lines 28 and 29, or left and right in lines 33 and 34), and then insets the radius of the particle from each edge to determine the allowable values for particle movement. If a particle collides with a horizontal plane (top or bottom stage edge), the angle of movement is turned into a negative of itself (multiplied by −1) (line 30). Table 7-1 shows a range of incoming angles (angles of incidence) and after-bounce angles (angles of reflection), off both bottom and top edges, using this formula.

*Table 7-1. Angles before and after bounce off horizontal planes*

| Angle of incidence | Angle of reflection |
| --- | --- |
| 45 | −45 |
| 90 | −90 |
| 135 | −135 |
| 225 | −225 |
| 270 | −270 |
| 315 | −315 |

If a particle collides with a vertical plane (left or right stage edge), the angle of movement is turned into a negative of itself and 180 is added to that value (line 35). Table 7-2 shows a range of incidence and reflection angles, off both right and left edges, using this formula. Remember that you don't have to think in terms of radians because the conversion function takes care of that for you.

*Table 7-2. Angles before and after bounce off vertical planes*

| Angle of incidence | Angle of reflection |
| --- | --- |
| 45 | 135 |
| 135 | 45 |
| 180 | 0 |
| 225 | −45 |
| 315 | −135 |
| 360 | 180 |

The last step in handling the movement of each particle is to again call the **updateParticleVelocities()** method (lines 31 and 36), to update the particle's x and y velocities after the collision, and, in turn, its **x** and **y** properties

```
21  addEventListener(Event.ENTER_FRAME, onEnter, false, 0, true);
22  function onEnter(evt:Event):void {
23      g.clear();
24
25      for (var i:int = 0; i < particles.length; i++) {
26          var particle:Particle = particles[i];
27
```

```
28      if (particle.y + particle.velY < 0 + pR ||
29          particle.y + particle.velY > stage.stageHeight - pR) {
30          particle.angle = -particle.angle;
31          updateParticleVelocities(particle);
32      }
33      if (particle.x + particle.velX < 0 + pR ||
34          particle.x + particle.velX > stage.stageWidth - pR) {
35          particle.angle = -particle.angle + 180;
36          updateParticleVelocities(particle);
37      }
38
39      particle.x += particle.velX;
40      particle.y += particle.velY;
41
42      for (var j:int = i + 1; j < particles.length; j++) {
43          var nextParticle:Particle = particles[j];
44
45          var dX:Number = particle.x - nextParticle.x;
46          var dY:Number = particle.y - nextParticle.y;
47          var distance:Number = Math.sqrt(dX * dX + dY * dY);
48          if (distance < 100) {
49              g.lineStyle(0, 0x999999);
50              g.moveTo(particle.x, particle.y);
51              g.lineTo(nextParticle.x, nextParticle.y);
52          }
53      }
54  }
55 }
56
57 function updateParticleVelocities(p:Particle):void {
58     var radians:Number = deg2rad(p.angle);
59     p.velX = Math.cos(p.angle) * p.speed;
60     p.velY = Math.sin(p.angle) * p.speed;
61 }
62
63 function deg2rad(degree):Number {
64     return degree * (Math.PI / 180);
65 }
```

Finally, the loop in lines 42 through 53 checks the distance between every particle. Upon entering this nested loop, the current particle (*particle*, assigned in the outer loop in line 26) is compared with every other particle (*nextParticle*, assigned in the inner loop in line 43). By nesting the loop this way, each particle compares itself with the other remaining particles every time an enter frame event is received. This way, we can determine whether the distance between any two particles is less than 100 so we can draw a line between them. Note, too, that the counter variable of the inner loop is *j*, not *i*. This is necessary because if *i* were used again, it would conflict with the outer loop, get reassigned, and wreak havoc.

This nested loop structure is also more efficient than it could be, because the inner loop doesn't start with 0 every time. Instead, it starts at the next particle in line (*i* + 1), after the current particle (*i*). This is possible because the relationships between the previous particles have already been examined. Put another way, when the outer loop reaches 19, the inner loop need only compare particle 19 (*i*) with particle 20 (*i* + 1).

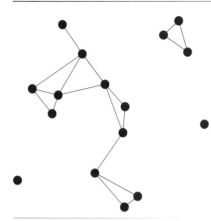

*Figure 7-14. During movement, particles in close proximity to each other will be connected.*

When making the comparisons, the loop checks the distance between every two particles. If less than 100 (line 48), it readies a gray hairline stroke (line 49), moves to the location of the first point (line 50) and draws a line to the location of the second point (line 51) being compared. We'll discuss drawing vectors with code in the next chapter, but the effect is that only those particles within close proximity of each other will be connected. As the positions of the particles change, so do their connections. Figure 7-14 shows the file in action.

## Circular Movement

Now that you know how to determine x and y coordinates from an angle, circular movement is a snap. It will now be relatively trivial for you to move an object in a circle, the way a moon revolves around a planet. With circular movement, we are not interested in the velocity derived from direction and magnitude, because the display object will not be traveling along that vector. Instead, we want to calculate the x and y coordinates of many consecutive angles. By plotting the sine and cosine of many angles, you can move the ball in a circle.

If you think of the sine and cosine values of various angles, this technique is easy to understand. (For simplicity, all angles will be discussed in degrees, but assume the calculations are performed with radians.) The values of both cosine and sine are always between −1 and 1. The x component, or cosine, of angle 0 is 1, and the y component, or sine, of angle 0 is 0. That describes an x, y point (1, 0), or straight out to the right. The cosine of 90 degrees is 0 and the sine of 90 is 1. That describes (0, 1), or straight down.

This continues around the axes in a recognizable pattern. Remembering that we're discussing degrees but calculating in radians, the cosine and sine of 180 degrees are −1 and 0, respectively (point (−1, 0), straight to the left), and the cosine and sine of 270 degrees are 0 and 1, respectively (point (0, 1), straight up).

You must do only two more things to plot your movie clip along a circular path. Because all the values you're getting from your math functions are between −1 and 1, you must multiply these values by the desired radius of your circle. A calculated value of 1 times a radius of 100 equals 100, and multiplying −1 times 100 gives you −100. This describes a circle around the origin point of the axes, which spans from −100 to 100 in both horizontal and vertical directions.

Figure 7-15 illustrates these concepts in one graphic. Each color represents a different angle shown in the legend in both degrees and radians. The x and y values of the radians are expressed in the legend in standard cosine and sine units (between −1 and 1). The resulting x and y coordinates determined by multiplying these values by 100 are shown in the graph.

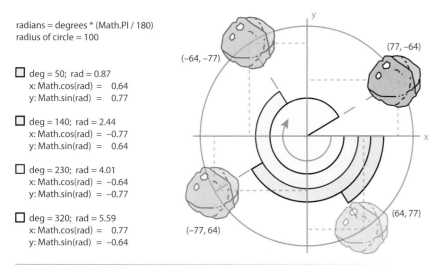

radians = degrees * (Math.PI / 180)
radius of circle = 100

☐ deg = 50;  rad = 0.87
   x: Math.cos(rad) =   0.64
   y: Math.sin(rad) =   0.77

☐ deg = 140;  rad = 2.44
   x: Math.cos(rad) =  −0.77
   y: Math.sin(rad) =   0.64

☐ deg = 230;  rad = 4.01
   x: Math.cos(rad) =  −0.64
   y: Math.sin(rad) =  −0.77

☐ deg = 320;  rad = 5.59
   x: Math.cos(rad) =   0.77
   y: Math.sin(rad) =  −0.64

*Figure 7-15. Four angles around a circle, expressed in degrees, radians, and as x and y points on a circle with a radius of 100 pixels*

Finally, you can position your invisible circle wherever you want it on the stage. If you take no action, the object will rotate around the upper-left corner of the stage, or x, y coordinates (0, 0). The following script centers the circle on the stage.

The following example is found in the *circular_movement.fla* source file. The first nine lines of the script initialize the important variables. Specified are a starting angle of 0, a circle radius of 100, an angle increment of 10, and a circle center that matches the center of the stage (its width and height divided by 2, respectively). Also created is the satellite that will be orbiting the center of the stage, derived from the **Asteroid** linkage class assigned to a library symbol (line 7). It's initially placed offstage in line 8 before becoming a part of the display list in line 9.

```
1    var angle:Number = 0;
2    var radius:Number = 100;
3    var angleChange:Number = 10;
4    var centerX:Number = stage.stageWidth / 2;
5    var centerY:Number = stage.stageHeight / 2;
6
7    var satellite:MovieClip = new Asteroid();
8    satellite.x = satellite.y = -200;
9    addChild(satellite);
```

The last part of the script is the enter frame event listener and degree-to-radian conversion utility discussed earlier. The listener function sets the **x** and **y** properties of the asteroid by starting with the center of the circle, and multiplying its radius by the x and y values calculated by the **Math.cos()** and **Math.sin()** methods (lines 13 and 14). After each plot, the angle is incremented in line 15.

**NOTE**

*As discussed in Chapter 3, ActionScript will automatically adjust incoming rotation angles to create values most efficient for Flash Player to handle. Therefore, it doesn't matter if* **angle** *continues to increment and exceed 360. For example, if you set a display object's rotation property to 370 degrees, Flash Player will understand that this is equivalent to 10 degrees.*

```
10    addEventListener(Event.ENTER_FRAME, onLoop, false, 0, true);
11    function onLoop(evt:Event):void {
12        var radian:Number = deg2rad(angle);
13        satellite.x = centerX + radius * Math.cos(radian);
14        satellite.y = centerY + radius * Math.sin(radian);
15        angle += angleChange;
16    }
17
18    function deg2rad(deg:Number):Number {
19        return deg * (Math.PI / 180);
20    }
```

**NOTE**

*The companion website discusses additional ways to convert rotation angles to usable values. See the "Working with Rotation Angles" post at http://www. LearningActionScript3.com.*

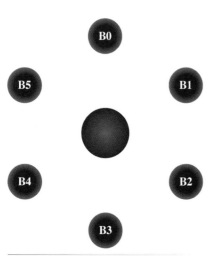

*Figure 7-16. A navigation system created by positioning buttons in a circle*

# A Circular Navigation System

Although this chapter is called *Motion*, you can do more with the skills you're accumulating than move objects around the stage. You can use the same math that animates an object along a circular path to position static elements along a circle. The following script, found in the *circle_navigation.fla* source file, automatically positions six buttons around a center draggable object, as shown in Figure 7-16. The buttons, complete with labels, are children of the center object. So, when the center object is dragged around, all the buttons follow making a movable navigation system. Such a system could be very useful for projects with large visual assets, or many user interface elements, because the navigation widget could be moved around as needed to expose underlying content.

Line 1 sets the number of satellite buttons positioned around the center object. Line 2 sets the radius of the hidden outer circle, effectively setting the distance each button rests from the center object. Line 3 sets the starting angle of the first button. Remember that ActionScript angles begin at 0 to the right (or 3:00 on a clock face) and increase clockwise. Therefore, the first button appears straight up, or 12:00 on a clock face. Line 4 sets the amount the angle will be incremented with each new button. The number of buttons needed determines this. Our example uses six buttons, so they are positioned 60 degrees apart (360/6).

Lines 6 through 9 create the center button from the FLA library using the **MainButton** linkage class, center the button in the middle of the stage, and add it to the display list.

```
1    var numButtons:int = 6;
2    var radius:Number = 100;
3    var angle:Number = 270;
4    var angleChange:Number = 360/numButtons;
5
6    var mainButton:MainButton = new MainButton();
7    mainButton.x = stage.stageWidth / 2;
8    mainButton.y = stage.stageHeight / 2;
9    addChild(mainButton);
```

The heart of this script is the **positionButtons()** function (lines 10 through 33). When called from line 34, it runs through a loop once for every button requested—6 times, in this example. For each button, the loop begins by storing the current angle in a variable (line 12) and incrementing the angle to the next button position (line 13). The value of the angle is converted from degrees to radians using **deg2rad()**, the utility function we've discussed before, at the end of the script.

The button is then created using the library symbol with the **SatelliteButton** linkage class, centered, and positioned on the circle defined by the *mainButton* center point and radius. The same technique to move an object along a circular path is used here. The cosine of the current angle times the radius of the circle determines the x coordinate, and the sine of the angle multiplied by the circle's radius calculates the y coordinate (lines 16 and 17).

Each button is then given a name in line 18, consisting of an uppercase "B," and the number of the button, taken from the loop counter. The first button, for example, will be B0, the second B1, and so on. the last line of this code block adds a mouse click listener to each button that calls the **onClick()** function found in lines 36 through 38. In this simple example, this function just traces the button name. However, as discussed in Chapter 6, you can change this instruction to update the playhead in a movie clip, and we'll teach you how to load external assets in Chapter 13.

**NOTE**

*Although not strictly necessary in this example, it's good practice to convert the* **int** *data type of the loop counter to a* **String** *data type before adding it to the button name.*

Because the buttons in this example have text labels, Line 21 is very important. Setting the **mouseChildren** property of an object to false prevents the content of that object from receiving mouse events. By default, the mouse will automatically interact with the text fields in this example that display the labels inside the buttons. This interaction includes text selection, cursor feedback, and more. With **mouseChildren** set to false for each button, the text field child of the button won't react to mouse events.

Line 22 is also important to this example because the navigation widget is draggable. By adding each button as a child of *mainButton*, rather than the main timeline, dragging the center button will also drag all its satellite button children.

The remainder of the function is consistent with our prior basic uses of text fields in the *Hello World!* applications presented in earlier chapters. Line 24 creates the text field, line 25 sets the field's width to the width of the button, and lines 26 and 27 center the button horizontally and vertically, respectively. Line 28 automatically scales the text field down to fit its text and is also a simple way to center the text prior to learning more advanced formatting options in Chapter 10. Line 29 is another formatting shortcut, making all text in the field white. Finally, the button name is added to the text field in line 30 and the field is added as a child of the button to serve as its label.

```
10   function positionButtons() {
11       for (var i:int = 0; i < numButtons; i++) {
12           var radian:Number = deg2rad(angle);
13           angle += angleChange;
14
15           var btn:SatelliteButton = new SatelliteButton();
16           btn.x = Math.cos(radian) * radius;
```

```
17          btn.y = Math.sin(radian) * radius;
18          btn.name = "B" + String(i);
19          btn.addEventListener(MouseEvent.CLICK, onClick,
20                               false, 0, true);
21          btn.mouseChildren = false;
22          mainButton.addChild(btn);
23
24          var tf:TextField = new TextField();
25          tf.width = btn.width;
26          tf.x = -btn.width / 2;
27          tf.y = -btn.height / 4;
28          tf.autoSize = TextFieldAutoSize.CENTER;
29          tf.textColor = 0xFFFFFF;
30          tf.text = btn.name;
31          btn.addChild(tf);
32      }
33  }
34  positionButtons();
35
36  function onClick(evt:MouseEvent) {
37      trace(evt.target.name);
38  }
```

Lines 39 through 51 are responsible for creating the drag behavior of *main-Button*. Lines 39 and 40 create a mouse down listener that triggers **onStart-Drag()**, and lines 41 through 44 assign mouse up listeners to both *mainButton* and the stage. The latter is important because it's possible while dragging for a mouse up event to not register on the button. Without allowing the stage to catch that event, the draggable object would be stuck to your mouse.

The **onStartDrag()** function (lines 46 through 48) is a great example of how using **currentTarget** in an event listener function can be very helpful. As discussed in Chapter 3, the **target** property will tell you which button received the mouse down event, but it will also make that single button draggable. The **currentTarget** property, on the other hand, refers to the object to which the listener is attached. That means that no matter which button you mouse down upon, *mainButton* will move, dragging all its child buttons along.

Finally, the **onStopDrag()** function (lines 49 through 51) stops all dragging.

```
39  mainButton.addEventListener(MouseEvent.MOUSE_DOWN, onStartDrag,
40                               false, 0, true);
41  mainButton.addEventListener(MouseEvent.MOUSE_UP, onStopDrag,
42                               false, 0, true);
43  stage.addEventListener(MouseEvent.MOUSE_UP, onStopDrag,
44                               false, 0, true);
45
46  function onStartDrag(evt:MouseEvent):void {
47      evt.currentTarget.startDrag();
48  }
49  function onStopDrag(evt:MouseEvent):void {
50      stopDrag();
51  }
52
53  function deg2rad(degree):void {
54      return degree * (Math.PI / 180);
55  }
```

This example shows how a little math can spice up even a simple navigation system, but without being too difficult to master. Best of all, this script automatically positions your satellite buttons for you, even if the number of buttons changes. If you'd rather have nine buttons instead of six, so be it! Just change the value in line 1 and the script will evenly space the buttons around the circumference of the circle.

## Rotation Toward an Object

Determining points on a circle when you start with an angle requires sine and cosine, as seen in the previous example. However, the opposite of that task requires a different trigonometric method. Determining an angle when starting with point data requires **atan2()**. The **atan2()** method is a variation on the arctangent method and is especially useful when you want to use rotation to point something at another location. For instance, the next code example uses a frame event to continuously point a movie clip at the mouse location, no matter where the mouse is on the stage, as simulated in Figure 7-17.

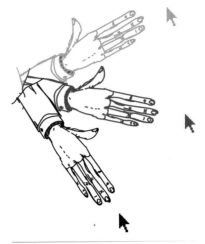

*Figure 7-17. Using* atan2()*, you can continuously point a movie clip at the mouse no matter where it's on the stage*

The formula used to calculate the angle for the rotating object is:

```
Math.atan2(y2 - y1, x2 - x1)
```

There are two important issues to be aware of when using **atan2()**. As you can see, the method always takes **y** point data as its first parameter (instead of **x**, which is more commonly placed in the first position). Second, the method returns its angle in radians, not degrees.

With that in mind, let's take a look at the following script, found in the *point_at_mouse.fla* source file. It begins by creating a new instance of the **Hand** linkage class from the library, placing the hand and forearm shown in Figure 7-17 in the center of the stage, and adding it to the display list. The listener that follows in lines 6 through 11 calculates the angle of rotation in radians, and then converts it to degrees, the unit required by the movie clip's **rotation** property. The conversion takes place in the utility function **rad2deg()** at the end of the script.

The **atan2()** method in line 8 subtracts the mouse location from the hand location (in y and x components) to get the angle the hand must use to point at the mouse. Think of the location at which you want to point as the origin of the system. In other words, point back to home base. That will help you remember that the rotating object is point 2, and the mouse (in this case) is point 1.

```
1   var hand:MovieClip = new Hand();
2   hand.x = stage.stageWidth / 2;
3   hand.y = stage.stageHeight / 2;
4   addChild(hand);
5
```

```
6    addEventListener(Event.ENTER_FRAME, onLoop, false, 0, true);
7    function onLoop(evt:Event):void {
8        var rotationRadians:Number = Math.atan2(hand.y - mouseY,
9                                                hand.x - mouseX);
10       hand.rotation = rad2deg(rotationRadians);
11   }
12
13   function rad2deg(rad:Number):Number {
14       return rad / (Math.PI / 180);
15   }
```

This example points one movie clip at the mouse, but the effect can be adapted in many ways. One obvious variant is to point a movie clip at another movie clip. Another visually interesting adjustment is to point many instances of a movie clip at the same object. A grid of such pointers, for example, looks interesting because each pointer rotates independently based on its location. This can be seen in Figure 7-18, and will be demonstrated in the next script. Finally, the ultimate effect need not be visual. You can use this technique simply to track things, such as planning the trajectory of a projectile toward a target.

## Creating a grid using modulus

The following script, found in the *grid_point_mouse.fla* source file, points several independent objects at the mouse, but it also lays out the objects in a grid. Using `atan2()` to point at the mouse has already been discussed in the prior example, so let's focus on how to create the grid.

Line 1 stores the y position of the first row in the grid, and the variable in line 2 will hold instances of the FLA library linkage class, **Arrow**. Line 3 starts a loop that increments 70 times to build a grid with as many arrows. Each arrow is created in line 4 and added to the display list in line 10. But the grid layout occurs in lines 5 through 9 through the magic of the *modulo* operator (%).

The *modulo* operator, often refer to as "mod," returns the remainder of a division—any partial value left over when a number can't be divided into equal parts. For example, 4 divided by 2 is 2, with no remainder. However, 5 divided by 2 leaves a remainder of 1. Modulo can be used to test when a specific number of iterations has occurred, without the need for another variable.

*Figure 7-18. Detail of grid_point_mouse. fla. Using* atan2()*, you can continuously point a movie clip at the mouse no matter where it is on the stage*

It's tidy to arrange 70 items in a grid that contains 10 columns and 7 rows. To do this, we can loop over a process 70 times, but we need to know when the end of a row is reached if we are to advance down to the next row. We can't rely solely on the loop counter because it increments from 0 to 70. However, dividing the loop counter by 10, there will be no remainder at counter values 0, 10, 20, and so on. Therefore, using the modulo operator, we can tell when the remainder is 0 and when we've reached the end of a row. The header of Table 7-3 shows the remainders of all numbers 0 through 69. For example, the numbers in the first column all have a remainder of 0, the numbers in the second column all have a remainder of 1, and so on.

*Table 7-3. 70 values (i) listed by their remainder when dividing by 10 (i % 10)*

| 0 | 1 | 2 | 3 | 4 | 5 | 6 | 7 | 8 | 9 |
|---|---|---|---|---|---|---|---|---|---|
| 0 | 1 | 2 | 3 | 4 | 5 | 6 | 7 | 8 | 9 |
| 10 | 11 | 12 | 13 | 14 | 15 | 16 | 17 | 18 | 19 |
| 20 | 21 | 22 | 23 | 24 | 25 | 26 | 27 | 28 | 29 |
| 30 | 31 | 32 | 33 | 34 | 35 | 36 | 37 | 38 | 39 |
| 40 | 41 | 42 | 43 | 44 | 45 | 46 | 47 | 48 | 49 |
| 50 | 51 | 52 | 53 | 54 | 55 | 56 | 57 | 58 | 59 |
| 60 | 61 | 62 | 63 | 64 | 65 | 66 | 67 | 68 | 69 |

Line 6 sets the x coordinate of the arrow based on the grid column number, derived using modulo ($i$ % 10). All columns start with an initial offset of 50, and an additional offset of 50 pixels per column is added. The first arrow will be positioned at 50 (based on 50 + (0 * 50)), the second will be positioned at 100 (based on 50 + (1 * 50)), and so on. If $i$ % 10 is 0 (line 6) a new row is required and 50 is added to **rowY**.

```
1    var rowY:Number = 0;
2    var myArrow:Arrow;
3    for (var i:int = 0; i < 70; i++) {
4        myArrow = new Arrow();
5        myArrow.x = 50 + ((i % 10) * 50);
6        if (i % 10 == 0) {
7            rowY += 50;
8        }
9        myArrow.y = rowY;
10       addChild(myArrow);
11       myArrow.addEventListener(Event.ENTER_FRAME, onLoop,
12                               false, 0, true);
13   }
14
15   function onLoop(evt:Event):void {
16       var thisArrow:Arrow = Arrow(evt.target);
17       var rotationRadians:Number = Math.atan2(thisArrow.y - mouseY,
18                                   thisArrow.x - mouseX);
19       thisArrow.rotation = rad2deg(rotationRadians);
20   }
21
22   function rad2deg(rad:Number):Number {
23       return rad / (Math.PI / 180)
24   }
```

# Programmatic Tweening

Scripting your own animations from scratch gives you a lot of control and freedom, but it can be time-consuming, too. You may also discover that you're frequently rewriting similar equations in project after project. If you find yourself spending too much time in this manner, you may want to look into ActionScript tweening classes. A *tween* is an animation sequence in which the computer interpolates all relevant settings between starting and ending property values. For example, just like you would create a motion tween in Flash Professional's timeline, you might write a programmatic tween that moves a movie clip from an x position of 100 to an x position of 400.

## Adobe's Tween Class

Until you are comfortable using third-party ActionScript packages, you may want to get up to speed with tweening using Adobe's **Tween** class. Built into the ActionScript language, the **Tween** class is fairly limited but also easy to understand. Here is a look at the class's signature, and the seven parameters into which you send data when instantiating a tween object:

```
Tween(obj:Object, prop:String, func:Function, begin:Number,
      finish:Number, duration:Number, useSeconds:Boolean):Tween
```

The class takes the following arguments (in this order):

- **obj**: The object to animate
- **prop**: A relevant property to manipulate
- **func**: A preexisting easing function to add expressiveness to the animation
- **begin**: The beginning value of the property
- **finish**: The finishing value of the property
- **duration**: The duration of the tween
- **useSeconds**: Whether to use seconds or frames as the desired time unit

It also returns a **Tween** object, so you can store a reference to the tween for additional manipulation. For example, you can stop or start the tween at a later point.

The following script, found in the *tween_class.fla* source file, provides a simple example of how to use the **Tween** class. It moves a movie clip from one side of the stage to the other, bouncing the clip into its final destination. Lines 1 through 4 tell the compiler where to find the required classes. Lines 6 through 8 create a movie clip from the FLA library using the **Ball** linkage class, place it at point (100, 100), and then add it to the display list.

```
1   import fl.transitions.Tween;
2   import fl.transitions.easing.Bounce;
3   import fl.transitions.easing.None;
4   import fl.transitions.TweenEvent;
5
6   var ball:MovieClip = new Ball();
7   ball.x = ball.y = 100;
8   addChild(ball);
9
10  var ballXTween:Tween = new Tween(ball, "x", Bounce.easeOut,
11                                   100, 400, 3, true);
12
```

```
13   ballXTween.addEventListener(TweenEvent.MOTION_FINISH,
14                               onMotionFinish);
15   function onMotionFinish(evt:TweenEvent):void {
16       var ballAlphaTween:Tween = new Tween(ball, "alpha",
17                                   None.easeOut,
18                                   1, 0.3, 1, true);
19   }
```

Lines 10 and 11 create a Tween instance to animate ball's **x** property. Pay particular attention to the fact that the property is specified in string format. That can take a little getting used to.

The tween will use the **Bounce** easing function to add expressiveness to the animation while moving the movie clip horizontally from 100 to 400 pixels. As a result, the ball will appear to bounce against its final position. Finally, the tween will conclude in 3 seconds—indicated by the time unit 3, and the **true** value of the last parameter, **useSeconds**, ensuring the tween is timed with seconds, not frames.

Lines 13 and 14 add an event listener to the **ballXTween** object, to trigger the listener function when the animation is finished and the **TweenEvent. MOTION_FINISH** event is fired. At that point, a new tween is created, to fade the alpha property of the same object from 1 to 0.3. The second tween will take 1 second, and uses no easing to complete the task.

Only the last parameter of the **Tween** class is optional. (When omitted, **useSeconds** will be false and will use frames to time the tween, rather than seconds.) Therefore, if you don't want to use easing, you must specify the **None** easing class, and either the **easeIn** or **easeOut** property. Which you choose will not matter, as no easing will be applied. The names and descriptions of other available easing classes can be found in Table 7-4. All easing classes allow easing in, easing out, and easing both in and out of the tween.

*Table 7-4. Easing types found in the fl.transitions.easing package*

| Easing Class | Description |
| --- | --- |
| Back | Easing in begins by backing up and then moving toward the target. Easing out overshoots the target and backtracks to approach it. |
| Bounce | Bounces in with increasing speed, or out with decreasing speed. |
| Elastic | Undulates in an exponentially decaying sine wave, accelerating in and decelerating out. |
| None | Linear motion without easing. |
| Regular | Normal easing, like that found in the timeline's simple easing feature, accelerating in and decelerating out. |
| Strong | Emphasized easing, stronger than that found in the timeline's simple easing feature, but without additional effects. Accelerates in and decelerates out. |

# GreenSock's TweenLite

After gaining a little experience with third-party packages, you'll very likely want to stop using the built-in **Tween** class and find a tweening package that you like. Invariably, these heavily optimized products are smaller, faster, and more robust, offering quite a bit that is worthy of your experimentation.

Our favorite is the Tweening Platform by GreenSock. The platform contains several great products, but the one we want to focus on is TweenLite. The tweening library comes in two variations: TweenLite, which is the smallest possible size and is optimized by making a wide array of features optional, and TweenMax, which is basically TweenLite with all of its features pre-enabled, as well as a handful of additional advanced features.

We'll introduce TweenLite by recreating the tween example from the "Adobe's Tween Class" section for comparison, and then building an example banner as an additional project. The main tools of TweenLite are a pair of nice, simple methods: **to()** and **from()**. As their names imply, they allow you to tween an object's properties from their current values *to* final values, or *from* initial values to their current values, respectively.

Our first TweenLite example will demonstrate the **to()** method, which has the following signature:

```
to(target:Object, duration:Number, vars:Object):TweenLite
```

It begins with the object to tween, then includes the duration of the tween, and finishes up with an object that contains all other variables you may want to use to manipulate your tween. We'll show you a few options for the variables object in a moment, but a relevant example is the **useFrames** property. The duration of the tween is measured in seconds by default, but you can set **useFrames** to true if you prefer, and the tween duration will be based on the file's frame rate. The method also returns a **TweenLite** instance if you want to store a reference to the tween for later use.

All TweenLite examples are found in the *tweenLite* directory in the source archive, and the following script is in the *tweenLite.fla* source file. The first six lines are very similar to the **Tween** class example from the prior section—importing required classes and creating a movie clip to manipulate. Because this is an external library, you must have the Greensock Tweening Platform package in a known class path for the imports to work. For this example, you can place the package's *com* folder in the same directory as your FLA file.

**NOTE**

*With the developer's kind permission, we've included the Tweening Platform with the sample source code from the companion website. As with any software product, however, you would be wise to check periodically with the Greensock website (http://www.greensock.com) to see if any changes to the packages have been made, and update your files accordingly.*

```
1    import com.greensock.TweenLite;
2    import com.greensock.easing.Bounce;
3
4    var ball:MovieClip = new Ball();
5    ball.x = ball.y = 100;
6    addChild(ball);
7
8    TweenLite.to(ball, 3, {x:400, ease:Bounce.easeOut,
9                          onComplete:fadeBall});
```

```
10   function fadeBall():void {
11       TweenLite.to(ball, 1, {alpha:0.3});
12   }
```

In lines 8 and 9, TweenLite **to()** method is used to tween ball for 3 seconds, from whatever the current location is (100, as set in line 5) to 400. It uses the **Bounce** easing class and calls the **fadeBall()** function when the animation is complete.

The way TweenLite handles methods is quite different from the **Tween** class. Instead of having to create all your own listeners, TweenLite uses callbacks. An ActionScript *callback* is similar to the everyday use of the term. It's a mechanism where you can essentially leave a message for an object and ask it to call you back at the function specified when an event occurs. In this case, you're asking TweenLite to call the **fadeBall()** function when the tween is complete. When the function is called, another tween is created, this time fading the ball movie clip to 30 percent.

TweenLite also makes it very easy to build a sequence of tweens by using the **delay** property. In the prior example, the first tween spanned 3 seconds and, upon finishing, called another tween. Rather than relying on events, you can simply create both tweens but delay the second one to occur when the first finishes. This will produce the same effect as the previous example, but illustrates the ability to start your tweens whenever it suits you. To see this in action, simply use the following code to replace lines 8 through 12 of the prior example. This modification can be found in the *tweenLite_to_delay.fla* source file.

```
8    TweenLite.to(ball, 3, {x:400, ease:Bounce.easeOut});
9    TweenLite.to(ball, 1, {alpha:0.3, delay:3, overwrite:false});
```

Note that when taking this approach, you're essentially asking the tween to reassign itself. Just like for a variable, you may want a new behavior, or you may not. If you don't want a tween to cancel out a prior tween referencing the same object, you must use a property called **overwrite** to control how the tweens interrelate. Setting the property to false will treat the tweens independently. The result is a sequence of tweens but without relying on events. The next example uses this technique.

## Creating a simple banner using TweenLite

With a little experience under your belt, let's make a banner. We'll explore two key TweenLite concepts in this exercise: the **from()** method, and the ability to add advanced features through a plug-in mechanism.

The nice thing about using the **from()** method is that you can precreate a layout and TweenLite will automatically build it up using your specified *from* settings. For example, Figure 7-19 shows what the FLA file looks like when you write your script. This is actually the *final* state of the banner, so you can adjust your layout until you're satisfied. Once you're happy with the

**NOTE**

*The object syntax for the third parameter of TweenLite's* **to()** *method makes it very easy to tween many properties at once. For example, you could write a tween like this:*

```
TweenLite.to(ball, 3, {x:10,
    y:10, alpha:1, rotation:90,
    ease:Bounce.easeOut});
```

*This tween would alter the* **x**, **y**, **alpha**, *and* **rotation** *properties all in a single structure, making it much easier to use than Adobe's* **Tween** *class. You can kill all properties, or even select properties, any time so you can change the behavior of the tween after creating it.*

*Figure 7-19. A mock banner advertisement animated with TweenLite*

banner, it's time to itemize the properties you want to work with and their initial values. The following script is found in the *tweenLite_from_banner.fla* source file.

The first property we'll use is called **tint**, and it's not part of the TweenLite default configuration. It is part of TweenLite's bigger brother package, TweenMax, but TweenLite is optimized to be as small as possible and doesn't include any non-essential features. However, you don't need to move up to TweenMax if you only want to use a few features and keep everything really small. TweenLite has a plug-in system that allows you to activate specific plug-ins on an as-needed basis. You have to do this only once and the plug-in features will be available to the rest of your file thereafter.

Lines 1 through 4 import the needed classes, including the **TweenPlugin** class that manages plug-ins, and the specific plug-in we need, **TintPlugin**. Line 6 activates the **TintPlugin**. It will then be available throughout the life of the project. Lines 9 through 17 are the **from()** tweens, each of which lasts for 1 second.

Line 8 fades the background up from black. Lines 9 through 16 scale up the four balls from 0 to final size. They use an **Elastic** ease so the tweens spring forward and back a few times around their final scale values. However, each tween is delayed a bit to build a sequence. The first ball starts a half-second after the tint fade begins, the second tween starts one and one-half seconds later, and so on. The last ball springs into place three seconds after the process begins. This timing is amassed from a two-second delay and a one-second duration. At the same time, the word "AS3" finishes sliding in from the left.

```
1    import com.greensock.TweenLite;
2    import com.greensock.plugins.TweenPlugin;
3    import com.greensock.plugins.TintPlugin;
4    import com.greensock.easing.Bounce;
5
6    TweenPlugin.activate([TintPlugin]);
7
8    TweenLite.from(bg, 1, {tint:0x000000});
9    TweenLite.from(ball0, 1, {scaleX:0, scaleY:0,
10                             ease:Elastic.easeOut, delay:0.5});
11   TweenLite.from(ball1, 1, {scaleX:0, scaleY:0,
12                             ease:Elastic.easeOut, delay:1.5});
13   TweenLite.from(ball2, 1, {scaleX:0, scaleY:0,
14                             ease:Elastic.easeOut, delay:1.75});
15   TweenLite.from(ball3, 1, {scaleX:0, scaleY:0,
16                             ease:Elastic.easeOut, delay:2});
17   TweenLite.from(as3, 1, {x:-100, ease:Elastic.easeOut, delay:2});
```

# Reproducing Timeline Tweens with ActionScript

The last thing we want to mention in this chapter is a companion website post about a feature that's a bit out of the ordinary. As such, we intend it to be an additional resource for your continued study outside this book. In addition to scripting motion solely with code, it's also possible to rebuild a Flash Professional timeline motion tween using ActionScript.

At the very least, this is an interesting workflow between designer and developer—allowing a designer to carefully tweak an animation using traditional interface tools, and then turning the file over to a developer that can make the entire process more dynamic with ActionScript. At best, it's a way for any Flash user to turn restrictive timeline tweens into code-based animations that are vastly easier to reuse and adapt.

This process requires that a traditional timeline tween be created first, and then Flash can break down the steps needed to reproduce the tween and write them to an XML document. ActionScript can then load the document, parse the instructions, and recreate the tween on the fly. The companion website (*http://www.LearningActionScript3.com*) has a full tutorial, including sample files, in a post called "Recreating Timeline Tweens with ActionScript," so be sure to check it out.

> **NOTE**
>
> *In this introduction, we've only scratched the surface of what the GreenSock Tweening Platform can do. Visit* http://www.greensock.com *for details, documentation, interactive examples, performance comparisons of other tweening engines, and more.*

## learningactionscript3 Packages

As discussed multiple times in prior chapters, one of the greatest benefits of learning object-oriented programming is the ability to quickly and easily reuse code. To that end, we're going to evolve a small library of code as the book progresses, to show you how to build reusable packages of your own.

In this and every subsequent chapter, we'll add a little code to this ongoing `learningactionscript3` project package. We won't stress this too heavily, and it won't get in the way of learning any of the syntax. However, by the time you finish the book, you will have amassed a small collection of classes that you can use in your own projects.

The contribution from this chapter is the `MotionUtils` class, which includes several of the basic formulas covered herein, including the degree-to-radian and radian-to-degree conversion, Zeno's paradox, Hooke's law, and more.

# What's Next?

Though this chapter details a variety of ActionScript animation techniques, it only begins to cover the subject of motion through code. The basic building blocks are here, however, and it's with these concepts (and related skills that grow from the ideas herein) that greater art and industry can be achieved.

Next on the to-do list is the ability to partially free yourself from the constraints of the Flash Professional interface and approach code-only projects with a little more latitude. When working with visual assets, we've so far relied heavily on symbols created within Flash and stored in a file's library.

It's true that we've sneaked a dynamically created vector in here and there, such as in the second particle system in this chapter, when lines were drawn between particles in close proximity. Despite that, thus far we've typically instantiated objects from a file's library using a linkage class. We'll continue to do that any time complex artwork warrants this practice, but we'll also begin to work with vectors and bitmaps created with code. In addition to giving you more freedom, this approach can also reduce file size and make your SWFs load faster.

**In the next chapter**, we'll discuss:

- Using the `Graphics` class to draw vectors to create assets on the fly without contributing to file size

- Calling methods of the `flash.geom` package to use rectangles and points in your scripts

- Using 9-slice scaling to achieve distortion-free symbol instance scaling

## CHAPTER 8

# DRAWING WITH VECTORS

Flash is well known for popularizing *vector graphics* on the Web. Put simply, vectors are composed of mathematically generated points, lines, curves, and shapes and are used to create artwork in computer software. Using vectors is optimal when you need to scale artwork because the vectors remain crisp and clean at any size. By contrast, bitmap graphics pixelate when scaled.

Drawing vectors graphics with code brings with it special benefits. Included among them is the freedom to create assets on the fly, rather than relying solely on art drawn or imported prior to publishing your file. Related to this is the additional bonus of reduced file size, because assets are created at run-time rather than occupying space in your SWF. Smaller files mean less time that your viewers spend waiting for your files to load.

In this chapter, we'll focus on drawing vectors, the first of two ways to originate visual assets with code. Over the next several pages, we'll cover:

- **The Graphics Class.** This class, often referred to as part of the *drawing API*, contains methods for drawing vectors. You have control over stroke and fill attributes, and can move a virtual pen around the screen, choosing where to draw lines, curves, and shapes like circles and rectangles.

- **The Geometry Package.** This utility package contains classes for creating points and rectangles, as well as transforming objects, and creating matrices (a special kind of number array) for complex simultaneous changes to rotation, scaling, and x and y translation. Using matrices, you can achieve effects for which no properties exist, including skew and shear.

- **9-slice Scaling.** Through the use of a dynamically assignable rectangle, 9-slice scaling can prevent the sides and corners of a movie clip from distorting when scaled.

- **Applied Examples.** Combining what you'll learn in this chapter, you'll write a custom button class that can be reused from project to project, and create the graphics for a color picker. You can then carry the color picker exercise into the next chapter, where you'll put it to work while composing and creating bitmaps.

## The Graphics Class

The **Graphics** class is the foundation for drawing vectors with code. You use methods of this class to define line and fill styles, and draw lines, curves, and shapes, similar to how you would by using the Flash interface.

Before we get started with syntax-specific discussions, however, here's a quick word of advice about where to draw your vectors. It is possible to draw vectors directly into the main timeline, but we recommend that you first create one or more movie clips or sprites to serve as canvases for your drawings. This is analogous to an artist drawing on a canvas instead of a studio wall—which makes it a lot easier to move a masterpiece around or exhibit it in a gallery. The same is true of virtual canvases in movie clips.

For example, if you draw into a movie clip, you can change its depth, assign it to a new parent, or change many properties to affect its appearance or functionality. Similarly, as you'll learn in the next chapter, you can apply special effects and filters to movie clips, which can't be applied directly to the stage.

This is particularly relevant because you don't create a new instance of the **Graphics** class when you want to start drawing. Instead, all methods of the class must be called from the **graphics** property of the movie clip or sprite you're drawing into, and it's useful to create a reference to this property, both as a shortcut and performance enhancement. For example, the following code creates a sprite canvas and stores its graphics object in the variable *g*. In this snippet, *⟨methodOrProperty⟩* is a placeholder for method or property syntax we are about to introduce.

```
var canvas:Sprite = new Sprite();
var g:Graphics = canvas.graphics;
g.<methodOrProperty>;
```

After creating *g*, you can manipulate all methods and properties of the **Graphics** class from that reference. This is not only less to type, but it's faster because the player doesn't have to retrieve the reference to the graphics object every time it's used. This isn't a requirement, and we may not use this method universally throughout this book, but it's a good habit to get into.

*Figure 8-1. The culmination of several Graphics class method calls*

To demonstrate styling and drawing lines, curves, and shapes, we're going to build the contents of Figure 8-1 over several examples. Continuing the same example over multiple snippets will also emphasize the fact that you can continue drawing from where you left off, move your virtual pen before drawing again, and restyle your stroke or fills while you draw. The finished script can be found in the *lines_curves_primitives.fla* source file.

# Drawing Lines

The first step in drawing lines is to set a line style using the **lineStyle()** method. This is equivalent to setting several stroke properties in the Properties panel of the Flash Professional interface. The typical syntax is as follows:

```
1   var canvas:Sprite = new Sprite();
2   addChild(canvas);
3   var g:Graphics = canvas.graphics;
4
5   g.lineStyle(2, 0x000000);
```

The first parameter of the **lineStyle()** method represents line thickness in points, and the second is color in 0xRRGGBB hexadecimal format, as described in Chapter 3. When a color is not included, black is used as the default. When a line thickness of 0 is specified, a hairline thickness is used. If you don't want to use a line at all, you can omit the method. If you want to switch to no line for future shapes, after you've already started drawing, call the method with no parameters to clear any existing line style.

The next step is to draw the line. The process of doing so is similar to physically drawing a line on a piece of paper. Ordinarily, you don't start drawing a line from the edge of the paper to the intended first point of the line, and then continuing to draw until you reach the second point of the line. Instead, you move your pen to the preferred starting point and then begin drawing. This is also true with the **Graphics** class. If you don't first *move* your virtual pen to the line's starting point, you will begin drawing from point (0, 0), the upper-left corner of your canvas. The **moveTo()** method moves the virtual pen to the x and y coordinate specified therein, and the **lineTo()** method draws from the previous virtual pen location to the x and y coordinates specified. Continuing our script from the prior code block, the following sequence will first move to point (150, 100) and then draw to point (400, 100):

```
6   //continued from prior section
7   g.moveTo(150, 100);
8   g.lineTo(400, 100);
```

To continue drawing straight lines, you can add more **lineTo()** methods. Each successive call will continue drawing the line from the previous location, as if you never lifted pen from paper. You can, however, change line styles at any time during the process.

The following script continuation draws another line 20 pixels down, and then another line back to the left to the x coordinate where we started. It then changes the line style from 2-pixel black to 4-pixel red, moves the pen to a new location 55 pixels below the prior line, and draws another line of the same length back to the right. When this script block finishes executing, it will have drawn the straight black and red line segments seen in Figure 8-1.

```
9   //continued from prior section
10  g.lineTo(400, 120);
11  g.lineTo(150, 120);
```

**NOTE**

*As described in Chapter 4, when you don't need a timeline, as in this example, you can work with a sprite instead of a movie clip. For more information about when to use* **MovieClip** *and when to use* **Sprite**, *see the "MovieClip versus Sprite" post at the companion website, http://www.LearningActionScript3.com.*

**NOTE**

*The* **lineStyle()** *method includes additional properties that are also found in the Properties panel, including alpha, stroke hinting, caps (end cap style: round, square, or none), join (joint style: round, bevel, or miter), and miter (miter limit: degree of joint pointiness). In cases like these, where the Flash Professional interface overlaps an ActionScript method so thoroughly, comparing the Properties panel with the ActionScript documentation can help jump-start your experimentation with these features.*

```
12  g.lineStyle(4, 0xFF0000);
13  g.moveTo(150, 175);
14  g.lineTo(400, 175);
```

# Drawing Curves

**NOTE**

*Although originally developed by Paul de Casteljau, vector curves are commonly called Bézier curves because they were famously used by French engineer Pierre Bézier in the design of automotive bodies during the early 1960s.*

As you might imagine, you're not limited to drawing straight lines. You can also draw curves like those created by vector drawing programs such as Adobe Illustrator. The syntax for drawing a curve requires the addition of a point that will act as a control point, effectively pulling the curve away from an ordinary straight-line appearance. This is equivalent to creating a control point in Illustrator.

ActionScript, however, uses the *quadratic* Bézier curve model. Quadratic curves use one control point (often referred to as a *handle*) for both end points of a line segment. By contrast, other drawing tools (including Illustrator) use the *cubic* Bézier model, which adds separate control handles for each point. A quadratic Bézier curve is illustrated in Figure 8-2, showing both end points and the control point used to manipulate the curve.

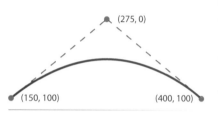

(275, 0)

(150, 100)    (400, 100)

*Figure 8-2. A quadratic Bézier curve with one control point for both end points of a line segment*

Though the algorithms used by ActionScript behind the scenes aren't paramount, remembering that only one control point is used to create a curve can help you remember the syntax of the **curveTo()** method, used to draw a curve with the drawing API. Here is the method's signature:

```
curveTo(controlX:Number, controlY:Number,
anchorX:Number, anchorY:Number):void
```

Unlike **lineTo()**, it uses four coordinates. The first two are the **x** and **y** values of the control point, and the second two are the **x** and **y** values of the destination point.

The following code continues our script by drawing the curve shown at the top of Figure 8-1. It starts by switching to a 2-point blue line and moving the pen to point (150, 100). It then draws a curve that ends at point (400, 100) but is affected by the control point at point (275, 0).

```
1  //continued from prior section
2  g.lineStyle(2, 0x0000FF);
3  g.moveTo(150, 100);
4  g.curveTo(275, 0, 400, 100);
```

It's also possible to draw simple shapes including a circle and a rectangle with or without rounded corners. Before we demonstrate drawing these basic shapes, let's introduce how to style fills.

# Adding Solid Fills

To add a solid-color fill to a drawing, you must use the **beginFill()** method. It accepts two parameters: color and alpha. Color is a **uint** (an unsigned integer, or nonnegative integer), and is typically specified in the 0xRRGGBB hexadecimal format. The alpha value is a **Number** in the percentage range of 0 to 1, with a default of 1 (100 percent).

After setting a fill style, you can continue drawing lines, curves, and shapes, and then conclude with the **endFill()** method, which uses no parameters. The following code demonstrates two things. First, it shows the benefit of drawing into a dedicated canvas, allowing you to position the display object (and therefore your drawing) anywhere on the stage (lines 20 through 23). It then demonstrates line and fill styling (lines 26 and 27) and moving to, and drawing, a triangle (lines 28 through 31). Finally line 32 ends the fill.

```
1    //continued from prior section
2    var triangle:Sprite = new Sprite();
3    triangle.x = 50;
4    triangle.y = 250;
5    addChild(triangle);
6
7    var tg:Graphics = triangle.graphics;
8    tg.lineStyle(0);
9    tg.beginFill(0xFF9900, 1);
10   tg.moveTo(50, 0);
11   tg.lineTo(100, 100);
12   tg.lineTo(0, 100);
13   tg.lineTo(50, 0);
14   tg.endFill();
```

**NOTE**

*Although the* **endFill()** *method can be omitted for simple drawings, doing so can produce unexpected results. See the "Using endFill() with the Drawing API" post at the companion website for more information.*

## Drawing Shapes

Drawing one line segment at a time is not the only method for drawing shapes. It's also possible to draw simple shapes using a trio of methods: **drawCircle()**, **drawRect()**, and **drawRoundRect()** (for drawing rectangles with rounded corners). The following code segment concludes our ongoing script by drawing three shapes—with varying fill colors and fill alpha values—into the same canvas, newly created in lines 34 through 37. Drawing multiple objects into one canvas reduces flexibility because you can't manipulate the objects separately thereafter. However, this is useful when drawing complex shapes that will be treated as a single object.

Lines 41 and 42 show how to use opacity for a special effect. Note that the stroke and fill both have an alpha value of 50 percent. The fill is red and the stroke is blue and 6 pixels thick. In Flash, strokes center on the edge to which they are applied, which, in this case, results in a 3-pixel overlap between stroke and fill edge. The partial opacity of both stroke and fill result in a red circle with the appearance of a 3-pixel purple outline surrounded by a 3-pixel blue outline. Line 43 creates the circle itself, using the **drawCircle()** method. This method requires the **x** and **y** values of the center of the circle (50, 50), and the circle's **radius** (50). The end result can be seen in the circle at the bottom of Figure 8-1.

```
1    //continued from prior section
2    var shapes:Sprite = new Sprite();
3    shapes.x = 150;
4    shapes.y = 250;
```

```
5    addChild(shapes);
6
7    var sg:Graphics = shapes.graphics;
8
9    sg.lineStyle(6, 0x0000FF, 0.5);
10   sg.beginFill(0xFF0000, 0.5);
11   sg.drawCircle(50, 50, 50);
12   sg.endFill();
13
14   sg.lineStyle();
15   sg.beginFill(0x0000FF, 0.2);
16   sg.drawRect(125, 0, 100, 100);
17   sg.endFill();
18
19   sg.beginFill(0x0000FF, 0.5);
20   sg.drawRoundRect(250, 0, 100, 100, 50);
21   sg.endFill();
```

Line 46 shows how to clear a previously existing line style. If you want to *begin* without a stroke, it's easy to omit the method. If a stroke already exists, however, and you want to clear it, you must invoke the **lineStyle()** method with no parameters. (If you use a value of 0, the method creates a hairline stroke.) Line 48 draws a rectangle using the **drawRect()** method, which accepts the x and y coordinates of the rectangle, followed by the width and height of the rectangle. The last shape method, **drawRoundRect()** in line 52, is the same as **drawRect()** but adds a fifth parameter for the corner radius used to draw all four corners of the rectangle. See Figure 8-1 to check the results of this finished script.

### NOTE

*An undocumented method called* **drawRoundRectComplex()** *allows you to control the corner radius of each corner independently. Here is the method signature:*

```
drawRoundRectComplex(x:Number, y:Number, width:Number,
    height:Number, topLeftRadius:Number, topRightRadius:Number,
    bottomLeftRadius:Number, bottomRightRadius:Number):void
```

*The following code, found in the draw_round_rect_complex.fla source file, creates a graphic that looks like a tab, which is convenient for tab-based navigation systems.*

```
var tab:Sprite = new Sprite();
tab.x = tab.y = 50;
addChild(tab);
tab.graphics.beginFill(0x333399);
tab.graphics.drawRoundRectComplex(0, 0, 100, 25,
                                  15, 15, 0, 0);
```

*As with all undocumented code, use at your own risk. Adobe may remove this method at any time. (The likelihood of that is probably low, however, because the method has been part of the Flex ActionScript documentation since Flex 2. Adobe has never made public why they chose not to document this method for Flash Professional users.)*

# Using Gradient Fills and Lines

ActionScript 3.0 doesn't restrict you to using solid colors for your fills or lines. You can also use gradients and bitmaps. Let's first discuss gradients, using the **beginGradientFill()** method for fills and the **lineGradientStyle()** method for lines.

## Gradient fills

Gradients can be linear (left to right, by default) or radial (radiating from the epicenter of the gradient outward). The content of the gradient is then determined by three parallel arrays (arrays with the same number of items in a corresponding order): colors, alpha values for each color, and *ratios*—values for each color that determine its weighting within the gradient.

The type of gradient is specified by the **GradientType** constants **LINEAR** or **RADIAL**. The colors of the gradient are specified as an array of color values, typically **uint** values in hexadecimal format, and listed within the array in the order in which they appear in the gradient. The alpha values for color are specified as an array of **Number** values between 0 and 1, and correspond with the order of the colors.

The ratio array contains a number for each color that places it within the gradient between 0 (far left, or center of radial) to 255 (far right or outer edge of radial). For simplicity, we'll use a linear gradient in our description, but the same ideas apply to radial gradients.

Think of the numeric span from 0 to 255 as a distance. If a gradient has only two colors, an evenly distributed gradient would have a ratio array of [0, 255]. In this example, the starting value of one color is at the extreme left and the starting value of the other color is at the extreme right. The mixture between these two colors creates the gradient, as you can see in the center of Figure 8-3.

However, you can also weight a color by skewing the ratio array. For example, to favor the right color, move its starting point further to the left—expanding the amount of the right color in the gradient, and reducing the amount of the left color, resulting in a ratio of [0, 127]. The top of Figure 8-3 shows this effect, skewing to black. Using a ratio of [127, 255] will have the reverse effect, favoring the color on the left and skewing red in the bottom of Figure 8-3.

Now let's put these values to work in the following example. Having shown the appearance of linear gradients in Figure 8-3, let's take a look at radial gradients. This exercise can be found in the *radial_gradient_1.fla* source file. Lines 1 through 3 create our drawing canvas and **Graphics** reference, line 10 creates the gradient fill using variables for each parameter, and line 11 draws a square. The heart of the gradient fill spans lines 5 through 8. Line 5 opts for a radial gradient. Line 6 identifies red and black as the gradient's colors. Line 7 provides an alpha value of 1 (100 percent) for each color. Finally, line 8 weights the colors evenly across the full distance of the gradient.

*Figure 8-3. Gradient color ratios*

**NOTE**

*Graphic symbols beneath each gradient in Figure 8-3 mark color positions for demonstration purposes only. Although these symbols make intentional allusions to the Flash Professional Color panel, the gradients in the figure were created solely with ActionScript.*

```
1   var canvas = new Sprite();
2   addChild(canvas);
3   var g:Graphics = canvas.graphics;
4
5   var gradType:String = GradientType.RADIAL;
6   var colors:Array = [0xFF0000, 0x000000];
7   var alphas:Array = [1, 1];
8   var ratios:Array = [0, 255];
9
10  g.beginGradientFill(gradType, colors, alphas, ratios)
11  g.drawRect(0, 0, 100, 100);
```

Figure 8-4. A radial gradient fill created with the Graphics class

Figure 8-4 shows the resulting gradient fill. To manipulate the gradient as a whole, such as moving the center of a radial gradient, rotating a linear gradient, or scaling a gradient to include more or less of the color span, you must use a *matrix*—a special kind of number array, which we'll introduce later in the chapter. Before that, let's look at gradient line styles, bitmap fills, and bitmap line styles. Then we'll revisit these topics to see how matrices can alter their appearance.

## Gradient line styles

Using a gradient line style is very much like combining a regular line style with a gradient fill. The only difference is that the gradient is applied to the line, not the fill. In fact, **lineGradientStyle()**, the method for applying a gradient line style, doesn't even replace the solid-color **lineStyle()** method. Instead, both methods work together to define a line style and then paint it with a gradient. If you omitted the basic **lineStyle()** method, no line would appear at all.

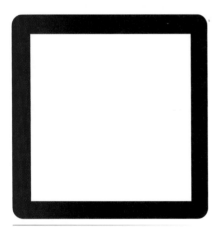

Figure 8-5. A linear gradient line style

The following script, found in *line_style_gradient.fla* source file, shows this medley in action. Lines 1 through 5 create and position a canvas, as well as create a reference to its **graphics** property. Line 6 applies a conventional line style, specifying a black, 20-pixel stroke. Lines 8 through 11 define the gradient properties, just as we did in the last example, specifying a linear gradient, from red to black, at full alpha, and evenly distributed between the two colors. Line 13 applies the gradient, also in a similar fashion to the last example, but this time to the line style, not the fill. Once the line is styled, line 14 draws a 200 × 200 rectangle. The effect is illustrated in Figure 8-5.

```
1   var canvas:Sprite = new Sprite();
2   addChild(canvas);
3   var g:Graphics = canvas.graphics;
4
5   canvas.x = canvas.y = 10;
6   g.lineStyle(20, 0x000000);
7
8   var gradType:String = GradientType.LINEAR;
9   var colors:Array = [0xFF0000, 0x000000];
10  var alphas:Array = [1, 1];
11  var ratios:Array = [0, 255];
12
13  g.lineGradientStyle(gradType, colors, alphas, ratios);
14  g.drawRect(0, 0, 200, 200);
```

**NOTE**

*As discussed in the "Gradient fills" portion of this section, transforming the line gradient also requires a special mathematical construct called a matrix, which we'll introduce in the upcoming section "The Geometry Package."*

# Using Bitmap Fills and Lines

In addition to applying gradients to fills and lines, you can use bitmaps to decorate your drawing's fills and lines. Both the **beginBitmapFill()** and **lineBitmapStyle()** methods we cover in this section use instances of the **BitmapData** class. This class handles pixel color and alpha data and allows low-level manipulation of bitmaps. Conveniently, **BitmapData** is also the data type of bitmaps instantiated from the Flash Professional library using a linkage class. So, any time we need such an instance in the following examples, using a linkage class with an imported bitmap will fit the bill.

## Bitmap fills

Using bitmap fills is an easy way to add art to a shape created with the drawing API. Instead of using the **beginFill()** method, simply substitute **beginBitmapFill()**. The method requires a **BitmapData** instance, such as a bitmap from the library, but all remaining parameters are optional. When using the default values, the bitmap will automatically tile. This is very useful for keeping file size down because you can fill large areas with custom bitmap art by using tiles.

In the following example, the 18 × 19 pixel tile in Figure 8-6 has been imported into the *bitmap_fill_tiled.fla* source file and been given a linkage class of **WeaveTile**. The following code fills a 200 × 200 rectangle with the tile resulting in what you see in Figure 8-7. Note in line 5 that you must pass in the size of the bitmap you want to use for your fill when creating the **BitmapData** instance.

```
1    var canvas:Sprite = new Sprite();
2    addChild(canvas);
3    var g:Graphics = canvas.graphics;
4
5    g.beginBitmapFill(new WeaveTile(18, 19));
6    g.drawRect(0, 0, 200, 200);
7    g.endFill();
```

If you don't want to tile the bitmap, you need only adjust an optional parameter of the **beginBitmapFill()** method. Here is the method signature:

```
beginBitmapFill(bitmap:BitmapData, matrix:Matrix=null,
repeat:Boolean=true, smooth:Boolean=false):void
```

The first optional parameter is for a matrix, used to rotate, scale, or adjust the location of a bitmap within your shape. We'll do that a little later in the chapter. We do need to provide a value here, however, to get to the remaining parameters, because the order of parameters is not arbitrary. So, in this case, we'll pass in **null** to make no change.

The second parameter controls tiling. By default, its value is true, but you can turn off tiling by setting its value to false. The third optional parameter smoothes the appearance of the bitmap when scaled, softening up the edges. Smoothing can adversely affect performance, so don't apply it arbitrarily, and usually not to fast-moving sprites.

**NOTE**

*In Chapter 13, we'll discuss how to load external images so you can use bitmaps that haven't already been imported into an FLA. For now, let's focus on the syntax required to use bitmaps, no matter where they originate.*

**NOTE**

*Flash Professional CS5 users can omit the width and height values in this usage. This will be discussed further in the next chapter, when covering the* **BitmapData** *class in greater detail.*

*Figure 8-6. A bitmap tile*

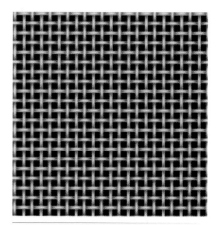

*Figure 8-7. A tiled bitmap fill*

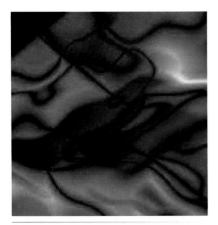

*Figure 8-8. A bitmap fill without tiling*

The following code, found in the *bitmap_fill.fla* source file, is nearly identical to the last example, only modifying the arguments in the `beginBitmapFill()` method. It uses a bitmap with a linkage class of **Texture**, no matrix, turns off tiling, and turns on smoothing to show you an example of the syntax for the optional parameters (all in line 5). The result is shown in Figure 8-8.

```
8    var canvas:Sprite = new Sprite();
9    addChild(canvas);
10   var g:Graphics = canvas.graphics;
11
12   g.beginBitmapFill(new Texture(550, 400), null, false, true);
13   g.drawRect(0, 0, 200, 200);
14   g.endFill();
```

## Bitmap line styles

Applying bitmaps to line styles will likely feel like familiar territory. It's similar to applying gradients to line styles, in that the basic `lineStyle()` method is still required to control things like thickness and alpha values for the line. The `lineBitmapStyle()` method is then used immediately thereafter to apply the bitmap. This method is similar to the `beginBitmapFill()` method in that it takes the same parameters: a **BitmapData** instance, a matrix for bitmap manipulation (null by default), and tiling and smoothing options (true and false by default, respectively).

*Figure 8-9. A tiled bitmap line style*

The only drawing API change the following code (found in the *line_style_bitmap_tiled.fla* source file) makes to the previous examples is substituting a bitmap line style for a fill style. It again uses the **WeaveTile** linkage class, putting the tile from Figure 8-6 to use one more time. Because tiling is enabled by default, the result of this simple code is seen in Figure 8-9.

```
1    var canvas:Sprite = new Sprite();
2    addChild(canvas);
3    var g:Graphics = canvas.graphics;
4
5    canvas.x = canvas.y = 10;
6    g.lineStyle(20, 0x000000);
7    g.lineBitmapStyle(new WeaveTile(18, 19));
8    g.drawRect(0, 0, 200, 200);
```

*Figure 8-10. A bitmap line style without tiling*

**NOTE**

*One very important thing to remember is that bitmap line styles are new to Flash Player as of version 10.1. Therefore, your viewers must have that version of the player or later for this feature to work.*

When tiling is turned off, you can apply larger bitmaps to line styles for a less geometric effect. The following code uses the previously mentioned **Texture** bitmap and sets tiling to false. The result is seen in Figure 8-10, and found in the *line_style_bitmap.fla* source file.

```
9    var canvas:Sprite = new Sprite();
10   addChild(canvas);
11   var g:Graphics = canvas.graphics;
12
13   canvas.x = canvas.y = 20;
14   g.lineStyle(40, 0x000000);
15   g.lineBitmapStyle(new Texture(550, 400), null, false)
16   g.drawRect(0, 0, 510, 360)
```

# Simulating the Pencil Tool

A good way to learn interactive drawing is to simulate the functionality of the Flash Professional Pencil tool. As when you use the Pencil tool in Flash, in ActionScript you select a line size and color, move the mouse to the drawing's starting point, then click and drag to draw. In both cases, you also release the mouse to move to a new location, and then start drawing again.

This process is outlined in the following script from the *pencil.fla* source file. Lines 1 through 3 prepare our usual canvas, and line 4 initializes a Boolean to keep track of whether the pencil is drawing. Line 6 sets the line style.

Lines 8 through 18 create a trio of listeners: Line 8 is added to the main time-line (the scope of the script) and updates the art every enter frame. Lines 9 through 11 are added to the stage and toggle the **drawing** Boolean based on the mouse activity. Finally, lines 21 through 25 move the drawing point with the mouse if the mouse button is up, and draw with the mouse if its button is down. Figure 8-11 is a simple graphic drawn with this code.

**NOTE**

*In lines 9 and 10 of the **pencil.fla** code, the mouse event listeners are added to the stage because the stage can easily react to mouse events. If you add a mouse event listener to a movie clip (which the main timeline is), the mouse events will register only if you click on visible content within the movie clip. As this example is a simple drawing application that begins with a blank canvas, attaching mouse events to the main timeline would mean that no mouse event would ever be heard.*

```
1    var canvas:Sprite = new Sprite();
2    addChild(canvas);
3    var g:Graphics = canvas.graphics;
4    var drawing:Boolean = false;
5
6    g.lineStyle(1, 0x000000);
7
8    this.addEventListener(Event.ENTER_FRAME, onLoop, false, 0, true);
9    stage.addEventListener(MouseEvent.MOUSE_DOWN, onDown,
10                          false, 0, true);
11   stage.addEventListener(MouseEvent.MOUSE_UP, onUp, false, 0, true);
12
13   function onDown(evt:MouseEvent):void {
14       drawing = true;
15   }
16   function onUp(evt:MouseEvent):void {
17       drawing = false;
18   }
19
20   function onLoop(evt:Event):void {
21       if (drawing) {
22           g.lineTo(mouseX, mouseY);
23       } else {
24           g.moveTo(mouseX, mouseY);
25       }
26   }
```

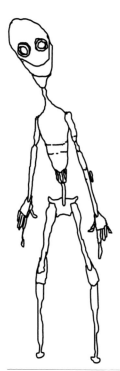

*Figure 8-11. Art created using the pencil.fla source file*

# Drawing Complex Shapes with drawPath()

If you want to push yourself a bit to use many of the skills you've learned throughout this book, you can take a sideline and look over this more advanced technique for drawing with vectors. Feel free to skip this section, if you're still finding your scripting legs. You can always come back to it when you're more comfortable with ActionScript 3.0.

This exercise is just a form of self-guided study, and introduces a new feature of Flash Player 10.1. Although it can really expand what you can do in combination with other new features discussed on the companion website, there's nothing here that you can't put off for now. In essence, all this feature does is allow you to draw a complex shape all at once, having stored the same drawing methods you've just learned, and corresponding points, for later recall.

The `drawPath()` method allows you to build a collection of drawing commands and draw a vector masterpiece all at once. From a comparison standpoint, `drawPath()` isn't very different from executing a list of individual drawing API commands. In the simplest terms, it collects `moveTo()`, `lineTo()`, and `curveTo()` commands into a single method, but it does a bit more if you delve deeper.

First, it stores both the commands and data points using the fast, efficient `Vector` class. An instance of the `Vector` class is very different from the vectors we've been drawing throughout this chapter. Essentially, the ActionScript construct *vector* is an array and, in most cases, working with a vector will be the same as working with an array. However, vectors are very fast because they are *typed* arrays. That is, normal arrays can contain a mixture of many data types, making it impossible for the array as a whole to be checked against a single data type. Each vector, on the other hand, can contain only one data type, so the compiler knows right away what the data type of everything in the vector will be. That makes them fast. If you haven't used vectors yet, take another look at Chapter 2.

The second, and most beneficial feature of the `drawPath()` method is that you can save the drawing commands and points for later use; you can recall them again and again to draw complex paths without having to rewrite the code every time. The companion website has more information about this process in a series of posts aptly prefixed "The Drawing API." For now, however, let's write a function that will collect polygon coordinates and `lineTo()` commands to draw finished polygons using the `drawPath()` method. Two example polygons created by the script, a hexagon and a triangle, are shown in Figure 8-12.

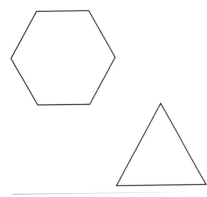

*Figure 8-12. Two shapes created with the* `drawPath()` *method*

The following script can be found in the *draw_path_polygons.fla* source file. Lines 1 through 7 create two canvases into which we will draw a triangle and hexagon, respectively. We're using two canvases because our function can draw polygons with three or more sides, and the script will demonstrate both a three-sided polygon (triangle) and a six-sided polygon (hexagon).

```
1    var hexagon:Sprite = new Sprite();
2    hexagon.x = hexagon.y = 100;
3    addChild(hexagon);
4
5    var triangle:Sprite = new Sprite();
6    triangle.x = triangle.y = 200;
7    addChild(triangle);
```

The **drawPolygon()** method, which we defined in lines 9 through 33, uses simple math to calculate points on an invisible circle, and then divides the circumference of that circle into equal segments to find the points of a polygon. In other words, if you divided a circle at two equidistant points along its circumference, you'd end up with two points that describe a straight line (the circle's diameter). If you divided the circumference into three segments, you'd end up with three points that form a triangle, and so on.

The **drawPolygon()** method takes as its arguments: a sprite to draw into, the radius and number of sides for the polygon, and the starting angle of the first point in the polygon (lines 9 and 10). Line 11 stores the graphics property of the desired canvas so we can draw into it, and line 12 stores the number of points of the polygon we want to draw to. (The number of points is one larger than the number of sides because we have to draw back to the first point again, to close the shape.)

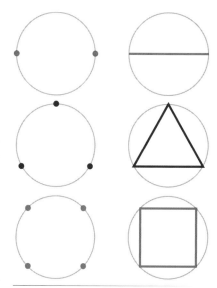

*Figure 8-13. Forming polygons by dividing a circle's circumference into equal sections and then connecting the equidistant points*

The number of polygon segments determines the amount by which the angle is incremented each time a line is drawn (line 13). A triangle touches our invisible circle three times, so the angle increment is 360/3 or 120 degrees. A hexagon has 6 sides, so its angle is incremented 60 degrees each time a side is drawn (360 / 6 = 60).

The last initialization steps, in lines 14 and 15, create empty vectors to contain the polygon points and commands. Note that the data type of the vector is added to the process, as discussed in Chapter 2. The points of the polygon will be stored in **Number** format, and the commands will be stored in **int** (integer) format. Line 16 adds the first drawing instruction, a **moveTo()**, to the *commands* vector. The constant **MOVE_TO** from the **GraphicsPathCommand** class contains the required integer, making it easier to remember because you don't have to recall which integer corresponds to which method. If you prefer to use integers to save space, however, **moveTo()** is 1, **lineTo()** is 2, and **curveTo()** is 3.

Lines 17 through 21 determine the point to which the first move is made. They use the basic circle math discussed in Chapter 7 to find the points of the polygon on our invisible circle. The current angle is first converted from degrees to radians (line 17, calling the function in lines 35 through 37), and then the x and y coordinates of the first point are calculated, using cosine and sine respectively, times the radius of the circle (lines 18 and 19). Finally, lines 20 and 21 push the point into the *points* vector. Note that the **x** and **y** values are stored separately and sequentially, rather than as x-y pairs, to take advantage of the speed boost that comes from processing numbers in a vector.

```
8   //drawing function
9   function drawPolygon(canvas:Sprite, radius:Number,
10                       numSegments:int, angle:Number=0):void {
11      var g:Graphics = canvas.graphics;
12      var numPoints:int = numSegments + 1;
13      var angleChange:Number = 360/numSegments;
14      var points:Vector.<Number> = new Vector.<Number>;
15      var commands:Vector.<int> = new Vector.<int>;
16      commands.push(GraphicsPathCommand.MOVE_TO);
17      var radians:Number = deg2rad(angle);
18      var xLoc:Number = Math.cos(radians) * radius;
19      var yLoc:Number = Math.sin(radians) * radius;
20      points.push(xLoc);
21      points.push(yLoc);
```

The **for** loop in lines 22 through 30 repeats this process for every point in the polygon, with two exceptions. First, line 23 increments the angle to determine the location of the next point. For each subsequent point, the **lineTo()** method is used to draw a line to the point, rather than move there.

The final part of the function sets a line style, and draws the polygon all at once by walking through each command and matching it with corresponding points (lines 31 and 32, respectively).

```
22      for (var i:int = 0; i < numPoints; i++) {
23          angle += angleChange;
24          radians = deg2rad(angle);
25          xLoc = Math.cos(radians) * radius;
26          yLoc = Math.sin(radians) * radius;
27          commands.push(GraphicsPathCommand.LINE_TO);
28          points.push(xLoc);
29          points.push(yLoc);
30      }
31      g.lineStyle(1, 0x000000);
32      g.drawPath(commands, points);
33  }
34
35  function deg2rad(deg:Number):Number {
36      return deg * (Math.PI/180)
37  }
38
39  drawPolygon(hexagon, 50, 6);
40  drawPolygon(triangle, 50, 3, 270);
```

The last step in the process occurs in lines 39 and 40 when the function is called. Each time, a minimum of three things is passed to the function: a movie clip canvas into which the art is drawn, the radius of the desired polygon, and the number of sides used to create the polygon. Line 40 demonstrates the optional parameter, dictating the starting position of the polygon's first point. By default, this is at angle 0, or to the right. (This is determined by the default value of 0 for the **angle** parameter in line 10.) To align the triangle upward, we must set the starting angle to 270 degrees.

Don't forget: there are additional discussions related to this process on the companion website. Two more drawing methods, for example, offer slightly modified syntax for the **moveTo()** and **lineTo()** drawing commands. They introduce no new functionality, but are designed to require fewer code edits, should you ever need to switch to drawing a curve later on. More importantly, additional features not covered here can be used to store and redraw graphics data again and again. Push yourself to learn and check out the site when you're ready.

# The Geometry Package

Regardless of whether you intend to use a lot of math in your programming, you will probably use more geometry than you think. You've already indirectly referenced points on many occasions, and you might also use rectangles for simple tasks like defining an area or checking to see if something is within a given boundary. Fortunately, simple tasks like these do not require that you calculate your own formulas. In fact, preexisting ActionScript classes can even replace some of the manual coding you're already doing, such as calculating the distance between two points, discussed in Chapter 7.

The `flash.geom` package contains a handy set of utility classes that help create and manipulate points, rectangles, and other data used to transform the appearance of objects. Here we'll focus on three of its classes that most closely relate to drawing with code: **Point**, **Rectangle**, and **Matrix**. We'll also revisit the **Geometry** package when discussing color in the next chapter.

## Creating Points

The **Point** class allows you to reference an x and y coordinate as a single point. An instance of the **Point** class contains **x** and **y** properties, and creating the instance is as easy as using the **new** operator, just as you've done many times so far. Using an empty constructor, as seen in the first line of the following code block, will automatically create a default point of (0, 0). You can reference another location, however, by passing **x** and **y** values into the constructor. The first syntax demonstration that follows creates a default point and traces the point's **x** and **y** properties separately. The second demonstration creates a specific point and traces the point as a whole.

```
var pt:Point = new Point();
trace(pt.x, pt.y);
//0 0

var pt2:Point = new Point(100, 100);
trace(pt2);
//(x=100, y=100)
```

In addition to its **x** and **y** properties, the **Point** class also has a handful of useful methods to make processing point data easier. These methods allow you to move a point, add or subtract the x and y values of two points, or determine whether two points are the same. It can even calculate the distance from one point to another, or find an interim location between two points.

**NOTE**

*Neither the* **Point** *nor the* **Rectangle** *class draws a shape. These classes define virtual points and rectangles for use with other coding needs.*

The following code is found in the *points.fla* source file. Traces are used throughout the code to show you the immediate results of each instruction. To start, lines 1 and 2 create two points to work with. Line 3 demonstrates the **offset()** method, moving the point 50 pixels in both the x and y directions.

Lines 6 and 8 demonstrate adding and subtracting points. These methods work on the point's **x** and **y** values independently, creating a *new point* that is calculated from the sum or difference of the two point coordinates. Line 10 checks to see if two points are the same using the **equals()** method. This is very handy for conditionals because you don't have to test for x and y values independently.

```
1   var pt1:Point = new Point(100, 100);
2   var pt2:Point = new Point(400, 400);
3   pt1.offset(50, 50);
4   trace(pt1);
5   //(x=150, y=150)
6   trace(pt1.add(pt2));
7   //(x=550, y=550)
8   trace(pt2.subtract(pt1));
9   //(x=250, y=250)
10  trace(pt1.equals(pt2));
11  //false
```

Two very convenient **Point** methods are **distance()** and **interpolate()**, which really simplify animation math. Essentially, **distance()** performs the work of the Pythagorean theorem discussed in the previous chapter, so you don't have to do it yourself. The **interpolate()** method calculates an interim location between two specified points. The method's third parameter determines how close to either point you want the new location to be. A value closer to 0 is nearer the proximity of the second point; a value approaching 1 is closer to the first point.

```
12  trace(Point.distance(pt1, pt2));
13  //353.5533905932738
14  trace(Point.interpolate(pt1, pt2, 0.5));
15  //(x=275, y=275)
```

## Creating Rectangles

Rectangles are defined in a way similar to defining points, but by using the **Rectangle** class. Like using point data, creating and manipulating rectangular areas via ActionScript can be very helpful when positioning objects. For example, a rectangle can be used to establish a boundary within which something must remain or occur—such as keeping a movie clip in a corner of the stage. You will also see in the next chapter that rectangles are valuable for defining areas of data—in much the way a marquee selection or cropping tool behaves in a drawing application.

Here's an example of creating a rectangle, and checking its location, width, and height. The first line of the following snippet shows the order of arguments that must be supplied when instantiating a rectangle. Comparing the

**NOTE**

*See the "Using Points and Rectangles" post on the companion website for additional information.*

sample output comments to this line shows how the properties and values are related.

```
//Rectangle(x:Number, y:Number, width:Number, height:Number)
var rect:Rectangle = new Rectangle(0, 0, 100, 100);
trace(rect.x, rect.y);
//0 0
trace(rect.width, rect.height);
//100 100
trace(rect);
//(x=0, y=0, w=100, h=100)
```

Three sets of properties also give you a more granular look at location and dimension values of the rectangle. For example, in the *rectangles.fla* source file, you'll find the following script, which shows how to find the rectangle's location, width, and height, just as you did with the **Point** class. Line 4 demonstrates the **left**, **top**, **right**, and **bottom** properties of the rectangle. You can use these properties to check for the location of an *edge* of a rectangle. Finally, line 6 uses the **topLeft** and **bottomRight** properties to retrieve the appropriately named bounding *points* of the rectangle.

```
1    var rect:Rectangle = new Rectangle(50, 50, 200, 100);
2    trace(rect.x, rect.y, rect.width, rect.height);
3    //50 50 200 100
4    trace(rect.left, rect.top, rect.right, rect.bottom);
5    //50 50 250 150
6    trace(rect.topLeft, rect.bottomRight);
7    //(x=50, y=50) (x=250, y=150)
```

As with the **Point** class, you can move a rectangle with one call to the **off-set()** method (shown in line 9 of the continuing script that follows), instead of changing both the rectangle's **x** and **y** properties. You can also create a larger rectangle by increasing the width and height on all sides surrounding the initial rectangle's center point. This is accomplished using the **inflate()** method and is another way of creating a quick frame around a rectangle. The first parameter of this method is added to the location of the rectangle's left and right dimensions (enlarging the rectangle horizontally), and the second parameter is applied to the top and bottom dimensions (enlarging the rectangle vertically).

```
8    //offset and inflate
9    rect.offset(10, 10);
10   trace(rect.left, rect.top, rect.right, rect.bottom);
11   //60 60 260 160
12   rect.inflate(20, 20);
13   trace(rect.left, rect.top, rect.right, rect.bottom);
14   //40 40 280 180
```

Next, you can use a handful of methods to compare rectangles with points and other rectangles. The following code block compares two new rectangles, *rect1* and *rect2*, and a new point, *pnt*. Lines 19, 21, and 23 determine whether an object is inside a rectangle. Line 19 checks to see whether x and y locations are both inside the rectangle. Line 21 performs the same test, but allows you to pass in a point instead of discreet x and y values. Line 23 checks to see whether an entire rectangle is within another rectangle. These methods can be handy for programming drag-and-drop exercises.

```
15  //contains
16  var rect1:Rectangle = new Rectangle(0, 0, 100, 50);
17  var rect2:Rectangle = new Rectangle(50, 25, 100, 50);
18  var pnt:Point = new Point(125, 50);
19  trace(rect1.contains(25, 25));
20  //true
21  trace(rect2.containsPoint(pnt));
22  //true
23  trace(rect1.containsRect(rect2));
24  //false
```

Line 26 of this ongoing example checks to see if two rectangles overlap, and line 28 returns any area shared by both rectangles. Line 30 returns the union of the two specified rectangles—a new rectangle created from the minimum-bounding area that fully encompasses both original rectangles.

```
25  //intersection and union
26  trace(rect1.intersects(rect2));
27  //true
28  trace(rect1.intersection(rect2));
29  //(x=50, y=25, w=50, h=25)
30  trace(rect1.union(rect2));
31  //(x=0, y=0, w=150, h=75)
```

These methods can be used in advanced collision detections, drawing tools, and other efforts. For example, you can rule that two objects collide only if a certain degree of overlap is achieved (rather than first contact). This can be determined by checking the size of the resulting intersection.

Because neither the **Rectangle** nor **Point** classes create display objects, Figure 8-14 visualizes the rectangles and points discussed. The blue rectangle represents *rect1*, the yellow rectangle represents *rect2*, the red dot represents *pnt*, and the black dot represents the explicit point (25, 25). The green area depicts the new rectangle created by the intersection of *rect1* and *rect2*, and the dashed line depicts the new rectangle created by the union of *rect1* and *rect2*.

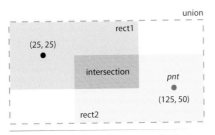

*Figure 8-14. Rectangle class methods demonstrated*

## Using Matrices

ActionScript offers predefined properties for affecting a display object's scale, rotation, and x and y locations, all of which are specified individually. However, there are certain types of objects to which these properties do not apply, such as the gradient fill and line style discussed previously and similar bitmap properties we'll introduce in a moment and cover in the next chapter.

To change these kinds of objects, you must use a *matrix*. A matrix is basically a special kind of array of numbers, expressed in a grid. It is not a multidimensional array, as the numbers are stored linearly. However, they relate to each other within the matrix in special ways. Matrix elements can be used independently or together to perform complex object transformations.

For example, combinations of elements, such as scale and rotation, can be applied at once, and matrices can even be used to achieve effects that are otherwise not possible with individual properties, such as skewing.

You can also use matrices for more advanced operations such as determining where a point ends up after an object has been transformed. In other words, the point (10, 10) near the upper-left corner of a rectangle will not be at point (10, 10) after a 90-degree rotation. The **Matrix** class can tell you the new location to which that point has moved, or even the change in location between the new and original points.

The **Matrix** class provides a basic 3 × 3 matrix for use in several transformation processes. Its structure can be seen in Figure 8-15. Built-in **Matrix** properties **a** and **d** affect scaling. Properties **b** and **c** will skew (or *shear*) an object. The **tx** and **ty** properties affect x and y location, respectively. Together, elements **a**, **b**, **c**, and **d**, affect rotation. The last three values in the matrix, $u$, $v$, and $w$, are not used in ActionScript and can be ignored.

[ a,  c,  tx
  b,  d,  ty
  u,  v,  w ]

*Figure 8-15. Matrix properties*

Table 8-1 shows the transformations possible with a matrix. The first column shows the type of transformation, the second column lists related properties and a simplified class method for accomplishing the goal (if one exists), and the third column shows the values that must be adjusted, if you need to do so manually. It is almost always more convenient to use existing methods, or the **a**, **b**, **c**, **d**, **tx**, and **ty** properties, but writing out the matrix explicitly is useful when you want to make several changes at once. Finally, the last column depicts a representative change in an object when the transformation is applied.

*Table 8-1. Matrix values and how they transform objects*

| Transformation | Properties/Methods | Matrix | Result |
|---|---|---|---|
| *Identity*<br><br>Default matrix, null transformation | `a, b, c, d, tx, ty`<br><br>`identity()` | [ 1,  0,  0<br>  0,  1,  0<br>  0,  0,  1 ] |  |
| *Translation*<br><br>Changes position, x and y, respectively, using pixels | `tx, ty`<br><br>`translate(tx, ty)` | [ 1,  0,  tx<br>  0,  1,  ty<br>  0,  0,  1 ] | 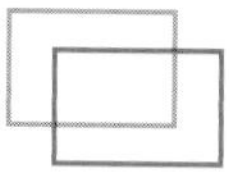 |
| *Scale*<br><br>Scales along the x and y axes, respectively, using percent | `a, d`<br><br>`scale(a, d)` | [ sx,  0,  0<br>  0,  sy,  0<br>  0,  0,  1 ] | 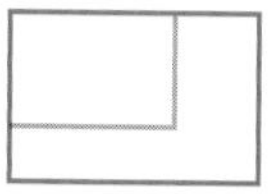 |
| *Rotation*<br><br>Rotates, using radians | `a, b, c, d`<br><br>`rotate(q)` | [ cos(q),  sin(q),  0<br>  −sin(q),  cos(q),  0<br>      0,      0, 1 ] |  |

*(continued)*

*Table 8-1. Matrix values and how they transform objects*   **(continued)**

| Transformation | Properties/Methods | Matrix | Result |
|---|---|---|---|
| *Skew (Shear)* <br><br> Skews along the x and y axes, respectively, using pixels | **b, c** <br><br> None. (See the **MatrixTransformer** note in the "Calculating changes in points after transformations" section.) | [      1, tan(zx),   0 <br> tan(zy),      1,  0 <br>     0,      0,  1 ] | |

## Skewing with matrices

To test this information, let's use the **Matrix** class to do something you can't do with a built-in property or method—skew a display object. The following script, found in the *matrix_skew_1.fla* source file, creates a rectangle with the **Graphics** class and then skews it.

To start with, lines 1 through 7 create a translucent green rectangular sprite with a 1-pixel black border and add it to the display list. The function spanning lines 9 through 10, originally discussed in Chapter 7, converts degrees to radians for use with the **Matrix** skewing code.

```
1   var rect:Sprite = new Sprite();
2   addChild(rect);
3   var g:Graphics = rect.graphics;
4   g.lineStyle(1, 0x000000);
5   g.beginFill(0x00FF00, 0.4);
6   g.drawRect(0, 0, 100, 50);
7   g.endFill();
8
9   function deg2rad(deg:Number):Number {
10  return deg * Math.PI / 180;
11  }
12
13  var matrix:Matrix = rect.transform.matrix;
14  matrix.c = Math.tan(deg2rad(20));
15  rect.transform.matrix = matrix;
```

Finally, lines 13 through 15 apply the skewing effect. Line 13 creates a matrix based on the existing object's matrix, by retrieving the value of the **matrix** property of the **transform** object. This makes sure you are starting from any current transformation, whatever that may be. That is, if an object has already been skewed, starting with a default matrix (also called an *identity* matrix) will effectively reset the prior skew with the new values.

Line 14 sets the **c** property of the matrix, which skews along the x-axis using the angle specified. It requires radians instead of degrees, so a value of 20 degrees is passed to the conversion function to get back the required radian value. Finally, the matrix is applied to the object's **matrix** property in line 15. The result is seen in the top illustration in Figure 8-16.

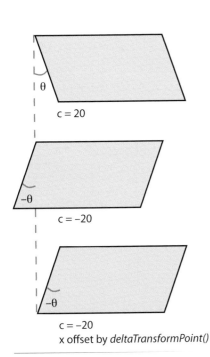

c = 20

−θ

c = −20

−θ

c = −20
x offset by *deltaTransformPoint()*

*Figure 8-16. A sprite skewed with the Matrix class*

Note that the skew is applied to the bottom edge of the sprite. This is important because if you wanted to give the sprite the appearance that it was slanted right rather than left, you need to compensate with the correct angle. Angles between 90 and 180 degrees and between 270 and 360 degrees will slant an object to the right but it's easier to use corresponding negative values. The following change to the existing script (indicated in bold) is found in *matrix_skew_2.fla* and uses −20 degrees instead of 20 degrees, and the result appears in the middle illustration of Figure 8-16.

```
16   var matrix:Matrix = rect.transform.matrix;
17   matrix.c = Math.tan(deg2rad(-20));
18   rect.transform.matrix = matrix;
```

## Calculating changes in points after transformations

The sprite slants to the right, but because horizontal skewing affects only the bottom edge, the sprite now appears offset to the left. That is, we successfully skewed the object −20 degrees, but it is no longer where we want it to be. To compensate, we can use the occasionally life-saving methods that calculate the change in a point's location as a result of a transformation. We'll demonstrate this feature first. Putting aside the correction we're seeking for a mometnt, let's trace the new position of a sprite point, as it exists after the skew.

Let's focus on the original location of the lower-left corner of the rectangle. We knew that to be (0, 50) because the rectangle had a height of 50 and was positioned at (0, 0) (per our **drawRect()** instruction in line 6). Therefore, we can pass a point of (0, 50) to the **transformPoint()** method to see the new value of that location:

```
19   trace(matrix.transformPoint(new Point(0, 50)));
```

The new point will trace as approximately (18, 50) because the prior point (0, 50) has been skewed to the left. Calculating this change can require fairly involved trigonometry, so this method is very handy.

If we stopped here, we could determine the difference between the two points and change the location of the sprite accordingly. However, there's already a method that eliminates the need to calculate the offset. The **deltaTransformPoint()** method determines the *change* in the before and after locations of a point, rather than the absolute old and new locations.

We know from the prior trace that the lower-left corner of the rectangle has moved approximately 18 points to the left, and did not move vertically. Therefore, passing (0, 50) to the **deltaTransformPoint()** method will return a point that is approximately (−18, 50). All we need to do is use that information to correct the location of the sprite. We can, therefore, subtract the x change in the point from the original x, and the sprite will be restored to its original position. Add lines 16 and 17 to the ongoing example (as in the *matrix_skew_2.fla* source file) and see the bottom illustration in Figure 8-16.

```
20   rect.x -= matrix.deltaTransformPoint(new Point(0, 50)).x;
```

**NOTE**

*If you're a Flash Professional user, check out the timesaving* **MatrixTransformer** *class. It's part of the* **fl.motion** *package, added to Flash to support recreating timeline animations with ActionScript.*

*This class makes matrix transformations even easier than the dedicated methods of the* **Matrix** *class. For instance, it has getters and setters for every matrix setting and both degrees and radians are supported, eliminating the need to convert angle values before use.*

*Here's an example of using the class to skew the mc movie clip 20 degrees:*

```
var matrix:Matrix = new Matrix();
MatrixTransformer.
    setSkewX(matrix, 20);
mc.transform.matrix = matrix;
```

*That's easier than transforming points, as described in the "Skewing with matrices" discussion of this chapter. The class can also automatically rotate a display object around any point, rather than just the object's transformation point. See the "Using the MatrixTransformer Class" post at the companion website for more information.*

## Manipulating gradient fills and line styles

Now that you know a little bit about matrices, you can exert greater control over gradient fills and line styles. The first time we introduced gradient fills, we filled a rectangle with a radial gradient. The center of the fill did not match the center of the object because we couldn't control the scale of the gradient. Similarly, the scale of the gradient applied to the line style was too large, not revealing full red on the left or full black on the right.

Using matrices, you can control a number of attributes, including the width, height, rotation, and translation of these fills and line styles. To simplify this process for you, Adobe added the **createGradientBox()** method to the **Matrix** class. This method allows you to affect all of these properties with a single method call, and accepts these parameters:

```
createGradientBox(width, height, rotation, tx, ty);
```

Let's see how the optional addition of a matrix to the **beginGradientFill()** method improves our gradient, by starting with the simplest use of the **createGradientBox()** method. The following code is derived from the prior radial gradient example and is found in the *radial_gradient_2.fla* source file. We've created a matrix in line 10, and then used the **createGradientBox()** method in line 11 to set the size of the matrix to match the size of the sprite. Finally, we added that matrix to the fill creation in line 12.

```
1    var canvas = new Sprite();
2    addChild(canvas);
3    var g:Graphics = canvas.graphics;
4
5    var gradType:String = GradientType.RADIAL;
6    var colors:Array = [0xFF0000, 0x000000];
7    var alphas:Array = [1, 1];
8    var ratios:Array = [0, 255];
9
10   var matrix:Matrix = new Matrix();
11   matrix.createGradientBox(100, 100, 0);
12   g.beginGradientFill(gradType, colors, alphas, ratios, matrix);
13
14   g.drawRect(0, 0, 100, 100);
```

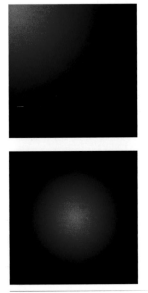

*Figure 8-17. A radial gradient before (top) and after (bottom) matrix transformations*

Figure 8-17 shows the original look of the gradient (top) and its appearance after matching its size to that of the rectangle. After the transformation, the radial gradient is now entirely visible.

By adding translation values to the method, you can also now reposition the center of the gradient. For example, using 30 pixels for **tx** and **ty** would place the epicenter of the gradient in the lower-right corner of the rectangle, demonstrated in the *radial_gradient_3.fla* source file.

```
15   var matrix:Matrix = new Matrix();
16   matrix.createGradientBox(100, 100, 0, 30, 30);
```

To demonstrate the rotation of a gradient, we'll change the script in two small ways. First, we'll switch the gradient type from radial to linear so the rotation is more noticeable (line 5). Then we'll send a rotation value into the `createGradientBox()` method (line 11). The degree-to-radian conversion function rounds out the changes in lines 16 through 18 of the following script. Figure 8-18 shows before and after rotating a linear gradient 90 degrees. This code can be found in the *linear_gradient_matrix.fla* source file.

**NOTE**

*The* linear_gradient_matrix.fla *source file contains additional code to create a second box with a gradient that is not rotated. Comparing the boxes next to each other, as seen in Figure 8-18, will show the effect of the matrix manipulation.*

```
17  var canvas = new Sprite();
18  addChild(canvas);
19  var g:Graphics = canvas.graphics;
20
21  var gradType:String = GradientType.LINEAR;
22  var colors:Array = [0xFF0000, 0x000000];
23  var alphas:Array = [1, 1];
24  var ratios:Array = [0, 255];
25
26  var matrix:Matrix = new Matrix();
27  matrix.createGradientBox(100, 100, deg2rad(90));
28  g.beginGradientFill(gradType, colors, alphas, ratios, matrix);
29
30  g.drawRect(0, 0, 100, 100);
31
32  function deg2rad(deg:Number):Number {
33      return deg * (Math.PI / 180);
34  }
```

Figure 8-18. A linear gradient after (top) and before (bottom) rotation with the Matrix class

## Adjusting gradient line styles

The same matrix adjustment can improve the gradient line style example from earlier in the chapter. The following example, from the *line_style_gradient_matrix.fla* source file, uses the changes indicated in bold to display the full size of the gradient—exposing full red and full black at the left and right sides, respectively. The result appears in Figure 8-19, which can be compared with Figure 8-5 to see the change.

```
1   var canvas:Sprite = new Sprite();
2   addChild(canvas);
3   var g:Graphics = canvas.graphics;
4
5   canvas.x = canvas.y = 10;
6   g.lineStyle(20, 0x000000);
7
8   var gradType:String = GradientType.LINEAR;
9   var colors:Array = [0xFF0000, 0x000000];
10  var alphas:Array = [1, 1];
11  var ratios:Array = [0, 255];
12
13  var matrix:Matrix = new Matrix();
14  matrix.createGradientBox(200, 200, 0);
15
16  g.lineGradientStyle(gradType, colors, alphas, ratios, matrix);
17  g.drawRect(0, 0, 200, 200);
```

## Adjusting bitmap line styles

So far, we've adjusted the size of gradients to improve their appearance in fills and line styles. Now let's look at using a matrix to translate the location of a bitmap line style or fill. When a bitmap tiles, it initially tiles relative to

Figure 8-19. A gradient line style transformed with a matrix to show the full range of colors in the gradient. Compare with Figure 8-5.

*Figure 8-20. Bitmap line style with no transformation matrix*

*Figure 8-21. Bitmap line style corrected with transformation matrix*

a global positioning point. That is, point (0, 0) of your tile won't necessarily line up with point (0, 0) of your object. The following code, found in *line_style_bitmap_tiled_heart.fla*, uses a heart tile to fill a 20-pixel line. The initial result, shown in Figure 8-20, demonstrates what can happen when the tile and object don't initially line up properly.

```
1   var canvas:Sprite = new Sprite();
2   addChild(canvas);
3   var g:Graphics = canvas.graphics;
4
5   canvas.x = canvas.y = 10;
6   g.lineStyle(20, 0x000000);
7
8   g.lineBitmapStyle(new HeartTile(20, 19));
9   g.drawRect(0, 0, 200, 209);
```

However, we can use a matrix to translate the x and y coordinates of the bitmap so that it better matches our shape. The following adjustments appear in the *line_style_bitmap_tiled_heart_matrix.fla* source file. The changes to the previous script add a matrix (line 9), use the **translate()** method to move the bitmap 10 pixels to the left and 9 pixels up, and then apply the matrix when creating the line's bitmap style (line 11). (To prevent this particular tile from showing an extra pixel at the bottom, we also reduced the height of the rectangle. Be prepared to fiddle with your values a bit, to achieve your goal.) The result can be seen in Figure 8-21.

```
10   var matrix:Matrix = new Matrix();
11   matrix.translate(-10, -9);
12
13   g.lineBitmapStyle(new HeartTile(20, 19), matrix);
14   g.drawRect(0, 0, 200, 209);
```

## Gradient Spread Method

For our last word on gradients, let's talk about the available *gradient spread methods*. Using these options, you can control the way a gradient behaves when it fills an area larger than its own dimensions. In Flash Professional's Color panel this feature is called *overflow* (or *flow* in version CS5), but in ActionScript it is called the spread method. The default behavior is *extend* in the Color panel, which is called *pad* in ActionScript—specified by the **SpreadMethod.PAD** constant. This setting continues the last color in the gradient throughout the remaining visible area to which the gradient is applied. This can be seen in all prior figures depicting gradients, as well as in the first illustration of Figure 8-22.

**NOTE**

*The change in nomenclature for the gradient fill spread method was required because overflow and extend both have important separate meanings in ActionScript.*

The other two ActionScript options, `SpreadMethod.REFLECT` and `SpreadMethod.REPEAT`, share the same names and functionality with the Color panel. The former reverses the colors as many times as is needed to occupy the available space filled by the gradient, as if the gradient was held against a mirror. The latter fills the visible area in a similar fashion but starts over at the first color as if tiled. Figure 8-22 shows these effects in the middle and bottom illustrations, respectively.

To control this feature, we must add another optional parameter to the `beginGradientFill()` call. The following code is found in *spread_method.fla*, and is based on the code from the *linear_gradient_matrix.fla* source file. The changes in bold, reflect the gradient. Commented lines are included for testing the pad and repeat options, as well. You can switch the comments to see the varying results.

Remember that a gradient needs to spread only when it is smaller than the canvas it is trying to fill. Therefore, this example reduces the width and height of the gradient using the `createGradientBox()` method to show the effect in action. If both the gradient and rectangle were 100 × 100 pixels, no spreading would occur.

*Figure 8-22. Gradient fill spread method options pad (top), reflect (middle), and repeat (bottom)*

```
1   var canvas:Sprite = new Sprite();
2   addChild(canvas);
3   var g:Graphics = canvas.graphics;
4
5   var gradType:String = GradientType.LINEAR;
6   var colors:Array = [0xFF0000, 0x000000];
7   var alphas:Array = [1, 1];
8   var ratios:Array = [0, 255];
9
10  var matrix:Matrix = new Matrix();
11  matrix.createGradientBox(50, 50, deg2rad(90), 0, 0);
12
13  //var spread:String = SpreadMethod.PAD;
14  var spread:String = SpreadMethod.REFLECT;
15  //var spread:String = SpreadMethod.REPEAT;
16  g.beginGradientFill(gradType, colors, alphas, ratios, matrix,
    spread);
17
18  g.drawRect(0, 0, 100, 100);
19
20  function deg2rad(deg:Number):Number {
21      return deg * (Math.PI / 180);
22  }
```

# 9-Slice Scaling

Scaling vectors is usually a pleasure because the crispness of the vector art isn't lost when it's resized. This is because the vectors are recalculated every time an object is scaled. However, one of the downsides of this default behavior is that certain visual characteristics, such as stroke weight and rounded corners, can become distorted during scaling. This phenomenon can be seen in the top two illustrations of Figure 8-23.

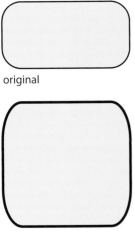

original

scaled with distortion

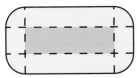

9-slice scaling enabled

scaled without distortion

*Figure 8-23. 9-Slice scaling reduces distortion during scaling*

**NOTE**

*It is possible to slice a display object into a different number of slices by repositioning the slice-defining rectangle, but unpredictable results may occur.*

To reduce distortion caused by scaling in many types of display objects, you can use a feature called *9-slice scaling*. This feature virtually slices a display object into nine pieces and controls scaling of these pieces independently. A typical grid of nine slices can be seen in Figure 8-23, marked with "9-slice scaling enabled." The four corners are not scaled. The top and bottom slices between the corners are scaled only horizontally, the left and right slices between the corners are scaled only vertically, and the center slice is scaled in both directions.

To enable this feature using ActionScript, you must set the corresponding **scale9grid** property to a rectangle that, in essence, defines the object's center slice. ActionScript then extrapolates the corners and perimeter slices by extending the sides of the virtual rectangle. The aforementioned "9-slice scaling enabled" illustration in Figure 8-23 shows this by darkening the center rectangle and outlining the slices with dashed lines. To demonstrate this feature, the following exercise, found in the *scale9.fla* source file, will create a sprite with rounded corners and then scale it using the mouse.

Lines 1 through 9 follow our familiar routine of creating a sprite, drawing vector assets, and positioning and adding the sprite to the display list. However, there's one new twist to this process. The **lineStyle()** method in line 6 contains an optional parameter we haven't discussed. The third parameter tells the method to give the line an alpha value of 100 percent. This parameter was discussed in the Drawing Shapes section of the chapter when we overlapped a 50-percent fill and a 50-percent line. (See the circle in Figure 8-1.) An alpha value of 1 is the default behavior, but we need to include it here to add our fourth parameter. (It's not possible to vary the order in which parameters are supplied to this method, so the first three must be present to use the fourth.)

The fourth parameter enables *stroke hinting*, which aligns strokes along whole pixels, improving legibility. Specifically, this parameter reduces the apparent loss of stroke thickness due to anti-aliasing and improves the look of rounded corners, which is central to this exercise.

```
1    var canvas:Sprite = new Sprite();
2    canvas.x = canvas.y = 50;
3    addChild(canvas);
4
5    var g:Graphics = canvas.graphics;
6    g.lineStyle(1, 0x000000, 1, true);
7    g.beginFill(0xFFFF00, 0.5);
8    g.drawRoundRect(0, 0, 100, 50, 15);
9    g.endFill();
10
11   var slice9rect:Rectangle = new Rectangle(15, 15, 70, 20);
12   canvas.scale9Grid = slice9rect;
13
14   addEventListener(Event.ENTER_FRAME, onLoop, false, 0, true);
15   function onLoop(evt:Event):void {
16       canvas.width = Math.max(mouseX - canvas.x, 30);
17       canvas.height = Math.max(mouseY - canvas.y, 30);
18   }
```

Lines 11 and 12 create a rectangle that is inset from all four sides of the sprite by 15 pixels, and sets the **scale9Grid** property of the sprite to the specified rectangle. An inset of 15 pixels is just enough to ensure that the rounded corners of the rectangle are positioned in the four corners of the grid, thus preventing scaling.

Finally, an event listener calls the **onLoop()** function every enter frame, resizing the sprite based on the mouse location. Lines 16 and 17 set the width and height, respectively, of the sprite to the mouse coordinates minus 50, which are the **x** and **y** values of the sprite assigned in line 2. So, if the mouse is at point (150, 150), the sprite will have a size of 100 × 100.

One new element, introduced in lines 16 and 17, limits how small the rectangle can become. The **max()** method of the **Math** class determines which of the two values provided to it is larger and uses that value. Therefore, if the distance of the mouse from the sprite registration point's x or y value is greater than 30, that value is used. Conversely, if the mouse is closer than 30 pixels to the sprite's registration point, 30 will be used. This allows the rectangle to scale but prevents it from getting any smaller than 30 × 30 pixels.

If you want to see a live comparison between using and not using 9-slice scaling, add the bold lines in the following code to your script, or see the source file, which already includes this code. Every time you click the mouse, the feature toggles between on and off by alternately applying or removing the rectangle to the sprite's **scale9Grid** property.

```
19  //switch between default and 9-slice scaling
20  function onLoop(evt:Event):void {
21      canvas.width = Math.max(mouseX - sp.x, 30);
22      canvas.height = Math.max(mouseY - sp.y, 30);
23  }
24
25  stage.addEventListener(MouseEvent.CLICK, onClick, false, 0, true);
26  function onClick(evt:Event):void {
27      if (canvas.scale9Grid) {
28          canvas.scale9Grid = null;
29      } else {
30          canvas.scale9Grid = slice9rect;
31      }
32  }
```

# Applied Examples

Now let's use much of what we've covered in this chapter in two applied examples. In the first exercise, we'll create the artwork for a basic color picker. Then we'll create a custom button tool that can serve as a lightweight, code-only alternative to components. In both cases, let's build the examples in classes to practice using object-oriented programming.

**NOTE**

*Remember that providing left-, top-, right-, and bottom-edge coordinates does not specify a Flash rectangle. Instead, the x and y coordinates of the upper-left corner, width, and height of the rectangle are specified. So, a rectangle that insets 15 pixels from a 100 × 50-pixel sprite, must start at the sprite's point 15, 15, and have dimensions of 70 × 20 pixels.*

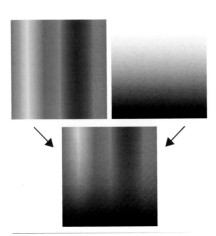

*Figure 8-24. Two layers of the color picker*

# Starting a Color Picker

Let's start by writing a class that will build the display portion of a simple color picker. In the next chapter, we'll show you how to retrieve values from the picker using your mouse. To preview this exercise, test the *color_picker_graphics_example.fla* source file, which simply instantiates the class we're about to discuss, and adds it to the display list.

The picker will contain two separate pieces: a color spectrum in vertical blended stripes, and a transparent-to-black gradient overlay, as seen in Figure 8-24. The overlay will allow you to vary how much black is added to a color.

First we'll create the color spectrum and add it to the display list. Then we'll create the transparent-to-black overlay and add it to the display list. Adding it after the color spectrum gradient will position it on top. Because both sprites will be added to the class, all you need to do is add an instance of the finished class to the display list of your project and your color picker artwork will be self-contained and ready for the functional enhancements planned in Chapter 9.

Now take a look at the following code. Lines 1 through 10 cover the basic syntax found in many classes. Line 1 defines the package, including a package location. This means that the **ColorPickerGraphics** class will be found inside a directory called *color*, which is inside *learningactionscript3*, which is inside *com*.

Lines 3 through 6 import the necessary classes, line 8 defines the class, and line 10 defines the constructor that will be executed immediately when the class is instantiated. Note in line 8 that the class extends **MovieClip**. This means that this class will inherit the public and protected properties and methods found in **MovieClip**. It also means that we can add the class to the display list as if it were a movie clip itself.

Our gradient method requires arrays for colors, alpha values, and color ratios, as previously described. The colors array includes red, yellow, green, cyan, blue, purple, and red again. The alphas array contains a 1 for every color, rendering each step in the gradient at full alpha. The ratios array evenly distributes each color across the 0–255 span, without weighting any one color over another.

The spectrum is next created and added to the display list in lines 18 through 20. The process is then repeated for the overlay. The overlay includes two evenly distributed colors, black at 0 percent alpha, and black at 100 percent alpha (lines 22 through 24). It's then created and added to the display list. We'll explain the calls to **drawGradientBox()**, in lines 18 and 26 when we discuss the method. Review the following code and then we'll look at the method that creates the artwork.

```
1    package com.learningactionscript3.color {
2
3        import flash.display.Sprite;
4        import flash.display.GradientType;
5        import flash.geom.Matrix;
6        import flash.display.Graphics;
7
8        public class ColorPickerGraphics extends Sprite {
9
10           public function ColorPickerGraphics() {
11
12               var colors:Array = [0xFF0000, 0xFFFF00, 0x00FF00,
13                                   0x00FFFF, 0x0000FF, 0xFF00FF,
14                                   0xFF0000];
15               var alphas:Array = [1, 1, 1, 1, 1, 1, 1];
16               var ratios:Array = [0, 42, 84, 126, 168, 210, 255];
17
18               var spectrum:MovieClip = drawGradientBox(100, colors,
19                                                 alphas, ratios);
20               addChild(spectrum);
21
22               colors = [0x000000, 0x000000];
23               alphas = [0, 1];
24               ratios = [0, 255];
25
26               var overlay:Sprite = drawGradientBox(100, colors,
27                                               alphas, ratios,
28                                               deg2rad(90));
29               addChild(overlay);
30           }
```

In addition to the aforementioned arrays, the method also requires a size for the artwork (100 for both components) and, optionally, a rotation (90 degrees, in the case of the overlay, sent to the method in line 28). The rotation value can be omitted from the method call that creates the spectrum (lines 18 and 19), not just because it isn't needed, but also because the `matrixRotation` parameter of the method (line 34) has a default value.

Lines 35 and 36 create a sprite and reference to its graphics property, but the movie clip is not yet added to the display list. Instead, it is returned by the method in line 48 and added to the display list by the constructor, as discussed previously.

Because the gradient data is sent to the method through its parameters, all that remains in lines 38 through 41 is to specify a linear gradient, create the matrix, and modify the matrix with the specified size and rotation, if any. The matrix is then applied using the `createGradientBox()` method (lines 40 and 41), a 1-pixel black line is specified in line 43, and all the gradient values are passed to the `beginGradientFill()` method in lines 44 and 45. Finally, lines 46 through 48 draw the rectangle, close the fill, and return the sprite to the constructor.

**NOTE**

*Because the rotation angle is easier to specify in degrees, the value is converted to radians using the function at the end of the class.*

```
31              //creating the gradient artwork
32              private function drawGradientBox(size:Number, colors:Array,
33                                  alphas:Array, ratios:Array,
34                                  matrixRotation:Number=0):Sprite {
35                  var canvas:Sprite = new Sprite();
36                  var g:Graphics = canvas.graphics;
37
38                  var fill:String = GradientType.LINEAR;
39                  var matrix:Matrix = new Matrix();
40                  matrix.createGradientBox(size, size,
41                                      matrixRotation, 0, 0);
42
43                  g.lineStyle(1, 0x000000);
44                  g.beginGradientFill(fill, colors, alphas,
45                                      ratios, matrix);
46                  g.drawRect(0, 0, size, size);
47                  g.endFill();
48                  return canvas;
49              }
50
51              private function deg2rad(deg:Number):Number {
52                  return deg * (Math.PI/180);
53              }
54          }
55  }
```

To add this first step of our color picker to your project, all you need to do is create an instance of the class and add it to the display list. The source file *color_picker_graphics_example.fla* has already been created for this purpose.

```
import com.learningactionscript3.color.ColorPickerGraphics;

var picker:ColorPickerGraphics = new ColorPickerGraphics();
addChild(picker);
```

Don't forget that this example just demonstrates the dynamic creation of the picker. (No assets—all code!) In the next chapter, we'll show you how to retrieve color values from the picker so you can use it in your own projects.

## A Custom Button Class

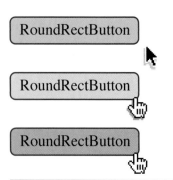

Figure 8-25. A custom button created by the RoundRectButton class

The next applied example is a class that creates functioning buttons entirely with code, and it's based on your work with the **Graphics** class in this chapter. The *RoundRectButton_example.fla* source file shows the class at work. This example introduces two new concepts. The first is the use of the **SimpleButton** class, which allows you to dynamically create traditional buttons that have up, over, down, and hit states, as well as cursor feedback. As such, they will behave just like buttons you create manually on the stage using Flash Professional's drawing and symbol tools. The button's behavior is simulated in Figure 8-25, showing not only cursor feedback in the over and down states (middle and bottom) showing up, over, and down states, but also the use of a brighter color in the over state, and darker color in the down state.

This color change is a result of the other new concepts discussed in this example: the ability to automatically interpolate a color that falls between two given color values. For example, given red and blue, the code will return purple. This is accomplished through the **Color** class, which is part of the **fl.motion** package.

Our custom button class starts with the standard package syntax through line 19, declaring the package, importing classes, and declaring the class and class properties. Note, again, the custom package path. See the introduction to "Starting a Color Picker" earlier in this chapter for more information.

**NOTE**

*As mentioned previously, the* **Color** *class is available to Flash Professional users only. However, we have reproduced the functionality in the* **com.learningactionscript3.color.ColorUtils** *class for users of other ActionScript editors. The sample source code for this chapter includes notes on its use.*

```
1   package com.learningactionscript3.ui {
2
3       import flash.display.Graphics;
4       import flash.display.MovieClip;
5       import flash.display.Shape;
6       import flash.display.SimpleButton;
7       import flash.text.TextField;
8       import flash.text.TextFieldAutoSize;
9       import fl.motion.Color;
10
11      public class RoundRectButton extends MovieClip {
12
13          private var _w:Number;
14          private var _h:Number;
15          private var _rad:Number;
16          private var _linW:Number;
17          private var _col:uint;
18          private var _txt:String;
19          private var _txtCol:uint;
```

The constructor begins with lines 21 through 31, populating the class variables with the parameter values passed in when instantiating the class. These include values for width, height, corner radius, line weight, color, text, and text color. It follows with the creation of a button and text field (both of which we'll discuss in just a moment), and adding both to the display list of the class instance.

```
20          //constructor
21          public function RoundRectButton(w:Number, h:Number,
22                                  rad:Number, linW:Number,
23                                  col:uint, txt:String,
24                                  txtCol:uint){
25              _w = w;
26              _h = h;
27              _rad = rad;
28              _linW = linW;
29              _col = col;
30              _txt = txt;
31              _txtCol = txtCol;
32
33              var btn:SimpleButton = createBtn();
34              addChild(btn);
35              var labl:TextField = createLabel();
36              addChild(labl);
37          }
```

The **createBtn()** method assembles the button using the **SimpleButton** class. The **createBtn()** method calls **createRoundRect()** (reviewed in just a moment) to create a shape that serves as the background for each button state. The latter method requires only one parameter, which is the color used for the background shape.

We determine these colors in lines 40 and 41 using the static method **interpolateColor()** from the **Color** class. Given two colors, the method calculates a color between the two. A third parameter indicates how close to either color the new value should be. For example, if you provided black and white and a weighting of 0.1, the new color would be closer to the first, or a charcoal gray. A weighting of 0.9 would be closer to the second color, or near white.

To create the over-state color (lines 40 through 42), we calculate a value 30 percent between the main button color (visible in the button's up state) and white. To determine the down state color (lines 43 through 45), we calculate a value 30 percent between the main button color and black. Accordingly, the over state is lighter than the up state, and the down state is darker than the up state. After each state is added to the **SimpleButton** instance (lines 47 through 50), the button is returned to the constructor.

> **NOTE**
>
> *Static methods are called from the class, not an instance of the class. As such, the **new** keyword is not used to create an instance before invoking the method.*

```
38        //create all button states
39        private function createBtn():SimpleButton {
40            var ovCol:uint = Color.interpolateColor(_col,
41                                                    0xFFFFFF,
42                                                    0.3);
43            var dnCol:uint = Color.interpolateColor(_col,
44                                                    0x000000,
45                                                    0.3);
46            var btn:SimpleButton = new SimpleButton();
47            btn.upState = createRoundRect(_col);
48            btn.overState = createRoundRect(ovCol);
49            btn.downState = createRoundRect(dnCol);
50            btn.hitTestState = btn.upState;
51            return btn;
52        }
```

The **createRoundRect()** method (lines 54 through 62) presents no new material, but reviews an idea discussed in Chapter 4 about display lists. Notice that the method returns a shape instead of a sprite or movie clip. You can now create shapes with code, an improvement over prior versions of ActionScript. Unlike sprites and movie clips, shapes don't support interactivity like mouse event listeners. However, they do require fewer resources to create. Because these shapes will be used inside a **SimpleButton** instance, which provides all the necessary interactivity, they are well suited for this situation.

```
53          //create background shape for button states
54          private function createRoundRect(col:uint):Shape {
55              var rRect:Shape = new Shape();
56              var g:Graphics = rRect.graphics;
57              g.lineStyle(_linW, _col);
58              g.beginFill(col, 0.5);
59              g.drawRoundRect(0, 0, _w, _h, _rad);
60              g.endFill();
61              return rRect;
62          }
```

Finally, the **createLabel()** method in lines 64 through 74 adds text to the button. Line 65 creates the text field, line 66 sets the width of the field to the width of the button, and line 67 sets the y location to slightly above the midpoint of the button, centering the text vertically. The text is centered horizontally in line 68, and line 69 sets the color of the text to the value passed into the class during instantiation. Finally, the specified button's text is added to the field in line 70, all mouse interaction with the field is disabled in line 71, and the field is returned to the constructor in line 73.

```
63          //create text overlay for button
64          private function createLabel():TextField {
65              var txt:TextField = new TextField();
66              txt.width = _w;
67              txt.y = _h / 2 - 6;
68              txt.autoSize = TextFieldAutoSize.CENTER;
69              txt.textColor = _txtCol;
70              txt.text = _txt;
71              txt.mouseEnabled = false;
72
73              return txt;
74          }
75      }
76  }
```

**NOTE**

*As discussed in prior chapters, disabling mouse interaction with the text field is vital because if this step is omitted, the field will interfere significantly with the operation of the button. The cursor will change to an I-beam text editing cursor, the text will be selectable, and the field will intercept mouse events.*

Using this class is one way to present interface buttons to the user without having to precreate them in the Flash Professional interface. This restricts the ability to use custom artwork for individual buttons but keeps file size to a minimum. This is a simple demonstration, so the class is not very feature-rich when it comes to button styling options. However, that fact presents an ideal opportunity for you to practice what you've learned. Try to improve on this class by drawing specialized button shapes or, perhaps, by offering a choice between circular, rectangular, or rounded button shapes.

> ## learningactionscript3 Package
>
> The project package for this chapter includes ColorUtils, which provides color interpolation and tinting options to those using an ActionScript editor other than Flash Professional. *ColorUtilsExample.fla*, the example file in this chapter's source archive, demonstrates its use. Also included is RoundRectButton, a custom code-only button class, and ColorPickerGraphics, the beginnings of a color picker that we'll expand in Chapter 9. We will make use of one or more of these classes in future chapters to create small exercise files without building custom assets, and to increase your comfort with using classes.

## What's Next?

Manipulating visual assets with ActionScript is one of the most fun and most satisfying ways to learn the language. Drawing vectors does more than minimize file size. It also provides nearly limitless possibilities for creating generative art. Combining data from other corners of the ActionScript world (user input, sound, mathematical calculations, random numbers, and so on) with vectors opens the door to compelling and instructional experiments. Vectors, however, are only half of the puzzle. Flash also provides an impressive range of classes for manipulating pixel-based assets at runtime.

**In the next chapter,** we'll look at working with bitmaps, including:

- Drawing bitmaps at runtime

- Applying blend modes such as lighten, screen, and Flash-specific options

- Using simple filters like drop shadow, bevel, and blur, to enhance assets

- Using complex filter techniques like convolution, color mixing, and displacement maps for special effects

- Encoding custom bitmap data and saving those graphics to your hard drive

## CHAPTER 9

# DRAWING WITH PIXELS

Though largely known for its focus on vector assets, ActionScript also has an impressive arsenal of *bitmap compositing* features—options that work by layering, blending, and filtering pixel-based assets. ActionScript can even take a snapshot of vectors and manipulate the snapshot—behind the scenes with no loss in vector quality—giving you additional compositing options and, in many cases, performance gains.

Although it's unrealistic to expect ActionScript to achieve the feature breadth and depth of a pixel-editing application like Adobe Photoshop, you really can accomplish quite a bit with it. Among others, ActionScript features include a set of blend modes (darken, lighten, multiply, screen, and others that closely resemble Photoshop blend modes), basic filters (like drop shadow, bevel, and blur, akin to Photoshop layer styles), and advanced filter effects (like convolution and displacement mapping, similar to Photoshop filters).

Today, ActionScript 3.0's speed and efficiency make bitmap manipulation practical in more processor-intensive scenarios than ever before. In this chapter, we'll discuss several ways to add pixel pushing to your projects, including:

- **Bitmap Caching.** Moving pixels on screen is a lot more efficient than recalculating the math required to display moving vectors every time a frame renders. Temporarily caching a bitmap representation of a vector asset can reduce this strain and increase performance.

- **The `BitmapData` Class.** Just as you use the `Graphics` class to draw with vectors, you can use the `BitmapData` class to draw with pixels.

- **Blend Modes.** ActionScript can blend assets together to alter the appearance of one or more assets. Included are a standard set of blend modes, which you might find in a typical bitmap editing application, such as Darken, Multiply, Lighten, Screen, and so on. We'll also discuss a few ActionScript-specific blend modes that use transparency to great effect.

- **Bitmap Filters.** Advanced filtering techniques such as blurring, sharpening, embossing, and distorting images can also be applied at runtime. They can even be applied to vector symbol instances, as well as bitmaps, without losing any fidelity or access to vector properties.

- **Color Effects.** ActionScript 3.0 offers a few ways to manipulate color, ranging from applying simple tints to full manipulation of red, green, blue, and alpha channels of bitmap data.

- **Image Encoding.** Bitmap data can even be encoded and saved in an external graphics format like JPG or PNG, using additional ActionScript libraries.

## Bitmap Caching

First, we need to clear up a misconception: manipulating bitmaps in ActionScript does not mean you'll lose all the advantages of crisp, clean vectors. ActionScript offers multiple ways to work with bitmap information, and, as you'll see, vectors and bitmaps can work together well. In fact, using bitmaps judiciously can help you improve the look and performance of your vector animations.

Vector animations can sometimes lag behind comparable bitmap animations because they're much more processor intensive to manipulate. The resources needed to render all the vectors every time an update is required is invariably more demanding than moving and compositing bitmaps.

With that in mind, ActionScript has the capability of *caching*, or temporarily storing, a version of a vector asset as a bitmap. It can then work with the bitmap instead of the original vector until it's no longer optimal to do so. For example, consider a complex vector background over which other vectors are changing. If the background is unchanging, there's no need to redraw the vector background repeatedly. Instead, it's more efficient to work with the changing foreground elements on top of a bitmap. This situation is ideal for bitmap caching, the syntax for which is shown here:

```
displayObject.cacheAsBitmap = true;
```

By setting the **cacheAsBitmap** property to **true**, you can tell Flash Player to create a *surface*, a cosmetically identical bitmap representation of a symbol, to use for display purposes. Viewers won't notice the difference, because the bitmap snapshot of the symbol is always kept current, through any changes, to prevent degradation of image quality. For example, if the symbol is scaled, the original cached bitmap is discarded and a new version is generated.

Because of this automatic updating feature, knowing when, and when not, to use bitmap caching is important. For example, if you're moving several complicated vector assets around the stage, but doing little to alter their appearance, bitmap caching can dramatically improve performance. However, it's usually unwise to enable caching if you'll be scaling, rotating, or changing the opacity of a display object frequently. These operations change the appearance of the display object, and it must be composited again with any surrounding elements. Therefore, a new cache is created each time such a change is made, so making many changes (and therefore caching frequently) in quick succession can slow things down.

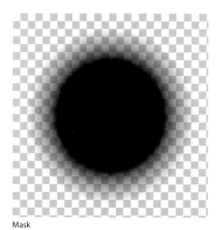
Mask

## Soft-Edged Masks

Optimizing performance isn't the only reason to use `cacheAsBitmap`. Some features require this property to be true in order to function. For example, although you can use ActionScript to assign one display object to mask another, the mask has sharp edges by default because it can't use varying degrees of alpha transparency. That is, any nontransparent pixel, no matter what its alpha value, is considered opaque when added to the mask.

**NOTE**

*A mask is used to reveal a portion of a display object. Only the areas of the display object that overlap with the mask area are visible.*

If you use bitmap caching for both the masker (the display object that will serve as the mask) and maskee (the display object that will be masked), however, ActionScript can composite the two elements as bitmaps. This allows alpha masks to composite semitransparent pixels using their actual alpha values to create a soft edge. Figure 9-1 illustrates this effect. The top image is of the mask itself, showing a soft edge. The middle image is the default appearance of an ActionScript mask, even when the mask contains varying degrees of opacity. The bottom image shows the same mask in use, but this time both the mask and revealed display object have their `cacheAsBitmap` property set to `true`.

Mask applied without bitmap caching

The following code snippet can be found in the *as_mask.fla* source file, which has two movie clips on the stage, with instance names of *maskee* and *masker*.

```
1  masker.cacheAsBitmap = true;
2  maskee.cacheAsBitmap = true;
3  maskee.mask = masker;
```

Mask applied with bitmap caching

*Figure 9-1. The same alpha mask applied without bitmap caching (above) and with bitmap caching (below)*

# The BitmapData Class

The **BitmapData** class is the real workhorse when it comes to ActionScript pixel-based manipulations. As its name implies, an instance of the **BitmapData** class contains not a bitmap, but the pixel color and alpha data that often comprise a bitmap. As with bitmap caching, you need not be confined to working with actual bitmaps to create a bitmap data instance. You can draw bitmap data from scratch or derive it from vector assets just as easily as from bitmap assets. Think of the latter process as working with a screenshot. Whether the display object contains a bitmap or a vector shape is immaterial. You can capture the bitmap data of that object in either case. Let's start by looking at creating bitmap data from scratch and highlighting the difference between bitmap data and a bitmap.

## Creating Opaque Bitmaps

There are two parts to creating a bitmap. One is the bitmap display object, and the other is the bitmap data. The *bitmap display object* is the picture you see on stage, and the *bitmap data* is a detailed description of the number of pixels used, their individual colors and alpha values, and so on. Your ultimate goal may be to display a bitmap, but you may also find it advantageous to work with bitmap data without ever actually displaying the pixels in question! (You'll do just that later in the chapter when we demonstrate using a displacement map.)

In our next example, we want to see the fruit of our labors, so we'll work with both bitmap data and a bitmap. The following script, found in the *bitmap_from_scratch.fla* source file, creates an instance of the **BitmapData** class, creates a bitmap using that data, and adds the bitmap to the display list. Without setting the **x** or **y** property of the bitmap, it appears at (0, 0).

```
1   var bmd:BitmapData = new BitmapData(100, 100, false, 0xFF0000FF);
2   var bm:Bitmap = new Bitmap(bmd);
3   addChild(bm);
```

The first two arguments sent to the **BitmapData** class are the dimensions of the instance (100 × 100 pixels, in this example), and are required. If you intend only to create an empty **BitmapData** instance into which you'll add content later, you need not add the remaining arguments. If you want to add visible pixels to your data instance at this stage, however, you can dictate the transparency and color of the data.

The third parameter tells the class that this instance will not be transparent. The last parameter is the color desired, but it uses a format we haven't discussed previously. Instead of using the familiar 0xRRGGBB format, this class parameter must communicate alpha values, and thus requires the 32-bit 0xAARRGGBB hexadecimal format. This format adds two digits for alpha data at the beginning of the number. Line 1 of this code specifies FF, or full

**NOTE**

*The maximum size of a **BitmapData** object in Flash Player 10 is determined by a combination of total number of pixels and dimensions. It can't exceed 16,777,215 pixels. When creating a bitmap, square dimensions can't exceed 4095 × 4095 pixels, and a single side can't exceed 8,191 pixels. Currently, it's possible to load bitmaps that exceed these side restrictions, as long as the total pixel count doesn't exceed 16,777,215 pixels. This may change in the future. For more information, see http://kb2.adobe.com/cps/496/cpsid_49662.html.*

*Flash Player 9 limits are considerably more restrictive. **BitmapData** instances can't exceed 8,294,400 pixels (2880 × 2880) or 2880 pixels on any side.*

*If you exceed the maximum value in either dimension, in either player version, an instance is not created.*

opacity, and then 0000FF, or blue, for the color. The result of this script is a 100 × 100–pixel, 100-percent opaque, blue square positioned at (0, 0).

## Creating Bitmaps with Transparency

To create a bitmap data object with transparency, you must change the third parameter of the class constructor to **true** and then reduce the opacity of the color value. The first pair of characters in the hexadecimal number (from left to right) represents alpha (AA in the 32-bit format listed previously). The acceptable alpha range is 00 (fully transparent) to FF (fully opaque). For example, the following code, found in the *bitmap_from_scratch_transparency. fla* source file, creates a green square that is 50-percent transparent. The alpha value is 80, or half of the alpha range. The color that follows is then 00FF00, or green, corresponding with the RRGGBB format.

```
1  var bmd:BitmapData = new BitmapData(100, 100, true, 0x8000FF00);
2  var bm:Bitmap = new Bitmap(bmd);
3  addChild(bm);
```

## Using a Bitmap from the Library

If you need to work with an actual bitmap image, rather than originating your own **BitmapData** object, you can add an imported bitmap dynamically from the library. You can use the *bitmap_from_library.fla* file from the accompanying source code for this exercise, or use your own image. You must have an image already imported into the library and have given it a class name in the Linkage Properties dialog.

In our sample source file, a 550 × 400–pixel image of penguins has been given the linkage class name **Penguins**. Discussed briefly in Chapter 8, the base class for a library bitmap is **BitmapData**. This allows you to easily access the data without requiring that you first create an instance of the **Bitmap**. If you want to display a bitmap, objects for both **BitmapData** and **Bitmap** must be created.

The following three lines, found in the *bitmap_from_library.fla* source file, create both objects, and add the bitmap to the display list.

```
1  var penguinsBmd:BitmapData = new Penguins(550, 400);
2  var penguinsBm:Bitmap = new Bitmap(penguinsBmd);
3  addChild(penguinsBm);
```

In the section "Creating Opaque Bitmaps" earlier in this chapter, we said that the first two parameters of the **BitmapData** constructor, width and height, are required. This makes sense when you're creating bitmap data from scratch, but is a bit inconsistent when instantiating a bitmap from the library. Thinking about your past experience with creating movie clips and text fields, for example, it may be more intuitive to try this:

```
var penguinsBmd:BitmapData = new Penguins();
```

**NOTE**

*The hexadecimal value 0x80 is equivalent to 128, or half of the 0–255 range for red, blue, green, and alpha channels of a color.*

**NOTE**

*When adding a linkage class name to a symbol, you needn't actually create a class file first. The compiler will create an internal placeholder for you, which will automatically be replaced by an actual class should you later decide to create one. For more information, see the "Adding Custom Symbol Instances to the Display List" section of Chapter 4.*

**NOTE**

*Loading a bitmap from an external source is discussed in Chapter 13.*

**NOTE**

*Typing your bitmap data instance as* **BitmapData**, *rather than the linkage class name (***Penguins**, *in this case) is more flexible because any bitmap data can be put into the variable. However, if you want your data type checking to be stricter, you can type to the linkage class name, instead:*

```
var penguinsBmd:Penguins = new
    Penguins(550, 400);
```

*This will restrict the variable to accepting only the* **Penguins** *data.*

However, in earlier versions of most ActionScript editors, including Flash Professional CS3 and CS4, this will cause the compiler to generate the error: *Incorrect number of arguments. Expected 2*. This behavior has been improved in Flash Professional CS5, which will no longer issue this error, allowing you to create a **BitmapData** instance from a library bitmap in a manner consistent with the instantiation of many other objects.

Fortunately for users of older ActionScript compilers, the exact width and height values are not required when using a preexisting bitmap (as in the preceding penguins example). The **BitmapData** class will update these values and the data will be placed into the instance variable without scaling. If you're uncertain about the dimensions of the bitmap you want to instantiate, just use (0, 0).

## Copying Pixels

In the previous example, you populated an instance of the **BitmapData** class with a bitmap. But what if you want to work with only a portion of a bitmap? You can simply copy pixels from one **BitmapData** instance to another. The exercise that follows uses the **copyPixels()** method to create a new penguin bitmap by copying a segment from another bitmap. The method is called from a new **BitmapData** instance (into which you're copying) and requires three parameters: the source object, a rectangle defining the pixels to be copied, and the destination point in the new object to which the pixels should be copied.

The following code is found in the *copy_pixels_stage_click.fla* source file. Lines 1 through 3 create the original penguin bitmap, as seen in the prior example. Line 4 adds a listener to the stage to call the **onClick()** function when the mouse is clicked. This is where the pixel copying takes place, which we'll explain after the code.

```
1   var penguinsBmd:BitmapData = new Penguins(550, 400);
2   var penguinsBm:Bitmap = new Bitmap(penguinsBmd);
3   addChild(penguinsBm);
4   stage.addEventListener(MouseEvent.CLICK, onClick, false, 0, true);
5
6   function onClick(evt:MouseEvent):void {
7       var rect:Rectangle = new Rectangle(290, 196, 95, 170);
8       var penguinCopyBmd:BitmapData = new BitmapData(95, 170);
9       penguinCopyBmd.copyPixels(penguinsBmd, rect, new Point());
10
11      var penguinCopyBm:Bitmap = new Bitmap(penguinCopyBmd);
12      penguinCopyBm.x = 385;
13      penguinCopyBm.y = 196;
14      addChild(penguinCopyBm);
15  }
```

*Figure 9-2. A detail of the source image with the area to be copied marked in red*

Line 7 defines the rectangle required to specify the area you want to copy. The **Rectangle** class requires the rectangle's x and y location, and width and height. Figure 9-2 shows these values in a detail of the source material. We want to reference the area outlined in red, which is 95 × 170, but begins at (290, 196) from the upper-left corner of the bitmap.

Line 8 creates a new **BitmapData** instance the size of the desired rectangle. Line 9 concludes the copy process by copying the pixels into the new **BitmapData** instance, using the original source (*penguinsBmd*), the area to be copied (*rect*), and the destination for the copied pixels. We want to copy the pixels into a new bitmap, so for the last parameter, we just use a default **Point** instance to copy into (0, 0) of the new bitmap.

Finally, lines 11 through 14 create a new bitmap from the copied pixels, position it next to the original penguin, and add the new bitmap to the display list so it appears atop the original. The result is seen in detail view in Figure 9-3.

By design, this exercise demonstrates that not all display objects are interactive. The preceding code attached the mouse listener to the stage because we can't attach a listener to a bitmap.

If you want a bitmap to serve as a button, however, you can place the bitmap into an interactive display object, such as a sprite. In the code excerpt that follows, found in the *copy_pixels_sprite_click.fla* source file, note that the step to add the bitmap to the stage, and the stage listener (lines 3 and 4 from the preceding script), have both been removed. In their place (indicated by the bold code), the bitmap is placed inside a new sprite and a listener is attached to that sprite, rather than the stage.

```
16   var penguinsBmd:BitmapData = new Penguins(550, 400);
17   var penguinsBm:Bitmap = new Bitmap(penguinsBmd);
18   var sp:Sprite = new Sprite();
19   sp.addChild(penguinsBm);
20   addChild(sp);
21   sp.addEventListener(MouseEvent.CLICK, onClick, false, 0, true);
```

## Drawing into a Bitmap

Sometimes it's simpler to draw the entire contents of a bitmap data source into another, rather than copying pixels. For example, this is often true when you want to draw into a bitmap repeatedly or build bitmaps from multiple sources. Let's demonstrate this by actually painting on a canvas. In the *paint_tool.fla* source file, we'll create two simple, one-color circular brushes and the user will be able to switch between them by pressing the Shift key. In this section, we'll match the color of one brush to the color of the canvas for a simple eraser effect. Figure 9-4 shows an example of a painted area with a swatch of color "erased" in the middle.

The no-interface functionality of this simple example calls for a dual role for the mouse—both painting and erasing. So we'll start the following script by declaring a Boolean variable to track the mouse state. We then create an empty canvas to hold our bitmap painting and add it to the display list (lines 3 and 4). Lines 6 through 10 prepare the drawing surface by creating an empty white **BitmapData** object the size of the stage, populating a bitmap with that data, and adding the bitmap to the canvas sprite. Each time the bitmap data is updated, the display bitmap will reflect the change.

**NOTE**

*For more information about the* **Rectangle** *or* **Point** *classes, see Chapter 7.*

**Figure 9-3.** *A detail of the SWF after the pixels have been copied*

**Figure 9-4.** *A detail of drawing into a BitmapData object with brush and eraser*

**NOTE**

*In the next section, we'll use a blend mode to add true eraser functionality to this basic drawing application.*

```
1    var mouseIsDown:Boolean;
2
3    var canvas:Sprite = new Sprite();
4    addChild(canvas);
5
6    var w:Number = stage.stageWidth;
7    var h:Number = stage.stageHeight;
8    var bmd:BitmapData = new BitmapData(w, h, false, 0xFFFFFFFF);
9    var bm:Bitmap = new Bitmap(bmd);
10   canvas.addChild(bm);
11
12   var brush:Sprite = createBrush(0x000099);
13   var eraser:Sprite = createBrush(0xFFFFFF);
14   var tool:Sprite = brush;
15
16   function createBrush(col:uint):Sprite {
17       var sp:Sprite = new Sprite();
18       sp.graphics.beginFill(col);
19       sp.graphics.drawCircle(0, 0, 20);
20       sp.graphics.endFill();
21       return sp;
22   }
```

**NOTE**

*In this painting example, note that neither brush nor eraser is added to the display list. A display object does not need to be in the display list to draw it into a bitmap data instance.*

Lines 12 through 22 finish the tool setup by creating a brush and an eraser. Both tools are created by the same function, each passing in a different color; blue for the brush and white for the eraser. The **createBrush()** function returns a new sprite with an opaque circle of the color requested, with a 20-pixel radius. Line 14 initializes the tool's default state to using the brush, rather than eraser.

In the next script segment, a trio of listeners controls the brush/eraser functionality. The mouse down event listener function (lines 30 through 37) first sets the **mouseIsDown** Boolean to **true** so the app will know to alter the canvas. Then in line 32, a conditional checks to see if the **shiftKey** property of the incoming mouse event is **true**, indicative of whether the user is holding down the Shift key when the mouse is clicked. If so, the **tool** variable is set to **eraser**. Otherwise, **tool** is set to **brush**. The mouse up listener (lines 39 through 41) resets **mouseIsDown** to **false**, as the user is neither painting nor erasing. This combination of listeners toggles the paint/erase functionality with every mouse click.

The enter frame listener function, **onLoop()** (lines 43 through 49), starts by placing the tool at the mouse location so the user is ready to draw or erase. It then uses a conditional to determine whether the mouse is down. If so, the appropriate tool is drawn into the **BitmapData** instance used by the canvas. We'll talk about the matrix used by the second parameter of the **draw()** method after the code.

```
23   canvas.addEventListener(MouseEvent.MOUSE_DOWN, onDown,
24                         false, 0, true);
25   canvas.addEventListener(MouseEvent.MOUSE_UP, onUp,
26                         false, 0, true);
27   canvas.addEventListener(Event.ENTER_FRAME, onLoop,
28                         false, 0, true);
29
```

```
30  function onDown(evt:MouseEvent):void {
31      mouseIsDown = true;
32      if (evt.shiftKey) {
33          tool = eraser;
34      } else {
35          tool = brush;
36      }
37  }
38
39  function onUp(evt:MouseEvent):void {
40      mouseIsDown = false;
41  }
42
43  function onLoop(evt:Event):void {
44      tool.x = mouseX;
45      tool.y = mouseY;
46      if (mouseIsDown) {
47          bmd.draw(tool, tool.transform.matrix);
48      }
49  }
```

In line 47, we added a second argument to the **draw()** method: a matrix used to transform the pixels drawn.

By default, no transformations of the source or destination **BitmapData** instances are performed by the **draw()** method. The resulting effect is that the bitmap data from the source object at point (0, 0) will be drawn into the canvas at point (0, 0). That wouldn't make a very interesting painting program because changes would only appear at x, y coordinate point (0, 0) in the canvas.

For this exercise, therefore, we can't merely copy the tool bitmap data; we also need the location of the brush (or eraser) relative to point (0, 0). The second parameter of the **draw()** method is designed to process any such changes by using a matrix. In this case, we care about the translation values for x and y, meaning the degree to which the x and y values of the source differ from (0, 0). Using the matrix, pixel data that was offset from the origin of the source **BitmapData** instance will be drawn into the destination source **BitmapData** instance using the same offset from its origin. The **tx** and **ty** values of the matrix will be updated when the **x** and **y** values of the tool are changed with the mouse movement. In other words, if the brush is used at (100, 100), it will be drawn into the canvas at (100, 100).

**NOTE**

*For more information about matrices, see Chapter 7.*

## Blend Modes

Not every bitmap manipulation requires building **BitmapData** objects from the ground up. Sometimes you may need to just apply a quick effect—to bitmaps and vectors alike—to get the result you want. One of the most basic, yet very useful, effects you can apply is a *blend mode*—a means of blending two or more sets of visual data to create a unique appearance. ActionScript supports a set of these compositing behaviors similar to the blending modes used in Adobe Photoshop (in the Layers panel, for instance). Though ActionScript's set of blend modes is understandably smaller than Photoshop's, many of the most widely used modes (such as Darken, Multiply, Lighten, Screen, Overlay, and Hard Light) are available.

The syntax required to apply a blend mode to a display object or `BitmapData` object is very simple. The object's `blendMode` property is set to one of the blend mode values, typically via a constant of the `BlendMode` class that identifies each mode by name. Here's an example:

```
dispObj.blendMode = BlendMode.DARKEN;
```

Let's take a look at a practical example that combines a couple of blend modes. One of the modes used is Darken, which preserves the darker value of each of the red, green, and blue color components of every overlapping (foreground and background) pixel. This mode is typically used for removing a light background in an overlapping image. Figure 9-5 shows a bitmap of the word Waikiki, on a white background, overlapping a blue sky. When a Darken blend mode is applied to the overlaying image, the white will drop out because the underlying blue sky in the bottom image is darker.

*Figure 9-5. Two overlapping images (word and photo) prior to the use of blend modes*

The second mode used in this example is Overlay, which adjusts the compositing method of the foreground element dynamically, based on the darkness of the background. If the background is lighter than 50 percent gray, the elements are screened, resulting in a bleaching effect. If the background is darker than 50 percent gray, the elements are multiplied, resulting in a darkening effect.

Figure 9-6 shows the resulting effect of the Darken blend mode applied to the "Waikiki" image, and the Overlay blend mode applied to an orange gradient, which turns reddish after blending with the blue sky. The gradient alters the color of the blue sky to hint at the color-rich sunsets typical of tropical areas.

*Figure 9-6. The finished composition with the Darken blend mode applied to the word, and the Overlay blend mode applied to a red gradient*

The code for this example is found in the *blend_modes_darken_overlay.fla* source file. The FLA contains the bitmaps shown in Figure 9-5, with linkage classes **Beach** and **Waikiki**.

Lines 1 through 3 of this script review the process of adding library bitmap symbols to the display list, described earlier in this chapter. The beach image is the first to be added to the stage. Lines 5 through 16 review the steps required to create a gradient fill, as described in Chapter 8. This fill is linear, evenly distributed with an orange color from 100-percent opaque to 100-percent transparent, measures 310 × 110 pixels, and is rotated 90 degrees. The rotation is specified in degrees and converted to radians, thanks to the conversion function in lines 24 through 26.

The blend modes are applied in lines 14 and 21. The *canvas* sprite, into which the gradient is drawn, is assigned the Overlay mode, changing a harsh orange gradient to a simulated sun-saturated skyline, in which the orange is applied based on the darkness of the clouds and the sky. The text is assigned the Darken mode, so only the word "Waikiki" remains visible after compositing, the white background having dropped out because white is lighter than all red, green, and blue color components of the background.

```
1   var beachBmd:BitmapData = new Beach(310, 256);
2   var beach:Bitmap = new Bitmap(beachBmd);
3   addChild(beach);
4
5   var gradType:String = GradientType.LINEAR;
6   var matrix:Matrix = new Matrix();
7   matrix.createGradientBox(310, 110, deg2rad(90), 0, 0);
8   var colors:Array = [0xFF6600, 0xFF6600];
9   var alphas:Array = [1, 0];
10  var ratios:Array = [0, 255];
11  var canvas = new Sprite();
12  canvas.graphics.beginGradientFill(gradType, colors, alphas,
13                                    ratios, matrix);
14  canvas.graphics.drawRect(0, 0, 310, 110);
15  canvas.blendMode = BlendMode.OVERLAY;
16  addChild(canvas);
17
18  var waikikiBmd:BitmapData = new Waikiki(310, 76);
19  var waikiki:Bitmap = new Bitmap(waikikiBmd);
20  addChild(waikiki);
21  waikiki.blendMode = BlendMode.DARKEN;
22  waikiki.y = 10;
23
24  function deg2rad(deg:Number):Number {
25      return deg * (Math.PI / 180);
26  }
```

## ActionScript Compositing Blend Modes

Even if you only glance at Figure 9-6, you'll probably recognize the effects of these traditional blend modes. However, we'd like to call your attention to three ActionScript-specific blend modes that aren't as easy to grasp: Layer, Alpha, and Erase.

### Layer

Layer is an extremely useful and welcome problem solver. In brief, Layer creates a transparency group for a display object container. It precomposes any contents of the container into a virtual layer so that an effect applied to the container will alter the container as a whole, rather than altering each individual element. This can be made clearer by demonstrating this effect.

The top of Figure 9-7 shows a movie clip that contains three additional movie clips: two adjacent squares, red and blue, and a green square of the same dimensions centered on top of the underlying red and blue squares. If you were to apply a 50-percent alpha value to the parent movie clip, you might expect the parent movie clip opacity to be reduced by 50 percent, producing a lighter version of exactly what you saw on the stage. Unfortunately, ActionScript effectively goes into the parent clip and applies a 50-percent alpha reduction to each of the children individually.

container 100% opacity; no blend mode

container 50% opacity; no blend mode

container 50% opacity; Layer blend mode

*Figure 9-7. Original (top), default 50% opacity (middle), and 50% opacity after applying the Layer blend mode (bottom)*

*Figure 9-8. The Alpha (above) and Erase (below) blend modes*

The result, shown in the middle of Figure 9-7, is what you'd expect to see when applying a 50-percent alpha value to each square. However, when you want the entire container to fade, the default behavior produces an unpleasant effect. Because each of the squares is partially transparent, their colors blend, creating four bands. Left to right, the first is 50-percent red, the second is 50-percent green overlapping 50-percent red, the third is 50-percent green overlapping 50-percent blue, and the fourth is 50-percent blue.

When applying the Layer blend mode, however, the children of the parent movie clip are composited together as a single item and the alpha value is correctly applied to the container, not separately to each child within. As a result, you see the expected appearance of the original three colors all at 50 percent, as seen in the bottom of Figure 9-7.

**NOTE**

*The blend_mode_layer.fla source file includes an interactive example toggling the application of the Layer blend mode to the three color boxes, as seen in Figure 9-7.*

## Alpha and Erase

Layer mode also facilitates the use of two more blend modes, Alpha and Erase. The functionality of each is straightforward. Given a foreground display object with alpha data, such as a movie clip with a partially transparent PNG inside, the two modes behave this way: Alpha knocks out a background element using the foreground element's alpha channel, and Erase does the opposite, knocking out the background using the nontransparent pixel data of the foreground element. The effects of each can be seen in Figure 9-8. The overlying image is an opaque star on a transparent background. The white areas are actually missing from the underlying image, showing the stage beneath.

The important item to note, however, is that these effects work only when applied to display objects that are inside a display object container (such as a movie clip) and only when the Layer blend mode is applied to the container. The child elements must be composited together first for the effect to be visible.

In other words, if you used the same movie clip with semitransparent star PNG therein, and placed it on top of the same background beach image on the stage (rather than inside a movie clip), the beach image would not be affected even if the Alpha or Erase blend modes were applied to the star. Instead, it would cause the foreground element to disappear altogether.

**NOTE**

*Push Yourself: Try to apply what you've learned and create a dynamic version of the example described in the "Alpha and Erase" section of this chapter. The blend_mode_alpha_erase_assets.fla source file contains the beach and star images. After giving this a try, look at the blend_mode_alpha_erase.fla source file. It includes an interactive example toggling the Alpha and Erase blend modes shown in Figure 9-8.*

## Using Blend Modes with BitmapData Instances

Blend modes can also modify other ActionScript objects, including instances of the **BitmapData** class. Earlier, we created a drawing program that used brush and eraser tools to paint on a canvas. In that simple example, the eraser tool was nothing more than a brush set to the color of the canvas, giving the illusion of erasing what you painted.

However, the **draw()** method used in that example takes, as its fourth argument, a blend mode, and we can use the Erase blend mode to erase brush-strokes instead of paint over them. Remember that the Erase blend mode uses the foreground content to erase the background content. In the example paint program, this means it will use the eraser tool pixels to erase the bitmap data of the canvas.

The following modification to the earlier example is found in the *paint_tool_erase.fla* source file. All we have to do is replace the use of the single **draw()** method in the prior script, at line 44, with a conditional statement. The conditional checks to see if the current tool is the brush. If so, it uses the same code as the previous example, drawing into the canvas bitmap data without using a blend mode (line 45). However, if the current tool is not the brush (which means the user is erasing content) the modified **draw()** method is used, with the Erase blend mode (lines 47 and 48).

```
1   function onLoop(evt:Event):void {
2       tool.x = mouseX;
3       tool.y = mouseY;
4       if (mouseIsDown) {
5           if (tool == brush) {
6               bmd.draw(tool, tool.transform.matrix);
7           } else {
8               bmd.draw(tool, tool.transform.matrix, null,
9                       BlendMode.ERASE);
10          }
11      }
12  }
```

**NOTE**

*The third parameter of the* **draw()** *method is used to transform the color of the bitmap data, which is not a part of this example. However, to use the fourth parameter, arguments for the first three parameters must be provided. The first is mandatory, and is the* **BitmapData** *instance we're drawing. The second is optional, and is the transform matrix we're using. The third is a* **colorTransform** *instance, which we aren't using. In its place, we send in the parameter's default value,* **null**. *Supplying these three values then allows us to provide the fourth value, our blend mode.*

# Bitmap Filters

Filters have been a mainstay of graphics editing programs for years, adding special effects to images and illustrations with a minimum of effort. ActionScript has a number of filters for your number-crunching manipulation. Although there are no official classifications for filters, we've divided the filters we discuss into two sections: basic and advanced. Using Adobe Photoshop for comparison, basic filters are like Layer Styles—quick, easy-to-apply effects with limited functionality—and advanced filters are more robust and are more like the features found in Photoshop's Filters menu.

**NOTE**

*There's no class in the* `flash.filters` *package for the Adjust Color filter found in Flash Professional's Properties panel. However, Flash Professional users can use the* `AdjustColor` *class found in the* `fl.motion` *package. If you're not using Flash Professional, advanced filter classes that appear a little bit later in the chapter can mimic Adjust Color's filter results.*

*Figure 9-9. An interactive element with* **DropShadowFilter** *applied (above) and removed (below) to simulate the pressing of a raised button*

# Basic Filters

A good place to start when learning how to control filter effects with code is with a subset of filters found both in Flash Professional's Properties panel and in their own ActionScript classes. These filters include DropShadow, Blur, Glow, Bevel, GradientGlow, and GradientBevel. This convenient overlap lets you play around with Flash Professional's interface to see how various properties affect the appearance of the filter. You can then apply that understanding to your code settings later on. The advantages to using ActionScript over the Flash Professional interface include the ability to apply changes dynamically at runtime and reuse your code more easily.

For the most part, the properties of the ActionScript filter classes correlate closely with the properties found in the Properties panel for the same filter, providing a smooth transition to ActionScript without much effort. Let's use the `DropShadowFilter` class in the next example, to create button artwork without custom graphics.

## Creating dynamic button art with the DropShadowFilter

The following script, found in the *drop_shadow_button.fla* source file, simulates a two-state button by using a drop shadow. At rest, the button has a small drop shadow, but when a user clicks the button, the drop shadow is removed as if the button is being pressed down to the screen. This effect is shown in Figure 9-9.

The script begins by creating the drop shadow filter. Once created, it can be applied to objects at any time. An instance of the aptly named class is created in line 1. Individual properties are then set in lines 2 through 4. In this case, the degree of blur in the x and y directions is set to 10, and the opacity of the shadow is set to 60 percent. Other properties, including the angle of the shadow and its distance offset from the display object, use their default values.

Lines 6 through 11 use the `Graphics` class discussed in Chapter 8 to create a basic, yellow rectangle with rounded corners and add it to the display list. Line 13 is where the shadow is applied. The display object property, `filters`, accepts an array of filter instances so that more than one filter can be applied. In this example, only `DropShadowFilter` is used so only the `ds` filter instance is placed into the array. At this point, the application of the filter is complete, and the sprite is added to the display list in line 14. However, this example changes with mouse interaction, so let's look at its interactive elements in the next code block.

```
1    var ds:DropShadowFilter = new DropShadowFilter();
2    ds.blurX = 10;
3    ds.blurY = 10;
4    ds.alpha = 0.6;
5
6    var sp:Sprite = new Sprite();
7    var g:Graphics = sp.graphics;
8    g.lineStyle(1, 0x000000);
```

```
 9   g.beginFill(0xFFFF00, 1);
10   g.drawRoundRect(0, 0, 200, 50, 20);
11   g.endFill();
12
13   sp.filters = [ds];
14   addChild(sp);
```

Because we went the simple route of using a sprite for our interactive element (rather than building a multistate button with the **SimpleButton** class, as seen in the applied example at the end of Chapter 8), we need to set the **buttonMode** property of the sprite to **true** in line 15. This won't create the up, over, and down states of a button symbol, but it will provide visual feedback by changing the cursor to the hand cursor when over the sprite.

The listeners in lines 16 through 18 trigger functions based on mouse behavior. The mouse down listener function, **onDown()** (lines 20 to 22) removes the drop shadow effect from the sprite by clearing the **filters** array. Both the mouse up and mouse out listeners point to the **onUp()** function in lines 23 to 25, which repopulates the **filters** array with the drop shadow. This restores the elevated "up" appearance to the sprite.

**NOTE**

*For information about creating arrays with bracket syntax ([]), see Chapter 2.*

```
15   sp.buttonMode = true;
16   sp.addEventListener(MouseEvent.MOUSE_DOWN, onDown, false, 0, true);
17   sp.addEventListener(MouseEvent.MOUSE_UP, onUp, false, 0, true);
18   sp.addEventListener(MouseEvent.MOUSE_OUT, onUp, false, 0, true);
19
20   function onDown(evt:MouseEvent):void {
21       sp.filters = [];
22   }
23   function onUp(evt:MouseEvent):void {
24       sp.filters = [ds];
25   }
```

Another way to handle this task would be to leave the **ds** filter active, but change some of its properties. For example, rather than eliminating the shadow, you could reduce its distance value when the button is pressed. When the shadow appears closer to the object, the object's virtual elevation appears to be reduced.

**NOTE**

*Filters can be used in creative ways. If you wanted to simulate casting a shadow from a moving light source, you could vary the distance, angle, and alpha values of the **DropShadowFilter**. See the "Animating Filters" post at the companion website, http://www. LearningActionScript3.com, for more information.*

## Using the BlurFilter to create an airbrush

With just a couple of lines of additional code, you can turn the brush from the drawing tool developed previously in this chapter into an airbrush. The following ActionScript excerpt shows new code in bold, and can be found in the *paint_tool_erase_blur.fla* source file. The first new line (30) creates an instance of the **BlurFilter** that blurs 40 pixels in the x and y direction. The second new line (39) applies the filter to the current tool. Figure 9-10 shows the result of softening the brush and eraser with these modifications.

```
26   canvas.addEventListener(MouseEvent.MOUSE_DOWN,
27                           onDown, false, 0, true);
28   canvas.addEventListener(MouseEvent.MOUSE_UP, onUp,
29                           false, 0, true);
30   canvas.addEventListener(Event.ENTER_FRAME, onLoop,
31                           false, 0, true);
```

```
32
33  var blur:BlurFilter = new BlurFilter(40, 40);
34
35  function onDown(evt:MouseEvent):void {
36      mouseIsDown = true;
37      if (evt.shiftKey) {
38          tool = eraser;
39      } else {
40          tool = brush;
41      }
42      tool.filters = [blur];
43  }
```

*Figure 9-10. A Blur filter applied to the drawing tool in the ongoing paint application*

## Advanced Filters

A number of more advanced ActionScript filters allow you to mimic some of the special effects features in pixel-editing applications like Photoshop. We'll focus on the convolution, displacement map, and Perlin noise filters in this section, and then group a trio of color filters together in the following section.

### Convolution filter

Convolution filtering is typically a part of many visual effects in most, if not all, pixel-editing applications. Photoshop offers direct access to a convolution filter (renamed to *Custom* some years ago, and found in the Filters→Other menu), but usually the filter works quietly behind the scenes.

Put simply, a convolution filter calculates pixel color values by combining color values from adjacent pixels. Combining these colors in different ways (using different values in the matrix) produces a wide variety of image effects. These effects include, but are not limited to, blurring, sharpening, embossing, edge detection, and brightness.

Using the filter effectively requires at least a working knowledge of matrices so, if you haven't read Chapter 8, do so now. Although still a matrix, visualized as a grid of numbers, the **ConvolutionFilter** doesn't use the same matrix format discussed in Chapter 8. Instead, you can define any number of rows and columns in a convolution matrix, and the structure of the matrix determines how each pixel is affected.

Unless you plan to delve deeply into writing your own filters, you probably don't need to learn the algorithms behind how a convolution matrix works. In most circumstances, you'll use an existing matrix for a specific effect and use experimentation to determine a satisfactory setting.

To give your experimenting some focus, let's look at three parts of the matrix: the center grid element, the grid symmetry, and the sum of all grid elements. Consider a 3 × 3 matrix. The center value in the matrix represents the current pixel (all pixels in an image are analyzed), while the remaining elements are the eight adjacent pixels. The numbers in each matrix position determine how the color values of that pixel affect the current pixel. The basic idea is that each of the nine pixels is given a weight, or importance, that affects how they are altered.

Blur

Brightness

Edges

Emboss

Original

Sharpen

*Figure 9-11. Example convolution filter effects*

A convolution matrix of all zeros will turn an image black because no color values are used for *any* pixel, including the current pixel in the center of the grid. Using a 1 in the center of an all-zero grid won't change the image because the current pixel is unchanged (default value of 1), and no color values from surrounding pixels are used. Placing a 2 in the center of an all-zero grid will brighten the image because no colors from surrounding pixels are used, but the weight of the color values of the current pixel are increased.

The `ConvolutionFilter` constructor appearing on line 8, 14, and 20 in the following code example requires two parameters, the number of rows and the number of columns. A third, optional parameter is the matrix used to affect the image. If no matrix is furnished a default (no change) matrix is used. Applying a default matrix allows you to remove any changes made by prior convolution filters, as seen in the event listener that follows. This code is found in the *convolution_filter_basics.fla* source file.

```
1    var black:ConvolutionFilter;
2    var noChange:ConvolutionFilter;
3    var brightness:ConvolutionFilter;
4
5    var blackArr:Array = [0, 0, 0,
6                          0, 0, 0,
7                          0, 0, 0];
8    black = new ConvolutionFilter(3, 3, blackArr);
9    mc0.filters = [black];
10
```

```
11   var noChangeArr:Array = [0, 0, 0,
12                            0, 1, 0,
13                            0, 0, 0];
14   noChange = new ConvolutionFilter(3, 3, noChangeArr);
15   mc1.filters = [noChange];
16
17   var brightnessArr:Array = [0, 0, 0,
18                              0, 2, 0,
19                              0, 0, 0];
20   brightness = new ConvolutionFilter(3, 3, brightnessArr);
21   mc2.filters = [brightness];
22
23   stage.addEventListener(MouseEvent.CLICK, onClick,
24                          false, 0, true);
25
26   function onClick(evt:MouseEvent):void {
27       for (var i:int = 0; i < 3; i++) {
28           var mc:MovieClip = MovieClip(getChildAt(i));
29           mc.filters = [noChange];
30       }
31   }
```

Now let's focus on the symmetry of the surrounding grid elements. The remainder of the code in this section is found in the *convolution_filter_more. fla* source file, and demonstrates centralizing the filter creation into a function called **convFilter()** to reduce repeating code. The function appears at the end of the discussion so you can focus on the matrices we're discussing.

The **embossUp** example uses reduced values for the three pixels to the upper left of the current pixel, and increased values for the three pixels to the lower right of the current pixel. The result is a traditional embossing effect (see Figure 9-11). By contrast, the **embossDown** example reverses this effect, seemingly stamping into the image.

```
32   var embossUp:Array = [-1, -1, 0,
33                         -1,  1, 1,
34                          0,  1, 1];
35   convFilter(mc0, embossUp);
36
37   var embossDown:Array = [1,  1,  0,
38                           1,  1, -1,
39                           0, -1, -1];
40   convFilter(mc1, embossDown);
```

As our third area of interest, we want to focus on the fact that overall image brightness is affected by the sum of all elements in the matrix. In each of the prior examples, all the matrix elements add up to 1, except *brighter* (which adds up to 2) and *black* (which adds up to 0). The following example is a matrix that uses the left, top, right, and bottom adjacent pixel color values to affect the current pixel. The result is a blurring effect. However, a dramatic brightening of the image occurs because the sum of the matrix elements is 5, not 1. The affected image is five times brighter.

If this is not desired, you can compensate by using an optional fourth parameter of the **ConvolutionFilter** class, called a *divisor*. The sum of the matrix will be divided by this value and the result will affect the brightness. If the result is 1, the brightening effect of the matrix will be eliminated. The first filter instance here uses only the first three parameters without compensating for brightness. The second instance adds the divisor as the fourth parameter, bringing the brightness back to the original state, leaving only the blur effect.

```
41  var blurBright:Array = [0, 1, 0,
42                          1, 1, 1,
43                          0, 1, 0];
44  convFilter(mc2, blurBright);
45
46  var blurOnly:Array = [0, 1, 0,
47                        1, 1, 1,
48                        0, 1, 0];
49  convFilter(mc3, blurOnly, 5);
```

As a summary of what we've learned, we'll look at how sharpen and find edges filters differ. The *sharpen* instance that follows uses negative values for the left, top, right, and bottom pixels, which is the opposite of blur and causes the pixels to pop. The sum of the matrix is 1, meaning there is no increase or decrease in brightness.

The *edges* instance uses the same values for the surrounding pixels, but the sum of the array is 0. This has a sharpening effect but reduces the brightness, leaving only the emphasized edges visible.

```
50  var sharpen:Array = [ 0, -1,  0,
51                       -1,  5, -1,
52                        0, -1,  0];
53  convFilter(mc4, sharpen);
54
55  var edges:Array = [ 0, -1,  0,
56                     -1,  4, -1,
57                      0, -1,  0];
58  convFilter(mc5, edges);
```

The function that applies these matrices differs from the prior source file in only one major respect: It provides for the use of the fourth optional parameter, *divisor*, to compensate for accumulated brightness.

```
59  function convFilter(dispObj:DisplayObject, matrix:Array,
60                      divisor:int=1):void {
61      var conv:ConvolutionFilter =
62          new ConvolutionFilter(3, 3, matrix, divisor);
63      dispObj.filters = [conv];
64  }
```

## Perlin noise and displacement map

Two other very useful and entertaining effects supported by ActionScript are the Perlin noise generator and the displacement map filter. Perlin noise is widely used for generating naturalistic animated effects like fog, clouds, smoke, water, and fire, as well as textures like wood, stone, and terrain. Displacement maps are used to translate (or displace) pixels to add extra dimension to surfaces. They are commonly used to add realism to textures (such as a pitted or grooved surface) as well as distort images to appear as if seen through a refracting material like glass or water.

**NOTE**

*Ken Perlin developed the Perlin noise algorithm while creating the special effects for the 1982 film* Tron. *At the time, the extensive use of effects in that film may have been cost-prohibitive using traditional multi-exposure film compositing techniques. Perlin noise was used to manipulate the near-constant computer-generated glows and shadings, among other effects. Mr. Perlin won an Academy Award for Technical Achievement in 1997 for his contributions to the industry.*

Figure 9-12. Perlin noise texture

Figure 9-13. Elements of the Perlin noise and displacement map filter exercise

The following exercise, found in the *perlin_displacement.fla* source file, will create an animated Perlin noise texture that will then be used as the source for a displacement map. In our example, the Perlin noise will include random areas of blue, as shown in Figure 9-12. These blue areas will cause the displacement in a photo of a reef aquarium, and the combined effect will cause soft corals in the scene to undulate as if experiencing the effect of water currents.

The source material we'll use is a picture of a reef aquarium, as seen in Figure 9-13. The sea life are the sole elements in a foreground image, and will be affected by the filters so that they will appear to be moving in the water current. The rock is in a separate background and will not be affected.

## Perlin noise

The first step in building our aquarium simulation is to create a **BitmapData** object to contain the Perlin noise. Our image will cover the stage, so we'll pass the stage width and height into the object to size it appropriately (line 1). Lines 3 and 4 create a bitmap using the bitmap data, and then add that bitmap to the display list. However, the lines are commented out because we do not want to see the Perlin noise in the final product. We need access only to the bitmap data to drive the displacement map. However, it's often helpful to see the Perlin noise as you work so you can experiment with various settings. By uncommenting these lines, you can adjust the Perlin noise values until you're satisfied with the effect, and then comment out these lines again when moving on to the displacement filter.

```
1    var bmpData:BitmapData = new BitmapData(stage.stageWidth,
2                                     stage.stageHeight);
3    //var bmp:Bitmap = new Bitmap(bmpData);
4    //addChild(bmp);
5    //comment out lines 3 and 4 to see Perlin noise
```

The Perlin noise generator has a number of settings that will produce dramatically different results when adjusted. As we discuss these settings, we'll reference natural phenomena, like water and smoke. We'll first discuss the settings of the filter and then simply pass these settings into the **perlin-Noise()** method later on in lines 30 through 32.

Lines 7 and 8 set the scale of the texture in the x and y directions. Think of this as influencing the number of waves you can see at one time in water. A very large scale might result in the look of a swelling sea, and a small scale might look like a babbling brook.

Line 7 determines the number of *octaves* in the texture, which are discreet layers of noise that function independently of each other. A single-octave noise will not be as complex as a multi-octave noise and, during animation, you can move a single-octave noise in only one direction at a time. You can create basic animations with single octaves, like the look of running water or, in our case, underwater current. But the ability to move each octave in a different direction makes multi-octave noise better suited for effects like colliding waves moving in multiple directions, or fire, or smoke.

Line 10 creates a *random seed* to influence the starting point for the creation of the texture. A random seed allows you to randomize the effect but also call back that same result by using the same seed at a later time. In our case, we only care about the randomization, so we'll use a random number, between 0 and 100, for the seed as well.

```
6    //perlin noise settings
7    var baseX:Number = 50;
8    var baseY:Number = 50;
9    var numOctaves:Number = 1;
10   var randomSeed:Number = Math.random() * 100;
11   var stitch:Boolean = true;
12   var fractalNoise:Boolean = true;
13   var channelOptions:Number = BitmapDataChannel.BLUE;
14   var grayScale:Boolean = false;
15   var offsets:Array = new Array(new Point());
```

**NOTE**

*Perlin noise layers are called* octaves *because, like musical octaves, each one doubles the frequency of the previous octave, increasing detail within the texture. It's also important to note that the processor power required to generate noise patterns increases with the number of octaves used.*

Line 11 determines whether the edges of the area defined when creating the noise pattern are stitched together in an attempt to create a seamless tile. When creating static textures, this "stitching" is not usually needed, but it's recommended when animating the effect.

Whether fractal noise or turbulence techniques are used when generating the effect is determined by line 12. Fractal noise (used when the `fractalNoise` property is true) generates a smoother effect; turbulence (used when the `fractalNoise` property is false) produces more distinct transitions between levels of detail. For example, fractal noise might be used to create a terrain map of rolling hills or an oceanscape, and turbulence might be better suited to a terrain of mountains or crevices in a rock.

Line 13 chooses which channels of bitmap data are used when generating the texture: red, green, blue, and/or alpha. These can be indicated by constants from the `BitmapDataChannel` class or with integers. You can also use a special operator called the *bitwise OR* operator (|) to combine channels to create multicolor effects or combine color with alpha. For example, combining alpha with noise can create fog or smoke with transparent areas through which a background can be seen.

*Figure 9-14. Perlin noise detail without alpha data*

In this exercise, because we are generating a pattern only to provide data for a displacement map, we need only one channel. (Blue was chosen arbitrarily.) However, experimenting with the Perlin noise settings can make it difficult to visualize the texture's effect. To improve these efforts a bit, you can add alpha data to the mix, so you can see the underlying image through the pattern. Figure 9-14 shows the visible noise texture and the reef beneath it. In our finished example, the anemones will be displaced to a greater degree where blue is more visible.

To see the background image as you experiment with the noise settings, you just have to add an alpha channel to the `channelOptions` property. To do this, replace line 13 with this:

```
13   var channelOptions:Number = BitmapDataChannel.BLUE |
     BitmapDataChannel.ALPHA ;
```

The **grayscale** parameter in line 14 desaturates the texture so it generates only grays. In our exercise, the texture won't be visible, so this isn't relevant, but it's ideal when visible fog or smoke is required.

Finally, line 15 uses an array of offset points, one for each octave, to control the location of the noise pattern generated. We need only one octave in this example, so this is a single-item array. Because the texture will not be visible, its starting point is arbitrary, so we'll use a default point of (0, 0). During animation, we'll alter the position of this point to move the pattern.

You've now set all the values required to create a Perlin noise texture. If you want to see the noise before moving on to the next section, look at the *perlin_noise_only.fla* source file. Later, we'll animate these values by changing the offset values upon every enter frame event. First, however, we need to set up the displacement map settings.

## Displacement map

The displacement map filter is a bit simpler. Lines 18 and 19 of the script that follows determine which color channel will affect the distortion in each direction. We used the blue channel when creating our Perlin noise texture, so we'll use the same channel here.

Next, lines 20 and 21 set the scale of displacement in the x and y directions. Think of these values as the size of the waves when looking through water, or the degree of refraction when looking through glass, in each direction.

```
16  //displacement map settings
17  var displaceMap:DisplacementMapFilter;
18  var componentX:uint = BitmapDataChannel.BLUE;
19  var componentY:uint = BitmapDataChannel.BLUE;
20  var xScale:Number = 10;
21  var yScale:Number = 10;
22  displaceMap = new DisplacementMapFilter(bmpData, new Point(),
23                  componentX, componentY, xScale, yScale,
24                  DisplacementMapFilterMode.CLAMP);
```

Finally, lines 22 through 23 determine how the edges of the displacement map will behave. When set to *clamp*, any displacement will be confined by the edges of the source data. If *wrap*, is used, the distortion will wrap around from edge to edge. The *wrap* option is great for tiled patterns but not useful for affecting a realistic image of a recognizable object. You don't want to see the top of a person's head appearing beneath their feet as a displacement wraps from top to bottom edge.

Now that our settings are complete, we create the **DisplacementMapFilter** in lines 22 through 24. The source for the displacement data is the same **BitmapData** object that is being affected by the Perlin noise pattern, so the degree of displacement will be determined by that bitmap data, passed into the class in the first parameter. The second parameter is the *map point*—the location at which the upper-left corner of the displacement map filter will be applied. This is useful for filtering only a portion of the image. We want to filter the entire image, however, so we'll pass in a default point to begin filtering at (0, 0). The remainder of the parameters correspond directly to the settings previously created.

## Animating the effect

To animate the Perlin noise, and therefore the displacement map effect, we start with a listener that triggers the **onLoop()** function upon every enter frame event. The first thing the function does is update the offset point for the Perlin noise octave, seen in lines 28 and 29. This example sets the offset point of the octave, not the location of a display object (see the adjacent note for more information). Lines 28 and 29 move the first octave (the only octave used in our example) up and to the right, 2 pixels in each direction.

With each change to the offset point, the **perlinNoise()** method is called (line 30), applying all the previously set parameters along with the offset update. Finally, with the call of the Perlin noise method, the **DisplacementMap** filter source data is updated, so the **DisplacementMap** filter must be reapplied to the display object in line 33.

```
25  //enter frame update of both filters
26  addEventListener(Event.ENTER_FRAME, onLoop, false, 0, true);
27  function onLoop(evt:Event):void {
28      offsets[0].x -= 2;
29      offsets[0].y += 2;
30      bmpData.perlinNoise(baseX, baseY, numOctaves, randomSeed,
31                      stitch, fractalNoise, channelOptions,
32                      grayScale, offsets);
33      tank_mc.filters = [displaceMap];
34  }
```

**NOTE**

*Animating an octave with the offset property is not the same as moving a display object. Instead, think of adjusting the offset position of an octave as adjusting that octave's registration point.*

*If you move a movie clip five pixels in the x and y directions, it will move down and to the right. However, if you adjust the movie clip's registration point, down and to the right, the clip won't move on stage, but its contents will move up and to the left.*

# Color Effects

You can apply color effects using ActionScript in multiple ways, and we'll look at three. The first is relatively straightforward: Alter the emphasis of individual color channels (red, green, blue, and alpha) in an image using the **ColorTransform** class. The second is a more powerful technique that uses the **ColorMatrixFilter** to apply a detailed matrix to simultaneously change all color and alpha channels. The last method discussed is the simplest, using the **Color** class to apply a tint to a display object.

## The ColorTransform Class

Although we'll focus exclusively on color, you can use the **ColorTransform** class to adjust the alpha channel as well as the individual color channels of a display object or **BitmapData** object. In the examples that follow, we'll be using the class to invert an image (create a color negative) and apply a simple saturation effect.

Original

Saturation

Invert

*Figure 9-15. ColorTransform filter effects*

The class offers two ways to change color. First, you can multiply a color channel to increase or decrease its effect. For example, you can double the weight of the color by using a multiplier of 2, and you can reduce the weight of the color by half by using 0.5 as a multiplier. Second, you can offset a color channel from –255 to 255. For example, assuming a default multiplier of 1 (no change from the multiplier), an offset value of 255 would maximize the red channel, 0 would apply no change, and –255 would remove all red from the image.

The following code, found in the *color_transform.fla* source file, manipulates three movie clips instantiated as `mc0`, `mc1`, and `mc2`. Lines 1 through 10 show the default `ColorTransform` instance, which makes no change to the source material. Also, by using this default configuration (with a multiplier of 1 and an offset of 0 on each channel), you can effectively reset any prior color transformation. Despite the example's focus on color, we've included alpha multiplier and offset values to show the complete syntax of a reset.

Note that the `ColorTransform` class is not a filter, so it's not applied to the `filters` property of a display object. Instead, the color transformation is applied to the `colorTransform` property of a display object's `transform` object (line 10). Similar to the filtering process, however, every time a change is made to the color transformation, it must be reapplied to the `colorTransform` property.

Lines 12 through 19 provide for an increase in saturation. The offset values of all colors are unchanged, but the color multipliers increase the color for each channel. To emphasize the image, the values used increase red more than green and blue. This effect can be seen in the "Saturation" example in Figure 9-15. You could also partially desaturate an image using the same technique but applying a multiplier value of less than 1 to each color channel.

Finally, lines 21 through 28 invert all color in the image. The multiplier for all color channels is set to –1, which effectively turns the image black, and then the offset values are set to full to revert back to color. This effect can be seen in the "Invert" example from Figure 9-15.

```
1   var noChange:ColorTransform = new ColorTransform();
2   noChange.redOffset = 0;
3   noChange.greenOffset = 0;
4   noChange.blueOffset = 0;
5   noChange.alphaOffset = 0;
6   noChange.redMultiplier = 1;
7   noChange.greenMultiplier = 1;
8   noChange.blueMultiplier = 1;
9   noChange.alphaMultiplier = 1;
10  mc0.transform.colorTransform = noChange;
11
12  var saturation:ColorTransform = new ColorTransform();
13  saturation.redOffset = 0;
14  saturation.greenOffset = 0;
15  saturation.blueOffset = 0;
16  saturation.redMultiplier = 1.3;
17  saturation.greenMultiplier = 1.1;
18  saturation.blueMultiplier = 1.1;
19  mc1.transform.colorTransform = saturation;
20
```

```
21  var invert:ColorTransform = new ColorTransform();
22  invert.redOffset = 255;
23  invert.greenOffset = 255;
24  invert.blueOffset = 255;
25  invert.redMultiplier = -1;
26  invert.greenMultiplier = -1;
27  invert.blueMultiplier = -1;
28  mc2.transform.colorTransform = invert;
```

## The ColorMatrixFilter Class

The next color effect uses the `ColorMatrixFilter` class. This class uses a 4 × 5 matrix to transform red, green, blue, and alpha values of the image, and can be used to create advanced hue, saturation, and contrast changes, among other effects. The following example demonstrates using luminance constants to desaturate an image to create a color grayscale.

The identity matrix (the default matrix, as discussed in Chapter 8) for the `ColorMatrixFilter` class is as follows:

```
        Rs, Gs, Bs, As, Os
Rnew =  1,  0,  0,  0,  0,
Gnew =  0,  1,  0,  0,  0,
Bnew =  0,  0,  1,  0,  0,
Anew =  0,  0,  0,  1,  0
```

The rows represent the sum of changes in red, green, blue, and alpha values for each pixel. The first four columns are the multipliers for red, green, blue, and alpha values of the source (s), and the fifth column is the offset value for each row. The identity matrix shows a default multiplier of 1 and offset of 0 for each color channel, and no change to the other source color multiplier or offset values for that channel—that is, *Rnew* equals *Rs*, *Gnew* equals *Gs*, and so on.

By introducing changes to the other color values, the appearance of each pixel will change. A good way to make this clear is to demonstrate the creation of a color grayscale image. When creating the new red value for a pixel, instead of using a multiplier of 1 for red and 0 for green and blue, you can use a *partial* value of 1 for all colors (with no change in alpha or offset). There will be no change in brightness because the sum of each row will still be 1. The alpha row receives no change to R, G, or B values, and the standard alpha multiplier of 1 is used with no offset.

The only question is, what partial values should be used for each color? Knowing that hexadecimal values of gray are created with equal values of each color (0x666666, for example), it's common to see a value of 0.33 used for each R, G, and B component of every pixel. However, it turns out that unequal values of red, green, and blue combine to create better grayscale images. We can take advantage of prior research to achieve color grayscales that are more pleasing to the eye, using what are known as *luminance constants*—constant red, green, and blue brightness values used for color calibration.

**NOTE**

*Luminance is the amount of light that is reflected or emitted by a color. In lay terms, luminance is brightness (which is more of a human perception than a measured quantity). NTSC broadcast luminance constants (TV grayscale) published in 1954 were replaced by values better tuned to CRT monitors and computer displays.*

*For many years, Paul Haeberli's luminance vectors of 0.3086 for red, 0.6094 for green, and 0.0820 for blue, published in 1993, were used for color grayscale. Recently, these values have been adjusted for HDTV standards and are now slightly different. Red has reduced slightly, and green and blue have increased slightly, over previous values. The current standard is 0.2126 for red, 0.7152 for green, and 0.0722 for blue. Experiment to see which combination you prefer.*

Original

Grayscale

*Figure 9-16. Grayscale created by the ColorMatrixFilter*

**NOTE**

*Discussed in Chapter 8, the* **Color** *class was written to support converting time-line animations into ActionScript and is only available to Flash Professional users. However, we have reproduced a subset of these features, to support the material covered in this book, in the* **com.learningactionscript3.color. ColorUtils class**. *This will allow users of other ActionScript editors to use the scripts in this book with minor modification. The class is included in the source material for this chapter, and its use in sample source code for Chapter 8 includes notes on its use.*

By applying these constants to the source R, G, and B values, the new red, green, and blue values for each pixel will be optimized for grayscale display (Figure 9-16). The newly created matrix is passed to the filter constructor (line 8), and the result is applied to the filters array of the display object (line 12). The following code is found in the *color_matrix_filter.fla* source file.

```
1   //ITU-R BT.709-5 Parameter Values for the HDTV
2   //  Standards for Production, 2002
3   var lumRd:Number = .2126;
4   var lumGr:Number = .7152;
5   var lumBl:Number = .0722;
6
7   var grayscale:ColorMatrixFilter =
8       new ColorMatrixFilter([lumRd, lumGr, lumBl, 0, 0,
9                              lumRd, lumGr, lumBl, 0, 0,
10                             lumRd, lumGr, lumBl, 0, 0,
11                                 0,     0,     0, 1, 0]);
12  mc1.filters = [grayscale];
```

## The Color Class

The last color manipulation is the simplest. It uses the **Color** class, from the **fl.motion** package to set the tint of a display object. The tint is set the same way line and fill styles are set using the **Graphics** class. Two parameters, color and alpha, are used to define the tint. Once the tint is created, it's applied to the **colorTransform** property of the display object's transform object, as in previous examples.

The following code is found in the *set_tint.fla* source file:

```
1   import fl.motion.Color;
2
3   var blueTint:Color = new Color();
4   blueTint.setTint(0x0000FF, 1);
5   mc.transform.colorTransform = blueTint;
```

## Image Encoding and Saving

Now that you know how to create bitmap data, let's talk about how to save it! We'll discuss encoding a **BitmapData** object and saving the image as a JPG. At the end of the chapter, you'll see how to add encoding and saving to our ongoing painting application, as well as save to PNG format, complete with transparency.

The encoding process involves sending the bitmap data to an image encoding class. Fortunately, Adobe provides both JPG and PNG encoders as part of Adobe's AS3 Core Library. At the time of this writing, information can be found at *https://github.com/mikechambers/as3corelib*, where you can download the library.

The saving portion of the exercise is accomplished using the `FileReference` class. This class allows you to upload and download files. Some features, including the `save()` method for saving to your hard drive, require Flash Player 10.

## Saving JPG Images

The heavy lifting of this exercise is performed during the encoding process by Adobe's image encoder classes. The inner workings of these classes are a bit outside the scope of this book, but they're very easy to use. The following script is found in the *encode_and_save_jpg.fla* source file, and it demonstrates the handy feature of taking a screen capture of everything on the stage. We'll review Chapter 8 by drawing a button dynamically and adding it to the stage. Clicking that button will copy anything on the stage into a `BitmapData` instance, and then provide a prompt to save that image as a JPG. Later on, we'll use a button to save the contents of a preexisting `BitmapData` instance—namely, the output of the paint program we developed earlier in this chapter.

This exercise starts routinely with line 1 importing the `JPGEncoder` class, and lines 3 through 11 drawing a button and adding it to the display list. Notice that lines 8 and 9 center the button by determining the horizontal and vertical center of the stage, and line 10 sets the `buttonMode` property of the sprite to true to enable hand cursor feedback when rolling over the sprite.

```
1    import com.adobe.images.JPGEncoder;
2
3    var saveBtn:Sprite = new Sprite();
4    var g:Graphics = saveBtn.graphics;
5    g.beginFill(0x990000, 1);
6    g.drawCircle(0, 0, 40);
7    g.endFill();
8    saveBtn.x = stage.stageWidth/2;
9    saveBtn.y = stage.stageHeight/2;
10   saveBtn.buttonMode = true;
11   addChild(saveBtn);
```

Lines 12 and 13 add a mouse click event listener to the button, which calls the function in lines 14 through 24 when the button is clicked. Lines 15 and 16 create a `BitmapData` object the size of the stage, and line 17 draws into the object everything on the stage, effectively taking a screen shot of the stage.

Line 19 creates an instance of the `JPGEncoder` class, and passes an image quality setting of 100 into the constructor when doing so. If no value is passed into the class during instantiation, a 50-percent quality setting is used. Line 20 encodes the bitmap data into bytes that can be understood as a JPG. It also stores the bytes in a special array called a `ByteArray`. A `ByteArray` is a heavily optimized array with its own properties and methods for reading and writing data at the byte level.

> **NOTE**
>
> *An ActionScript 3.0 package called ZaaIL, developed by Aaron Boushley and Nate Beck of ZaaLabs, adds support for 40 additional image formats! See http:// www.zaalabs.com/2010/04/introducing-zaail-40-image-format-support-for-flash/ for more information.*

> **NOTE**
>
> *When using a Flash Player 10–specific feature, be sure your file is set to publish to Flash Player 10 in the File→Publish Settings→Flash→Player menu. (Flash Professional CS5 users can get to this setting immediately by clicking the Profile→Edit button in the Publish section of the Properties panel.)*

> **NOTE**
>
> *The companion website includes information about using a server and PHP to accomplish the same goal in Flash Player 9. See the post "Saving Data in Flash Player 9 Using PHP" for more information.*

> **NOTE**
>
> *See Chapter 8 if you need to review drawing vectors with the `Graphics` class.*

NOTE

*Prior to Flash Player 10.1, saving a file using the **FileReference** class required active involvement, such as a mouse click, from the user. You can't invoke the **save()** method from a timer or enter frame event, for example, because that is considered a passive experience from the viewpoint of the user. This has been relaxed in Flash Professional CS5.*

Finally, line 22 creates an instance of the **FileReference** class, and line 23 invokes the **save()** method from this instance. In doing so, it passes in the bytes for the JPG and a default file name. The user's operating system prompts for a location to save the file and the JPG is written to your local directory of choice.

```
12    saveBtn.addEventListener(MouseEvent.CLICK, onSaveImage,
13                             false, 0, true);
14    function onSaveImage(evt:Event):void {
15        var stageCapture:BitmapData =
16            new BitmapData(stage.stageWidth, stage.stageHeight);
17        stageCapture.draw(stage);
18
19        var jpgEncoder:JPGEncoder = new JPGEncoder(100);
20        var jpgBytes:ByteArray = jpgEncoder.encode(stageCapture);
21
22        var fileRef:FileReference = new FileReference();
23        fileRef.save(jpgBytes, "stageCapture.jpg");
24    }
```

## Push Yourself!

# Adding Functionality to Your Color Picker

Now it's time to exercise the gray cells and put what you've learned into practice. The first example makes the color picker art you created in Chapter 8 functional. In the process, you'll learn how to get and set pixel color values in a **BitmapData** instance. Then we'll end with an exercise that uses many of the skills you've developed over the past few chapters. We'll expand the drawing application you created by adding the color picker to change the color of your brush. We'll also use the **RoundRectButton** class from Chapter 8 to create a button that triggers a save method, saving your artwork to your hard drive in PNG format.

## Getting and Setting Pixels

*Figure 9-17. The color picker created in Chapter 8*

NOTE

**ColorPickerGraphics**, *the display portion of the color picker exercise created in Chapter 8, is in the same directory as this class, so your new code will function without importing that class. However, doing so allows you to see all class dependencies at a glance.*

In Chapter 8, we created the visual component of a color picker (shown in Figure 9-17), but didn't add any functionality to the exercise. In this chapter, we'll expand this class-based example and create a **ColorPickerCustom** class (named as such to differentiate it from the ColorPicker component in Flash Professional). This class will add an instance of the **ColorPickerGraphics** class you created in Chapter 8 to serve as the color graphic in the picker. We'll also add a simple text display and a "current color" chip to the picker, and then show you how to get and set pixels using methods of the **BitmapData** class. The class is found in the book code library, at *com/learningactionscript3/ color/ColorPickerCustom.as*, and we'll put it to use in the next section.

Lines 1 through 10 define the package and import all the classes required by this class. Lines 12 through 18 declare the class (which extends **MovieClip** so you can easily treat the picker as a display object) and declare a small number of variables. Lines 14 and 15 contain the picker (**_pickerArt**) and a **BitmapData** instance (**_bmd**) that will contain the pixel data from the picker. This will allow us to get the color value of a pixel during the actual color picking process.

The _col variable in line 16 will hold the picked color, and the _tf variable in line 17 will contain a text field that we'll use to display the color value in string hexadecimal notation (#FFFFFF rather than 0xFFFFFF). The final variable, _chip, in line 18, will contain a movie clip that we'll tint to match the selected color. The text and color chip will provide valuable feedback for the user when picking colors.

```
1    package com.learningactionscript3.color {
2
3        import flash.display.BitmapData;
4        import flash.display.Graphics;
5        import flash.display.MovieClip;
6        import flash.events.MouseEvent;
7        import flash.text.TextField;
8        import flash.text.TextFieldAutoSize;
9        import fl.motion.Color;
10       import com.learningactionscript3.color.ColorPickerGraphics;
11
12       public class ColorPickerCustom extends MovieClip {
13
14           private var _pickerArt:ColorPickerGraphics;
15           private var _bmd:BitmapData;
16           private var _col:uint = 0x000000;
17           private var _tf:TextField;
18           private var _chip:MovieClip;
```

Lines 20 through 50 make up the class constructor. Lines 21 and 22 create an instance of the **ColorPickerGraphics** class to create the spectrum artwork, and add it as a child of the new class instance. Lines 23 and 24 add a mouse click event listener to the picker art inside the class. The private method **onClick()** (lines 52 through 59) will be used for visual feedback inside the picker (setting the text and "current color" chip values) and to populate a class property with the selected color. What we do with that color will be determined outside the **ColorPickerCustom** class when the picker is put into use by a project. We'll look at that process later in this section.

Lines 26 through 28 create a **BitmapData** instance the size of the picker art and draw the picker art into the bitmap data. Once we have the color spectrum in pixel data, we can retrieve the color values of a pixel clicked on by the mouse.

Lines 30 through 37 create a text field to display the chosen color's hexadecimal value. It's the width of the picker art, 14 pixels tall, and positioned just under the picker art. Note its initial content of "#FFFFFF" (white) is in line 34. In a moment, we'll also apply an initial white color to the selected color chip. In line 35, the field's background (with a default color of white) is turned on so the picker won't let the stage color show beneath the field. Also, line 36 disables mouse interaction so that the cursor won't change into a text cursor upon rolling over the field and the text won't be selectable.

Lines 39 through 45 draw a small movie clip using the **Graphics** class discussed in Chapter 8, to serve as the selected color chip. It's white (set in line 41), 100 × 14 pixels (line 42) and is positioned just under the text field (line

**NOTE**

*In this example, no bitmap is created from the bitmap data or added to the display list. Because the spectrum art has already been stored in the _pickerArt property and added to the display list, we need only the BitmapData instance for accessing color data. It need not be a part of the display list.*

44). Also, using the **Graphics** class, lines 47 through 50 draw a 1-pixel black border for the entire picker, as a finishing touch to the picker's appearance.

```
19      //class constructor
20      public function ColorPickerCustom() {
21          _pickerArt = new ColorPickerGraphics();
22          addChild(_pickerArt);
23          _pickerArt.addEventListener(MouseEvent.CLICK,
24                                      onClick, false, 0, true);
25
26          _bmd = new BitmapData(_pickerArt.width,
27                                _pickerArt.height);
28          _bmd.draw(_pickerArt);
29
30          _tf = new TextField();
31          _tf.width = 100;
32          _tf.height = 14;
33          _tf.y = 100;
34          _tf.text = "#000000";
35          _tf.background = true;
36          _tf.mouseEnabled = false;
37          addChild(_tf);
38
39          _chip = new MovieClip();
40          var g:Graphics = _chip.graphics;
41          g.beginFill(0x000000);
42          g.drawRect(0, 0, 100, 14);
43          g.endFill();
44          _chip.y = 114;
45          addChild(_chip);
46
47          var border:MovieClip = new MovieClip();
48          border.graphics.lineStyle(1, 0x000000);
49          border.graphics.drawRect(0, 0, 100, 128);
50          addChild(border);
51      }
```

## getPixel()

Three things happen within the class when the picker is clicked. First, the **getPixel()** method is used in lines 54 and 55 to retrieve the color value from the pixel at the mouse location. This color is stored in the private property **_col**. Second, line 56 places the hexadecimal value of the color into the text field, using the **prependZeros()** method in lines 67 through 75. We'll cover that method in a moment. Finally, the **setTint()** method (line 59) is used to apply the selected color to the color chip, as discussed previously in the section "The Color Class."

```
52      //listener function
53      private function onClick(evt:MouseEvent):void {
54          _col = _bmd.getPixel(_pickerArt.mouseX,
55                               _pickerArt.mouseY);
56          _tf.text = prependZeros(_col);
57
58          var col:Color = new Color();
59          col.setTint(_col, 1);
60          _chip.transform.colorTransform = col;
61      }
```

At this point, the color picker is completely functional, but only as a self-contained widget. We can't yet use the picker for its intended purpose, because the **_col** property is private, so we can't retrieve the selected color from outside the class. Therefore, the last functionality we need to put in place is a getter, **color**, in lines 63 through 65, to provide access to the **_col** property.

```
62        //getter for access to _col
63        public function get color():uint {
64            return _col;
65        }
```

Finishing the explanation of this class, the aforementioned **prependZeros()** method takes a numeric color value and converts it to a string for display in the picker's text field. However, when converting to a string, leading zeros are dropped. As such, if blue was selected, a string converted from its hexadecimal value would read FF instead of the far more typical 0000FF equivalent. So we need to add the number of leading zeros required to fill out the color value.

The method starts with an empty string, **zeros**, in line 68, and then converts the numeric value to a string in line 69 using the **toString()** method. If we used this method without an argument, it would convert the number to decimal, or base 10. White, therefore, would appear as 16777215, which isn't very useful for most people. By passing 16 into the method, it will convert the value to hexadecimal, or base 16. Using this argument, the result for white would be ffffff—acceptable, but not ideal. By using the **toUpperCase()** method, the string will be converted to uppercase and display as FFFFFF. All that remains is adding any necessary leading zeros and the preceding hash mark (#).

Because the hexadecimal color string we want has six characters, line 70 determines how many zeros are needed by subtracting the current length of the string from 6. Using blue (0000FF) as an example again, 6 minus 2 (for the two characters in FF) is 4, so we need 4 zeros. Lines 71 through 73 loop the determined number of times and build the **zeros** string. Finally, the return string is assembled by concatenating the hash mark, leading zeros, and color string.

```
66        //text formatting for hex string display in picker
67        private function prependZeros(hex:uint):String {
68            var zeros:String = "";
69            var hexString = hex.toString(16).toUpperCase();
70            var cnt:int = 6 - hexString.length;
71            for (var i:int = 0; i < cnt; i++) {
72                zeros += "0";
73            }
74            return "#" + zeros + hexString;
75        }
76    }
77 }
```

## Using the picker with setPixel()

Now that you know how to get the color values from a pixel, let's do the reverse. To set the color values of a pixel in a **BitmapData** object, you need to again provide an x and y coordinate, but you also need to furnish the color you want the pixel to display. In the *color_picker_set_pixel.fla* source file, we'll use the picker we just created to set the color of pixels in a small bitmap.

Lines 1 through 5 import the **ColorPickerCustom** class, instantiate the picker, place it at point (10, 10), and add it to the display list. Lines 7 through 12 create a 100 × 100–pixel black **BitmapData** object, create a bitmap from that data, position it just to the right of the picker, and add it to the display list. The enter frame event listener in lines 14 through 19 manipulates the bitmap data, which we'll explain after the code.

```
1    import com.learningactionscript3.color.ColorPickerCustom;
2
3    var colorPicker:ColorPickerCustom = new ColorPickerCustom();
4    colorPicker.x = colorPicker.y = 10;
5    addChild(colorPicker);
6
7    var canvasBmd:BitmapData = new BitmapData(100, 100,
8                                          false, 0xFF000000);
9    var canvasBm:Bitmap = new Bitmap(canvasBmd);
10   canvasBm.x = 120;
11   canvasBm.y = 10;
12   addChild(canvasBm);
13
14   addEventListener(Event.ENTER_FRAME, onLoop, false, 0, true);
15   function onLoop(evt:Event):void {
16       var rndX:int = Math.random() * 100;
17       var rndY:int = Math.random() * 100;
18       canvasBmd.setPixel(rndX, rndY, colorPicker.color);
19   }
```

Lines 16 and 17 of the listener select random pixel locations between 0 and 100, the size of the **BitmapData** instance. These values are then passed to the **setPixel()** method, along with the value from the color property of the picker. Figure 9-18 shows the file in action.

If you want to get a better view of the pixels changing, add the following bold line to your script after line 11. This will scale the bitmap 300 percent, enlarging the pixels so they are easier to see. The source file already has this line in place, so you can compare your file with the source file, if you prefer.

```
10   canvasBm.y = 10;
11   canvasBm.scaleX = canvasBm.scaleY = 3;
12   addChild(canvasBm);
```

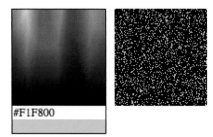

*Figure 9-18. Setting pixels in a canvas*

**NOTE**

*The **setPixel()** method takes integer pixel values but ActionScript will automatically truncate a **Number** (lop off the decimal value) when passed into any object typed as an **int**.*

## Expanding Your Paint Program

This exercise picks up where our paint tool left off, and can be found in the *paint_tool_erase_blur_pick_save_png.fla* source file. At this point, the paint program can paint using a blue color and air brush effect, as well as erase what you create. We're going to add the most recent color picker, to allow you to pick the color for your brush, and a custom button and image encoder to save your artwork as a PNG.

Although you may want to reorganize your file later (to consolidate import statements, for example), we're going to add the new code to the end of the existing script for consistency and simplicity. Lines 56 through 58 import the required classes, including the color picker, button, and image encoder classes. Lines 60 through 62 create and position the color picker, and add it to the display list, as in the **setPixel()** example.

Lines 64 through 68 add a mouse click event listener to the color picker to supplement its functionality. In addition to its self-contained behavior (like populating its text field and tinting its color chip), clicking on the picker widget will also query its color property and recreate the brush tool with the newly selected color. This will change the color of your airbrush.

```
56  import com.learningactionscript3.color.ColorPickerCustom;
57  import com.learningactionscript3.ui.RoundRectButton;
58  import com.adobe.images.PNGEncoder;
59
60  var colorPicker:ColorPickerCustom = new ColorPickerCustom();
61  colorPicker.x = colorPicker.y = 10;
62  addChild(colorPicker);
63
64  colorPicker.addEventListener(MouseEvent.CLICK,
65                               onPickColor, false, 0, true);
66  function onPickColor(evt:MouseEvent):void {
67      brush = createBrush(colorPicker.color, 1);
68  }
```

The final section of code allows you to save your artwork to a PNG file. Lines 70 through 72 create a single instance of the **RoundRectButton** class introduced in Chapter 8. The button is 60 × 20 pixels, with a rounded corner radius of 6. A single-pixel border and button color based on a dark blue color theme, offsets the white button label, "Save." The button is positioned below the picker in lines 73 and 74, and added to the display list in line 75.

Lines 77 through 84 add a mouse click event listener to the button, and the three simple lines of code therein are all it takes to save your art as a PNG. Line 80 encodes the bitmap data into bytes, just like the **JPGEncoder** class that you used in the "Saving JPG Images" section of this chapter, with two small exceptions. The **PNGEncoder** class requires no quality setting or instantiation. Instead, the **encode()** method is static and can be called by the class itself, not by an instance of the class. Lines 82 and 83 are essentially the same in both examples, with the very minor change of the default file name.

```
69  //encode and save
70  var saveBtn:RoundRectButton =
71      new RoundRectButton(60, 20, 6, 1, 0x000066,
72                          "Save", 0xFFFFFF);
73  saveBtn.x = 10;
74  saveBtn.y = 150;
75  addChild(saveBtn);
76
```

*Figure 9-19. A detail of the save-capable painting application*

```
77  saveBtn.addEventListener(MouseEvent.CLICK, onSaveImage,
78                              false, 0, true);
79  function onSaveImage(evt:Event):void {
80      var byteArray:ByteArray = PNGEncoder.encode(bmd);
81
82      var fileRef:FileReference = new FileReference();
83      fileRef.save(byteArray, "myArt.jpg");
84  }
```

Congratulations! Your modifications are complete. Figure 9-19 shows a detail of the application at work. In this figure, we set the stage color to a pale yellow to emphasize that the erasing is actually removing color, instead of painting over it with white.

# What's Next?

One of the most surprising things to come to light after each major Flash upgrade is how small the engineering team manages to keep Flash Player. The bitmap manipulation and compositing features discussed in this chapter are by no means an exhaustive look at everything Flash Player can do with pixels. If you spent some time and effort on the project, you could make a fairly respectable graphics-editing application using only Flash (and, perhaps, a server technology like PHP for file management). The best examples of this that we can think of are the image editing applications available in the Aviary suite at *http://www.aviary.com*. Yet despite these capabilities, Flash Player still remains small and easy to install and update. Bravo, past and present Flash Professional and Flash Player engineers, and congratulations to the creative and programming team at Aviary!

Now it's time to change direction and focus on the oft-overlooked workhorse of the Flash family: text. Text can be as fruitful a subject for experimentation and eye-candy as vectors and bitmaps, but it also serves a very important utilitarian purpose. Creating, styling, and parsing text are fundamental needs that you'll frequently encounter.

**In the next chapter**, we'll look at ways to work with text, including:

- Creating text fields on the fly

- Initializing basic text field appearance and behavioral attributes

- Formatting text, including default formats for text fields, as well as changing formats across entire fields or partial text selections

- Using HTML and Cascading Style Sheets (CSS) for limited HTML rendering and global styling

- Embedding ActionScript triggers in HTML anchor tags

- Parsing paragraph, line, and character data from text fields using points and indices

# TEXT

Part III focuses exclusively on text, and covers a variety of text uses. Chapter 10 begins with the dynamic creation of text fields and the styling of text elements using `TextFormat` objects. Using this approach, text styles can be precreated and applied to individual text fields at any time. For global styling, you can use a combination of HTML and Cascading Style Sheets (CSS). Both the HTML content and the CSS styles can be created internally or loaded from external sources. By using HTML and CSS, you can establish styles that apply to an entire project, if desired. Further, CSS styles can be edited easily in one central location, and all text to which the styles are applied will be automatically updated.

We finish the chapter with a look at Adobe's new text technology, the Text Layout Framework (TLF). Built atop Flash Player's new text engine, TLF was officially released both as part of the Flash Professional CS5 interface and as a set of ActionScript 3.0 classes, and offers Flash Platform users unprecedented typographic control.

## CHAPTER 10

# TEXT

Working with text can be a basic affair, such as displaying a simple text string in a default text field, or as complex as your needs require, perhaps creating individual text fields for every character in a string to build an animated text effect. Learning how to create and manipulate text objects at runtime with ActionScript can increase flexibility and make it much easier to reuse code from project to project.

In this chapter, we'll focus mostly on how to display, populate, and format text data. We'll discuss two kinds of text: the traditional Flash Platform text technology, available for many years and newly christened Classic text; and text created using the Text Layout Framework (TLF)—a significantly more robust text technology introduced with Flash Player 10. TLF offers improved typographical control, support for multiple columns, flowing text among multiple linked containers, and more.

We'll cover:

- **Creating Text Fields.** Text fields can be created with ActionScript like any display object, freeing you from the Flash Properties panel and allowing you to create fields on the fly.

- **Setting Text Field Characteristics.** How you set up your text field will determine how the field will appear and function.

- **Selecting Text.** You can select segments of text using ActionScript by specifying the start and end of a selection block.

- **Formatting with TextFormat.** Text can be formatted easily by creating a formatting object that can be applied to one or more text fields at any time, including partial content of these fields.

- **Formatting with HTML and CSS.** It's also possible to use a limited subset of supported Hypertext Markup Language (HTML) and

Cascading Style Sheets (CSS) features to format and style your text globally or on a field-by-field basis.

- **Triggering ActionScript from HTML.** In addition to standard links in HTML text that might open a website, you can also use links to trigger ActionScript. This makes it easier to use HTML data to control your project and provides another way of dynamically triggering functions. For example, rather than creating buttons to drive an interface, a text field could contain links to serve the same purpose.

- **Push Yourself**. Concluding this chapter is an example of how to load HTML and CSS data from external files, and an introduction to the Text Layout Framework (TLF).

## Creating Text Fields

Creating text fields dynamically is as simple as creating any other display object, and we'll be using this method in most of the examples in this chapter. The code that follows creates a text field and adds it to the display list. It also uses the **text** property to populate the field, as seen in the *text_field_1.fla* source file.

```
1    var txtFld:TextField = new TextField()
2    txtFld.text = "Hello Skinny";
3    addChild(txtFld);
```

Without your setting additional properties of the field, default values will shape most of its characteristics. These defaults are fairly straightforward, such as black text, dimensions of 100 × 100 pixels, no field styling (such as background or border use), and single-line display without text wrapping. In other words, no assumptions are made by ActionScript about the way you want to display the text.

By default, a text field created with ActionScript will be a *dynamic* field type. This type supports programmatic control, in contrast to the *static* field type you might create by hand using Flash Professional's Text tool. Later on we'll show you how to create an *input* text field type, which also supports user input at runtime.

## Setting Text Field Attributes

It's almost certain that you'll need to customize text fields to suit your needs, so we'll modify a typical set of properties to demonstrate the most common adjustments made to a field. Whether you need fields that simply display text or accept input at runtime, ActionScript offers ample control over the appearance and functionality of a text field. It's a simple matter to control color, wrap text, limit acceptable input characters, and more.

# Dynamic Text Fields

Dynamic text fields are the go-to field type because they support ActionScript control but not user input. When displaying text in typical scenarios, for example, you're unlikely to want the user to edit your content. This first example can be found in the *text_field_2.fla* source file, and includes syntax for setting the most common properties of a text field. If you've been reading this book linearly, you've used several of these properties in the Hello World! examples as well as a few other exercises in past chapters. Collecting the properties here, however, will help you focus on them in the context of other text manipulations.

Lines 1 and 2 create a text field and position it at (20, 20), while lines 3 and 4 set the width of the field to 200, and automatically size the height of the field to fit its content, while justifying left. This means the field will remain 200 pixels wide, but will resize from the upper-left corner to whatever height is required to accommodate all the text you add to the field.

```
1   var txtFld:TextField = new TextField();
2   txtFld.x = txtFld.y = 20;
3   txtFld.width = 200;
4   txtFld.autoSize = TextFieldAutoSize.LEFT;
5   txtFld.border = true;
6   txtFld.borderColor = 0x000033;
7   txtFld.background = true;
8   txtFld.backgroundColor = 0xEEEEFF;
9   txtFld.textColor = 0x000099;
10  txtFld.multiline = true;
11  txtFld.wordWrap = true;
12  txtFld.selectable = false;
13
14  for (var i:Number = 0; i < 25; i++) {
15      txtFld.appendText("word" + String(i) + " ");
16  }
17
18  addChild(txtFld);
```

Lines 5 through 9 enable and set the color of the border, background, and text of the field. By default, a field is transparent with black text. To show a border or background of any color, the corresponding properties must first be enabled, as shown in lines 5 and 7. Once enabled, the default colors of the border and background are black and white, respectively. Line 6 sets the field's border to a dark blue, and line 8 sets its background to light blue. Finally, line 9 sets the color of the text to a medium blue.

Lines 10 through 12 control text behavior. Line 10 supports more than one line of text (allowing carriage returns or line feeds in the text, for example), and line 11 supports wrapping text to the next line. Line 12 prevents the user from selecting text within the field. Even if a field is of *dynamic* type, rather than *input* type, the user can still select and copy text by default. However, you may not want a text field to allow selection, or you may not want the mouse cursor to switch to the corresponding *I-beam* text edit cursor that comes with the selection process. In these cases, set the **selectable** property to false.

**NOTE**

*The* **appendText()** *method executes faster than using the* **+=** *compound operator (*`txtFld.text += "new value"`*) and is recommended for this purpose.*

Lines 14 through 16 populate the field using a **for** loop. This loop puts multiple occurrences of the text "word" into the field, adding the loop counter number to the text as it goes, ending with a space each time through the loop. The result will be "word0 word1 word2 " and so on. The **appendText()** method is used to add text to the field incrementally.

This is a simple example that fills a text field quickly with minimal code, but adding new text to a populated field is quite common. You may want to build a list based on user selections, for example. Imagine a to-do list application in which a user can create a running list by adding new items when needed. Without appending text to the end of a list, every new item would replace all current items. In fact, you've already added text incrementally in previous chapters, including the opening script of Chapter 3 when you animated the string, "Hello World!".

## Input Text Fields

To allow the user to input text in a field at runtime, all you need to do is to set the field's **type** property to **INPUT** using the **TextFieldType** class. Using default input field properties will suffice for things like a user typing a name or email address into a form. For more specific tasks, additional features are available.

Consider, for example, a password field. When entering passwords, you usually want to obscure the password by replacing its characters with symbols. You may also want to limit input in a field to a specific number of characters or range of allowable input. To demonstrate, consider the following script, seen in the *text_field_3.fla* source file:

```
1    var txtFld:TextField = new TextField();
2    txtFld.x = txtFld.y = 20;
3    txtFld.width = 100;
4    txtFld.height = 20;
5    txtFld.border = txtFld.background = true;
6    txtFld.type = TextFieldType.INPUT;
7    txtFld.maxChars = 10;
8    txtFld.restrict = "0-9";
9    txtFld.displayAsPassword = true;
10   addChild(txtFld);
11   stage.focus = txtFld;
```

Lines 1 through 4 and line 10 create, position, and size the field, and add it to the display list. Line 6 sets the field to an input field, and lines 7 through 9 define the password-related behavior. The **maxChars** property limits the number of characters that can be entered. The **restrict** property limits the valid characters that can be entered. These characters can be expressed individually or in ranges, such as the 0 through 9 number range used in this example. For example, you could allow uppercase and lowercase letters, the dollar sign ($) and underscore (_), and numbers 0 through 5, this way:

```
txtFld.restrict = "A-Za-z$_0-5";
```

Line 9 performs the task of automatically switching the typed character for an asterisk at runtime to hide the password. Finally, line 11 gives the field focus so the user can begin typing without first selecting the field with the mouse.

# Selecting Text

Your control over text and text fields is not limited to styling or input. You can also track user selections or even select portions of a field programmatically and replace its content.

The following example, found in the *text_field_4.fla* source file, uses the button creation class discussed in Chapter 8 to create two buttons that allow you to select and replace a word of text. The first block of code consists only of material discussed previously in this and prior chapters. Line 1 imports the **RoundRectButton** class, lines 3 through 11 create and setup a dynamic text field, and lines 12 through 28 create two buttons and add event listeners to trigger the functions at the end of the script.

```
1   import com.learningactionscript3.ui.RoundRectButton;
2
3   var txtFld:TextField = new TextField();
4   txtFld.x = txtFld.y = 20;
5   txtFld.width = 500;
6   txtFld.autoSize = TextFieldAutoSize.LEFT;
7   txtFld.multiline = true;
8   txtFld.wordWrap = true;
9   txtFld.selectable = false;
10  txtFld.text = "Lorem ipsum dolor sit amet, elit, sed.";
11  addChild(txtFld);
12
13  var selBtn:RoundRectButton = createButton("Select");
14  selBtn.x = 300;
15  selBtn.y = 20;
16  selBtn.addEventListener(MouseEvent.CLICK, onSelectWord,
17                          false, 0, true);
18  addChild(selBtn);
19
20  var repBtn:RoundRectButton = createButton("Replace");
21  repBtn.x = 300;
22  repBtn.y = 60;
23  repBtn.addEventListener(MouseEvent.CLICK, onReplaceWord,
24                          false, 0, true);
25  addChild(repBtn);
26
27  function createButton(labl:String):RoundRectButton {
28      return new RoundRectButton(110, 20, 10, 2, 0x000099,
29                              labl, 0xFFFFFF);
30  }
```

The new functionality is introduced in the pair of functions shown below. The first function, **onSelectWord()** in lines 31 through 34, defines the selection behavior. Line 32 selects characters bound by indices 6 and 11. Counting characters begins with 0, and the **setSelection()** method includes the first

**NOTE**

*If you have trouble using the Backspace/Delete key when testing your movie in Flash Professional, it's not because the* **restrict** *property prohibits its operation. This is a function of keyboard behavior in Flash's built-in player. You can either test in a browser or disable keyboard shortcuts via the Control menu while in the player. This will remove the functional limitation on the Backspace/Delete key. Just remember to reenable keyboard shortcuts when returning to Flash.*

**NOTE**

*You can select text content with code when using either dynamic or input text fields.*

character up to, but not including the last character. So, in this example, the second word, "ipsum," is selected. Setting the `alwaysShowSelected` property in line 33 to true ensures that the selection highlight remains visible even when the field no longer has focus. When false (the default), the selection highlight will disappear when the user interacts with any other part of the SWF.

```
31  function onSelectWord(evt:MouseEvent):void {
32      txtFld.setSelection(6, 11);
33      txtFld.alwaysShowSelection = true;
34  }
```

The `onReplaceWord()` function replaces the selected word with another. The first line is a form of error check that ensures that a selection has been made. This prevents an error if the user clicks the second button before making a selection with the first button. The error is avoided by checking that the start and end of the current selection are not equal.

If, as a hypothetical example, you selected the first five characters of text in any field, the start of the selection would be different from the end of the selection. If, however, you made no selection, both values would be 0, and if you just clicked in the field without selecting any text, both values would reflect the *caret*, or text edit cursor, location. Either way, both values would be the same, allowing you to use this information to confirm an attempted selection.

**NOTE**

*It's also possible to select text field content interactively using mouse input. See the companion website, http:// www.LearningActionScript3.com, for more information, specifically the post "Parsing Text Data with Mouse Interaction."*

If this error check passes, line 37 uses the `replaceSelectedText()` method to replace the previously selected text with the string argument of the method.

```
35  function onReplaceWord(evt:MouseEvent):void {
36      if (txtFld.selectionBeginIndex != txtFld.selectionEndIndex) {
37          txtFld.replaceSelectedText("LOREM");
38      }
39  }
```

## Formatting Text

Now that you can create, style, and populate text fields, as well as select their contents, you're ready to learn how to format the text the field contains. This is accomplished with another class called `TextFormat`. The process is to set up a `TextFormat` instance that controls all the desired formatting, and then apply that object to all or part of a field.

You can apply the object in two ways: by establishing it as the default format for the field, affecting all *future* input or by applying it on a case-by-case basis, affecting all or part of *existing* text. Only the application of the format varies in these cases. Creating the `TextFormat` instance is unchanged. In the upcoming example, we'll create a source file that uses a format to style future text, and then we'll modify that file to style text after it's been added to the field.

## Establishing a format for new text

In the following code, found in the *text_format_1.fla* source file, lines 1 through 7 create the format. It's instantiated in line 1, and settings for font, color, size, leading (line spacing), left and right margins, and paragraph indent are established.

The **font** property is the name of the font you wish to use. The following syntax shows the use of a *device font*—a font that must be in the operating system of the user's device (computer, handheld) to display correctly. System fonts can be specified by name, such as "Verdana," but there's no certainty that a user will have that particular font installed. To account for this variance, Flash Player can work with a user's operating system to specify its default font (whatever that may be) in one of three categories.

serif

sans serif

afgy

*Figure 10-1. Serif (top) and sans-serif (bottom) fonts*

Using "_serif" for the **font** property will use a font with *serifs*—the flourishes usually found at the top and bottom of most characters, as shown in Figure 10-1. Typically this means Times or Times New Roman, but anyone can customize an operating system, so the actual font used isn't guaranteed. All that's reasonably sure to happen is that a serif font will be chosen. Using "_sans," as in the following script, will specify a *sans-serif* font (without serifs), such as Arial or Helvetica. Finally, using "_typewriter" will specify a *fixed-width* font, in which all characters share the same width to ensure that they line up nicely. This usually means that Courier or Courier New will be used.

The **color** property is a hexadecimal color value in the 0xRRGGBB format. The **size**, **leftMargin**, and **rightMargin** properties are measured in pixels. The **leading** property is also measured in pixels but is based on the space *between* lines, rather than including the line height as in some typography-centric applications. For example, if you wanted 10-point type on 12-point leading, **size** would be set to 10 and **leading** would be set to 2. Finally, **indent** indents the first line of every paragraph by a measure of pixels.

**NOTE**

*The **blockIndent** property (not used in this example), will indent the entire paragraph rather than the first line—typical when formatting block quotes in text display.*

```
1  var txtFmt:TextFormat = new TextFormat();
2  txtFmt.font = "_sans";
3  txtFmt.color = 0x000099;
4  txtFmt.size = 10;
5  txtFmt.leading = 4;
6  txtFmt.leftMargin = txtFmt.rightMargin = 6;
7  txtFmt.indent = 20;
```

Lines 8 through 13 create and setup a text field. Lines 14 though 18 apply the format to the field. Line 14 uses the **defaultTextFormat()** method to format future text. This must be applied while the field is empty, or it will have no effect. Lines 16 through 18 use a **for** loop and the **appendText()** method to add 25 words to the field, and line 19 adds the field to the display list.

```
8   var txtFld:TextField = new TextField();
9   txtFld.x = txtFld.y = 20;
10  txtFld.width = 200;
11  txtFld.autoSize = TextFieldAutoSize.LEFT;
12  txtFld.multiline = true;
13  txtFld.wordWrap = true;
```

```
14   txtFld.defaultTextFormat = txtFmt;
15
16   for (var i:Number = 0; i < 25; i++) {
17       txtFld.appendText("word" + String(i) + " ");
18   }
19   addChild(txtFld);
```

## Applying a format to existing text

If you need to format existing text, you must use the **setTextFormat()** method. This method can apply a TextFormat instance to an entire field just like the **defaultTextFormat** property, but only after the text has been added to the field. To format an entire field, the only argument you must supply to the method is the format you want to use:

```
txtFld.setTextFormat(txtFmt);
```

To format selected text within the field, you can add two additional arguments to the method call, specifying the characters to be formatted. The first integer value is the starting character index and the second integer value is one more than the last character index. In other words, the span includes the character at the first index, but not the character at the second index.

The *text_format_2.fla* source file demonstrates this by adding the following new five lines of code to the prior example. Lines 20 through 23 create a new format that will style the changed text as red, bold, and underline, and lines 25 and 26 format the first and last word in the field. Line 25 formats from character 0 up to 5, to include "word0." Line 26 uses the text field property **length** to determine the number of characters in the field and uses that value for the last index. The first index is 7 characters less to include the last characters added to the field, "word24 "—created by line 17 of the last example in the "Establishing a format for new text" section.

```
20   var txtFmt2:TextFormat = new TextFormat();
21   txtFmt2.color = 0xFF0000;
22   txtFmt2.bold = true;
23   txtFmt2.underline = true;
24
25   txtFld.setTextFormat(txtFmt2, 0, 5);
26   txtFld.setTextFormat(txtFmt2, txtFld.length-7, txtFld.length);
```

## Adding text after using setTextFormat()

One important issue is worthy of note when adding text to a field *after* applying a format with **setTextFormat()**. Using the recommended **appendText()** method to add text to a field will maintain the formatting of the last character as expected. Using the compound assignment operator (**+=**) to add text, however, will reset the field to its default text format. As a proof of concept, add the following lines to the end of the current example (or look at *text_format_3.fla*), and test your file twice, using each line in turn.

```
27   txtFld.appendText("new");
28   //txtFld.text += "new";
```

> **NOTE**
>
> *Remember that character counting starts with 0 and the **length** property tells you how many characters are actually in the field. So, if a text field contains five characters, the indices of the characters would be 0, 1, 2, 3, and 4, and the **length** of the field would be 5.*
>
> *The **setTextFormat()** method uses an ending index one higher than the characters you want to format in order to support the use of the **length** property in the method's last argument.*

Using the first line, the extra word, "new" will be red, bold, and underlined because that's the format when the text was added. Commenting out line 27 and using line 28, however, will remove all the red, bold, underline formatting from the field because the field will revert to its default format.

## Tab Stops

Another handy feature made possible by the **TextFormat** class is tab stops. If you find formatting text columns difficult using the Flash Professional interface, you'll be relieved to find how easy it can be to create simple columns with tab stops using ActionScript. The next example uses the **TextFormat** class to set two tab stops so that text including tab characters will line up at these stops, forming columns. See file *text_format_4.fla* to try this yourself.

Let's get to the code. The first 13 lines of this script include only previously discussed material—creating and configuring **TextFormat** and **TextField** objects. We didn't include the tab stops in the format initially, because we want to show you how to edit and use a **TextFormat** object after it's been created. Take a look at the setup first, and then we'll discuss the application of the tab stops:

```
1   var txtFmt:TextFormat = new TextFormat();
2   txtFmt.font = "_sans";
3   txtFmt.size = 10;
4   txtFmt.leading = 4;
5   txtFmt.leftMargin = txtFmt.rightMargin = 6;
6
7   var txtFld:TextField = new TextField();
8   txtFld.x = txtFld.y = 20;
9   txtFld.width = 400;
10  txtFld.autoSize = TextFieldAutoSize.LEFT;
11  txtFld.border = txtFld.background = true;
12  txtFld.multiline = txtFld.wordWrap = true;
13  txtFld.defaultTextFormat = txtFmt;
```

Lines 14 through 17 populate the field, **txtFld**, which you just set up in lines 7 through 13. Notice the inclusion of the **\t** escape character in line 15. Its backslash prevents this character from being understood as the letter "t." Instead, it's interpreted as a tab. Another escape character, **\n**, appears in line 16. In this case, the "n" is a new line character, moving the new text insert point down to the next line in the field. Therefore, each time through the loop, new text is added on a new line.

All we need to do now is add our tab stops to ensure that the columns line up nicely. These are applied in line 20, using an array of pixel values to indicate the location of each tab stop. We applied this property later, in line 20, for demonstration purposes. You may go back and edit a **TextFormat** instance at any time. After you make such a change, however, you must *reapply* the format to the text field, as seen in line 21, for the change to be reflected in the field.

**NOTE**

*As a nicety, Flash Professional will warn you that using the compound assignment operator (+=) is slower than using the* **appendText()** *method.*

**NOTE**

*At the end of this chapter, we'll show you a way to create true column-based layouts using a new Flash Platform text technology. Unlike simple tab-based columns, text using this technology can flow into columns, wrap from one column to the next, and adjust when the text is changed.*

```
14   for (var i:Number = 0; i < 10; i++) {
15       txtFld.appendText("product:\t" + String(i) + "\tin stock:\t"
16                         + "yes\n");
17   }
18   addChild(txtFld);
19
20   txtFmt.tabStops = [120, 200];
21   txtFld.setTextFormat(txtFmt);
```

# Using Embedded Fonts

Up to this point, we've been using system fonts in our examples. When a custom font is required, you must *embed* that font to ensure that it displays properly on all machines. Embedding adds just enough vector information to the SWF for the Flash Player to display the font, even if it's not in a user's operating system. The embedding process has changed through the evolution of Flash Professional, so we'll cite versions where appropriate.

## Flash Professional CS3 and CS4

The first step to embedding a font in Flash Professional CS3 or CS4 is to create a new font symbol from the Library panel's menu, seen in Figure 10-2. In the resulting Font Symbols Properties dialog—Figures 10-3 (CS3) and 10-4 (CS4)—choose the font and font style you wish to embed.

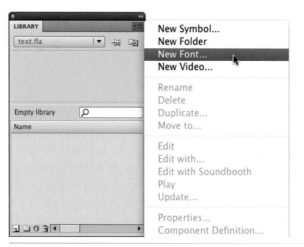

*Figure 10-2. Creating a new font from the Library menu (CS4 pictured)*

In Flash Professional CS3, you select the bold, italic, or combination bold/italic styles by using the checkboxes below the font name (see Figure 10-3). In Flash Professional CS4, support for font families was introduced. You select these styles using the font family's dedicated bold, italic (oblique), or bold/italic font in the Style menu. Older fonts that don't have individual style variants may support the checkboxes for faux bold and italic found below the Style menu.

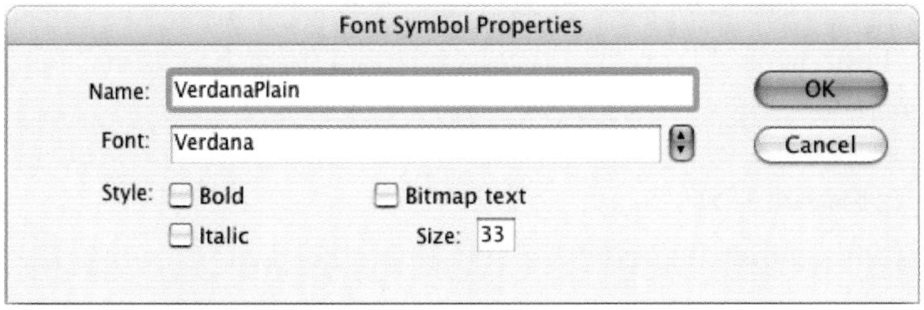

*Figure 10-3. Font Symbol Properties (CS3 pictured)*

Each font symbol can style text in a preset manner only: plain, bold, italic, or a combination thereof, and they can't be combined at runtime. So, to include separate bold and italic font styles, for example, you need a font symbol for bold and a font symbol for italic.

As with other symbols, such as movie clips, we need to use a linkage class to instantiate a font symbol. So the name of the symbol itself should be useful and descriptive, but need not follow any specific conventions. When creating a linkage class, on the other hand (using the same Library menu shown in Figure 10-2), the class name should follow the same naming conventions applied to other classes throughout earlier chapters. For example, the name should contain no spaces and start with a capital letter. Figure 10-4 shows a class name for the font symbol in the exercise we're building, `VerdanaPlain`.

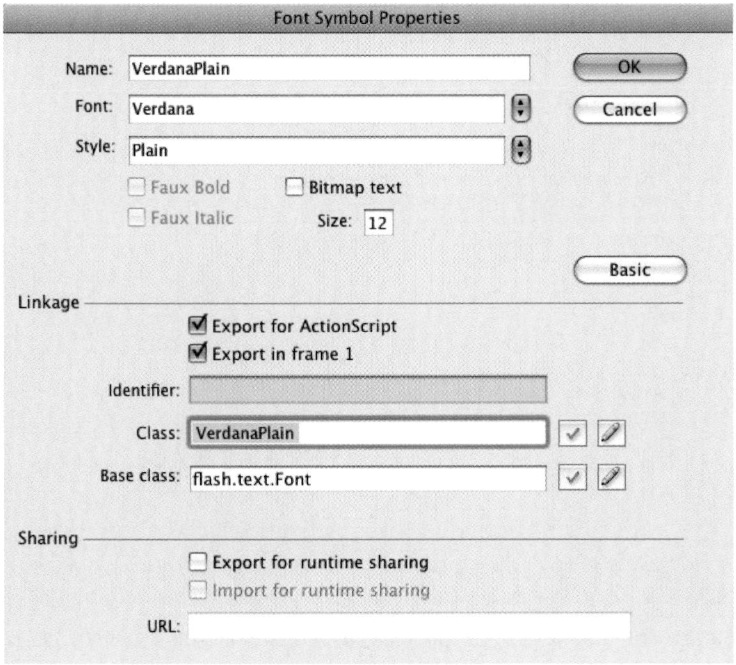

*Figure 10-4. Font Symbol Properties (CS4 pictured)*

In both Flash Professional CS3 and CS4, the Linkage information can be found in the Font Symbol Properties dialog, accessed from the Library menu after the Font symbol has been created.

## Flash Professional CS5

The process for embedding fonts in Flash Professional CS5 has been improved and simplified. All of the steps discussed in the CS3/CS4 section are accessed in one dialog box in version CS5. This dialog box is accessed by the Text→Font Embedding menu command. Figure 10-5 shows the Options tab of this dialog box. At the top, selecting a font is similar to the process used in CS4, choosing a name, picking a family, and selecting a style.

As of CS5, however, you can specify which glyphs (characters) should be embedded with the font, just like you can when you embed fonts into a specific text field using the Flash Professional Properties panel. This allows you to select only a subset of the glyphs in a particular font family, which reduces file size. In Figure 10-5, only uppercase, lowercase, numerals, and punctuation characters are being embedded.

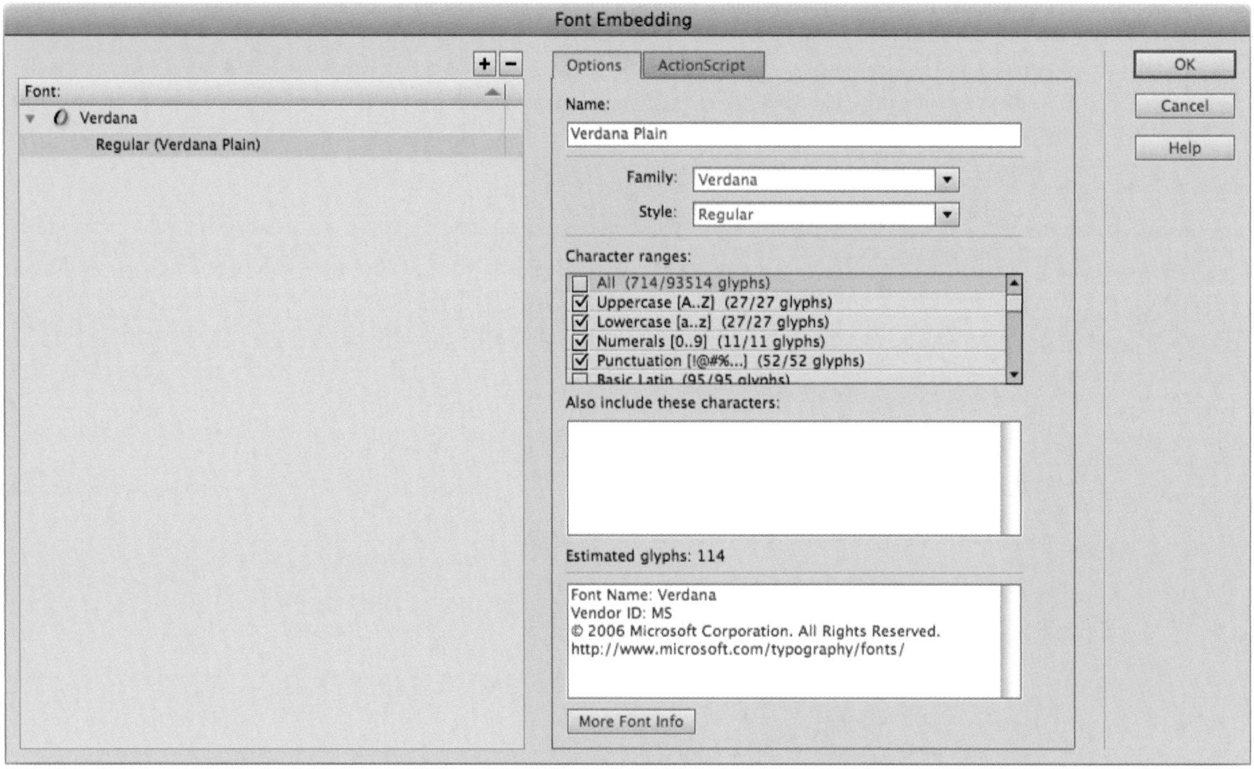

*Figure 10-5. Flash Professional CS5's Font Embedding dialog, showing the Options tab*

Next to the Options tab in the dialog box is the ActionScript tab, as shown in Figure 10-6. Under this tab, you can export for ActionScript use and set a linkage class name, as is possible in previous versions of Flash Professional. At the top of this dialog box, you'll notice an Outline format section with options for Classic and TLF text. Classic text includes dynamic and input text fields, and TLF is a new text field type that stands for Text Layout Framework, which we'll discuss at the end of the chapter. If you embed an OpenType or TrueType font, you can choose the appropriate outline format for the kind of field you intend to use: Classic for Classic text fields, and TLF for Text Layout Framework fields.

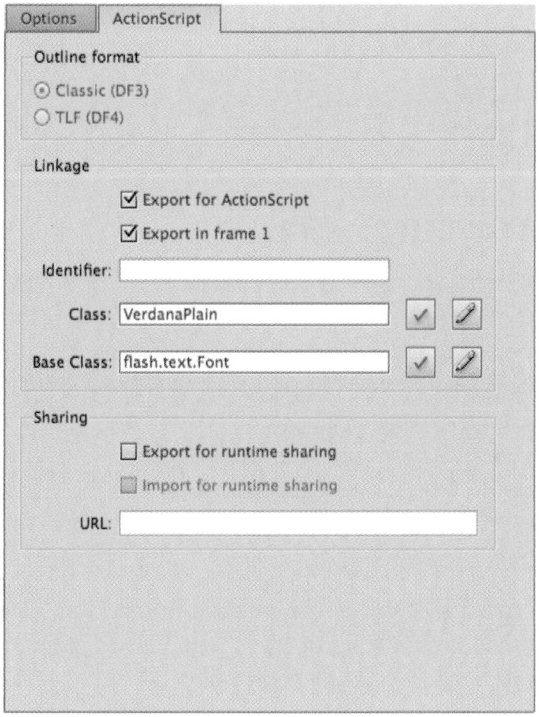

*Figure 10-6. A detail of the ActionScript tab from Flash Professional CS5's Font Embedding dialog*

Regardless of which version of Flash Professional you use, you end up with the same thing at this point: a Font Symbol that can be instantiated at runtime using ActionScript.

## ActionScript

Once your symbol has been embedded and given a linkage name, you're ready to use it in a **TextFormat** instance. The following code, found in the *embed_font.fla* source file, uses embedded fonts and the **VerdanaPlain** font symbol created in the previous sections. Line 1 instantiates the font symbol, and line 4 applies the embedded font to the **font** property of the text format.

This is a very important step because it can be counterintuitive. You can't set the property to the class or instance reference from line 1, and you can't use a string, like "Verdana." You must specify the **fontName** property of the font symbol instance. Finally, line 14 sets the **embedFonts** property to true.

```
1   var verdanaPlain:Font = new VerdanaPlain();
2
3   var txtFmt:TextFormat = new TextFormat();
4   txtFmt.font = verdanaPlain.fontName;
5   txtFmt.size = 8;
6   txtFmt.bold = true;
7
8   var txtFld:TextField = new TextField();
9   txtFld.x = txtFld.y = 20;
10  txtFld.width = 300;
11  txtFld.defaultTextFormat = txtFmt;
12  txtFld.text = "Hello World!";
13  txtFld.selectable = false;
14  txtFld.embedFonts = true;
15  addChild(txtFld);
```

## Using Custom Anti-Aliasing

Once you use an embedded font, you can take advantage of custom anti-aliasing options. By setting the **antiAliasType** property to **ADVANCED** using the **AntiAliasType** class, you can control the thickness of the text (using a range of −200 to 200, thinner to thicker) and its sharpness (using a range of −400 to 400, blurrier to sharper). Custom anti-aliasing can be used on any type size and is one way to achieve an effect that is more pronounced than a plain font, but not quite as strong as a bold font. It's also good for softening the edges of fonts to better meld with background art, and it's particularly useful for improving the legibility of small type sizes.

The following code, when added to the example in the prior section, will adjust the text to maximum thickness and a little less sharp. This adaptation is found in the *embed_font_custom_anti-alias.fla* source file.

```
1   txtFld.antiAliasType = AntiAliasType.ADVANCED;
2   txtFld.thickness = 100;
3   txtFld.sharpness = -100;
```

# Formatting with HTML and CSS

The **TextFormat** class is great for case-by-case uses. But managing a large ActionScript project this way might become unwieldy if several formats are required and all must be manually applied. An alternative to this approach is to use HTML and CSS to style the project globally.

# Hypertext Markup Language (HTML)

Flash supports a limited subset of HTML tags, as seen in Table 10-1.

*Table 10-1. The HTML tags supported by Flash Player*

| HTML Tag | Notes |
|---|---|
| `<font>` | Supported attributes include: `color`, `face`, `size`. |
| `<b>` | Bold version of font must exist to work. |
| `<i>` | Italic version of font must exist to work. |
| `<u>` | Underlines text. |
| `<span>` | Supported attributes include: `class`. |
| `<p>` | `multiline` must be enabled to work; supported attributes include: `align` and `class`. |
| `<br>` | `multiline` must be enabled to work. |
| `<li>` | All lists are bulleted; ordered and unordered qualifiers are ignored. |
| `<img>` | Supported attributes include: `src`, `width`, `height`, `align`, `hspace`, `vspace`, and `id`; can embed external images (JPG, GIF, PNG) and SWF files with automatic text flow around the images. |
| `<a>` | Supported attributes include: `href` and `target`. |
| `<textformat>` | Used to apply a limited subset of `TextFormat` properties to text; supported attributes include: `blockindent`, `indent`, `leading`, `leftmargin`, `rightmargin`, and `tabstops`. |

To use HTML in a text field, you need only switch from using the **text** property to using the **htmlText** property. For example, the following code will put the word "ActionScript," in bold, into a text field:

```
txtFld.htmlText = "<b>ActionScript</b>";
```

If you are seeing unexpected results, you should look closely at Table 10-1 for anything that might vary from what you have written, and to ensure Flash-specific requirements have been fulfilled for a particular tag to function. For example, it should make sense that line breaks (through use of `<p>` or `<br>` tags) require a **multiline** field, because you can't have a line break if more than one line isn't supported. However, it may not be obvious that `<ol>` and `<ul>` have no effect on list items, resulting in bullets for all lists.

**NOTE**

*The efficient **appendText()** method does not work with HTML, so you must use traditional compound addition (**+=**) to append HTML text to a field.*

# CSS

ActionScript also supports a limited subset of CSS properties, as seen in Table 10-2. Style sheets require a bit more setup than just using the **htmlText** property to populate fields. We'll begin by demonstrating how to create style objects with code, and then the last section of the chapter will describe how to load both the HTML and CSS data from external files.

*Table 10-2. The CSS properties supported by Flash Player*

| CSS Property | AS3 Property | Notes |
|---|---|---|
| color | color | Font color in "#RRGGBB" format. |
| display | display | Controls display of an item. Values include: **none**, **block**, and **inline**. |
| font-family | fontFamily | Font name in comma-separated list to indicate priority; device fonts also supported using the following conversions: **mono** = _typewriter, **sans-serif** = _sans, and **serif** = _serif. |
| font-size | fontSize | Font size in pixels. |
| font-style | fontStyle | Font style. Values include: **italic** and **normal**. |
| font-weight | fontWeight | Font style. Values include: **bold** and **normal**. |
| kerning | kerning | Turns kerning on or off. Value can be **true** or **false**. |
| leading | leading | Number of pixels added after each line. A negative value condenses the space between lines. |
| letter-spacing | letterSpacing | Specified in pixels. |
| margin-left | marginLeft | Specified in pixels. |
| margin-right | marginRight | Specified in pixels. |
| text-align | textAlign | Aligns text. Values include: **left**, **right**, **center**, and **justify**. |
| text-decoration | textDecoration | Underlines text. Values include: **underline none**. |
| text-indent | textIndent | First-line paragraph indent specified in pixels. |

The process of building a style sheet involves creating an instance of the **StyleSheet** class, and then adding styled objects for each tag or class to the instance. For each tag or class, you create a custom object to which the relevant CSS properties are added. Once complete, each object is associated with the tag or class and added to your style sheet using the **setStyle()** method.

In the following example, seen in *html_css.fla*, line 1 creates the style sheet, lines 3 through 21 create styles for the **body** HTML tag, **heading** CSS class, **byline** CSS class, and **a** (anchor) HTML tag respectively. Finally, lines 23 through 26 add each style to the **css** instance of the **StyleSheet** class.

```
1   var css:StyleSheet = new StyleSheet();
2
3   var body:Object = new Object();
4   body.fontFamily = "Verdana";
5   body.textIndent = 20;
6
7   var heading:Object = new Object();
8   heading.fontSize = 18;
9   heading.fontWeight = "bold";
10  heading.textIndent = -20;
11  heading.letterSpacing = 1;
12  heading.color = "#FF6633";
13
14  var byline:Object = new Object();
15  byline.fontSize = 14;
16  byline.fontStyle = "italic";
17  byline.textAlign = "right";
```

```
18
19   var a:Object = new Object();
20   a.color = "#990099";
21   a.textDecoration = "underline";
22
23   css.setStyle(".heading", heading);
24   css.setStyle(".byline", byline);
25   css.setStyle("body", body);
26   css.setStyle("a", a);
```

The remainder of the script creates and sets up a text field, and then populates it with HTML. Remember, the **appendText()** method will not work when using the **htmlText** property. Instead, you must use the compound assignment operator for addition.

More importantly, however, we must stress that the style sheet must be applied *before* the HTML is added to the field. If you don't follow this rule, the style sheet won't be applied. In this example, the style sheet is applied in line 33, before the HTML is added to the field beginning at line 34.

```
27   var txtFld:TextField = new TextField();
28   txtFld.x = txtFld.y = 20;
29   txtFld.width = 500;
30   txtFld.autoSize = TextFieldAutoSize.LEFT;
31   txtFld.multiline = true;
32   txtFld.wordWrap = true;
33   txtFld.styleSheet = css;
34   txtFld.htmlText = "<body>";
35   txtFld.htmlText += "<span class='heading'>ActionScript 10.0 Adds
     Time Travel</span><br><br>";
36   txtFld.htmlText += "<span class='byline'>by Walter Westinghouse</
     span><br><br>";
37   txtFld.htmlText += "<p>January 1, 2015. The rumors swirling around
     the tech community recently have been confirmed today as lead Flash
     Player engineer, Dr. Eldon Tyrell, announced that ActionScript 10.0
     will support time travel. Ever since the concept of time travel was
     popularized by H. G. Wells in 1895, humans have yearned for the
     ability to travel through time, and now it's a reality.</p><br>";
38   txtFld.htmlText += "<p>Flash Player QA lead Roy Batty, agreed.
     \"We're happy to add this feature to human BioChips everywhere using
     the standard Express Install Opt-In process. Flash Player has long
     been a leader in bringing immersive experiences to humans. Just
     search <a href=\"http://www.google.com\" target=\"_blank\">Google</
     a> for your favorite feature and you'll likely find that it's
     supported.\"</p><br>";
39   txtFld.htmlText += "<p>Users of the antiquated \"desktop computing\"
     model can't take advantage of this feature, nor can users of the
     recently standardized HTML5.</p>";
40   txtFld.htmlText += "</body>";
41   addChild(txtFld);
```

## Escaping quotation marks

Finally, note that lines 38 and 39 contain quotes within quotes. This would ordinarily be a problem because the second quotation mark would balance the first quotation mark and close a string. Typically, prematurely closing a string will cause a syntax error of some kind, but it virtually always results in unexpected behavior.

However, this file has no problem because the nested quotes have been escaped just like the tab and new line characters in the "Tab Stops" section of this chapter. The backslashes, when used as part of a string, prevent the characters from functioning like quotation marks and make them behave instead like any other character. It's also possible to nest single quotes within double quotes when a double-quote is not required. This is demonstrated in lines 35 and 36.

## Triggering ActionScript from HTML Links

**NOTE**

*If you are familiar with prior versions of ActionScript, the* **event:** *protocol replaces the* **asfunction:** *protocol.*

In addition to supporting standard HTML links, ActionScript can trigger functions from anchor tags. Simply replace the Internet protocol **http://** with **event:** and ActionScript will fire a **TextEvent.LINK** event that can trigger a listener function.

The following example, seen in *text_event_link.fla*, shows both a conventional **http://** link and ActionScript **event:** link in action. The traditional link is in line 10. The ActionScript **event:** link is in line 12. The link is still constructed using the *anchor* tag and *href* attribute but, instead of pointing to a URL, a string is specified—in this case, "showMsg." An event listener is added to the field in line 11, listening for the **TextEvent.LINK** event.

When a user clicks the conventional link, the normal behavior ensues automatically. Flash Player launches or switches to the default browser and navigates to the site. However, when the user clicks the "Show Message" link, the listener traps the event and calls the **linkHandler()** function, passing the link information into the argument. To demonstrate one way to handle many links, a conditional queries the text passed in from the event. If the incoming text matches a specific string, the listener traces a message to the Output panel.

```
1    var txtFmt:TextFormat = new TextFormat();
2    txtFmt.size = 18;
3    txtFmt.bullet = true;
4    txtFmt.color = 0x990099;
5
6    var txtFld:TextField = new TextField();
7    txtFld.autoSize = TextFieldAutoSize.LEFT;
8    txtFld.multiline = true;
9    txtFld.defaultTextFormat = txtFmt;
10   txtFld.htmlText = "<a href='http://www.google.com'>Search</a>";
11   txtFld.htmlText = "<br />";
12   txtFld.htmlText += "<a href='event:showMsg'>Show Message</a>";
13   txtFld.addEventListener(TextEvent.LINK, linkHandler,
14                           false, 0, true);
15   addChild(txtFld);
16
17   function linkHandler(evt:TextEvent):void {
18       if (evt.text == "showMsg") {
19           trace("Dynamic links are useful");
20       }
21   }
```

Now we come again to a point where you should stretch the mental muscles and try to take what you've learned one step further. The first topic of this section will give you a peak at what we'll be covering in Chapter 13: loading external assets. You'll learn how to load and apply external HTML and CSS files.

The second topic of this section will give a brief overview of the new Text Layout Framework that brings some advanced typographic support to ActionScript. We'll list a few pros and cons of this new technology and then show you a few examples of how to use TLF fields that differ from uses of ordinary text fields.

## Loading HTML and CSS

This exercise uses the same HTML, CSS, and some of the ActionScript from the prior HTML and CSS example but loads the content from external files. We'll discuss loading again in Chapter 13, but here we'll just focus on loading text files.

The assets you'll need for this exercise are included with the source code from the companion website, but here are the setup files in case you wish to recreate them on your own. The following files should go in the same directory as your host *.fla* file. In case you want to try the sample files, they're found in the *LoadHTMLCSS_Example* directory of the source archive, and the FLA uses the class as a document class.

HTML (*demo.html*)

```
<body>
    <p class='heading'>ActionScript 10.0 Adds Time Travel</p>
    <p class='byline'>by Walter Westinghouse</p>
    <p>January 1, 2015. The rumors swirling around the tech
        community recently have been confirmed today as lead
        Flash Player engineer, Dr. Eldon Tyrell, announced that
        ActionScript 10.0 will support time travel. Ever since
        the concept of time travel was popularized by
        <a href="event:author of early science fiction novel,
        The Time Machine">H. G. Wells</a> in 1895, humans have
        yearned for the ability to travel through time, and now
        it's a reality.
    </p>
    <p>Flash Player QA lead Roy Batty, agreed. "We're happy to
        add this feature to human BioChips everywhere using the
        standard Express Install Opt-In process. Flash Player has
        long been a leader in bringing immersive experiences to
        humans. Just search <a href="http://www.google.com"
        target="_blank"> Google</a> for your favorite feature and
        you'll likely find that it's supported."
    </p>
    <p>Users of the antiquated "desktop computing" model can't
        take advantage of this feature, nor can users of the
        recently standardized HTML5.
    </p>
</body>
```

**NOTE**

*When text resides in an external file and you're not assigning strings to variables in ActionScript, nested quotes are typically not a problem and don't have to be escaped with a backslash character.*

CSS (*demo.css*)

```css
body {
    font-family: Verdana;
    text-indent: 20px;
}

.heading {
    font-size: 18px;
    font-weight: bold;
    text-indent: -20px;
    letter-spacing: 1px;
    color: #FF6633;
}

.byline {
    font-size: 14px;
    font-style: italic;
    text-align: right;
}

a:link {
    color: #000099;
    text-decoration: underline;
}

a:hover {
    color: #990099;
}
```

ActionScript (*LoadHTMLCSS_Eample.as*)

Loading HTML and CSS from external files requires use of the **URLLoader** and **URLRequest** classes. The loading process is the same for both HTML and CSS, so we'll focus on one and discuss the other briefly. You'll also use the **Event. COMPLETE** event to continue after the loading is complete.

Lines 1 through 12 set up the class by creating the package, importing required classes, and creating the class. Lines 14 through 17 create four private properties that reference two loaders, the CSS data, and a text field used to display a definition when the user clicks on a term in a link.

```actionscript
1    package {
2
3        import flash.display.MovieClip;
4        import flash.events.Event;
5        import flash.events.TextEvent;
6        import flash.net.URLLoader;
7        import flash.net.URLRequest;
8        import flash.text.StyleSheet;
9        import flash.text.TextField;
10       import flash.text.TextFormat;
11
12       public class LoadHTMLCSS_Example extends MovieClip {
13
14           private var _cssFile:URLLoader;
15           private var _htmlFile:URLLoader;
16           private var _css:StyleSheet;
17           private var _definitionField:TextField;
```

The constructor sets up the CSS loading, so we'll focus on that in detail. Line 19 creates an instance of the **URLLoader** class that you can monitor. Lines 20 through 22 add a listener to that instance, which calls the **onLoadCSS()** function when the load is complete. Line 23 creates an instance of the **URLRequest** class for the URL that points to our external CSS file. A **URLRequest** object is used for all loads and allows for consistent handling of URLs throughout ActionScript 3.0. Line 24 loads the CSS.

```
18          //constructor
19          public function LoadHTMLCSS_Example() {
20              _cssFile = new URLLoader();
21              _cssFile.addEventListener(Event.COMPLETE, onLoadCSS,
22                                        false, 0, true);
23              var req:URLRequest = new URLRequest("demo.css");
24              _cssFile.load(req);
25          }
```

When the CSS document loads, the function in the following code block is called. Line 28 creates a new **StyleSheet** instance, and line 29 parses the CSS data sent to the listener function. Note the use of the **data** property to retrieve this information from the event's target (in this case, the **cssFile** instance responsible for the loading). The style sheet is now ready to be applied, but neither the HTML nor the text field exist yet.

Next on the to-do list is the exact same procedure for the HTML file. Line 30 creates the **URLLoader** instance, a listener is added to the instance in lines 31 and 32, a **URLRequest** instance is created in line 33, and the file is loaded in line 34.

```
26          //loading style sheet
27          private function onLoadCSS(evt:Event):void {
28              _css = new StyleSheet();
29              _css.parseCSS(evt.target.data);
30              _htmlFile = new URLLoader();
31              _htmlFile.addEventListener(Event.COMPLETE, onLoadHTML,
32                                         false, 0, true);
33              var req:URLRequest = new URLRequest("demo.html");
34              _htmlFile.load(req);
35          }
```

Once the HTML is fully loaded (triggering the listener function in the following code block), it's put into the **htmlString** variable (line 38). In line 40, a text field is created that will hold the body copy from the story in the loaded HTML. Lines 41 through 52 do nothing that we haven't already covered, but it warrants repeating that the CSS is applied *before* the HTML is added to the field (lines 47 and 48, respectively). Also, a listener is added to trap any link-based ActionScript triggered by an HTML anchor tag's **event:** protocol. This event will be used to show a definition of a term clicked on in the main body text.

Lines 54 through 57 create a **TextFormat** instance to format any definition displayed, and lines 59 through 66 create the field to hold that definition. The last thing the function does is clean up a bit by removing the listeners from the two **URLLoader** instances, because everything has loaded successfully at that point in the code.

The last functions in the class, **onTextEvent()** places the definition sent by any **event:** link click to the **_definitionField** text field.

```
36          //loading html
37          private function onLoadHTML(evt:Event):void {
38              var htmlString:String = evt.target.data;
39
40              var storyField:TextField = new TextField();
41              storyField.x = storyField.y = 20;
42              storyField.width = 500;
43              storyField.height = 330;
44              storyField.multiline = true;
45              storyField.wordWrap = true;
46              storyField.selectable = false;
47              storyField.styleSheet = _css;
48              storyField.htmlText = htmlString;
49              storyField.addEventListener(TextEvent.LINK,
50                                          onTextEvent,
51                                          false, 0, true);
52              addChild(storyField);
53
54              var definitionFormat:TextFormat = new TextFormat();
55              definitionFormat.font = "_sans";
56              definitionFormat.size = 12;
57              definitionFormat.italic = true;
58
59              _definitionField = new TextField();
60              _definitionField.x = 20;
61              _definitionField.y = 360;
62              _definitionField.width = 500;
63              _definitionField.height = 20;
64              _definitionField.mouseEnabled = false;
65              _definitionField.defaultTextFormat = definitionFormat;
66              addChild(_definitionField);
67
68              _cssFile.removeEventListener(Event.COMPLETE,
69                                          onLoadCSS);
70              _htmlFile.removeEventListener(Event.COMPLETE,
71                                          onLoadHTML);
72          }
73
74          private function onTextEvent(evt:TextEvent):void {
75              _definitionField.text = evt.text;
76          }
77      }
78  }
```

With this exercise as a basis for future work, you can control the text formatting for very large projects by applying a project-wide CSS document to every applicable text field. This also makes your development process much easier because you can edit the external CSS file and its styles will be updated everywhere the file is used. The document in Figure 10-7 was created using external HTML data and formatted using a CSS document.

## ActionScript 10.0 Adds Time Travel

*by Walter Westinghouse*

January 1, 2015. The rumors swirling around the tech community recently have been confirmed today as lead Flash Player engineer, Dr. Eldon Tyrell, announced that ActionScript 10.0 will support time travel. Ever since the concept of time travel was popularized by <u>H. G. Wells</u> in 1895, humans have yearning for the ability to travel through time, and now it's a reality.

Flash Player QA lead Roy Batty, agreed. "We're happy to add this feature to human BioChips everywhere using the standard Express Install Opt-In process. Flash Player has long been a leader in bringing immersive experiences to humans. Just search <u>Google</u> for your favorite feature and you'll likely find that it's supported."

Users of the antiquated "desktop computing" model can't take advantage of this feature, nor can users of the recently standardized HTML5.

*Figure 10-7. Text loaded and styled from external HTML and CSS data*

# Text Layout Framework

Integrated in Flash Professional CS5 and Flash Builder 4, a new text mechanism called Text Layout Framework (TLF) brings unprecedented control over type to the Flash Platform. TLF requires Flash Player 10 and the following are just a few of things that TLF offers:

- Added character styles including subscript, superscript, underline, strikethrough, case conversion, enhanced leading, ligatures, highlight color, and more.

- Added paragraph styles including multicolumn support with gutter width, last line justification options, enhanced margins and indents, paragraph spacing, padding, and more.

- Text flow across multiple linked text containers.

- Support for alpha and rotation transformations when using device fonts.

- Support for 3D rotation, color effects, and blend modes without first placing the field into a movie clip or sprite.

- Support for right-to-left text for languages like Arabic and Hebrew.

- Support for bidirectional text, or right-to-left text that can contain elements within it that flow left-to-right. This is important for embedding English words or numbers within Arabic or Hebrew text, for example.

Along with TLF's extensive feature set comes complexity. We want to stress that we consider TLF to be an intermediate to advanced feature, depending on how deeply you want to delve into its inner workings. Documentation, in particular, is still in its infancy. However, we thought it important to discuss

**NOTE**

*TLF was first introduced to Flash Professional users in beta format as a component for Flash Professional CS4 and to other ActionScript editors (such as Adobe's Flash Builder 4 and Powerflasher's FDT) via the beta version of the Flex 4 SDK.*

*At the time of this writing, it's still available on Adobe Labs: http://labs.adobe. com/technologies/textlayout/. However, there is no guarantee that it will remain available for Flash Professional CS4, nor is it certain that the beta release is stable enough to use in production.*

*If you are interested in using TLF, we recommend using Flash Professional CS5, Flash Builder 4, or another editor built around the release version of the Flex 4 SDK.*

TLF in this book because it offers several useful text features not supported by the traditional Flash Platform text technology (now called Classic text, and covered throughout this chapter).

For basic use, the ActionScript syntax for creating and manipulating TLF fields is very similar to that of Classic text fields, so we'll avoid straight repetition wherever possible. For the following exercises, we've chosen a practical subset of TLF's features that are likely to be useful in a variety of situations and apply to the widest range of possible users. We're just discussing the tip of the proverbial iceberg, however. Please consider this section an introduction to TLF—a trial run that will, at best, encourage you to explore additional capabilities and, at minimum, provide you with a set of code blueprints that you can adapt for your own use.

## Rotating device fonts

Using Classic text fields, rotating a field will cause device fonts to disappear. The workaround for this issue is to embed the font in your SWF—after which the text will display correctly. The problem is, every font symbol you embed contributes to file size, and adding TLF fields to your files requires only a one-time file size increase for each user (which we'll discuss at the end of this section). So, if you intend to use many device fonts, or even several variants of a small number of device fonts, you may be better served by using TLF.

The following code, found in the *tlf_rotation.fla* source file demonstrates rotation of both Classic and TLF text fields. The Classic field is positioned at x, y coordinates (20, 20), and the TLF field is placed at (100, 100). In the former case, the rotation causes the device font text to disappear. However, the same device font used in the TLF field remains visible.

```
1   import fl.text.TLFTextField;
2
3   var txtFld:TextField = new TextField();
4   txtFld.x = txtFld.y = 20;
5   txtFld.text = "Hello World!";
6   txtFld.rotation = 45;
7   addChild(txtFld);
8
9   var tlfFld:TLFTextField = new TLFTextField();
10  tlfFld.x = tlfFld.y = 100;
11  tlfFld.text = "Hello World!";
12  tlfFld.rotation = 45;
13  addChild(tlfFld);
```

## Improved typographic controls

In many ways, the core of the Text Layout Framework is the **TextFlow** class (contained in the **flashx.textLayout.elements** package provided by Adobe) and its TextFlow markup syntax. TextFlow markup is a bit like a cross between XML and HTML. It's structured like XML but has predefined tags and attributes, and controls display features. Manipulating this class is your ticket to improved typographic control, columnar layout, and more.

Although you can populate a `TextFlow` instance incrementally using string input, it requires creating each paragraph, span, and so on individually with a collection of classes and a fair amount of additional syntax. Sometimes it's simpler to write the `TextFlow` content as one string containing markup syntax, which is structured much like HTML. Understanding the syntax is not difficult, but explaining HTML-style syntax is outside the scope of this book.

Unfortunately, no clear documentation of the `TextFlow` markup syntax currently exists. At the time of this writing, Adobe recommends an understanding of `TextFlow` markup tags (Table 10-3) to learn how to structure the content and consulting the documentation of the `TextLayoutFramework` class (*http://help.adobe.com/en_US/FlashPlatform/reference/actionscript/3/flashx/textLayout/formats/TextLayoutFormat.html*) to learn how to lay out and format the content within the field.

**NOTE**

*See the post "Building a TLF TextFlow" at the companion website for an example of writing TextFlow content incrementally.*

*Table 10-3. TextFlow markup tags*

| Element | Notes |
|---|---|
| div | A division of text; can contain only **div** or **p** elements |
| p | A paragraph; can contain any element except **div** |
| br | A break character; text continues on the next line but does not start a new paragraph |
| a | A hypertext link (anchor); can contain **span**, **img**, **br**, **tab**, and **tcy** elements |
| span | A run of text in a paragraph; cannot contain other elements |
| img | An image in a paragraph element |
| tab | A tab character; (not included in this chapter's examples) |
| tcy | A run of horizontal text, used within vertical text (such as Japanese) used, for example, to include English text within Japanese text. can contain the **a**, **span**, **img**, **tab**, or **br** elements; (not included in this chapter's examples) |

Figure 10-8 shows the hierarchical relationship among `TextFlow` elements, which is also illustrated in the following sample markup structure.

```
<div>
    <p>
        text<br />
        <a>link text</a>
    </p>
    <p>
        <span>text</span><br />
        <img />
    </p>
</div>
```

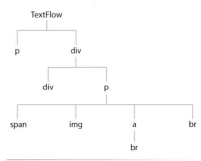

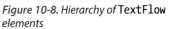

*Figure 10-8. Hierarchy of `TextFlow` elements*

Div elements (**div**) can be used to organize copy into separate sections and commonly apply block styling that might apply to multiple paragraphs. Paragraph elements (**p**) are used (unsurprisingly) to define discrete paragraphs and contain paragraph-wide styling. They need not be limited to text, however. It's common, for example, to enclose images (**img**) or lists of links (**a**) in paragraph tags, as shown previously. Span elements are used to style segments of a paragraph because they don't force a line break. Finally, if a line break (**br**) is desired, you can add them anywhere within a paragraph or link element.

Table 10-4 describes a selection of TextFlow formatting options, all of which are used in the following example.

*Table 10-4. Select TextFlow formatting options*

| Element | Notes |
|---|---|
| fontFamily | Font family; can contain a comma-separated list of font families; the first font in the list found will be used. |
| fontSize | Font size from 1 to 720, or **inherit**. |
| fontWeight | Font weight; values include **normal**, **bold**, and **inherit**; applies only to device fonts, as embedded fonts use one font family, including weight and style, per font symbol. |
| fontStyle | Font style; values include **normal**, **italic**, and **inherit**; applies only to device fonts, as embedded fonts use one font family, including weight and style, per font symbol. |
| typographicCase | Case; values include **default** (mixed case), **upper**, **lower**, **smallCaps**, and **inherit**. |
| textDecoration | Underline; values include **none**, **underline**, and **inherit**. |
| color | Color in string hexadecimal format (#FF0000 for red, for example). |
| lineThrough | Character strike-through; values include **true**, **false**, and **inherit**. |
| textAlign | Text alignment; values include **left**, **right**, **center**, **justify**, **start**, **end**, and **inherit**; **start** and **end** are designed to accommodate alignment in text that can be right-to-left or left-to-right; **start** represents left in left-to-right text and right in right-to-left text; **end** represents right in left-to-right text and left in left-to-right text. |
| textAlpha | Opacity from 0 to 1 and **inherit**. |
| trackingRight | Letter spacing in pixels or percent of font size (with % symbol), and **inherit**; number values for both pixels and percent range from −1000 to 1000;. |
| textRotation | Character rotation; values include **rotate0**, **rotate90**, **rotate180**, **rotate270**, **auto**, and **inherit**. |
| lineHeight | Leading in pixels (−720 to 720), percent of font size (−1000 to 1000, with % symbol), or **inherit**. |
| baselineShift | Distance from baseline in pixels (−1000 to 1000) percent of font size (−1000 to 1000 with % symbol), **subscript**, **superscript**, or **inherit**. |
| alignmentBaseline | Aligns baseline of specified text to baseline; values include **roman**, **ascent**, **descent**, **ideographicCenter**, **ideographicTop**, **ideographicBottom**, **useDominantBaseline**, and **inherit**; ideographic baselines used by Asian fonts; **useDominantBaseline** used when Asian fonts enabled, determining baseline of text explicitly selected, not by paragraph. See Figure 10-9. |

**NOTE**

*Elements without a balancing closing tag, such as* **img** *and* **br**, *must be applied as self-closing tags to conform to XML specifications. This means you must add a slash as the last character inside the tag:* **<br />**.

*Figure 10-9. TLF text baselines*

The following code is found in the *tlf_typography.fla* source file. It demonstrates many of the most common formatting options used in a **TextFlow** string, including some of those listed in Table 10-4. This example shows the simplest way to apply a **TextFlow** string to a **TLFTextField** class instance. The field's **tlfMarkup** property will automatically populate the field's internal **TextFlow** instance without first having to process the incoming string. Figure 10-10 shows the outcome of this file.

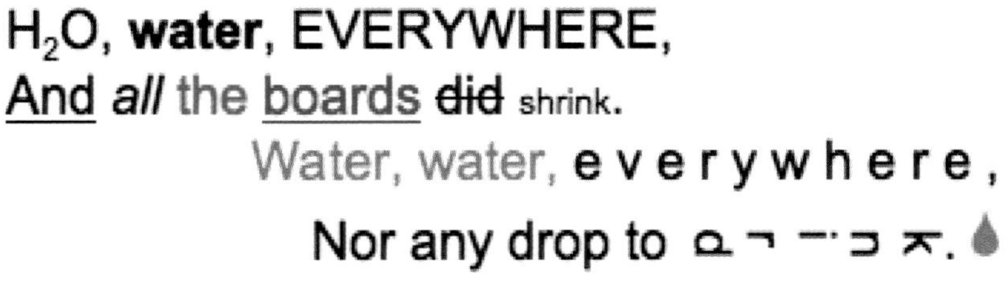

H$_2$O, **water**, EVERYWHERE,
And *all* the boards did shrink.
Water, water, **e v e r y w h e r e ,**
Nor any drop to ם ר ־־ כ א.

*Figure 10-10. A TLF field formatted by a TextFlow markup string*

**NOTE**

*The text in this example is a modified excerpt of "The Rime of the Ancient Mariner" by Samuel Taylor Coleridge.*

```
1    import fl.text.TLFTextField;
2
3    var tlfTxt:TLFTextField = new TLFTextField();
4    tlfTxt.x = tlfTxt.y = 100;
5    tlfTxt.width = 350;
6    tlfTxt.multiline = true;
7    tlfTxt.wordWrap = true;
8    tlfText.selectable = false;
9    addChild(tlfTxt);
10
11   tlfTxt.tlfMarkup = "<TextFlow xmlns='http://ns.adobe.com/
     textLayout/2008' fontFamily='Arial' fontSize='18'><div><p>H<span
     baselineShift='subscript' alignmentBaseline='descent'>2</
     span>0, <span fontWeight='bold'>water</span>, <span typ
     ographicCase='uppercase'>everywhere</span>,<br /><span
     textDecoration='underline'>And</span> <span fontStyle='italic'>all</
     span> <span color='#009900'>the</span> <a href='http://
     en.wikipedia.org/wiki/The_Rime_of_the_Ancient_Mariner'>boards</
     a> <span lineThrough='true'>did</span> <span fontSize='12'>shrink</
     span>.</p></div><p textAlign='right'><span textAlpha='0.5'>Water,
     water,</span> <span trackingRight='5'>everywhere</span>,<br
     /><span lineHeight='150%'>Nor any drop to</span> <span
     textRotation='rotate90' baselineShift='10'>drink</span>. <img
     width='10' height='16' source='water_drop.jpg' /></p></TextFlow>";
```

One side effect of this approach, however, is that the **TextFlow** instance is tied to the field. In the last example of the chapter, we'll look at an alternative approach that creates an independent **TextFlow** instance first, and then translates a string to populate it.

**NOTE**

*If when testing your file you get no errors but the text does not display, check the syntax of your **TextFlow** string. Look for single tags that are not self-closing (**<br>**, for example), tags that are not balanced (such as a **** with no ****), incorrect or misspelled format properties, and improperly nested tags (such as text within a **<div>** rather than within a **<p>** inside that **<div>**).*

## Columnar layout

The following code, found in *tlf_columns.fla*, builds on the prior source file. Adding this code to the end of the prior example provides a simple demonstration of columnar layout. Arranging TLF text in columns requires direct manipulation of a `TextFlow` instance. In the prior example, however, working directly with a `TextFlow` instance was not required, thanks to the field's `tlfMarkup` property. This code demonstrates a simple way of gaining access to a populated TLF field's `TextFlow` instance through its `textFlow` property:

```
12  //addition to previous example
13  import flashx.textLayout.elements.TextFlow;
14
15  var tlfTextFlow:TextFlow = tlfTxt.textFlow;
16  tlfTextFlow.columnCount = 1;
17  tlfTextFlow.columnGap = 30;
18
19  stage.addEventListener(MouseEvent.CLICK, onClick, false, 0, true);
20  function onClick(evt:MouseEvent):void {
21      if (tlfTextFlow.columnCount == 1) {
22          tlfTextFlow.columnCount = 2;
23      } else {
24          tlfTextFlow.columnCount = 1;
25      }
26      tlfTextFlow.flowComposer.updateAllControllers();
27  }
```

Line 13 adds an import statement for the `TextFlow` class. Line 15 creates a `TextFlow` instance by referencing the field's `textFlow` property. All that remains is to set the `columnCount` and, optionally, the `columnGap` properties. In this example, a mouse click will change the column count at runtime to demonstrate the automatic reflow of text. Line 16 sets the initial number of columns to 1, to match the appearance of the prior example. Line 17 sets the gap between columns to 30 pixels. This has no immediate effect on the layout of the text.

**NOTE**

*Although code is consolidated in this book into logical blocks, import statements can be moved to the top of the collected script if you prefer. This optional edit will organize all your import statements in one place for clarity but will not affect the file in any other way.*

However, lines 19 through 27 create a mouse click listener and add it to the stage. With each mouse click, the conditional beginning in line 20 checks the number of columns in the field and toggles between 1 and 2 columns. Finally, Line 26 instructs the flow composer (which controls the flow of text) of the `TextFlow` instance to update the text flow of the field. Because the field is already populated, the layout reflows between 1 and 2 columns on the fly. Figure 10-11 shows the two-column layout of the file.

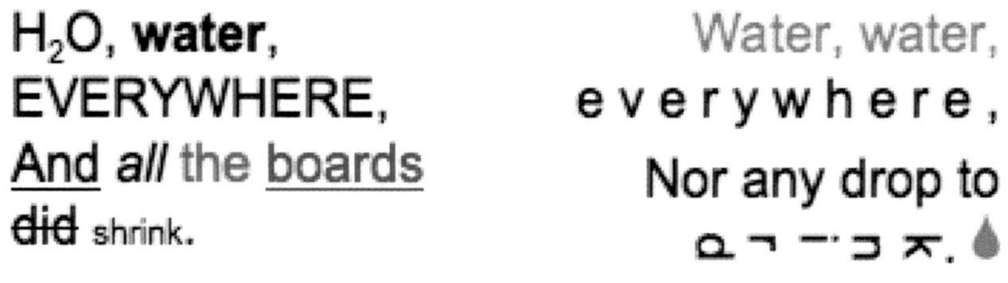

*Figure 10-11. The same TLF field from Figure 10-10, reflowed into two columns*

## Flowing text across multiple containers

The last example of the chapter is the most advanced and demonstrates one of TLF's most powerful features: the ability to flow text across multiple containers. This is called *linked text*, or *threaded text*, because the text is not broken apart when populating more than one text field. Instead, it flows through linked text fields, threading its way through your layout. This is further demonstrated with selectable linked text and the ability to scroll within a field while selecting text—just like you can in a text editor.

One of the first things you're likely to notice, is that this script contains no direct reference to TLF text fields. Instead, it uses the concept of *TLF containers*—sprites or movie clips that are automatically populated with TLF text by Flash Player. This approach is very powerful because it means that anywhere you can create a sprite, you can fill it with TLF text, and even link it up as part of a chain of TLF text.

For example, you could create many text fields across the stage and size them all to accommodate one line of text. You could then link them together, flow "The Rime of the Ancient Mariner" through them, and animate them up and down like undulating waves of water. Best of all, you can easily reflow the text along the linked chain whenever required.

The following code is found in the *tlf_containers.fla* source file. Lines 1 through 6 import all the classes required to complete this exercise.

```
1  import flashx.textLayout.compose.StandardFlowComposer;
2  import flashx.textLayout.container.ContainerController;
3  import flashx.textLayout.container.ScrollPolicy;
4  import flashx.textLayout.conversion.TextConverter;
5  import flashx.textLayout.edit.SelectionManager;
6  import flashx.textLayout.elements.TextFlow;
```

Lines 8 through 16 fill the field with text. Lines 8 through 12 create a string of TLF markup. Lines 9 and 12 open and close the **TextFlow** content, and lines 10 and 11 use the **dummyText()** function (found in lines 49 through 55) to fill the two paragraphs with dummy text.

Lines 14 through 16 demonstrate how to create an independent **TextFlow** instance. They use the **TextConverter** class's static method **importToFlow()** to convert the TextFlow markup into layout format. Not only does this allow you to separate the **TextFlow** from a text field for easy reuse, but it's also particularly important here because we're not making direct use of a TLF text field.

```
7   //create TextFlow instance
8   var textMarkup:String =
9       "<TextFlow xmlns='http://ns.adobe.com/textLayout/2008'>" +
10          "<p>" + dummyText() + "</p><br />" +
11          "<p>" + dummyText() + "</p>" +
12      "</TextFlow>";
13
14  var textFlow:TextFlow =
15      TextConverter.importToFlow(textMarkup,
16      TextConverter.TEXT_LAYOUT_FORMAT);
```

Lines 18 through 25 do nothing more than create sprites for cosmetic purposes. They will lie under the TLF containers to provide a border for each. This process uses the **borderedBox()** function, in lines 57 through 63, to draw borders into the sprites.

**NOTE**

*It's possible to draw directly into TLF containers, but if they are designed to scroll, they may cover one or more sides of the border. By placing self-contained border objects beneath the TLF containers, this issue is avoided.*

```
17   //create border shapes for cosmetic purpose
18   var box1:Sprite = borderedBox();
19   box1.x = box1.y = 10;
20   addChild(box1);
21
22   var box2:Sprite = borderedBox();
23   box2.x = 240;
24   box2.y = 10;
25   addChild(box2);
```

Lines 27 through 44 set up containers for the TLF text. Lines 27 through 29, and 31 through 34, create two sprites and position them side by side. Lines 36 through 39 turn these sprites into TLF containers using the **ContainerController** class. The containers and the width and height of each are passed to the class constructor. The class then does everything required to support TLF text display, all automatically.

The last part of the container code occurs in lines 41 through 44. These lines link the containers together and ready them for TLF text. Line 41 adds a new **StandardFlowComposer** instance to the **TextFlow** object's **flowComposer** property. Lines 42 and 43 add the two containers to the flow composer using the **addController()** method, and line 44 updates all the controllers, flowing the text among them.

```
26   //create TLF containers
27   var container1:Sprite = new Sprite();
28   container1.x = container1.y = 20;
29   addChild(container1);
30
31   var container2:Sprite = new Sprite();
32   container2.x = 250;
33   container2.y = 20;
34   addChild(container2);
35
36   var controllerOne:ContainerController =
37       new ContainerController(container1, 200, 200);
38   var controllerTwo:ContainerController =
39       new ContainerController(container2, 200, 200);
40
41   textFlow.flowComposer = new StandardFlowComposer();
42   textFlow.flowComposer.addController(controllerOne);
43   textFlow.flowComposer.addController(controllerTwo);
44   textFlow.flowComposer.updateAllControllers();
```

Finally, lines 46 and 47 control the selection and scrolling options. Line 46 populates the **interactionManager** of the **TextFlow** with a **SelectionManager** instance. The **interactionManager** controls how a user can interact with a container. It can enable selection, editing, or both. In this case, the resulting TLF containers will allow users to select, but not edit, their content.

Line 47 concludes our discussion by enabling vertical scrolling, but only for the second container. Because the two containers are linked and selectable, users will be able to select text across both containers. Because the second container is scrollable, dragging your mouse through the text will scroll up or down as long as content exists outside the bounds of the container in that direction. Figure 10-12 shows the result of this exercise, with a selection in progress.

```
45  //enable selection and scrolling
46  textFlow.interactionManager = new SelectionManager();
47  controllerTwo.verticalScrollPolicy = ScrollPolicy.AUTO;
48
49  function dummyText():String {
50      var str:String = "";
51      for (var i:int = 0; i < 60; i++) {
52          str += "dummy text ";
53      }
54      return str;
55  }
56
57  function borderedBox():Sprite {
58      var sp:Sprite = new Sprite();
59      var g:Graphics = sp.graphics;
60      g.lineStyle(1, 0x000000);
61      g.drawRect(0, 0, 220, 220);
62      return sp;
63  }
```

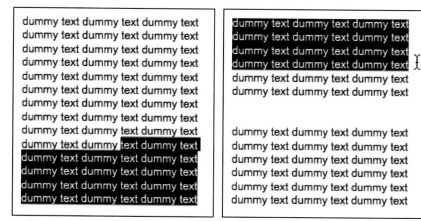

Figure 10-12. Text flowed across two TLF containers with selection in progress

## Distributing SWFs that use TLF

TLF is significantly different from Classic text when it comes to distributing your SWFs. TLF works as a *runtime shared library* (RSL)—an external archive of code (and sometimes assets) that must be distributed with your SWF.

When you publish your file, you will notice in the same directory as your SWF, that a document with the extension *.swz* has been created. This is the extension for a compressed runtime library. At the time of this writing, the

**NOTE**

*Although technically a component, this is virtually transparent to the Flash Professional CS5 user. TLF is tightly integrated into the Properties panel and, unlike other components, does not need to be in the Library of your FLA before it can be used.*

file is called *textLayout_1.0.0.595.swz*, but the numbers used in this filename may change with future releases.

Unlike the classes and packages that are compiled into your SWF when you publish your projects, runtime shared libraries remain external. They must be distributed with your SWFs, and their location relative to your SWF should be maintained. For example, if the RSL is in the same directory as your SWF, this should be true when distributing your project, as well.

In the case of the TLF, Flash Player will attempt to download the RSL from the Adobe website, but it's still a good idea to keep your own copy with your SWF in case the Adobe site is unavailable.

As external files, runtime shared libraries must be downloaded by the user, so using TLF adds about 160K to your overall project size. The good news is that you need to download each RSL only once. For example, if you create 10 projects that use TLF, and a reader views all 10 projects, the first project will initiate the download of the TLF RSL, but all remaining projects will use the library already on the reader's hard drive.

TLF also causes a problem when a parent SWF loads a child SWF that uses a TLF text field. We'll discuss this in Chapter 13 when we discuss loading external assets.

> **NOTE**
>
> *When authoring a TLF project, Flash Player will attempt to connect to the Internet to retrieve the RSL from Adobe's site. If you do not have an active connection, you will see an error something like this: "Error opening URL 'http://fpdownload.adobe.com/pub/swz/ crossdomain.xml'." If you then activate a connection later, your code will work without this error.*

## What's Next?

Text is fundamental to most ActionScript projects, and this chapter should give you the starting knowledge you need to explore text usage further. Once you've become more comfortable with using text (including tasks like displaying and formatting), start to delve deeper into the raw data that makes up text. Look at strings and break them into their constituent parts. Learn how to build and parse the paragraphs, words, and characters you see every day. Try to think of imaginative ways of generating, deconstructing, and otherwise manipulating text, such as combining string methods and properties with arrays and other ActionScript elements.

**In the next chapter**, we'll look at many ways of using sound in ActionScript, including:

- Understanding the new granular components of sound management, including individual sound channels and a global sound mixer

- Playing, stopping, and pausing internal and external sounds

- Controlling the volume and pan of sounds

- Working with microphone input

- Parsing data from sounds, including ID3 tags from MP3 files

- Visualizing frequency amplitudes

# SOUND AND VIDEO

PART **IV**

Part IV covers sound and video, the media types that arguably contributed most significantly to the ubiquitous use of Flash on the web. Chapter 11 covers the use of internal and external sound, and features examples of controlling sound playback, as well as manipulating volume and stereo panning. The chapter also includes a brief overview of parsing ID3 metadata from MP3 sounds, for display during audio playback. Also featured is a sound visualization exercise that uses the `Graphics` class from Chapter 8 to draw a waveform in real time. The chapter concludes with new features that allow access to incoming microphone data, allowing you to record, play back, and even save microphone input.

Chapter 12 contains information about encoding video using the free Adobe Media Encoder. The chapter also discusses two approaches to authoring video playback. By using components, you're able to focus more on the balance of your design and application as most of the ActionScript is taken care of for you. However, this chapter also includes the information necessary to code your own video player, so you can keep file size down if you choose not to rely on the video components. Finally, Chapter 12 provides true full-screen video examples, and covers accessibility and multilanguage projects through the use of video captioning.

## CHAPTER 11

# SOUND

As the ActionScript language has evolved, it's interesting to see how far its sound capabilities have come. Although many audio and ActionScript experts alike will say that many issues still must be overcome before the Flash Platform truly conquers sound, few will deny that the current audio features far surpass anything available in ActionScript before.

As of Flash Player 9 you can control multiple discrete channels of audio, gain direct access to the bytes of data that make up the actual sound file, process that data in several ways, and visualize its content. Flash Player 10 adds the ability to extract data from audio files, generate sound from scratch, save audio files, record microphone input without a server, and more.

If you want to be inspired before beginning your journey into ActionScript sound control, visit *http://www.audiotool.com* and play with the incredibly impressive Audiotool. This amazing project replicates a feature-rich electronic music studio and allows you to pick from many sound synthesizers, process them through a host of effects, sequence them in a near infinite number of ways, and even save and share your compositions with others.

Make no mistake: Audiotool is a very advanced project created by programming experts that have long led the way in ActionScript sound manipulation. In fact, much of what ActionScript can do today in this area is possible partially because of the efforts of this team—forever pushing the limits of the language—and the Flash Player engineers who were inspired to add greater sound features to Flash Player as a result.

Will you be able to create anything of Audiotool's complexity and quality after only working through this chapter? Realistically, no; such a project takes great skill, effort, and time to achieve. You will, however, have a good foundation of techniques on which you can build and evolve creative sound toys of your own.

To get you started, we'll look at the following introductory topics in this chapter:

- **ActionScript Sound Architecture.** Depending on what you want to do, you're likely to work with a handful of sound-related classes in ActionScript 3.0. This section provides a quick overview of the most commonly used classes.

- **Internal and External Sounds.** We'll show you how to work with internal sounds found in your library, as well as load external MP3 sounds on the fly.

- **Playing, Stopping, and Pausing Sounds.** In addition to playing and stopping sounds, you'll learn how to pause and resume playback, as well as stop sound playback in all active channels at once.

- **Buffering Streaming Sounds.** To optimize playback across slower connections, you can buffer, or preload, sounds. This ensures that sounds play longer without interruption while data continues to download.

- **Changing Sound Volume and Pan.** The `SoundTransform` class gathers volume and panning features, allowing you to increase or decrease volume, as well as move sounds between the left and right speakers.

- **Reading ID3 Metadata from MP3 Sounds.** When creating MP3 files, it's possible to embed metadata, including artist name, track title, and so on, into the file. The `ID3Info` class allows you to parse this information, if available, for use in your application.

- **Visualizing Sound Data.** Using ActionScript 3.0, you can dynamically poll the amplitude and frequency spectrum data of a sound during playback. You can use the information gathered to display visualizations of the sound, such as waveforms, peak meters, and artistic interpretations while the sound plays.

- **Working with Microphone Data.** You can also access the microphone to check the activity level periodically to visualize the amplitude of a live sound source. Depending on the version of the Flash Player you want to target, and your ActionScript compiler, you can also access the raw microphone data.

- **Recording, Playing, and Saving Microphone Input.** To end this chapter, we'll use features introduced in Flash Player versions 10 and 10.1 to record microphone input, generate sound dynamically (rather than playing an MP3, for example), and save the result as a WAV file.

## ActionScript Sound Architecture

The ActionScript 3.0 sound architecture, found in the `flash.media` package, is composed of several classes that contribute to a finer degree of control over sound data and sound manipulation than previously available. You'll be using several of these classes, so before moving on to specific examples, let's take a quick look at each.

## Sound

The **Sound** class is the first required to work with sound. It's used to load and play sounds, and manage basic sound properties.

## SoundChannel

This class is used to create a separate channel for each discrete sound file. In this context, we're not referring to the left or right channel of a stereo sound. Audio playing in an ActionScript sound channel can be either mono or stereo. Instead, an instance of this class is analogous to a channel in a recording studio mixing desk. By placing each sound in its own channel, you can work with multiple audio files but control each separately.

## SoundMixer

As the name implies, the **SoundMixer** class creates a central mixer object through which all sound channels are mixed. Changes to the mixer will affect all playing sounds. For example, you can use this class to stop all sounds that are playing.

## SoundLoaderContext

In conjunction with the **load()** method of the **Sound** class, you can use the **SoundLoaderContext** class to specify how many seconds of a sound file to buffer.

## SoundTransform

This class is used to control the volume and panning between left and right stereo channels of a source. With it, you can also affect a single sound channel, the **SoundMixer** object (to globally affect all playing sounds), the microphone, and even the sound of a video.

## ID3Info

The **ID3Info** class is used to retrieve metadata written into ID3 tags found in an MP3 file. ID3 tags store information about the MP3, including artist name, song name, track number, and genre.

## Microphone

Using the **Microphone** class, you can control the gain, sampling rate, and other properties of the user's microphone, if present. You can check the activity level of the microphone (and create simple visualizations of microphone amplitude values) in all versions of ActionScript. In Flash Player 10 and later, you can also access raw microphone data to visualize, process, and even save recorded input.

Although we'll demonstrate many capabilities of these classes, experimenting with sound is one of the most rewarding ways to learn more about what ActionScript has to offer. Be sure to carry on your learning after working through this chapter!

# Internal and External Sounds

Typically, ActionScript control of sound in your projects will include loading sounds from external sources. Keeping your sounds external to your primary SWF has many benefits. As two simple examples, external audio can keep the file size of your SWF from becoming too large, and it's easy to change the sound files without having to recompile your SWF.

Most of the examples we'll cover in this chapter use external sound files, but it's still possible to use internal sounds without having to rely on the timeline. To prepare for the remaining examples, we'll show you how to store a reference to both an internal and an external sound. Thereafter, you can adapt any exercise to use internal or external audio sources.

## Working with Sounds in Your Library

Creating an instance of a sound from your Flash Professional library is consistent with creating an instance of a display object, as described in Chapter 4 and used throughout the book. After importing a sound, you'll find it in the Library panel of your FLA file. Select the sound in the Library panel and open the Symbol Properties dialog. Click the Export for ActionScript check box and give the sound a class name. Flash Professional will automatically create a class name for you, but look at it carefully, as you may want to edit the provided text.

For example, consider a sound in your library called *claire elmo.mp3*. When exporting this symbol for ActionScript, Flash Professional will remove the space for you (all class names must be one word) giving you claireelmo.mp3. However, you must still remove the period, which is also not allowed in a class name, and omit the file extension. Finally, it's a good idea to capitalize the first character of class names and use camel case (uppercase letter for each new word) if you want to follow best practices. This gives you ClaireElmo, as shown in Figure 11-1. Appropriately, the Base class automatically assigned is the **Sound** class, so your class inherits all the accessible properties, methods, and events of the **Sound** class upon instantiation.

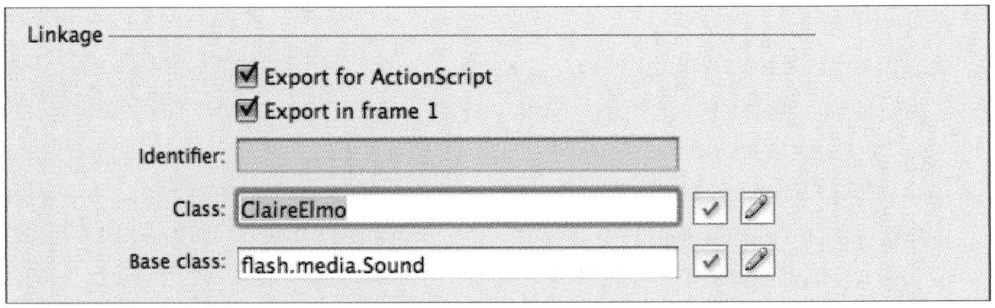

*Figure 11-1. Detail of the sound symbol's Properties dialog; choosing a linkage class name for instantiating a sound symbol with ActionScript*

Once you've provided a linkage class name, you can create an instance of the sound the same way you instantiate a movie clip:

```
var snd:Sound = new ClaireElmo();
```

Thereafter, you can manage the instance of this sound by referring to the variable **snd**. This creation of a **Sound** class instance and the use of one method to load a sound file are the only basic differences between using internal and external sounds. All play, pause, stop, and transform operations are identical, regardless of the sound source.

If you prefer to use internal sounds, the *using_internal_sound.fla* source file demonstrates the playing and stopping of a short imported sound using the basic syntax explained in the "Playing, Stopping, and Pausing Sounds" section later in this chapter. However, we recommend using external sounds for most uses.

## Loading External Sounds

Using internal sounds, creating an instance of the **Sound** class and populating it with audio occur in one step. To load a sound from an external MP3, we need to use the **load()** method of the **Sound** class, so we must first explicitly create an instance of the class. This is shown in line 1 of the following code, found in the *loading_external_sound.fla* source file.

```
1   var snd:Sound = new Sound();
2
3   var req:URLRequest = new URLRequest("song.mp3");
4   snd.load(req);
```

As discussed in prior chapters, you also need to create an instance of the **URLRequest** class (line 3) any time you load something. Although it has additional purposes for advanced URL processing, the **URLRequest** class is also used to standardize the loading process. This allows you to load many asset types in a consistent manner. Finally, we load the sound in line 4.

Once you've completed this process, you're again ready to start manipulating the **snd** instance. When working with external sounds, however, there are additional factors that warrant a little extra attention. The steps we'll describe aren't required, but they're recommended. You'll find that they improve not only your own development efforts (such as when listening for errors when loading a sound), but also the user experience (such as providing feedback during loading).

It's not uncommon when loading external assets to encounter a missing file problem. The path to the file may be old or incorrect, or the loaded asset or your SWF may have been moved. In this case, a runtime error like this may occur:

```
Error #2044: Unhandled IOErrorEvent:.
text=Error #2032: Stream Error.
```

**NOTE**

*Another difference between working with internal and external sounds is that you can buffer a loaded sound to improve playback experience. Buffering a sound means that your playback won't begin until a specified amount of sound data has loaded. This allows the background loading of the rest of the sound to stay ahead of your playback and is discussed in the "Buffering Sounds" section later in this chapter.*

So, it's a good idea to plan for this possibility and listen for an **IO_ERROR** (input/output error). If you do encounter an error, you can present it to the viewer as part of the user experience (through an alert or warning icon, for example), or just try to correct it during the authoring process by tracing to the Output panel. The following listener function traces a message, as well as the descriptive text sent with the event.

```
5   //listen for error
6   snd.addEventListener(IOErrorEvent.IO_ERROR, onIOError,
7                       false, 0, true);
8   function onIOError(evt:IOErrorEvent):void {
9       trace("Error occurred when loading sound:", evt.text);
10  }
```

The next enhancement to include when working with external sounds is to provide feedback to the user during the loading process. Again we add a listener to the sound instance, this time listening for a **PROGRESS** event, which is dispatched whenever loading progress occurs. When this happens, you can update the user by, for example, increasing the width of a sprite to create a progress bar.

Lines 12 through 24 of the following code create the progress bar. Line 12 passes a color to the **drawBar()** function (lines 17 through 24), which creates a sprite, draws a rectangle that is 1 pixel wide and 10 pixels tall, and returns the sprite. Lines 13 and 14 position the progress bar and line 15 adds it to the display list.

**NOTE**

*In this example, the progress bar will reach 100 pixels wide when the process finishes or will stay at its original 1-pixel width if the function fails. Keeping these start and finish sizes in mind when testing locally is useful because loading even very large files from a local hard drive happens very quickly, and it's quite common not to see the progress bar move at all with small sound files.*

Lines 26 through 30 contain the listener function. The event captured by the listener function carries with it information, including the total number of bytes in the target object (in this scenario the sound being loaded), as well as the number of bytes loaded at the moment the event was fired. By dividing the latter by the former, you end up with a fraction. For example, if 500 bytes of a total 1,000 bytes have loaded, the progress is 500/1,000 or 0.5, indicating that the object is 50-percent loaded. By multiplying with a desired width of the progress bar, the bar will increase to the final desired size when the file is 100-percent loaded.

```
11  //track loading progress
12  var loadBar:Sprite = drawBar(0x000099);
13  loadBar.x = 20;
14  loadBar.y = 15;
15  addChild(loadBar);
16
17  function drawBar(col:uint):Sprite {
18      var bar:Sprite = new Sprite();
19      var g:Graphics = bar.graphics;
20      g.beginFill(col, 1);
21      g.drawRect(0, 0, 1, 10);
22      g.endFill();
23      return bar;
24  }
25
26  snd.addEventListener(ProgressEvent.PROGRESS, onLoadingProgress,
27                      false, 0, true);
```

```
28  function onLoadingProgress(evt:ProgressEvent):void {
29      loadBar.width = 100 * (evt.bytesLoaded / evt.bytesTotal);
30  }
```

The last option we'll introduce here is for responding to the completion of the sound loading process. The structure is similar to the prior two event listener examples, this time using the **Event.COMPLETE** event to trigger the listener function.

```
31  //react to successful load
32  var sndLength:Number = 0;
33  snd.addEventListener(Event.COMPLETE, onCompleteLoad,
34                      false, 0, true);
35  function onCompleteLoad(evt:Event):void {
36      sndLength = snd.length;
37      trace("Sound length:", sndLength);
38  }
```

After creating the variable in line 32, this example stores the length of the sound in milliseconds in **sndLength**, and traces that value as a quick indication that the process is complete. This code is the starting point for an audio player exercise that runs throughout the chapter. Soon, we'll use the sound's length to update a progress bar during playback of the sound. First, however, let's look closely at the playback syntax.

# Playing, Stopping, and Pausing Sounds

The simple syntax of the **Sound** class's **play()** method can be a bit deceiving because it's only part of the picture. To play a sound, all you need to do is call the method from the **Sound** class instance. However, all this does is start playback and, without additional infrastructure, you can't do much else. Instead, you should play the sound into an instance of the **SoundChannel** class, which allows you to stop, pan, or adjust the volume of the channel. This is different from prior versions of ActionScript, in which all sound control rested with the **Sound** object.

To emphasize this idea, let's think again about a recording studio. To move a sound from the left speaker to the right speaker in a mix, a sound engineer would twist a knob at the mixing desk, not ask a musician to run from one side of the studio to another. Similarly, although musicians often handle volume subtleties, fading a sound up or down is typically accomplished by adjusting a sound channel's volume slider. In other words, the playback of the sound is typically separated from the manipulation of that sound in the mixing process. The same is true in ActionScript 3.0.

We'll begin with simple examples and then we'll add these features to our ongoing audio player.

## Playing a Sound

To place a sound into a channel, all you need to do is create the channel and then set it equal to the result of the sound's **play()** method.

```
var channel:SoundChannel; = new SoundChannel();
channel = snd.play();
```

This associates the sound with the specified channel, the same way you would plug a guitar into a channel in our metaphorical recording studio's mixing desk. Once the sound is in the channel, you'll be able to adjust its volume, set its pan, and stop its playback—all of which we'll discuss in a moment.

But how soon can you play the sound? If you're using imported audio files, you can typically play the sound right away. However, when working with external files, you must consider the loading process. If you invoke the **load()** method to start loading an external sound file and then immediately attempt to play the sound, your attempt will likely fail because the sound will probably still be loading. However, we saw in the previous section that a **COMPLETE** event is dispatched when a **Sound** instance's MP3 is finished loading. So, an event listener listening for that event can play the sound without any problem.

The following snippet shows syntax for playing a sound immediately after it's loaded. This snippet assumes a **Sound** instance of *snd*, and a **SoundChannel** instance of *channel*.

```
snd.addEventListener(Event.COMPLETE, onLoadComplete,
                     false, 0, true);
function onLoadComplete(evt:Event):void {
    channel = snd.play();
}
```

This approach is used to play a sound as soon after loading as possible. This is useful for things like background audio that begins playing right away. Perhaps the most common way to play a sound, however, is by clicking a button or through similar user interaction. We'll set up just such a button when we return to our ongoing sound player project.

## Stopping a Sound

Stopping a single sound in a channel requires only the **stop()** method. Unlike playing the sound, however, this method is invoked from the channel, not from the sound itself. Again assuming you've previously created a new instance of the **SoundChannel**, named *channel*, the syntax looks like this:

```
channel.stop();
```

It's also possible to stop *all* sounds using the **SoundMixer** class. As in the real world, multichannel playback funnels through a master sound mixer. Just as you can kill that master channel in a studio, you can stop all sounds using the **SoundMixer** class and it's **stopAll()** method.

Unlike the previous methods discussed, **stopAll()** is static. This means an instance of the **SoundMixer** class does not need to be created using the **new** keyword. Instead, the method is called directly from the class. Therefore, to stop playing the sounds in all channels, you need only write:

```
SoundMixer.stopAll();
```

**NOTE**

*You can control the volume and pan of the master mix by using the* **SoundMixer** *class, which we'll demonstrate later on. We'll also use the* **SoundMixer** *to visualize a sound during playback later in the chapter.*

## Pausing Sounds and Resuming Playback

Pausing a sound is a bit different. Currently, there is no dedicated pause method in ActionScript 3.0. Instead, you must rely on an optional parameter of the **play()** method that allows you to play the sound starting from a particular number of seconds offset from the beginning of the sound.

To use this feature to pause playback, you must first store the current position of a sound as it's playing. Having retrieved this value from the channel's aptly named **position** property, you can then stop playback in that channel. Later, you can resume playback by playing the sound from the stored position. Assuming the ongoing use of the *snd* and *channel* instance names, here are the first and second steps of the process:

```
var pausePosition:Number = channel.position;
channel.stop();
```

Then, at some later point, you can resume playback from where you left off:

```
channel = snd.play(pausePosition);
```

## Applying the Syntax

Now let's put these concepts into practice and pick up from the source file we started in the "Loading External Sounds" section. The following code, added to the previous example, forms the *player_basic.fla* source file.

If you want to look ahead, here's a quick description of all the code related to playing a sound, spanning lines 40 through 75, so we know what we're trying to accomplish. Lines 44 through 54 contain an event listener that will be triggered when a user clicks on the play button we'll soon create. Lines 56 through 65 include the code required to show a progress bar during playback. Finally, lines 67 through 75 contain the function triggered when the playback is complete.

Now let's focus on the function that plays the sound and its accompanying variables. Line 40 creates a Boolean variable that we'll use to check whether the sound is already playing. Because we'll be using a button to play our sound, it will now be possible to play the sound multiple times. However, this also means that rapid repeated clicks of the button will play the sound over and over itself, layering the sound. This is fine for simulating a musical instrument or an echo, for which multiple simultaneous occurrences of the sound are acceptable, but it's less desirable for playing spoken dialog or other sounds that typically would not be layered over themselves.

Line 41 creates a variable that will store the most recent playback position of the song in its channel, when the pause button is pressed. Remember that we're adding extra functionality to the play process to support pausing playback, so we'll need to pass this value to the **play()** method. Because we're using one **play()** method to play from a stop and from a pause, it's very important to initialize the value of this variable to zero so that the sound starts playing at the beginning when first played. Similarly, when we code the stop behavior later on, we'll need to reset this variable to zero after stopping the sound, to avoid restarting from any previous pause position when replaying.

Lines 44 through 54 make up the **onPlaySound()** function, which will be called by a play button that we'll add later on. Line 45 checks to see whether the sound is *not* already playing. If that test passes, the **isPlaying** variable is set to true to prevent the sound from playing more than once simultaneously. Lines 47 and 48 add a listener to the main timeline (the scope of the script) that will fire upon every enter frame event. We'll use this listener to update the playback progress bar in just a moment. Lines 49 through 51 add a listener to the channel to trigger when the sound playback is complete. We'll use that to reset things so the sound can be played again. Finally, line 52 plays the sound. The first time it plays, it will play from the beginning because of the initial 0 value of the **soundPosition** variable in line 41.

```
39  //play
40  var isPlaying:Boolean = false;
41  var soundPosition:Number = 0;
42  var channel:SoundChannel = new SoundChannel();
43
44  function onPlaySound(evt:MouseEvent):void {
45      if (!isPlaying) {
46          isPlaying = true;
47          addEventListener(Event.ENTER_FRAME, onPlayProgress,
48                          false, 0, true);
49          channel.addEventListener(Event.SOUND_COMPLETE,
50                                  onPlayComplete,
51                                  false, 0, true);
52          channel = snd.play(soundPosition);
53      }
54  }
```

Next, we'll setup the playback progress bar. Lines 56 through 59 create the bar, position it and add it to the display list. The **drawBar()** function is the same function found earlier in the file, spanning lines 17 through 24 and discussed in the "Loading External Sounds" section earlier in this chapter. It simply creates a sprite and draws a 1 × 10-pixel rectangle.

The function in lines 61 through 65 updates the width of the progress bar. It's called every enter frame event because of the listener created in lines 47 and 48. Dividing the playback position of the sound in the channel by the total length of the sound gives us a percentage. For example, if the position is 5000 and the length of the sound clip is 10,000 milliseconds (10 seconds), the playback is

50-percent complete. That percentage is then multiplied by the desired width of the bar, 100 pixels, and the width of the bar is set to this value.

Later on in the chapter, we'll drop two function calls into lines 63 and 64 to control the volume and pan of the sound, and we'll update peak meter graphics on the stage that show the amplitude of the sound during playback.

```
55   //play progress bar
56   var playBar:Sprite = drawBar(0x0000FF);
57   playBar.x = 20;
58   playBar.y = 15;
59   addChild(playBar);
60
61   function onPlayProgress(evt:Event):void {
62       playBar.width = 100 * (channel.position / sndLength);
63       //future home of volume and pan adjustment
64       //future home of amplitude meter adjustment;
65   }
```

The **onPlayComplete()** listener function (added in line 48) is triggered after the sound has finished playing. Lines 68 and 69 remove both listeners added when playback began. Once the sound is finished playing, there is no longer a need to update its playback progress or listen for a **SOUND_COMPLETE** event. Removing the listeners is not only efficient, but also allows us to set the playback progress bar width to 0. If not removed, the enter frame event would continue to set the bar's width to 100. (The position of the sound is at the end of the file when playback is complete.)

The remainder of the function stops the sound, resets the **soundPosition** variable to 0, the width of the play progress bar to 0, and the **isPlaying** variable to false. All of this allows us to play the sound anew.

```
66   //playback complete listener function
67   function onPlayComplete(evt:Event):void {
68       removeEventListener(Event.ENTER_FRAME, onPlayProgress);
69       channel.removeEventListener(Event.SOUND_COMPLETE,
70                                   onPlayComplete);
71       channel.stop();
72       soundPosition = 0;
73       playBar.width = 0;
74       isPlaying = false;
75   }
```

Now that we have the play functionality complete, we need a button to trigger it. We'll be creating three buttons by the time we're done, so rather than repeating the button creation code three times, let's set up a function to do the work for us. This takes less code but, more importantly, it means that if a future edit is required, you have to edit the code in only one place, not three.

We're going to draw our buttons dynamically, using the **RoundRectButton** class we created in Chapter 8, so line 77 imports the class. Remember that this material is presented in chunks for clarity. Import statements are typically consolidated at the top of your script and you should feel free to reorganize your code any way you see fit.

**NOTE**

*One idea behind using the* **RoundRectButton** *class to draw buttons dynamically is to give you continued practice using packages and classes. However, you'll also find when we're done that this entire file will contain no imported assets. As such, the entire audio player is less than 5 KB! This is a best-case scenario because we kept the interface simple—both so you didn't need to rely on library assets and so a more complex interface didn't intrude on the sound tutorial. The idea, however, is good. You could use the* **Graphics** *class to draw additional interface artwork, for example, and still keep the file size low.*

The **createButton()** function in lines 79 through 87 instantiates a button, positions it on the stage, adds a mouse click event listener, and adds the button to the display list. This later lets us create buttons with only one line of code, as seen with the first button in line 89. With three or more buttons, this approach can really be economical.

The function takes three arguments: the y coordinate to place the button on the stage, the label for the button, and the function that will be triggered when the user clicks on the button. Although this book has shown how to pass numbers and strings into functions, this is the first time we've used a function as an argument. This is a handy process that's not only expedient, but also emphasizes the fact that functions are objects too, just like numbers and strings.

As mentioned, line 89 creates the first button, passing a y-position of 40, a label of "Play" and the **onPlaySound()** function, created earlier, as the function to execute when the button is clicked.

```
76  //playback complete listener function
77  import com.learningactionscript3.ui.RoundRectButton;
78
79  function createButton(yLoc:Number, labl:String,
80                        func:Function):void {
81      var btn:RoundRectButton =
82          new RoundRectButton(100,20,10,2,0x000099,labl,0xFFFFFF);
83      btn.x = 20;
84      btn.y = yLoc;
85      btn.addEventListener(MouseEvent.CLICK, func, false, 0, true);
86      addChild(btn);
87  }
88
89  createButton(40, "Play", onPlaySound);
```

The remainder of the script is dedicated to the pause and stop buttons. Lines 91 through 98 create the pause button, setting its y location to 65 and adding the **onPauseSound()** function as its mouse click listener. In line 93, the function checks to see whether the sound is playing and, if so, stores the current playback position in the **soundPosition** variable. It then stops the sound and sets the **isPlaying** variable to false so the sound can play again later.

Lines 99 through 102 follow the same process but are even simpler. The stop button is created in line 99, which places the button below the previously created play and pause buttons, and adds the **onStopSound()** method as the button's mouse click listener. The functionality required by manually stopping the sound is the same as the functionality required when the sound stops on its own in the **onPlayComplete()** function (lines 67 through 75). Therefore, all that's required here is to call that function.

However, because **onPlayComplete()** is a listener function, it expects an event argument. Calling the function without supplying the expected event argument will cause an argument count mismatch error. We can get around this by sending **null** to the function to stand in for the event. The **null** value will satisfy the type checking at the listener function because **null** is the default value for all events. As long as your listener function doesn't rely on specific information from the event, such as mouse coordinates or keyboard key code values, this technique makes it possible to use listener functions not only when an event occurs, but also manually.

**NOTE**

*For more information about listener functions and the argument count mismatch error, see the "Using Event Listeners" section of Chapter 3.*

```
90   //playback complete listener function
91   createButton(65, "Pause", onPauseSound);
92   function onPauseSound(evt:MouseEvent):void {
93       if (isPlaying) {
94           soundPosition = channel.position;
95           channel.stop();
96           isPlaying = false;
97       }
98   }
99   createButton(90, "Stop", onStopSound);
100  function onStopSound(evt:MouseEvent):void {
101      onPlayComplete(null);
102  }
```

At this point, you should be able play, pause, and stop your sound, and both the load and play progress bar should reach 100 pixels in width upon their respective completions.

# Buffering Sounds

Waiting to play a sound until it's fully loaded will prevent errors or stutters that might otherwise occur during the loading process. This method, however, does suffer from the drawback of having to wait. An alternative approach is to preload only a portion of the sound prior to playback, and then play the sound while it continues to download progressively to Flash Player in the background. The principle behind this approach is to preload a buffer that can stay ahead of playback during the time required to download the remainder of the sound. You'll still need to wait, but not as much.

How much of the sound should you buffer? That depends on how you plan to distribute your project. Theoretically, if you have no load time, you need no buffer time because the sound loads instantly. This is usually true of local files, when you are not loading the sound from the Internet. For remote files, connection speeds can dictate how much sound needs to be preloaded. If you know you'll only encounter broadband connection speeds, you can buffer less of the sound. If you're worried about slower connections, you may want to buffer more of the sound to prevent the playback from catching up with the loading process and stalling playback.

To specify the buffer time, you must use the **SoundLoaderContext** class at the time of sound loading. The number of milliseconds of sound to buffer is passed to the constructor when instantiating the class; otherwise, a default value of 1000 is used. After instantiating the class, you then pass the resulting instance into the sound **load()** method, as a second parameter following the **URLRequest** object.

The following example adapts the start of our audio player by inserting line 2, and modifying line 4. It buffers 5 seconds of the loaded sound before the **play()** method will execute. This modification can be found in the *player_buffering.fla* source file.

```
1  var snd:Sound = new Sound();
2  var context:SoundLoaderContext = new SoundLoaderContext(5000);
3  var req:URLRequest = new URLRequest("song.mp3");
4  snd.load(req, context);
```

NOTE

*Remember that buffering will have little effect when testing locally because the loading process will complete very quickly. You may wish to upload your test files to a server, and perhaps even use a very large sound file, to test your efforts.*

## Changing Sound Volume and Pan

During playback, it's possible to manipulate the volume and pan of individual channels, as well as the global mixer containing all sounds. Doing so requires the **SoundTransform** class.

The process involves starting with a **SoundTransform** instance (either by creating a new instance or by storing a reference to the existing transform object of the channel or mixer), setting the volume and/or pan setting of that instance, and then applying the transformation to the channel. For example, this snippet will set the volume of a **SoundChannel** instance called *channel* to 50 percent.

```
var trans:SoundTransform = new SoundTransform();
trans.volume = 0.5;
channel.soundTransform = trans;
```

This syntax will set the volume of a channel to half of what it currently is:

```
var trans:SoundTransform = channel.soundTransform;
trans.volume *= 0.5;
channel.soundTransform = trans;
```

Notice that the first example sets the volume of a new **SoundTransform** instance to 0.5, while the second example multiplies the volume of an existing **SoundTransform** instance by 0.5. The first example will set the volume to 50 percent, regardless of its prior setting, but the second example will cut the current volume in half. For example, if the second volume was originally 50 percent, it would then be 25 percent.

Most ActionScript 3.0 settings that require percentage values use a unit range of 0 to 1. For example, volume is expressed as a range of 0 (muted) to 1 (full volume) with any interim value expressed as a percentage of full volume.

To determine a value that describes a pan setting between left and right stereo channels, both a percentage left and a percentage right are required. Therefore, the units are expressed as a range of −1 (full left) through 0 (centered) to 1 (full right). Negative interim values reflect some degree of pan left, and positive interim values reflect some degree of pan right. The following script sets the *channel* instance to a pan setting of full left:

```
var trans:SoundTransform = new SoundTransform();
trans.pan = -1;
channel.soundTransform = trans;
```

To transform all playing sounds at once, substitute the specified channel with the master **SoundMixer** class. For example, the following script mutes all sounds:

```
var trans:SoundTransform = new SoundTransform();
trans.volume = 0;
SoundMixer.soundTransform = trans;
```

Now let's apply what we've learned to our ongoing player example. The following code can be found in the *player_transform.fla* source file, and demonstrates both volume and pan by using mouse coordinates. Figure 11-2 shows how the mouse will affect the sound transformation. Moving the mouse left and right pans the sound left and right. Moving the mouse up and down fades the volume up and down.

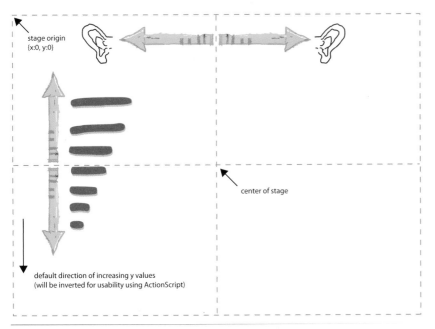

*Figure 11-2. How the mouse affects sound volume and panning in the adaption made to the sound player project*

Line 104 creates a **SoundTransform** instance and lines 105 through 109 contain the **onPlayProgress()** function that will set and apply the transformations. This function will be called from the enter frame event listener function created earlier, which we'll adapt in a moment.

To set these changes with the mouse in a natural and intuitive way, we need to think about ActionScript mouse coordinates and apply a little math. Line 106 sets the volume based on the y-coordinate of the mouse. By dividing the current vertical mouse coordinate (mouseY) by the stage height, we get a percentage change. For example, if the mouse were in the middle of the stage, the value would be 50 percent (0.5). This suits us just fine because the volume setting should be between 0 and 1.

```
103  //transformations
104  var trans:SoundTransform = new SoundTransform();
105  function updateMouseTransform():void {
106      trans.volume = 1 - mouseY / stage.stageHeight;
107      trans.pan = mouseX / (stage.stageWidth / 2) - 1
108      channel.soundTransform = trans;
109  }
```

However, y-coordinates in ActionScript increase by moving *down*, and we typically think of the values of a volume slider increasing as they go *up*. Therefore, we must subtract our percentage from 1 to get the correct value. For example, let's say the mouseY is 100, and the stage is 400 pixels tall. Dividing 100 by 400 gives us 25 percent, but the mouse is near the top of the stage, which we think of as a higher volume when imagining a volume slider. By subtracting 0.25 from 1, we end up with 0.75, or 75 percent, which is what we want. Next, let's look at calculating pan.

Line 107 affects the pan. This calculation is similar to the volume calculation, but we need a value between −1 for full left and 1 for full right, and a value in the center of the stage should equate to 0. To find the middle of the stage, we need to divide the stage width by 2, and if we continually divide the horizontal location of the mouse (mouseX) by that value, we get a range of 0 to 2. For example, using the default stage width of 550, the center would be 275. Far left is 0/275 (0), center is 275/275 (1) and far right is 550/275 (2). Because, we need a range of −1 to 1, we subtract 1 from the entire formula.

**NOTE**

*Again, if you want to transform every sound playing at a given moment, simply substituting **SoundMixer** for the specific channel in line 108 will accomplish the task.*

After calculating the volume and pan values based on the mouse position, and altering the corresponding properties of the **trans** transform object you created (lines 106 and 107), all that remains is updating the **soundTransform** property of the desired channel (line 108).

Now all we have to do is amend the **onPlayProgress()** function earlier in the script, to update the transform. The function spans lines 60 through 64 and we need to replace the earlier sound transformation placeholder comment with a call to the **updateMouseTransform()** function (shown in bold in the following example). Now when you test your movie, you should be able to vary the volume and pan of the playing sound by moving the mouse around the stage.

```
60  function onPlayProgress(evt:Event):void {
61      playBar.width = 100 * (channel.position / sndLength);
62      updateMouseTransform();
63      //future home of amplitude meter adjustment;
64  }
```

# Reading ID3 Metadata from MP3 Sounds

When *encoding* MP3 files (compressing and saving the audio in the MP3 format), most sound applications can inject metadata into the file, storing this data in tags established by the ID3 specification. The amount of metadata included is decided during the encoding process, usually by whomever is doing the encoding. The software itself, however, can add some information, such as the name and/or version of the encoding software.

Accessing this information is accomplished via the **ID3Info** class. The simplest way to query a sound's main ID3 tags is by using the named properties of the **ID3Info** instance found in every **Sound** object. This is found in every sound's **id3** property. For example, you can query the artist and song names of an MP3 file this way (again assuming a **Sound** instance called *snd*):

```
snd.id3.artist;
snd.id3.songName;
```

There are seven tags supported in this direct fashion, as seen in Table 11-1.

*Table 11-1. The most common ID3 tags and their corresponding ActionScript property names*

| ID3 2.0 tag | ActionScript property |
| --- | --- |
| COMM | `Sound.id3.comment` |
| TALB | `Sound.id3.album` |
| TCON | `Sound.id3.genre` |
| TIT2 | `Sound.id3.songName` |
| TPE1 | `Sound.id3.artist` |
| TRCK | `Sound.id3.track` |
| TYER | `Sound.id3.year` |

The remainder of the supported tags can be accessed through the same **id3** property of the **Sound** class, but using the tag's four-character name. Table 11-2 shows supported tags that do not also have accompanying property names of their own. Accessing the beats-per-minute data, for example, would require the following syntax:

```
snd.id3.TBPM;
```

If you prefer a consistent approach, it's also possible to access all ID3 tag information using the four-character tag names, including the seven tags that have their own dedicated property names. However, for quick access to the most commonly used properties, you will likely find the descriptive names to be more useful.

**NOTE**

*Many audio applications can add ID3 tags to sounds, both during and after the encoding process. Apple's free iTunes can tag and encode, and Pa-software's shareware ID3 Editor can inject tags into existing MP3s. Both are available for the Macintosh and Windows platforms.*

*Table 11-2. Supported ID3 tags without dedicated ActionScript property names*

| ID3 2.0 tag | Description |
| --- | --- |
| TBPM | Beats per minute |
| TCOM | Composer |
| TFLT | File type |
| TIT1 | Content group description |
| TIT3 | Subtitle/description refinement |
| TKEY | Initial key |
| TLAN | Languages |
| TLEN | Length |
| TMED | Media type |
| TOAL | Original album/movie/show title |
| TOFN | Original filename |
| TOLY | Original lyricists/text writers |
| TOPE | Original artists/performers |
| TORY | Original release year |
| TOWN | File owner/licensee |
| TPE2 | Band/orchestra/accompaniment |
| TPE3 | Conductor/performer refinement |
| TPE4 | Interpreted, remixed, or otherwise modified by |
| TPOS | Disc/position in set |
| TPUB | Publisher |
| TRDA | Recording dates |
| TRSN | Internet radio station name |
| TRSO | Internet radio station owner |
| TSIZ | Size |
| TSRC | ISRC (international standard recording code) |
| TSSE | Software/hardware and settings used for encoding |
| WXXX | URL link frame |

Finally, it's possible to output all ID3 tags using a type of **for** loop. The following code, found in the *player_id3.fla* source file, continues our player example by first creating a text field to display the data (lines 111 through 118). Lines 120 through 127 then add a listener to the sound instance to listen for the **Event.ID3** event. Line 122 pulls the ID3 information from the event argument.

The **for...in** loop in lines 123 through 126 is a little different than the **for** loop discussed in Chapter 2. Instead of looping through a finite number of times, it loops through all the properties of an object. It uses the property name as a key, and pulls the property value from the object using that string. Lines 124 and 125 add each tag to the end of the field by concatenating a string and ending it with a new line character to jump down to the next line.

```
110 //id3
111 var id3Field:TextField = new TextField();
112 id3Field.x = 140;
113 id3Field.y = 15;
114 id3Field.width = 340;
115 id3Field.height = 95;
116 id3Field.border = true;
117 id3Field.background = true;
118 addChild(id3Field);
119
120 snd.addEventListener(Event.ID3, onID3Info, false, 0, true);
121 function onID3Info(evt:Event):void {
122     var id3Properites:ID3Info = evt.target.id3;
123     for (var propertyName:String in id3Properites) {
124         id3Field.appendText("ID3 Tag " + propertyName + " = " +
125                         id3Properites[propertyName] + "\n");
126     }
127 }
```

When ID3 information is detected and the listener function is triggered, an **ID3Info** object is created to store the incoming data. The **for...in** loop in lines 123 through 126 walks through all the properties stored and, in this case, adds them to a text field on stage. The data could also be displayed in a custom MP3 player interface, placed into a database to rank most often played songs, and so on.

**NOTE**

*In all cases, if a tag has not been encoded into the MP3, querying the tag directly will return* **undefined** *as a value.*

## Visualizing Sound Data

Mastering any language depends heavily on motivating yourself to practice it. This is especially true with programming languages, because code is difficult to work into day-to-day conversation. Finding as little as 15 minutes a day to experiment with ActionScript 3.0 will hasten your progress considerably, however, and visualizing sound data will make that practice time fly by.

ActionScript 3.0 gives you access to raw sound data during playback, allowing you to synchronize visuals to amplitude or frequency spectrum information. Using the former, you might easily create peak meters, or animated speaker illustrations, that bounce or throb to the beat. With spectrum data, on the other hand, you can draw a waveform of the sound or depict the low-, mid-, and high-range frequency bands of a sound much like an equalizer display.

### Amplitude

The terms *amplitude* and *volume* are often used interchangeably, but understanding just a bit about these concepts can help clarify our task. Volume is probably a familiar idea. It's a measure of the loudness or intensity of

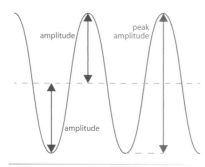

*Figure 11-3. Amplitude and peak amplitude of a sound wave*

a sound, and is somewhat subjective. Amplitude, on the other hand, is a physics property that more directly applies to a sound wave. It measures the distance of the peak of a sound wave from its baseline.

Because a waveform can contain positive and negative values, amplitude can also be positive or negative, as a waveform's peaks can be above and below its baseline. *Peak amplitude* is a specific measurement of amplitude, measuring from one peak of a sound wave to the next. Because it's measuring between peaks, and not from a baseline, its value is always positive. In other words, peak amplitude is the *absolute value*, or nonnegative value, of amplitude, and is the kind of amplitude information ActionScript 3.0 will deliver in this example. Figure 11-3 shows both amplitudes in a hypothetical sound wave.

Getting the amplitude of a sound channel requires only that you read its **leftPeak** and/or **rightPeak** properties depending on which stereo channel you want to visualize. These properties will be equal when mono sounds are playing. Assuming a **SoundChannel** instance called *channel*, the syntax is:

```
channel.leftPeak;
channel.rightPeak;
```

These properties will return a value between 0 and 1 to represent the current amplitude. Conveniently, this is also the range of values used by such properties as **alpha**, **scaleX**, and **scaleY**. Therefore, to create a basic amplitude meter, you need only manipulate the height of a movie clip. Imagine two movie clips that look like vertical bars 100 pixels high, with instance names *leftMeter* and *rightMeter*. Because the **leftPeak** or **rightPeak** values are always a fraction of 1, multiplying the full size of the meters by these values will cause the meter to vary between a height of 0 (at minimum volume) and 100 (at full volume). A **leftPeak** value of 0.5 will set the left meter to half-height, or 50 pixels. The following snippet shows this process in code. We'll also use this same technique in our sound player project in just a moment.

```
leftMeter.height = 100 * channel.leftPeak;
rightMeter.height = 100 * channel.rightPeak;
```

If you wanted something slightly less conventional, you might manipulate the scale of a graphic, rather than the height of a bar, with the amplitude values. For example, you could create a picture of a speaker that increased in size based on the amplitude values. Unlike a peak meter, however, you don't want the speaker icons to disappear at 0 volume—a possible byproduct of setting the scale of the graphic to a dynamic value between 0 and 1, inclusive. Therefore, you can *add* the amplitude value to the graphic's original scale of 1 (100 percent, or full size). The speakers, therefore, will remain unchanged during silence and potentially grow to twice their size at 100 percent amplitude—that is, a scale of 1 + 1, or 2. This approach is shown in the following code snippet, and a complete implementation of the code is found in the *speakers_peak.fla* source file.

```
leftSpeaker.scaleX = leftSpeaker.scaleY = 1 + channel.leftPeak;
rightSpeaker.scaleX = rightSpeaker.scaleY = 1 + channel.rightPeak;
```

## Adding peak meters to the sound player

Let's add a pair of peak meters to the sound player project we've been developing. The following code is found in *player_peak.fla*.

Lines 129 through 139 create two sprites using the **drawBar()** method discussed earlier—with one important difference. The bars are rotated –90 degrees so that they will expand upward, instead of to the right. Lines 141 through 144 update the **scaleX** of each peak meter. Note that we're updating **scaleX**, even though it will look like the height of the meters is changing due to the rotation in lines 130 and 136. Figure 11-4 illustrates this idea.

```
128  //peak meters
129  var lPeak:Sprite = drawBar(0x009900);
130  lPeak.rotation = -90;
131  lPeak.x = 500;
132  lPeak.y = 110;
133  addChild(lPeak);
134
135  var rPeak:Sprite = drawBar(0x009900);
136  rPeak.rotation = -90;
137  rPeak.x = 520;
138  rPeak.y = 110;
139  addChild(rPeak);
140
141  function updatePeakMeters():void {
142      lPeak.scaleX = channel.leftPeak * 100;
143      rPeak.scaleX = channel.rightPeak * 100;
144  }
```

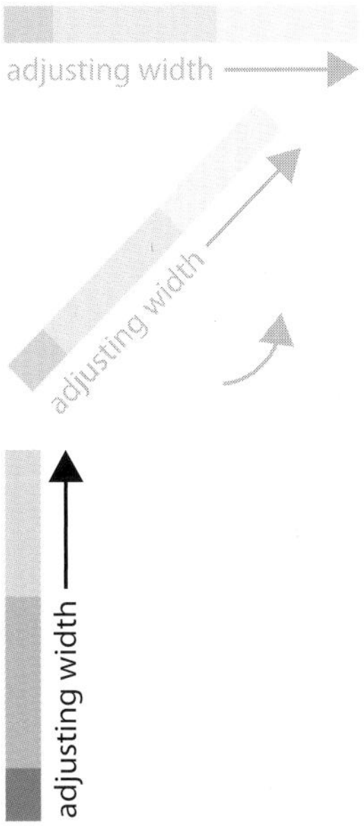

*Figure 11-4. Adjusting the width of a sprite rotated –90 degrees appears to affect the height of the sprite*

As with the **updateMouseTransform()** function call in the "Changing Sound Volume and Pan" section, we must now update our peak meters in the **onPlayProgress()** function found earlier in the script. We'll again replace a function placeholder comment, this time the amplitude meter adjustment comment found in line 63 with a call to the **updatePeakMeters()** function.

```
60   function onPlayProgress(evt:Event):void {
61       playBar.width = 100 * (channel.position / sndLength);
62       updateMouseTransform();
63       updatePeakMeters();
64   }
```

Now when you test your file, you should see two peak meters in the upper-right corner of the stage, moving in sync with the music and visualizing the peak amplitude of the sound during playback. You may also notice that this visual feedback reflects the sound transformations made with your mouse.

If, for example, you move the mouse to the upper-left corner of the stage, you will see larger peaks in the left meter. If you move your mouse across the top of the stage, you will see the peaks move from the left meter to the right meter to correspond with the panning of the sound. Finally, if you then move your mouse down the right side of the stage, you will see the peaks steadily diminish in size as the amplitudes of the sound diminish.

# Creating More Expressive Peak Meters Using Masks

Just for fun, we're going to show you a slightly more expressive peak meter, based on a meter that you might see on a home stereo. In case you've never seen a peak meter before, it's usually a series of 6 to 10 consecutive lights, stacked vertically or placed end to end, which glow in sequence depending on the amplitude of the sound. Typically, low amplitudes reveal cool colors (green or blue) for acceptable amplitudes. Additional lights reveal warm colors (yellow or amber) as amplitudes increase to possible distortion levels. Finally, hot colors (red) are revealed when the amplitude exceeds acceptable levels. A representation of this type of meter is shown in the top illustration of Figure 11-5.

Because of the color changes, we can't simply adjust the `width`, `height`, `scaleX`, or `scaleY` properties of the meter. If we did that, we would invalidate the purpose of the color bands because all the colors would be visible all the time, even at low amplitudes. This can be seen in the bottom left illustration of Figure 11-5. We need, instead, to show only those colors representative of the amplitude, be they cool or hot, as seen in the bottom-right illustration of Figure 11-5.

You can reveal only specific colors by creating a mask for the color bars, and scaling only the mask. The entire peak meter is a movie clip, within which are two discrete elements: the color bands and another movie clip used as a mask. (In our file, a third element serves as an outline but is not affected by ActionScript.) Because a mask dictates which part of the content is seen (rather than hiding that content), altering the size of the mask will reveal the desired portion of the color bars, as seen in Figure 11-6.

The following code is included in *multicolor_peak_meters.fla*, which contains two instances of a movie clip that serves as our meter. The instances are called *lPeak* and *rPeak*, and the symbol contains the outline, mask, and color bars seen in Figure 11-6. The mask has an instance name of *barMask*.

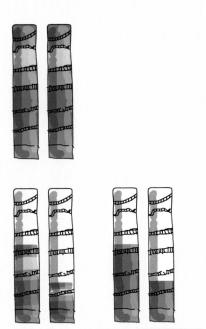

*Figure 11-5. The color peak meter in use*

The first five lines cover the basic sound loading and playing tasks discussed earlier in the chapter. The code inside the listener function sets the vertical scale of the mask inside each meter to match the peak amplitudes of the left and right channels.

```
var snd:Sound = new Sound();
snd.load(new URLRequest("song.mp3"));

var channel:SoundChannel = new SoundChannel();
channel = snd.play();

addEventListener(Event.ENTER_FRAME, onLoop,
                false, 0, true);

function onLoop(evt:Event):void {
    lPeak.barMask.scaleY = channel.leftPeak;
    rPeak.barMask.scaleY = channel.rightPeak;
}
```

Unlike the speaker example discussed earlier, we *do* want the colors in the peak meter to disappear during silent passages, so we can set the `scaleY` property directly to the values generated by the `leftPeak` and `rightPeak` properties.

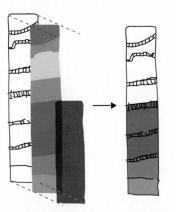

*Figure 11-6. The component parts of the color peak meter*

Though this example uses assets found in the library of an FLA, the learningactionscript3 package contains the `PeakMeter` class for creating multicolor peak meters entirely from code. The *PeakMeter_Example.as* document class, and the corresponding *PeakMeter_Example.fla* file for Flash Professional users, demonstrate how to use the class.

# Sound Spectrum Data

So far, we've been able to synchronize visuals with sound data by using the values returned by the **leftPeak** and **rightPeak** properties of the **SoundChannel** instance. With this information, we've already created peak meters to visualize the amplitude of a sound during playback—but there's a lot more you can do. We discussed scaling a speaker, and you can just as easily change the **alpha**, **x**, **y**, or **rotation** properties of a display object. The *peak_visualizations* directory in the accompanying source code includes examples of each of these tasks.

Even with a lot of creativity behind your efforts, however, you still only have two simultaneous values to work with when using peak amplitudes. Fortunately, ActionScript 3.0 provides another way to visualize sound by giving you access to *spectrum data* during playback. Audio spectrum data typically contains a mixture of frequency and amplitude information and can give you a visual snapshot of a sound at any moment. You can use this information to draw a sound wave or you can preprocess the information to look at amplitudes in the low, mid, and high frequency ranges—much like the visual feedback a home-stereo equalizer can give you.

We'll support both kinds of data, and we'll do so in a class so that it's easy to add waveform visualization to your own projects. Figure 11-7 shows an example of what our class can draw. It depicts the left stereo channel waveform in green and the right stereo channel waveform in red.

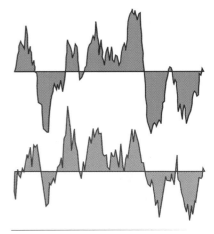

*Figure 11-7. A visualization of left and right channel waveforms*

## Storing and retrieving sound spectrum data

Before we discuss the new class, let's talk a little bit about how much data we'll be using and how we'll handle the load. Each time we retrieve the sound spectrum data, we're going to do so using the **computeSpectrum()** method of the **SoundMixer** class. This method retrieves data from the sound in real time and places that data into a special kind of array called the **ByteArray**, which we'll explain in a moment. Every time the method is called, we'll be using 512 data values from the sound—256 for the left channel and 256 for the right channel—to draw our waveform.

We're going to use an enter frame event listener to call the method so, assuming the default Flash Professional frame rate of 24 frames per second, that means we'll be using 12,288 values per second. What's more, the **computeSpectrum()** method returns *bytes*, which are very small units of data. We need to work with decimal values like 0.5, which are also called *floating-point numbers* or *floats*. It takes 4 bytes to make a single float, and we need 12,288 floats per second. Therefore, our file will need to process 49,152 bytes per second!

You don't need to worry about any of this math, because you'll soon see that it's all handled for you. But it does help to understand the magnitude of what we're going to be doing. Working your way through nearly 50,000 values per second isn't trivial, so this is a potential performance issue.

Storing the data and retrieving it quickly are challlenges handled by the **ByteArray** class. A byte array is an optimized array that can be used to store any kind of bytes. For example, we used the **ByteArray** as part of the process that saved an image in Chapter 9. It can also be used to read external file data, like the ZaaIL library mentioned in the same chapter, that reads unsupported image formats. In this case, we're going to use a **ByteArray** instance to store sound data.

The **ByteArray** class has special methods that make retrieving data fast and efficient. These methods will process a series of bytes and turn them into the data format you need, so you don't have to. For instance, we need float values, rather than bytes. The **readFloat()** method will read four sequential bytes, translate them into a float, and return the data we need. What's more, the method will automatically increment through the bytes so that you don't have to update a loop counter when parsing the contents of the array.

For example, think of an array called *myByteArray* that contains 12 bytes. If this data were stored in a normal array, you'd likely work through it using a **for** loop, and you'd have to increment the loop counter after each query. Using a byte array, however, the first time you execute **myArray.readFloat()**, it will read the first four bytes, return a float, and remain poised at byte 5 to continue parsing the array. With the next call of **myArray.readFloat()**, bytes 5 though 8 will be returned as a float—again with no manual incrementing of the array—and you're now at byte 9 ready to continue.

The **computeSpectrum()** method will populate our **ByteArray** for us, and the **readFloat()** method will automatically translate the bytes into the data format we need, so we're ready to go. However, a second, optional parameter of the **computeSpectrum()** method will allow us to choose between two ways to analyze our sound.

## Drawing a waveform or frequency spectrum

By default, the **computeSpectrum()** method will fill a byte array with values that will translate to floats between −1 and 1. These values will plot a waveform as it ascends above or descends below its baseline, as shown in Figure 11-7.

However, a second, optional parameter called **FFTMode** will return the amplitude of individual frequencies, with values between 0 and 1. An FFT plot distributes positive amplitudes of different frequencies across the baseline, much like the visual feedback a home-stereo equalizer can give you. Low frequencies of each channel appear on the left, and high frequencies appear on the right, as seen in Figure 11-8.

As previously described, our example exercise will draw a waveform. However, after you've successfully tested your code, experiment with setting the second parameter of the **computeSpectrum()** method to true to plot FFT frequency amplitudes.

**NOTE**

*FFT refers to "Fast Fourier Transform," a method for efficiently computing the component frequencies that make up a signal like a sound or light wave.*

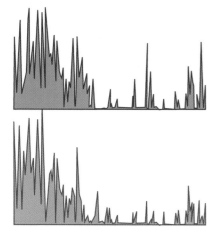

*Figure 11-8. Visualizing frequency values with an FFT display*

## The Waveform class

The first dozen or so lines of the **Waveform** class will be familiar to you if you've been reading this book linearly. Line 1 declares the class's package path as this class is part of the learningactionscript3 code library developed throughout this book. Lines 3 through 7 import all the other classes required by this class. Line 9 declares the class and extends **Sprite** so it can inherit all accessible properties, methods, and events from the **Sprite** class. As discussed extensively in Chapter 6, this is important for things like being able to access properties like **graphics**, use event listeners, and add instances of this class to the display list.

```
1    package com.learningactionscript3.sound {
2
3        import flash.display.Graphics;
4        import flash.display.Sprite;
5        import flash.events.Event;
6        import flash.media.SoundMixer;
7        import flash.utils.ByteArray;
8
9        public class Waveform extends Sprite {
10
11           private var _bytes:ByteArray = new ByteArray();
12           private var _fft:Boolean;
13           private var _g:Graphics;
14
15           public function Waveform(fft:Boolean=false) {
16               _fft = fft;
17               _g = this.graphics;
18
19               this.addEventListener(Event.ENTER_FRAME, onVisualize,
20                                     false, 0, true);
21           }
22
23           private function onVisualize(evt:Event):void {
24               SoundMixer.computeSpectrum(_bytes, _fft);
25               _g.clear();
26               plotWaveform(0x009900, 50);
27               plotWaveform(0xFF0000, 100);
28           }
29
30           private function plotWaveform(col:uint,
31                                        chanBaseline:Number):void {
32               _g.lineStyle(1, col);
33               _g.beginFill(col, 0.5);
34               _g.moveTo(0, chanBaseline);
35               for (var i:Number = 0; i < 256; i++) {
36                   _g.lineTo(i, (chanBaseline -
37                               _bytes.readFloat() * 50));
38               }
39               _g.lineTo(i, chanBaseline);
40               _g.endFill();
41           }
42       }
43   }
```

Lines 11 through 13 create three class properties. The **_bytes** property stores an instance of the **ByteArray** class to hold the sound data. The Boolean **_fft** determines whether the class draws a waveform or frequency peaks. Finally, **_g** stores a reference to the **graphics** property, as described in Chapter 8, so we can draw the waveform with vectors.

The class constructor in lines 15 through 21 does only three simple things. Line 16 sets the Boolean class property **_fft** to the value passed into the **FFTMode** parameter during instantiation. Note that the parameter has a default value of false. Therefore, if true is passed into the parameter, **computeSpectrum()** will use its FFT mode, and only positive values will be calculated. If nothing is passed into the parameter, **computeSpectrum()** will return values between −1 and 1, drawing a waveform.

Line 17 stores a reference to the **graphics** property of the class so we can draw the sound's waveform at runtime. Remember that this class extends **Sprite**, so it already has its own **graphics** property. Furthermore, because you'll be adding an instance of this **Waveform** class to the display list anyway, there's no benefit to creating another sprite within that instance just to serve as a canvas for your drawing.

Finally, lines 19 and 20 add an event listener to the class that calls the **onVisualize()** method every time it hears an enter frame event. This method draws one waveform for each stereo channel.

The first task of the **onVisualize()** method is to extract the waveform data from the sound using the **computeSpectrum()** method (line 24). The data is stored in the **_bytes** property and **_fft** determines if wave or frequency spectrum data is returned. Line 25 then clears all prior drawing to the graphics property to show only the current waveform and prevent an ongoing layering of vectors. Finally, lines 26 and 27 call the **plotWaveform()** method to draw a waveform for the left and right stereo channels, respectively. These calls pass the color and y coordinate of the baseline of each waveform to the method.

The first two lines of the method create a hairline stroke (line 32) and 50-percent transparent fill (line 33) of the requested color. Line 34 moves the virtual drawing pen to an x coordinate of 0, and a y coordinate that matches the requested baseline. The loop that follows in lines 35 through 41 will draw the waveform from this point.

**NOTE**

*Using two loops of 256 values, rather than 1 loop of 512 values, makes it easier for us to draw the left and right channels separately. For example, because the loop counter (i) ranges from 0 to 255, we can use it as an x coordinate for each point of our waves. If we used a single loop from 0 to 511, the x coordinate of the right channel waveform would begin at 256, after the left channel waveform ended, and the two waveforms would appear next to each other, rather than stacked vertically.*

Earlier we mentioned that the **ByteArray** is populated with 512 data values each time the **computeSpectrum()** method is called. Note, however, that the **for** loop starting in line 35 iterates only 256 times. This is because the class is designed to draw the waveform for the left and right stereo channels consecutively. That is, the method call in line 26 draws a waveform using the first 256 values, which correspond to the left channel. Line 27 calls the method to draw a waveform using the next 256 values, representing the right channel. Therefore, each time **onVisualize()** is executed all 512 values are retrieved. Because the **ByteArray** instance automatically increments itself when a value is retrieved, it returns to its first position ready for the next request of 256 values.

Lines 36 and 37 call the **lineTo()** method of the **Graphics** class. The repeated call of the method by the loop draws a line that connects all 256 samples of each waveform. The x coordinates increment from 0 to 255, and the y coordinates are based on the values stored in the byte array. Each float, or decimal value, returned from the byte array is multiplied by the maximum waveform height of 40 pixels.. Therefore, at full amplitude (1 or −1), the waveform height at that point is 40 or −40, at minimum amplitude (0), the height of the waveform is 0, and with an interim amplitude the waveform height will fall somewhere in between.

The resulting waveform height is then subtracted from the desired baseline. A positive sample amplitude is subtracted from the baseline position, causing a peak to rise above the baseline. Negative sample amplitudes are effectively added to the baseline position (subtracting a negative value is equivalent to adding that value) causing a peak to appear below the baseline. (Increasing y values in the Flash Coordinate system move down the y axis.) Figure 11-9 shows a few sample values and their resulting position in the waveform.

Finally, lines 39 and 40 return the drawing point of the waveform to its baseline, and then close the fill, respectively.

The best part of this visualization is that it operates independently of any sound playback code. As we discussed previously, the **SoundMixer** class is equivalent to the main channel on a recording studio mixing desk. As such, our **Waveform** class will automatically visualize any sound running through that master mixer—in other words, any sound in any **SoundChannel** instance. We'll show this in action by demonstrating how easy it is to add the visualization to a project that already plays sound.

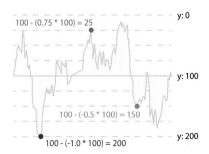

*Figure 11-9. A few sample amplitude calculations, and where they appear in an example waveform*

## Adding the Waveform Visualization to Our Sound Player

The following code completes our ongoing sound player project, and appears in the *player_complete.fla* source file. Because the visualizer plots waveforms for all sounds, and because the player is already capable of playing sound, all we need to do is add an instance of **Waveform** to the player's display list.

Line 146 imports the class we just created, line 148 creates the instance we need, lines 149 and 150 position the visualization sprite, and line 151 adds it to the display list. For cosmetic purposes, line 152 doubles the scale of the visualization so it spans 512 pixels to fill the stage, rather than its default 256-pixel width.

```
145 //waveform visualization
146 import com.learningactionscript3.sound.Waveform;
147
148 var vis:Waveform = new Waveform();
149 vis.x = 20;
150 vis.y = 100;
151 vis.scaleX = vis.scaleY = 2;
152 addChild(vis);
```

This is just one example visualization, with a simple display. The kind of art you can create is limited only by what you can manipulate with numbers in real time and, of course, your imagination.

# Visualizing Microphone Input

Prior to Flash Player 10, accessing input from the microphone was very limited. Only an overall activity level, somewhat akin to the amplitude of the input, was available. As of Flash Player 10, extensive manipulation of mic input is now possible. You can draw a waveform of the input, capture the input, alter it, and even save it to a WAV file with the help of additional classes.

For maximum compatibility, we'll start our discussion about microphone input by visualizing the mic's `activityLevel` property. This is compatible all the way back to the introduction of ActionScript 3 (which also means versions CS3 through CS5 of Flash Professional support this technique). We'll then follow with additional features that require Flash Player 10.

## Activity Level

The following code is found in the *microphone_activity_level.fla* source file. After granting Flash Player permission to use the microphone, this file will continually react to microphone input, drawing a line across the screen that corresponds to microphone activity level. The relationship between activity and time makes the file look a bit like an EKG read out. The line perpetually draws to the right and the line draws up and down with mic activity.

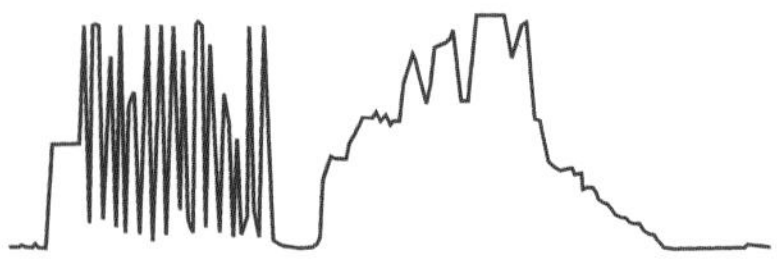

Figure 11-10 shows a sample of the file output. The first segment of the plot was created with staccato whistling. The sharp rise and fall of activity is characteristic of this type of sound. The second segment was created by a human voice steadily increasing the amplitude of a single tone to crescendo and then diminishing again to silence. The fact that the rise and fall of the tone are not represented by straight lines is attributed to the natural wavering of the average human voice when attempting this exercise.

*Figure 11-10. A visualization of a microphone's activity level*

The first six lines of this script are important as they initialize the microphone for use. Line 1 stores a reference to the current microphone using the static method, `getMicrophone()` of the `Microphone` class. This will activate the microphone, but it won't yet provide any data to ActionScript. In order to work with the microphone input, you'll need to feed that data back to ActionScript, as seen in line 2.

When doing so, it's best to use echo suppression, shown in line 3, to minimize feedback from your speakers during recording. As an added measure against feedback, we'll set the volume of the microphone to 0 later on, as we don't need to hear the input in this example. Line 4 sets the *gain* of the microphone—the amount by which the microphone data is multiplied before transmitting. It's a little like the volume of the microphone's throughput.

0 transmits nothing, 50 is the default value, and 100 amplifies the input to its maximum degree.

Line 5 sets the *sample rate* of the microphone—the number of samples taken from the source audio during the encoding process. The higher the sample rate, more samples are taken, and the better the sound quality is. Possible values include 5, 8, 11, 22, and 44, which correspond to 5.512 and 8.000 kHz, (both poor quality), 11.025 kHz (good for basic voice input), 22.050 kHz (mid quality), and 44.100 kHz (maximum quality, and the rates at which audio CDs are sampled).

Line 6 sets the silence level—a kind of activity threshold. In order for the microphone to sense any activity, a noise level above the first value (5 in this case) must be sustained for a specified number of milliseconds (1,000, or 1 second, in this case). This helps reduce the amount of background noise captured by the microphone.

```
1   var mic:Microphone = Microphone.getMicrophone();
2   mic.setLoopBack(true);
3   mic.setUseEchoSuppression(true);
4   mic.gain = 80;
5   mic.rate = 11;
6   mic.setSilenceLevel(5, 1000);
```

Despite echo suppression, if your microphone is close to your speakers (particularly when using a laptop with a built-in microphone), feedback can still occur. Therefore, if you don't need to hear the input, you may wish to set the volume of the mic throughput to zero, as seen in lines 8 through 10. This is not the same as muting, or deactivating, the microphone; it merely sets the volume of the data recorded to an inaudible level.

```
7   //transformation
8   var trans:SoundTransform = mic.soundTransform;
9   trans.volume = 0;
10  mic.soundTransform = trans;
```

The next two dozen lines are optional and provide feedback about the mic to the Output panel. If you're not getting any results from your code, it's helpful to know what your microphone settings are. You may find that the mic is muted, or has a 0 gain, or a high silence threshold.

You may also be able to check on the microphone's responsiveness by checking its **silenceTimeout** property. This is the number of milliseconds between the time the microphone stops sensing input, and the time an inactivity event is sent. (The event **ActivityEvent.ACTIVITY** is dispatched both when the microphone starts and stops sensing activity.)

The listener created in lines 12 through 20 responds to the event, **StatusEvent. STATUS**, which is triggered by any microphone status updates, such as when the mic is muted or unmuted. Each time the listener function is triggered, it checks to see whether the user has granted access to the mic, which would be reflected by a **Microphone.Unmuted** status code (line 15). If so, the `showMicInfo()` function is called. If the received code is **Microphone. Muted** (line 17), a trace says that access was denied.

```
11   //mic status
12   mic.addEventListener(StatusEvent.STATUS, onMicStatus
13                        false, 0, true);
14   function onMicStatus(evt:StatusEvent):void {
15       if (evt.code == "Microphone.Unmuted") {
16           showMicInfo();
17       } else if (evt.code == "Microphone.Muted") {
18           trace("Microphone access denied.");
19       }
20   }
21
22   function showMicInfo():void {
23       var sndInputs:Array = Microphone.names;
24       trace("Available sound input devices:");
25       for (var i:int = 0; i < sndInputs.length; i++) {
26           trace("--", sndInputs[i]);
27       }
28       trace("Selected sound input device name:", mic.name);
29
30       trace("Muted:", mic.muted);
31       trace("Echo suppression:", mic.useEchoSuppression);
32       trace("Gain:", mic.gain);
33       trace("Rate:", mic.rate, "kHz");
34       trace("Silence level:", mic.silenceLevel);
35       trace("Silence timeout:", mic.silenceTimeout);
36   }
```

Another reason that you may not get the results you expect from microphone input is if the wrong input has been selected, when multiple inputs are available. Lines 23 through 28 of the **showMicInfo()** function retrieve an array of all available microphones, loop through the list and trace them, and finish with the name of the currently selected microphone. This allows you to verify that the desired mic is active.

Next, we begin to get into the visualization section of the file. This example will plot a graph of microphone activity levels over time. To do this, we need to use the **Graphics** class and draw lines from point to point, as discussed earlier when covering the **Waveform** class. Lines 38 through 46 create a sprite into which we can draw, clear the canvas, set a line style, and move the virtual drawing pen to the far left of the stage at the y coordinate 300.

Notice that lines 43 through 45, the methods responsible for initializing the canvas, are placed into a function and then called right away in line 47. This may seem like an unnecessary step but the **initCanvas()** function will be called again and again to reinitialize the canvas.

```
37   //creating a canvas to draw into
38   var canvas:Sprite = new Sprite();
39   var g:Graphics = canvas.graphics;
40   addChild(canvas);
41
42   function initCanvas():void {
43       g.clear();
```

```
44      g.lineStyle(0, 0x6600CC);
45      g.moveTo(0, 300);
46  }
47  initCanvas();
```

As our last task, we draw the graph. We want this exercise to plot continually, even if there is no activity, much like an EKG will run until it is stopped. So, we'll use a Timer event firing every 50 milliseconds to visualize the mic activity (lines 49 through 52). Line 54 initializes a variable that will be used for the x coordinate of each point in the line.

**NOTE**

*See the "Timer Events" section of Chapter 3 for more information.*

The graph is drawn from point to point in line 56, using the same technique discussed in the **Waveform** class. The x coordinate is advanced across the screen, and the y coordinate is determined by subtracting the mic activity level from a baseline. A maximum line height is not required here, however, because the values output from the **activityLevel** property are between 0 and 100.

Finally, a conditional in lines 57 through 62 determines the x coordinate of each point to which a line is drawn in the graph. Line 57 checks to see if the x coordinate has exceeded the right side of the stage. If so, the **xPos** property is reset to 0, the graph is cleared, and the graphing process begins anew from the left side of the stage. If not, the graph continues to advance across the stage 2 pixels at a time.

```
48  //drawing the activity graph
49  var myTimer:Timer = new Timer(50);
50  myTimer.addEventListener(TimerEvent.TIMER, onTimer,
51                           false, 0, true);
52  myTimer.start();
53
54  var xPos:int = 0;
55  function onTimer(ev:TimerEvent):void {
56      g.lineTo(xPos, 300 - mic.activityLevel);
57      if (xPos > stage.stageRight) {
58          xPos = 0;
59          initCanvas();
60      } else {
61          xPos += 2;
62      }
63  }
```

# SampleDataEvent

Flash Player 10 significantly improves ActionScript's sound processing capabilities through the use of the **SampleDataEvent.SAMPLE_DATA** event. This event is dispatched in two ways. The first is when a sound object requests sound data. We'll look at this circumstance at the end of the chapter when we play back recorded input.

The second way this event is used is when the microphone receives input. Every time audio samples become available to the microphone, the event is dispatched and you can process the incoming data. The following example, found in the *microphone_sample_data_event.fla* source file, visualizes microphone input by drawing a waveform at runtime.

Lines 1 through 5 create a sprite canvas into which we'll draw our visualization. Line 3 positions it horizontally, 20 pixels from the left of the stage, and line 4 centers the visualization vertically. Line 5 scales the canvas to 25 percent of its original size. We'll tell you why in a moment when we discuss the size of the waveform we're drawing.

Line 8 creates an instance of the microphone, and line 9 sets its sample rate to 44.100 kHz. Lines 10 and 11 create a microphone event listener that responds to the **SAMPLE_DATA** event. Each time sample data is received by the microphone, the **onMicData()** function (lines 13 through 22) is called. This function uses the same techniques described when visualizing spectrum data and microphone activity level, with a few notable exceptions that we'll explain after the code.

```
1    var canvas:Sprite = new Sprite();
2    var g:Graphics = canvas.graphics;
3    canvas.x = 20;
4    canvas.y = stage.stageHeight / 2;
5    canvas.scaleX = canvas.scaleY = 0.25;
6    addChild(canvas);
7
8    var mic:Microphone = Microphone.getMicrophone();
9    mic.rate = 44;
10   mic.addEventListener(SampleDataEvent.SAMPLE_DATA, onMicData,
11                        false, 0, true);
12
13   function onMicData(evt:SampleDataEvent):void {
14       var xPos:Number = 0;
15       g.clear();
16       g.lineStyle(1, 0x0000FF);
17
18       while(evt.data.bytesAvailable) {
19           g.lineTo(xPos, evt.data.readFloat() * 200);
20           xPos++;
21       }
22   }
```

First, we're not calculating sound bytes using the **computeSpectrum()** method. Instead, bytes are being provided by the event, and we're referencing the byte array in which they're stored through the event's **data** property.

Second, we've simplified access to the byte array by looping through all available bytes. This is possible because the byte array **readFloat()** method automatically increments through the data, as discussed in the "Sound Spectrum Data" section of this chapter. So, as long as the event has bytes that have not yet been read, the loop will continue. When all bytes have been checked, the loop concludes and the next event is processed.

Finally, although the actual drawing of the waveform (line 19) is consistent with prior examples, it does influence the scale setting we used in line 5. There's nothing different about the use of the **lineTo()** method in this example. We're still incrementing the x coordinate of each point every time through a loop, and we're still determining the y coordinate of each point by multiplying an amplitude float from the byte array by a maximum possible wave height.

However, the number of samples used by the microphone dictates how many points are drawn. When recording or generating audio, you can typically work with between 2048 and 8192 samples (bytes) per **SAMPLE_DATA** event. The higher the number of samples, the better your sound. The number of samples used is determined by the **rate** property of the microphone. Table 11-3 shows the correlation between the digital sample rate and the number of samples used.

We set the mic **rate** property to 44 in line 9, which means 8192 samples are used every time **onMicData()** is called. Because we need floats, not bytes, the **readFloat()** method advances through the available bytes four at a time. This means that we end up with 2048 points each time the waveform is plotted. So, to fit the waveform within the default stage width of 550 pixels, we scale the canvas sprite down to 25 percent.

When testing your file, after you grant access to the microphone, the SWF will draw a single waveform in the center of the screen when microphone input is received, as shown in Figure 11-11.

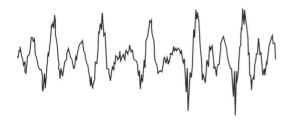

*Figure 11-11. A microphone input waveform, using SampleDataEvent*

# Recording, Playing, and Saving Microphone Input

The following exercise covers new features introduced with Flash Players 10 and 10.1 and requires Flash Player 10.1 or later to function. In this example, you'll capture mic input and play it back without a sound file to work from. You'll also use the ByteArray to save the data as a WAV file.

The source code consists of two classes: **RecordMicrophone**, which is part of the learningactionscript3 package (in the *sound* directory), and **RecordMicrophone_Example**, which is a document class that accompanies the *RecordMicrophone_Example.fla*. The document class simply sets up a user interface with five buttons that are used to control the **RecordMicrophone** class. The **RecordMicrophone** class contains the core functionality of the exercise and is where we'll start.

**NOTE**

*When recording microphone input, you can actually work with 1024 samples per* **SAMPLE_DATA** *event, by using a microphone* **rate** *of 8 or 5. However, we recommend against it. We suggest using a* **rate** *of 44, resulting in 8192 samples per event, but a* **rate** *of 11, for 2048 samples per event, should be a minimum.*

*Notably, the fewer samples you use, the higher the likelihood of introducing audio artifacts like clicks and pops into your sound. In fact, when generating sounds from code, you can't even use fewer than 2048 samples.*

*Table 11-3. Microphone sample rates and the number of samples recorded per* **SAMPLE_DATA** *event*

| Mic rate | Sample Rate | Samples Used |
|----------|-------------|--------------|
| 44 | 44.100 kHz | 8192 |
| 22 | 22.050 kHz | 4096 |
| 11 | 11.025 kHz | 2048 |
| 8 | 8.000 kHz | 1024 |
| 5 | 5.512 kHz | 1024 |

**NOTE**

*See "Storing and retrieving sound spectrum data" earlier in the chapter for more information about the* **ByteArray** *class and* **readFloat()** *method.*

Flash Professional users can try the exercise by testing the FLA, but you'll need version CS5 to compile. If you're using another ActionScript editor, we've written the `RecordMicrophone_Example` class to extend `MovieClip` so it can easily be used as an application class.

# RecordMicrophone Class

Relying heavily on event-driven sample processing, `RecordMicrophone` is a utility class that provides the minimum required to effectively record, play, and save microphone input. During recording, it adds an event listener to the microphone to listen for the `SAMPLE_DATA` event, and will capture any input that is fed to the mic.

During playback, it again creates an event listener to listen for the `SAMPLE_DATA` event but, this time, the listener is added to the `Sound` object. In this case, the listener plays any sample data that is sent to the sound object, generating the sound dynamically at runtime.

Because both processes are event-driven, adding and removing these listeners essentially switches on and off the two functions. Stopping recording or playback, for example, removes the corresponding listener, and listeners are recreated each time the record or play button is used. Now let's look at the code.

Lines 1 through 10 establish the package path of the class, and import all required additional classes. Note that we're using another class from Adobe's as3corelib package, and the `FileReference` class, discussed in the "Image Encoding and Saving" section of Chapter 9. The `WAVWriter` class encodes bytes of sound data as a WAV file and, as of Flash Player 10 and later, the `FileReference` class saves a file to your hard drive.

Lines 12 through 17 declare the class and class properties. The _mic_ property holds an instance of the microphone. The _sndBytes_ property contains a byte array of all microphone input, _snd_ is a `Sound` instance that we can use to play back what we record, and _channel_ references the sound channel into which the `Sound` object is played.

Lines 19 through 28 include the class constructor and `setupMicrophone()` method. The latter is a basic microphone initialization method that creates an instance of the microphone and sets three simple mic properties discussed previously in the chapter.

**NOTE**

*As you look over the* `RecordMicrophone` *class in the coming pages, note which methods are public and which are private. Their designation will affect which methods we can call from our second class, which builds the example interface.*

**NOTE**

*The* `RecordMicrophone` *class doesn't extend anything because no inheritance is required. We don't need to add instances of this class to the display list, for example, or inherit the accessible properties, methods or events of a parent class.*

```
1    package com.learningactionscript3.sound {
2
3        import flash.events.Event;
4        import flash.events.SampleDataEvent;
5        import flash.media.Microphone;
6        import flash.media.Sound;
7        import flash.media.SoundChannel;
8        import flash.net.FileReference;
9        import flash.utils.ByteArray;
10       import com.adobe.audio.format.WAVWriter;
11
```

```
12      public class RecordMicrophone {
13
14          private var _mic:Microphone;
15          private var _sndBytes:ByteArray;
16          private var _snd:Sound = new Sound();
17          private var _channel:SoundChannel = new SoundChannel();
18
19          public function RecordMicrophone() {
20              setupMicrophone();
21          }
22
23          public function setupMicrophone():void {
24              _mic = Microphone.getMicrophone();
25              _mic.rate = 44;
26              _mic.setSilenceLevel(0);
27              _mic.setUseEchoSuppression(true);
28          }
```

## Recording microphone input at runtime

Lines 30 through 45 contain the code needed to start and stop recording. When the public **startRecording()** method is called from a button we'll create later, a new byte array is created to hold the new recording. Lines 33 and 34 add a **SAMPLE_DATA** event listener to the mic to prepare it for capturing input. First, however, line 32 checks to see if the listener doesn't already exist. This is a very useful technique to prevent the accidental creation of redundant listeners and makes it easier to remove listeners and manage memory and performance issues.

The **getMicData()** method in lines 38 through 40 is the aforementioned listener method and does nothing more than write incoming bytes to the byte array. It's private because it's only accessed by the listener, not from outside the class. The last method in this block, **stopRecording()** in lines 42 through 45, removes the **SAMPLE_DATA** listener, to stop the recording process. This, too, is public so a stop recording button in a user interface can call the method.

```
29          //start and stop recording
30          public function startRecording():void {
31              _sndBytes = new ByteArray();
32              if(!_mic.hasEventListener(SampleDataEvent.SAMPLE_DATA)){
33                  _mic.addEventListener(SampleDataEvent.SAMPLE_DATA,
34                                      getMicData, false, 0, true);
35              }
36          }
37
38          private function getMicData(evt:SampleDataEvent):void {
39              _sndBytes.writeBytes(evt.data);
40          }
41
42          public function stopRecording():void {
43              _mic.removeEventListener(SampleDataEvent.SAMPLE_DATA,
44                                      getMicData);
45          }
```

**NOTE**

*Note that the **RecordMicrophone** constructor does nothing but call the method **setupMicrophone()**. Why, then, isn't the content of the latter method just placed inside the constructor?*

*Remember that a constructor executes immediately upon instantiation but is not typically called again. By moving the setup routine to its own method, you can setup your microphone any time you like. What's more, by making the method public, you can setup the mic from another part of your project, such as a button or frame script, if desired. The constructor calls this method, too, to enable recording the moment the **RecordMicrophone** class is instantiated.*

**NOTE**

*Although helpful when adding listeners, checking to see if a listener is present before removing it is not required. The **removeEventListener()** method is designed to have no effect if the listener doesn't already exist.*

NOTE

*When using higher numbers of samples, the chance of latency—the delay between interacting with a sound and hearing the result—also increases. Unfortunately, latency is the hardest thing to conquer when processing sound in Flash Player, and the problem is related to your computer operating system performance. We recommend starting with 8192 samples when generating audio and scaling back when required. See http://help.adobe.com/en_US/as3/dev/WSE523B839-C626-4983-B9C0-07CF1A087ED7.html for more information.*

The next three methods control recording playback. The **playSound()** method in lines 47 through 58 starts the process. After checking to see if a **SAMPLE_DATA** listener doesn't already exist in line 48, the listener is added in lines 49 through 51. This is the mechanism used to enable playback of a dynamically generated sound. When we used this event with the microphone, the listener listened for incoming data to record. When we use the event to generate a new sound, the sound object listens for data to play.

The byte array is then reset in line 52 to enable playback. Remember that the byte array automatically increments itself as its used. So, when you finish populating or playing a byte array, its position will be at the end of the file. If not reset, the byte array will have nothing to play.

The sound is then played into a channel in line 53, and a **COMPLETE** event listener is added to the channel in lines 54 through 56.

## Writing sound data dynamically at runtime

The **playbackData()** method is an example of generating sound at runtime. Instead of playing an internal audio file, or a loaded MP3, bytes from the captured microphone input are fed to the **Sound** object in real time.

When generating sound dynamically, you must feed the **Sound** object between 2048 and 8192 samples at a time. The greater the number of samples, the less likely you are to hear pops, clicks, or other audio artifacts.

Because you can't be sure of the amount of microphone input you'll receive, you need to process as many samples as are required to play back the sound. As a safeguard against running out of data prematurely and generating an error, we need to be sure we have enough data to accomplish our immediate goal. In this case, we need to write floats from the mic to a **Sound** object, so we'll be using the **writeFloat()** method to turn 4 bytes into a float.

So before proceeding, line 62 first checks to be sure there are at least 4 bytes in the mic data to create a float. If so, line 63 creates the sample. Because the mic input is mono, and the sound object contains stereo channels, the sample must be written twice—once for each channel. This will create a mono sound with the same data in both left and right channels. As the mic data is written to the sound object, we hear the sound play. Next we need to understand two circumstances under which playback is halted.

## Stopping playback

The **onPlayComplete()** method in lines 70 through 75 remove the listeners from the sound and sound channel objects, readying them for reuse. This function is triggered when the sound has played fully and stops on its own. We need similar behavior when the user stops playback.

This is accomplished with the **stopPlaying()** function in lines 77 through 80. In addition to stopping the channel playback manually, it also calls the **onPlayComplete()** method to remove the active listeners. Rather than repeating this code, the event listener method is called, passing the default event value of **null** to avoid an argument count mismatch error. (See the "Pausing Sounds and Resuming Playback" section for more information.)

```
46    //play recording
47    public function playSound():void {
48        if(!_snd.hasEventListener(SampleDataEvent.SAMPLE_DATA)){
49            _snd.addEventListener(SampleDataEvent.SAMPLE_DATA,
50                                  playbackData,
51                                  false, 0, true);
52            _sndBytes.position = 0;
53            _channel = _snd.play();
54            _channel.addEventListener(Event.SOUND_COMPLETE,
55                                      onPlayComplete,
56                                      false, 0, true);
57        }
58    }
59
60    private function playbackData(evt:SampleDataEvent):void {
61        for (var i:int = 0; i < 8192; i++) {
62            if (_sndBytes.bytesAvailable >= 4) {
63                var sample:Number = _sndBytes.readFloat();
64                evt.data.writeFloat(sample);
65                evt.data.writeFloat(sample);
66            }
67        }
68    }
69
70    private function onPlayComplete(evt:Event):void {
71        _snd.removeEventListener(SampleDataEvent.SAMPLE_DATA,
72                                 playbackData);
73        _channel.removeEventListener(Event.SOUND_COMPLETE,
74                                     onPlayComplete);
75    }
76
77    public function stopPlaying():void {
78        _channel.stop();
79        onPlayComplete(null);
80    }
```

Finally, lines 82 through 96 contain the **saveFile()** method, which we'll use for encoding and saving the recording as a WAV file. Line 83 first checks to be sure the byte array contains content to save. If it does, line 84 again resets the byte array's position to the beginning of the sound data, and line 86 creates a byte array to contain the newly encoded data. Line 88 creates an instance of Adobe's **WAVWriter** class to initialize a new WAV file, and line 89 sets its encoding channel count to 1 (mono) instead of the default 2 (stereo).

Line 90 encodes the data from the recording byte array **_sndBytes** and stores it in the new byte array, **outputStream**. It also specifies the incoming sample rate and number of channels for the encoding process. You must match the incoming sample rate and number of channels with the corresponding values used for the **WAVWriter** instance to avoid resampling or errors during the encoding process.

> **NOTE**
>
> *WAVWriter uses a default bit depth of 16-bit, and a default sample rate of 44.100 kHz. If you use a different sample rate in your microphone settings, you must assign the* **samplingRate** *property of the* **WAVWriter** *class to match.*
>
> *For example, if your mic* **rate** *property were 22, you would set the* **WAVWriter** *instance* **samplingRate** *property to 22050. (It's measured in Hz, not kHz.) If you save a stereo sound you can use the default* **numOfChannels** *value of 2, but remember that the ActionScript* **Microphone** *class records in mono.*

The last part of the function is to instantiate the **FileReference** class and use its **save()** method to save the newly WAV-encoded byte array data with a default file name of *recording.wav*. The user's operating system will prompt for a save location during the save. This is the same process we used to save a PNG in the "Image Encoding and Saving" section of Chapter 9, and requires Flash Player 10.

```
81        //save recording to WAV
82        public function saveFile():void {
83            if (_sndBytes.length > 0) {
84                _sndBytes.position = 0;
85
86                var outputStream:ByteArray = new ByteArray();
87
88                var wavWriter:WAVWriter = new WAVWriter();
89                wavWriter.numOfChannels = 1;
90                wavWriter.processSamples(outputStream, _sndBytes,
91                                         44100, 1);
92
93                var fileRef:FileReference = new FileReference();
94                fileRef.save(outputStream, "recording.wav");
95            }
96        }
97    }
98 }
```

## RecordMicrophone_Example Class

This class sets up a simple five-button interface to put the **RecordMicrophone** class to work. It extends **MovieClip** so it can be used as a document class or application class so that an FLA is not mandatory to try the exercise.

Lines 1 through 9 are standard fare, with the only additional notable mention being that we're using the **RoundRectButton** class to create our buttons. Lines 11 and 12 declare class properties to store an instance of the **RecordMicrophone** class and microphone, respectively.

Line 15 creates the **RecordMicrophone** instance, and lines 17 through 34 create five buttons to record, stop recording, play, stop playing, and save the recording, respectively. Using a method to create multiple buttons is the same approach used in the "Playing, Pausing, and Resuming Sounds" section of this chapter.

The remainder of the class consists of event listener methods triggered by the buttons. They do nothing but call the equivalent public methods of the **RecordMicrophone** class.

```
1  package {
2
3      import flash.display.MovieClip;
4      import flash.media.Microphone;
5      import flash.events.MouseEvent;
6      import com.learningactionscript3.ui.RoundRectButton;
7      import com.learningactionscript3.sound.RecordMicrophone;
8
```

```
9    public class RecordMicrophone_Example extends MovieClip {
10
11       private var _sm:RecordMicrophone;
12       private var _mic:Microphone;
13
14       public function RecordMicrophone_Example() {
15          _sm = new RecordMicrophone();
16
17          createButton(25, "Record", startRecording);
18          createButton(50, "Stop Recording", stopRecording);
19          createButton(75, "Play", playRecording);
20          createButton(100, "Stop Playing", stopPlaying);
21          createButton(125, "Save Recording", saveRecording);
22       }
23
24       private function createButton(yLoc:Number, labl:String,
25                                     func:Function):void {
26          var btn:RoundRectButton =
27             new RoundRectButton(120, 20, 10, 2, 0x000099,
28                                  labl, 0xFFFFFF);
29          btn.x = 20;
30          btn.y = yLoc;
31          btn.addEventListener(MouseEvent.CLICK, func,
32                               false, 0, true);
33          addChild(btn);
34       }
35
36       private function startRecording(evt:MouseEvent):void {
37          _sm.startRecording();
38       }
39
40       private function stopRecording(evt:MouseEvent):void {
41          _sm.stopRecording();
42       }
43
44       private function playRecording(evt:MouseEvent):void {
45          _sm.playSound();
46       }
47
48       private function stopPlaying(evt:MouseEvent):void {
49          _sm.stopPlaying();
50       }
51
52       private function saveRecording(evt:MouseEvent):void {
53          _sm.saveFile();
54       }
55    }
56 }
```

# What's Next?

This chapter covered quite a bit of ground regarding ActionScript control of sound, but there is much left to explore and many fun experiments left to try. The companion website for this book can serve as a starting point for this ongoing study. The website includes a more elaborate object-oriented example akin to a desktop sound mixer, in which you can mix three sound files.

## learningaction-script3 Package

This chapter's contribution to the learningactionscript3 package includes the `Waveform` visualization class discussed in the "Sound Spectrum Data" section of this chapter, the `PeakMeter` class, mentioned in the "Creating More Expressive Peak Meters Using Masks" sidebar, and the `RecordMicrophone` class covered in this chapter's "Push Yourself" section.

The site also includes examples of how to generate sound from scratch and how to extract sound from MP3 files and use the extracted sample.

Next, we make the logical jump to another media type: video. We'll not only demonstrate how to deliver Flash video in a number of ways—including both with components and ActionScript-only solutions—but we'll also briefly discuss how to encode videos into a Flash-compatible format.

**In the next chapter**, we'll discuss:

- Using components for video playback requiring little to no ActionScript
- Writing your own simple ActionScript-only video player to reduce file size
- Displaying video in a browser in true full-screen resolution
- Adding captions to video playback

CHAPTER 12

# VIDEO

These days, you have to live under a rock not to repeatedly hear how prevalent Flash Platform video solutions are. Video playback is largely responsible for dramatic increases in Flash Player use over the past several years, and Flash Player is now the first choice for the world's largest video delivery site, Google's YouTube. Flash is estimated to drive more than 75 percent of all Internet video playback, in part because Flash Player is installed on more than 99 percent of computers in the world market, and in part because it's among the most reliable and easy to use cross-platform video technologies.

At the time of this writing, Flash video has also been the subject of much debate as it faces challenges from emerging interest in the next phase of HTML development, HTML5. Although HTML5 is not expected to be ratified as an official standard for some time (many theorize that wide browser adoption may not happen until 2011 or 2012, but that ratification could happen as late as 2022), the allure of video playback without reliance on a browser plug-in is already attracting attention.

In this debate much has been made of replacing the proprietary Flash video format, FLV, with other open video formats. However, although support for video playback within HTML5 is improving, no video file format is currently part of the HTML5 specification. At present, which *codec* (the software algorithm used to compress and decompress video) to support is decided by the makers of software that renders HTML5, such as the developers of today's web browsers. This potential incompatibility risks continuing some of the decidedly *non*standard ways of creating rich media that have plagued developers for years and, some believe, make the consistency of ActionScript development even more compelling.

Furthermore, in addition to the FLV format, Flash Player can play one of today's most widely used video standards, H.264—the codec most commonly used in the MP4 video format popularized by personal video players. This flexibility makes the Flash Platform even more enticing as a playback technology independent of the available video format used.

In this chapter, we'll leave the fortune telling and politics for another forum and focus instead on using ActionScript to play both FLV- and H.264-encoded videos. We'll discuss:

- **Encoding.** Encoding is the process of converting video assets to a format compatible with your delivery system, in this case Flash Player, and typically involves compressing the video to reduce its file size. The scope of this book doesn't allow us to delve extensively into video encoding, but a little background will be enough to get you started.

- **Components.** It's easy to get going with Flash video by using the FLVPlayback component. Components combine user interface assets with ActionScript to create ready-to-use widgets for specific tasks. The FLVPlayback component contains everything you need for basic video playback.

- **Full-Screen Video.** We'll discuss the steps required to present your video in a true full-screen environment, where your video fills the screen entirely—rather than just filling a browser window.

- **Captions.** Adding captions to your video becomes a basic task with another component and a basic XML file. The FLVPlaybackCaptioning component simplifies accessibility efforts by supporting external caption files that can be loaded at runtime. We'll introduce the Timed Text caption file format and show you how to use it to easily add captions to videos controlled by the FLVPlayback component.

- **Writing Your Own Player.** Although components are valuable tools, we also want to show you how to create simple video playback functionality strictly with code. Eliminating the use of components means you can make use of video content without any internal assets and reduce your SWF file size in the process.

## Encoding

Before you can control video with ActionScript, you need to encode video source material into a format that's compatible with Flash Player. Encoding is a big topic that entails finding a sometimes complex balance between quality, video dimensions, and file size. As we are focusing on ActionScript, any in-depth discussion of encoding subtleties is beyond the scope of this book, but we'll show you how to create a video that's compatible with Flash Player.

Three popular encoding applications are Adobe Media Encoder (AME), Wildform Flix Pro, and Sorenson Media Squeeze. In this text, we'll focus on Media Encoder, as it is installed free with the purchase of Adobe Flash Platform tools. However, the commercial products from Wildform and Sorenson Media offer additional features, and the book's companion website contains information about both products.

**NOTE**

*The correct terminology is to say that the title element is **nested** within the head element. We'll talk about nesting more in later chapters.*

**NOTE**

*For comprehensive discussions about encoding and all things Flash video, consult the excellent Video with Adobe Flash CS4 Professional Studio Techniques (Adobe Press), by Robert Reinhart.*

Let's start with the basics of Media Encoder. The application's interface is quite simple, opening to little more than a field that holds a list of files for encoding and a single active Add button. Media Encoder supports batch encoding, allowing you to add several files to a queue for processing. You can add to the queue by dragging the source into the field or using the Add button to browse for your file.

Once you've added a file to the queue, you can immediately choose an output file format from the Format menu, one of many encoding presets from the Preset menu, and the location of the output file by clicking on the link in the Output File column. Figure 12-1 shows a detail of the initial interface, including a single file in the encoding queue.

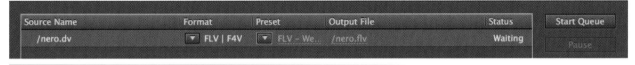

*Figure 12-1. Detail of the Adobe Media Encoder CS5 encoding queue*

# Formats

Media Encoder supports encoding to a wide array of video file types for use with other applications as well as Flash Player. The two file types optimized for Flash Player are FLV and F4V. Supported by Flash Player for several years, FLV is a proprietary video format (also sometimes called a *container* or *wrapper*). Two codecs can be used within an FLV container, Spark and VP6, but we'll focus on VP6-encoded FLVs in our discussions. F4V is the file format for H.264-encoded video in an MP4 container. This format is an adaptation of MPEG-4, based on Apple's QuickTime container (see *http://en.wikipedia.org/wiki/MPEG-4_Part_14* for more information), and was introduced with Flash Player 9 Update 3 (version 9,0,115,0) in December 2007.

The first consideration when choosing a video format is which Flash Player you wish to target. If you must target a Flash Player version prior to 9,0,115,0, you will need to use FLV. If you plan to publish for later Flash Player versions, you have the freedom to choose FLV or F4V.

Another deciding factor is whether or not you need cue points. Embedded within the video during encoding or assigned with ActionScript, *cue points* are markers that can trigger events when reached during playback. Although both video formats now support cue points, this again comes down to which version of Flash Player you want to target. Cue points have been supported in FLV files since Flash Player 8, but were added to F4V files in Flash Player 10.

Beyond the constraints of Flash Player compatibility, each file format has its strengths. FLV supports alpha channels for transparency in your video and performs better on weaker computers. The H.264 codec and MP4 container

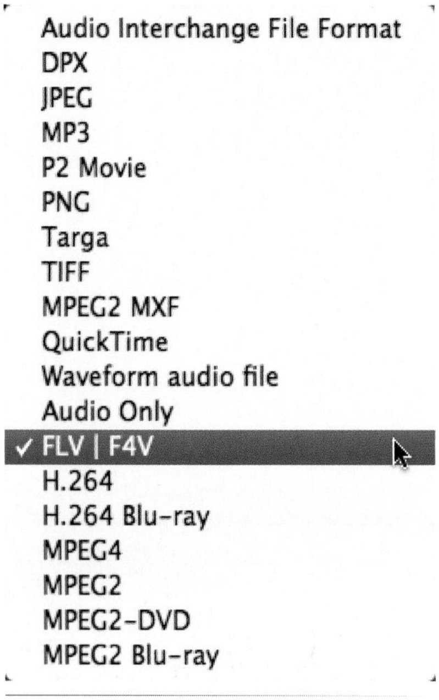

Audio Interchange File Format
DPX
JPEG
MP3
P2 Movie
PNG
Targa
TIFF
MPEG2 MXF
QuickTime
Waveform audio file
Audio Only
✓ FLV | F4V
H.264
H.264 Blu-ray
MPEG4
MPEG2
MPEG2-DVD
MPEG2 Blu-ray

*Figure 12-2. Selecting a video format from Media Encoder's format menu*

**NOTE**

*Robert Reinhart has created a very useful bitrate calculator for compressing FLV files. You can enter concrete data like dimensions, audio sample rate, and whether you're using stereo or mono sound, as well as qualifying information like how much motion is in the video, and it will give you a recommended bitrate to use when encoding. The calculator can be found at http://blogs.flash-support.com/robert/?p=138.*

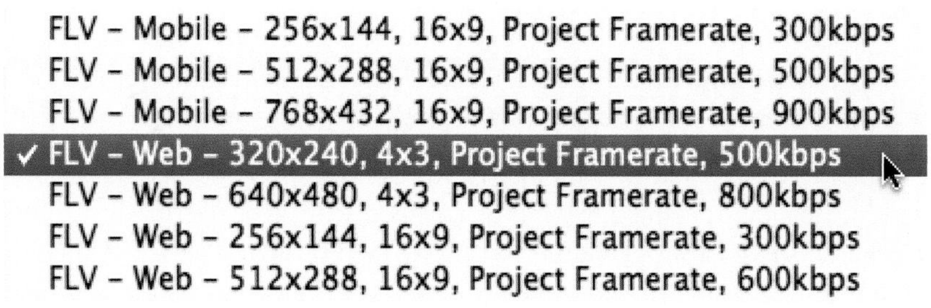

used when encoding F4V files are very widely implemented making it easier to reuse videos with non-Flash projects. This latter point is especially important if you work with a large library of existing MP4 video assets, as they most likely won't need to be reencoded to be compatible with Flash Player.

**NOTE**

*An H.264-encoded video need not have an .f4v extension to work in Flash Player. Extensions such as .mp4, .m4v, and .mov will work as long as the video is encoded correctly. It's a good idea to test your videos for compatibility as early as you can because it's possible to use the H.264 codec without encoding into a compatible MP4 container. This is particularly important when you haven't encoded the video files yourself.*

For maximum compatibility with Flash Professional CS3 through CS5 and support for all versions of Flash Player 9, we'll work with FLV files in this chapter, but feel free experiment with whichever one you choose. You can make that decision in a moment, when we get to encoding presets. For now, after adding your source video to the interface, select FLV | F4V from the Format menu, as shown in Figure 12-2.

## Presets

The next step is to pick an encoding preset. There are almost 50 presets that apply to FLV or F4V files, configured to suit multiple quality settings, resolutions, frame dimensions, and even playback mediums (web or mobile, for example). Figure 12-3 shows a detail of the Preset menu, and selecting a preset that will encode the video to dimensions of 320 × 240, maintain a 4 × 3 aspect ratio, use the source material's frame rate, and compress to a data *bitrate* (the recommended minimum amount of data used when encoding the video) of 500 kilobits per second. This is a pretty good starting point for your first encoding test. It's also a good idea to compare your results with output encoded with other presets if you require a smaller file size or better quality.

FLV – Mobile – 256x144, 16x9, Project Framerate, 300kbps
FLV – Mobile – 512x288, 16x9, Project Framerate, 500kbps
FLV – Mobile – 768x432, 16x9, Project Framerate, 900kbps
✓ FLV – Web – 320x240, 4x3, Project Framerate, 500kbps
FLV – Web – 640x480, 4x3, Project Framerate, 800kbps
FLV – Web – 256x144, 16x9, Project Framerate, 300kbps
FLV – Web – 512x288, 16x9, Project Framerate, 600kbps

*Figure 12-3. Detail from the Preset menu; selecting an encoding preset from the approximately four dozen that ship with Media Encoder*

# Customizing Settings

If you're not content with a preset, or if you have additional needs (such as resizing the source), you can click on the Settings button to customize the settings. (You can even save your customizations as a preset of your own.) Figure 12-4 shows the Settings interface. The upper left quadrant allows you to see various sizes of the source material, as well as crop the source prior to encoding. The bottom left quadrant allows you to create cue points that will be embedded in the video during encoding. Between those areas is the video timeline, which you can use to preview the video and set in and out points if you wish to compress only a portion of the video.

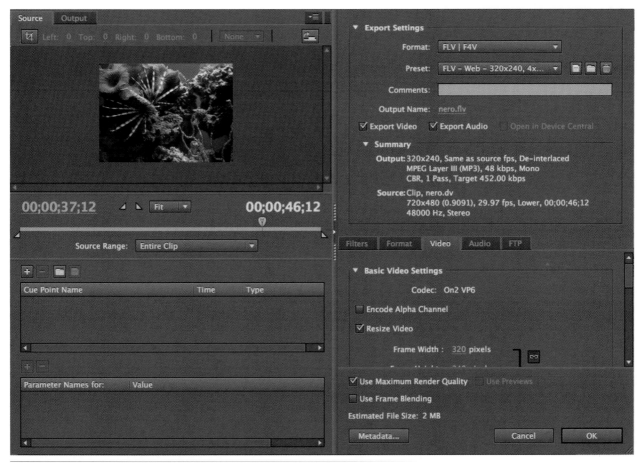

*Figure 12-4. The Settings interface of Adobe Media Encoder (CS5 pictured)*

The upper right quadrant is a general settings area that allows you to choose the file format, encoding preset, and output directory, as well as show a summary of the settings applied by the chosen preset. The lower right quadrant contains more specific settings including video and audio encoding options, and the ability to apply a blur during encoding.

For more information about Adobe Media Encoder, see the Using Adobe Media Encoder CS5 resource at *http://help.adobe.com/en_US/mediaencoder/cs/using/index.html*. Information about embedding cue points during encoding can be found in the "Encoding and exporting" section of this resource. The companion website has additional information about creating cue points—both during encoding and at runtime through ActionScript when using the FLVPlayback component.

## Starting the Queue

Once a preset is selected, all you need to do is press the Start Queue button. Adobe Media Encoder will encode the file and save it in the location specified in the Output File column. (The default location for the output is the same directory in which the source file resides.)

# Components

Components offer designers and coders alike a chance to speed up the development process by using precreated widgets. Components usually combine ActionScript and assets to make it easier to achieve a specific goal. Components can be dropped onto the stage like a movie clip or button symbol and often function with little or no intervention. When effort is required, most components can be configured using the Flash Professional CS5 Properties panel or Flash Professional CS3 or CS4 Components Inspector panel.

Most components can also be manipulated with ActionScript, which is what we'll focus on in this section. Before working with any component, however, Flash Professional users must place the component in the library of the FLA file that will compile to SWF. Simply drag any component from the Components panel to the Library panel, or drag it to the stage and delete it immediately. In this chapter, we'll work with three different components. First, we'll add the FLVPlayback component as a prefabricated video player. Next, we'll add captioning support to the player with the FLVPlaybackCaptioning component. Finally, we'll add a Button component to satisfy a simple user interface need.

## Working with the FLVPlayback Component

The fastest way to add video to your ActionScript application is by using the FLVPlayback component (Figure 12.5). The component is available in two flavors. FLVPlayback is available to Flash Professional users of version CS3 and later, and FLVPlayback 2.5 was introduced with version Flash Professional CS4 and is also available for Flex.

---

*By default, Adobe Media Encoder will start processing the assets in the encoding queue after two minutes of idle time. This behavior can be adjusted in the application preferences.*

---

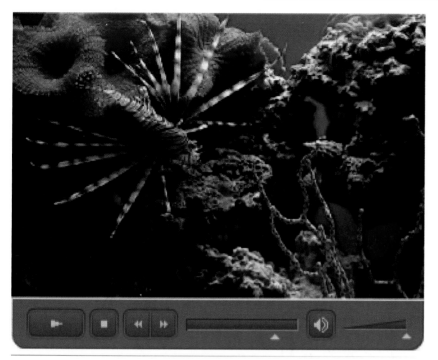

*Figure 12-5. The FLVPlayback component simplifies adding video to projects*

In addition to Flex compatibility, FLVPlayback 2.5 was designed to take advantage of features introduced in version 3.5 of Flash Media Interactive Server—Adobe's streaming media and real-time communication server software. It improves performance for video on demand and live streaming and supports live DVR functionality (pausing, rewinding, and recording live streams) introduced in FMS 3.5.

If you prefer to avoid components—perhaps because you want to design your own player interface, or because components increase the size of your SWF (the FLVPlayback component contributes between 50k and 65k)—we'll show you how to play video entirely with ActionScript shortly. If you're open to the use of components, however, FLVPlayback has a few useful benefits.

First, you can pick from several preconfigured controllers, or *skins*, or you can use the component without a skin and create your own custom controller. This lets the component handle all the heavy lifting in the video display area, but allows you to control playback with your own code and your own design. (We'll show you a very simple implementation of this approach later in the chapter.)

More importantly, the code in the FLVPlayback component takes care of some important behind-the-scenes tasks that you would have to recreate. For example, the component will automatically determine if you're using a streaming server by parsing the URL of the video source. If so, it will then handle the necessary initial communication with the streaming server for you so you don't have to script those connections yourself.

We advise starting out with the FLVPlayback component, even if you choose to create your own controller. Then you can move on to coding your own player to replace the component after you're comfortable with the relevant classes.

### Scripting the component

The following example, found in the *video_comp.fla* source file, demonstrates the minimum code necessary to play a video.

```
1    import fl.video.FLVPlayback;
2
3    var vid:FLVPlayback = new FLVPlayback();
4    vid.source = "nero.flv";
5    addChild(vid);
```

Note in line 1 that the **FLVPlayback** class must be imported even in the timeline because it's not part of the **flash** package. (Most component classes are found in the **fl** package and are not automatically part of the Flash Player to keep the player size small.) Line 3 types the instance variable and instantiates the component. Line 4 populates the **source** property (telling the component which video to play), and line 5 adds the instance to the display list.

**NOTE**

*If you test the video_comp.fla file, you may wonder how it can play without any instruction to do so. The component has an* **autoplay** *property that's set to true by default.*

### Skinning the component

To add controls simply, we can use a skin that ships with the component. FLVPlayback skins are external SWFs that are loaded at runtime. Therefore, to add a skin with ActionScript, you must know the path to the skin.

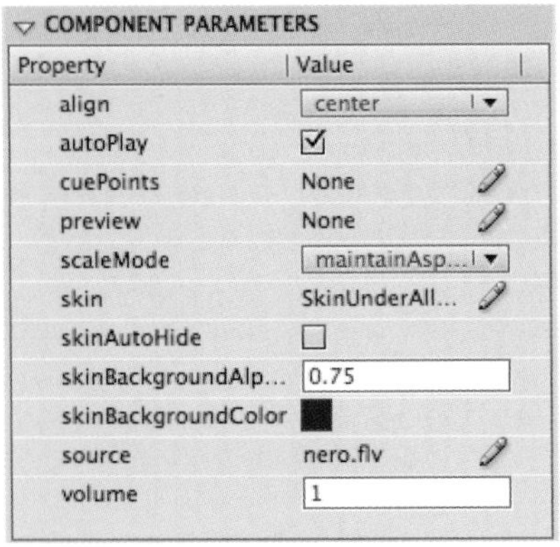


*Figure 12-6. The Component Parameters section of the Properties panel (CS5 pictured)*

Fortunately, Flash Professional users can take advantage of the fact that Flash will move your chosen skin to the same directory as your SWF when you test your file. To choose a skin, save your FLA, or create a new temporary file and save that, to the directory you're using for your project. Temporarily drag the component from your file's library to the stage and select it. Flash Professional CS5 users can then look in the Component Parameters section of the Properties panel (shown in Figure 12-6) to customize the component. Flash Professional CS3 and CS4 users will need to open the Component Inspector panel to see the same content.

Next, click on the UI element next to the *skin* option. (In Flash Professional CS5 there's a pencil button, while other versions show a magnifying glass button after clicking on the field.) This will open a dialog box that allows you to preview all the available skins, collected into groups that display the controller under your video or over your video. Flash Professional CS5 users will also see an additional grouping of new skins called Minima. You can choose which functionality to include in your controller by looking at the name of the skin and previewing its appearance when displayed in the dialog box.

**NOTE**

*Users of Flex Framework authoring tools can download the component, skins, sample files, component source, and several additional related tools at http://www.adobe.com/products/flash-mediaserver/tool_downloads/.*

For the following exercise, found in the *video_comp_skin.fla* source file, choose the SkinUnderAllNoFullNoCaption skin and test your movie. Don't worry about the fact that it won't work. After all, you didn't select a video source. All that matters is that Flash copies the skin to the same directory in which you published your SWF. You should see *SkinUnderAllNoFullNoCaption.swf* in that directory. (If not, be sure you save the FLA you were using for this task and retest.) Once you have your skin in place, you can remove the FLVPlayback component from the stage, or discard any temporary file you created.

Once the skin is in place, all that remains is to add one or more of the following three lines to your existing script. Line 6 specifies your skin choice, and the optional lines 7 and 8 specify the color and alpha of the skin. Now, when you test your movie, you'll see a skin that you can use to control video playback.

```
6   vid.skin = "SkinUnderAllNoFullNoCaption.swf";
7   vid.skinBackgroundColor = 0x003366;
8   vid.skinBackgroundAlpha = 0.75;
```

If you don't want to store the skin file in the same directory as your main SWF (for example, if you want to store multiple skins in a directory), you can specify another path for the skin property. Also, remember that the skin you see is an external SWF that's loaded at runtime. Therefore, just like the video file, the skin must be deployed with your main SWF and HTML files.

## Full-Screen Video

One of the most entertaining Flash video features is true full-screen video—video that occupies the entire screen, rather than a maximized browser or player window, hiding other computer operating system interface elements for a fully immersive experience. Both the FLVPlayback component and pure ActionScript can launch into full-screen mode, both of which we'll cover. Before we get to implementation, however, we need to cover two preliminary steps.

The first step is to start with optimal source material for final assets. This includes the highest quality source, the largest size your interface will allow, and careful attention during encoding. Beyond those common sense suggestions, you'll probably want to experiment with such encoding options as different bitrates and deinterlacing your content if you're using a DV source. *Deinterlacing* is the process of converting the two fields of a DV source (which are like video frames but each contain half the horizontal lines and are displayed twice as fast) into the frames used by the FLV format. One common artifact that is more pronounced when working with interlaced source material is jagged lines visible along sharp edges in your videos. Deinterlacing the source during encoding significantly reduces this effect.

The second step is to instruct Flash Player to allow the switch to full-screen display. If you think about it for a moment, you certainly don't want the decision to switch to full-screen mode left in the hands of content creators. If that were the case, every Flash advertisement would take over your screen, leaving you no control. Instead, the developer must make the feature possible, and the user must be responsible for switching back and forth between normal and full-screen modes.

To enable the feature, you must add the **allowFullScreen** parameter, with a value of true, to the file's host HTML file. One way to do this is to add this parameter manually to the object and embed tags, as seen in the following excerpt.

```
<object>
    ...
    <param name="allowFullScreen" value="true" />
    <embed ... allowfullscreen="true" />
</object>
```

Flash Professional users can also use the quick and easy solution (particularly handy during testing) of choosing the "Flash Only – Allow Full Screen" publishing template in the Publish Settings dialog (File→Publish Settings→HTML→Template).

After adding support for full-screen video in your HTML host file, you're ready to enable the full-screen button in the FLVPlayback component. To do so, choose any skin that supports full screen, such as SkinUnderAll or SkinOverPlayFullscreen, to cite two examples. These and other skins add the Full Screen button shown in Figure 12-7.

The following change to line 6 of the previous example, found in the *video_comp_skin_full.fla* source file, changes the skin to one that supports full screen mode.

```
6    vid.skin = "SkinUnderAllNoCaption.swf";
```

Once you have a video and have supported full screen mode in your host HTML file and skin, you can test your file in a browser. Full screen mode will not work when testing within Flash Professional, so Flash users can select the default Publish Preview command, File→Publish Preview→HTML. Pressing the Full Screen button in the skin will switch to full-screen mode, and you can press the Escape key to return to normal mode. Later in this chapter, we'll show you how to add full-screen playback using your own ActionScript.

*Figure 12-7. The Full Screen button used by select FLVPlayback skins (color and alpha may differ)*

**NOTE**

*If HTML is not available for Flash Professional users, go to the File→Publish Settings menu dialog and add HTML as a publishable format.*

## Captions

Captions, also referred to in some contexts as subtitles, consist of text that is displayed synchronously during video playback. Captions are useful for providing alternate language tracks to bring your video to a wider audience. Captions are also appreciated by the deaf and hearing impaired, as they provide a much needed accessible alternative for audio tracks when it comes to dialog and descriptive audio services.

Captions help satisfy requirements imposed by the United States Rehabilitation Act of 1973, Section 508, which establishes accessibility mandates for content developed for government use, or financed by federal funds. Many private entities, particularly those serving the educational markets, also require accessible content. As the demand for this requirement increases, captions will play an increasingly more important role in digital video.

## Using the FLVPlaybackCaptioning Component

Flash supports captioning via the FLVPlaybackCaptioning component, when used in conjunction with the FLVPlayback component. Adding the FLVPlaybackCaptioning component to the stage at authoring time, or dynamically at runtime with ActionScript, opens the door for caption use.

The simplest way to display captions is to use the FLVPlayback component. In fact, with only one FLVPlayback instance on the stage the captioning component will automatically detect the playback component, and use its internal text element for caption display. You can also manually specify any FLVPlayback component as the target for the captions (in case you require more than one at any given time), or even your own target for the captions (in the event that you want to use another text element—perhaps integrated into your interface, rather than the video).

*Figure 12-8. The Captions button used by select FLVPlayback skins (color and alpha may differ)*

To use the FLVPlayback, you'll need to choose any skin that supports captions, such as SkinUnderAll or SkinOverPlayCaption, among others. These skins feature the Captions button shown in Figure 12-8.

The following edit to line 6 of the previous example, found in the *video_comp_skin_full_captions.fla* source file, uses a skin that supports all skinned features, including captions.

```
6    vid.skin = "SkinUnderAll.swf";
```

Once the FLVPlayback component is configured to display captions, we must add the FLVPlaybackCaptioning component to the stage.

The following code continues the example first by importing the component class in line 10, and instantiating the component in line 11. Line 12 assigns the caption file for loading at runtime (which we'll discuss in a moment), and line 13 adds the component to the display list.

```
10   import fl.video.FLVPlaybackCaptioning;
11   var cap:FLVPlaybackCaptioning = new FLVPlaybackCaptioning();
12   cap.source = "nero_timed_text.xml";
13   addChild(cap);
```

Note that we're not placing the component at a particular location on the stage. Although it appears as a small rectangle when dragged to the stage in

**NOTE**

*As with the FLVPlayback component, Flash Professional users must have the component in the library of their FLA to instantiate it with ActionScript. See the "Working with the FLVPlayback Component" section of this chapter for more information.*

authoring mode, this is merely to simplify selecting the component. At runtime, it will be invisible, so its position is irrelevant.

Now both components are ready to display captions, so we need to create the caption file. You can create a captioned video in two ways. You can embed the caption data in the video using cue points. Embedding means they'll always be with the video, but it also means that you have to reencode the video just to edit the text. A far more flexible option is to load a caption file at runtime. This approach also allows you to switch caption files dynamically—ideal for offering subtitles in multiple languages, a task we'll look at later in the chapter. First, however, we need to know how to format the captions.

## Creating Captions with Timed Text

To create a caption file to load at runtime, you need to write an XML (Extensible Markup Langauge, discussed in Chapter 14) file using the World Wide Web Consortium (W3C) Timed Text Markup Language (TTML or, familiarly, TT)—also sometimes referred to by its format name, Distribution Format Exchange Profile (DFXP). We'll cover a portion of Timed Text features here, but you can learn more about the language by visiting the W3C page at *http://www.w3.org/AudioVideo/TT/*. More importantly, you can learn about the subset of features supported by the FLVPlaybackCaptioning component from Adobe's ActionScript 3.0 Language and Components Reference at *http://www.adobe.com/livedocs/flash/9.0/ActionScriptLangRefV3/TimedTextTags. html*.

**NOTE**

*MAGpie is a free captioning tool developed by accessibility leaders at the National Center for Accessible Media (NCAM). For more information, see http://ncam.wgbh.org/invent_build/ web_multimedia/tools-guidelines/magpie. You can find the Manitu Group's Captionate at http://www.captionate. com, and Adobe's Flash Developer Center features a tutorial on using Captionate with the FLVPlayback and FLVPlaybackCaptioning components (http://www.adobe.com/devnet/flash/ articles/video_captionate.html).*

Several tools can create Timed Text files, including the pair listed in the adjacent note. However, you can also write your own Timed Text files. The example XML that follows is an edited excerpt of the *nero_timed_text.xml* source file provided in this chapter's source archive. (For brevity, two captions are shown and minor edits have been made to use all features from the source file.)

```
1   <?xml version="1.0" encoding="UTF-8"?>
2   <tt xmlns="http://www.w3.org/2006/04/ttaf1"
3     xmlns:tts="http://www.w3.org/2006/04/ttaf1#styling">
4     <head>
5       <styling>
6         <style id="1"
7           tts:textAlign="center"
8           tts:fontFamily="_sans"
9           tts:fontSize="18"
10          tts:fontWeight="bold"
11          tts:color="#FFFF00FF" />
12        <style id="2" tts:backgroundColor="#00000000" />
13        <style id="3" tts:backgroundColor="#000000FF" />
14        <style id="trans" style="1 2" />
15        <style id="opaq" style="1 3" />
16      </styling>
17    </head>
18    <body>
19      <div>
20        <p begin="00:00:05.00" dur="00:00:04.00" style="opaq">
```

```
21          Nero is a Lionfish<br /> (<span tts:fontStyle="italic">
22          Pterois volitans</span>),
23       </p>
24       <p begin="00:00:09.00" dur="00:00:02.00" style="trans">
25          in his reef aquarium.
26       </p>
27    </div>
28  </body>
29 </tt>
```

We'll discuss custom XML solutions in Chapter 14, but Timed Text is a predefined format so conforming to its specification is pretty straightforward. We'll occasionally point out things that we'll cover in greater detail in Chapter 14, but you should feel comfortable simply editing an existing Timed Text file until you gain a little experience with XML.

Lines 1 through 3 include two default tags used to validate the file. The first tag (also called a *node*) is `<?xml... ?>` and is the XML declaration tag. We'll discuss this in Chapter 14 but, essentially, it declares the version of XML in use and the character encoding used when writing the document.

The second tag, `<tt>`, is the document's root node. All XML documents must have a root node that encloses all other nodes, and we'll discuss this further in Chapter 14, as well. Be sure to see the accompanying note describing the use of attributes in this tag.

**NOTE**

*Character encoding just maps text characters to specific codes (usually numeric), so that software responsible for parsing the text know which character to use based on a given code. It's a way of bringing platform, hardware, and software neutrality to the process of rendering text. We recommend using UTF-8, which includes a wide range of characters, such as those used in different languages around the world.*

*For more information about character encoding, see http://en.wikipedia.org/ wiki/Character_encoding. For more information about UTF-8, see http:// en.wikipedia.org/wiki/UTF-8.*

**NOTE**

*The ActionScript 3.0 Language and Components Reference entry "Timed Text Tags", found at http://www.adobe.com/livedocs/flash/9.0/ActionScriptLangRefV3/ TimedTextTags.html, specifies that all attributes of the `<tt>` tag are ignored. However, this is not the case if you style your captions. If you omit the `xmlns` attribute, your captions will not be styled, and if you omit the `xmlns:tts` attribute, the use of the tts namespace in styles will result in errors. When using styles, consider both of these attributes required.*

A `<head>` tag (spanning lines 4 through 17) is optional, but we recommend its use because it makes styling your captions much easier. Within it, a `<styling>` tag (spanning lines 5 through 16) is also optional but necessary if you intend to create styles. *Styles* are Cascading Style Sheet (CSS) entities for the Timed Text document and are itemized in lines 6 through 15. You can have as many styles as you like, but each must have a unique **id** attribute. The style attributes that are actually responsible for the formatting are very similar to CSS properties, but are preceded by the **tts:** prefix.

It's possible to assign multiple styles directly by their alphanumeric id, but it's also possible to manage formatting efficiently by creating new styles consisting of other styles. Take a look at the styles in our example. We wanted to achieve two looks for our captions: one with a black background, for use over light areas of video, and one with a transparent background, to allow more of the video to show through the text.

**NOTE**

*Be sure to consult the "Timed Text Tags" ActionScript 3.0 Language and Components Reference resource, mentioned earlier in this section, for a complete list of supported and unsupported properties. Here are a few noteworthy mentions:*

- *fontFamily supports device fonts, as seen in our example.*

- *fontSize supports only the first size found; supports absolute and relative sizes but not percentages.*

- *lineHeight, padding, and overflow, although potentially useful for captions, are among several options that are not supported.*

**NOTE**

*If you've spent some time with Chapter 9 in this book, you may recall that the color notation that included alpha was specified as 0xAARRGGBB. The difference between this BitmapData color notation, and the #RRGGBBAA used with Timed Text, can lead to confusion. If you see an unpredictable color behind your caption text, check to see if you've used the wrong format.*

**NOTE**

*In our main Timed Text example, we used full clock format for clarity and consistency, even when the duration matched the time at which the next caption appeared. However, you can simplify this by using partial clock format, and omitting any duration or end attributes when the caption is to remain on screen until replaced. As an illustration, we have formatted our Spanish-language example this way, which we'll discuss shortly.*

Style *1* consists of all styling attributes common to both treatments, which means that the background alpha information appears in other styles. Styles *2* and *3* itemize only the background color and specify transparent and opaque, respectively. The Timed Text format uses #RRGGBBAA color notation, where AA is alpha. However, the ActionScript components support only opaque and transparent settings. All zeros will be seen as transparent, but *any* value other than zero will be opaque. We've used the opposite of zero for alpha, FF, to remind us that this is opaque. The resulting value of #000000FF is, therefore, an opaque black background.

Once you've created these individual styles, you can then apply more than one style at a time. It's possible to do so at the caption level by using syntax like `id="1 2"`, but it's also possible to create a new style the same way. For example, you can create a new style combining styles 1 and 2 and, because the style names can be alphanumeric, you can give it a descriptive name. We've done this in lines 14 and 15, specifying that *trans* is centered, sans-serif, 18-point, bold, yellow text on a transparent (because it uses styles *1* and *2*), and *opaq* shares the same font attributes but is atop an opaque background because it uses styles *1* and *3*.

A `<body>` tag (lines 18 through 28) is required and is used to hold all the caption data. Within the body tag, one `<div>` tag (lines 19 through 27) is required, and paragraph tags `<p>` are required for each line of caption (lines 20 through 26).

The ActionScript documentation doesn't say that `<div>` is required but neither `<p>` nor `<span>` tags can appear in the `<body>` tag. Similarly, the documentation says zero or more paragraph tags are supported, but we didn't find a logical way of applying time or style attributes to individual captions without them. For example, `<span>` tags (lines 21 and 22) are supported, but not in the `<body>` or `<div>` tags. Therefore, we suggest you consider `<div>` and `<p>` tags required.

For each caption (in our case, in each `<p>` tag), a `begin` attribute is required to set the time of the caption. The attributes `dur` (duration) and `end` (the time at which the caption should end) are optional. If omitted, the caption will remain onscreen until the next caption appears. Time can be specified in full clock format (HH:MM:SS.m, where m is milliseconds), partial clock format (MM:SS.m or SS.m), or offset time (with units, such as "1s" for one second). Frames are not supported as a measure of time.

Now that you know how to create a Timed Text file, you can run the previous source file, *video_comp_skin_full_captions.fla*, (discussed in the "Captions" section of this chapter) which makes use of the *nero_timed_text.xml* caption source file.

# Providing Captions in Multiple Languages

Feature-rich DVD titles frequently have multiple caption programs available, each in a different language. This broadens the reach of the title across cultures and supports a wider audience with accessibility needs. It's possible to achieve the same thing using the FLVPlaybackCaptioning component.

All you need to do is prepare multiple Timed Text files, one for each language, and switch among them when needed. Off the shelf, however, the FLVPlaybackCaptioning component does a couple of things that make this an odd experience.

First, if you change the caption content between times specified in a Timed Text document, the component will *overwrite* the caption field only if the current caption is empty or contains only white space (tab, return, or space). If that's not the case (such as when switching captions from one language to another at any moment), it *adds* the new text to the existing caption. Only when the next Timed Text caption time comes along will the field contents be replaced correctly. Second, the method it uses to determine whether or not the Timed Text file has already been loaded results in no immediate change. Therefore, you must wait for the next caption to come along to see a language update.

Fortunately, there's an easy workaround. All you have to do is turn off caption display before making the caption source switch, and then turn the display back on again. The example file, *video_comp_skin_full_captions_multilingual.fla*, demonstrates this using the Button component to toggle the caption source files.

**NOTE**

*As with the FLVPlayback and FLVPlaybackCaptioning components, you must have this component, found in the User Interface category of the Components panel, in your library.*

```
15  import fl.controls.Button;
16  var capsLangBtn:Button = new Button();
17  capsLangBtn.label = "English/Spanish";
18  capsLangBtn.x = vid.x + vid.width + 20;
19  capsLangBtn.y = vid.y + vid.height;
20  addChild(capsLangBtn);
21  capsLangBtn.addEventListener(MouseEvent.CLICK, switchTTCaps,
22                               false, 0, true);
23
24  function switchTTCaps(evt:MouseEvent):void {
25      cap.showCaptions = false;
26      if (cap.source == "nero_timed_text.xml") {
27          cap.source = "nero_timed_text_sp.xml";
28      } else {
29          cap.source = "nero_timed_text.xml";
30      }
31      cap.showCaptions = true;
32  }
```

Line 15 imports the **Button** class so we can instantiate the Button in line 16. Lines 17 through 20 set the buttons label, position it next to the lower-right corner of the FLVPlayback component, and add it to the display list. Lines 21 and 22 add an event listener to call the **switchTTCaps()** function upon each mouse click event. Finally, the **switchTTCaps()** function (lines 24 through 32) turns off caption display, checks to see which caption source is in use and switches to the other file, and then turns caption display back on again.

# Writing Your Own Player

Wrapping up the chapter, we want to introduce you to some of the ActionScript required to create a customized player. We'll start with coding your own controls for the FLVPlayback component, to give you freedom to design your own controller bar. Then we'll show you how to write your own player to eliminate reliance on the FLVPlayback component altogether.

In both cases, we'll create play, pause, and stop buttons using the **RoundRectButton** class discussed in Chapter 8. While not a fully functional controller, this will give you the foundation necessary to set properties and call methods in the **FLVPlayback** and **NetStream** classes. You can then decide which features you want to implement in your custom controllers.

## Scripting Buttons to Control the FLVPlayback Component

This exercise, found in the *video_comp_custom_buttons.fla* source file, builds on the first example in the chapter. That example showed that you can use the FLVPlayback component without having to use a skin. This exercise will add custom buttons to the file to control video playback.

Lines 1 and 2 import the **FLVPlayback** and **RoundRectButton** classes. Lines 4 through 7 initialize the FLVPlayback component, as previously discussed. In this exercise, however, we've added line 6 to set the **autoPlay** property to false. This will prevent the video from playing automatically and let the user choose when to play it.

Lines 9 through 24 create three buttons using the **RoundRectButton** class. The class was introduced in Chapter 8, and we've used this technique in several chapters. Briefly, a function is used to create an instance of the class, as well as position the button and assign a function to the event listener. This approach is designed to minimize the number of lines required to create the buttons, and it can be customized to fit your needs. We'll discuss the functions that control the video after the code.

```
1    import fl.video.FLVPlayback;
2    import com.learningactionscript3.ui.RoundRectButton;
3
4    var vid:FLVPlayback = new FLVPlayback();
5    vid.source = "nero.flv";
6    vid.autoPlay = false;
7    addChild(vid);
8
9    createButton(50, "Play", playVideo);
10   createButton(130, "Pause", pauseVideo);
11   createButton(210, "Stop", stopVideo);
12   createButton(240, "Full Screen", fullScreenVideo);
13
14   function createButton(xLoc:Number, labl:String,
15                         func:Function):void {
16       var btn:RoundRectButton =
```

```
17          new RoundRectButton(60, 20, 10, 2, 0x000099,
18                         labl, 0xFFFFFF);
19    btn.x = xLoc;
20    btn.y = 240;
21    btn.addEventListener(MouseEvent.CLICK, func,
22                    false, 0, true);
23    addChild(btn);
24  }
25
26  function playVideo(evt:MouseEvent):void {
27      vid.play();
28  }
29
30  function pauseVideo(evt:MouseEvent):void {
31      vid.pause();
32  }
33
34  function stopVideo(evt:MouseEvent):void {
35      vid.stop();
36      vid.seek(0);
37  }
38
39  function fullScreenVideo(evt:MouseEvent):void {
40      stage.displayState = StageDisplayState.FULL_SCREEN;
41  }
```

Lines 26 through 41 contain the functions used to control the video. The functions and methods used are self-explanatory, with two exceptions. First, in addition to stopping the video in the **stopVideo()** function, we also use the **seek()** method to seek through the video to a specific point in time. Seeking to 0 returns the video to its starting point. This is a user-experience consideration that differentiates the functionality of the pause and stop buttons. Second, to switch to full screen, you set the **displayState** property of the stage to **StageDisplayState.FULL_SCREEN**.

By default, changing the stage's display state to full screen mode when an FLVPlayback component is in use mimics the behavior of the component. The video will fill the screen and show only the video regardless of any other user interface elements. In this case, however, we're not using a skin that's designed to show the controller on top of the video. As a result, the control buttons disappear. To show the control buttons, you can prevent the video from taking over the stage after resizing by setting the **fullScreenTakeOver** property of the **FVLPlayback** instance to false.

One side effect of this is that you can then see the Full Screen button and it won't do anything because the display state will already be in full screen mode. So, you can write a simple **if** statement that will toggle between the display states as needed. The script below replaces the **fullScreenVideo()** function in the previous example and appears in the *video_comp_custom_buttons_full.fla* source file.

```
39  vid.fullScreenTakeOver = false;
40  function fullScreenVideo(evt:MouseEvent):void {
41      if (stage.displayState == StageDisplayState.NORMAL) {
42          stage.displayState = StageDisplayState.FULL_SCREEN;
```

```
43        } else {
44            stage.displayState = StageDisplayState.NORMAL;
45        }
46    }
```

Finally, you can even control how much of the stage is visible in full screen mode by setting the stage's **fullScreenSourceRect** property to a rectangular area. The following line is included in the *video_comp_custom_buttons_full.fla* source file, and specifies a rectangle that encloses the video and buttons.

```
stage.fullScreenSourceRect = new Rectangle(0, 0, 320, 270);
```

This line is initially commented out in the source file, so you publish to HTML multiple times and comment this line in and out to see its effect.

# A Code-Only Solution

Up to this point, we've relied on components for video display. Creating your own player exclusively with ActionScript can reduce file size and allow you to customize functionality. In this exercise, you'll write a class called **BasicVideo** to create a simple video player that does not use the FLVPlayback component. As a result, the generated SWF file is less than 4K.

If you want to preview this exercise before going over the code, it uses a document class called **BasicVideo_UI** in the main directory of the chapter source archive. Flash Professional users can open the *code_only_player.fla* source file, which already makes use of this class. **BasicVideo** is in the *com. learningactionscript3.video* package. We'll discuss **BasicVideo** first, and then talk about the document class that creates the user interface.

## The main video class

Line 1 declares the package, and lines 3 through 9 import the required classes. Line 11 declares the class and extends **MovieClip** so we can use its accessible properties, methods, and events of that class. Lines 13 through 17 declare private class properties—available throughout the class.

```
1    package com.learningactionscript3.video {
2
3        import flash.display.MovieClip;
4        import flash.events.AsyncErrorEvent;
5        import flash.events.MouseEvent;
6        import flash.events.NetStatusEvent;
7        import flash.net.NetConnection;
8        import flash.net.NetStream;
9        import flash.media.Video;
10
11       public class BasicVideo extends MovieClip {
12
13           private var _conn:NetConnection;
14           private var _stream:NetStream;
15           private var _vid:Video;
16           private var _vidPlaying:Boolean;
17           private var _source:String;
```

Lines 19 through 36 contain the class constructor. It accepts one string parameter for the video path to allow you to select a video when instantiating the class. Later, we'll add a getter and setter to let you to do this by setting a property instead.

Lines 22 through 24 use the two main classes required to play videos with ActionScript. Line 22 creates an instance of the **NetConnection** class, which establishes a bi-directional connection between the user's player and a server delivering data, such as a video streaming server. It's a bit like the cable running between your house and the cable television company. You connect to the server using the **connect()** method in line 23. In this example, however, we're not using a server, so we'll pass null into this method. In this case, the class is designed to connect to a local file.

Line 24 creates an instance of the **NetStream** class and is associated with the **NetConnection** instance by passing the latter into the former's constructor. A **NetStream** instance is a channel of a **NetConnection** instance, a little like a single cable channel, and transmits data in one direction. For example, a server can send data and a client can receive data.

Line 26 creates an instance of the **Video** class, which is the display object used to show the video. This is a bit like a television set. The **NetStream** instance is then attached to the video in line 27, a little like picking the cable channel you want to watch. Line 28 adds the video instance to the main class instance so it can become part of the display list.

Lines 30 through 33 create a custom object that will serve as a data client for the class. Select data will automatically be sent out when playing the video and if this object (or a similar object like a custom class created for the same purpose) does not exist, errors will occur. For example, any metadata that exists in the video, either by default or that was added during encoding, will be sent soon after the video begins loading. Similarly, any cue points that were embedded in the video will be sent when encountered. Lines 31 and 32 assign the **onMetaData()** and **onCuePoint()** methods to their corresponding properties so Flash Player knows where to send the appropriate information. This association is formalized when the object is assigned to the **client** property of the **NetStream** instance in line 33. Finally, event listeners are added to the class in line 35, which we will talk about after the code block.

```
18          //constructor
19          public function BasicVideo(path:String="") {
20              _source = path;
21
22              _conn = new NetConnection();
23              _conn.connect(null);
24              _stream = new NetStream(_conn);
25
26              _vid = new Video();
27              _vid.attachNetStream(_stream);
28              addChild(_vid);
29
30              var _infoClient:Object = new Object();
```

```
31            _infoClient.onMetaData = this.onMetaData;
32            _infoClient.onCuePoint = this.onCuePoint;
33            _stream.client = _infoClient;
34
35            addEventListeners();
36        }
```

Lines 38 through 47 add two event listeners each to the **NetConnection** and **NetStream** instances. The **NET_STATUS** event is dispatched when status updates become available from either instance. Similarly, the **ASYNC_ERROR** event is dispatched when an asynchronous error occurs in either instance. An *asynchronous error* is an error that's not dependent on a specific (synchronized) order of execution. That is, it need not be the sequential result of another task performed by the class. This event is typically dispatched when a server calls a method that's not defined in the client.

When either event is received, the methods in lines 49 through 60 are called. Both trace information so you can see what's going on, but **onNetStatus()** also toggles the value of the **_vidPlaying** property. When a status update indicates that the video has started, the **_vidPlaying** property is set to true. When the status indicates that the video has stopped it sets the property to false.

```
37        //event listeners
38        private function addEventListeners():void {
39            _conn.addEventListener(NetStatusEvent.NET_STATUS,
40                            onNetStatus,false,0,true);
41            _conn.addEventListener(AsyncErrorEvent.ASYNC_ERROR,
42                            onAsyncError,false,0,true);
43            _stream.addEventListener(NetStatusEvent.NET_STATUS,
44                            onNetStatus,false,0,true);
45            _stream.addEventListener(AsyncErrorEvent.ASYNC_ERROR,
46                            onAsyncError,false,0,true);
47        }
48
49        private function onAsyncError(evt:AsyncErrorEvent):void {
50            trace(evt.text);
51        }
52
53        private function onNetStatus(evt:NetStatusEvent):void {
54            trace(evt.info.level + ": " + evt.info.code);
55            if (evt.info.code == "NetStream.Play.Start") {
56                _vidPlaying = true;
57            } else if (evt.info.code == "NetStream.Play.Stop") {
58                _vidPlaying = false;
59            }
60        }
```

Lines 62 through 74 contain the methods triggered by the metadata and cue points received during video playback. Line 63 traces the duration metadata field to demonstrate reacting to incoming information. You can add metadata during the encoding process, and encoding software can also automatically create metadata for you. Available metadata fields range from such basic items as duration, creation and modified date, width, height, and so on, to the highly specialized, like the DICOM collection of medical fields, depending on the encoder. Adobe Media Encoder supports an impressive array of available metadata.

Lines 67 through 69 trace the time, name, and type properties of any cue point received, and lines 70 through 73 trace any parameters added to that cue point when it was created.

```
61      //client methods
62      private function onMetaData(info:Object):void {
63          trace("MetaData duration:", info.duration);
64      }
65
66      private function onCuePoint(info:Object):void {
67          trace("CuePoint time:", info.time);
68          trace("CuePoint type:", info.type);
69          trace("CuePoint name:", info.name);
70          for (var prop in info.parameters) {
71              trace("Cue point parameter " + prop + ": " +
72                  info.parameters[prop]);
73          }
74      }
```

Finally, lines 76 through 101 contain the public methods, getters, and setters available outside the class. Lines 76 through 93 contain methods to play, pause, and stop the video, all of which are configured to receive mouse events. However, they also all include default values for the event, making it possible to call the methods directly, rather than as a result of an event. We'll see this demonstrated in the main document class.

The **playVideo()** method in lines 76 through 83 first checks to see if the **_vid-Playing** property is true. If so, it calls the **resume()** method of the **NetStream** instance. This is because the class changes this property value when a status event indicates that the stream has been started or stopped, but not paused. Therefore, if a play button is clicked and the property is true, the video has been paused and should be resumed. If the property is false, the **play()** method is called, using the path in the **_source** property to indicate which video to play. In either case, the **_vidPlaying** property is set to true to record the fact that the video is playing.

The **pauseVideo()** method in lines 85 through 87 calls the **togglePause()** method. This is a nice feature because it will automatically pause the video if it's playing and play the video if it's paused.

Lines 89 through 93 contain the **stopVideo()** method. This method closes the stream (which is a bit like turning off your cable set top box), clears the **Video** instance (which is akin to turning off your television), and sets the **_vidPlaying** property to false.

Finally, lines 95 through 101 provide a getter and setter to allow the retrieval and assignment of the **_source** property from outside the class.

**NOTE**

*For more information about getters and setters, see the "Encapsulation" section of Chapter 6.*

```
75      //public player methods and getter/setter
76      public function playVideo(evt:MouseEvent=null):void {
77          if (_vidPlaying) {
78              _stream.resume();
```

```
79              } else {
80                  _stream.play(_source);
81              }
82              _vidPlaying = true;
83          }
84
85          public function pauseVideo(evt:MouseEvent=null):void {
86              _stream.togglePause();
87          }
88
89          public function stopVideo(evt:MouseEvent=null):void {
90              _stream.close();
91              _vid.clear();
92              _vidPlaying = false;
93          }
94
95          public function set source(path:String):void {
96              _source = path;
97          }
98
99          public function get source():String {
100             return _source;
101         }
102     }
103 }
```

## The document class

The **BasicVideo_UI** class is a document class that instantiates **BasicVideo** and creates a simple interface with a play, pause, and stop button. Lines 1 through 7 declare the package and import the required classes. Lines 9 through 12 declare the class (which extends MovieClip so it can easily function as a document class) and declare two private properties. The first is a movie clip container to hold the video and buttons, so you can easily position the video interface anywhere on the stage. The second stores a reference to the **BasicVideo** instance so it can be used throughout the class.

Lines 14 through 27 contain the class constructor. Lines 15 through 17 create a container to hold the video and buttons, but also use the **drawBackground()** method (lines 29 through 36) to draw a black background the size of the video into the container. This is so, when clearing the video object after stopping playback, the video doesn't look like it's disappearing. (The function simply creates a movie clip, draws a black rectangle into it, and returns it to the point in the script where the function was called.)

Lines 19 through 21 create an instance of the **BasicVideo** class, assign the source property of the instance to the appropriate video path, and add the **BasicVideo** instance to the container. Line 22 demonstrates how to call the **BasicVideo** public method **playVideo()** directly, rather than from an event. This means you can automatically start the video playing without requiring a mouse click from the user.

The remainder of the class creates three buttons and assigns a listener to each to control the video, just like we did in the "Scripting Buttons to Control the FLVPlayback Component" section of this chapter. The only difference between the two examples is that listeners in this class call the methods in the **BasicVideo** class, while the previously cited example called methods of the FLVPlayback component.

```
1   package {
2
3       import flash.display.Graphics;
4       import flash.display.MovieClip;
5       import flash.events.MouseEvent;
6       import com.learningactionscript3.ui.RoundRectButton;
7       import com.learningactionscript3.video.BasicVideo;
8
9       public class BasicVideo_UI extends MovieClip {
10
11          private var _container:MovieClip;
12          private var _vidPlayer:BasicVideo;
13
14          public function BasicVideo_UI() {
15              _container = drawBackground();
16              _container.x = _container.y = 20;
17              addChild(_container);
18
19              _vidPlayer = new BasicVideo();
20              _vidPlayer.source = "nero.flv";
21              _container.addChild(_vidPlayer);
22              _vidPlayer.playVideo();
23
24              createButton(20, "Play", playVideo);
25              createButton(120, "Pause", pauseVideo);
26              createButton(220, "Stop", stopVideo);
27          }
28
29          private function drawBackground():MovieClip {
30              var sp:MovieClip = new MovieClip();
31              var g:Graphics = sp.graphics;
32              g.beginFill(0x000000);
33              g.drawRect(0, 0, 320, 240);
34              g.endFill();
35              return sp;
36          }
37
38          private function createButton(xLoc:Number, labl:String,
39                                        func:Function):void {
40              var btn:RoundRectButton =
41                  new RoundRectButton(80, 20, 10, 2, 0x000099,
42                                      labl, 0xFFFFFF);
43              btn.x = xLoc;
44              btn.y = 250;
45              btn.addEventListener(MouseEvent.CLICK, func,
46                                   false, 0, true);
47              _container.addChild(btn);
48          }
49
50          private function playVideo(evt:MouseEvent=null):void {
51              _vidPlayer.playVideo();
52          }
53
54          private function pauseVideo(evt:MouseEvent=null):void {
```

```
55              _vidPlayer.pauseVideo();
56          }
57
58          private function stopVideo(evt:MouseEvent=null):void {
59              _vidPlayer.stopVideo();
60          }
61      }
62  }
```

## Project Package

This chapter's contribution to the learningactionscript3 package is the **BasicVideo** class. With this class, you can add a video display to any project and be free to customize the access controls to fit any design.

Although this exercise doesn't create a full-featured video controller, it demonstrates the basics required to create the remaining functionality on your own, with help from the ActionScript 3.0 Language and Component Reference. Having completed this exercise, try to build a progress bar or a seek option. Try to combine what you've learned here with what you learned in Chapter 11 and create a volume or mute button. How you design your controller is up to you.

## What's Next?

This chapter discussed a few ways to add video features to your projects. You can now decide, typically on a project-by-project basis, whether to use prebuilt components, or your own custom ActionScript player. You also have the ability to add full screen support and captions, if your project calls for these features.

**In the next chapter**, we'll begin Part V of book, covering input and output. Chapter 13 discusses the basics of loading external assets, including:

- Using the universal **URLRequest** class

- Loading visual assets, including graphics and other SWF files

- Loading text and variables

# INPUT/OUTPUT

Part V homes in on two of the possible input and output methods used for transferring data and assets in the Flash world. Chapter 13 covers several ways to load external assets. It also includes a discussion of text, with an in-depth look at loading variables. Similar to the text-loading example, the chapter takes a close look at best practices for loading external SWF and image formats. The chapter wraps up with a look at communicating with loaded SWFs.

Chapter 14 provides a detailed look at what may be the most common format for structured data exchange: XML. In addition to the creation of XML documents in their own right, the chapter discusses reading, writing, and editing XML on the fly. Finally, the chapter covers XML communication between client and server.

## CHAPTER 13

# LOADING ASSETS

You don't always need to load external assets at runtime, but the ability to do so is extremely important. Loading assets on the fly reduces initial file size and, therefore, load times. It also increases the degree to which a Flash experience can change—not only through the all-important dynamic nature of runtime content updates, but also by streamlining the editing process. For example, you can alter external assets easier and faster than you can republish an FLA file every time an update occurs.

Augmenting prior discussions regarding sound, video, and plain text, this chapter will teach you how to load external SWFs and images. You'll also take a peek at loading variables and binary data, and see how to increase your error checking efforts. Specifically, we'll look at:

- **Loading SWFs and Images.** Right out of the gate, it's fairly easy to load SWFs and JPG, PNG, and GIF images. Third-party ActionScript libraries support loading even more asset types. We'll look at simple syntax examples and then build a multipurpose class that can handle some error checking and reporting for you automatically.

- **Loading Data.** Next we'll discuss loading text, URL variables, and binary data. We discussed loading text from external sources in Chapter 10 but limited our coverage to loading HTML and CSS information. In this chapter, we'll expand the scope of our discussion to loading URL-encoded variables and binary data. We'll also write a multipurpose class you can use to load data. In Chapter 14 you'll use that class to load XML.

- **Communicating with Loaded SWFs.** After a SWF is loaded, the parent and child SWFs can communicate. We'll discuss communication in both directions, and demonstrate a variety of tasks you may want to perform in the process.

- **Additional Online Resources**. We'll wrap up the chapter by referencing two additional loading-related topics discussed online. First we'll describe problems caused by loading SWFs that use Text Layout Framework (TLF) assets (featured in Chapter 10). TLF assets use a custom preloader at run-time, which presents its own unique difficulties. We'll point to two solutions, including Adobe's new **SafeLoader** class, designed to successfully load SWFs that use TLF. Finally, we'll introduce a great new ActionScript 3.0 loading library called LoaderMax, created by GreenSock, the makers of TweenLite.

# Loading SWFs and Images

There are a few ways to load SWFs or images at runtime, but you'll commonly use the **Loader** class in one way or another. To simplify the process of loading these visual assets, the **Loader** is also a display object. This makes it much easier to load and display visual assets because the **Loader** itself can be added to the display list, rather than waiting for its content to finish loading. In addition, because it's a display object, you can use a variety of properties and methods shared with other display objects, affecting position (**x**, **y**), transformation (**alpha**, **rotation**), event management (**addEventListener()**) and more.

## Loading SWFs

The following example is found in the *load_swf.fla* source file. Line 1 creates an instance of the **Loader** class, line 2 loads a SWF using a **URLRequest** instance, and line 3 adds the **Loader** instance to the display list. Even if it takes some time for the remote SWF to load, the **Loader** is already waiting, a little bit like a TV waiting for a program to begin.

```
1   var swfLoader:Loader = new Loader();
2   swfLoader.load(new URLRequest("swfToLoad.swf"));
3   addChild(swfLoader);
```

One important difference between the **Loader** class and other display object classes, such as **MovieClip**, is that event listeners are usually attached to the **contentLoaderInfo** property of the **Loader** instance, rather than the instance itself. The property references an instance of the **LoaderInfo** class, which traffics all information about the *content* of the **Loader**.

For example, if you attached an event listener to the **Loader** instance that listened for the **COMPLETE** event, it would work without error, but would respond to the fact that the **Loader** itself had loaded, not its content. As this is virtually instantaneous and doesn't relate to the content you're trying to load, it's not very helpful. If you attached the same listener to the **contentLoaderInfo** property of the **Loader** instead, it would trigger its function when the *content* finished loading.

The following code, added to the prior example, stresses two concepts. First, it demonstrates attaching an event listener to the **contentLoaderInfo** property, as discussed (lines 5 through 7), showing that the target of the listener is the **LoaderInfo** instance described (line 10). Second, it shows that you can access the **Loader** instance from the data sent with the event, as well as the content of the **Loader**, as seen in lines 11 and 12, respectively. Note, too, that the example cleans up after itself by removing the **COMPLETE** event listener in line 9, once the loading is finished.

```
4    //use contentLoaderInfo for listeners
5    swfLoader.contentLoaderInfo.addEventListener(Event.COMPLETE,
6                                                 onComplete,
7                                                 false, 0, true);
8    function onComplete(evt:Event):void {
9        evt.target.removeEventListener(Event.COMPLETE, onComplete);
10       trace(evt.target);
11       trace(evt.target.loader);
12       trace(evt.target.loader.content);
13   }
```

## Loading Images

Waiting for the content of the **Loader** to finish loading is important when you need to work with the content rather than just display it. For example, we discussed working with bitmaps in Chapter 9, both with and without adding them to the display list. For example, if you just want to load the bitmap data from the bitmap, you don't need to add it to the display list. In this case, you can't pull bitmap data from a **Loader** instance and, even if you do want to add the **Loader** content to the display list, you can't add something that hasn't yet loaded.

The following example, found in the *load_jpg.fla* source file, uses the same basic syntax as the previous example, but with two significant differences. First, it loads a JPG rather than a SWF. Second, it adds the JPG directly to the display list (line 9) instead of adding the **Loader** instance. The result is a single child in the display list that is of type **Bitmap**. As a demonstration of using **Loader** properties, it also traces the **bytesLoaded** and **bytesTotal** of the loaded asset in lines 11 and 12. (After loading is complete, both numbers should be the same, no matter what the asset's size.)

```
1    var jpgLoader:Loader = new Loader();
2    jpgLoader.load(new URLRequest("imageToLoad.jpg"));
3
4    jpgLoader.contentLoaderInfo.addEventListener(Event.COMPLETE,
5                                                 onComplete,
6                                                 false, 0, true);
7    function onComplete(evt:Event):void {
8        evt.target.removeEventListener(Event.COMPLETE, onComplete);
9        addChild(evt.target.content);
10
11       trace(evt.target.bytesLoaded);
12       trace(evt.target.bytesTotal);
13   }
```

# Writing a Multiuse SWF and Image Loading Class

The previous examples presented the simplest syntax for loading visual assets. Typical loading tasks are more involved, because they include additional features such as error checking and tracking loading progress.

Unfortunately, this can result in long scripts and become tedious quickly. So we'll write a multipurpose class that will not only load SWF and image files, but will also report errors, monitor loading progress, and provide other diagnostic options, if you desire. The class will also mimic some of the features of the **Loader** class, allowing you to use much of the same syntax you would use if writing the code from scratch each time using that class. This is helpful because one of the drawbacks of a do-it-all approach like this is less flexibility. If the new class resembles the existing **Loader** class in useful ways, you can use the new class instead when you want a diagnostic environment rolled into a simple load, but revert to **Loader** when you want more control.

**NOTE**

*You can even type the new class as* **Loader** *when creating instances, so your code can be more flexible.*

## Writing the CustomLoader Class

The class we want to write is called **CustomLoader** and is in the in the *loading* directory of the learningactionscript3 package we've been developing throughout the book. We'll be using this class with the *load_swf_custom.fla* and *load_jpg_custom.fla* source files, if you want to test it before proceeding.

Lines 1 through 9 declare the package and import all required classes. We'll discuss classes from the **flash.events** package that we haven't mentioned before.

**NOTE**

*See Chapter 6 for more information about inheritance.*

Line 11 declares the class and extends the **Loader** class. This makes the accessible properties, methods, and events of the **Loader** class available to our custom loader through inheritance. Lines 13 through 16 declare four private properties that will contain: a reference to the **LoaderInfo** instance of the class inherited from **Loader** (line 13), the path to the asset you want to load (line 14), a flag used to enable and disable trace statements (line 15), and a number between 0 and 1 representing the percentage of the asset's bytes that have already been loaded (line 16).

```
1   package com.learningactionscript3.loading {
2
3       import flash.display.Loader;
4       import flash.display.LoaderInfo;
5       import flash.events.Event;
6       import flash.events.HTTPStatusEvent;
7       import flash.events.IOErrorEvent;
8       import flash.events.ProgressEvent;
9       import flash.net.URLRequest;
10
11      public class CustomLoader extends Loader {
12
13          private var _ldrInfo:LoaderInfo;
14          private var _path:String;
15          private var _verbose:Boolean = false;
16          private var _loadedPercent:Number = 0;
```

The constructor is pretty simple. It takes two arguments: the asset path and flag to show trace output, as mentioned previously, both with default values. Lines 20 and 21 populate class properties with data provided to the constructor during instantiation. Line 23 calls the **addListeners()** method, which adds all the listeners used internally by the class (more on this in a moment).

The last lines of the constructor (25 through 31) load the requested asset if a path is passed into the constructor during instantiation. Providing a default value for **path**, and checking **path** before calling the **load()** method, means that you can load assets in two ways. First, you can pass a simple string to the constructor during instantiation. In this case, **path** will contain a **String**, and **load()** will be called in the constructor. Or, you can pass nothing to the class during instantiation (in which case **path** will remain null, and **load()** will not be called in the constructor) and use the **load()** method from the class instance with a **URLRequest**, just as you do with the **Loader** class. We'll demonstrate both techniques when we show usage examples.

Before we talk about the **try..catch** block that surrounds the **load()** method, note that no **Loader** instance is created before loading. This is because the class you're writing extends the **Loader** class and, through inheritance, we can use its accessible methods, which include **load()**. Therefore, the **this** keyword is used instead, so the class loads the asset without having to create an additional **Loader**.

A **try..catch** block, discussed at the end of Chapter 2, allows you to try something but suppress a resulting error to prevent it from being seen by those viewing your SWF in the wild. You can use a **try..catch** block in many ways. For example, you could try to load an asset from a remote server and, upon receiving an error, load a local version of the asset instead. More generically, you can use a **try..catch** block when a runtime error is possible so the error doesn't reach the user. It's helpful to trace these errors and add descriptive messages, so it's easier to track them down during development.

```
17        //constructor
18        public function CustomLoader(path:String=null,
19                                     verbose:Boolean=false) {
20            _path = path;
21            _verbose = verbose;
22
23            addListeners();
24
25            if (path != null) {
26                try {
27                    this.load(new URLRequest(path));
28                } catch (err:Error) {
29                    trace("Cannot load", _path, err.message);
30                }
31            }
32        }
```

The **addListeners()** and **removeListeners()** methods do nothing but add and remove listeners, respectively, but there are a few things worthy of note.

First, in line 35 the listeners are added to the **contentLoaderInfo** property of the class (again, inherited from **Loader**), as explained in the "Loading SWFs" section of this chapter.

Second, we're adding several new events, including some that come from event classes we haven't previously discussed. For completeness, let's briefly go over when each event is dispatched.

- **Event.OPEN**: When the loading process is initiated. If this event is never received, you know loading never even started.

- **ProgressEvent.PROGRESS**: Each time data is received during the load. This allows you to update a loading progress bar.

- **HTTPStatusEvent.HTTP_STATUS**: When an HTTP request is made (such as fetching an asset from a server) and a status code is detected. For more information see *http://en.wikipedia.org/wiki/ List_of_HTTP_status_codes*.

- **Event.INIT**: When enough of the loading process is complete to have access to the properties of the object. If, for example, you try to query the width of a loaded asset before this event is dispatched, it will likely be 0. After properties are accessible, the correct width will be available.

- **Event.COMPLETE**: When loading is finished. This occurs after **Event. INIT**.

- **IOErrorEvent.IO_ERROR**: When an input/output error occurs. One example of such an error is when the asset can't be found at the URL provided.

- **Event.UNLOAD**: When the asset is unloaded. This is usually the last event to be dispatched.

Lastly, notice that the **removeListeners()** method is public. This allows you to remove all listeners from outside the class, when you're through using the class instance you created. In some cases, you want to remove listeners right away, such as when you only need your listener once, as demonstrated in the examples earlier in this chapter. In other circumstances, you may want to use the same **Loader** instance repeatedly to load asset after asset, in which case you want the listeners to remain active. The **removeListeners()** method allows you to remove the listeners any time you like.

**NOTE**

*New to Flash Player version 10.1 is the* **uncaughtErrorEvents** *property of the* **Loader** *and* **LoaderInfo** *classes. This allows you to trap any errors not caught by other means (such as a* **try..catch** *block) in your code. For more information, see the "Trapping Uncaught Errors" post at the companion website,* *http://www.LearningActionScript3.com.*

**NOTE**

*Another way to maintain your listeners is to add them before every load and remove them every time the load is complete. To keep your class as self-reliant as possible, you want to add the listeners when calling the* **load()** *method. This requires that you override the* **load()** *method, as discussed in the "Polymorphism" section of Chapter 6. The post, "Overriding the load() Method in Custom Loader Classes," found at the companion website shows how this is done.*

```
33      //listeners
34      private function addListeners():void {
35          _ldrInfo = this.contentLoaderInfo;
36          _ldrInfo.addEventListener(Event.OPEN,
37                                    onOpen, false, 0, true);
38          _ldrInfo.addEventListener(ProgressEvent.PROGRESS,
39                                    onProgress, false, 0, true);
40          _ldrInfo.addEventListener(HTTPStatusEvent.HTTP_STATUS,
41                                    onStatusEvent,
42                                    false, 0, true);
43          _ldrInfo.addEventListener(Event.INIT,
```

```
44                                  onInit, false, 0, true);
45          _ldrInfo.addEventListener(Event.COMPLETE,
46                                  onComplete, false, 0, true);
47          _ldrInfo.addEventListener(IOErrorEvent.IO_ERROR,
48                                  onIOError, false, 0, true);
49          _ldrInfo.addEventListener(Event.UNLOAD,
50                                  onUnloadContent,
51                                  false, 0, true);
52      }
53
54      public function removeListeners():void {
55          _ldrInfo.removeEventListener(Event.OPEN, onOpen);
56          _ldrInfo.removeEventListener(ProgressEvent.PROGRESS,
57                                  onProgress);
58          _ldrInfo.removeEventListener(HTTPStatusEvent.HTTP_STATUS,
59                                  onStatusEvent);
60          _ldrInfo.removeEventListener(Event.INIT, onInit);
61          _ldrInfo.removeEventListener(Event.COMPLETE,
62                                  onComplete);
63          _ldrInfo.removeEventListener(IOErrorEvent.IO_ERROR,
64                                  onIOError);
65          _ldrInfo.removeEventListener(Event.UNLOAD,
66                                  onUnloadContent);
67      }
```

The remainder of the class contains the listener methods, one getter, and one setter. The listener methods all trace specific feedback during the loading process, only if you pass true into the verbose flag during instantiation. Note, however, that the trace in the **onIOError()** method is not wrapped in a conditional that uses the **_verbose** Boolean. This is because we only want to turn on and off the logging feature, not any valid error reports. If the error were included in the list of items shown only when **_verbose** is true, we would have to see all diagnostic text all the time just to see any input/output errors.

The **onProgress()** method also calculates the percent that an asset has loaded. This way, if you want to create a progress bar, you can simply check the related property, **percentLoaded**, via the getter at the end of the class, instead of calculating the value yourself. The **onInit()** method also traces a few properties of the asset to help you in your loading diagnostics. The first is the asset's URL (line 89) and, if the asset is a SWF, lines 93 through 96 trace the version of the Flash Player and ActionScript that the SWF was compiled for, and the SWF's frame rate.

The **percentLoaded** getter provides access to the **_loadedPercent** property previously described, and the **verbose** setter allows you to optionally turn on or off debugging through a property, rather than in the constructor.

**NOTE**

*In this class, enabling debugging through the constructor parameter or the verbose setter is entirely a matter of preference. The setter was provided to allow the instantiation of the class to more closely resemble the instantiation of the **Loader** class.*

```
68          //listener methods, getter, and setter
69          private function onOpen(evt:Event):void {
70              if (_verbose) { trace("Loading begun:", _path); }
71          }
72
73          private function onProgress(evt:ProgressEvent):void {
74              _loadedPercent = evt.bytesLoaded / evt.bytesTotal;
75
76              if (_verbose) {
```

```
 77                          trace("Loading", _path,
 78                                "-- progress (0-1):", _loadedPercent);
 79                      }
 80                  }
 81
 82          private function onStatusEvent(evt:HTTPStatusEvent):void {
 83              if (_verbose) { trace("HTTP status:", evt.status); }
 84          }
 85
 86          private function onInit(evt:Event):void {
 87              if (_verbose) {
 88                  trace("Content initialized. Properties:");
 89                  trace("url:", evt.target.url);
 90                  trace("Same Domain:", evt.target.sameDomain);
 91                  if (evt.target.contentType ==
 92                      "application/x-shockwave-flash") {
 93                      trace("SWF Version:", evt.target.swfVersion);
 94                      trace("AS Version:",
 95                              evt.target.actionScriptVersion);
 96                      trace("Frame Rate:", evt.target.frameRate);
 97                  }
 98              }
 99          }
100
101          private function onComplete(evt:Event):void {
102              if (_verbose) { trace("Loading complete:", _path); }
103          }
104
105          private function onUnloadContent(evt:Event):void {
106              if (_verbose) { trace("Unloaded:", _path); }
107          }
108
109          private function onIOError(evt:IOErrorEvent):void {
110              trace("CustomLoader loading error:\n", evt.text);
111          }
112
113          public function get percentLoaded():Number {
114              return _loadedPercent;
115          }
116
117          public function set verbose(bool:Boolean):void {
118              _verbose = bool;
119          }
120      }
121 }
```

# Using the CustomLoader Class

Because we extended the **Loader** class when writing **CustomLoader**, both class-es use similar syntax. The following examples replicate the previous examples closely to demonstrate this benefit of inheritance.

## Loading SWFs

The first example, found in the *load_swf_custom.fla*, loads a SWF. After importing the class in line 1, line 3 passes the SWF's path to the constructor during instantiation, and the class takes care of the **URLRequest** and call to the

**load()** method. The only other difference between this script and the example shown in the "Loading SWFs" section is in line 11. Because the example makes no further use of the **CustomLoader** class, all its listeners are removed.

```
1    import com.learningactionscript3.loading.CustomLoader;
2
3    var swfLoader:CustomLoader = new CustomLoader("swfToLoad.swf", true);
4    addChild(swfLoader);
5
6    swfLoader.contentLoaderInfo.addEventListener(Event.COMPLETE,
7                                                 onComplete,
8                                                 false, 0, true);
9    function onComplete(evt:Event):void {
10       evt.target.removeEventListener(Event.COMPLETE, onComplete);
11       evt.target.loader.removeListeners();
12       trace(evt.target);
13       trace(evt.target.content);
14       trace(evt.target.loader);
15   }
```

**NOTE**

*The event listeners in the example FLA files are not the same as the event listeners inside the class. All the internal listeners are at the class level, and are private so nothing outside the class is aware of their existence. The listeners in the example FLA files are applied to class instances.*

## Loading images

The second example, found in the *load_jpg_custom.fla*, uses **CustomLoader** much the same way **Loader** is used. The instantiation process in line 3 passes no values to the constructor, the verbose flag is enabled in line 4, and loading is accomplished via the **load()** method and a **URLRequest** instance in line 5. Like the previous JPG loading example, this script also loads the JPG directly to the display list in the last instruction of the **onComplete()** method.

This example also adds the use of the **percentLoaded** getter to increase the horizontal scale of a progress bar. In line 7 the progress bar is created using the **createProgressBar()** function found at the end of the script. The function creates a sprite, draws a green rectangle, and returns the sprite to the **progressBar** variable. The sprite is then added to the display list in line 8.

Two listeners are then added to the **contentLoaderInfo** property of the **CustomLoader** instance, so the property is stored in a variable for efficiency. In addition to the **COMPLETE** event listener found in the prior JPG loading example, a **PROGRESS** event listener is added in lines 13 through 15. It calls the **onProgress()** function in lines 17 through 19, which updates the **scaleX** property of the progress bar sprite every time asset data is received during the loading process.

```
1    import com.learningactionscript3.loading.CustomLoader;
2
3    var jpgLoader:CustomLoader = new CustomLoader();
4    jpgLoader.verbose = true;
5    jpgLoader.load(new URLRequest("imageToLoad.jpg"));
6
7    var progressBar:Sprite = createProgressBar();
8    addChild(progressBar);
9
10   var jpgLoaderInfo:LoaderInfo = jpgLoader.contentLoaderInfo;
11   jpgLoaderInfo.addEventListener(Event.COMPLETE, onComplete,
12                                  false, 0, true);
```

*If you want your usage of the* **Loader** *and* **CustomLoader** *classes to be as similar as possible, so you can switch between them with as few edits as possible, you can still enable verbose tracing without loading the asset immediately. You can set up your code like the custom JPG loading example, so the* **load()** *method is used separately—just like using the* **Loader** *class. However, when instantiating* **CustomLoader** *(line 3 in the example), just pass in null and true as the parameter values:*

```
new CustomLoader(null, true);
```

*This will enable verbose logging, but will not invoke the* **load()** *method in the class constructor.*

*Loading XML is just like loading text. We'll cover loading XML in detail in Chapter 14 and make use of the* **CustomURLLoader** *class you'll write in this chapter.*

```
13  jpgLoaderInfo.addEventListener(ProgressEvent.PROGRESS,
14                              onProgress,
15                              false, 0, true);
16
17  function onProgress(evt:Event):void {
18      progressBar.scaleX = evt.target.loader.percentLoaded;
19  }
20
21  function onComplete(evt:Event):void {
22      evt.target.removeEventListener(Event.COMPLETE, onComplete);
23      evt.target.loader.removeListeners();
24      addChild(evt.target.content);
25  }
26
27  function createProgressBar():Sprite {
28      var sp:Sprite = new Sprite();
29      var g:Graphics = sp.graphics;
30      g.beginFill(0x00FF00);
31      g.drawRect(0, 0, 100, 10);
32      g.endFill();
33      sp.x = sp.y = 10;
34      return sp;
35  }
```

## Loading Data

While the **Loader** class will load visual assets, data such as text, URL variables, and even binary data, is loaded with the **URLLoader** class. Using the **URLLoader** class is similar in many ways to using the **Loader** class. In fact, we'll write a custom class for loading data that will closely resemble the programming design and syntax of the **CustomLoader** class we wrote previously.

Just like the **Loader** class can load more than one kind of object (SWF and image), **URLLoader** can load three kinds of data, selected with the **dataFormat** property of the **URLLoader** instance. Plain text (such as text, HTML, CSS and so on) returns a string. URL-encoded variables (such as HTML form data and server responses) returns an instance of the **URLVariables** class with a collection of variables and corresponding values. Binary data (such as image or sound data) returns a **ByteArray**.

We introduced loading plain text in the "Loading HTML and CSS" section of Chapter 10, but we'll cover it again here for completeness. We'll also include examples of loading variables and binary data, including a beyond the basics look at how you can use binary data.

### Loading Text

The default behavior of the **URLLoader** class is to load text. The following example, found in the *load_text.fla* source file, is the simplest implementation of the **URLLoader** class. All you need to do is instantiate the class (line 1), and load the text file using a **URLRequest** instance. This example uses a **COMPLETE** event listener to initialize a text field when the loading is finished (lines 4 through 15), populate the field with the text data sent with the event (line 13), and add the field to the display list (line 14).

```
1    var ldrText:URLLoader = new URLLoader();
2    ldrText.load(new URLRequest("lorem.txt"));
3
4    ldrText.addEventListener(Event.COMPLETE, onComplete,
5                             false, 0, true);
6    function onComplete(evt:Event):void {
7        evt.target.removeEventListener(Event.COMPLETE, onComplete);
8        var txtFld:TextField = new TextField();
9        txtFld.x = txtFld.y = 20;
10       txtFld.width = 500;
11       txtFld.height = 350;
12       txtFld.multiline = txtFld.wordWrap = true;
13       txtFld.text = evt.target.data;
14       addChild(txtFld);
15   }
```

## Loading Variables

One of the ways to send data between client and server is by using *name-value pairs* (also called attribute-value pairs). These are assembled in a URL like those sent from an HTML form or returned from some web applications like search tools. An example is *firstname=Liz&lastname=Lemon*.

If your project requires communication using URL variables, you must set the **dataFormat** property of the **URLLoader** class to **URLLoaderDataFormat.VARIABLES** before loading. This automatically changes the data returned from the loading process to a **URLVariables** object. Names and values are created in the object to match the names and values from the loading result. You can then access those properties to retrieve their values.

Web-based applications change frequently, so we've demonstrated this syntax using a local file written as URL variables. (Local URLs are no different to **URLLoader** than remote server URLs.) The file *vars.txt* contains the following data:

```
name=Joe&age=25
```

This data will be loaded by the following example, found in *load_vars.fla*. The example assigns the **dataFormat** property in line 2, and the property values are traced from the event target's data property in lines 9 and 10.

```
1    var ldrVars:URLLoader = new URLLoader();
2    ldrVars.dataFormat = URLLoaderDataFormat.VARIABLES;
3    ldrVars.load(new URLRequest("vars.txt"));
4
5    ldrVars.addEventListener(Event.COMPLETE, onComplete,
6                             false, 0, true);
7    function onComplete(evt:Event):void {
8        evt.target.removeEventListener(Event.COMPLETE, onComplete);
9        trace("name property:", evt.target.data.name);
10       trace("age property:", evt.target.data.age);
11   }
```

The following is the trace output:

```
//name property: Joe
//age property: 25
```

## Loading Binary Data

It's also possible to load binary data from a URL, which is stored in a **ByteArray**. In this book, we've already used the **ByteArray** to load frequency spectrum data from sounds at runtime. ActionScript 3.0 has also been used to create FTP clients, VNC clients, and image loaders, just to name a few examples.

To send or load binary data with the **URLLoader** class, you must set the **dataFormat** property to **URLLoaderDataFormat.BINARY**. The following example, found in the *load_binary.fla* source file, sets the property in line 2, loads an image in line 3, and, upon completing the load, creates a **Loader** instance to read the bytes of data returned from the **URLLoader** instance, and adds the instance to the display list (lines 9 through 11).

```
1    var imgLoader:URLLoader = new URLLoader();
2    imgLoader.dataFormat = URLLoaderDataFormat.BINARY;
3    imgLoader.load(new URLRequest("imageToLoad.jpg"));
4
5    imgLoader.addEventListener(Event.COMPLETE, onComplete,
6                                    false, 0, true);
7    function onComplete(evt:Event):void {
8        evt.target.removeEventListener(Event.COMPLETE, onComplete);
9        var ldr:Loader = new Loader();
10       ldr.loadBytes(evt.target.data);
11       addChild(ldr);
12   }
```

This example was designed to be simple to introduce the syntax for loading binary data. Later in the chapter, a beyond-the-basics example will use this technique to load a Pixel Bender filter to process an image.

**NOTE**

*Pixel Bender is an Adobe technology that lets you use a programming language based on C to write your own image filters.*

## Writing a Multiuse Data Loading Class

Just as our **CustomLoader** class extended the **Loader** class, we want to extend the **URLLoader** class and add similar automatic diagnostic features. We'll call the new class **CustomURLLoader** and, as before, we'll design it to use familiar syntax so you can switch between **URLLoader** and **CustomURLLoader** relatively easily. This class is very similar to **CustomLoader** in design and syntax, so our discussion will focus primarily on what makes it unique.

## Writing the CustomURLLoader Class

Lines 1 through 9 declare the package, and import all the required classes. The classes required are similar to those required by **CustomLoader**, with the addition of the **SecurityErrorEvent** class and the substitution of the **URLLoader** class for **Loader**. We'll discuss the **SecurityErrorEvent** class when we cover the listeners. Line 11 declares the class and extends **URLLoader**. Again, this makes available the accessible properties and methods of the **URLLoader** class. Lines 13 through 15 contain private properties also used in **CustomLoader** to contain the asset path, the logging **Boolean**, and a number that reports what percentage of the asset has loaded.

```
1   package com.learningactionscript3.loading {
2
3       import flash.events.Event;
4       import flash.events.HTTPStatusEvent;
5       import flash.events.IOErrorEvent;
6       import flash.events.ProgressEvent;
7       import flash.events.SecurityErrorEvent;
8       import flash.net.URLLoader;
9       import flash.net.URLRequest;
10
11      public class CustomURLLoader extends URLLoader {
12
13          private var _path:String;
14          private var _verbose:Boolean;
15          private var _loadedPercent:Number = 0;
```

The constructor is nearly identical to that of the **CustomLoader** class. Starting with their similarities, this class accepts the asset path string and Boolean for verbose logging as arguments during instantiation (lines 17 and 18), populates the related properties (lines 20 and 21), adds the needed listeners (line 24), and tries to load the asset if a path was provided (lines 26 through 31). The big difference between the two classes is that this class also accepts the **format** string argument, with a default value of "text" (line 19), and assigns that value to the **dataFormat** property of the class, inherited from **URLLoader**, (line 22).

```
16          //constructor
17          function CustomURLLoader(path:String=null,
18                                   verbose:Boolean=false,
19                                   format:String="text") {
20              _path = path;
21              _verbose = verbose;
22              this.dataFormat = format;
23
24              addListeners();
25
26              if (path != null) {
27                  try {
28                      this.load(new URLRequest(path));
29                  } catch (err:Error) {
30                      trace("URL load error:", err.message);
31                  }
32              }
33          }
```

The remainder of the class is also nearly identical to that of **CustomLoader**. Starting with the event listeners, the **addListeners()** and removeListeners() methods also add and remove listeners, respectively (lines 35 through 63). The **INIT** and **UNLOAD** listeners are absent, as they do not apply to **URLLoader**, and the **SecurityErrorEvent.SECURITY_ERROR** has been added (lines 47 through 49, and 61 through 62). The latter is dispatched when you attempt

Loading Data

**NOTE**

*When doing anything that might cause a possible security concern, including loading assets, test your work in a browser as often as is practical. Flash Professional is considered a trusted zone that is not susceptible to most Flash Player security issues. As a result you may think your file is working without security problems throughout development, only to find out at the last minute that restrictions do apply in the browser. The default settings of Flash Professional allow you to test in a browser easily using the Ctrl+F12 (Windows) or Cmd+F12 (Mac) keyboard shortcut.*

to load data from a URL outside the security sandbox used by the SWF, and calls the method in lines 85 through 87.

Flash Player security is a big topic, which is discussed in greater detail on the companion website. Put simply, however, not every asset can be loaded without permission. Notably, a SWF can't readily access the user's local file system and remote URLs at the same time unless permission is granted, nor can you load content from different domains without permission—typically granted with a cross-domain policy file, which is an XML file on the remote server, listing any IP addresses that are allowed access. As your experience grows, and you start to work on projects where either of these needs arise, you'll want to leave ample time to study security issues. See the post "Security Overview" on the companion website for more information.

Finally, the getter and setter (lines 93 through 99) are identical to those found in the **CustomLoader** class, returning the percentage of bytes loaded, and enabling or disabling the verbose logging feature, respectively.

```
34      //listeners
35      private function addListeners():void {
36          this.addEventListener(Event.OPEN,
37                              onOpen, false, 0, true);
38          this.addEventListener(ProgressEvent.PROGRESS,
39                              onProgress, false, 0, true);
40          this.addEventListener(HTTPStatusEvent.HTTP_STATUS,
41                              onStatusEvent,
42                              false, 0, true);
43          this.addEventListener(Event.COMPLETE,
44                              onComplete, false, 0, true);
45          this.addEventListener(IOErrorEvent.IO_ERROR,
46                              onIOError, false, 0, true);
47          this.addEventListener(SecurityErrorEvent.SECURITY_ERROR,
48                              onSecError,
49                              false, 0, true);
50      }
51
52      public function removeListeners():void {
53          this.removeEventListener(Event.OPEN, onOpen);
54          this.removeEventListener(ProgressEvent.PROGRESS,
55                              onProgress);
56          this.removeEventListener(HTTPStatusEvent.HTTP_STATUS,
57                              onStatusEvent);
58          this.removeEventListener(Event.COMPLETE, onComplete);
59          this.removeEventListener(IOErrorEvent.IO_ERROR,
60                              onIOError);
61          this.removeEventListener(SecurityErrorEvent.SECURITY_ERROR,
62                              onSecError);
63      }
64
65      private function onOpen(evt:Event):void {
66          if (_verbose) { trace("Loading begun:", _path); }
67      }
68
69      private function onProgress(evt:ProgressEvent):void {
70          _loadedPercent = evt.bytesLoaded / evt.bytesTotal;
71          if (_verbose) {
72              trace("Loading", _path,
```

```
73                    "-- progress (0-1):", _loadedPercent);
74              }
75        }
76
77        private function onStatusEvent(evt:HTTPStatusEvent):void {
78              if (_verbose) { trace("HTTP status:", evt.status); }
79        }
80
81        private function onComplete(evt:Event):void {
82              if (_verbose) { trace("Loading complete:", _path); }
83        }
84
85        private function onSecError(evt:SecurityErrorEvent):void {
86              trace("Security error:", evt.text);
87        }
88
89        private function onIOError(evt:IOErrorEvent):void {
90              trace("Loading error:", evt.text);
91        }
92
93        public function get percentLoaded():Number {
94              return _loadedPercent
95        }
96
97        public function set verbose(bool:Boolean):void {
98              _verbose = bool;
99        }
100    }
101 }
```

**NOTE**

*As with the* **CustomLoader** *class, the companion website includes an alternate version of* **CustomURLLoader** *that overrides the* **load()** *method. This simplifies the use of both classes because their internal listeners—those responsible for the verbose logging— are added and removed automatically. See the post, "Overriding the load() Method in Custom Loader Classes," at the companion website,* http://www. LearningActionScript3.com.

## Using the CustomURLLoader Class

As you might imagine from their complementary design, using the CustomURLLoader class is very similar to using the CustomLoader class. We'll show examples for loading text, variables, and binary data.

### Loading text

The following example, found in the *load_text_custom.fla* source file, is a simple use of the class. It passes the path of the text file into the class constructor to let the class handle the loading (lines 3 and 4), and it uses verbose logging so you can see what's going on. Other than using our custom class and removing its internal listeners (line 10), it's the same in every other respect as the basic text-loading example explained earlier in the chapter.

```
1   import com.learningactionscript3.loading.CustomURLLoader;
2
3   var ldrText:CustomURLLoader = new CustomURLLoader("lorem.txt",
4                                                     true);
5
6   ldrText.addEventListener(Event.COMPLETE, onComplete,
7                            false, 0, true);
8   function onComplete(evt:Event):void {
9       evt.target.removeEventListener(Event.COMPLETE, onComplete);
10      evt.target.removeListeners();
11      var txtFld:TextField = new TextField();
12      txtFld.x = txtFld.y = 20;
```

```
13    txtFld.width = 500;
14    txtFld.height = 350;
15    txtFld.multiline = txtFld.wordWrap = true;
16    txtFld.text = evt.target.data;
17    addChild(txtFld);
18  }
```

## Loading variables

The next example, found in the *load_vars_custom.fla* source file, employs syntax similar to what you used with the **URLLoader** class. The class is instantiated with no arguments (line 3), the **dataFormat** property is set separately (line 4), and the **load()** method is called using a **URLRequest** instance (line 5).

Two things that are different than the previous variable loading example are the removal of the self-contained class listeners (line 11) and the fact that the event listener method demonstrates using a **for..in** loop (lines 12 through 14) to iterate through all variables, rather than retrieving their values by name.

```
1   import com.learningactionscript3.loading.CustomURLLoader;
2
3   var ldrVars:CustomURLLoader= new CustomURLLoader();
4   ldrVars.dataFormat = URLLoaderDataFormat.VARIABLES;
5   ldrVars.load(new URLRequest("vars.txt"));
6
7   ldrVars.addEventListener(Event.COMPLETE, onComplete,
8                             false, 0, true);
9   function onComplete(evt:Event):void {
10      evt.target.removeEventListener(Event.COMPLETE, onComplete);
11      evt.target.removeListeners();
12      for (var prop in evt.target.data) {
13          trace(prop + ": " + evt.target.data[prop]);
14      }
15  }
```

**NOTE**

*You can learn more about Pixel Bender from the Pixel Bender Developer Center: http://www.adobe.com/devnet/ pixelbender/.*

## Loading binary data

The final use of our **CustomURLLoader** class will again demonstrate loading binary data. This time, however, we'll load a Pixel Bender filter. Adobe developed Pixel Bender to allow users to program image processing filters using a C-based language. Filters are typically written using the Pixel Bender Toolkit (an integrated development environment created expressly for this purpose) and then used by other Adobe applications like Photoshop, AfterEffects, and Flash Player.

You don't have to be able to write the filters to use them, however. Many filters exist under a variety of licenses, including open source, freeware, shareware, and commercial. One place to find Pixel Bender filters is the Adobe Pixel Bender Exchange. Visit *http://www.adobe.com/cfusion/exchange/*, select the Pixel Bender exchange, and then browse or search for filters that can be used with Flash.

In this example, we'll use the SquarePattern filter created by the talented Flash Platform evangelist, teacher, and developer Lee Brimelow. You can read about it at Lee's blog, The Flash Blog, at *http://blog.theflashblog.com/?p=432*.

In ActionScript, this process begins by creating a *shader* using the `Shader` class. A shader defines a function that executes on all the pixels of an image, one pixel at a time. Shaders can be used for filters, fills, blend modes, and even numeric calculations. The benefit of these efforts is that Pixel Bender shaders can improve performance of these processor-intensive tasks. In this example, we'll create a filter using the `ShaderFilter` class.

The following class, *CustomLoadBinaryExample.as*, is a document class used by the accompanying *CustomLoadBinaryExample.fla* source file. It will use the `CustomLoader` class to import an image and add it to the display list, then load the `SquarePattern` filter using the `CustomURLLoader` class, and finally animate the filter using an enter frame event listener.

Lines 1 through 11 declare the package and import all the required classes. Line 13 declares the class, which extends `MovieClip` so it can be used as a document class, if desired. Lines 15 through 20 declare a set of private properties that will hold the `CustomLoader`'s `LoaderInfo` instance (line 15), the loaded image (line 16), a `CustomURLLoader` instance (line 17), the Pixel Bender `Shader` and `ShaderFilter` (lines 18 and 19), and a property to hold the changing filter values during animation (line 20).

The constructor (lines 22 through 29) then uses the `CustomLoader` class to load an image (lines 23 and 24) and create an event listener to respond to the `COMPLETE` event (lines 25 through 28).

**NOTE**

*Lee Brimelow also created the Pixel Bender Viewer, a tool that allows you to load Pixel Bender filters, experiment with their settings, and export them in a format compatible with Flash Player. For more information, see http://blog. theflashblog.com/?p=385.*

```
1    package {
2
3        import flash.display.Bitmap;
4        import flash.display.LoaderInfo;
5        import flash.display.MovieClip;
6        import flash.display.Shader;
7        import flash.filters.ShaderFilter;
8        import flash.events.Event;
9        import flash.net.URLLoaderDataFormat;
10       import com.learningactionscript3.loading.CustomLoader;
11       import com.learningactionscript3.loading.CustomURLLoader;
12
13       public class CustomLoadBinaryExample extends MovieClip {
14
15           private var _ldrInfo:LoaderInfo;
16           private var _penguins:Bitmap;
17           private var _ldrBinary:CustomURLLoader;
18           private var _shader:Shader;
19           private var _shaderFilter:ShaderFilter;
20           private var _val:Number = 0;
21
22           public function CustomLoadBinaryExample() {
23               var jpgLoader:CustomLoader =
24                   new CustomLoader("penguins.jpg");
```

```
25              _ldrInfo = jpgLoader.contentLoaderInfo;
26              _ldrInfo.addEventListener(Event.COMPLETE,
27                                    onImgLoaded,
28                                    false, 0, true);
29          }
```

Once the image has loaded, the **onImgLoaded()** method (lines 31 through 44) is called. The **COMPLETE** event listener is removed from the **CustomLoader**'s **LoaderInfo** instance (lines 32 and 33), the class's internal listeners are removed (line 34), and the loaded bitmap is then added to the display list (lines 35 and 36). Next, the **CustomURLLoader** class is used to load the Pixel Bender filter file as binary data (lines 38 through 40), and another **COMPLETE** listener is created (lines 41 through 43)—this time calling its method when the filter is completely loaded.

```
30          //load filter
31          private function onImgLoaded(evt:Event):void {
32              evt.target.removeEventListener(Event.COMPLETE,
33                                    onImgLoaded);
34              evt.target.loader.removeListeners();
35              _penguins = Bitmap(evt.target.content);
36              addChild(penguins);
37
38              _ldrBinary =
39                  new CustomURLLoader("squarepattern.pbj", true,
40                                    URLLoaderDataFormat.BINARY);
41              _ldrBinary.addEventListener(Event.COMPLETE,
42                                    onFilterLoaded,
43                                    false, 0, true);
44          }
```

When the filter file is loaded, the **onFilterLoaded()** method (lines 46 through 55) is called. The **COMPLETE** event listener is removed from the **CustomURLLoader** (lines 47 and 48), and the class's internal listeners are removed on line 49. Next a **Shader** instance is created from the loaded Pixel Bender data, and a **ShaderFilter** instance is derived from the **Shader** instance. The last task of the method sets up the filter animation by creating an enter frame event listener (lines 53 through 54).

```
45          //create Shader and ShaderFilter
46          private function onFilterLoaded(evt:Event):void {
47              _ldrBinary.removeEventListener(Event.COMPLETE,
48                                    onFilterLoaded);
49              evt.target.removeListeners();
50              _shader = new Shader(evt.target.data);
51              _shaderFilter = new ShaderFilter(shader);
52
53              this.addEventListener(Event.ENTER_FRAME, onEnter,
54                                    false, 0, true);
55          }
```

Finally, the enter frame event listener method **onEnter()** (lines 57 through 66) animates the filter. First, the filter is assigned to the **Bitmap** instance's **filters** property, as discussed in Chapter 9. Next the **_val** property is incremented (line 60). Then the **_val** property is used to update the SquarePattern's **amount** property value. The property takes an array of three numbers: minimum, maximum, and default. We've set the maximum to 50, and the default to 0, and we're incrementing the minimum by 1 every enter frame. When the value reaches 50, the event listener is removed, halting the animation (lines 62 through 65).

```
56        //adjust filter values
57        private function onEnter(evt:Event):void {
58            _penguins.filters = [_shaderFilter];
59
60            _val++;
61            _shader.data.amount.value = [_val, 50, 0];
62            if (_val >= 50) {
63                this.removeEventListener(Event.ENTER_FRAME,
64                                         onEnter);
65            }
66        }
67    }
68 }
```

# Communicating with Loaded SWFs

Now that you know how to load SWFs, let's talk about communicating between them. For this discussion, we'll reference the **Loader** class, but the ideas in this section apply equally to the **CustomLoader** class.

The key to communicating between a parent SWF created with ActionScript 3.0 and a loaded SWF created with ActionScript 3.0 is understanding the position of the **Loader** instance between the two SWFs. Within the parent, accessing the child SWF is straightforward because you need only do so through the **Loader** instance. The same is true in the other direction, from child to parent, but is less obvious to some. Just like when traversing the display list, you can use **this.parent** within a loaded child SWF to talk to its parent. However, this will refer to the **Loader** instance, not the SWF's main timeline (or document class) scope.

The following examples, found in the *communication_parent.fla* and *communication_child.fla* source files, demonstrate several tasks you may need to perform when communicating between parent and child SWFs, including getting or setting properties, calling methods, and calling functions. This exercise shows communication in both directions. Both SWFs contain a simple movie clip animation, a function, and a variable. They both trace information to help you understand what's happening when the parent SWF loads the child SWF into a **Loader** instance.

## The child SWF

Lines 1 through 7 provide the code that is self-contained within the child SWF, which the parent will manipulate. Line 1 initially stops the animation so we can demonstrate the parent calling the **MovieClip play()** method. We'll show you when this occurs in the parent script, but after loading, the animation should play. Line 3 creates and populates a string variable, the content

**NOTE**

*To see the* **CustomLoader** *class used in this context, consult the nearly identical source files,* communication_child_custom.fla *and* communication_parent_custom.fla. *For these examples to work, the child SWF must exist before testing the parent SWF.*

**NOTE**

*SWFs created with ActionScript 3.0 cannot talk directly to SWFs created with ActionScript 2.0 or ActionScript 1.0. If you must do this, such as when showcasing legacy projects in a new portfolio site, you can do so with a workaround that establishes a* **LocalConnection** *channel between the SWFs. For more information, see the "Sending Data from AVM2 to AVM1" post on the companion website.*

of which states that it exists inside the child SWF. Lines 5 through 7 define a function that traces a string passed to it as an argument. This string will originate in the parent SWF to demonstrate calling a function in the child SWF.

Lines 9 through 25 contain the inter-SWF communication, but the conditional beginning in line 9 is necessary to prevent errors when testing the SWF prior to loading. The conditional simply checks to see if the parent of the SWF's main timeline is the stage. As we discussed in Chapter 4 when covering the display list, there is only one stage and, when a SWF is on its own, its parent is the stage. If this is true, the child will trace [object Stage] in line 11, and show that the stage has no other parent by tracing null in line 12. We'll discuss what happens when the SWF's parent is not the stage after the code.

```
1    childAnimation.stop();
2
3    var stringMsg:String = "STRING INSIDE CHILD";
4
5    function childFunction(msg:String):void {
6        trace("traced from function within child:", msg);
7    }
8
9    if (this.parent == this.stage) {
10       trace("child without being loaded:");
11       trace("  my parent:", this.parent);
12       trace("  my parent's parent:", this.parent.parent);
13   } else {
14       trace("child communicating with parent:");
15       var parentLoader:Loader = Loader(this.parent);
16       var parentApp:MovieClip = MovieClip(this.parent.parent);
17       trace("  my parent:", parentLoader);
18       trace("  getting my parent's property:", parentLoader.x);
19       trace("  my parent's parent:", parentApp);
20       parentApp.stringMsg = "NEW STRING INSIDE PARENT";
21       trace("  my parent's parent's redefined variable:",
22           parentApp.stringMsg);
23       parentApp.parentFunction("message from child");
24       parentApp.parentAnimation.play();
25   }
```

If the child SWF's parent is not the stage, lines 15 and 16 cast the parent to a **Loader** instance and the parent's parent (which is the main timeline of the SWF doing the loading) to a **MovieClip** instance. Line 17 then traces the **Loader** instance, and line 18 traces a property of that **Loader**. Line 20 demonstrates *setting* a variable in another SWF by changing the string variable in the parent. (We'll see that variable in a moment, but it's equivalent to line 3 in the child). Lines 21 and 22 then *get* and trace that variable. Finally, line 23 calls a function in the parent (passing a string argument in the process), and line 24 plays the movie clip in the parent.

## The parent SWF

The parent SWF requires no conditional, but is responsible for loading the child SWF. Lines 1 through 7 perform similar roles to the corresponding lines in the child SWF—initially stopping a movie clip animation, declaring and populating a string variable, and defining a function that accepts a string as an argument. The variable in line 3 is the same one redefined by the child SWF in its line 20, and the function in line 5 is the same one called by the child SWF in its lines 21 and 22.

Lines 9 through 15 should be familiar territory by now. They create a **Loader** instance, add it to the display list, load the child SWF, and create a **COMPLETE** event listener that calls the function in line 16 when the event is heard. Line 17 casts the content of the **Loader** (the child SWF) as a **MovieClip**, line 19 traces the child SWF's variable, line 21 calls the child SWF's function, and line 22 plays the child SWF's movie clip.

```
1    parentAnimation.stop();
2
3    var stringMsg:String = "STRING INSIDE PARENT";
4
5    function parentFunction(msg:String):void {
6        trace("traced from within parent:", msg);
7    }
8
9    var ldr:Loader = new Loader();
10   addChild(ldr);
11   ldr.load(new URLRequest("communication_child.swf"));
12
13   ldr.contentLoaderInfo.addEventListener(Event.COMPLETE,
14                                          onComplete,
15                                          false, 0, true);
16   function onComplete(evt:Event):void {
17       var childSWF:MovieClip = MovieClip(ldr.content);
18       trace("\nparent communicating with child:");
19       trace("  getting my child's variable:",
20             childSWF.stringMsg);
21       childSWF.childFunction("message from parent");
22       childSWF.childAnimation.play();
23   }
```

> **NOTE**
>
> *The source files communication_parent_custom.fla and communication_child_custom.fla replicate the scripts in this section but use the* **CustomLoader** *class for all loading.*
>
> *The companion website also contains an example of communication between parent and child SWF without using a* **Loader** *instance. See the post "SWF Communication without Going Through Loader."*

# Additional Online Resources

We want to wrap up by drawing attention to two important loading-related issues that we've documented in detail online. The first is a workaround for a problem that occurs when loading SWFs that contain Text Layout Framework (TLF) assets (discussed in Chapter 10). The second is a third-party ActionScript package called LoaderMax that brings a lot of power and convenience to the loading process.

## Loading SWFs with TLF Assets

TLF uses a *Runtime Shared Library* (*RSL*)—an external library of code with an *.swz* extension that's loaded at runtime. If a user doesn't already have the correct version of the RSL on his or her computer, the TLF asset will try to download it from the Adobe website. Failing that, a version of the RSL from the same directory as the SWF will be loaded.

> **NOTE**
>
> *Runtime shared libraries can have a .swz extension if compressed, and a .swc extension if not compressed.*

**NOTE**

*If you ever see an animated line of five dots before a TLF asset displays, that's its preloader at work.*

**NOTE**

*Flash Professional CS5 users can see an example of a self-preloader in the templates that ship with the application. Select the File→New menu option, and then select the Templates tab in the dialog box that appears. Choose the Sample Files category and select the Preloader for SWF template. You can then see the preloading code in frame 1.*

*If you are not using Flash Professional CS5, you can search the web using the phrase "AS3 preloader internal" for many examples to find one that suits your coding style. Because links change often, the companion website will provide a link to both a class-based and timeline-based example in the cited post.*

Because RSLs are external, it's possible to experience a short delay when viewing TLF assets. (Ideally this occurs only the first time, as RSLs should be cached on your computer thereafter.) To compensate for this possible delay, Adobe included a preloader that's automatically added to any SWF that uses TLF.

Unfortunately, this setup causes problems after loading SWFs with TLF assets. The most common problem is that you can't communicate between parent and child, as described in the "Communicating with Loaded SWFs" section of this chapter, because of the extra layers of loaders that are inserted into the display list by the TLF asset.

There are essentially two solutions to this problem, both of which are discussed on the companion website in the "Loading SWFs that Use TLF" post. The first is to compile the TLF Runtime Shared Library code into your SWF. This makes the entire setup internal, but also increases your SWF's file size by about 120k. The second solution is to use Adobe's new `SafeLoader` class.

The `SafeLoader` class is a replacement for the `Loader` class (it doesn't extend Loader) and is available for download from the following Adobe Technote: *http://kb2.adobe.com/cps/838/cpsid_83812.html*. Its use is nearly identical to the `Loader` class, and you only really need to use it when you know you're loading TLF assets. Sample code is provided with the class in the cited download. We'll also use it in the XML navigation bar in Chapter 14.

The `SafeLoader` class was released soon after Flash Professional CS5 was released and may still have some issues to grapple with. We discuss such issues in the aforementioned companion website post, so be sure to review it before using the class.

TLF assets also affect preloading code designed to preload the SWF in which the code resides. That is, instead of loading an external asset, this kind of preloading code sits in frame 1 of the SWF and loops back to frame 1 until the SWF is fully loaded. Once the SWF is loaded, the code then moves the playhead on to the next frame.

## GreenSock's LoaderMax

A fitting end to this chapter is a quick blurb about LoaderMax. Brought to you by GreenSock, the makers of TweenLite, LoaderMax is the crème de la crème of ActionScript 3.0 loading libraries. Adding as little as 7k to your SWF (depending on which classes you need to use), LoaderMax loads SWFs, images, XML, videos, MP3s, CSS, data, and more. LoaderMax simplifies and enhances loading the way TweenLite simplifies and enhances tweening. For example, here are some of the things LoaderMax can do:

- Build loaders in a variety of ways, including single-item loaders from nothing more than a **String** path (LoaderMax can automatically determine which type of loader to use based on the file extension) and loader queues automatically assembled from XML documents

- Build a queue that intelligently loads assets in the order specified but that can easily reprioritize the queued assets on the fly

- Show progress of individual loaders or all loaders as a group

- Easily add robust event listeners, including multiple events in a single line of code

- Integrate subloaders (LoaderMax instances that exist inside an asset being loaded) with the overall progress and event model of the main loader

- Provide an alternate URL that will automatically be used in the event the first URL fails

- Pause and resume loads in progress

- Circumvent existing ActionScript loading and unloading issues with improved garbage collection, including properly loading SWFs with TLF assets

- Optionally manipulate many display characteristics include automatic scaling, image smoothing, centering registration points, and more

- Operationally control video and MP3 assets, including methods that play, pause, and go to specific time; properties that get or set volume, time, and duration; and events that monitor playback progress and more

- Provide a substantial number of shared properties, methods, and events to all loader types improving consistency and saving lots of manual labor.

LoaderMax is easy to learn and use, particularly after you're familiar with the ActionScript 3.0 loading process. Ideally, this chapter has provided you with the groundwork to get you started, and you can consider using LoaderMax for your next project. For more information, visit *http://www.LoaderMax.com*.

**NOTE**

*See the "Meet LoaderMax" post at the companion website for additional information and source code.*

## learningactionscript3 Package

The contributions from this chapter to our ongoing package of ActionScript classes include **CustomLoader** (for loading SWFs and images) and **CustomURLLoader** (for loading text, URL variables, and binary data).

# What's Next?

Throughout this book, we've demonstrated a few examples of loading external assets. Previously, we discussed loading HTML and CSS (Chapter 10), sound (Chapter 11), and video (Chapter 12). In this chapter, we focused on loading SWF and image assets, as well as text, URL variables, and binary data. We also extended the **Loader** and **URLLoader** classes to add some basic diagnostic features to make it easier to check on your loading efforts. Finally, we discussed communication with loaded SWFs and provided a few online resources that touch on additional loading-related topics. With this information as a head start, you should be able to begin working with just about any basic external asset, and begin explorations into intermediate and advanced loading issues.

Next we're going to cover XML, which is among the most important standard formats used for data exchange, and E4X, the dramatically simplified approach to working with XML in ActionScript. XML is very widely used and enables a significant leg up over name-value pairs when it comes to structured data and large data sizes.

**In the next chapter**, we'll cover:

- The basics of the XML format

- Reading, writing, and editing XML data

- Loading XML assets using the **CustomURLLoader** class from this chapter

- XML communication with servers and other peers

# XML

XML, which stands for Extensible Markup Language, is a structured, text-based file format for storing and exchanging data. If you've seen HTML before, XML will look familiar. Like HTML, XML is a tag-based language. However, it was designed to organize data, rather than lay out a web page. Instead of a large collection of tags that define the language (as found in HTML), XML is wide open. It starts with only a handful of preexisting tags that serve very basic purposes. This freedom allows you to structure data in a way that's most efficient for your needs.

In the past, traversing and working with XML within ActionScript has not been the most pleasant or efficient of experiences. Fortunately, E4X (which stands for ECMAScript for XML), is a part of ActionScript 3.0. E4X is the current standard for reading and writing XML documents and is maintained by the European Computer Manufacturers Association. It greatly reduces the amount of code and hoop-jumping required to communicate with XML. It allows you to treat XML objects like any other object with familiar dot syntax, and provides additional shortcuts for traversing XML data. You can use ActionScript's E4X implementation to create XML inside a class or the Flash timeline or, more commonly, load an XML file at runtime.

In this chapter you'll learn the essentials of E4X, and other XML-related concepts. We'll cover:

- **Understanding XML Structure.** The flexibility of XML means you can set up files in a manner that best serves your project's requirements. Unlike other tag-based languages, there's no library of tags to memorize—just a few simple rules to follow.

- **Creating an XML Object.** To learn how to read and write XML, you must first be able to create an XML object. We'll show you how to create an object directly from XML nodes and from parsing a string. Later, we'll show you how to load XML from an external file.

- **Using Variables with XML Nodes.** Both when creating an XML object and when writing XML on the fly, you can use variables when building nodes. This gives you the same latitude to manipulate XML on the fly using stored information that you enjoy when working with other data. We'll also review basic variable practice to build a string, which can then be *parsed*, or analyzed, as XML.

- **Reading XML.** Reading and parsing XML files is significantly easier using E4X than when using prior versions of ActionScript. You can find specific pieces of information, as well as sweep through the entire document, using properties and methods that are consistent with other ActionScript objects.

- **Writing XML.** You can also put the same power, clarity, and ease of use to work when creating XML. You can create XML for internal use or build data structures for use with servers or other clients.

- **Deleting XML.** Whether eliminating unwanted items during reading to simplify the final XML object or removing errant elements when writing, it is sometimes necessary to delete elements.

- **Loading External XML Documents**. Because you determine its structure, XML is highly efficient and often the format of choice for portable data. As a result, external XML documents are very useful for loading data at runtime.

- **Communicating with XML Servers**. After learning how to read and write XML, you can then use it in your communications between servers and other clients.

- **An XML Navigation System**. We'll enhance the navigation system created in Chapter 6, reading the menu content from XML instead of an array. We'll also populate a **Loader** instance so you can use the menu to load external SWFs and images.

## Understanding XML Structure

When working with large data sets, XML is a vast improvement over the name-value pairs that are used in simple web communications, such as HTML forms. An XML document can contain much more data, but can also convey an information hierarchy, detailing relationships among data elements. For example, you can organize a list of users—with names, emails, passwords, and similar information—much the way you would a traditional database. Records might be represented with tags (called *element nodes* in XML) that define a single user, similar to a database record; nested, or child, tags might serve as the equivalent of database fields, associating data with that user. Element nodes can contain text, which is also considered an XML node (a *text node*) for easy parsing. Once you establish a structure, you can duplicate a tag set any time a new record (or user, in this case) is added, and the consistent structure can be reliably navigated when retrieving the data.

Here is an example XML document:

```
<users>
  <user>
    <username>johnuser</username>
    <email>email1@domain.com</email>
    <password>123456</password>
  </user>
  <user>
    <username>janeuser</username>
    <email>email2@domain.com</email>
    <password>abcdef</password>
  </user>
</users>
```

Because you make up the tags as you go along, this document would be just as valid if you replaced the word "user" with "student" throughout. Neither the data nor the data structure would change. The document simply might be more meaningful if you were describing students instead of users.

The easiest way to understand this open format is to remember that XML simply structures your content. While HTML defines the layout of a web page and gives instructions for displaying that page to a browser, XML does nothing more than organize data. It's up to the application to correctly parse the data. Think of XML as you would any other structuring effort. For example, you might export text from a database or a spreadsheet using XML as a replacement for comma-delimited or tab-delimited formats (records separated by carriage returns, fields separated by commas or tabs, respectively).

There are only a few simple rules to remember when you're creating an XML document:

- Every XML document must have a root node that contains all other information. It doesn't have to have a specific name, but all XML data must be nested within one node.

- XML is case-sensitive. It doesn't matter whether you use lowercase or uppercase, but the case used in matching opening and closing tags must be consistent. There are two schools of thought when it comes to choosing a case. The first school advocates uppercase as a means of making it easier to separate tags from content when you glance at the document. The other school pursues lowercase as a de facto standard form used in programming, URLs, and other places where case sensitivity matters.

- All nodes must be closed—either with a balancing tag or as a self-closing tag. Balancing tags must be written as `<one>text</one>` versus `<one>text`. Single tags (such as a line break, `<br>`, in HTML), must use the self-closing format—preceding the last greater-than symbol with a slash (such as `<br />`).

- All tags must be properly nested. The following is incorrect: `<one><two>term</one></two>`. But this is correct: `<one><two>term</two></one>`.

**NOTE**

*As a personal preference, we opt for lowercase. You'll learn later in this chapter how you can address XML elements using dot syntax the same way you would create custom properties of objects, as described in the section "Custom Objects" section of Chapter 2. However, case sensitivity must be preserved. Therefore, a node called username in lowercase would be represented as `<username>`, while uppercase requires `<USERNAME>`. We prefer to reserve uppercase in ActionScript as a convention for representing constants.*

- All attributes must be enclosed within quotation marks. The following would generate an error: `<story class=headline>News</story>`. But this will not: `<span class="headline">News</span>`. This is important not only because the XML must be well formed, but because attributes are also XML nodes and can be parsed just like element and text nodes.

A few other items that warrant a bit more discussion are covered in the following sections.

## White Space

White space includes all returns, tabs, and spaces between tags, as indicated in the example below:

By contrast, the following example has no white space:

```
<users><user><username>richshupe</username><email>email1@domain.com
</email><password>123456</password></user></users>
```

Both are representations of the same document, and they each have their benefits. The file size of the version with no white space is a tiny bit smaller due to the reduced number of characters; however, in all but very large documents, this is usually negligible. The version with white space is much easier to read.

White space is important to understand because this information could be interpreted as text. Return, tab, and space characters are all legal text entities, so the XML parser must be told to ignore them or they will be counted as such when reading the document. This is because tags and text are separate objects when parsed. The tags are called *element nodes* and the text entries within the tags are called *text nodes*. Because the white space can be interpreted as text nodes, the previous XML examples would contain a different number of nodes with and without white space.

Readability usually prevails when formatting XML documents and, fortunately, ignoring white space is the default behavior of ActionScript's E4X implementation. To parse white space, you must add this static property setting to your script before creating your XML object.

```
XML.ignoreWhitespace = false;
```

# Declarations

You will likely see additional tags at the start of XML documents that you should be aware of. The first is the XML *declaration* tag, and it usually looks something like this:

```
<?xml version="1.0" encoding="UTF-8"?>
```

This may differ, depending on the source document, but the purpose of such a tag is usually the same. It tells parsers the version of the XML language specification and the type of encoding used when the file was written. Another example of a declaration tag is the *document type declaration* (DTD), which is used to identify a set of rules against which a parser will compare the XML when validating. An example can be seen here:

```
<!DOCTYPE note SYSTEM "note.dtd">
```

ActionScript does not validate XML using these declaration tags. If you plan to use an XML document with another parser, such as a server-side component of your project with which ActionScript will communicate, you may need to use these tags. However, ActionScript does not require their presence.

# Comments and Processing Instructions

XML comments use the same form as HTML comments: `<!-- comment -->`. In ActionScript, they are ignored by default but they can be parsed using E4X in the rare case that you may want to use them. For example, you may want to track version or date information that wouldn't otherwise appear in the structure of your data. To parse comments, you must add the following static property assignment to your script before creating your XML object:

```
XML.ignoreComments = false;
```

Processing instructions are strings typically used when working with style sheets to display XML, and ActionScript does not use them. They take the form: `<?instruction ?>`. They are ignored by default but can also be parsed using E4X and converted to strings if you wish to use them, though this, too, is exceedingly rare. To do so, you must add this static property setting to your script before creating your XML object:

```
XML.ignoreProcessingInstructions = false;
```

# Entities and the CDATA Tag

When writing your XML documents, you must be aware that it is possible to confuse a parser or even break your document by including restricted characters. For example, the following document would cause a problem:

```
<example topic="<, "">use entities for < and "</example>
```

In this case, the XML parser assumes the quotation mark within the attribute is closing the attribute prematurely, and it sees the two less than symbols (one within the attribute and one within the text node) as the start of XML tags. The quotation mark within the text node is fine, as it does not conflict with the quotation marks required for attributes. To be considered well formed, the offending characters must be represented by entities:

```
<example topic="&lt;, &quot;">use entities for &lt; and "</example>
```

There are only five entities included in the XML specification, as seen in Table 14-1.

*Table 14-1. The five entities included in the XML specification*

| Entity | Correct Form | Notes |
|---|---|---|
| < | &lt; | Less than |
| > | &gt; | Greater than |
| & | &amp; | Ampersand |
| ' | &apos; | Apostrophe |
| " | &quot; | Quotation mark |

To include other special characters, or preserve special formatting, you can use a **CDATA** (character data) tag. This tag wraps around the special content and tells the XML parser to consider everything therein as plain text. This is particularly useful when you want to include HTML, white space, or formatted text inside your XML document. The following example might be used to display a sample ActionScript function. The less than and greater than symbols will not cause a problem, and the white space will be preserved.

```
<stuff>
  <![CDATA[
    function styleBold(txt:String):String {
      return "<b>" + txt + "</b>";
    }
  ]]>
</stuff>
```

## Creating an XML Object

The first step in using XML in ActionScript 3.0 is typically to create an instance of the **XML** class. There are two ways of creating an **XML** instance from internal data. (We'll cover loading external XML files separately.) The first approach is to write the content explicitly, as XML nodes, when creating the object. The following example is found in the *xml_from_nodes.fla* source file:

```
1    var las3Data:XML = <authors>
2                         <author>
3                           <firstname>Rich</firstname>
4                           <lastname>Shupe</lastname>
5                         </author>
```

```
 6                      <author>
 7                        <firstname>Zevan</firstname>
 8                        <lastname>Rosser</lastname>
 9                      </author>
10                   </authors>;
11   trace(las3Data);
```

There are a couple of wonderful things about of this approach. First, the XML is automatically treated like XML, rather than like plain text. As a result, an instance of the **XML** class is automatically created, and you don't need to enclose the XML in quotes. Second, you don't need to worry about white space or line breaks until the next ActionScript instruction is encountered. In line 11, for example, a **trace** statement occurs. This makes it easy to format your XML in a nice, readable way.

**NOTE**

*This is a good example of where the semicolon at the end of a line significantly improves readability. The semicolon at the end of line 10 clearly indicates the end of the XML.*

The second approach is to create the **XML** instance from a string. This is handy for creating XML on the fly from user input, such as when a user types information into a field. In this case, you must use the **XML** class constructor explicitly, passing to it the string you want to convert to XML. This example is in the *xml_from_string.fla* source file.

```
1   var str:String = "<book><publisher>O'Reilly</publisher></book>";
2   var las3Data:XML = new XML(str);
3   trace(las3Data);
```

## Using Variables in XML

It's even possible to use variables when writing XML nodes by enclosing the variables in braces. This can be seen inside the tags in lines 7 and 8 in the following example, found in the *xml_from_nodes_variables.fla* source file.

```
 1   var author1First:String = "Rich";
 2   var author1Last:String = "Shupe";
 3
 4   var las3Data:XML = <authors>
 5                        <author>
 6                          <firstname>{author1First}</firstname>
 7                          <lastname>{author1Last}</lastname>
 8                        </author>
 9                      </authors>;
10   trace(las3Data);
```

If you choose to create XML from a string, you can also use standard variable syntax to build the string before parsing. Lines 2 and 3 join two strings with a variable before converting to XML. The following code is found in the *xml_from_string_variables.fla* source file.

```
1   var publisher:String = "O'Reilly";
2   var str:String = "<book><publisher>" + publisher +
3                    "</publisher></book>";
4   var las3Data:XML = new XML(str);
5   trace(las3Data);
```

# Reading XML

ActionScript 3.0 makes reading XML easier than ever before. You can now use syntax consistent with that of other ActionScript objects. Not only can you use basic properties and methods of an **XML** instance, you can also work with individual nodes and attributes using familiar dot syntax.

A familial relationship is used to describe nodes. Nested element nodes, text nodes, and comments are children of their parent element nodes. Nodes at the same level—meaning they have the same parent node—are known as *siblings*. Retrieving a node from an XML object is as easy as drilling down through the family tree of parent and child nodes—just like you would access a nested movie clip from the main timeline.

Before we continue, take care to note that the root node of an **XML** object is never included in dot syntax that references its child nodes. Consider this example:

```
var las3Data:XML = <book><publisher>O'Reilly</publisher></book>;
//trace(las3Data.book.publisher);
trace(las3Data.publisher);
```

The commented line is wrong, and the last line is correct. This is because the root node is synonymous with the XML instance. Every XML document must have a root node, so traversing it is an unnecessary extra step, and it should not be referenced.

## Element and Text Nodes, and the XMLList Class

As mentioned previously, element nodes are XML tags, and text enclosed in a pair of tags is a text node unto itself. Conveniently, accessing an element node allows you to work with the node as an object—such as when you want to copy or delete a node (both of which we'll do later in this chapter)—but it also *returns* useful context-sensitive data for immediate use.

When the queried node contains additional element nodes, they are returned so that you can work with a subset of the larger **XML** object. This is handy for working only with information you really need, as we'll see when working with individual menus in our XML-based navigation system project at the end of the chapter. When the queried node contains a text node, the text is returned as a **String**. This is convenient for populating variables or text fields with node content without first having to convert the data to a **String**.

In all cases, however, it's important to understand the difference between the node and what's returned when accessing the node. This is worth a few minutes of detailed focus, as it will save you time when you have to write code to parse XML for use at runtime. Let's look at how to work with text nodes first.

**NOTE**

*Including a root node in your syntax targeting XML nodes will not only produce no useable result, it typically won't generate an error and you'll be left scratching your head. Remember to omit it from all node references and use the* **XML** *class instance instead.*

## Text nodes and strings

The following example is found in the *text_nodes_and_strings.fla* source file and begins with the explicit creation of an **XML** instance called *las3Data*, in lines 1 through 15.

```
1   var las3Data:XML = <book>
2                       <publisher name="O'Reilly"/>
3                       <title>Learning ActionScript 3.0</title>
4                       <subject>ActionScript</subject>
5                       <authors>
6                         <author>
7                           <firstname>Rich</firstname>
8                           <lastname>Shupe</lastname>
9                         </author>
10                        <author>
11                          <firstname>Zevan</firstname>
12                          <lastname>Rosser</lastname>
13                        </author>
14                      </authors>
15                     </book>;
16
17  trace("- name of title node:", las3Data.title.name());
18  //- name of title node: title
19
20  trace("- data returned from title node:", las3Data.title);
21  //- data returned from title node: Learning ActionScript 3.0
22
23  var txtFld:TextField = new TextField();
24  txtFld.width = 300;
25  txtFld.text = las3Data.title;
26  addChild(txtFld);
```

Now take a look at line 17. This illustrates a simple example of working with a node object by using the **name()** method to return the node's name. The rest of the segment demonstrates working with data *returned* when querying a node. Line 20 traces the value to the Output panel, and lines 23 through 26 show a text field populated with the **String** returned.

Line 28 in the following code block further demonstrates the difference between these two concepts by showing that the **title** node, itself, is still an element node. Like an element node, a text node is also XML and can be accessed using the **text()** method shown in line 31. This, too, will return a **String** for your convenience, but line 34 shows that the node itself is a text node.

```
27  //node kind
28  trace("- kind of title node:", las3Data.title.nodeKind());
29  //- kind of title node: element
30
31  trace("- text node child of title:", las3Data.title.text());
32  //- text node child of title: Learning ActionScript 3.0
33
34  trace("- kind of text node:", las3Data.title.text().nodeKind());
35  //- kind of text node: text
```

**NOTE**

*Throughout the chapter, ActionScript comments are used to show* **trace()** *output to simplify our discussion, and have been included in the file so you can compare your own results.*

*The* **trace()** *statements will often use a comma to separate items output to a single line, but a newline and plus (+) operator for multiple line output. This is purely aesthetic. The comma adds a space between items in a trace and, when combined with a carriage return, it causes the first line of multiline input to be formatted with a leading space. Because white space plays a part in XML, we didn't want this to be a distraction, so we concatenated multiline items to avoid this cosmetic issue.*

**NOTE**

*It's not uncommon for ActionScript to return separate but related data that may be useful to you. For example, we discussed in Chapter 2 that the* **push()** *method of the* **Array** *class adds an item to an array. However, it also returns the new length of the array. The following snippet shows the most common use of the* **push()** *method—simply adding an item (banana) to an array (fruit). However, in the third line of this snippet, you'll see another* **push()** *that's inside a* **trace()** *statement. This displays a 4 in the Output panel, which is the new length of the array.*

```
var fruit:Array = ["apple",
    "orange"];
fruit.push("banana");
trace(fruit.push("grape"));
//4
```

*You don't have to use the returned information, as seen in the second line of the example, but it's there if you want it.*

When your goal is to work with text, you are most likely to use the **String** data returned when querying a text node or an element node that contains text. However, it's occasionally convenient to work with the text node instead because it's still XML. For example, you can use XML syntax to collect all occurrences of a particular node in an **XML** object. This is accomplished with the **XMLList** class, the real heart of E4X. We'll demonstrate the power of this class using element nodes.

## Element nodes and the power of XMLList

An **XMLList** instance is a list of all occurrences of a node at the same hierarchical level in the XML object—even if there is only one of those nodes. Let's start right away by pointing out that all XML nodes are of the **XMLList** data type. The following example is found in the *element_nodes_and_xmllist.fla* source file, and lines 1 through 15 again create a basic instance of the XML class. Lines 17 and 20 show that both element and text nodes are typed as **XMLList**.

```
1    var las3Data:XML = <book>
2                         <publisher name="O'Reilly"/>
3                         <title>Learning ActionScript 3.0</title>
4                         <subject>ActionScript</subject>
5                         <authors>
6                           <author>
7                             <firstname>Rich</firstname>
8                             <lastname>Shupe</lastname>
9                           </author>
10                          <author>
11                            <firstname>Zevan</firstname>
12                            <lastname>Rosser</lastname>
13                          </author>
14                        </authors>
15                      </book>;
16
17   trace("- XMLList element node:", las3Data.title is XMLList);
18   //- XMLList element node: true
19
20   trace("- XMLList text node:", las3Data.title.text() is XMLList);
21   //- XMLList text node: true
```

Now let's take a closer look at how wonderful **XMLList** can be. First, you can isolate a segment of your **XML** object to make it easier to parse. Lines 23 and 24 show that you can place a subset of *las3Data* into an **XMLList** instance (**<authors>**, in this case).

```
22   //isolation of XML subset
23   var authors:XMLList = las3Data.authors;
24   trace("- authors:\n" + authors);
25   /*- authors:
26   <authors>
27     <author>
28       <firstname>Rich</firstname>
29       <lastname>Shupe</lastname>
30     </author>
31     <author>
32       <firstname>Zevan</firstname>
33       <lastname>Rosser</lastname>
```

```
34     </author>
35   </authors>
36   */
```

But that's just the beginning. What **XMLList** excels at is pulling together all occurrences of a node at the same hierarchical level. We'll first show this at work by collecting both **<author>** nodes within the **<authors>** node.

```
37   //collecting siblings into an XMLList instance
38   trace("- author:\n" + las3Data.authors.author);
39   /*- author:
40   <author>
41     <firstname>Rich</firstname>
42     <lastname>Shupe</lastname>
43   </author>
44   <author>
45     <firstname>Zevan</firstname>
46     <lastname>Rosser</lastname>
47   </author>
48   */
```

Note that line 38 references simply **<author>**, but two of these nodes are returned, evidenced by the **trace()** output. This is **XMLList** collecting the relevant nodes for you. If an additional **<author>** node appeared on another level, perhaps as a parent, child, or grandchild, it would not be included.

Collecting siblings for you is great, because you don't have to loop through the siblings and build an array yourself. Using **XMLList**, for example, you could automatically generate a list of all sibling news items from an XML news feed. What's *really* great, however, is that **XMLList** will *traverse nodes* for you to collect all nodes at the same hierarchical level. Continuing the news feed example, you could collect all headline nodes from each parent news node.

Using our book example, line 50 of the following script collects both **<firstname>** nodes, even though they are in separate **<author>** parent nodes. Furthermore, you can use bracket syntax to retrieve specific data from the list. For example, line 56 retrieves only the first **<firstname>** node.

```
49   //collecting nodes at the same level into an XMLList instance
50   trace("- firstname:\n" + las3Data.authors.author.firstname);
51   /*- firstname:
52   <firstname>Rich</firstname>
53   <firstname>Zevan</firstname
54   */
55
56   trace("- firstname[0]:\n", las3Data.authors.author.firstname[0]);
57   //- firstname[0]: Rich
```

## Using the descendant accessor operator and wildcards

Two more powerful tools make traversing **XML** and **XMLList** instances easier: the descendant accessor operator and the wildcard. The *descendant accessor operator* is a pair of dots (**..**) and allows you to query a node or nodes in any hierarchical level at or below the specified node, without using a complete path to that element. This is convenient for retrieving deeply nested nodes,

**NOTE**

*Using the same name for nodes that are not siblings with the same purpose is bad XML design because of the possible confusion this structure may cause. If something akin to this is required (such as listing primary authors at one level and contributing authors at another, to follow our example), it's best to use separate names for each node purpose (such as* **<primary>** *and* **<contributor>***).*

**NOTE**

*Although you can use bracket syntax, an* **XMLList** *instance is not an array. One of the most common mistakes developers make when working with* **XMLList** *results is using the array* **length** *property to see how many items are in the list. This will not work, either failing silently or returning a null object reference error depending on usage. The* **XMLList** *equivalent to this property exists as a method:* **length()***.*

as long as no other nodes bear the same name. (Again, this would probably be bad XML design, and all nodes of the same name would be collected.) The following is an alternate way to retrieve only the **<firstname>** nodes that reside within separate parent nodes, anywhere in the *las3Data* instance.

```
58  //descendant accessor operator
59  trace("- ..firstname:\n" + las3Data..firstname);
60  /*- ..firstname:
61  <firstname>Rich</firstname>
62  <firstname>Zevan</firstname>
63  */
```

The *wildcard* is an asterisk (*) that allows you to include *every* node at one hierarchical level. The following will retrieve both **<firstname>** and **<lastname>** nodes, even traversing multiple parent nodes.

```
64  //wildcard operator
65  trace("- author.*:\n" + las3Data.authors.author.*);
66  /*- author.*:
67  <firstname>Rich</firstname>
68  <lastname>Shupe</lastname>
69  <firstname>Zevan</firstname>
70  <lastname>Rosser</lastname>
71  */
```

## Using Attributes

XML element nodes can include attributes the same way HTML nodes can. For example, an HTML image tag might contain a width attribute, and the **<publisher>** node of our *las3Data* XML object contains an attribute called **name** with "O'Reilly" as its content. To access an attribute by name, you first treat it like a child of the node in which it resides, and then precede its name with an *at* symbol (@). The following code is found in the *xml_attributes.fla* source file and contains a simplified adaptation of our *las3Data* example.

```
1  var las3Data:XML = <book>
2                        <publisher name="O'Reilly" state="CA"/>
3                     </book>;
4
5  trace("- dot syntax:", las3Data.publisher.@name);
6  //- dot syntax: O'Reilly;
```

Because an element node can contain multiple attributes, you can also access all attributes as an **XMLList**. You can create the list using the **attributes()** method (line 8) or a wildcard (line 11). And, as the result of both queries is an **XMLList**, you can again use array syntax to select one attribute by index number. (This syntax is shown in line 11, though only one attribute exists in this simple example).

```
7   //collecting attributes using XMLList
8   trace("- attributes():", las3Data.publisher.attributes());
9   //- attribute(): O'ReillyCA
10
11  trace("- @*:", las3Data.publisher.@*[0]);
12  //- @*: O'Reilly
```

Collecting attributes using one of these methods is particularly important when you have to work with XML that uses node names that aren't legal in ActionScript. The most common example is a node name that contains a dash. The following example creates a simple XML instance in lines 14 through 16 and then repeats two ways to retrieve an attribute: by name and by the **attributes()** method. The first approach (line 18) would generate an error if uncommented. The second (line 21) will work correctly.

**NOTE**

*The output from the* **trace()** *statement in line 8 reads "O'ReillyCA" but the data is returned as an* **XMLList**. *You can still work with a single item, as shown in line 11.*

```
13   //querying attribute names illegal in AS3
14   var example:XML = <file creation-date="20071101">
15                         <modified-date>20100829</modified-date>
16                     </file>;
17
18   //trace("- bad attribute name", example.@creation-date);
19   //causes an error
20
21   trace("- attribute(name):", example.attribute("creation-date"));
22   //- attribute(name): 20071101
```

## Coping with element node names that are incompatible with ActionScript

Finally, on a related note, using a method to retrieve all nodes of a specified type can also be used to retrieve element nodes with illegal names. This is seen in line 24 of the following code, which has been appended to the *xml_attributes.fla* source file for side-by-side comparison.

Note, however, that there is an inconsistency here. The **attributes()** (plural) method collects all attributes in a given scope, while the **attribute()**, (singular) method is used to query a single attribute. The **elements()** (plural) method, however, is used for *both* purposes.

```
1   //querying node names illegal in AS3
2   trace("- elements(name):", example.elements("modified-date"));
3   //- elements(name): 20100829
```

## Finding Elements by Content

Another convenient feature of E4X is the ability to use conditionals when querying a node. For example, instead of walking through the contents of an XML document with a loop and a formal **if** structure, you can simply start with the conditional directly inside the dot-syntax address, and create an **XMLList** automatically. Consider the following information, which can be seen in *find_by_content.fla*:

```
1   var phones:XML = <phones>
2                       <model stock="no">
3                         <name>T2</name>
4                         <price>89.00</price>
5                       </model>
6                       <model stock="no">
7                         <name>T1000</name>
8                         <price>99.00</price>
9                       </model>
```

## Finding Elements by Relationship

Although it's a bit less common, it's also possible to parse XML using familial relationships like asking for all the children of a node or the parent of a node. This sidebar will give you a quick overview of a handful of ways to do this, and the "Parsing XML Using Familial Relationships" post at the companion website (*http://www. LearningActionScript3.com*) discusses this further.

There are four ways to access descendents of a node, all of which return an **XMLList** instance. The first is using the **children()** method. This will return all immediate children, including comments and processing instructions, if you've chosen to override the default behavior of ignoring these node types. See the "Comments and Processing Instructions" section of this chapter for more information. The second and third ways to access node descendants are using the **elements()** and **text()** methods to return only the element node children or text node children, respectively.

All three of these methods return only the first level of child nodes within the specified node and will preserve their familial relationships. In some cases, particularly for diagnostic or analysis purposes, you may instead want an **XMLList** of every node nested within a parent node—not only children but grandchildren, great grandchildren, and so on, element nodes and text nodes alike—which flattens everything into one linear list.

To do this, you can use the **descendants()** method, which drills down completely through each child in turn. For example, it starts by collecting the first child of the specified node, then goes through its first child, and then its first child, and so on, until it reaches the last element or text node in the chain. It then moves on to the next child, and continues.

```
10          <model stock="yes">
11            <name>T3</name>
12            <price>199.00</price>
13          </model>
14        </phones>;
```

Line 15 checks to see if any phone model has a price that is below $100. Only the first two models are listed because they are the only models with a price less than 100.

```
15   trace("< 100:\n" + phones.model.(price < 100));
16   /*
17   <model stock="no">
18     <name>T2</name>
19     <price>89.00</price>
20   </model>
21   <model stock="no">
22     <name>T1000</name>
23     <price>99.00</price>
24   </model>
25   */
```

Line 26 looks for any element one level down that has an attribute named stock with a value of "yes." Both implicit and explicit casting are also represented here, with the same results of both instructions listed only once.

```
26   trace("in stock:\n" + phones.*.(@stock == "yes"));
27   /*
28   <model stock="yes">
29     <name>T3</name>
30     <price>199.00</price>
31   </model>
32   */
```

### A limitation when filtering by attribute

Another important thing to know about the aforementioned @ versus **attribute()** choice is that filtering content using @ works only if all of the queried elements have the attribute. Note, in the following example, found in the *xml_attributes_filtering_issue.fla* source file, that one of the element nodes is missing the *price* attribute. Matching nodes using **@price** will generate an error, but using **attribute("price")** will not.

```
1   var catalog:XML = <stock>
2                       <product name="one" price="100" />
3                       <product name="two" price="200" />
4                       <product name="three" />
5                       <product name="four" price="100" />
6                     </stock>;
7
8   //trace(catalog.product.(@price == 100));
9   //error
10
11  trace(catalog.product.(attribute("price") == 100));
```

# Writing XML

You've already seen how to write XML when creating an instance of the **XML** class, but you may also have to write to the instance over time. For example, you may need to add to XML based on user input or as data changes. The majority of techniques for adding content to XML mirror the process of reading the data, except this time you're assigning information to a node rather than retrieving it.

In this section, you'll re-create the data used throughout the "Reading XML" section of this chapter. For simplicity, we'll create element nodes, text nodes, and attributes in one example, and build an **XML** instance as if we were writing it over time. In a real scenario you would not assemble XML in multiple steps in the same script. However, assuming the premise that we're writing the object in stages will allow us to demonstrate the most common XML writing methods.

Because we're intentionally writing the XML out of order to demonstrate methods like **insertChildBefore()** that will alter the order of nodes, we'll show the progress of the XML as we go. The code that follows can be found in the *write_xml.fla* source file. For clarity, only the last **trace()** statement is used in the source file, to show the final XML content, but you can uncomment any trace along the way to see interim results.

To begin, we must have an **XML** instance and a root node, so line 1 creates both. Note that, when adding element nodes without content, you must specify a self-closing tag so the XML remains well formed. As soon as you add content to a self-closing node, ActionScript will replace it with balanced open and closing tags. For example, we're initially adding **<book />** as the root node but, after adding the next element node, the root node will become **<book> </book>**.

Line 2 demonstrates the simplest technique for creating both an element node and a text node. When assigning a value to a node, if the node does not already exist, it will be created. If you assign another element node to the new node, a nested element will be created. If you assign a **String** to the new node, a text node will be created. Line 2, therefore, creates an element node called **<title>** and a text node that contains "Learning ActionScript 3.0." The result appears in lines 5 through 7.

```
1   var las3Data:XML = <book />
2   las3Data.title = "Learning ActionScript 3.0";
3   trace(las3Data);
4   /*
5   <book>
6       <title>Learning ActionScript 3.0</title>
7   </book>
8   */
```

We started with the **<title>** node intentionally to demonstrate the next method. The **prependChild()** method will add a node to the beginning of the XML object specified. In this case, line 9 creates the **<publisher>** element node and positions it before the **<title>** node so it's the first node of *las3Data*. Line 10 demonstrates the creation of an attribute node adding the **name** attribute to the publisher element node just created. The cumulative result appears in lines 13 through 16.

```
9    las3Data.prependChild(<publisher />);
10   las3Data.publisher.@name = "O'Reilly";
11   trace(las3Data);
12   /*
13   <book>
14     <publisher name="O'Reilly"/>
15     <title>Learning ActionScript 3.0</title>
16   </book>
17   */
```

The opposite of **prependChild()**, **appendChild()** adds a node to the end of an **XML** object. Therefore, line 18 adds the **<authors>** node after the **<title>** node. Up to this point, we've only added objects to the **XML** instance, which is equivalent to the root node. However, you can also use **appendChild()** to add a child to another node. Line 19 adds the first **<author>** node as a child of **<authors>**. Lines 20 and 21 again demonstrate the simultaneous creation of element and text nodes, adding **<firstname>** and **<lastname>** nodes and assign a **String** to each. The cumulative result appears in lines 24 through 33.

**NOTE**

*It's not possible, using this method, to add more than one node with the same name to an **XMLList**. For example, we have to add another author to the **<authors>** node, but if we repeat lines 19 through 21, we'll receive this error:*

```
Error #1089: Assignment to lists
    with more than one item is
    not supported.
```

*Instead, we must copy the first author node and change its contents. We'll show you how to do that in just a moment.*

```
18   las3Data.appendChild(<authors />);
19   las3Data.authors.appendChild(<author />);
20   las3Data.authors.author.firstname = "Zevan";
21   las3Data.authors.author.lastname = "Rosser";
22   trace(las3Data);
23   /*
24   <book>
25     <publisher name="O'Reilly"/>
26     <title>Learning ActionScript 3.0</title>
27     <authors>
28       <author>
29         <firstname>Zevan</firstname>
30         <lastname>Rosser</lastname>
31       </author>
32     </authors>
33   </book>
34   */
```

Line 35 demonstrates the **insertChildAfter()** method, the first of a pair that allows you to provide an existing node as a reference point for where the new node should be added. The first argument of the method is the existing node, and the second argument is the node you want to create. In this case, the **<subject>** node is being inserted after the **<title>** node. Line 36 adds a text node to **<subject>**, and the cumulative result is seen in lines 39 through 49.

```
35   las3Data.insertChildAfter(las3Data.title, <subject />);
36   las3Data.subject = "ActionScript";
37   trace(las3Data);
38   /*
39   <book>
40     <publisher name="O'Reilly"/>
```

```
41    <title>Learning ActionScript 3.0</title>
42    <subject>ActionScript</subject>
43    <authors>
44      <author>
45        <firstname>Zevan</firstname>
46        <lastname>Rosser</lastname>
47      </author>
48    </authors>
49  </book>
50  */
```

The next block of code demonstrates **insertChildBefore()**, the other method that uses an existing node as a reference. However, it also demonstrates how to copy a node and change its values. Line 51 uses the **copy()** method to copy the previously created **<author>** node, and lines 52 and 53 change the text nodes in **<firstname>** and **<lastname>**. After the edits, the new node is inserted before the existing **<author>** node to match the order of the original data we're trying to recreate. Using the **copy()** method is a real timesaver when tags with many children must be reproduced over and over again with few changes.

The final result is shown in lines 57 through 71, and matches the original *las3Data* object to achieve our goal.

```
51  var firstAuthor:XMLList = las3Data.authors.author.copy();
52  firstAuthor[0].firstname = "Rich";
53  firstAuthor[0].lastname = "Shupe";
54  las3Data.authors.insertChildBefore(las3Data.authors.author,
      firstAuthor);
55  trace(las3Data);
56  /*
57  <book>
58    <publisher name="O'Reilly"/>
59    <title>Learning ActionScript 3.0</title>
60    <subject>ActionScript</subject>
61    <authors>
62      <author>
63        <firstname>Rich</firstname>
64        <lastname>Shupe</lastname>
65      </author>
66      <author>
67        <firstname>Zevan</firstname>
68        <lastname>Rosser</lastname>
69      </author>
70    </authors>
71  </book>
72  */
```

# Deleting XML

We've placed deleting XML elements in a separate section because you may delete elements when reading or writing XML. When parsing XML, you're likely to ignore small sections of unwanted content, but deleting large segments of unneeded material can sometimes simplify your task. When writing

XML, you may find the need to delete an element added in error or that is no longer needed.

To delete something, simply use the **delete** operator on the desired item. Here are a few examples showing how to delete attributes, element nodes, and text nodes from a simplified version of our ongoing *las3Data* example. This code can be seen in the *delete_xml.fla* source file. Line 7 deletes an attribute, line 8 deletes an element node and all its children (which deletes the text node therein), and line 9 deletes only a text node, leaving the parent element node intact. The final result is seen in lines 12 through 15.

```
1   var las3Data:XML = <book>
2                        <publisher name="O'Reilly" />
3                        <title>Learning ActionScript 3.0</title>
4                        <subject>ActionScript</subject>
5                      </book>;
6
7   delete las3Data.publisher.@name;
8   delete las3Data.subject;
9   delete las3Data.title.text()[0];
10  trace(las3Data);
11  /*
12  <book>
13    <publisher/>
14    <title/>
15  </book>
16  */
```

Note that the delete operator won't work with **text()**, **elements()**, **attributes()**, **children()**, or **descendents()** to delete all of the nodes returned by these methods. Rather, you must specify which item within the **XMLList** returned that you want to delete. This can be counterintuitive if you just want to delete a single text node, as in line 9.

## Loading External XML Documents

Often when you work with XML, you're using data that's being retrieved from an external source. Even when you need only a local data source, however, it's almost always easier to work with an external XML document because it's easier to edit the XML as you project evolves.

We'll use the **LoadURL** class developed in Chapter 13 to load data for our XML navigation system at the end of this chapter, but right now we'd like to stress the basic syntax of loading XML. The code in this section can be found in the *load_xml.fla* source file.

Before we get started with the syntax, let's create a very simple XML document called *toLoad.xml*. It contains the mandatory root node, one element node called **<stuff>**, and one text node with the string, "XML loaded!"

```
<main>
  <stuff>XML loaded!</stuff>
</main>
```

With that in hand, let's start our script by creating a text field to display our results (lines 1 through 5). This is a handy alternative to tracing loaded content because it's easier to test in a browser. Next, create a **URLRequest** instance for the XML file (line 7), and a **URLLoader** instance to load the document (line 9). Then create two event listeners to react to a possible I/O error (lines 10 and 11), and the completion of the loading process (lines 12 and 13). The **onIOError()** function in lines 16 through 18 places any error text (if an I/O error occurs) into a text field, and we'll discuss the **onComplete()** function after the first code block. Next, the XML document is loaded in line 14.

```
1   var txtFld:TextField = new TextField();
2   txtFld.width = 500;
3   txtFld.height = 350;
4   txtFld.multiline = txtFld.wordWrap = true;
5   addChild(txtFld);
6
7   var req:URLRequest = new URLRequest("toLoad.xml");
8
9   var urlLoader:URLLoader = new URLLoader();
10  urlLoader.addEventListener(IOErrorEvent.IO_ERROR,
11                             onIOError, false, 0, true);
12  urlLoader.addEventListener(Event.COMPLETE,
13                             onComplete, false, 0, true);
14  urlLoader.load(req);
15
16  function onIOError(evt:IOErrorEvent):void {
17      txtFld.text = "XML load error.\n" + evt.text;
18  }
```

The **onComplete()** function (lines 19 through 28) is triggered when the XML file has completely loaded. The function first removes the listeners because the XML document was both found and loaded. It then uses a **try..catch** block to create an **XML** instance from the loaded data, and places the **<stuff>** node into a text field. If unsuccessful, an error message is placed into the same field, often allowing you to locate something that may cause the XML to be malformed.

```
19  function onComplete(evt:Event):void {
20      urlLoader.removeEventListener(IOErrorEvent.IO_ERROR, onIOError);
21      urlLoader.removeEventListener(Event.COMPLETE, onComplete);
22      try {
23          var loadedXML:XML = new XML(evt.target.data);
24          txtFld.text = loadedXML.stuff;
25      } catch (err:Error) {
26          txtFld.text = "XML parse error:\n" + err.message;
27      }
28  }
```

Before we demonstrate populating menus with XML in our navigation system project, let's look at sending data to a server and loading the result.

# Sending to and Loading from a Server

Another frequent use of XML data is for transmission to and from a server. XML is often the data format used by news feeds (RSS, ATOM), Web services, and database output. While some of these uses require only loading information, other tasks, including application logins, game high score submission, and so on, also require sending data. In this chapter, we'll cover the basic send and load method of communicating with a server.

## Send and Load

The send-and-load approach is a form of traditional server communication, be it a browser retrieving an HTML file or a user submitting data via a form. Essentially, the client sends data to the server and waits for a response. The server processes the incoming information, formulates a reply, and sends information back to the client.

For simplicity, this example sends a short XML object to a PHP script, which then writes data to a text file on the server and sends back a short reply. Writing a text file on the server may not be the most common use of XML submissions, but it's basic enough to illustrate in this context. This example uses two files: *send_load_xml.fla* and *save_xml.php*. Let's look at the FLA file first.

### The client source

This example is nearly identical to the *load_xml.fla* source file discussed in the preceding "Loading External XML Documents" section. All we need to do is substitute the following eight lines of code for line 7 of that example. These lines both create XML to send, and customize the **URLRequest** instance to send data, as well as load it.

Lines 7 through 9 create the **XML** object to send to the server. Like ActionScript, our PHP script does not require the XML declaration tag in line 7 but, for maximum flexibility, it's not a bad idea to prepend this to any XML you send to a server. You may find that it's required in a future configuration of your project and, since it makes no difference in ActionScript, there's no good reason not to include it.

Lines 11 through 14 create a **URLRequest** instance for submitting the data. *Note that you'll need to put the correct path to your server in line 11*. As discussed in Chapter 13, line 12 assigns the outgoing XML to the **data** property of the request, and lines 13 and 14 specify "text/xml" as the **contentType**, and POST as the **method**, of the request object, respectively.

```
7   var str:String = "<?xml version='1.0' encoding='utf-8'?>";
8   str += "<value>Sent from ActionScript</value>";
9   var xmlToSend:XML = new XML(str);
10
```

```
11   var req:URLRequest = new URLRequest("save_xml.php");
12   req.data = xmlToSend;
13   req.contentType = "text/xml";
14   req.method = URLRequestMethod.POST;
```

## The server source

The next code block is the server-side PHP script. This is the server destination of your simple XML data and, as specified in line 11 of the ActionScript code, should be called *save_xml.php*. The script first checks to be sure POST data has been received (line 3), and then populates the **$data** variable with that data (line 4). In lines 6 through 8, it creates and opens for writing a file called *data.txt*, writes the data to the file, and then closes the open file instance. Lastly, it checks to make sure the file was written successfully and sends a simple XML object back to ActionScript.

If successful, you'll see the message "File saved." in the text field. If not, you'll see "Server unable to create file." There may be a permissions issue on the server preventing write access to the directory in which the PHP script has been placed, for example, or another error preventing file creation.

```
1    <?php
2
3    if (isset($GLOBALS["HTTP_RAW_POST_DATA"])){
4        $data = $GLOBALS["HTTP_RAW_POST_DATA"];
5
6        $file = fopen("data.txt", "wb");
7        fwrite($file, $data);
8        fclose($file);
9
10       if (!$file) {
11           echo("<stuff>Server unable to create file.</stuff>");
12       } else {
13           echo("<stuff>File saved.</stuff>");
14       }
15   }
16
17   ?>
```

# An XML-Based Navigation System

If you haven't done so already, you may want to read the last exercise in Chapter 6, before continuing with this project. Chapter 6 discusses object-oriented programming and uses a simplified version of this exercise without XML, populating the menus with an array. By comparing this exercise with the more basic version in Chapter 6, you can see how incorporating XML changes the system. The result of this exercise will be a five-button navigation bar with submenus, the labels and partial functionality of which are populated through XML.

## The Directory Structure and Source Files

Before looking at the ActionScript for this exercise, we need to explain a couple of quick things about the project's directory structure and source files. We've tried to use several of the key topics that we've learned throughout the book to approximate an average use of an XML-driven menu system. Highlights include: object-oriented design, embedded fonts, text formatting, TweenLite animations, loading external assets, drawing with vectors, filter effects, and, of course, parsing XML.

The project directory, *nav_bar_xml*, includes the primary FLA file, *LAS3Lab.fla*, and document class, *LAS3Main.as*. The exercise also uses classes from the learningactionscript3 package (in the *com* directory) that we've been building throughout the book:

`com.learningactionscript3.loading.LoadURL`

> Created in Chapter 13, this class can load text from a URL, and includes error checking, making it convenient for loading XML.

`com.learningactionscript3.ui.NavigationBarXML`

> This class is the backbone of the system and is a new version of the **NavigationBar** class used in Chapter 6. It replaces that chapter's array data with XML, adds submenus, and puts the whole system to work by adding a loader that the menu items can target for loading SWFs and images.

`import com.learningactionscript3.ui.MenuButtonMain`

> This simple class essentially provides a text field and text formatting for the **MenuButtonMain** movie clip in the *LAS3Main.fla* library.

`import com.learningactionscript3.ui.MenuButtonSub`

> This class dynamically creates submenu buttons that will be clicked to load visual content at runtime.

In addition, the exercise uses classes that are developed by others and are not part of any default ActionScript 3.0 distribution, including a few classes from TweenLite (the ActionScript tweening platform discussed in Chapter 7), and a modified version of Adobe's **SafeLoader** class (the class designed to load SWFs that contain TLF instances without error, discussed in Chapter 13).

The last parts of the exercise directory are the XML data and content for loading. The XML file that populates the menus is called *nav.xml* and is found inside a directory called *data*, and the content ready for loading, and specified in paths in the XML data, is found inside the *projects* directory.

**NOTE**

*The navigation menu system in this chapter is an enhancement of the version in Chapter 6. We elected, however, not to replace the older classes to allow you to compare the classes and see the evolution of the code. Instead, we placed the new and revised classes in the* **com. learningactionscript3.ui** *package.*

# The Library of the FLA

The main FLA file requires three symbols in its library:

**ArialBold**

**ArialRegular**

These are embedded font symbols containing bold and plain versions of the Arial font with linkage class names of **ArialBold** and **ArialRegular**, respectively. Although embedded fonts in a SWF ensure that viewers don't need to have the fonts installed in their computer, this is not true of editing an FLA. If you prefer, you can substitute your own fonts and then either use the same linkage class names or update the code accordingly.

**MenuButtonMain**

This is a movie clip that looks like a tab-shaped button. The class of the same name provides the text field and text formatting needed to display the tab's text label.

# The XML and Classes

Now we'll being looking at the code behind the project. We'll start by showing you an excerpt of the XML data file, and then discuss each of the classes that you'll write. We'll also explain the usage of related, third-party classes.

## XML

You can look at the XML document any time, but the following excerpt is representative of the data:

```
<nav>
  <menus>
    <button label="MOTION">
      <project label="flocking" path="projects/motion/worm.swf">
        Flocking with Zeno's paradox
      </project>
      <project label="point at" path="projects/motion/point.swf">
        Pointing at the mouse position
      </project>
    </button>
  </menus>
</nav>
```

The root node, **<nav>**, has a child node, **<menus>**, which contains the data for all menus. Each menu is delineated by a **<button>** node, which corresponds to the main menu button. This node has a **label** attribute, which holds the text used for the main menu button text label.

Within each **<button>** node are multiple child nodes called **<project>** (two are shown in the excerpt for brevity). Collectively, these make up the submenu for each menu. Each **<project>** node corresponds with one button in the submenu, and has an attribute called **label**. This is used to populate the text label of the submenu button. It also has a **path** attribute, used to load the corresponding content, and a text node, which we'll use in Chapter 15 to display a brief blurb about the loaded asset.

## LAS3Main (document class)

The document class is pretty straightforward. It loads the XML data, creates a **SafeLoader** for loading content and a mask for masking the content to an area below the menus, and initializes the menus.

Lines 1 through 10 declare the package and import required classes, including **SafeLoader**, and two custom classes, **CustomURLLoader** and **NavigationBarXML**. Line 12 declares the class, including extending **MovieClip** so it can easily be used as a document class. Finally, lines 14 through 16 create three private properties for the **CustomURLLoder**, **XML**, and **SafeLoader** instances, respectively.

```
1    package {
2
3        import flash.display.Graphics;
4        import flash.display.MovieClip;
5        import flash.events.Event;
6        import flash.filters.DropShadowFilter;
7        import flash.net.URLRequest;
8        import fl.display.SafeLoader;
9        import com.learningactionscript3.loading.CustomURLLoader;
10       import com.learningactionscript3.ui.NavigationBarXML;
11
12       public class LAS3Main extends MovieClip {
13
14           private var _menuLdr:CustomURLLoader;
15           private var _xml:XML;
16           private var _loader:SafeLoader;
```

The class constructor occupies lines 18 through 22 and creates an instance of the **CustomURLLoader** class to load the external data. Discussed in Chapter 13, this class does all the loading work for us and dispatches an **Event.COMPLETE** event when the loading is finished. Line 20 adds an event listener to trap this event and call **onLoadXML()**.

Once the XML is loaded, the **onLoadXML()** method uses a **try..catch** block to attempt to parse the XML. It retrieves the data from the **data** property of the **CustomURLLoader** instance and tries to instantiate an **XML** object using that data (line 26). If successful, it calls the **initLoader()** and **initMenus()** methods (lines 27 and 28, respectively). If the data can't be parsed as XML, it traces an error (lines 30 and 31).

```
17           //constructor and xml load
18           public function LAS3Main() {
19               _menuLdr = new LoadURL("data/nav.xml");
20               _menuLdr.addEventListener(Event.COMPLETE, onLoadXML,
21                                         false, 0, true);
22           }
23
24           private function onLoadXML(evt:Event):void {
25               try {
```

```
26              _xml = new XML(_menuLdr.data);
27              initLoader();
28              initMenus();
29          } catch (err:TypeError) {
30              trace("Can't parse loaded content as XML:",
31                  err.message);
32          }
33      }
```

The **initLoader()** method creates an instance of the **SafeLoader** class (line 36), positions it below the future location of the menus (line 37), and adds it to the display list (line 38). It also draws a 750 × 450 pixel movie clip (lines 40 through 44), adjusts its y position to 100, the same location as the **SafeLoader** instance (line 45), and uses it to mask the loaded content (line 46).

**NOTE**

*Using a mask prevents loaded content from appearing outside the area dedicated for its display—something that frequently happens when assets follow the mouse, for example. If you want to see what the project looks like without a mask at any point, simply comment out line 46 when testing.*

```
34          //loader and mask
35          private function initLoader():void {
36              _loader = new SafeLoader();
37              _loader.y = 100;
38              this.addChild(_loader);
39
40              var loaderMask:MovieClip = new MovieClip();
41              var g:Graphics = loaderMask.graphics;
42              g.beginFill(0x000000, 1);
43              g.drawRect(0, 0, 750, 450);
44              g.endFill();
45              loaderMask.y = 100;
46              _loader.mask = loaderMask;
47          }
```

**NOTE**

*See Chapter 13 for information about a modification made to Adobe's **SafeLoader** class.*

The **initMenus()** method creates an instance of the **NavigationBarXML** class (lines 50 and 51) and adds it to the display list (line 52). In doing so, it passes the scope of the document class into the constructor, as well as the **<menus>** **XMLList**. This makes all of the menu XML data available to the class so it can create the necessary buttons. The method also creates a **DropShadowFilter** instance (line 54), sets its alpha to 25 percent, and adds it to the *_navBar* instance. This will give the entire menu system, including the submenus that appear interactively, a drop shadow.

```
48          //navigation menu bar
49          private function initMenus():void {
50              var _navBar:NavigationBarXML =
51                  new NavigationBarXML(this, _xml.menus);
52              this.addChild(_navBar);
53
54              var ds:DropShadowFilter = new DropShadowFilter();
55              ds.alpha = 0.25;
56              _navBar.filters = [ds];
57          }
58
59          public function get assetLoader():SafeLoader {
60              return _loader;
61          }
62      }
63  }
```

Finally, a getter is provided to return the **SafeLoader** instance when required. Despite not processing the information returned, a getter is used here instead of a public property because the value should be read-only. By contrast, we'll use public properties later on in the **MenuButtonSub** class, to give you more experience with both approaches to controlling information access in classes. For more information, see the "Encapsulation" section in Chapter 6.

## NavigationBarXML

The **NavigationBarXML** class is the longest class in the project, and the real workhorse. Although its functionality isn't particularly complex, a little more detail is warranted to cover some of its inner workings.

Lines 1 through 15 declare the package and import the necessary classes. In this case, note that three TweenLite classes that we haven't discussed before are imported: **TweenPlugin**, **ColorTransformPlugin**, and **VisiblePlugin**. We'll discuss those when we go over the constructor. Also, note that **MenuButtonMain** and **MenuButtonSub** are imported. It's in this class that we'll be using both button types.

Line 17 declares the class and extends **MovieClip** so the navigation bar instance inherits the accessible properties and methods of the **MovieClip** class. Lines 19 through 21 create three private properties, preventing access from outside the class. The first property (line 19) will hold an instance of the document class (remember that it extended **MovieClip**, as well) passed into the constructor during instantiation. This will allow us to get the **SafeLoader** instance when one of the menu buttons needs to load content.

The second property (line 20) will hold an **XMLList** of all the button data loaded in the document class—also passed into the constructor during instantiation. The last property (line 21) will contain the currently active submenu when the user rolls his or her mouse over a menu button. This will allow us to reference the same menu in another method when the user rolls the mouse away and we must hide the menu.

```
1    package com.learningactionscript3.ui {
2
3        import flash.display.Graphics;
4        import flash.display.MovieClip;
5        import flash.events.Event;
6        import flash.events.MouseEvent;
7        import flash.geom.Matrix;
8        import flash.net.URLRequest;
9        import flash.text.TextField;
10       import com.greensock.TweenLite;
11       import com.greensock.plugins.TweenPlugin;
12       import com.greensock.plugins.VisiblePlugin;
13       import com.greensock.plugins.ColorTransformPlugin;
14       import com.learningactionscript3.ui.MenuButtonMain;
15       import com.learningactionscript3.ui.MenuButtonSub;
16
17       public class NavigationBarXML extends MovieClip {
18
```

```
19        private var _app:MovieClip;
20        private var _navData:XMLList;
21        private var _subMenu:MovieClip;
```

The class constructor occupies lines 23 through 41. It accepts two arguments: the movie clip in which the navigation bar was instantiated (to allow us to get a reference to the **SafeLoader** instance), and the button data loaded from XML. This information is immediately stored in the aforementioned private properties, in lines 25 and 26, so we can use the references in multiple methods within the class.

Line 28 calls the **addMenus()** function, which builds the menu system and which we'll discuss in just a moment. Lines 30 through 37 dynamically draw the thick black line that serves as the lower bound of the main menu tabs. This improves upon the original version of the menu system in Chapter 6, which used a symbol for this purpose, because the code can easily be altered without having to create new artwork in the FLA.

The last two lines in the constructor activate the TweenLite plugins. The TweenLite tweening package is kept staggeringly small by only integrating the bare animation essentials. It doesn't skimp on bells and whistles, however, because it allows you to add individual features as needed by activating plugins. This project uses two TweenLite plugins: **VisiblePlugin**, which turns an asset invisible after a tween, and **ColorTransformPlugin**, which allows us to tween color values. The uses of both plugins will be explained in context. This is a one-time process. Once the plugins are activated, their features will be available throughout your SWF, and any SWFs loaded from the same domain.

```
22        //constructor
23        public function NavigationBarXML(app:MovieClip,
24                                         navData:XMLList) {
25            _app = app;
26            _navData = navData;
27
28            addMenus();
29
30            var line:MovieClip = new MovieClip();
31            var g:Graphics = line.graphics;
32            g.beginFill(0x000000);
33            g.drawRect(0, 0, _app.stage.stageWidth, 4);
34            g.endFill();
35            line.y = 100;
36            line.mouseEnabled = false;
37            this.addChild(line);
38
39            TweenPlugin.activate([VisiblePlugin]);
40            TweenPlugin.activate([ColorTransformPlugin]);
41        }
```

The **addMenus()** method is the workhorse of this class, and it's responsible for parsing the XML data, instantiating each main menu button, creating their submenus, and instantiating all submenu buttons. Line 44 uses the XML

**length()** method to determine how many main menu buttons are included in the XML. (The project source XML contains five menus.)

The remainder of the function is inside a loop that iterates five times, once for every menu. Line 46 starts the process by excerpting only the XML relevant to the current menu. Lines 49 through 59 then initialize the main menu button. Lines 49 and 50 create a **MenuButtonMain** instance, passing the label attribute from the XML into the class constructor to create the button's text label.

Line 51 positions the button horizontally, beginning at 20 pixels and then offsetting a distance equivalent to the buttons width and a 2-pixel space, for each button in the loop. As the button is 120 pixels wide, this means the first button is placed at an x position of 20 pixels **(20 + 0 * (120 + 2))**, the second at 142 **(20 + 1 * (120 + 2))**, and so on. Line 52 positions each button at a y coordinate of 75.

Lines 53 through 58 create two event listeners, one for the **MOUSE_OVER** event and another for the **MOUSE_OUT** event. When these events occur, they call the methods starting at lines 83 and 90, respectively. We'll discuss these methods in a few minutes. Finally, line 59 adds each main menu button to the display list.

```
42    //building the menus
43    private function addMenus():void {
44        var mainButtonLength:uint = _navData.button.length();
45        for (var i:int; i < mainButtonLength; i++) {
46            var buttonXML:XML = _navData.button[i];
47
48            //main button
49            var mainBtn:MovieClip =
50                new MenuButtonMain(buttonXML.@label);
51            mainBtn.x = 20 + i * (mainBtn.width + 2);
52            mainBtn.y = 75;
53            mainBtn.addEventListener(MouseEvent.MOUSE_OVER,
54                                     onMainBtnOver,
55                                     false, 0, true);
56            mainBtn.addEventListener(MouseEvent.MOUSE_OUT,
57                                     onMainBtnOut,
58                                     false, 0, true);
59            this.addChild(mainBtn);
```

Still within the primary loop that iterates once for each main menu button, lines 61 through 64 create the *subMenu* **MovieClip** instance to hold all submenu buttons. The submenu is added as a child to the main button (line 64), so their locations start out at the same point. In line 62, the submenu's y coordinate is set to the bottom of the main button (using the button's height plus a 2-pixel margin to account for the black line that will lay on top of the navigation bar).

Line 67 next determines the number of *project* nodes in the current menu. This will determine how many submenu buttons are required. Lines 68 through 79 make up a loop that iterates once for every submenu button. Line 69 parses the current project node from the parent menu XML data.

Lines 70 and 71 create an instance of the **MenuButtonSub** class, passing the **label** attribute of the **<project>** node into the constructor to serve as the button's text label. Line 72 sets the button's public property **projectPath** to the **path** attribute of the project, and Line 73 sets the button's public property **projectDescription** to the text within the **<project>** node.

Lines 75 through 77 add an event listener for the **CLICK** event so the submenu button will load the asset at the path associated with the button. Note that no other mouse event listeners are created. The **ROLL_OVER** and **ROLL_OUT** behavior of the button is cosmetic and is not customizable, so we'll build it in the **MenuButtonSub** class.

The last line of the loop, line 78, adds the button to the submenu.

```
60          //sub menu
61          var subMenu:MovieClip = new MovieClip();
62          subMenu.y = mainBtn.height + 2;
63          subMenu.visible = false;
64          mainBtn.addChild(subMenu);
65
66          //sub buttons
67          var subButtonLength:uint = buttonXML.project.length();
68          for (var j:int = 0; j < subButtonLength; j++) {
69              var projectNode:XML = buttonXML.project[j];
70              var subButton:MovieClip =
71                  new MenuButtonSub(projectNode.@label);
72              subButton.projectPath = projectNode.@path;
73              subButton.projectDescription = projectNode;
74              subButton.y = ((subButton.height) * j);
75              subButton.addEventListener(MouseEvent.CLICK,
76                                          onSubBtnClick,
77                                          false, 0, true);
78              subMenu.addChild(subButton);
79          }
80      }
81  }
```

Called each time the main menu button is rolled over, the **onMainBtnOver()** method shows the submenu. Line 84 first determines which button was rolled over by checking the **currentTarget** property of the event. Next, the button must show its submenu. Because the main menu button contains both a sprite background and a text field (explained in the next section), line 85 references the submenu by querying the third child of the button. Line 86 sets the visibility of the menu to true, and then line 87 uses TweenLite to fade from an alpha of 0 (transparent) to 1 (opaque), in one-quarter of a second.

Rolling off the main menu button calls the **onMainBtnOut()** method so we can again hide the menu. The first line of the method uses the **relatedObject** property of mouse events to determine if the mouse has rolled onto anything but a submenu button. We don't want to hide the menu if one of its buttons is in use. If that's not the case, the submenu's visible property is set to true so you can see the submenu when it fades in. TweenLite is used to fade the submenu up to an alpha of 1 over one-quarter second.

**NOTE**

*If the contents of the button were less uniform, you might prefer to set the **name** property of the submenu in the creation process (perhaps after line 64 in this class) and then us the **getChildByName()** method to retrieve a reference to the submenu.*

*Hiding and revealing the submenus could be simplified by just popping the menus in and out when the value of their visible property changes. But TweenLite makes this so easy that only three extra lines of code are required— line 87 does the work and lines 12 and 39 enable the* **VisiblePlugin**. *(Line 11 is still required to support the* **ColorTransformPlugin**, *and line 92 will still be required in another form.)*

*If you prefer that the submenus pop in and out (perhaps because the quarter-second tween up and down makes the system feel less responsive), that's easy to change. First comment out lines 87 and 92 and then add the following after line 92 to hide the menu:*

```
_subMenu.visible = false;
```

*(You may also comment out line 12 and 39, but their effect on the project will be negligible. To remove all alpha tweening of the submenus entirely, you can remove lines 12, 39, 87, and the original line 92, but they will not hinder performance if the appropriate lines remain commented, and this allows you restore the functionality later if you change your mind.)*

Also, the visibility of the menu is set to false using TweenLite's **VisiblePlugin**. When the **visible** property of the TweenLite object is set to false, this plugin automatically sets the visibility of the target to false *after* the tween is complete. In other words, the menu fades out and then becomes invisible. This is vital to the success of the menu because we can't rely solely on alpha to hide our menus.

Despite being transparent, display objects with an alpha value of 0 can still receive mouse events. If we just faded the submenu out, rolling the mouse over its prior location would cause it to fade back into view without ever going near its main menu button. Instead, the menus must be invisible because invisible assets won't respond to mouse events. So, the menus must start as invisible, become visible but tween their alpha property from 0 to 1 when rolled over, tween their alpha back to 0 and become invisible again upon mouse out.

```
82    //menu button mouse roll behavior: appearance
83    private function onMainBtnOver(evt:MouseEvent):void {
84        var mainBtn:MovieClip = MovieClip(evt.currentTarget);
85        _subMenu = mainBtn.getChildAt(2);
86        _subMenu.visible = true;
87        TweenLite.to(_subMenu, 0.25, {alpha:1});
88    }
89
90    private function onMainBtnOut(evt:MouseEvent):void {
91        if (!(evt.relatedObject is MenuButtonSub)) {
92            TweenLite.to(_subMenu, 0.25, {alpha:0, visible:false});
93        }
94    }
```

The last method in the class is called when a submenu button is clicked. Line 97 determines which button was clicked and retrieves the values from its public properties **projectPath** and **projectDescription**. The path is used to load the content associated with that button, and the description (included here only as an example) might be used to show information about the asset in a caption field, if you thought it necessary.

Line 100 *or* 101 will unload any content from the **SafeLoader** instance (retrieved from the document class **assetLoader** getter), depending on which platform you're targeting. As discussed in Chapter 13, **unloadAndStop()** is preferable because it closes all sound and video streams, stops all timers, and removes all relevant listeners, so the asset can be properly unloaded. This method, however, requires Flash Player 10 or later. If you must target Flash Player 9, you must use the **unload()** method and take all necessary steps yourself to close open streams, stop timers, and remove listeners within the loaded asset. After any content is unloaded, line 102 then loads the content at the path contained in the local **path** variable.

```
95    //menu button click behavior: loading
96    private function onSubBtnClick(evt:MouseEvent):void {
97        var subBtn:MovieClip = MovieClip(evt.target);
98        var path:String = subBtn.projectPath;
99        var description:String = subBtn.projectDescription;
```

```
100         //_app.assetLoader.unload(); //FP 9
101         _app.assetLoader.unloadAndStop(); //FP 10
102         _app.assetLoader.load(new URLRequest(path));
103     }
104   }
105 }
```

This actually concludes the main functionality of the navigation bar, including the XML loading and parsing, and the content loading triggered by using the system. However, we must still discuss the classes that create the main menu buttons and submenu buttons.

## MenuButtonMain

The `MenuButtonMain` class works hand in hand with the corresponding movie clip symbol in the main FLA's Library. The movie clip contains artwork resembling a tab, and a linkage class of `com.learningactionscript3.ui.MenuButtonMain`. This class resides in that location and creates the button's text field and text format.

Lines 1 through 8 declare the package and import the required classes. Line 10 declares the class and extends `MovieClip` to work with the aforementioned symbol. Line 12 opens the class constructor, and receives a `String` as its only argument to serve as the text label for the button. It has a default value of an empty `String`, so an instance of the class can still be created even without passing in any text.

Line 13 sets the `buttonMode` property of the button to true, so the cursor will change from a pointer to a finger when rolling over the button.

Lines 15 through 22 initialize the button's text field, and lines 24 through 31 initialize and apply a text format. Much of this is self-explanatory, but a few things are worthy of note. Lines 17 and 18 set the width and height of the text field to fill the button. This exposes the possibility that the button will cease working because the text field will trap incoming mouse events. To prevent this, line 21 disables mouse interaction with the field.

Also of note, line 19 sets the field to use embedded fonts, allowing us to use the font symbols in the library of the FLA. Line 24 instantiates the `ArialBold` symbol, line 26 ensures that we're using the embedded font, and, finally, line 31 applies the text format using the `setTextFormat()` method, after the text has been added to the field.

```
1   package com.learningactionscript3.ui {
2
3       import flash.display.MovieClip;
4       import flash.text.Font;
5       import flash.text.TextField;
6       import flash.text.TextFieldAutoSize;
7       import flash.text.TextFormat;
8       import flash.text.TextFormatAlign;
9
10      public class MenuButtonMain extends MovieClip {
11
```

```
12        public function MenuButtonMain(labl:String="") {
13            this.buttonMode = true;
14
15            var btnLabel:TextField = new TextField();
16            btnLabel.y = 5;
17            btnLabel.width = this.width;
18            btnLabel.height = 20;
19            btnLabel.embedFonts = true;
20            btnLabel.text = labl;
21            btnLabel.mouseEnabled = false;
22            this.addChild(btnLabel);
23
24            var btnFont:Font = new ArialBold();
25            var labelFormat:TextFormat = new TextFormat();
26            labelFormat.font = btnFont.fontName;
27            labelFormat.size = 12;
28            labelFormat.bold = true;
29            labelFormat.color = 0xFFFFFF;
30            labelFormat.align = TextFormatAlign.CENTER;
31            btnLabel.setTextFormat(labelFormat);
32        }
33    }
34 }
```

## MenuButtonSub

The **MenuButtonSub** class is responsible for creating a submenu button and controlling only its appearance when the mouse rolls over or out of the button. The click behavior is controlled from the **NavigationBarXML** class. This makes the button more flexible and reusable. It also uses two public properties to store the path and description of the asset the button will load.

Lines 1 through 13 declare the class package and import the required classes, including TweenLite. Line 15 declares the class and extends **MovieClip** to inherit its accessible properties and methods. Lines 17 through 19 declare the class properties. Note that both *projectPath* and *projectDescription* are public, meaning they can be both set and retrieved from outside the class. As a result, no getter or setter is used.

```
1  package com.learningactionscript3.ui {
2
3      import flash.display.GradientType;
4      import flash.display.Graphics;
5      import flash.display.MovieClip;
6      import flash.display.Sprite;
7      import flash.events.MouseEvent;
8      import flash.geom.Matrix;
9      import flash.text.Font;
10     import flash.text.TextField;
11     import flash.text.TextFormat;
12     import flash.text.TextFormatAlign;
13     import com.greensock.TweenLite;
14
15     public class MenuButtonSub extends MovieClip {
16
17         private var _background:Sprite;
18         public var projectPath:String;
19         public var projectDescription:String;
```

Lines 21 through 30 contain the class constructor. The **String** that will serve as the button label is passed into the constructor, and the argument uses an empty **String** as a default value so the button can still be instantiated even without text input. Lines 22 and 23 call functions to draw the button's background and create its text label, both of which we'll look at in a moment. (Note that the **String** passed into the constructor is passed on to the **addTextLabel()** method.)

Line 24 disables mouse interaction with the button's *children*. This is not only an alternative to disabling mouse interaction directly on the text field (as seen in **MenuButtonMain** class); it also disables interaction with the background sprite. Finally, lines 26 through 29 add event listeners for mouse roll over and roll out events.

```
20        //constructor
21        public function MenuButtonSub(labl:String="") {
22            addBackground();
23            addTextLabel(labl);
24            this.mouseChildren = false;
25
26            this.addEventListener(MouseEvent.ROLL_OVER,
27                                onOver, false, 0, true);
28            this.addEventListener(MouseEvent.ROLL_OUT,
29                                onOut, false, 0, true);
30        }
```

The **addBackgound()** method in lines 32 through 43, create the button's background sprite using the gradient fill technique discussed in Chapter 8. The colors used in the gradient both have alpha values of 80 percent, making the buttons translucent. The **addTextLabel()** method receives the button's label **String** from the constructor, and uses the same technique seen in the **MenuButtonMain** class to create and format a text field.

```
31        //background and text label
32        private function addBackground():void {
33            _background = new Sprite();
34            var g:Graphics = _background.graphics;
35            var matrix:Matrix = new Matrix();
36            matrix.createGradientBox(120, 25, deg2rad(90));
37            g.beginGradientFill(GradientType.LINEAR,
38                            [0x64788C, 0x2C4054],
39                            [0.8, 0.8], [0, 255], matrix);
40            g.drawRect(0, 0, 120, 25);
41            g.endFill();
42            addChild(_background);
43        }
44
45        private function addTextLabel(btnLabelText:String):void {
46            var btnLabel:TextField = new TextField();
47            btnLabel.x = btnLabel.y = 2;
48            btnLabel.width = this.width;
49            btnLabel.height = 20;
50            btnLabel.embedFonts = true;
51            btnLabel.text = btnLabelText;
52            this.addChild(btnLabel);
53
```

```
54                    var btnFont:Font = new ArialRegular();
55                    var labelFormat:TextFormat = new TextFormat();
56                    labelFormat.font = btnFont.fontName;
57                    labelFormat.size = 12;
58                    labelFormat.color = 0xDDDDEE;
59                    labelFormat.align = TextFormatAlign.LEFT;
60                    btnLabel.setTextFormat(labelFormat);
61                }
```

Although the actions invoked by a button click are invoked from the **NavigationBarXML** class, each **MenuButtonSub** instance updates its own appearance based on mouse interaction. Specifically, TweenLite is used to tint the button a slate blue using TweenLite's **ColorTransformPlugin** (activated earlier in the **NavigationBarXML** class). When rolling over the button with the mouse, TweenLite changes the tint from 0 to 100 percent, tinting it blue. When rolling off the button, the tint changes from 100 to 0 percent.

```
62              //submenu button mouse behavior
63              private function onOver(evt:MouseEvent):void {
64                  TweenLite.to(_background, 0.3, {colorTransform:
65                              {tint:0x223355, tintAmount:1}});
66              }
67
68              private function onOut(evt:MouseEvent):void {
69                  TweenLite.to(_background, 0.3, {colorTransform:
70                              {tint:0x334466, tintAmount:0}});
71              }
72
73              private function deg2rad(deg:Number):Number {
74                  return deg * (Math.PI/180);
75              }
76          }
77  }
```

Finally, the **deg2rad()** method in lines 73 through 75 supports the **createGradientBox()** method in line 36, allowing us to convert degrees to radians so we can rotate the gradient.

## Tying it all together

When you tie it all together, you end up with Figure 14-1. The document class creates the loader, loader mask, and navigation bar, and loads the XML. The **NavigationBarXML** class instantiates each **MenuButtonMain** instance, submenu, and **MenuButtonSub** instance based on the XML data. It also sets the click behavior of the submenu buttons to load content into the **SafeLoader** instance in the document class. The result is that new content is loaded every time the user clicks a submenu button.

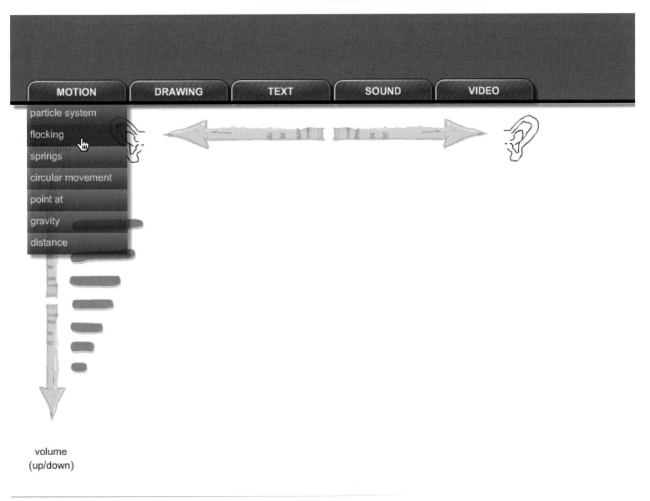

*Figure 14-1. A simple navigation system that loads button properties from an external XML file*

This simple navigation system brings a lot of power to a project because it allows you to quickly and easily change the main and submenu button names, modify project descriptions, and update what's loaded from each button—all by configuring an external XML file. In other words, you don't have to edit and republish the SWF every time you want to make a change.

**NOTE**

*The companion website contains additional examples that use XML for a variety of tasks, including driving an image gallery, and populating text fields.*

# What's Next?

A nice rest and a beverage, that's what. Reward yourself for all the progress you've made learning a new language. You've made your way through 14 chapters of new material; you've earned a break. Then, after putting your feet up for a while, get back to work. Spend 15 minutes a day experimenting. Adapt every exercise in the book to accomplish something new. Create mini-projects that combine topics, using the skills you've learned in each area to create something new. For example, create a particle system of text fields, or use the microphone activity level to start playing a video.

Write a class for every timeline example. Start just by converting each timeline script to document classes and compare your efforts to the supplemental source files provided. Then start writing classes that you can reuse.

Don't forget the companion website! Start reading its posts and explore the additional resources. Visit those and other ActionScript-related websites regularly, and subscribe to their news feeds, if available.

Finally, look for a **bonus chapter** on the companion website. In it, we'll examine the basic 3D capabilities that are integrated into ActionScript 3.0 as of Flash Player 10 and later. In the bonus chapter, we'll discuss rotating and translating (moving) objects in 3D space, perspective angle, vanishing point, and more.

We hope you enjoyed this book, and that you continue your learning. Please visit the companion website at your leisure and use the contact form to let us know how you're doing!

# INDEX

## Symbols and Numbers

**classes**
accessing stages in, 130–131
"Adding Classes to Pre-Existing
Symbols" post, 82
class constructors, 13, 118, 320
classpaths, 118–121
creating in Flash Professional, 10
defined (OOP), 114
display lists, 75–78
document. *See* document class
extending, 114
linkage, 82
naming, 83, 118
overview, 115–116
Square class (example), 124
subclasses, 122, 139
superclasses, 122, 139
symbol base, 124
tweening, 183
Vehicle class (example), 125–128
classic text, 273
classpaths, defined, 117
client source (XML send-and-load),
404–405
code
for playing videos, 342
organizing, 100
selecting text with, 265
codecs, defined, 335
coefficients, friction, 160–161
coercion, defined, 89
collision detection, 166–168
colors
Color class, 221, 250
color effects (bitmaps), 247–250
ColorMatrixFilter class, 249–250
color parameter (beginFill() method),
194
color peak meter, 316
color picker exercise, 218–220,
252–256
color property (text), 267
ColorTransform class, 247–249
ColorTransformPlugin, 411
ColorUtils package, 224
custom button class exercise, 222
expressing as numbers, 52
gradient fills and lines, 197
gradient spread methods, 214–215
#RRGGBBAA color notation, 348
solid-color fills, 194–195
columnar layout (TLF), 287–288

command-line compilers, 4
commas, tracing multiple items with,
22, 104
comments in XML, 389
ignoring. *See* ignoreComments
comparison operators
comparison equality operator (==),
29
defined, 30
listed, 27
compatibility with legacy code
(ActionScript 3.0), 5, 14
compilation, 3–4
compiler software (Flash Professional),
3
components, video, 336, 340–343
compositing blend modes
(ActionScript), 235–236
composition
adding sound system to vehicle
through, 145–147
basics (OOP), 131–133
defined (OOP), 114
compound assignment operators, 29,
54
computeSpectrum() method, 317, 318
concatenate (+) operator, 42
conditional statements, 20
conditional structures
if statements, 30–32
logical operator precedence, 32–33
overview, 29–30
switch statements, 33–34
constants, defined, 56
constructors
class, 118
defined, 13, 123
containers
ContainerController class, 290
TLF, 289
contentLoaderInfo property, 362, 369
convFilter() function, 242
ConvolutionFilter (bitmaps), 240–243
copying
copy() method, 401
pixels, 230–231
cos() method (Math class), 170
createBtn() method, 222
createButton() function, 306
createGradientBox() method, 213, 215,
219, 418
createLabel() method, 223

createRoundRect() method, 222
CSS (Cascading Style Sheets)
formatting text with, 274–277
loading, 279–283
for Timed Text document, 347
cubic Bézier model, 194
cue points (video), 337
currentLabels, 104–106
currentTarget event property, 64
currentTarget property, 180
curves
curveTo() command, 202
curveTo() method, 194
drawing, 194–195
customized video player, creating
code-only solution, 352–358
overview, 350
scripting buttons to control
FLVPlayback component,
350–352
customizing
adding custom symbol instances to
display lists, 82–84
custom anti-aliasing (text), 274
custom button class exercise,
220–223
CustomURLLoader Class, writing,
372
encoding settings, 339
CustomLoader class
using, 368–370
writing, 364–368
custom objects
creating, 44–45
defined, 20
CustomURLLoader Class
using, 375–379

**D**

Darken blend mode, 234
data
bitmap, 228
casting, 25
dataFormat property, 371
loading, 370
"Sending Data from AVM2 to AVM1"
post, 379
data types
defined, 15
of display objects, changing, 88–89
variables and, 23–27

eraser tool, creating, 232
error reporting in ActionScript 3.0, 6
Essential ActionScript 3.0 (O'Reilly), 21, 69
European Computer Manufacturers Association, 385
event listeners
  defined, 6
  removing, 67–69
  using, 55–58
events
  controlling properties with mouse events, 58–60
  defined, 51
  Event.COMPLETE event, 301
  frame, 65
  keyboard, calling methods with, 60–62
  MouseEvent class, 56
  overview, 54–55
  propagation of, 62–64
  timer, 66–67
extend, defined (ActionScript), 214
extending classes, 114
external sounds, loading, 299–301

## F

F4V format, 337
fadeBall() function, 187
FFT (Fast Fourier Transform) method, 318
FileReference class, 252, 328, 332
fills
  bitmap, 199–200
  gradient, 197–198
  solid-color, 194–195
filtering by attribute (XML), 398
filters, bitmap
  BlurFilter, 239–240
  ColorMatrixFilter class, 249–250
  ConvolutionFilter, 240–243
  displacement map filter, 246–247
  DropShadowFilter, 238–239
  overview, 237–238
  Perlin noise filter, 243–246
fixed-width fonts, 267
Flash
  Coordinate system, 321
  Developer Center (Adobe), 346
  Document class feature, 5
  FLA files, 3, 128–130

flash.geom package, 205
FLV (Flash video) format, 335, 337
FLVPlaybackCaptioning component, 336, 345–346
FLVPlayback component, 336, 340–343, 350–352
Platform, 4, 8–9
Professional library, sounds from, 298–299
Flash Player
  CSS properties supported by, 276
  frame rates and, 66
  HTML tags supported by, 275
  keyboard shortcut conflicts and, 61
  popularity of, 335, 337
  rotation angles and, 177
  "Saving Data in Flash Player 9 using PHP" post, 251
  security and, 374
Flash Professional
  creating classes in, 10
  CS5 features for custom classes, 121
  embedded fonts in CS3/CS4, 270–271
  embedded fonts in CS5, 272–273
  fl.motion package, 238
  fl.transitions.easing package, 185
Flex
  projects, ActionScript in, 4
  technology, defined, 8
floating point numbers, 317
flowComposer property, 288–290
flowing text across multiple containers (TLF), 289–292
fonts
  device, 267
  embedded, 270–274
  Font Symbol Properties dialog, 272
  font symbols, 270–271
  Font Symbols Properties dialog, 270
  rotating device fonts (TLF), 284
  System, 267
for...in loops, 312–313
for loops, 35–36, 204, 264
  appendText() method, 264
formatting text
  adding text after using setTextFormat(), 268–269
  applying format to existing text, 268
  with CSS, 274–277
  custom anti-aliasing, 274
  embedded fonts, 270–274
  establishing format for new text, 267–268

with HTML, 274–275
  tab stops, 269–270
  TextFlow formatting options (TLF), 286–288
  TextFormat class, 269
  TextFormat instance, 266
format type(data), 25
fractal noise, 245
frame events, 64, 65
frame labels (timelines), 101–106
  currentLabels, 104–106
frame loops, defined, 36
frame numbers, 101
  currentFrame, 100
  totalFrames, 100
frame rates
  adjustment example, 97–98
  frameRate property, 107
  maximum range of, 98
  runtime reassigning of, 106–107
frequency spectrum, drawing, 318–319
friction coefficients, 160–161
from() method (TweenLite), 187
full-screen video
  defined, 336
  fundamentals, 343–344
functions
  defined, 20
  local variables, 41
  overview, 40–41
  parameters and arguments, 42–43
  returning values from, 43–44

## G

gain, microphone, 322
garbage collection, 69
geometry package
  gradient spread methods, 214–215
  matrices, 208–214
  points, creating, 205–206
  rectangles, creating, 206–208
getChildAt() method, 78, 88
getChildByName() method, 413
getChildIndex() method, 88
getDistance() function, 171
getFrame() function, 105, 106
getMicData() method, 329
getPixel() method, 254
getter/setter methods, 134–138
glyphs (characters), 272
go() method, 126

tweening *(continued)*
  timeline tweens, rebuilding with
    ActionScript, 189
  TweenLite plugins, 411
  TweenLite/TweenMax (GreenSock),
    186–189
  tweens, defined, 157, 183
typed arrays (vectors), 39–40
type(data) casting format, 25

## U

uncaughtErrorEvents property (Flash
  Player), 366
unconditional alternative code, 31
unloadAndStop() method, 414
updateMouseTransform() function,
  310, 315
updateParticleVelocities() function, 173
updateParticleVelocities() method, 174
URLLoader class, 280–281, 371
URLLoaderDataFormat, 371
URLRequest class, 280–281
useCapture parameter (listener events),
  69
"Using endFill() with the Drawing API"
  post, 195
UTF-8, 347

## V

values
  returning from functions, 43–44
  syntax for setting (properties), 54
variables
  basics of, 23–27
  Boolean, 24
  data types and, 20
  int, 24
  loading, 371–372, 376
  local, 41–42
  Number, 24
  Object, 24
  String, 24
  uint, 24
  using in XML, 391
vectors
  defined, 39–40, 191
  drawing with. *See* drawing with
    vectors
  Vector class, 202
  vector quantities, 155

Vehicle class (example), 125–128,
  135–137, 139
velocity of objects, 155–156
video
  captions. *See* captions, video
  components, 340–343
  customized video player, creating.
    *See* customized video player,
    creating
  encoding. *See* encoding videos
  Flash video. *See* Flash video
  full-screen video, 343–344
  overview, 336–337
  video_comp.fla file, 342
  video display object class, 76
  videos as display objects, 74
  Video with Adobe Flash CS4
    Professional Studio Techniques
    (Adobe Press), 336
VisiblePlugin, 411
visualization of waveforms, 321–322
volume, sound (ActionScript), 308–310

## W

waveforms (sound)
  drawing, 318–319
  visualization of, 321–322
  Waveform class, 319–321
WAVWriter class, 328, 331
weak references, 69
web sites, for downloading
  Adobe AS3 Core Library, 250
  Adobe Pixel Bender Exchange, 376
  Audiotool, 295
  Aviary suite, 258
  bitrate calculator, 338
  Captionate software, 346
  MAGpie captioning tool, 346
  SafeLoader class, 382
  ZaaIL package, 251
web sites, for further information
  ActionScript 3.0 operators, 29
  character encoding, 347
  Collision Detection Kit, 167
  CSS, 274
  Flash Blog, 377
  Grant Skinner blog, 69
  GreenSock Tweening Platform, 189
  HTML, 274
  HTTP status codes, 366
  learning ActionScript, 8

LoaderMax, 383
MPEG-4 format, 337
Pixel Bender Developer, 376
sizing BitmapData objects, 228
source code for examples, 16
Timed Text Markup Language, 346
Timed Text Tags, 347
Using Adobe Media Encoder CS5
  resource, 340
while loops, 36–37
white space in XML documents, 388
  ignoring. *See* ignoreWhitespace
wildcards (*) in XML, 396
Wildform Flix Pro, 336
writing XML, 399–401

## X

XML-based navigation bar
  directory structure/source files, 406
  FLA library symbols, 407
  LAS3Main (document class),
    408–410
  MenuButtonMain class, 415–416
  MenuButtonSub class, 416–418
  NavigationBarXML class, 410–415
  overview, 405
  XML document, 407–408
XML (Extensible Markup Language)
  attributes, using, 396–397
  CDATA tags, 389–390
  comments in, 389
  creating XML objects, 390–391
  declaration tags, 389
  deleting, 401–402
  descendant accessor operator (..),
    395–396
  documents, handling in ActionScript
    3.0, 6
  element nodes in, 392–396
  entities in XML specification, 390
  finding elements by content, 397–398
  finding elements by relationship, 398
  loading external XML documents,
    402–403
  overview, 385–386
  "Parsing XML Using Familial
    Relationships" post, 398
  processing instructions in, 389
  reading, 392
  rules for creating documents in,
    387–388

send and load server communication, 404–405

structure overview, 386–388

text nodes in, 392–396

using variables in, 391

white space and, 388

writing, 399–401

XMLList class, 394–395

# Z

ZaaIL library, 318

ZaaIL package, 251

zeno() function, 158

Zeno's paradox, 157–158

zero-based arrays, 38